COURVOISIER'S
BOOK OF THE
BEST

C ognac Courvoisier is renowned worldwide for its unique Napoleonic connection.

The story dates back to the early 19th century when the enterprising Emmanuel Courvoisier became a supplier of cognac to Emperor Napoleon I. By 1811, when Napoleon visited Courvoisier's warehouses in Bercy, Paris, the association was proving a commercial success.

Soon after this, Napoleon tried to escape to America in a ship stocked with his favourite cognac, Courvoisier. However, he had to abandon his plans, and surrendered to the British. While the ship was being unloaded, British naval officers sampled the haul of cognac and were so impressed that they referred to it as the 'Emperor's Cognac', or 'Le Cognac de Napoleon'.

By 1869, the much-expanded business was proclaimed, by special appointment, purveyor to the court of another Emperor and Courvoisier aficionado, Napoleon III. From this association evolved the famous Courvoisier trademark, the silhouette of Napoleon, and the slogan 'Le Cognac de Napoleon'. To complement the cognac, Courvoisier created the distinctive 'Josephine' bottle.

Today, the bust of Napoleon appears on the bottle of all styles of Courvoisier cognac, and is the recognized symbol of cognac excellence throughout the world.

🜚 The silhouette of Napoleon has been used in this book to denote a person or establishment that has been highly recommended by several of our contributors.

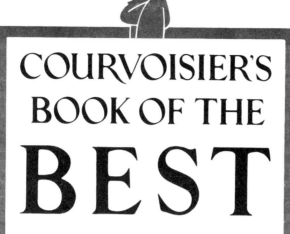

COURVOISIER'S
BOOK OF THE
BEST

Edited by
LORD LICHFIELD

Written by
SUE CARPENTER

NEW YORK

First edition for the United States,
its dependencies and the Philippines
published 1990 by Barron's Educational
Series, Inc.

First published by Ebury Press
Division of The National Magazine
Company Ltd
Colquhoun House
27-37 Broadwick Street
London W1V 1FR

All inquiries should be addressed to:
Barron's Educational Series, Inc.
250 Wireless Boulevard
Hauppauge, New York 11788

Library of Congress Catalog Card
No. 90-1174

International Standard Book
No. 0-8120-4490-8

Library of Congress Cataloging-in-
Publication Data

Carpenter, S.M.
    Courvoisier's book of the best /
edited by Lord Lichfield; written by
Sue Carpenter.
        p.   cm.
    Includes index.
    ISBN 9-8120-4490-8
    1. Voyages and travels—1981—
Guide-books.   2. Travel.
I. Lichfield, Patrick.   II. Title.
G153.4.C37   1990   90-1174
910'.2'02—dc20   CIP

PRINTED IN THE UNITED STATES
OF AMERICA

0123   8800   987654321

Contents

·

FOREWORD
—— by ——
LORD LICHFIELD

As *Courvoisier's Book of the Best* goes into its third updated edition, I am delighted to say that it is still growing, evolving and flourishing. It is becoming more and more well known and respected internationally. Since the last edition, when we invited your comments and recommendations, we have received letters from all over the world. I also meet frequent travellers who, like me, make *Courvoisier's Book of the Best* their constant travelling companion and their bible (at the very bottom line, it makes a brilliant telephone directory!). Of course, you don't have to be a globetrotter to enjoy the book – it's a great read for the bedside traveller who wants to keep in touch with what's best around the world.

I can't check out every single establishment myself (there are over 2,000 listed!), but I do have more opportunity than most. More than half my year is spent abroad, travelling 250,000 miles and staying 150 nights in hotels. I eat out virtually every day of the year.

People often ask me how I decide what is the best. The answer is I am not the only arbiter. What is best for me may differ from what is best for you. Best for me represents quality and uncompromising attention to detail. But, however you define it, opinions will vary as to what deserves the accolade 'the best'.

That is why we form our editorial opinion by consensus. My personal view does not always win the day. For example, I am still an avid supporter of the Mandarin Oriental in Hong Kong, but according to the consensus, the Regent has now reached the pinnacle. This book is a collection of ideas and views from over 200 style-setters and experts, whose opinions are informed and respected. Together these thoughts form a unique international record of the best – where else can you find word-of-mouth recommendations in volume form?

As always, they make riveting reading. Discover, for example,

---
♟ ——
World's Best Fashion Designers

1	YVES SAINT LAURENT · Paris
2	KARL LAGERFELD for CHANEL · Paris
3	GIORGIO ARMANI · Milan
4	DONNA KARAN · New York
5	ROMEO GIGLI · Milan
6	CLAUDE MONTANA · Paris
7	CALVIN KLEIN · New York
8	REI KAWAKUBO for COMME DES GARCONS · Tokyo
9	JEAN-PAUL GAULTIER · Paris
10	RIFAT OZBEK · London

LORD LICHFIELD was educated at Harrow and spent 7 years in the Grenadier Guards. In the Sixties he became a photographer, working for *Life, Queen* and then American *Vogue* under Diana Vreeland. Advertising and editorial work now takes him all over the world. He lives in London and Shugborough, Staffordshire. His books include the autobiographical *Not the Whole Truth; Lichfield in Retrospect;* and, a tribute to his great aunt, *Queen Mother – The Lichfield Selection.*

where Barry Humphries is off to if you see him on a bicycle in Holland; Beirut's answer to a candlelit dinner; where to see Tony Curtis's underwear; and the best advice ever given to Dudley Moore, Joan Collins, Peter Ustinov, Barbara Taylor Bradford, Jeffrey Archer and Simon Williams.

However, this remains, above all, a guide. Each entry has been recommended, selected (on merit alone – we accept *no* payment) and thoroughly researched. Full addresses and telephone numbers are supplied.

We have rearranged this edition to make it more practical and easy-to-use than ever. The book is now organized country by country, in alphabetical order. Cities are then listed alphabetically within each country, and under each city come the listings: art galleries and museums, bars and cafés, hotels, music, restaurants, shopping and much more. At the end of the book you will find the Travel Directory, with addresses and essential information about tour and villa companies, travel agents, cruises, rail trips, yacht charter and the best airlines.

There are other additions to the book. Our horizons are expanding – this year there's news from Our Men (and Women) in Belize, Guatemala, Botswana, Dubai, Oman, Hungary, Czechoslovakia, Poland, Yugoslavia and Taiwan – plus much greater coverage of such places as Austria, the Netherlands, Russia and Spain. You'll find plenty of new restaurants to try out, new ways to combat jetlag, the hotel with the best bathrooms (and the one that provides the best bedtime treat...that moreish chocolate truffle on your pillow).

I am always at pains to stress that the best need not be élitist. Quality is paramount, and it doesn't necessarily come with a prohibitively high price tag. As well as frequent bargains, there are many things to experience that are entirely free: not only great national art collections but also lesser-known galleries and churches containing some of the best art in existence (Masaccio's frescos in the Brancacci Chapel in Florence, for example); contemporary buildings that will become the classics of

World's Best Opera Companies

1	LA SCALA · Milan
2	ROYAL OPERA HOUSE · London
3	METROPOLITAN OPERA · New York
4	ENGLISH NATIONAL OPERA (ENO) · London
5	PARIS OPERA · Paris
6	LYRIC OPERA OF CHICAGO · Chicago
7	BAVARIAN STATE OPERA · Munich
8	NEW YORK CITY OPERA · New York
9	DEUTSCHE OPER · Berlin
10	VIENNA STATE OPERA · Vienna

World's Best Ballet Companies

1	L'OPERA BALLET · Paris
2	KIROV BALLET · Leningrad
3	ROYAL DANISH BALLET · Copenhagen
4	ROYAL BALLET COMPANY · London
5	NEW YORK CITY BALLET · New York
6	BOLSHOI BALLET · Moscow
7	AMERICAN BALLET THEATER · New York
8	NATIONAL BALLET OF CANADA · Toronto
9	AUSTRALIAN BALLET · Melbourne
10	JOFFREY BALLET · New York

tomorrow (such as the Institut du Monde Arabe in Paris); the best beaches; the best waters for scuba diving; scenic journeys (a celebration of the best stretches of road you may ever find yourself rolling along – from the A30 in the West Country of England to the Big Sur Coast of California); glorious gardens; colourful local markets (in Thailand, Portugal and Madeira, Guatemala, Greece, Austria...) and dazzling designer stores.

Long-standing 'bests' are balanced with what is trendsetting, innovative and currently fashionable. As our readers already know, we go way beyond simply listing Establishment 'bests'. Wonderful places constantly crop up; new young chefs, hoteliers and fashion designers emerge. Our experts have their ears to the ground. They spot the latest trends.

You may therefore find some surprises in our top 10 ratings. We give relative newcomers the chance to shine – Isaac Mizrahi, the American fashion designer, enters the charts above some of his more established compatriots; JJ's nightclub in Hong Kong shoots to top slot in the Far East. However, change has not been made for change's sake. Take the Paris restaurant Jamin (or Robuchon, as it is otherwise known), still No 1 after all these years. Just read the comments – nowhere else is raved about with such unqualified conviction. As before, entries with many recommendations have been awarded the familiar Courvoisier symbol, the silhouette of Napoleon.

Last time we presented Britain's best establishments with brass plaques, which I often see proudly displayed. The plaques will continue to be presented, but this year we have gone one step further. In our own version of the 'Oscars' ceremony, Courvoisier bestowed awards

World's Best Hotels

1	THE REGENT · Hong Kong
2	HOTEL BEL-AIR · Los Angeles
3	THE ORIENTAL · Bangkok
4	CLARIDGE'S · London
5	HOTEL SEIYO · Tokyo
6	MANDARIN ORIENTAL · Hong Kong
7	CIPRIANI · Venice
8	THE CONNAUGHT · London
9	HYATT ON COLLINS · Melbourne
10	MANSION ON TURTLE CREEK · Dallas

World's Best Galleries and Museums

1	MUSEE DU LOUVRE · Paris
2	MUSEO DEL PRADO · Madrid
3	GALLERIA DEGLI UFFIZI · Florence
4	KUNSTHISTORISCHES MUSEUM · Vienna
5	THE HERMITAGE · Leningrad
6	METROPOLITAN MUSEUM OF ART · New York
7	RIJKSMUSEUM · Amsterdam
8	NATIONAL GALLERY · London
9	MUSEI VATICANI · Rome
10	MUSEE D'ORSAY · Paris

World's Best Restaurants

1	JAMIN (ROBUCHON) · Paris
2	LAI CHING HEEN · The Regent, Hong Kong
3	GUY SAVOY · Paris
4	GIRARDET · Crissier, Switzerland
5	LE MANOIR AUX QUAT' SAISONS · Great Milton, England
6	LE BERNARDIN · New York
7	ESPERANCE · St Père, France
8	LEMON GRASS · Bangkok
9	STEPHANIE'S · Melbourne
10	DA FIORE · Venice

on 10 British establishments which were voted best in their category.

As the producers of the best and most stylishly presented cognac in the world, it was only natural for Courvoisier to initiate and support this book with such enthusiasm. Connoisseurs in one area are able to appreciate fine things on a broader scale: those who savour Courvoisier's fine cognac are attuned to the best things in life.

There can be no greater demonstration of the Courvoisier style than the Cognac Courvoisier Collection Erté, a limited edition with decanters designed by the great art deco illustrator. I have always loved Erté's work and had the honour of photographing him; so it was with sadness that I heard of his death, at the age of 97. The series of designs for Courvoisier were one of his last artistic creations. As a collector of Courvoisier Collection Erté (only three designs have been released so far), I have been intrigued to see prices soar at auction since his death. The Courvoisier Collection Erté is now truly a collector's item.

Courvoisier's Book of the Best will continue to be regularly updated. While some establishments are undoubtedly timeless, many fluctuate. We will constantly be assessing what is best, rating new entries and sifting out dead wood – and we welcome your ideas again. Meanwhile, as I have advised before, dispense with those weighty Michelins, Gault Millaus, Fodors, Good Food and Hotel Guides, for all you need is one all-encompassing guide: *Courvoisier's Book of the Best.*

_____ *written by* _____

SUE CARPENTER, a freelance writer and journalist, whose world travels have provided a rich source of material for *Courvoisier's Book of the Best*. Formerly with *Harpers & Queen*, she helped write the Official Sloane Ranger books, edited *St Moritz* magazine, and is author of *The Good Wedding Guide*.

_____ *with contributions from* _____

ROY ACKERMAN Food expert, chef, restaurateur and publisher, with a finger in many pies. Author of *The Ackerman Guide* to British restaurants.

MARION VON ADLERSTEIN Travel editor of *Vogue Australia*, based in Sydney.

LADY ELIZABETH ANSON Founder of Party Planners, which has organized parties for most of the British royals. Her latest book is *Lady Elizabeth Anson's Party Planners*.

JEFFREY ARCHER Bestselling author and playwright.

GIORGIO ARMANI Italy's No 1 fashion designer, a master of tailoring.

TONY ASPLER Canadian wine writer and consultant.

FREDERIC BEIGBEDER French socialite, club-owner and party organizer. He is also a social commentator for radio.

JEAN-PAUL BELMONDO Internationally acclaimed French actor who starred in many films including *Breathless*, and recently appeared in *Cyrano* on the Paris stage.

ROSS BENSON Social columnist and former foreign correspondent for the *Daily Express*. Educated at Gordonstoun, where he was a contemporary of Prince Charles.

PIERRE BERGE Director of the Paris Opéra, and of the fashion house of Saint Laurent.

JOSEPH BERKMANN French-based British wine expert and traveller, and owner of the London restaurant Au Jardin des Gourmets.

LIZ BERRY MW Owner of the London-based wine merchants La Vigneronne.

BIJAN Persian-born menswear designer based in America.

PETER BLAKE British artist best known for his Pop Art of the 1960s.

RAYMOND BLANC French chef-owner of the acclaimed Le Manoir aux Quat' Saisons in Oxfordshire.

BILL BLASS Top American fashion and furnishings designer, based in New York.

FRANK BOWLING British-born manager of The Carlyle hotel in New York.

BARBARA TAYLOR BRADFORD Novelist and journalist whose bestselling books include *A Woman of Substance*.

DAVID BRAY Food editor for *The Courier-Mail* in Brisbane.

SEYMOUR BRITCHKY American author of the annual guide *The Restaurants of New York* and the periodical *Seymour Britchky's Restaurant Letter*.

MICHAEL BROADBENT MW Head of Christie's Wine Department in London. President of International Wine & Food Society and author of the *Great Vintage Wine Book*.

BONNIE BROOKS Socialite and Vice President of merchandising at Holt Renfrew in Canada.

JOHN BROOKE-LITTLE CVO, Norroy & Ulster King of Arms British heraldry and genealogy expert and author at the College of Arms in London.

TYLER BRULE Canadian TV journalist based in England with BBC's *Reportage*.

MARIO BUATTA Top New York-based interior designer and chairman of the Winter Antiques Show. He recently redecorated Blair House, the Presidential guest house.

JAMES BURKE British broadcaster, scientist, traveller and writer. His latest TV series is called *Complexity*.

JOAN BURSTEIN Owner and chief buyer of Browns, the directional London fashion store.

SHAKIRA CAINE Guyanan beauty, jewellery designer and wife of Michael Caine.

JOAN CAMPBELL Food editor of *Vogue Australia*, based in Sydney.

EDWARD CARTER American traveller, hotel expert and international delegate for Relais & Châteaux, he publishes the monthly journal *Edward Carter's Travels*.

BARBARA CARTLAND The most famous romantic novelist in the world. She has written over 450 books and sold over 500 million copies, making her the world's bestselling author.

MARINA CHALIAPIN Daughter of the Russian bass singer, Fiodor Chaliapin, she is Rome editor of *Harpers & Queen*.

JEAN-PHILIPPE CHATRIER French actor and journalist for *Elle* and *Le Point* in Paris.

GLYNN CHRISTIAN New Zealand-born television chef and food writer, based in England. His many books include *Edible France* and *The Gourmet's Freezer*.

KIRSTIE CLEMENTS Fashion and beauty writer for *Vogue Australia*.

JOAN COLLINS British-born TV and film star. International traveller, author and socialite.

RICHARD COMPTON-MILLER Senior feature writer at the *Daily Express* in London, and former editor of the William Hickey column. Author of the insider's guide *Who's Really Who*.

JILLY COOPER Journalist and author of many books including the bestselling novels *Riders* and *Rivals*.

LEO COOPER London-based publisher specializing in military books.

OLIVIER COQUELIN Paris-born hotelier and club-owner, based in New York.

CLAUDIA CRAGG Journalist and Tokyo editor of *Harpers & Queen*. Far East editor of *Courvoisier's Book of the Best*.

CANDIDA CREWE British journalist and author. Soon to be published is her latest novel, *Mad About Bees*.

QUENTIN CREWE British writer, restaurateur and traveller. His books include *Great Chefs of France*, *The Last Maharaja*, and *Touch the Happy Isles*.

QUENTIN CRISP British-born author of *The Naked Civil Servant*, based in New York.

ALAN CROMPTON-BATT Leading food and restaurant consultant, based in London.

TESSA DAHL Daughter of Roald Dahl and Patricia Neal, her books include *Babies, Babies, Babies, The Same but Different* and *Working for Love*. Based mainly in America.

BEATRICE DALLE French actress who made her name in the film *Betty Blue*.

WILLIAM DAVIES British screenwriter of *Twins* and other Hollywood movies, based in Los Angeles and London.

LORD DONOUGHUE British economist, historian, politician, lecturer and author.

ALISON DOODY Irish actress based in London, she starred in *Indiana Jones and the Last Crusade*.

VICTOR EDELSTEIN Fashion couturier and socialite working in London.

ROBERT ELMS London-based style writer and journalist who contributes to BBC Radio 4's *Loose Ends*. His first novel is *In Search of the Crack*.

ROLAND ESCAIG French food expert and journalist based in Paris. He contributes to Radio TFL and hosts the TV programme *National 7*.

LEN EVANS OBE British-born wine producer and writer based in Australia, where he co-owns Rothbury Estate winery in the Hunter Valley.

DOUGLAS FAIRBANKS JR Son of silent-film star Douglas Fairbanks, he has acted in over 75 films himself. Also a film, TV and theatre producer, writer and businessman.

SERENA FASS British founder of Serenissima, she now arranges private tours for groups of clients in conjunction with Cox & Kings Travel.

FENDI SISTERS Paola, Anna, Franca, Carla and Alda, daughters of the original Adele Fendi, who founded the famous fur and fashion empire. All 5 work in the Rome-based family business.

CLARE FERGUSON New Zealand-born cookery writer, traveller, consultant and television personality. Her books include *Creative Vegetarian Cookery*.

MARCHESA FIAMMA DI SAN GIULIANO FERRAGAMO Eldest child of the renowned Italian shoe designer Salvatore Ferragamo, she follows in her father's footsteps as head of shoe production, based in Florence.

DUGGIE FIELDS Artist whose work has evoked controversy and cult admiration. He lives in London and is an avid nightclubber.

KEITH FLOYD Flamboyant food enthusiast whose BBC TV series and books include: *Floyd on Fish*, *Floyd on France, Floyd on Britain and Ireland* and *Floyd's American Pie*.

CLAUDE FORELL Food editor of *The Age* and co-editor of Melbourne's *The Age Good Food Guide*.

MATTHEW FORT Food critic for *The Guardian*.

CLARE FRANCIS Famous as a skilled yachtswoman – she crossed the Atlantic single-handed and sailed around the world – she is now a bestselling author of novels such as *Night Sky* and *Red Crystal*.

DIANE FREIS American fashion designer based in Hong Kong.

MARCHESA BONA FRESCOBALDI Italian aristocrat whose Tuscany estates yield some of Italy's best wines.

ANIKO GAAL Fashion/PR director for the top fashion store Garfinckel's in Washington, DC.

JOHN GALLIANO Fashion Designer of the Year in 1988, he is one of Britain's most original and influential designers.

CATHERINE GAYNOR Journalist and arts and fashion editor for *The Peak* magazine in Hong Kong.

DAVID GLEAVE MW A director of Winecellars, the London wine merchants.

JOHN GOLD British co-founder and host of Tramp nightclub in London.

HARVEY GOLDSMITH Top rock promoter whose clients have included Bruce Springsteen, the Rolling Stones, Stevie Wonder and Madonna.

LORD GOWRIE Chairman of Sotheby's in London and former Minister for the Arts.

MICHAEL GRADE Chief Executive of Channel 4 TV.

SOPHIE GRIGSON Cookery columnist for the *Evening Standard*, and writer for major magazines. Her books include *Food for Friends*.

LOYD GROSSMAN American-born restaurant critic, design expert, restaurateur and television writer and presenter.

MICHEL GUERARD Top French chef and restaurateur. He created cuisine minceur at the spa, Les Prés et Les Sources d'Eugénie, home also to his world-famous restaurant.

HELEN GURLEY BROWN Editorial Director of *Cosmopolitan*, she has guided its expansion from one edition in America to 13 worldwide.

VISCOUNT HAMBLEDEN The only European to have migrated with the Bacciari in Persia. Former colleague of Prince Philip for the World Wildlife Fund.

ROBIN HANBURY-TENISON Traveller and writer whose books include *A Ride Along the Great Wall*, *Worlds Apart*, *A Question of Survival* and the most recent, *Spanish Pilgrimage*.

ANTHONY HANSON MW Wine expert and a director of Haynes Hanson & Clark wine merchants. Author of *Burgundy*.

MARGARET HARVEY New Zealand wine expert, she runs Fine Wines of New Zealand in London.

MARCELLA HAZAN Italian food expert. Based in Venice, she has a cookery school in Bologna and a home in New York. Her books include *The Classic Italian Cookbook* and *Marcella's Kitchen*.

MARIE HELVIN An American top model, originally from Hawaii, now based in London. She has written on fashion and beauty and is the author of *Catwalk*. She is also a television presenter and actress.

MARGAUX HEMINGWAY Actress and former model turned documentary film-maker. She is the granddaughter of the legendary Ernest.

JEAN-MICHEL HENRY The leading hairdresser at Carita, the No 1 salon in Paris.

DON HEWITSON New Zealand-born wine expert and writer who owns several top London wine bars. His books include *Enjoying Wine* and *The Glory of Champagne*.

PATRICIA HODGE British film and television actress, appearing in *Life and Loves of a She-Devil* and *Jemima Shore*. Her most recent West End theatre success was *Noël and Gertie*.

TERRY HOLMES Vice-President and Managing Director of Cunard Hotels, based at The Ritz in London.

KEN HOM American cookery expert and food consultant with bases in California and Hong Kong. He wrote the bestselling *Ken Hom's Chinese Cookery* and *Ken Hom's East Meets West Cuisine*, and presented a cookery series on BBC TV.

NIGEL HOPKINS Food editor of *The Advertiser* in Adelaide.

SIMON HOPKINSON Head chef at Bibendum, Sir Terence Conran's restaurant in the Michelin building in London.

MELISSA HOYER Fashion editor for Sydney's *Sunday Telegraph*.

BARRY HUMPHRIES Australian comedian whose outrageous alter egos, Sir Les Patterson and Dame Edna Everage, entertain TV and theatre audiences around the world.

CAROLINE HUNT Based in Texas, she is the head of the Rosewood Corporation which runs some of the most exclusive hotels in America.

MADHUR JAFFREY Indian actress, cook and writer based in New York. Her latest book is *Food for Family and Friends*.

TAMA JANOWITZ New York-based author of the bestselling *Slaves of New York*. Her other books include *Cannibal in Manhattan* and *American Dad*.

IAN JARRETT British-born freelance journalist and public relations consultant, based in Perth, Australia.

JEAN-MICHEL JAUDEL International businessman based in Paris. He is a member of all the best clubs and collects contemporary art.

IAIN JOHNSTONE British film critic for *The Sunday Times* and author of the novel *Cannes*.

STEPHEN JONES British milliner who has created collections for fashion designers such as Claude Montana. He has also designed a cosmetics range for Shiseido in Japan.

JOSEPH Moroccan-born Joseph Ettedgui is a leading fashion retailer and designer in London.

BARBARA KAFKA American food expert and author. President of her

own New York-based food consultancy, she travels extensively.

KAREN KAIN Prima Ballerina of the National Ballet Company of Canada based in Toronto.

ANGELA KENNEDY Fashion editor for *Good Housekeeping* magazine in London.

BETTY KENWARD Social editor of *Harpers & Queen*. At 84, she still attends every social event in Jennifer's Diary, which she has written since 1945.

LARRY KING Radio and TV host based in Washington, DC, and star of the chat show *The Larry King Show*.

MILES KINGTON British humourist whose column appears in *The Independent*. Author of many books, including *Let's Parlez Franglais*.

JUDITH KRANTZ American novelist and francophile. Her many bestsellers include *I'll Take Manhattan* and *Till We Meet Again*.

IRVING SMITH KOGAN 'Smitty' Kogan is Director of the Champagne News and Information Bureau, based in New York.

NICO LADENIS Half Greek Tanzanian-born chef-owner of top restaurant Chez Nico in London.

MAX LAKE Australian writer, food expert and owner of Lakes Folly winery in the Hunter Valley.

ELEANOR LAMBERT Head of her own top fashion PR company based in New York, she initiated the Best Dressed Lists.

ELISABETH LAMBERT ORTIZ London-born food writer of award-winning cookery books such as *The Book of Latin American Cooking*, and *The Food of Spain and Portugal – The Complete Iberian Cuisine*. She contributes to *Gourmet* magazine.

KENNETH J LANE American costume jewellery designer. He has shops throughout America and in London and Paris. His many illustrious clients include Barbara Bush.

KARL LAGERFELD Fashion designer under his own name and for Chanel in Paris.

MARQUIS DE LASTOURS Businessman and pretender to the throne of France.

ALEXANDRE LAZAREFF Food adviser to the Minister for Culture, and director of the National Council of Culinary Arts. Author of the guides *Paris Rendez-Vous* and *Europe Rendez-Vous*, he writes a weekly food column in *Le Figaro*.

PRUE LEITH London-based food expert and author. She runs the prestigious Leith's Cookery School of Food and Wine, Leith's Restaurant and Leith's Good Food caterers. Cookery editor of *The Guardian*.

DAVID LITCHFIELD Writer for and publisher of the *Ritz Newspaper*.

JANE LINDQUIST Expert skier and executive producer of a ski series for Screensport and Super Channel television, based in London.

MAUREEN LIPMAN British television and stage actress, comedienne and bestselling author and columnist.

ALASTAIR LITTLE Top British chef whose namesake restaurant is among the most fashionable in London.

ANDREW LLOYD WEBBER Acclaimed composer of such box-office blockbuster musicals as *Evita*, *Cats*, *Starlight Express*, *The Phantom of the Opera* and *Aspects of Love*.

JULIAN LLOYD WEBBER Accomplished cellist who has played with all the major British orchestras, and tours worldwide.

SAUL LOCKHART An American writer who has lived in Hong Kong for over 20 years. His books include the *Insight Guide to Hong Kong* and *A Diver's Guide to Asian Waters*.

SIMON LOFTUS Director of top wine merchants Adnams of Southwold, and author of their wine list.

SARAH LONSDALE Tokyo-based fashion writer and social figure.

FRANK LOWE British chairman and founder of top international advertising group Lowe Howard-Spink & Bell.

SEAN MACAULAY British journalist and avid club-goer, he is features editor of *Punch*.

JUNE MCCALLUM Editor-in-Chief of *Vogue Australia*.

MARK MCCORMACK Chairman of International Management Group, the world's biggest sports management and sponsorship group.

LADY MACDONALD OF MACDONALD Author of many cookery and entertaining books, including *The Harrods Book of Entertaining* and *Celebrations*. She and her husband run the acclaimed Kinloch Lodge Hotel in Scotland.

SKYE MACLEOD National PR Manager for top Australian department store David Jones.

STEVEN HENRY MADOFF Executive editor of *Art News* in New York.

DEREK MALCOLM Film critic for *The Guardian* and *Cosmopolitan*.

MARIUCCIA MANDELLI Italian head of design at Krizia, Milan, and well-known society figure.

STANLEY MARCUS American chairman emeritus of top Dallas store Neiman-Marcus. He is also a lecturer and marketing consultant.

GEORGE MELLY Professional blues singer and modern art enthusiast, based in London. He presents the arts show *Gallery* on Channel 4.

YEHUDI MENUHIN Violinist and conductor, born in New York of Russian parents. President and Associate Conductor of the Royal Philharmonic Orchestra, he also conducts with the Warsaw Sinfonia and Berlin Philharmonic. Books include his autobiography *Unfinished Journey*.

RODNEY MILNES Editor of *Opera* magazine.

FREDERIC MITTERRAND Nephew of the French President, and a writer, TV presenter and producer. He also produces films such as *Love Letters from Somalia*.

ROBERT MONDAVI Internationally renowned California winemaker and wine expert.

LORD MONTAGU OF BEAULIEU Chairman of the Historic Buildings & Monuments Commission for England. He created the National Motor Museum at his seat at Beaulieu.

DUDLEY MOORE British actor, comedian, pianist and restaurateur, based in California.

ANTON MOSIMANN Swiss-born chef-owner of the private dining club Mosimann's in London. He regularly travels the world giving lectures.

STIRLING MOSS Former British motor racing champion. A car and gadget fanatic, he is motoring editor of *Harpers & Queen*.

ANNE-ELISABETH MOUTET French editor of *Courvoisier's Book of the Best*, based in Paris. She is a writer and journalist who contributes regularly to British, French and American newspapers and magazines including *The Sunday Times*, *Tatler* and *Harper's Bazaar*.

JEAN MUIR CBE Top British fashion designer.

MICHAEL MUSTO Nightlife columnist for *The Village Voice* in New York.

ROBERT NOAH American food writer living in Paris. He runs Paris en Cuisine, a company specializing in gastronomic tours of France.

BRUCE OLDFIELD Top British fashion designer whose clients include the Princess of Wales. He designed for Dior and Saint Laurent before opening his own shop in London.

BENNY ONG Chinese fashion designer brought up in Singapore. He now lives in London, running his own fashion business.

ELISE PASCOE Australian food writer, consultant and lecturer. She writes for *The Sydney Morning Herald*, is food editor of *Belle Entertaining* and appears weekly on TV's *Network 10*.

BOB PAYTON American restaurateur, writer and broadcaster whose Chicago Pizza Pie Factory is famous in London and across Europe. Now based in Leicestershire, he is the proprietor of Stapleford Park country house hotel.

ELLEN PECK New York editor of *Courvoisier's Book of the Best* and Associate Editor of *Entertainment Weekly*.

PALOMA PICASSO Daughter of Pablo Picasso, she is an international name in jewellery design, accessories and perfume.

DOMINIQUE PIOT French media executive based in Paris.

STEVE PODBORSKI A World Cup downhill ski champion and president of Pod Enterprises. He is a TV celebrity in Canada and author of 2 books on skiing.

MADELEINE POULIN A Radio-Canada television personality based in Montreal.

ANDRE PREVIN World famous conductor based in New York State.

WOLFGANG PUCK Innovative Californian chef-owner of Los Angeles restaurants Chinois on Main and Spago.

CHARLOTTE RAMPLING British actress and former model, she lives in Paris with her children and musician husband Jean-Michel Jarre.

ROBERT RAMSAY President of Remarkable Communications, a special events and PR firm in Canada. He is also on the board of the Festival of Festivals in Toronto.

FREDERIC RAPHAEL British/American novelist and writer of screenplays, biographies and reviews. Novels include *The Glittering Prizes* and *After the War*, both adapted for TV. He lives in England and the Dordogne in France.

JANE ROARTY Sydney-based fashion editor of Australian *Cosmopolitan*.

GEOFFREY ROBERTS Pioneer of California wines in Britain, he runs Les Amis du Vin in London.

MICHEL ROBICHAUD Top Canadian fashion designer based in Montreal.

CLEMENCE DE ROCH French writer and journalist who writes for *Le Journal du Dimanche* and *The European*.

CATHERINE ROUSSO Fashion editor for French *Elle*.

HILARY RUBINSTEIN Literary agent and editor of *The Good Hotel Guide*.

ROBERT SANGSTER British racehorse owner and breeder. Son of

pools founder Vernon Sangster and director of the family business, he now lives on the Isle of Man.

VIDAL SASSOON British-born founder of the worldwide hairdressing empire, he is now based in California.

LEO SCHOFIELD Australia's best-known public stomach, a PR and advertising expert, food and travel writer. He edits *The Sydney Morning Herald Good Food Guide*.

SEBASTIAN SCOTT Former New York and European correspondent for the BBC programme *Eyewitness*, he is now editor of the BBC *Rough Guide to the World*.

FIONA SCOTT ROBERTS Paris-based editor of *Boulevard*, an English-language magazine about contemporary France.

ROSEMARY SEXTON Toronto-based socialite and social columnist for *The Globe & Mail* in Canada.

GILES SHEPARD Managing Director of the Savoy Group of hotels in London.

JANE SEYMOUR British actress, based partly in Los Angeles, starring in films and TV series such as *War & Remembrance*.

NED SHERRIN Film, theatre and TV producer, director and writer. Host of BBC Radio 4's *Loose Ends*.

DAVID SHILLING A British milliner, he also designs clothes, fabric and china.

JOSETTE SIMON British actress who is a leading member of the Royal Shakespeare Company and appeared in *Cry Freedom*.

DREW SMITH British food writer, former editor of *The Good Food Guide* and co-editor of *The Good Food Directory*. He now works in media development. His latest book is *Modern Cooking*.

YAN-KIT SO London-based Chinese cookery expert from Hong Kong. Among her bestselling books are the award-winning *Yan-Kit's Classic Chinese Cook Book* and *Wok Cookbook*.

HECTOR SOLANAS Argentinian film director, based partly in Paris and partly in Buenos Aires.

STEVEN SPURRIER British wine expert. Founder of L'Académie du Vin, Paris's first wine school, his books include *Wine Course* and *French Country Wines*.

PETER STRINGFELLOW Nightclub owner based in London, with clubs in New York, Miami and Los Angeles.

SERENA SUTCLIFFE MW International wine consultant and writer for *Decanter* and *Lloyd's Log*. Her books include *The Wine Drinker's Handbook*, *The Pocket Guide to the Wines of Burgundy* and *A Celebration of Champagne*. She is a Chevalier dans l'Ordre des Arts et des Lettres.

TAKI THEODORACOPULOS Greek journalist known for his acerbic column, High Life, in *The Spectator*. Based in London, he travels frequently around Europe and to New York, where he writes for *Esquire*.

EDWARD THORPE Ballet critic for *The Standard* in London.

JEFFERY TOLMAN Deputy chairman of the international advertising agency Saatchi & Saatchi.

DAN TOPOLSKI British journalist, former international rower and Olympic coach. Son of the late Feliks Topolski, the Polish artist, he has travelled extensively in South America, Africa, Eastern Europe and the Far East and has written books on his expeditions.

JOHN TOVEY Chef-owner of top English country-house hotel, Miller Howe in Cumbria. He makes frequent television and radio appearances and his books include *The Miller Howe Cookbook* and *John Tovey's Country Weekends*.

JEREMIAH TOWER Top American chef and pioneer of new Californian cuisine. Brought up in Europe, he owns the acclaimed restaurants Stars and Postrio in San Francisco and Peak Café in Hong Kong.

SHIZUO TSUJI Japanese food expert who is head of the prestigious cookery school Ecole Technique Hotelière Tsuji in Osaka.

MARCUS TUSCH Australian fashion designer based in Sydney.

TWIGGY An internationally famous model of the Sixties, Twiggy Lawson is now a successful stage and screen actress.

PETER USTINOV Multi-talented international actor, author, traveller, director and producer, star of countless films and plays. He lives in Switzerland and Paris.

FRANCOISE VERNY A French publishing diva, she works for the respected independent publishing house Flammarion in Paris.

ED VICTOR American literary agent who divides his year between London, New York and LA.

NICHOLAS VILLIERS British-based international banker who travels constantly and has lived in America and Switzerland.

LISE WATIER President of Lise Watier Cosmetics, based in Montreal.

AUBERON WAUGH British author, wine expert and editor of the *Literary Review*. Son of Evelyn Waugh and former diarist for *Private Eye*.

JOSHUA WESSON Editor of the *Wine & Food Companion* based in New York.

DORIAN WILD Australian editor of *Courvoisier's Book of the Best*. Former political journalist and social columnist, he is now a freelance journalist, broadcaster and media consultant.

LESLEY WILD Publisher of *Vogue Australia*, based in Sydney and married to Dorian Wild.

ANNE WILLAN Writer on French cooking and President of Ecole de Cuisine La Varenne in Paris and at the Château du Fey in Burgundy.

SIMON WILLIAMS British actor famous for his role in the long-running *Upstairs, Downstairs* and the BBC comedy *Don't Wait Up*.

FAITH WILLINGER Freelance journalist based in Italy. Her latest book is *Eating in Italy*.

CAROL WRIGHT British journalist specializing in travel and cookery. Travel writer for *House & Garden*, she is Chairman of the British Guild of Travel Writers.

LYNN WYATT Texan socialite and patron of the arts, she is a key figure on the international society and charity circuit.

PETER YORK Founder-partner of SRU business strategy consultancy and well-known style watcher and writer. Co-author of the Official Sloane Ranger books.

BEVERLEY ZBITNOFF Vancouver-born fashion expert who has worked in London and San Francisco for Boboli and MaxMara. She is also a gourmet cook.

ACKNOWLEDGEMENTS

Lord Lichfield, Sue Carpenter and the publishers would especially like to thank the following people for their invaluable help in compiling this book:

Val Archer, Joanna Bailey, Elizabeth Belton, Wes Benson, Denis Bowman, Ivar Braastad, Priscilla Chen, Lionel Craven, Victoria Crawley, Yvonne De Valera, Daniel de Villeneuve, Elena Geuna, Fred and Kathie Gill, Brenda Glover, Jacki Gray, Stephen Harthog, Victor Hazan, Andrew Higgins, Michael John Holloway, Louise Jeffrey, Ian Jesnick, Roger Jupe, Susanna Little, Alice Mackenzie, Deborah MacMillan, Elizabeth Martyn, Yvonne McFarlane, Philip Moore, Lynne Morton, Masha Nordbye, Ian Roberts, Joel Selvin, Nicola and Robert Swift, Andrea Violante, Tim Zagat.

AMERICA

BOSTON

—— Art and museums ——

**BOSTON INSTITUTE OF
CONTEMPORARY ART, 955 Boylston St,
MA 02115 ☎ (617) 266 5152**
A space for displaying new painting, sculpture,
video, music, dance, photography, film and performance art.

**ISABELLA STEWART GARDNER
MUSEUM, 2 Palace Rd, MA 02115
☎ (617) 566 1401**
A charming European microcosm – Italian Renaissance and 17C Dutch paintings, tapestries
and sculptures, set in a replica of a Venetian
palazzo with leafy courtyard. Also the odd Sargent and Whistler (both were pals of Mrs Gardner). Appeals to LOYD GROSSMAN, LORD GOWRIE
and TESSA DAHL.

**🖋 MUSEUM OF FINE ARTS, 465
Huntington Ave, MA 02115 ☎ (617) 267 9300**
The best art gallery in Boston: French Impressionists, the largest collection of Asiatic works
under one roof, classical and contemporary
works, decorative arts. Lively exhibitions such
as New American Furniture and Monet's Series.

—— Ballet ——

**BOSTON BALLET, Wang Center, 533
Tremont St, MA 02117 ☎ (617) 964 4070**
Under artistic director Bruce Marks (ex-Met,
ABT and Royal Danish Ballet), the company has
a reputation for both classics and innovative
modern works. Home-grown talent is spiced up
by international dancers, choreographers and
designers.

—— Clubs ——

**AVENUE C, 120 Boylston St, MA 02116
☎ (617) 423 3832**
The old Links reincarnated as a New York loft
– minimal, open and interesting – with progressive dance music.

**HUB CLUB, 533 Washington St, MA 02111
☎ (617) 451 6999**
Restaurant by day, club by night. This renovated
historic 3-storey building has won many restaurant and architectural awards. There's a
black floor and blue bar both inlaid with silver,
a vast beaten-copper display over the bar and a
cave area cut into the wall with triangular red

tables – their idea of hell. Progressive music
(Wed), live jazz (Thurs), international and house
(Fri), retro (Sat) and live bands (Sun).

**VENUS DE MILO, 11 Lansdowne St, MA
02215 ☎ (617) 421 9595**
Latterday gods and goddesses love this fusion
of psychedelic rococo-a-go-go and funeral party
baroque – all red and black velvet and brocade.
Get on down to house and urban international
music.

**ZANZIBAR, 1 Boylston Place, MA 30216
☎ (617) 451 1955**
Tropical-style club with palm trees and a terracotta dance floor in the basement. Jacket-and-tie set groove to contemporary dance music, top
40 hits. Adjoining is the **Crescent Club** for
billiards, drinking and private functions.

—— Hotels ——

**THE CHARLES HOTEL, 1 Bennett St,
Cambridge, MA 02138 ☎ (617) 864 1200**
A privately owned suave hotel in the trendy $90
million Charles Square development of shops and
restaurants. Rooms are a mixture of neo-Folk
Art (patchwork quilts, pine-frame four-posters)
and functional. GLYNN CHRISTIAN is impressed
by the Le Pli health spa, **Courtyard Café** and
the excellent **Rarities**, for adventurous, creative, modern cuisine – Long Island duck with
ginger and oak mushrooms, native scallops
escarole, roast partridge in pear cider.

**🖋 RITZ-CARLTON, 15 Arlington St, MA
02117 ☎ (617) 536 5700**
The uncontested best in Boston. Recently expanded to include private dining rooms and a
ballroom, it has the highest staff:guest ratio in
town. Lauren Bacall, Warren Beatty, Liz
Taylor, Katharine Hepburn, the Prince of Wales
and a cluster of Euroroyals have stayed. It gets
the nod from NED SHERRIN and ELEANOR LAMBERT. *"At the end of any trip around the States,
I always end up here to put myself in a civilized
frame of mind before I fly back to England"* –
LEO COOPER. The **Dining Room** is an institution.

—— Music ——

**🖋 BOSTON SYMPHONY ORCHESTRA,
Symphony Hall, 301 Massachusetts Ave,
MA 02115 ☎ (617) 266 1492**
While the 110-year-old Boston Symphony remains a revered institution, music director Seiji
Ozawa is active in commissioning new works
from contemporary composers. Highlights are
the Boston Pops (May to mid-July) for lighter
music, and summer at Tanglewood.

**HANDEL & HAYDN SOCIETY, 295
Huntington Ave, MA 02115 ☎ (617) 266 3605**
The oldest continuously active performing music

Boston Airs

If it matters that Junior grows up to be a refined, gracious citizen with social skills that Miss Manners could not fault, then send him before it's too late to **The Judith Ré Académie**, 328 Dartmouth St, Boston ☎ (617) 267 0107. In a series of programmes presented at the Ritz-Carlton, young ladies and gentlemen can learn the 'genteel arts of poise, confidence and grace in social situations'. 13- to 15-year-olds learn social conversation and behaviour, skin and nail care, diction and wardrobe planning; 13- to 17-year-olds graduate to the decorum of the dinner party – proper table manners, polite conversation, appropriate use of utensils and 'the gentle management of special foods that require additional grace'. Not for them the Dilemma of the Quail's Egg.

society in the country. Orchestral and choral pieces by various composers (not just H & H).

🐟 TANGLEWOOD FESTIVAL OF CONTEMPORARY MUSIC, Tanglewood, Lenox, MA 01240 ☎ (617) 266 1492; July/Aug ☎ (413) 637 1600
The BSO's summer abode, where you can hear old and modern classical music, from Mozart and Tchaikovsky to Copland and Knussen. Frequent guest artists include James Galway, John Williams, Jessye Norman and Midori. No 1 in America for ANDRE PREVIN: *"The ideal musical atmosphere because it divides right down the middle between the world's great professionals and the world's top-rank students, so that you have an atmosphere of learning and teaching – plus all the concerts. I just don't know of a more remarkable atmosphere."*

——— *Restaurants* ———

See also Hotels.

🐟 AUJOURD'HUI, Four Seasons Hotel, 200 Boylston St, MA 02116 ☎ (617) 338 4400
Under chef Mark Baker, this deluxe dining room continues to wow Bostonians. French-rooted cuisine using local produce and Oriental spices.

BIBA, 272 Boylston St, MA 02216 ☎ (617) 426 5684
One of the hottest places in town, run by Lydia Shire, protégée of Jasper White, and something of a law unto herself. Inventive, eclectic American nosh of the first order.

🐟 JASPER'S, 240 Commercial St, MA 02109 ☎ (617) 523 1126
The best restaurant in Boston. Chef-owner Jasper White, now a prominent culinary star, has injected verve and excitement into New England food (which to New Englanders is a feat in itself). Upscale inventive dining, from pan-roasted lobster with chervil and chives to the renowned New England boiled dinner – corned beef with fresh horseradish and mustard pickles.

LEGAL SEA FOODS, 35 Columbus Ave, MA 02116 ☎ (617) 426 4444
One of a chain whose catch phrase is 'if it ain't fresh, it ain't legal'. Always packed, always a long wait, but always worth it. *"A people's fish café. The food is very fresh and beautifully done"* – CLARE FERGUSON.

🐟 LE MARQUIS DE LAFAYETTE, 1 Ave de Lafayette, MA 02150 ☎ (617) 451 2600
The best French restaurant in Boston, the elegantly chandeliered American outpost of French chef Louis Outhier (who acts as consultant and sends his protégés over to spread the word). Seasonal menu.

SEASONS, Bostonian Hotel, 1 Faneuil Hall, MA 02101 ☎ (617) 523 4119
One of the very best in town, an outstanding American rooftop diner with a seasonal menu – caraway venison with wood mushrooms and cheddar, roast chunk tuna with peppers and juniper, grilled lobster with charred onions in romescu sauce.

798 MAIN, 798 Main St, Cambridge, MA 02139 ☎ (617) 492 9500
Panache has had a name-change but remains a zippy bistro under chef-owner Bruce Frankel. Creative, hearty menu – New England clam chowder, a mean mako shark with apple cider vinaigrette, venison chilli, wild mushroom stew, maple-barbecued baby chicken with white corn bread. Fine wine list, including best local wines.

——— *Shopping* ———

The best shopping areas for high fashion and hip boutiques are **Newbury St, Boylston St** in the Back Bay, ye olde **Beacon Hill** (cobbles and gaslights galore); and **Harvard Square** and **Brattle St** in Cambridge.

CHARLES SUMNER, 16 Newbury St, MA 02116 ☎ (617) 536 6225
Bijou department store in the Bergdorf's mould. Valentino boutique, Donna Karan clothes and shoes, plus more footwear by Ferragamo, Jourdan and Saint Laurent.

FILENE'S, 426 Washington St, MA 02101 ☎ (617) 357 2698
The knock-down to beat all knock-downs – designer garb at bargain prices, from Dior jackets

to Ferragamo shoes. Turnover is swift and prices are repeatedly slashed to keep it that way.

SARA FREDERICKS, Copley Place, MA 02116 ☎ (617) 536 8766
High-class clothes for the carriage trade. Good, old-fashioned service (a team to fit and alter) with a rather more go-ahead image (oozing with Beene, Blass, Lagerfeld, Valentino and Ungaro). 3 more stores in New York, Palm Beach and Sarasota.

Theatre

AMERICAN REPERTORY THEATRE, Loeb Drama Center, 64 Brattle St, Cambridge, MA 02138 ☎ (617) 547 8300
A lively company that performs classic and contemporary drama. They have premièred works that have gone on to wow Broadway.

CHICAGO

Art and museums

🐟 THE ART INSTITUTE OF CHICAGO, Michigan Ave at Adams St, IL 60603 ☎ (312) 443 3624
One of the best national art museums in the USA. *"There are a great many beautiful galleries, but I think the ones I enjoy the most in America are this and MOMA"* – ANDRE PREVIN. A collection of almost 200,000 works, covering European painting from the Middle Ages to 1900 (a fine set of French Impressionist works), Oriental and classical art, photographs, architectural draw-

---

Turndown Treats

🐟

You're a guest in one of the world's best hotels. It's time to turn in. You pad towards the bed. Can you deny that tremor of anticipation as you look to see what little bedtime treat lies in store? Here's a rundown of the best pillow booty: at the **Mansion on Turtle Creek**, Dallas, home-made chocs, 'imported water', and the next day's weather forecast (knowing whether it's to be 'hot' or 'very hot' should take the stress out of choosing tomorrow's wardrobe). At the **Mayfair Regent**, Chicago, Marshall Field's fabuloso Frango Mints. At the **Oriental**, Bangkok, a chocolate truffle so moreish that guests raid the trolley for more.

---

ings and textiles. The $23 million Rice Building adds one-third more space for European decorative arts and sculpture, 17C-19C American arts and 20C American painting and sculpture. Important exhibitions such as Poussin to Matisse, part of a cultural exchange with the USSR.

Bars and cafés

POPS FOR CHAMPAGNE, 2934 N Sheffield St, IL 60657 ☎ (312) 472 1000
Champagne bar on the far reaches of Chicago, in an area where you would least expect to find nightlife. *"When people finish dinner they say 'Well, where do we go now?' And where they go is Pops. It's a special place, with live jazz and about 100 champagnes – by the glass, by the bottle. The charm of it is the informality"* – IRVING SMITH KOGAN.

Clubs

BAJA BEACH CLUB, 401 E Illinois, IL 60611 ☎ (312) 222 1992
Yuppie restaurant/nightclub/game emporium with state-of-the-art sound, light and video shows, games room and piano bar.

ESOTERIA, 2247 N Lincoln Ave, IL 60614 ☎ (312) 549 4110
Hot nightclub, whose front bar has been described as 'a throwback to Michelangelo with an 80s twist', while the dance room is pure Brazilia. Up-to-the-second dance music and videos.

KINGSTON MINES, 2548 N Halsted, IL 60631 ☎ (312) 477 4646
No 1 stop for authentic Chicago blues fans. Get your teeth into acts like Carlos Johnson, Sugar Blue, the Casey Jones Band, Zora Young, plus a pizza or a corn dog.

SECOND CITY, 1616 N Wells, IL 60610 ☎ (312) 337 3992
The place for comedy – stand-up comics, stage revues and shows. Where Gilda Radner, Dan Aykroyd and John Belushi kicked off.

Hotels

THE DRAKE, 140 E Walton Place, IL 60611 ☎ (312) 787 2200
"Surely one of the finest hotels in America. I think it's underrated, an old-fashioned classic" – BOB PAYTON. The British royal family agree. Great lake views and a recent renovation keep it on top. *"Richly decorated, fabulous rooms... wonderful view,"* confirms ELISE PASCOE.

🐟 FOUR SEASONS, 120 E Delaware Place, IL 60611 ☎ (312) 280 8800
A high point of hoteldom – rooms occupy floors 30 to 46 of one of Chicago's most striking skyscrapers (though the hotel lobby is on the 7th

floor). *"Absolutely wonderful, couldn't have looked after us better"* – ANDREW LLOYD WEBBER. *"Indescribable. There is more marble in that hotel than I've seen in all of Italy"* – BOB PAYTON.

LE MERIDIEN CHICAGO AT 21 EAST KEMPINSKI, 21 E Bellevue Place, IL 60611 ☎ (312) 266 2100
The hippest thing to hit Chicago, all granite and matt black, young trendy staff, and a mix of CDs and videos to end all thoughts of sleep. John Malkovich, La Toya Jackson and Harrison Ford check in. **Café 21** is *the* place for creative American cuisine.

MAYFAIR REGENT, 181 E Lake Shore Drive, IL 60611 ☎ (312) 787 8500
At the best address in town, with scintillating views over sandy-shored Lake Michigan. Billed as European-style, it's actually US eclectic – a Chinese mural here, a classical frieze there, a touch of Queen Anne elsewhere. Top-notch, friendly service. Elevated locals dine à la française at the penthouse **Le Ciel Bleu**.

⚓ RITZ-CARLTON, 160 E Pearson St at Water Tower Place, IL 60611 ☎ (312) 266 1000
Confusingly a Four Seasons hotel, this occupies floors 10 to 31 of the incredible 74-storey Water Tower Place complex of shops, restaurants and cinemas. **The Carlton Club** is for chic private dining, with a health spa, indoor pool and sun terrace. You can take the pampered pet, who can board in luxury kennels. Votes from STANLEY MARCUS (*"the best thing is its location"*) and MARK MCCORMACK. The sumptuous **Dining Room** serves impeccable French cuisine.

Music

CHICAGO OPERA THEATER, 20 E Jackson Blvd, IL 60604 ☎ (312) 663 0555
Contemporary and trad opera sung in English. Known for visually exciting theatre (eg the fantasy opera *Where the Wild Things Are*, with set and costumes by Maurice Sendak).

⚓ CHICAGO SYMPHONY ORCHESTRA, Orchestral Hall, 220 S Michigan Ave, IL 60604 ☎ (312) 435 8122
Celebrating its centenary this year, this orchestra is one of the best in the States, under the new directorship of Daniel Barenboim (who succeeds the great Sir Georg Solti). Or, in the words of BOB PAYTON, *"the best, no doubt about that"*.

⚓ LYRIC OPERA OF CHICAGO, 20 N Wacker Drive, IL 60606 ☎ (312) 332 2244
Widely regarded as the best opera company in America. *"It's extremely well run. They have a very remarkable general director, Ardis Krainik – she's as tough as old boots and very, very, very good"* – RODNEY MILNES. Some 8 operas in the Sept-Feb season, with English surtitles.

Restaurants

See also Hotels.

AMBRIA, 2300 N Lincoln Park W, IL 60614 ☎ (312) 472 5959
"The most elegant and stylish restaurant in town. Very plugged-in food" – ELISE PASCOE. Nouvellish French cuisine with a daily-changing menu and catch-of-the-day fish and seafood. Art deco setting.

CHARLIE TROTTER'S, 816 W Armitage St, IL 60614 ☎ (312) 248 6228
Viennese-style restaurant with a granite bar and a wine rack extending to the ceiling. Eclectic menu – French twisted with American with hints of Asia.

Payton Praise

BOB PAYTON lassoes his personal bests. "In Chicago, the best **barbecue ribs** are still at **Carson's**, 612 N Wells…The best **steakhouse** in America is still **Mortons**, 1050 N State St [for hulking slabs of prime beef]…The best **pizza** is at **Due's**, 619 N Wabash…The best **steak and cheese** is at the **Billy Goat**, 430 N Michigan Drive (still the best down and dirty café in the universe)…**Ed Debevic's**, 640 N Wells, is *the* ultimate diner in the whole world… The best **potato chips** in America are **Eagle Brand Hawaiian Kettle** …The best **popcorn** is **Popeye White Kernel** (I always get down to the nitty gritty, don't I?)…The best **hamburger** is at **Jackson Hole Wyoming**, 232 E 64th St, New York…and the best **frogs' legs** are at **Phil Schmidt's**, 1205 N Calmut Ave, Hammond, Indiana…"

THE EVEREST ROOM, 40th Fl, 440 S La Salle, IL 60605 ☎ (312) 663 8920
Outstanding French restaurant for serious power dining, with great views over West Chicago. Fresh, light cuisine from Alsace.

PIZZERIA UNO, 29 E Ohio St, IL 60611 ☎ (312) 321 1000
Traditional Chicago deep-dish pizzas – *the* one is deep-dish with sausage.

SHAW'S CRAB HOUSE, 21 E Hubbard St, IL 60611 ☎ (312) 527 2722
Fresh fish and seafood restaurant with occasional jazz trios playing.

The Inn Thing

As boutique hotels are to cities, inns are to the country – done-up, individual little home-from-homes with the accent on personal attention. *"The book 'America's Wonderful Little Hotels' is getting fatter all the time; not because they are lowering their standards, but because there are more and more people, mainly amateurs, who are creating upmarket guest houses that they call 'inns'"* – HILARY RUBINSTEIN. According to our inn-house expert EDWARD CARTER, **The Inn at Little Washington** (see listing) gets it all right, while others get it all wrong. *"A certain inn may be a highly touted place ... but who wants black and white marbleized corridors in Nantucket? You want wainscoting. You don't want mass-produced carved swans from Melrose Avenue in LA, or rooms that were small to start with and then because they didn't have enough bathrooms they built them inside the room as a sort of add-on feature. On the other hand, one of the most attractive places in the area is* **The Summer House**, *Siasconset* ☎ *(508) 257 9976, a little cluster of rose-covered – literally covered – cottages and a lovely swimming pool right on the ocean. The* **Charlotte Inn**, *27 S Summer St, Edgartown, Martha's Vineyard* ☎ *(508) 627 4751, has, perhaps, the most attractive rooms in an American inn – they've been done so well you wouldn't think they were done at all."* And therein lies the secret ...

Shopping

The Magnificent Mile, stretching along **Michigan Ave** from Wacker to Oak, is a browser's dream – gaze into Bloomingdale's, Lord & Taylor, Chanel, I Magnin and Hammacher Schlemmer; turn into **Oak St** for more international labels such as Armani. The best shopping mall is **Watertower Place**.

MARSHALL FIELD, 111 N State St, IL 60602 ☎ (312) 781 5000
The best department store in town. All the top designers – Lacroix, Rykiel, Dior, Lauren, Karan, Klein – plus their own sporty/exec line, Field Manor. Also bedding, china, crystal, furniture and food, including their famous Frangos in mouth-watering mint, raspberry ... or peanut butter.

STANLEY KORSHAK, 940 N Michigan Ave, IL 60611 ☎ (312) 280 0520
A Chicago institution that blossomed from a couture house and still carries the all-American stylebusters, de la Renta, Blass, Klein, Kors. Also Krizia and Steiger (shoe) boutiques, Genny, Basile and Cerruti.

ULTIMO, 114 E Oak St, IL 60611 ☎ (312) 787 0906
The upmarket designer hunting ground for fashion-conscious men and women. Not only their own Sonia Rykiel boutique at 106 E Oak and Armani at 113 E Oak, but the best of Ungaro, Valentino, Gigli, Ferre, Gaultier, Mugler, Alaïa, the Jap big 3, and the stylewise US boys such as Mizrahi.

DALLAS

Art and museums

DALLAS MUSEUM OF ART, 1717 N Harwood, TX 75201 ☎ (214) 922 1200
"A new and beautiful building – they have re-created Wendy Reves's Mediterranean villa with all the original contents. Also impressive collections of Pre-Columbian, South Pacific and modern art" – CAROLINE HUNT. *"A very exciting place under the direction of Rick Brettell, who has breathed new life into it"* – STANLEY MARCUS. Special shows too.

KIMBELL ART MUSEUM, 3333 Camp Bowie Blvd, Fort Worth, TX 76107 ☎ (817) 332 8451
Looking less like an art gallery than a series of farm sheds, the Kimbell is acclaimed for its classical modern design by Louis Kahn. With some $8 million a year at its disposal, it is the second richest museum in the land after the Getty. Mainly European and some Oriental art. Exhibitions from great collections, eg Windsor Castle, the Thyssen Collection.

Clubs

Deep Ellum (that's Elm with a Texas drawl, y'all) is the hip downtown area around Main St, Elm St and Commerce St. Originally the Bohemian blues area, it's now being gentrified with shops, galleries, restaurants, and nightclubs (eg **Club Clearview** on Elm).

BILLY BOB'S TEXAS, 2520 Rodeo Plaza, Fort Worth, TX 76106 ☎ (817) 624 7117
The world's largest country 'n' western club. Live music by the greats, and bullriding on Fri and Sat.

DALLAS ALLEY, Market at Monger, TX 75202 ☎ (214) 988 0581
An incredible 9-nightclub complex in 2 restored buildings in the West End historic district. Go full-tilt for **Tilt** – a games room; **Alley Cats** – duelling piano bar; **Alley Oops** – sports bar with TVs and pool; **Take 5** – dance room with live music; **Foggy Bottoms** – R&B, blues, jazz; **Bobby Sox** – 50s and 60s music; **Backstage** – quiet bar; **Plaza Bar** – country 'n' western bar; the **Boiler Room** – a massive techno-pop disco.

Hotels

HOTEL CRESCENT COURT, 400 Crescent Ct, TX 75201 ☎ (214) 871 3200
The executive stopover, centrepiece of The Crescent shopping mall and part of the Rosewood fold. Here you're not at the mercy of the air-con – windows actually *open*. Great dining at the **Beau Nash**, billed as 'restaurant as theatre'. A dozen chefs, working in an open kitchen (shades of consultant Wolfgang Puck) produce seasonal/Mediterranean/northern Italian/southwestern cuisine – lots of char-grilling, pizzas, calzone, home-baked breads.

Pei Check

I M Pei's latest essay in modernist monumentality is the **Morton H Meyerson Symphony Center**, 2301 Flora, TX 75201 ☎ (214) 954 1700, a firm move to put Dallas on the international cultural map. At $106 million, the sleek geometric limestone and glass structure cost double the original budget, and the original 2-year building plan stretched to 9. It appears to be worth it. *"One of the most extraordinary buildings of the 20C. It's very exciting for both the architecture and the acoustics ...one of the great symphony halls in the world"* – STANLEY MARCUS. Pei worked alongside acoustician Russell Johnson on the hall itself; credos clashed and resignations wavered, but an entente was reached. The result is a room of uncharacteristic warmth and intimacy – wood panelling, terracotta terrazzo floor and a trompe-l'oeil dome. Home to the Dallas Symphony Orchestra.

MANSION ON TURTLE CREEK, 2821 Turtle Creek Blvd, TX 75219 ☎ (214) 559 2100
The blueprint of Caroline Hunt's Rosewood Hotels, it wins ever more accolades each year (*"she is the shrewdest woman hotelier in the US"* – ELISE PASCOE). Cleverly converted 1925 Italian Renaissance-style mansion with domes, arcades, marble floors and leaded windows, plus an adjacent tower of guest rooms. More than 2 staff per guest. *"A small intimate hotel, beautifully decorated. The ambience is probably one of the most positive that I know of"* – STANLEY MARCUS. He also rates highly the superb **restaurant** ☎ (214) 526 2121 where pioneering chef Dean Fearing *"is doing great food,"* says ELISE. WOLFGANG PUCK seconds that. Adventurous and accomplished New American/southwestern cuisine, and a crème brûlée like duchesse satin.

Restaurants

ACTUELLE, 2800 Routh St, TX 75201 ☎ (214) 855 0440
Top-quality restaurant in a glass-enclosed pavilion with a muted colour scheme. New American cuisine with ethnic influences – grilled black bass with tomatillo sauce, Texas pheasant with wild mushroom strüdel, fresh fruit cobbler with rum-spiked whipped cream, lemon-lime tart and raspberry sauce.

ADOLPHUS HOTEL, 1321 Commerce St, TX 75202 ☎ (214) 742 8200
The elegantly muralled French Room, with its Venetian chandeliers and Louis XIV chairs, is, according to STANLEY MARCUS, a *"fine café with extraordinarily good food"*. Fixed-price menu for wild game terrines, salmon, stuffed quail, lobster.

THE RIVIERA, 7709 Inwood Rd, TX 75209 ☎ (214) 351 0094
Romantic restaurant of the candlelit variety, for seasonal Continental cuisine with hints of the Med. Gnocchi tart, escargots and tortelloni, garlicky rack of lamb, Norwegian salmon with sea scallops.

ROUTH STREET CAFE, 3005 Routh St, TX 75201 ☎ (214) 871 7161
True American foodie stuff, with a prix-fixé menu that changes daily. *"One of the best restaurants in the country. Original cuisine, based on southwestern condiments and flavouring. Very creative, it gives you a new experience in eating"* – STANLEY MARCUS. *"Stephan Pyle's food is fabulous. It's my favourite restaurant in Dallas"* – ELISE PASCOE. Its progeny, **Baby Routh**, 2708 Routh St ☎ (214) 871 2345, continues in the same vein, playing to a younger, noisier bunch. Howsabout a grilled prawn and apple-smoked bacon club sandwich followed by pumpkin-ginger crème brûlée with snickerdoodle cookies?

Shopping

The Crescent is the most stupendous and exclusive mall, with **The Galleria** hot on its heels for serious spenders.

THE GAZEBO, 8300 Preston Rd, TX 75225 ☎ (214) 373 6661
Where to get kitted out in designer wear from head to toe. Over 150 names include Karan, Kors, Genny and Ozbek. They call you to let you know when a suitable little something has come in, and they hold frequent 'trunk' shows where designers show their entire collection at the store, so customers can buy from them direct.

LADY PRIMROSE'S SHOPPING ENGLISH COUNTRYSIDE, 2200 Cedar Springs, TX 75201 ☎ (214) 871 8333
An experience not to be missed (unless you're English, in which case it'll bring a lump to your throat): antique furniture and decorative little bits and pieces have been whisked from the manors and cottages of England to...a street of thatched cottages and a Baronial Hall in Dallas. Fall for Lady P's own line of foodie fare; dig into tea with scones and clotted cream. Also **Shopping Texas Country Style**, for silver buckles, decoy ducks and other handcrafted Texana.

LOU LATTIMORE, 4320 Lovers Lane, TX 75225 ☎ (214) 369 8585
Where lovers of the latest and greatest looks wander, to buy Saint Laurent Rive Gauche, Mugler, Lolita Lempicka, Lacroix, Moschino, Ferré, plus Shoes...Walter Steiger (his bootique) and Carla Francis Gems & Jewelry.

NEIMAN MARCUS, 1618 Main St, TX 75201 ☎ (214) 741 6911
The world-famous store continues to bedazzle its Christmas clientele with indispensable little trinkets. What would you do without your his 'n' hers Texas-reared ponies complete with hand-tooled saddles ashine with silver conchos and gold detailing? Or your $1,800 glass-bottomed boat for two? Diamonds are standard stocking-fillers, furs a mere bagatelle (slink into a lynx for $150,000). Designer collections feature all the top Euro and home-grown talents.

HAWAII

Hotels

COLONY SURF HOTEL, 2895 Kalakaua Ave, Honolulu, HI 96815 ☎ (808) 923 5751
Set on the beach at the foot of Diamond Head, a dormant volcano. Overlook décor (a blend of pastel, bamboo and multi-patterned kitsch) and head to **Michel's** restaurant (voted the most romantic in America), an "*elegant French res-*

"*Maui is the prettiest island in the world. What is extraordinary is that one side is desert and the other is jungle, yet it's terribly small. One of the most incredible experiences I've ever had was a helicopter ride over the volcano* "**

 LORD LICHFIELD

taurant; during the day quiet and relaxing, at night romantic – you look out on to the Pacific" – MARIE HELVIN. Best accommodation: at their adjacent **Colony East** hotel, the Penthouse East, an apartment with balcony on 3 sides.

🏆 HALEKULANI, 2199 Kalia Rd, Honolulu, HI 96815 ☎ (808) 923 2311
If Halekulani ('house befitting heaven') means a spectacularly sky blue and dazzling white setting on Waikiki Beach, this hotel is well named. Here, holiday resort (large balconies, vast pool, beach sports) meets business-class (3 phones per room). A big hotel with the taste and service of a small one. Bette Midler stays.

HOTEL HANA-MAUI, Maui, HI 96713 ☎ (808) 248 8211
A Rosewood resort hotel with 66 bungalows sprinkled around 4,500 acres of ranch land.

Helvin on Hawaii

🏆

"*I have always held the belief that Hawaii is a place with special qualities and powers. The best scenic drives are on Kalanianiole Highway, Oahu, from Hanauma Bay to the North Shore, with the Koolau Mountains on one side; and the drive above Maalea Bay, Maui, to see the humpback whales arrive in November from Alaska and the Arctic to give birth.*

"*In Honolulu,* **Keo's**, *625 Capahulu Ave* ☎ *(808) 737 8240, is the most famous Thai restaurant in Hawaii, and* **Ray's**, *2250 Kalakaua Ave* ☎ *(808) 923 5717, the most famous chef – and the best! The best beauty treatment is at* **Les Beaux**, *Waikiki Parkway, 1660 Kalakaua Ave* ☎ *(808) 941 0325, where Candi Arita does the most incredible herbal facials and Jean does the body exfoliation using fresh aloe vera and Hawaiian rock salt. 1½ hours of total bliss*" – MARIE HELVIN.

Riding, hiking, biking, surfing, kayaking, jeep adventures, and cook-outs on the beach. Unsurprisingly, CAROLINE HUNT likes it: *"It's unusual, very small, one of the few places where the old Hawaii life still exists. It has the most beautiful beach [Hamoa] in the Pacific."* Best suites: the Sea Ranch Cottages, with spectacular views.

🏊 **KAHALA HILTON, 5000 Kahala Ave, Honolulu, HI 96816 ☎ (808) 734 2211**
Tip-top beachside hotel with its own dolphin lagoon and superlative rooms, dining, sports and entertainment.

MAUNA KEA BEACH HOTEL, 19 Queen Kaahumanu Highway, Kohala Coast, HI 96743 ☎ (808) 882 7552
On a vast stretch of unspoilt coastline beneath Mauna Kea, the highest volcano in the world, this superb resort boasts a velvety smooth Trent Jones golf course, 13 tennis courts and a fitness centre. Décor benefits from the Rockefeller collection of art from the Pacific Rim.

MAUNA LANI BAY, Kohala Coast, HI 96743 ☎ (808) 885 6622
The consummate resort, with lagoons, pools, acres of verdant land and white beaches, an oceanside golf course built on lava, 10 ace tennis courts and activities galore.

HOUSTON

— Art and museums —

THE MENIL COLLECTION, 1511 Branard, TX 77006 ☎ (713) 525 9400
Renzo (Centre Pompidou) Piano's low-key structure houses Dominique de Menil's $150 million private art collection of about 10,000 pieces – antiquities, Byzantine and Mediterranean art, tribal art and modern art, including Picasso, Ernst, Warhol and numerous Magrittes.

— Ballet —

HOUSTON BALLET FOUNDATION, 1921 W Bell, TX 77019 ☎ (713) 523 6300
One of the best regional companies in the States. The Royal Ballet-trained director Ben Stevenson, choreographer Christopher Bruce and artistic associate Kenneth MacMillan make sure it is not just another New York/Ballanchine clone. A fount of dancers from their own school plus international talent, backed by B-I-G Texan funding. Performances at the Wortham.

— Hotels —

🏊 **RITZ-CARLTON, 1919 Briars Oak Lane, TX 77027 ☎ (713) 840 7600**
A new face for the Remington on Post Oak Park,

but still the same impeccable surroundings and service. *"I was really impressed. It has a peculiar Englishness about it – very well-decorated rooms. It also has a very good American steakhouse. I'm not a great meat eater but sometimes there is nothing like a great American steak"* – LORD LICHFIELD. This and the Bel-Air are *"the only ones in America I look forward to going to"* – FRANK LOWE.

— Music —

WORTHAM THEATER CENTER, 510 Preston Ave, TX 77002 ☎ (713) 237 1439
Slick home to the highly regarded Houston Grand Opera and Houston Ballet Foundation. 2 theatres – the Brown and the Cullen. Also symphonic and pop concerts.

— Restaurants —

CADILLAC BAR, 1802 Shepherd St, TX 77007 ☎ (713) 862 2020
A great bar/diner aswamp with Spaghetti Western extras. Forget chicken-in-a-basket – here you get fantastic mesquite-barbecued quail, replenished as fast as you can tuck them in, swilled down by beer and margaritas.

— Shopping —

THE GALLERIA, 5075 Westheimer, TX 77056 ☎ (713) 621 1907
The most exclusive shopping mall, complete with the ubiquitous ice rink and nearly 300 well-heeled boutiques and stores – Lord & Taylor, Gucci, Macy's, Neiman Marcus, Tiffany, Marshall Field.

STELZIG'S, 3123 Post Oak Blvd, TX 77056 ☎ (713) 629 7779
The Stelzig family's store has been running for 120 years, selling saddles, harnesses, exotic boots (python belly, backcut boa, kangaroo, ostrich, iguana...) – the whole ranching/riding scene. *"A wonderful Western store for cowboy boots and hats, and the world shoeshine champion, TC, who will have your boots looking like glass in 15 minutes. Absolute perfection. People send in their boots from all over the world"* – LORD LICHFIELD. Michael Jackson sports a 5-in high silver and jade Stelzig's buckle emblazoned with a golden J.

— Theatre —

ALLEY THEATER, 615 Texas Ave, TX 77002 ☎ (713) 228 9341
Classic, modern classic and some new plays. The theatre's international Alley Award, presented to a person outstanding in theatre or the arts, continues to cause waves of interest in dramatic circles.

Hail Caesar

'I, Caesar, bid you welcome to my Palace of Pleasure,' says the brochure for **Caesars Palace**, 3570 Las Vegas Blvd, Las Vegas ☎ (702) 731 7222. You get the idea. This is fantasyland on the classical Roman scale, with 1,668 rooms and suites, 2 pools, a mass of marble statuary, giant stage, sports arena (top boxing events), 3 casinos, a domed Omnimax cinema and a $2.5 million mini-city of ancient Rome. *"Totally miraculous. I had an enormous circular bath that I could have done lengths in, but...it took an hour to fill"* – STEPHEN JONES. Now lend your ears to

SIMON WILLIAMS: *"My least favourite hotel in the whole world. Downstairs it's like Armageddon, the size of Wembley Stadium with all this ozone-injected air to keep the poor gamblers awake and they do nothing but just scandalously waste money, great pots of it. The bed, I mean I like a good big bed, but one the size of a small football pitch is just too big...you don't know where you are in it. Instead of a bath I had a Jacuzzi, which has terrible jets of water squirting you in unspeakable places. They also have no clocks, so you can't tell what time it is. I hated Las Vegas."*

LOS ANGELES

—— *Art and museums* ——

CALIFORNIA MUSEUM OF SCIENCE AND INDUSTRY, 700 State Drive, Exposition Park, CA 90037 ☎ (213) 744 7400
The scientifically illiterate should hotfoot it here. Participation exhibits include the latest in cinemagic, earthquakes, air and space, electronic media, health (check out your own) and the environment. Lots of exhibitions, its own theatre group, Science on Stage, and a vast Imax screen (progs ☎ (213) 744 2014).

J PAUL GETTY MUSEUM, 17985 Pacific Coast Highway, Malibu, CA 90265 ☎ (213) 459 7611
Known worldwide for its incomparable wealth, the museum is strong on Greek and Roman antiquities, including the famous Getty bronze. Also European master drawings, sculptures and paintings; decorative works; photographs. Ever on the look-out for ways to spend its chunk of the $90 million-a-year Getty Trust, the museum shelled out a record $26.4 million on a Manet, *La Rue Mosnier*, and bought Van Gogh's *The Irises* for an undisclosed amount. In 1995, a second showcase will open in the hills of west LA, part of the new campus-like Getty Center designed by Richard Meier. Antiquities will remain at the present home, a peaceful classical villa. Visitors with cars must book ☎ (213) 458 2003.

🐾 LOS ANGELES COUNTY MUSEUM OF ART, 5905 Wilshire Blvd, CA 90036 ☎ (213) 857 6211
Like the citizens of California, LACMA is into rejuvenation programmes. Added to the new shiny structures that encase the original 1960s

blocks are the new Robert O Anderson building (devoted to 20C art) and the Japanese Pavilion (hundreds of screen and scroll paintings and netsuke). Fine collections of Indian and 18C-19C American works, plus earlier European art.

🐾 MUSEUM OF CONTEMPORARY ART, 250 S Grand Ave at California Plaza, CA 90012 ☎ (213) 621 2766
MOCA's exciting shows (Frank Stella, 50s furniture presented in room sets, funky automobiles) attract a well-heeled thirtysomething crowd with bundles of pose value. Classy rose sandstone building by Japanese architect Arata Isozaki, supplemented by Frank Gehry's **Temporary Contemporary**, 152 N Central Ave, CA 90013 (on a 50-year lease which takes us appropriately up to the year two-thousand-and-thirtysomething). Despite general acclaim, DUGGIE FIELDS was *"shocked at how bad Isozaki's building was. Absolutely dreadful."*

> **❝The LA art scene keeps growing and establishing itself more. It's very hip and brings in a lot of wealthy people. Environmentally, the galleries have fantastic light – so the whole feeling is wide open ❞**
>
>  STEVEN HENRY MADOFF

MUSEUM OF NEON ART, 704 Traction Ave, CA 90013 ☎ (213) 617 1580
Adazzle with neon, electric and kinetic art, MONA is the only permanent institution of its kind. Major exhibitions each year, showing works of contemporary artists. Also night-time tours to see the bright lights of LA.

NORTON SIMON MUSEUM OF ART, 411 W Colorado Blvd, Pasadena, CA 91105 ☎ (818) 449 6840
Arguably the finest collection of Old Masters on the West Coast (unhappily mostly behind 'denglas' to protect them from UV rays). Also Impressionists, Post-Imps and Asian sculpture. Artists wield the quill too – peruse recently acquired letters by Rubens, Matisse, Gauguin, Van Gogh....

Arts centres

LA COUNTY MUSIC CENTER, 135 N Grand Ave, CA 90012 ☎ (213) 972 7200
3 buildings connected by a plaza with a fountain. The Dorothy Chandler Pavilion is the most elaborate hall (huge chandeliers, lots of mirrors), where the LA Philharmonic plays and the Academy Awards Ceremony is habitually held. The Mark Taper Forum is an experimental theatre in the round: new plays, new directors. The Ahmanson Theater is the baby: musicals and small plays.

Bars and cafés

The trendiest, WASPiest shopping/snacking area is **Brentwood Mart**, 225 26th St, Santa Monica. A bijou farmers' market in an upscale part of town, it draws the likes of Randy Newman, Mickey Rourke, Meryl Streep, Dean Stockwell and Michael Keaton. See 'em browsing in the **Book Nook**, sipping cappuccinos outside the **Mart Coffee & Juice Bar** (the best in LA), or grabbing a take-away from **Reddi Chick**.

Deli-cious

The 2 old greats, **Nate 'n' Als**, 414 N Beverly Drive and **Art's Deli**, 12224 Ventura Blvd, Studio City, have to contend with 2 arrivals from New York. **Carnegie Deli** has been cloned at 300 N Beverly Drive, Beverly Hills, by multi-multi-millionaire Marvin Davis (he couldn't get by without his smoked salmon near to hand). The Carnegie's pastrami, corned beef and chicken soup is an institution. **Stage Deli**, Market Place, Century City Mall, is a fairly happening scene, with movie moguls buzzing in and out for their sarnis...an after-theatre hang-out. The sawdust-floored **Jerry's Famous Deli**, 12655 Ventura Blvd, is a hip young Valley haunt, open 24 hours a day.

CAFFE LATTE, 6254 Wilshire Blvd, CA 90048 ☎ (213) 936 5213
Delicious cappuccinos, using home-roasted coffee beans. Great lunch spot habituated by the likes of Michael Keaton.

GORKY'S CAFE & RUSSIAN BREWERY, 536 E 8th St, CA 90014 ☎ (213) 627 4060
Artsy, trendy, Bohemian pseudo-Russian café, open all night. Not only stuffed cabbage and other glasnostian delicacies, but cappuccinos, muffins and live music.

JAVA, 7286 Beverly Blvd, CA 90036 ☎ (213) 931 4943
A dark environment in which to loll on inviting couches, sip exotic coffees and nibble finger food.

PIK-ME-UP, 5437 W 6th St, CA 90036 ☎ (213) 939 9706
Hot place to get caffeined out till 3am in company with aspiring artists who lounge around on thrift-shop furniture. *"People go for coffee and minimal snacks. You see people sitting alone, reading books. It's very casual, very would-be Bohemian, very un-LA"* – DUGGIE FIELDS.

TRUMPS, 8764 Melrose Ave, CA 90069 ☎ (213) 855 1480
Despite great Pacific-Western cuisine (ELISE PASCOE sighs for a stunning Japanese-inspired salad she had there), this restaurant is used primarily by chic LA as an after-dinner bar. Ever-changing contemporary art sets the scene.

Clubs

PONANA SOUK, Speakeasy, 8531 Santa Monica Blvd, CA 90069 ☎ (213) 285 8200
Billed as the most elaborate club since the 40s glory nights, this one is Arabian Nights fantasyland. Downstairs goes somewhat awry with blackjack, rasta music and tropicana, but upstairs pulls out the Eastern stops – tenting, low tables, strewn cushions, belly dancers and a harem's worth of beautiful women, supplemented by the likes of Rod Stewart, Emilio Estevez and Rob Lowe. Thurs is cabaret night; Fri and Sat pure clubbing; Sun dinner.

RUBBER, 1026 S La Cienega Blvd, CA 90035 ☎ (213) 659 6467
Known as Mickey Rourke's club (he is an associate) or the Motorcycle Club, this nitery is not as fetishist as it sounds – it's actually rather civilized, with a VIP restaurant and expansive dance floor. Open Fri and Sat and for private parties (Madonna had her birthday hop here).

VERTIGO, 333 S Boylston St, CA 90069 ☎ (213) 747 4849
As fashionable as ever, Vertigo is now installed in a new metro-tech home, while a massive crowd wait nail-bitingly on the door for a nod of acceptance. Dine on nouvelle cuisine on Fri and Sat.

—— *Fashion designers* ——

BOB MACKIE, 8636 Melrose Ave, CA 90069
☎ **(213) 657 7377**
For spangles and sequins and showbiz pzazz, Mackie's still No 1. Cher grabs every opportunity to dazzle in his barely there stunners.

GALANOS ORIGINALS, 2254 S Sepulveda Blvd, CA 90064 ☎ **(213) 272 1445**
Beautifully handcrafted, impeccably finished, outrageously expensive outfits (a ready-to-wear dress could set you back $30,000). Dresses the thinnest of the thin – Nancy Reagan, Gloria Vanderbilt, Ann Getty. However, some feel that he's remained in his ivory tower too long, and has fizzled on original ideas.

LEON MAX, Max Studio, 2712 Main St, Santa Monica, CA 90405 ☎ **(213) 396 3963**
A young designer for disposable (or shall we say seasonal) clothing for the working girl and manful man. Trendy knits, relaxed weekend and active wear, wardrobe staples. Here are the Max facts: his aim is to take mediocrity and fetishism out of fashion, appealing to those who want to project 'purity, imagination and romanticism'.

NOLAN MILLER, 241 S Robertson Blvd, CA 90211 ☎ **(213) 655 7110**
Exclusive designer to Dynasty types. He of the uncompromising shoulders and the cleavage suit remains a hit with such old fans as JOAN COLLINS.

—————— *Film* ——————

Cinema-wise, **Fox Village**, Westwood, is *"the best for a big movie – the best speaker system, where they turn the sound up highest. A huge 30s auditorium"* – WILLIAM DAVIES. **Universal City 18 Cinemas**, Universal City Plaza, is the largest movie-theatre complex in the US, lavishly decorated in art deco style: *"The best complex in LA, like going into a cathedral – you can always get in and always park. Vast auditoria and a good spread of films"* – WD. After that it's **Cineplex Odeons** – there are 8 in LA, expensively kitted out with 10 to 18 screens, plus bars and restaurants.

OM/AFI WORLD FEST, American Film Institute, 2021 N Western Ave, CA 90027 ☎ **(213) 856 7707**
A mere fledgling festival, started in 1986, directed by Ken Wlaschin, ex-London Film Fest. International and non-competitive, its venue is the Cineplex Odeon Century Plaza Cinemas. Held at Oscar time around April, in order to nab the stars.

—————— *Hotels* ——————

🐾 **BEVERLY HILLS HOTEL, 9641 Sunset Blvd, Beverly Hills, CA 90210**
☎ **(213) 276 2251**
The 'Pink Palace', a magnificent Spanish villa in luscious lawnscape, legendary Hills landmark and hang-out of Hollywood heroes, from Clark Gable and Marlene Dietrich to Elizabeth Taylor and Tom Selleck. Despite wall-to-wall celebs, rooms are a little jaded (a refit is planned) and the **Polo Lounge** (erstwhile hot spot for le movie monde) is sometimes wickedly referred to as the Polio Lounge. It still serves a mean power breakfast, presided over by Bernice Philbin. ED VICTOR prefers the **Coffee Shop** in the basement: *"The short-order chef Gary makes the best breakfast in the world. The apotheosis of the American breakfast."* A hit with JEREMIAH TOWER and MARK MCCORMACK.

CHECKERS, 535 S Grand Ave, CA 90071 ☎ **(213) 624 0000**
This plushy new downtown pile wanted a 'spiffy, ready-for-the-nineties, clubby sort of name', and liked the associations with the British PM's country pad and Richard Nixon's dog. 500 tons of Italian marble were imported. Hooked yet? With such pulls as Belgian sheets, king-size down

🐾 **Buzzz** In Los Angeles, you judge a man by the jet from his hosepipe: **"How's your pressure?"** is a likely opening gambit, to which the answer should be, "Oh, we have great pressure where I live." Best area to ensure a **power shower**: Pacific Palisades 🐾 ...... Best **hotel sea view**: from the **Shangri-La**, 1301 Ocean Ave, Santa Monica, CA 90401 ☎ (213) 394 2791 (ship-shaped art decodom), over palm tree-lined Palisades Park to the ocean 🐾 ...... **Hip hideaways**: rock stars/trendy actors/models check in to the **Sunset Marquis** on Sunset Blvd (Peter Gabriel, *Breaking In* hero Casey Siemaszko) or **Le Dufy** on Westmount Drive, W Hollywood (PATRICIA HODGE and fellow British thespians). **Mondrian**, also on Sunset, thinks it's the ultimate in cool, but old LA hands give it the thumbs down (guests Sean Penn and Elvis Costello ought to know better). .... 🐾

pillows, pet pampering and openable windows, it's impressing the likes of Placido Domingo and violinist Midori. Big sister hotel is the renowned Campton Place in San Francisco. *"Pretty fabulous. A small hotel, extremely ritzy and quite wonderful"* – KEN HOM.

🐾 FOUR SEASONS, 300 S Doheny Drive at Burton Way, CA 90048 ☎ (213) 273 2222

The new in place to stay – it's gotta be, with such VIP devotees as President Bush, Meryl Streep and the Rolling Stones. On offer are 16 floors abundant with foliage, pool terrace with Jacuzzi, airline-ticketing, a 24-hour seamstress and a pledge of child-friendliness (the way to a thirty-something's heart). Robin Leach named it best in the US. *"A big contender in Beverly Hills"* – FRANK BOWLING.

🐾 HOTEL BEL-AIR, 701 Stone Canyon Rd, CA 90077 ☎ (213) 472 1211

Still in the very top league in the USA, this is one of the most influential addresses in town. Recently sold to a Japanese firm for a reputed $1 million a room, it remains under Rosewood management. An arcaded pink mission and terracotta-tiled villas, set in heavenly blossom-filled gardens, with no stinting on necessities like private outdoor Jacuzzis. Al fresco dining, fine Californian cuisine (stars who *don't* want to be seen dine here). *"Still the best"* – FRANK BOWLING. *"As gorgeous, friendly and California as you can get – a hideaway in that big teeming city. I have been returning to the swans and the bougainvillaea for 30 years"* – HELEN GURLEY BROWN. *"The only hotel in LA that I like. You don't really feel you're in a hotel – it's something rather more intimate"* – ROSS BENSON. *"I love it for its beauty and luxury, in an idyllic and peaceful setting away from the smog"* – ELISE PASCOE. *"I don't know any hotels in America which exceed the Bel-Air in quality of food, service and environment. Besides, it is very close by"* – WOLFGANG PUCK. More votes shower down from BARBARA TAYLOR BRADFORD, VISCOUNT HAMBLEDEN, TESSA DAHL, ANTON MOSIMANN, LORD MONTAGU OF BEAULIEU, FRANK LOWE and STANLEY MARCUS, while ANDREW LLOYD WEBBER adds this caveat: *"The best hotel you can stay in during the week and the worst at the weekend. In the week it is a really organized business hotel where nothing can go wrong. From Friday night till Monday morning, don't try to sleep because it's where everybody has their weddings, bar mitzvahs and coming-out parties."*

L'ERMITAGE, 9291 Burton Way, Beverly Hills, CA 90210 ☎ (213) 278 3344

The archetypal boutique hotel. Each suite has a sunken living room with blazing fire at the flick of a switch, original works of art and a delectable collection of freebies, including fresh strawberries, mineral water and wine. Roof garden with heated pool. Test out the multilingual front-office staff and gawp at the genuine Van Gogh and Renoir.

America's Best Hotels

🐾 THE REGENT BEVERLY WILSHIRE, 9500 Wilshire Blvd, Beverly Hills, CA 90212 ☎ (213) 275 5200

Renovated to the tune of $65 million, this historic Hollywood cache now boasts Hong Kong-style service complete with room attendants who hop to at the snap of a finger. Water pressure has been souped up, rooms enlarged, rare marble shipped in, and 1930s fittings (such as the bronze and crystal chandelier) restored. *"A very grand hotel, beautiful, very traditional. The most wonderful bathrooms I have ever seen in America"* – FRANK BOWLING. *"Improved a great deal – it*

Le Petit Ermitage

Post-nose-job paradise: Le Petit Ermitage, next to and part of L'Ermitage, is the place where celebs hot off the plastic surgeon's slab go for R&R, to see and *not* be seen. After checking into an exec suite at the big-sister hotel for a night of pre-op pampering, you are limo-whisked next morning to a local hospital (likely to sound more like a film studio) such as Cedars Sinai or Century City. Successfully remodelled, it's back to Le Petit E via the discreet underground entrance, lest anyone should suspect. Calls are screened, there's a 24-hour pharmaceutical service, spa cuisine, hair and make-up experts.

has become one of the best hotels" – LARRY KING. *"I like it – it's been made all flash. I was shown a room that was huge with a rose marble bath-room and they said this was one of their starter rooms – I thought it was a suite"* – PETER YORK. It scores with SHAKIRA CAINE and PETER STRING-FELLOW, but some locals feel it's lost its soul; Warren Beatty doesn't live here any more.

ST JAMES'S CLUB, 8358 Sunset Blvd, W Hollywood, CA 90069 ☎ (213) 654 7100
A members-only club/hotel that has carved its niche in chic LA life. Housed in the famous art deco Sunset Towers, it's like a ravishing 1930s film set. French/California cuisine at the **Members' Dining Room**, and a poolside terrace where filmy types drink in the view.

WESTWOOD MARQUIS HOTEL, 930 Hilgard Ave, CA 90024 ☎ (213) 208 8765
Famed for *"the best Sunday brunch on the West Coast"* – FREDERIC RAPHAEL, who rates the rooms too: *"An excellent hotel for people who don't own limousines – mind you that's a very small class."* Sensational afternoon teas – little sandwiches, home-baked scones with Devon-shire cream, butter cookies, a glass of sherry. Bob Hoskins and JEFFREY ARCHER stay.

Music

WILTERN THEATER, 3790 Wilshire Blvd, LA 90010 ☎ (213) 380 5005
A wonderful art deco music hall where you can hear everything from the Los Angeles Chamber Orchestra to Prince (though not simultaneously).

Restaurants

See also Hotels.

THE BISTRO GARDEN, 176 N Canon Drive, Beverly Hills, CA 90210 ☎ (213) 550 3900
A racier version of The Bistro (at No 246) where movie greats and Hollywood wives lunch in the Riviera-style garden. *"Still excellent"* – ROBERT SANGSTER. *"Don't miss the chicken quesadilla (the recipe supposedly cost thousands of dol-lars). It's heaven on a plate"* – ELISE PASCOE.

🐦 CHAMPAGNE, 10506 Little Santa Monica Blvd, CA 90025 ☎ (213) 470 8446
Elegant and refreshingly unstuffy French res-taurant with friendly staff, under sage chef Patrick Healy. Grilled salmon is their die-for dish, followed by a sigh-for vegetable plate and swoon-for desserts.

CHASEN'S, 9039 Beverly Blvd, CA 90048 ☎ (213) 271 2168
Impressive, expensive relic of the 30s, famous for its hobo steaks and chilli, consumed by Establishment wrinklies – fans Liz Taylor, ROBERT SANGSTER and MARK MCCORMACK are spring chickens compared to some of their fellow diners (James Stewart, Ron and Nance...).

CHAYA BRASSERIE, 8741 Alden Drive, CA 90048 ☎ (213) 859 8833
Incredibly in, incredibly good, incredibly LA. Designed by Grinstein-Daniels in slick Jap-French style, with knockout Jap-French cuisine to match. *"One of the most intensely art-directed interiors you'll ever see"* – WILLIAM DAVIES. Eddie Murphy is a fan. Check out the new branch at 110 Navy St, Venice ☎ (213) 396 1179.

🐦 CHINOIS ON MAIN, 2709 Main St, Santa Monica, CA 90405 ☎ (213) 392 9025
The Franco-Oriental brainchild of Wolfgang Puck, voted by many No 1 in LA. Exotic environ-ment created by Puck's wife Barbara Lazaroff. BIJAN goes for a fun atmos, DUDLEY MOORE goes for his pet dish, Mongolian lamb. *"If you're coming from abroad, book before you leave home and don't take anyone you want to talk to, because you'll never be heard. Just eat the most imaginative food and look at all the beautiful people!"* – ELISE PASCOE. *"Totally fashionable"* – ANDREW LLOYD WEBBER.

🐦 Buzzz Great locations: on winding mountainside, the timbered **Saddle Peak Lodge**, 419 Cold Canyon Rd, Calabasas ☎ (818) 340 6029 – for game and Sunday brunch; trendy **DC3**, Santa Monica Airport, 2800 Donald Douglas Loop North ☎ (213) 399 2323 – ordinary kitchen, but *what* a setting 🐦 ...... **Hidden location:** a little-known authentic French restaurant, with garden patio, **Café des Artistes**, 1534 N McCadden Place ☎ (213) 461 6889 🐦 ...... **Out-of-the-way location:** savour Chinois on Main flavours yet stay in pocket at **Café Jacoulet**, 91 N Raymond Ave, Pasadena ☎ (818) 796 2233; for LA's best cod salad, **Hal's**, 1349 W Washington Blvd, Venice ☎ (213) 396 3105, a low-decibel, high-art warehouse restaurant 🐦 ...... **Relocation:** formerly hidden and now more conspicu-ous, **Chez Helene**, 267 S Beverly Drive ☎ (213) 276 1558, for fine French-Canadian cuisine. . . . . 🐦

Joshua Wesson's Top 5 in LA

Locanda Veneta, 8638 W 3rd St ☎ (213) 274 1893 is "the best small Italian restaurant – a real Italian trattoria. **Chinois on Main**, my favourite in LA, defines the genre of French-Japanese-American cooking. **72 Market Street** is a wonderful restaurant, typically Venice. At **Matsuhisa**, 129 N La Cienega Blvd ☎ (213) 659 9639, the chef Nobu Matsuhisa is the king of raw and cooked fish. It is an anti-sushi bar – he invents sushi, he blows your mind. **Valentino** is the finest Italian restaurant in the city and in the country. The food is not *brilliant* but simply very good. The wine list is peerless."

🍴 **CITRUS, 6703 Melrose Ave, CA 90038 ☎ (213) 857 0034**
Chef-owner Michel Richard continues to wow LA with a combination of cool environment (reminiscent of a garage) and hot French-Californian cuisine – local shrimp and crab ravioli, terrine of endive and foie gras with brioche, and a good wine list. Open kitchen, dining on a patio (with canvas pull-over roof). *"Tremendous fun place, jolly good food, terrific California cooking"* – SERENA SUTCLIFFE.

CITY RESTAURANT, 180 S La Brea Ave, CA 90036 ☎ (213) 938 2155
The Madonna of LA restaurants – fun, good and satisfying (or so Los Angelinos say). Set in an airy space with rough cement walls and a high ceiling, it's one of the noisiest, hippest eateries in town. Modern, unusual dishes (Thai, Mexican, French, Indian...), artistic presentation (a different-coloured plate for each dish).

FENNEL, 1535 Ocean Ave, Santa Monica, CA 90401 ☎ (213) 394 2079
For sensational French cuisine – a rotation of 2-star Michelin chefs wing in to head the kitchen each month. Ever-changing menu.

🍴 **THE IVY, 113 N Robertson Blvd, CA 90048 ☎ (213) 274 8303**
One of the finest in town, set in a cottage with a picket fence. Masters of mesquite grilling with a menu rich in fish, chicken, veal and crab cakes, rounded off by some of the most divine desserts on the West Coast, and cappuccino in oversized hand-painted cups. Power lunchspot for producer Robert Shapiro and his wife Sandy, ED VICTOR, PETER STRINGFELLOW and KENNETH LANE (who also likes **Ivy at the Shore**, 1541 Ocean Ave, Santa Monica ☎ (213) 393 3113 *"for Sunday lunch, sitting outside. Californian cuisine with a little creole and Cajun spices. Very pleasant."*) At dinner, spot Tom Selleck, Michael Hutchence and Elton John.

KATSU, 1972 Hillhurst Ave, Los Feliz, CA 90027 ☎ (213) 665 1891
New Wave monochrome sushi bar, where SERENA SUTCLIFFE sampled *"the best Japanese meal of my life. The most unbelievable food. Frankly I think Katsu rivals the best in the world, let alone LA."* Your fish is the chef's command – just fill out the form. Katsu's progeny are **Café Katsu**, 2117 Sawtelle Ave (minimalist, stark; fab Franco-Jap nosh) and **Katsu 3rd**, 8636 W 3rd St (futuristic Pacific dining; no sign outside).

KOO KOO ROO, 83–93 Beverly Blvd, CA 90048 ☎ (213) 655 9045
"At last, a fast food restaurant that is a health food restaurant. The original skinless, charbroiled chicken with American herbs and spices" – VIDAL SASSOON. Take-away too.

LA SERRE, 12969 Ventura Blvd, Studio City, CA 91604 ☎ (818) 990 0500
The best in the Valley, beloved of LARRY KING and VIDAL SASSOON, who cuts along for *"a magnificent bouillabaisse"*.

LE CHARDONNAY, 8284 Melrose Ave, CA 90046 ☎ (213) 655 8880
Romantic, grown-up Parisian bistro setting and cuisine. *"A lovely restaurant with a brilliant menu and a fabulous wine list. Ask for the snail ravioli"* – ELISE PASCOE.

LE DOME, 8720 Sunset Blvd, CA 90069 ☎ (213) 659 6919
Ever-popular bar-bistro, recognized home of the power lunch (and also a good late-nighter as ANDREW LLOYD WEBBER notes). George Hamilton, Neil Simon, Julian Lennon, Jackie Collins, ROSS BENSON, PETER STRINGFELLOW, ROBERT SANGSTER (*"still excellent"*) and ED VICTOR: *"their food isn't world-beating, but it's very high quality...exquisite crab cakes. The location is fab and the clientele is everybody you want to run into. I like eating in the glassed-in terrace and watching everyone make their entrance."*

L'ORANGERIE, 903 N La Cienega Blvd, CA 90069 ☎ (213) 652 9770
A ravishing restaurant for superb International/French cuisine, with fish flown in from the Med. Dishes are sensational but portions small and prices off the wall. *"Unpretentious and wonderful,"* opines MICHAEL GRADE; *"very pretentious but quite beautiful décor and very good food,"* counters JEREMIAH TOWER.

MICHAEL'S, 1147 3rd St, Santa Monica, CA 90403 ☎ (213) 451 0843
The original Michael's (now in NY too), for M McCarty's ever-changing menu of New

Californian-cum-French cuisine. Some say he has peaked (note a slight reduction in the notoriously high prices). Weekend brunch is cheaper still and just as good.

MORTONS, 8800 Melrose Ave, CA 90069 ☎ (213) 276 5205
The place to see a galaxy of stars, such as Randy Newman, Chris (son of Jack) Lemmon, Catherine Oxenberg and Jackie Collins. Marinated and grilled meats, delectable puddings. Dinner only.

ORSO, 8706 W 3rd St, CA 90048 ☎ (213) 274 7144
A branch of the NY/London Orsos, in the guise of a North Italian villa, with a romantic, softly lit patio. One-off hand-painted pottery that you'd like left on the table for aesthetics; bread from heaven, and a great mixed salad. Not too expensive, either. *"Great thin pizzas and all Italian food"* – ROBERT SANGSTER.

PATINA, 5955 Melrose Ave, CA 90038 ☎ (213) 467 1108
The long-awaited return of intellectual chef Joachim Splichal (late of Max au Triangle). Surroundings are sophisticated but sterile, cuisine (nouvelle Californian/French) is spectacular.

ST ESTEPHE, 2640 N Sepulveda Blvd, Manhattan Beach, CA 90266 ☎ (213) 545 1334
A feast for sore eyes (if not for rumbling stomachs) – some of the best French/southwestern food in Los Angeles, cooked by John Sedler and presented in petite portions as a culinary art form.

Impenetrable Restaurants

The most fashionable restaurants in town have one thing in common: no one you know has ever been to them because they can't get near the premises. No but seriously, folks, these are the ones to line up for: **Maple Drive**, 345 N Maple Drive ☎ (213) 247 9800 where there's a waiting list to get a reservation. **Campanile**, 624 S Le Brea Ave ☎ (213) 938 1447, set up by Mark Peel (ex-Spago, Ma Maison) and his pastry-chef wife Nancy Silverton. **Authentic Café**, 7605 Beverly Blvd ☎ (213) 939 4626 – only 12 tables, BYO, no reservations (lines stretch around the block – you could wait an hour). Like a party if you get in. Eclectic taste (and texture) sensations such as *cactus*.

72 MARKET ST, 72 Market St, Venice, CA 90261 ☎ (213) 392 8720
Part-owned by DUDLEY MOORE and Liza Minnelli, this high-tech art setting is filled with picturesque celebs. Dud, who you may catch tinkling the ivories, loves the warm scallop salad, spinach salad, curried lentil soup with mint and yogurt, and the ubiquitous crab cakes.

SPAGO, 1114 Horn Ave, W Hollywood, CA 90069 ☎ (213) 652 4025
Wolfgang Puck's original nouvelle pizzeria, a long-running Hollywood hit for the likes of Jackie Collins, DUDLEY MOORE, Michael and SHAKIRA CAINE, BARRY HUMPHRIES, LARRY KING, BIJAN. *"I think it's wonderful. It hurls all these different tastes at you…Wolfgang Puck is blessed with that rarity – imagination. Every time you go, it's full of the heavy hitters of Tinseltown. Billy Wilder, Jane Seymour, Lee Radziwill were there last time I went"* – ROSS BENSON. *"Superb food and great atmosphere"* – VIDAL SASSOON. A tad too many Valley types have infiltrated, but it's a legend not to be missed.

VALENTINO, 3115 Pico Blvd, Santa Monica, CA 90405 ☎ (213) 829 4313
Since the revamp of Piero Selvaggio's Italian restaurant, some adore it, others find it cold and unoccupied. Cuisine, however, remains faultless – especially in the eyes of WOLFGANG PUCK and BARBARA KAFKA (*"for an elegant Italian meal, very creative"*). White truffles a speciality.

WEST BEACH CAFE, 60 N Venice Blvd, Venice, CA 90291 ☎ (213) 823 5396
Bruce Marder's restaurant (also owns DC3) draws young arty types off the beach to lap up fresh California cuisine and wonderful seafood. Exhibitions of contemporary paintings.

Shopping

Rodeo Drive is still the most famous drag in Beverly Hills – glossy, international, expensive and soulless. **Sunset Plaza** is the new sleek place to shop – at Gallay, Lisa Norman, Rosenthal Truitt, Joan Vass, Oliver Peoples. First get shop-shape at Sunset Plaza Fitness (regulars Dyan Cannon, Pia Zadora and Jamie Lee Curtis are old hands at Lotte Berk's jerks), then toddle off for a pedicure at the Yuki Salon, where Goro Uesugi kneads the tired pedal extremities of Jack Nicholson, Anjelica Huston and Michelle Phillips. The maxiest mall in LA is the **Beverly Center**, a glassy complex with 2 exterior escalators, 20 restaurants, 13 movie theatres and shops like Bullocks, Abercrombie & Fitch, Banana Republic. **Melrose** is still the beat of the young, zany crowd in LA, sons and daughters of the rich and famous. Designer boutiques like Ecru through Retail Slut (cult vendor of punk). **Montana Avenue** has a 'neighbourhood atmosphere' (ie you can walk along it); browse from trad (Lanz) to trendy (Savannah).

ECRU, 7428 Melrose Ave, CA 90046
☎ **(213) 653 8761**
Purveyors of European high fashion to an up-scale clientele. Dressy and avant-garde gear for girls (John Galliano, Sybilla, Dolce & Gabbana) and guys (Verri, Adolfo Dominguez).

FRANCES KLEIN, 310 N Rodeo Drive, Beverly Hills, CA 90210 ☎ (213) 273 0155
Prestigious bijou boîte for impressive antique jewellery. Spectacular estate pieces seduce Sly Stallone, DUDLEY MOORE and Elton John.

FREDERICK'S OF HOLLYWOOD, 6608 Hollywood Blvd, CA 90028 ☎ (213) 466 8506
This steamy lingerie shop is so much a Hollywood institution that they have opened a museum to present their tart chart hits since 1946 (peep-hole bras, peek-a-boo peignoir sets, slingback mules) and to salute lingerie-loving stars of stage and screen. Among offerings from Cher, Cybill Shepherd, Lana Turner, Judy Garland, Cyd Charisse and Tony Curtis, see Madonna's bustier from her world tour, Mae West's maribou peignoir and the very bra and pantie set that Zsa Zsa Gabor wore in *Lili*.

FRED HAYMAN, 273 N Rodeo Drive, Beverly Hills, CA 90210 ☎ (213) 271 3000
Since the selling of the name 'Giorgio' to Avon for $165 million, this society store has been expensively remodelled. International designer-dom still features highly, but Hayman's really an olfactory man. The new fragrance Hills wives can't be without is 273. Expect to bump in to Liz Taylor, Barbra Streisand, Diana Ross, Farrah Fawcett and other hirsute beauts.

FRED JOAILLIER, 401 N Rodeo Drive, Beverly Hills, CA 90210 ☎ (213) 278 3733
Zippy jewellery designs such as a diamond and ruby heart on a zipper, as worn by Fred fan Jackie Collins.

GALLAY, 8711 Sunset Blvd, W Hollywood, CA 90069 ☎ (213) 858 8711
'Beautiful clients, beautiful clothes – made for each other' is the Gallay philosophy. Only those with A1-certified bodies dare riffle through the Alaïas, Giglis and Kamalis. A suitably celebby clientele includes a toned-up Dyan Cannon.

California Clones

Image says it all in LA. We all knew that. But self-obsession starts younger and younger. Stylewise children are not averse to taunting and fighting each other in the playground over who's wearing what – so much so that one 'scrap' ended in *murder* and the body being stripped of its designer tennis shoes. Obsession doesn't stop at the label. Oh no, these schoolkids want neater noses, vacuumed thighs, flattened ears, stronger jaws. Adolescent girls demand Christie Brinkley's nose, Cher's cheeks and Kim Basinger's lips. So, if you get the feeling of déja vu when you next mosey down Melrose, you'll know why....

LINA LEE, 459 N Rodeo Drive, Beverly Hills, CA 90210 ☎ (213) 556 2678
Where Hollywood Wives swan in for the latest crème de la crème of famous and undiscovered French, Italian and American designer wear.

MAXFIELD, 8825 Melrose Ave, CA 90069 ☎ (213) 274 8800
One of the coolest stockpiles of designerdom on Melrose: Ozbek, Miyake, Mugler, Sybilla, Gigli, Byblos, Comme des Garçons, Alaïa, Gaultier, Hamnett, Joseph and Jean Muir are here.

TORIE STEELE, 414 N Rodeo Drive, Beverly Hills, CA 90210 ☎ (212) 271 5150
Luxe lair for the best international designers for men and women (Fendi, Krizia, Valentino, Maud Frizon shoes). ROBERT SANGSTER recommends.

TRASHY LINGERIE, 402 N La Cienega Blvd, CA 90048 ☎ (213) 652 4543
8,000 ways to undress, from virtuous Victoriana to lascivious leather. Think back to Kim Basinger in *9½ Weeks* or Sherilyn Fenn in *Two Moon Junction* – or virtually any other revealing movie (they add spice to about 20 films a month). Specialists of buttery leather bras and bustiers.

🐌 **Buzzz** Best **cult book** on LA is Richard Rayner's *Lost in Los Angeles Without a Map* 🐌...... The short-sighted are divided: some swear by **Oliver Peoples** on Sunset Blvd for their specs, others by **LA Eyeworks** on Melrose Ave (the best collection of unusual glasses) 🐌...... Thrills 'n' spills 1: **Splash Mountain**, Disneyland, is the best ride in the world – chug up a scenic mountain, then plunge over the summit down a near-vertical drop into a log-jammed lake. Yippee 🐌...... T 'n' S 2: the worst-taste ride in the world is **Earthquake: The Big One**, at Universal Studios ☎ (818) 777 3794 – take their tram tour round highlights of movieland (the house in *Psycho*, that mean ol' shark from Amity ...).............. 🐌

NEW ORLEANS
Bars and cafés

NAPOLEON HOUSE, 500 Chartres St, LA 70130 ☎ (504) 524 9752
A respite from the trumpets and clarinets. After-noon, pre-prandial and late-night drinking (try their Pimm's) to piped classical music. In the French Quarter.

PAT O'BRIEN'S, 718 St Peter St, LA 70116 ☎ (504) 525 4823
Civilized piano bar for jazz/pop music with sing-alongs. 2 more bars – one with a juke box and one outside on the patio.

TYLER'S, 5234 Magazine St, LA 70115 ☎ (504) 891 4989
One of the hottest jazz joints in town. All manner of jazzery in a characterful bar.

Clubs

4141, 4141 St Charles Ave, LA 70115 ☎ (504) 897 0781
The best disco in town, thronging with boppers and contemporary dance music.

PRESERVATION HALL, 726 St Peter St, LA 70116 ☎ (504) 522 2841
Home of New Orleans jazz, a smoky, sweaty, cramped room with sawdust on the floor and a clammy clamour of punters. But it's worth the queues and crowds to hear trad jazz played from the heart by wrinkly black musicians.

TIPITINA'S, 501 Napoleon Ave, LA 70115 ☎ (504) 895 8477
Tops for live music – Cajun, R&B, rock – where major performers check in. The usual laid-back atmosphere, with youngsters wandering in and out, beer in hand.

Festivals

NEW ORLEANS JAZZ AND HERITAGE FESTIVAL, PO Box 2530, LA 70176 ☎ (504) 522 4786
Over 4,000 musicians and cooks descend on the city at the end of April to give 300,000 hungry listeners an earful and a gutful of whatever suits their palate: Louisiana dishes such as filé gumbo, alligator piquante and jambalaya, washed down by jazz, country 'n' western, R&B, Gospel, blue grass, zydeco, Afro-Caribbean, Cajun, blues, folk, Latin and ragtime.

Hotels

🏊 WINDSOR COURT HOTEL, 300 Gravier St, LA 70140 ☎ (504) 523 6000
Though relatively young, this one has zipped into the forefront of US hotels, claiming No 1 slot in several surveys. Owner Jimmy Coleman has perfected the English/French country-house look, with knockout antiques and paintings (Van Dyck, Gainsborough). "*More and more people are saying it is one of the best hotels in America. It has this European style that they do so frightfully well*" – LORD LICHFIELD. Best tea in town, marrying English and French trads (deli-cate sandwiches, piquant lemon tart) and top-notch creole-inspired contemporary cuisine at the **Grill Room** (conceived by Mancunian Kevin Graham) – try roast Maine lobster in crawfish hollandaise or baked oysters in a béchamel, horseradish and Parmesan sauce.

Restaurants

🏊 BAYOU RIDGE CAFE, 5080 Pontchartrain Blvd, LA 70118 ☎ (504) 486 0788
One of the zippiest young dineries in town, using a new light approach to creole cooking. Wonder-fully exotic little pizzas (smoked duck, crawfish and spinach, shrimp with pesto and sun-dried

🏊 **Buzzz PG in Louisiana**: stay in a real ol' **plantation home** such as Madewood, Napoleonville ☎ (504) 524 1988 – full of charm and slightly dusty as if the original owners were still in residence. Details of other homes from Louisiana Dept of Culture, Recreation & Tourism, PO Box 44247, Baton Rouge, LA 70804 ☎ (504) 925 3884🏊......Chugging in to **Pittsburgh**: dine at the **Grand Concourse Restaurant**, 1 Station Square ☎ (412) 261 1717, "*the old railway station, now turned into a restaurant, is exceptionally good for seafood. It's beautiful and has been brilliantly converted. You sit in what was the booking hall...it has a great feeling of grandeur*" – JULIAN LLOYD WEBBER🏊......Alight in **Atlanta** and be spoilt rotten at the sensational **Ritz-Carlton, Buckhead**, 3434 Peachtree Rd NE ☎ (404) 237 2700: accolades galore and "*extremely good service*" – VISCOUNT HAMBLEDEN.. 🏊

tomatoes), crisp-fried oysters saltimbocca, and a superb crème brûlée with raspberries and blueberries.

BISTRO AT MAISON DE VILLE, 733 Toulouse St, LA 70130 ☎ (504) 528 9206
Chic little bistro, full of Noo Orluns character, where Susan Spicer (one of the top 10 new chefs in the USA) updates creole and Cajun with an eclectic touch. Soft-shell crab and creole mustard salad, grilled shrimp in coriander sauce with a cake of black-bean paste and duck breast.

BRENNANS, 417 Royal St, LA 70130 ☎ (504) 525 9713
Swankier than ever after a revamp, Brennans is a must for the best Creole breakfast (variations on an eggs benedict, grits and suchlike), plus superb seafood at dinner.

♠ BRIGTSEN'S, 723 Dante St, LA 70118 ☎ (504) 861 7610
Now that K'Paul's caters almost entirely to files of tourists, this simple little cottage restaurant under K'P-ex Frank Brigtsen might be a better bet. Contemporary Cajun cooking includes a superb shrimp and tomato bisque, grilled mahi-mahi with peppers and smoked corn sauce, and broiled amberjack with crabmeat basil croustade and lemon mousseline.

COMMANDER'S PALACE, 1403 Washington Ave, LA 70130 ☎ (504) 899 8221
One of the old guard, a lavish restaurant in the Garden District, with fitting oak-shaded patio and glass-walled Garden Room. High-flavoured creole creations – stuffed Louisiana quail, fillet of pompano in saffron and fennel sauce, and *"wonderful creole bread pudding, a soufflé, nice and light, with a whisky sauce"* – ELISE PASCOE.

GALATOIRE'S, 209 Bourbon St, LA 70130 ☎ (504) 525 2021
A taste of old New Orleans, with an evocative fin-de-siècle ambience. *"The best creole food imaginable. Quite simple but absolutely marvellous, in a restaurant that hasn't changed for nearly 100 years"* – KENNETH LANE.

GINO'S, 3019 Grand Caillou Rd, Houma, LA 70360 ☎ (504) 876 4896
Take Annie Miller's boat trip through the swamp to Gino's, which *"might well be the best shellfish restaurant in the world"* – MILES KINGTON. Specialities include shrimp and crab pizza, soft-shell crab, broiled alligator.

LA PROVENCE, US Highway 190 (exit 1-12), Meedanville (Lacombe), LA 70445 ☎ (504) 626 7662
On the shores of Lake Pontchartrain, Chris Kerageorgio's rustic restaurant blends classic French cuisine with a hint of Greece and more than a soupçon of Acadia. Spicy seafood-based dishes, crisp garlicky duck, and one hell of a jambalaya.

Vanderbilt's Folly

No need to go all the way to Europe for your culture shot – it's all here at George Washington Vanderbilt's **Biltmore Estate**, 1 N Pack Square, Ashville, NC 28801 ☎ (704) 255 1776. This 1890s 'Loire' château and modest 125,000-acre estate is packed with European treasures. *"The most astounding if not outstanding place. A fantastic, enormous, incredible house. It's about the size of Blenheim and has everything: one of the first ever indoor swimming pools, a dining room to end all dining rooms, and marvellous English-style gardens. It also has a winery or vinery or whatever they call it where you taste wine and usually decide not to buy any"* – JOHN BROOKE-LITTLE.

NEW YORK
— Art and museums —

♠ FRICK COLLECTION, 1 E 70th St, NY 10021 ☎ (212) 288 0700
A museum on the human scale. This Louis XV/XVI-style mansion (built 1913-14) is the former residence of industrialist Henry Clay Frick and home to his superb collection of Old Masters. Wander from French boudoir (Boucher, Fragonard, 18C furniture, Sèvres) through halls and galleries (Dutch portraits and landscapes, marble busts) to the cool pooled courtyard. LORD LICHFIELD, VISCOUNT HAMBLEDEN, MICHAEL GRADE and JEFFREY ARCHER get a kick out of the Frick.

♠ METROPOLITAN MUSEUM OF ART, 5th Ave/82nd St, NY 10028 ☎ (212) 879 5500
One of the richest art museums in the world. You could spend a week here and merely scratch the surface (HELEN GURLEY BROWN would prefer to spend a *year*); better to take it in small doses. A tour of the majestic building with its multi-domed Great Hall takes you through Egypt, ancient Greece and Rome, Islam, Africa, Oceania and the Americas. Endless European masterpieces (Rembrandt's *Toilet of Bathsheba*, Vermeer's *Woman with a Water Jug*, Cézanne's *Cardplayers*); and reconstructed rooms from Europe (walk from an Andalusian Renaissance patio to a French chapel to an Adam room from London). Also the celebrated 20C art wing run by William Lieberman. There's always a dazzling exhibition at the Costume Institute. One of ANDRE PREVIN's world top 3, and a sure-fire hit

with LORD MONTAGU OF BEAULIEU, JEFFREY ARCHER, BARBARA TAYLOR BRADFORD and LARRY KING. *"So beautifully lit and designed. I love it"* – VISCOUNT HAMBLEDEN. Good gift shop.

🐾 MUSEUM OF MODERN ART, 11 W 53rd St, NY 10019 ☎ (212) 708 9750
The best modern art museum in the world. MOMA boasts an unparalleled collection of over 100,000 works of 20C painting, sculpture, drawing, prints and photography, plus film, architecture, industrial and graphic design. A large number of Picassos, Matisses, Mirós and Mondrians; major works by Hopper, Wyeth, Johns, O'Keeffe, Pollock, Rothko, Rauschenberg, et al.

🐾 SOLOMON R GUGGENHEIM MUSEUM, 1071 5th Ave, NY 10218 ☎ (212) 360 3555
A remarkable Frank Lloyd Wright structure (1957-59) commissioned by Solomon Guggenheim to hold his collection of modern art. Works are viewed from a spiral ramp that descends into the museum. Impressionists and modern art – the largest Kandinsky collection in the world, Klee, Chagall, Delaunay, Léger, Mondrian and Braque; excellent film and photographic archives. Stunning exhibitions. For STEPHEN JONES, it's the most beautiful museum in the world. More support from MARGAUX HEMINGWAY and MICHAEL GRADE. NB Closed for renovations until Oct 1991 at the latest.

WHITNEY MUSEUM OF AMERICAN ART, 945 Madison Ave, NY 10021 ☎ (212) 570 3633
Dedicated to American contemporary art, this is the place to pore over thousands of works of 20C American art, and see bold, progressive, up-to-the-minute exhibitions. Film and video works, too. *"I love the Whitney"* – TESSA DAHL.

──── Arts centres ────

LINCOLN CENTER, Broadway btwn 63rd and 65th St, NY 10023 ☎ (212) 877 1800
A spectacular centre for the performing arts. On a site of 14 cultivated acres that can seat 13,666 avid artsies, it's the largest complex of its kind in the world. It encompasses: the Metropolitan Opera; the New York Philharmonic (housed at Avery Fisher Hall); the New York City Ballet and the New York City Opera – both housed in the New York State Theater; the Lincoln Center Theater Co; the Film Society; the Chamber Music Society (housed in Alice Tully Hall – with a sense of intimacy that JULIAN LLOYD WEBBER appreciates); the School of American Ballet and the Juilliard School (of music, drama and dance, with its own theatre). Oh, and a car park for 700.

──── *Ballet* ────

Apart from the 2 main New York companies, there is the bicoastal **Joffrey Ballet**, 130 W 56th St, NY 10019 ☎ (212) 265 7300; LA: ☎ (213) 972 7384. Catch them in autumn at the City Center Theater, New York, in spring in Los Angeles County Music Center, and the rest of the year on tour.

🐾 AMERICAN BALLET THEATER, 890 Broadway, NY 10003 ☎ (212) 477 3030
ABT is an eclectic company, producing everything from classics to the works of new young choreographers. Dynamic and progressive during its recent years under Mikhail Baryshnikov, the company is now awaiting strong direction (not least to clear their debts). A pool of excellent athletic dancers from the School of American Ballet to draw on.

🐾 NEW YORK CITY BALLET, New York State Theater, Lincoln Center, NY 10023 ☎ (212) 496 0600
Still regarded as the most important company in the States, founded by Lincoln Kirstein with the legendary George Balanchine, who brought ballet to America. His style, along with that of Jerome Robbins (who recently left) lives on under artistic director Peter Martins. Fine dancers, creamed mainly from the School of American Ballet. New York society flocks to the opening of the season.

──── *Clubs* ────

THE BIG HUNT CLUB, 804 Washington St, NY 10014 ☎ (212) 727 7616
Rock club with an industrial aura, all black with silver pipes and girders, and blue spotlights reflecting off them. The Rolling Stones had their opening-night party there.

THE BOTTOM LINE, 15 W 4th St, NY 10012 ☎ (212) 228 6300
Jazz, rock and pop venue for many major stars. Bruce Springsteen was discovered here by HARVEY GOLDSMITH.

🐾 **Buzzz** Cooper-Hewitt Museum, 2 E 91st St ☎ (212) 860 6868, set in the lovely former home of Andrew Carnegie (of the Hall fame), houses the Smithsonian's dec arts collection and serves as a design reference centre🐾...... Pillage and plunder: on a skyscraperless grassy hill in Fort Tryon Park are the Met's **The Cloisters** ☎ (212) 923 3700, constructed from the ruins of several European cloisters, and filled with medieval art, sculpture and architectural relics....🐾

CAROLINE'S AT THE SEAPORT, 89 South St, Pier 17, NY 10038 ☎ (212) 233 4900
The best comedy club-restaurant in the city, in its new home. Guaranteed gags from tried and tested talent – virtually all major US comedians have played here.

CBGB, 315 Bowery, NY 10003
☎ (212) 982 4052
Granddaddy of the punk/new wave scene in New York, where the likes of Blondie and Talking Heads started out (the Heads come back to try out new music). Catch new bands before they make it big. Great sound system; Sunday afternoon concerts for under-age teenies; record shop and folk club next door.

COPACABANA, 10 E 60th St, NY 10022
☎ (212) 755 6010
Go for Suzanne Bartsch's one-nighter on the last Thursday of the month. *"The only one that is innovative and fabulous. That is fun. You get everybody who is ex-Studio 54 or ex-Xenon coming out and doing their thing. Transvestites and people who have suppressed lives all day suddenly break out and go wild – and they do go wild"* – JOAN BURSTEIN. *"In 3 hours you can enjoy everything you heard is wild about New York – vogueing in one corner, weird strip acts, transvestites dancing, yuppies trying to pick up downtown artists ... it's like a compressed version of most New York movies you've ever seen"* – SEBASTIAN SCOTT. *"Suzanne throws the best parties – they attract the flashiest crowd, and she hires showgirls and body builders, go-go dancers and drag queens to parade around. It never gets tired"* – MICHAEL MUSTO.

CRANE CLUB, 408 Amsterdam Ave, NY 10024 ☎ (212) 877 3097
Dinner club with dancing. Yuppified and always packed. Frank Sinatra-style dance music till midnight; thereafter recognizable rock and retro.

DELIA'S, 197 E 3rd St, NY 10009
☎ (212) 254 9184
Dark, pocket-sized supper club run by *"a wonderful Irish lady, Delia Roche-Kelly. It's got a tiny dance floor and one of the waiters struggles with the CD player, but it is really good fun, gets a good [largely Irish/Eurotrash] crowd"* – SEBASTIAN SCOTT.

HORATIO 113, 113 Horatio St, NY 10014
☎ (212) 627 2080
Civilized club with an elegant restaurant, bar, lounge, 3 pool tables and contemporary music.

LE CLUB, 313 E 58th St, NY 10022
☎ (212) 308 5520
Enduring, dignified private club, based in a town house. Eurotrash in dark suits. *"A bit Annabellish and quite quiet compared to the other clubs in the big bagel"* – ROSS BENSON.

LIVINGROOM, 154 E 79th St, NY 10021
☎ (212) 772 8488
Arguably the most luxurious supper club in town, with all the hominess of a stately mansion – wing chairs, wood panelling, terracotta floor. Elegant restaurant with 'really intense' food. No dancing as such, but jazz and other vibes entice some diners on to the floor.

MK, 204 5th Ave, NY 10010 ☎ (212) 779 1340
Eric [Area] Goode's restaurant-club has several floors, a library, butlers and maids. Strict door policy, hard to get into (some clubbers have stopped trying). *"A lot of stuffed animals – Dobermans and freeze-dried roaches, stuff like that. Really kinda sick. Some of the people there fit in with the décor. The crowd is very chi-chi, a lot of Europeans"* – MICHAEL MUSTO. *"Probably still a stop ..."* – TAMA JANOWITZ; *"... a very ungenerous dance floor"* – DUGGIE FIELDS.

NELL'S, 246 W 14th St, NY 10011
☎ (212) 675 1567
The club that set the trend for cosy gentlemen's-club-cum-country-house décor. No longer queen of the night, 'Little' Nell's joint is still on the beat. *"I like Nell's on Sunday nights – it plays good music. The trouble is, it's the kind of place where people pick you up for having a bad English accent, because it is so overpopulated with Brits. Everyone you have ever met at a drinks party in SW3 will one day turn up at Nell's"* – SEBASTIAN SCOTT. *"Fun ... just wonderful"* – TAMA JANOWITZ.

RED ZONE, 440 W 54th St, NY 10019
☎ (212) 582 2222
High-activity zone – a 10,000 sq ft dance floor with frantic, high-energy music, lasers, strobes, fog, the works. Upstairs is more relaxed, with a restaurant. *"A big sprawling dance floor with an ethnic, very young crowd"* – MICHAEL MUSTO.

THE NEW RITZ, 254 W 54th St, NY 10019
☎ (212) 541 8900
The best venue for live music any night of the week. An old dance hall where touring and up-and-coming bands play rock and roll, reggae, country – all sorts of music – to hip kids. Suzanne Vega was a regular. Record companies talent-spot from upstairs.

6 BOND STREET, 6 Bond St, NY
☎ (212) 979 6565
Cool café/restaurant/nightclub in Greenwich Village with the usual attention-grabbing hotchpotch of decorative styles. The bistro (goat cheeseburgers, venison chilli) is shiny futuristic-art deco; above it is the more upmarket 1930s-style restaurant, **Venus**; on the 4th floor, set in classical ruins, is the dance club where funk and house rule.

S O B's, 204 Varick St, NY 10014
☎ (212) 243 4940
Salsa or bop to Sounds Of Brazil ... the place for

Life on Mars

🏃 MARS, 28-30 10th Ave, NY 10014 ☎ (212) 691 6262. The hot club as we rocket into the 90s, run by Rudolf (ex-Danceteria, Studio 54), *"the majordomo of nightlife in New York"* – MICHAEL MUSTO. Mars is (or was) a meat-packing plant, in case you didn't know. One room is a combination of high-tech machinery and tribal art; the meat-grinding room has been left intact with hooks hanging off the ceiling. The roof opens up in summer for barbecues and dancing. *"Fabulous, the best club I've been to in ages. An interesting environment with radically different themes. They haven't lavished a fortune on it, but they've lavished ideas on it – Chinese rococo, a* whole wall of lava lamps, psychedelic revolving lamps, a battered piano hanging from a staircase..."* – DUGGIE FIELDS. *"My favourite, although you do spend a lot of your time going up and down the fire escape, and it's incredibly hot so you have to squeeze between damp T-shirts and the walls, like some kind of rhythmic exercise"* – SEBASTIAN SCOTT. *"Youthful, energetic, very kitschy décor. Every floor has a different DJ, but they lean towards house music"* – MM. *"If you want to see the scene in New York, that's probably the first stop"* – TAMA JANOWITZ. *"A bit less glitzy than the rest, a bit scuzzy, but don't let that betray it – it is the trendiest"* – ROBERT ELMS.

top international Latin-American acts. Also reggae, African, ska, etc. Carnival atmosphere. Knock-out sugar-cane alcohol caipirinhas.

WETLANDS, 161 Hudson St, NY 10002
☎ (212) 643 0728
Back to hippydom. Latterday flower people drift along with their children to this environment-conscious club. Here, when you're not boogieing to 60s revival groups or R&B, you can log in to the Earth Station, a psychedelic VW bus with T-shirts and leaflets on various Green campaigns. Downstairs is the Inner Sanctum, a smoky bar with beanbags. Live bands 6 nights a week. Sunday is for lectures and discussions on the state of the planet.

—— *Fashion designers* ——

ADOLFO, 36 E 57th St, NY 10022
☎ (212) 688 4410
Perennially favoured by the petite for his natty little cross-Chanel suits. 'Darling Dolf' is still No 1 for the petitest of them all, Nancy Reagan, and he's one of the tops for HELEN GURLEY BROWN. At his shows, his following make a point of wearing the *same* latest suit, like a class in uniform.

ADRIENNE VITTADINI at major department stores ☎ (212) 921 2510
Easy sportswear and casual evening togs... wool leggings, a spangled sweater, a fringed suede jacket. *"Her forte is in knits – beaded knits, decorative knits. Her bodies are super"* – ANIKO GAAL. Also her own boutiques all over the States.

ARNOLD SCAASI COUTURE, 681 5th Ave, NY 10022 ☎ (212) 755 5105
The only true couturier in the Paris tradition. His métier is great-occasion dressing, triumphant trumpetings of taffeta and tulle. Clients are Social Register-meets-showbiz: Ivana Trump, Jackie Onassis, Barbra Streisand, Joan Rivers. Lots of deb and wedding dresses. Also ready-to-wear at 530 7th Ave ☎ (212) 245 2683.

🏃 BILL BLASS, 550 7th Ave, NY 10018
☎ (212) 221 6660
"Still one of the leaders for his design, choice of fabric and workmanship" – ELEANOR LAMBERT. America's No 1 fashion accessory himself, draped on the arm of the best society dames, Blass spells class. Gorgeous evening wear, embroidered and embellished, beaded and bugled ...or a seasonal dash of sparkling lurex and shimmering leopard print.

🏃 CALVIN KLEIN, 205 W 39th St, NY 10018 ☎ (212) 719 2600
With a total look that's body-conscious yet casual, Calvin remains *"amazingly on target for the 90s. He epitomizes the great American non-chalant style – perfectly put-together separates that look like it happened by accident. There is genius in that. It's signature American"* – ANIKO GAAL. As big a marketing phenomenon as Ralph Lauren, with an annual turnover of more than $1 billion, he does men's and women's wear plus perfume (*you* know his ads for Obsession and Eternity). Klein remains one of HELEN GURLEY BROWN's favourites: *"classic, sexy, sophisticated and young."*

CARMELO POMODORO, 575 7th Ave, NY 10018 ☎ (212) 398 9116
A young designer in the Klein/Karan vein of svelte city dressing. While still doing his elegant but casual thing, Carmelo is getting more and more into fashion politics, waving the avant-garde downtown banner in the face of trad Madison Ave... which, some say, doesn't do that much for his fashion.

CAROLINA HERRERA, 19 E 57th St, NY 10022 ☎ (212) 355 3055

Society queen turned dress designer to her peers, Herrera is *"truly an independent thinker in fashion"* – ELEANOR LAMBERT. Unhung up on the American sportswear look, she turns out refined, dressy little luncheon ensembles and accomplished evening luxuries. *"Superb for short little black dresses for all occasions,"* opines ROBERT SANGSTER.

CAROLYNE ROEHM, 8th Fl, 550 7th Ave, NY 10018 ☎ (212) 921 0399

Oscar de la Renta's former assistant is a confirmed hit with the best-dressed set. Her strength lies in cocktail and evening wear, beautifully cut and extravagantly detailed.

🚶 DONNA KARAN, 14th Fl, 550 7th Ave, NY 10018 ☎ (212) 398 0616

With her soft, pared-down separates (the draped skirt, the fluid pants, the body, the wrap-over top, the three-quarter length jacket) Karan has overtaken Klein and co to become everybody's No 1, dead right for the New Age 90s. A working mother herself, she *understands* what women need and want. *"She makes comfort and ease part of her design and women really appreciate that. Still very much at the top of the creative ladder. Her designs are a perfect expression of the 90s, where stylized simplicity, comfort and practicality converge"* – ANIKO GAAL. Bestselling Karan staples appear in her younger, more affordable line, DKNY. HELEN GURLEY BROWN, BRUCE OLDFIELD and MARIE HELVIN are admirers, as is ELEANOR LAMBERT: *"Natural talent and a fabulous training – that is the missing quantity in so many young designers. Donna was patient and when the time was right, she went out on her own and succeeded."*

🚶 GEOFFREY BEENE, 783 5th Ave, NY 10022 ☎ (212) 935 0470

Ensconced in his streamlined new shop at the Sherry-Netherland Hotel, Beene is now hailed the consummate American hero. *"The eternal leader in American fashion, the only one that stands aside and does his own thing"* – ELEANOR LAMBERT. *"Never been better. He is the quiet American master. His coats and jackets are masterpieces. Now he has evolved into a powerful force in evening wear as well – they are beautiful works of art. He invented new shaping*

❝I feel very strongly that there is an American point of view that has nothing to do with British, French or Italian fashion . . . a simplicity and a look that is really and truly totally American ❞

 BILL BLASS

America's Best Designers

1	DONNA KARAN
2	CALVIN KLEIN
3	ISAAC MIZRAHI
4	GEOFFREY BEENE
5	RALPH LAUREN
6	BILL BLASS

---

and cutting to accommodate sensuous cut-outs in the back. I have never seen cut-outs like that before" – ANIKO GAAL. Waft through an environment of marble, brushed aluminium, black lacquer and opaque glass, sifting through couture gowns, sportswear, cashmeres, stoles, scents and Diego della Valle shoes.

GORDON HENDERSON at major department stores ☎ (212) 354 2255

The critics' choice as hot designer last year ('Henderson's Hit Parade,' grooved WWD; *"classy modern clothes for the mass market. Strong but not too wild"* – ELEANOR LAMBERT; *"The best up-and-coming designer"* – HELEN GURLEY BROWN). Backed by World Hong Kong, he does affordable daywear in plummy, rusty colours – flowing cape-coats, gabardine blazers, slouchy knits. Less of a wow is the workmanship, however – there have been complaints of seams coming apart, faulty zips, *and* his sweaters have been spotted at Daffy's discount store . . . .

JOAN VASS, 485 7th Ave, NY 10018 ☎ (212) 947 3417

Vass has blossomed from knitwear into women's and men's sportswear with a spare, easy feel. Evening frocks and shoes too.

MICHAEL KORS, 119 W 24th St, NY 10001 ☎ (212) 620 4677

This young designer is now an establishment figure with a hot-selling line in sassy, sexy little separates. He believes in a minimal wardrobe of co-ordinates that can be dressed up or down. Some say he's the next Calvin Klein; others recognize his prowess at merchandising but feel his workmanship and originality don't compare.

🚶 NORMA KAMALI, 11 W 56th St, NY 10019 ☎ (212) 957 9797

Her shop is called OMO. It means On My Own. You get the picture. A free spirit, rather un-American, she has branched out from high-tech rubberized swimwear and body-clinging jersey to more worldly things. *"Fabulous – she works so hard. She has been using Indian fabrics, sari*

The Rise of Isaac Mizrahi

Hot new designers come, hot new designers go, but this one could stay for ever. *"Without question the young American designer to watch. He is firmly entrenched and the most likely not just to succeed but to survive"* – BILL BLASS. *"A potential leader of the same type as Geoffrey Beene. A very strong force; he'll keep going because he is very level-headed"* – ELEANOR LAMBERT. What is all the fuss about? Well, he gets under the skin rather than dealing with superficials. His hand and eye are guided by structure and form rather than sequins and gold thread. *"A great sense of classic shape and bold pattern – a cross* between ancient designs and Miró; he mixes these abstract designs with soft, gentle forms. Flowing lines in a modern way, with crisp outlines"* – ELEANOR L. *"There was a need to simplify after the over-designed 80s, and Mizrahi does this very well. Simple designs with spirit and wit. He gives you enough fabric to create your own look – for example, his oversized silk shirts and cropped pants in the most marvellous colours – oranges, yellows and fuchsias – which you could tie and wrap. He takes a basic shape and adds seasonal fashion relevance"* – ANIKO GAAL. Clothes available at major department stores.

materials with beading and embroidery, the Maharani look. Persian-looking coats and tight trousers. Motorcycle clothes too but terribly chic, and the cowgirl look – picturesque, great" – ELEANOR LAMBERT.

OSCAR DE LA RENTA, 550 7th Ave, NY 10018 ☎ (212) 354 6777
Long-standing darling of café society, known for his extravagant evening clothes that swank into balls and premières. Loves ornamentation, hand-beading. So do his clothes-horses, Marella Agnelli, Nancys Reagan and Kissinger, Lee Radziwill and Marie-Hélène de Rothschild.

♠ RALPH LAUREN, see Shopping

REBECCA MOSES, at Martha, Charivari, Neiman Marcus, I Magnin, Nordstrom's
Young Moses is not quite parting the waves, but she's certainly getting a following for classic day and evening wear that's not a million miles from Klein's and Karan's. *"She works beautifully with jerseys and knits. Her mohair dresses, almost like tunic sweaters, were almost the best I have ever seen"* – ANIKO GAAL.

——— Hotels ———

♠ THE CARLYLE, 36 E 76th St, NY 10021 ☎ (212) 744 1600
The most well-bred hotel in New York, under the caring management of Frank Bowling (who is *"legendary in the business"* – EDWARD CARTER). Loyal staff breed loyal guests such as the Fords and the Kennedys, ANDREW LLOYD WEBBER, DOUGLAS FAIRBANKS JR, BOB PAYTON, BARBARA TAYLOR BRADFORD and LARRY KING. *"It doesn't feel like a hotel at all. It's very, very, very discreet"* – ROSS BENSON. 35 storeys means gobsmacking city and park views; Mark Hampton design makes the interior pretty easy on the eye. *"Still has the nicest rooms of any hotel in New York"* – FRANK LOWE. *"It has charm, good service and the décor is very fine"* – VISCOUNT HAMBLEDEN.

THE LOWELL, 28 E 63rd St, NY 10021 ☎ (212) 838 1400
Classy boutique hotel based in an art deco landmark, now laced with French and Oriental antiques. Only 60 suites (all with kitchens and real log fires) mean truly personal service as VICTOR EDELSTEIN has discovered: *"I like it because it's so small. Excellent service...I'm very impressed. A well-kept secret in New York."* TESSA DAHL agrees. Ultra-elegant dining in the **Pembroke Room**, which non-residents in the know also head for.

♠ MAYFAIR REGENT, 610 Park Ave, NY 10021 ☎ (212) 288 0800
If you're after European dash, this is your hotel. *"A fabulous hotel, excellent for its personal attention, really well run, and small enough not to be overpowering"* – JOAN BURSTEIN. *"A particular favourite for its style and its attitude – one of personal service and warmth which is quite unusual in New York. A lady client said it's one of the few hotels where she feels perfectly happy on her own"* – JEFFERY TOLMAN. *"Combines European charm with American efficiency"* – WOLFGANG PUCK. *"The most European of New York hotels, the emphasis being on service and attention to the individual rather than being a number with a coded key"* – NICHOLAS VILLIERS. Known to its intimates as Dario's (Dario Mariotti is general manager), it can't go wrong as long as it houses Sirio's (**Le Cirque** – see Restaurants). Get acquainted with influential concierge Bruno Brunelli, too.

MORGANS, 237 Madison Ave, NY 10016
☎ (212) 686 0300

Minimal, monochrome Morgans is still a cool, cliquey option for the pop and fashion crowd – Azzedine Alaïa, Brooke Shields, Mick Jagger and Cher among them. Check out designer Andrée Putman's chequerboard fetish here – black and white squares run down the corridors, up the bathroom walls and over the outsize beds. That the Klein- and Armani-bedecked young staff comprises largely of resting actors and models has its advantages and disadvantages.

THE PENINSULA, 700 5th Ave, NY 10019
☎ (212) 247 2200

The old Gotham has been taken over by the Hong Kong-based group which can bode only well. *"Quite wonderful. Trying to do Hong Kong quality and service in New York . . . they're working on it and they'll soon get there. Great appointments and a pretty good location"* – KEN HOM. *"Superb,"* agrees FRANK BOWLING.

"One of the problems Far Eastern hotels face in the West is that labour is much more expensive, so they can't provide the thing that people expect most – marvellous quantities of staff hanging on your every word "

 GILES SHEPARD

🐾 THE PIERRE, 5th Ave at 61st St, NY 10021 ☎ (212) 838 8000

Hot contender for New York best, now under the auspices of Stan Bromley (Regional Vice-President of the Four Seasons group), who is considered by EDWARD CARTER to be *"the greatest hotelier in the US. I expect the Pierre to get up to, if not exceed, the Carlyle . . ."* The epitome of discretion and attentiveness. *"I love the location. Staying there is like having a supporting role in a film of the 1930s. It has very proper old-fashioned New York glamour"* – LOYD GROSSMAN. Tops for STANLEY MARCUS: *"First of all I like the construction. It's concrete; I saw it being built so I know how solid it is, which relieves you from worrying about fire. Secondly they have very little turnover in staff. I've been staying there since 1929 when it first opened."* Best view over Central Park is from the Presidential Suite. **Café Pierre**, designed by Valerian Rybar, continues to attract local and visiting glamorati; the **Rotunda** is good for light lunches and tea. A winner with LORD LICHFIELD, SHAKIRA CAINE and LORD MONTAGU OF BEAULIEU.

🐾 THE PLAZA, 768 5th Ave, NY 10019 ☎ (212) 759 3000

This great New York hotel (first opened in 1907), is set to trump them all since the Ivana Trump

facelift (to the hotel, that is). Stay to lap up the impeccable service, or just hang out at the famous **Oak Bar** and **Oak Room**. *"I think Trump has done a great job on it – I would rate it in the top class,"* trumpets LARRY KING. Further blasts from BILL BLASS and KENNETH LANE: *"This wonderful landmark hotel had become a bit shabby. Now it has been re-gilded, re-carpeted and re-chandeliered. A belle époque monument in top shape. Wonderful service, really snappy. It has become the place."*

PLAZA ATHENEE, 37 E 64th St, NY 10021
☎ (212) 734 9100

Chic little sister to the Paris hotel, done out in sophisticated French Empire style with a rather formal French ambience to match. Stars (Elizabeth Taylor, Princess Stephanie, George Hamilton) love it not least for its tight security. Executive chefs of **Le Régence** are the celebrated Rostangs of Antibes and Paris. *"My favourite New York hotel as the service is so good, and the restaurant is beautifully decorated and gracious"* – BETTY KENWARD. BILL BLASS rates it highly.

RITZ-CARLTON, 112 Central Park S, NY 10019 ☎ (212) 757 1900

Gentlemen's clubby atmosphere, echoed by the famous **Jockey Club** dining room (wood panelling, Old Masters, log fires). A fabulous view over the Park and personal service help earn a vote from LARRY KING.

THE ROYALTON, 44 W 44th St, NY 10036
☎ (212) 869 4400

A testament to the Designer Decade (the 80s, remember?) it's *"Morgans x 10. It's spartan space age, like living in the Comme des Garçons shop"* – ROBERT ELMS. Granite grey, gleaming steel, tinted glass, futuristic lighting, slicks of electric blue carpeting . . . or, in the words of another guest, 'surgical steel meets Frankenstein's Castle.' It's even got the most designer address (44 W 44). *"The pop sensation. A lot of pop and Hollywood rockers stay there"* – FRANK BOWLING. VCRs and cassette decks in every room go down well, as does the food: *"Actually really good. You eat almost in the lobby, so everyone can watch. Very tasty,"* adds ELMS. *"I love the Royalton. It's beautifully designed by Philippe Starck. One always finds somebody one knows"* – JOSEPH.

STANHOPE HOTEL, 995 Fifth Ave, NY 10028 ☎ (212) 288 5800

"Has always been my favourite in New York. The new management eliminated 58 out of 160 rooms to make the remaining ones bigger. Detailing is terrific down to the weighted notepad next to the telephone, 3 types of hangers in the closets. . . . Staff have been there for years. It's too far uptown for some people (at 81st), but there is a complimentary limo that will take you anywhere you want. To me that's terrific" – EDWARD CARTER.

Music

CARNEGIE HALL, 154 W 57th St, NY 10019
☎ (212) 247 7800
This much-loved concert hall celebrates its centenary in 1991. For ANDRE PREVIN, it is tops in
America, along with the Symphony Hall in Boston. However, the dramatic restoration of the
stage dome (a hole was cut out in the 1940s to
allow more light for the film *Carnegie Hall*) has
not been an unqualified success for AP: *"I was
hoping you wouldn't ask ... it is not quite what
it was, though it's still awfully good. A wonderful hall and great fun to play in."*

> **"As a city, without specifying
> which orchestra or which artist,
> you would have to go a long way to
> get past New York, because there
> are concerts of _every_ description
> _every_ night. With all it offers, New
> York is pretty unbeatable "**
>
> ANDRE PREVIN

♣ METROPOLITAN OPERA,
Metropolitan Opera House, Lincoln
Center, NY 10023 ☎ (212) 362 6000
A company of world renown, over 100 years old,
with an 800-strong company. A tradition of
producing no-holds-barred extravaganzas with
the very best, crowd-pulling performers. Tops
in the US for RODNEY MILNES, HELEN GURLEY
BROWN, AUBERON WAUGH and BILL BLASS, but
some opera devotees are not so impressed (one
complaint is that their concern lies more with big-
name singers than the production). However, it
plays to chock-a-block houses and no one can
deny the splendour of the opening gala, nor the
magic of the free operas in Central Park.

♣ NEW YORK CITY OPERA, New York
State Theater, Lincoln Center, NY 10023
☎ (212) 870 5570
A dynamic young company representing the best
contemporary artists for music, lyrics, set and
costume design. Also new productions of classics
like *The Magic Flute*, with English surtitles.
Highly recommended by ANDREW LLOYD WEBBER
and HELEN GURLEY BROWN. July-Nov season.

Restaurants

See also Hotels.

ALISON ON DOMINICK STREET, 38
Dominick St, NY 10013 ☎ (212) 727 1188
Known to its intimates as A on D, a small,
romantic restaurant with cream walls and velvet
banquettes. Cuisine from south-west France.
Signature dishes are braised lamb shank with
fava beans, white beans and chicory; roast guinea
fowl with black olive, thyme and roast tomato
risotto; ragout of mussels with mushrooms and
white beans. *"I'm pretty hot on Alison's,"* pants
DAVID SHILLING.

ARCADIA, 21 E 62nd St, NY 10021
☎ (212) 223 2900
Anne Rosenzweig set the pace, left (for the 21
Club), then came back. Now Arcadia is as hot as
ever, serving real New American cuisine. Fresh
produce, strong flavours – smoked lobster, quail.
MARIO BUATTA and MARC MCCORMACK approve.

ARIZONA 206, 206 E 60th St, NY 10022
☎ (212) 838 0440
Marilyn Frobuccino picks up where predecessor
Brendan Walsh left off. *"One of my 2 real
favourites. Great modern southwestern cookery.
Good if you like chilli, things that actually taste
of something. Very lively"* – LOYD GROSSMAN.
When feeling strapped for cash, GAEL GREENE
hits the cheaper **Arizona 206 Café**.

AUREOLE, 34 E 61st St, NY 10021
☎ (212) 319 1660
This newishcomer from chef Charles Palmer,
Nicolette Kotsoni and Steve Tzoh (River Café,
Il Cantinori) has an ardent following for French/
American cuisine. *"A very good new restaurant"*
– JOAN BURSTEIN. WOLFGANG PUCK's pick.

♣ BOULEY, 165 Duane St, NY 10013
☎ (212) 608 3852
Hailed as NY's most important newcomer, David
Bouley's restaurant offers a taste of la France –
modern cuisine and a warm, beautifully Gallic-
cum-Gothic setting. Daily arrivals of fresh fish,
exotic and organic produce.

CAFE LUXEMBOURG, 200 W 70th St, NY
10023 ☎ (212) 873 7411
McNally K's bustling bistro remains one of the
best diners on the West Side. Style-fiends pack
in for French cuisine – escargots, chicken liver
terrine, fine fish dishes, lemon tart.

CANAL BAR, 511 Greenwich St, NY 10013
☎ (212) 334 5150
*"One of the ultimate trendy places in New York.
I could not believe how packed it gets. You think
'how can they get another person in here?' The
food is good, not cheap, and the service is
appalling, but it is so crowded you can't blame
them"* – DUGGIE FIELDS. Even more remarkable
is it seems to have stayed that way for more than
a year. Could it be the McNally touch?

CHANTERELLE, 2 Harrison St, NY 10013
☎ (212) 966 6960
This old favourite has moved to luxy, romantic
premises in the landmark Mercantile Exchange
Building (all peachy-toned, beautiful architectural detailing, large fireplace). Opinions vary over

the post-nouvelle cuisine, but the home-made breads and baby profiteroles with coffee are sure-fire winners. A MARIO BUATTA favourite.

DAVID K'S, 1115 3rd Ave, NY 10021
☎ (212) 371 9090

Pure, clean, nouvelle Chinoise cuisine – minus the MSG. *"As good as ever"* – LORD LICHFIELD. GAEL GREENE recommends **David K's Café** for similar fare at half the dough.

DAWAT, 210 E 58th St, NY 10022
☎ (212) 355 7555

Indian country and street cooking comes to Manhattan. GAEL GREENE votes it tops: *"Feast on juicy goat in a haze of cardamom . . . vegetable cheese gratin, wholewheat paratha and a vegetable-studded biryani."*

ELAINE'S, 1703 2nd Ave, NY 10022
☎ (212) 534 8103

A somewhat hackneyed bastion of the Big Apple, packed with publishers and literati who are drawn by the matronly Elaine. To get a good table is a rare and valued prize. (Woody Allen's prized table is the one by the lavatory.) *"One of the best places to get a feed. Simple grilled meats and very good wines. She does the best veal chops"* – BARBARA KAFKA. *"Always good fun"* – KENNETH LANE. *"I love Elaine's still. I've known her for 25 years. It's like you have a barber and always go back to him"* – ED VICTOR.

ELIO'S, 1621 2nd Ave, NY 10028
☎ (212) 772 2242

Clannish café-bar for great fresh fish and seafood dishes. *"Fun, good Italian food"* – KENNETH LANE. *"The fun one in New York"* – BIJAN. *"I love Elio's"* – ED VICTOR.

�FOUR SEASONS, 99 E 52nd St, NY 10022 ☎ (212) 754 9494

Remains the sizzling hot spot for media/business lunches. *"The Establishment restaurant in New York . . . the food never varies – consistently sensational"* – HELEN GURLEY BROWN. *"The finest restaurant in the world"* – JOHN TOVEY. *"Always the best lunch – just excellent"* – ED VICTOR. *"Very, very good"* – ANDREW LLOYD WEBBER. *"You can't really beat it"* – SIMON WILLIAMS. And so says STANLEY MARCUS (though one food critic feels the food rating has slipped). If you thought you knew the distinction between the Bar Room (habitués) and the Pool Room (tourists), hark at habitué GAEL GREENE, who likes the *Pool* Room – it puts her in the mood for romance. ELISE PASCOE (who thinks the crab cakes are the best in town) explains the conventional wisdom: *"Book in to the Bar Room where you'll see New York's business dynamos lunching. If you find yourself beside the pool, you are no one."*

♠GOTHAM BAR & GRILL, 12 E 12th St, NY 10003 ☎ (212) 620 4020

Going from strength to strength, this glam restaurant boasts an eclectic menu in the hands of a gifted chef. *"Everything about it gives me a high: the architectural wit, the lively, good-looking crowd, electricity crackling, and the spectacular food emerging from Alfred Portale's kitchen, stunning to see, a revelation of flavour"* – GAEL GREENE. Duck breast carpaccio in pesto, grilled tuna with lemon-basil pasta.

IL CANTINORI, 32 E 10th St, NY 10003
☎ (212) 673 6044

Expensive Italiano with farmhouse décor and a foodie/trendy clientele. *"My favourite Italian. Its pasta dishes are unbeatable"* – BOB PAYTON.

LA COTE BASQUE, 5 E 55th St, NY 10022
☎ (212) 688 6526

"One of the best French restaurants in New York. Things are really done exactly like they are in France" – BARBARA CARTLAND. It's jolie and convivial, with seaside murals of la Côte. *"For me, the best of the French contenders"* – HELEN GURLEY BROWN.

Empire McNally

The McNally bros – that's Brian and Keith – were born with silver spoons, knives, forks, salt cellars, pepper mills and candelabras in their mouths. If a restaurant's been McNallied, you can bet it will succeed. It all began with a joint venture, **Odeon**, which was an instant draw for the hip, cool and trendy. A rift sent the brothers careering their separate ways. Brian opened the cult **Indochine**, 430 Lafayette St ☎ (212) 505 5111 (*"still has the best-looking staff"* – ROBERT ELMS; *"still the place to go"* – TAMA JANOWITZ),

the 50s-style diner **Jerry's**, 101 Prince St ☎ (212) 966 9464; the Crush Bar, sorry **Canal Bar**; and the biggest production number of them all, **150 Wooster**. Keith, lagging behind with only 3 crowd-thrilling, coffer-filling, model-milling, hip-hopping, chart-topping culinary victories, opened **Café Luxembourg**, **Nell's** (see Clubs) and, on target for the 90s, **Lucky Strike**, 59 Grand St ☎ (212) 941 0479, a cheaper re-run of Odeon with saloon-style décor and provençale-cum-brasserie fodder. No reservations – *everyone* waits.

Joshua Wesson's Top 5 in NY

Arcadia is "consistent, satisfying, innovative, delicious – everything a good restaurant should be. **Union Square Café** is the most comfortable American bistro in the city, with the kindest chef, Danny Meyer. **Bouley** is the most breathtakingly beautiful restaurant to have opened in NY in the last 20 years, the most heavily attended nouvelle French restaurant in the city, and the cheapest way to Provence. **Lafayette** provides a peek into the next century's cooking. Not only does the chef juxtapose great flavours, he invents techniques for cooking food. He's the most creative chef in New York. **Alison on Dominick** is a quiet refuge in a city that is too noisy, too flashy, too everything. Go for quiet conversation and enjoy tasty southwestern French-inspired food."

LAFAYETTE, Drake Hotel, 65 E 56th St, NY 10022 ☎ (212) 832 1565
Hushed and plush setting for French haute cuisine. *"Cooking of extraordinary drama, dazzling confrontations of flavour that for all their daring always work"* – SEYMOUR BRITCHKY.

LA GRENOUILLE, 3 E 52nd St, NY 10022 ☎ (212) 752 1495
Proving the old ones are the best, this refined dinery has been peaking for over 20 years. *"The most consistent fine-quality cuisine. I would rate it as the top classic French restaurant in New York"* – STANLEY MARCUS. At 100 bucks a pop, it should be good. While there is one report of 'middle-of-the-road food', recommendations are filed by LORD LICHFIELD, MARIO BUATTA and BARBARA TAYLOR BRADFORD: *"We love it for 2 reasons. The flowers are outstanding – very famous for these extraordinary giant arrangements done by Charles Masson, son of the owner. Also the food, of course."*

LA TULIPE, 104 W 13th St, NY 10011 ☎ (212) 691 8860
Parisian-style dinery with zinc-topped bar and tables, and artfully arranged dishes – herby, succulent snapper, game with spinach and pine kernels. *"A treat. It's almost as though you have been invited to dine privately with Sally and John Darr in their own house"* – ELISE PASCOE. EDWARD CARTER's sentiments exactly.

LE BERNARDIN, 155 W 51st St, NY 10019 ☎ (212) 489 1515
Remains No 1 for fish and seafood, and arguably tops for French cuisine. Hung with seascapes and fishy paintings, this tight ship is run by brother-sister duo Maguy and Gilbert LeCoze. *"At once the purest and most assertive expression of seafood through the whole spectrum of its flavours"* – SEYMOUR BRITCHKY. *"A breath of France in New York – vibrant and serious, the masterwork of professionals"* – GAEL GREENE. *"Good and unusual"* – CAROLINE HUNT. *"It has to be the best fish restaurant in New York"* – LORD LICHFIELD.

LE CIRQUE, 58 E 65th St, NY 10021 ☎ (212) 794 9292
As red-hot as ever, the Mayfair Regent's famous restaurant still has the most star quality and pzazz, not to mention sensational eclectic French and Italian cuisine (sea scallops and truffles, carpaccio of snapper, die-for crème brûlée). *"Being outrageously indulged by the prince of pamper, Sirio Maccioni, and Daniel Boulud's cuisinary high jinks make it my idea of heaven. I'm wild about the seared near-sashimi tuna on leeks"* – GAEL GREENE. *"Don't fall for a late luncheon booking. The food is so good and the scene so vibrant that no one wants to leave. Australians aren't used to waiting for tables, no matter how good"* – ELISE PASCOE. *"Very crowded with a good ambience"* – CAROLINE HUNT. Regulars (whose tables are earmarked) include Richard Nixon, DOUGLAS FAIRBANKS JR, Mick

Buzz Gastronomic gabble: Even GAEL GREENE will wait in line at **John's Pizza**, 278 Bleecker St ☎ (212) 243 1680, for *"the best pizza in the whole world. I like everything piled on except for anchovies"* – MARIO BUATTA ...... YAN-KIT SO plumps for the Italian **Palio**, 151 W 51st St ☎ (212) 245 4850 for *"breast of squab in a crispy artichoke shell – that for me was very unusual"* .. .... KENNETH LANE gauges **Gage & Tollner**, 374 Fulton St, Brooklyn ☎ (718) 875 5181, best for *"soft-belly broiled or steamed clams with toast, a little butter and cracker crumbs"* ...... TWIGGY LAWSON loves **Cantina**, 221 Columbus Ave ☎ (213) 873 2606: *"We adore Mexican food. This has great food (try the chicken fajitas), a casual atmosphere, and great margaritas!"* ....

Jagger, Woody Allen, Jerry Zipkin, Nancy Reagan, MARGAUX HEMINGWAY, BIJAN, WOLF-GANG PUCK and BARBARA TAYLOR BRADFORD (*"Always a circus! Full of celebrities"*).

LE MADRI, 168 W 18th St, NY 10011
☎ (212) 727 8022
Named after the 3 genuine Italian mammas who cook up genuine Italian food (under the auspices of a home-grown US chef). Opened by Pino Loungo, who used to own Il Cantinori. Its proximity to Barney's means you can flop down here after a hard day's credit card-flexing. *"You get real cooking. A good idea and tremendously successful"* – JOAN BURSTEIN.

LUTECE, 249 E 50th St, NY 10022
☎ (212) 752 2225
One of the top French restaurants in town, owned by the masterful chef André Soltner, with Marc Haberlin of Auberge de l'Ill, France, as consultant chef. Cosseted regulars and first-timers get the same star treatment. *"The most civilized eating place in New York. The trad-itional cooking has the character of the past, but refined, lightened and rarefied"* – SEYMOUR BRITCHKY.

METRO, 23 E 74th St, NY 10021
☎ (212) 249 3030
New feverishly hot diner, for American cuisine with classical French depths. Daily-changing menu. In a library-like setting filled with paint-ings, tuck in to warm poached Pine Island oysters, grilled black sea bass, sautéed Norwe-gian salmon steak, grilled squab or medallions of venison, trumped by crème brûlée or apple cake baked to order.

MONDRIAN, 7 E 59th St, NY 10022
☎ (212) 935 3434
Artful, luxy, new menu venue. *"I love Mon-drian. The food is complex but not convoluted, almost always as tasty as it is beautiful. Every-thing he does sings with flavour and textural surprise"* – GAEL GREENE. *"The food of the whole world integrated into one man's own visionary cooking, in the most smashing new restaurant setting to hit New York in a decade"* – SEYMOUR BRITCHKY. Feast on red snapper with lemon and deep-fried spinach, guinea hen with a compote of apple and potato, divine desserts.

MORTIMER'S, 1057 Lexington Ave, NY
10021 ☎ (212) 517 6400
Still *the* socialite 'club', run by Glenn Bernbaum for 'members' who lunch, such as Nan Kempner, Pat Buckley, BILL BLASS, Carolina Herrera, Jackie Onassis, Shirley MacLaine, Gloria Vanderbilt, JOAN COLLINS, King Juan Carlos, BARBARA TAYLOR BRADFORD. Only the most courageous unknowns dare enter. *"Remains the favourite"* – KENNETH LANE. *"Great for lunch, especially on the first day you arrive. You immediately feel you're in New York"* – JOAN BURSTEIN.

ODEON, 145 W Broadway, NY 10013
☎ (212) 233 0507
The McNallys' original, an American brasserie with tons of tubular chrome, fine French food and *bags* of ambience. Streetwise kids (and the not-so-kiddish) cram in late at night and for brunch.

150 WOOSTER, 150 Wooster St, NY 10013
☎ (212) 995 1010
Hot, hot *hot* – no self-respecting socialite or fashion hound hasn't been. Run by Brazilians Nessia Pope and Sylvia Martin, it's *"a real evening event. One of those places where I usually know most of the people...but even if you don't, you can get a glimpse of New York downtown society"* – TAMA JANOWITZ. Awash with people like Bianca Jagger, Diane Keaton, names ...*"Where else can I get close to Glenn Close"* quips DAVID SHILLING. *"Like every other trendy-wendy I rush down to 150 Wooster. I thought the food was excellent, the atmosphere 'so-what?', the room 'come again'"* – PETER STRINGFELLOW. *"The hot place in New York. Fun, very lively"* – ED VICTOR. MARIO BUATTA agrees. Others feel it's a case of the emperor's new clothes.

ORSO, 322 W 46th St, NY 10036
☎ (212) 489 7912
Papà to a bunch of Orsos (LA, Toronto, London), this North Italian diner is the best restaurant in the Theatre District (but book dinner with your tickets). A winner for MARIO BUATTA, ROBERT SANGSTER and TWIGGY LAWSON: *"The food is sensational – especially the pasta (very unusual sauces) and the garlic pizza bread. Most import-antly they don't hustle you out when it's late..."*

OYSTER BAR, Grand Central Terminal,
Lower Level, NY 10163 ☎ (212) 490 6650
So cacophonous you can't hear yourself eat (leav-ing some locals disenchanted), the legendary Oyster Bar is nevertheless a favourite. *"Don't go for a business lunch or a cosy lunch but a celebratory lunch with a greedy friend,"* advises LORD LICHFIELD. Alternatively, GAEL GREENE suggests arriving after the crowds have died down at 2pm, sitting at the bar, *"tasting one of each oyster, sharing a clam roast, sipping a great white wine...."* ELISE PASCOE declares: *"No serious seafood lover can honestly go to New York without dining there. I love the marvellous vaulted ceilings."* Tremendous atmosphere, with white-coated waiters whipping oysters from their shells; try also the clam chowder and scallop stew. *"Always fun"* – ANDREW LLOYD WEBBER.

PETROSSIAN, 182 W 58th St, NY 10019
☎ (212) 245 2214
Still the majestic best for caviare-plus. An art deco symphony in pink, with banquettes of mink-trimmed kid. *"For caviare, smoked sturgeon, fish roe and smoked fish of all kinds, this place has no peer"* – SEYMOUR BRITCHKY. Divine foie gras, too – and a mighty bill.

Grills, No Frills

Good, honest American bar/grills are the New Age rage. Expect good, honest décor – bare brick walls, original tiled or polished wood floors, a showpiece antique bar – and good, honest American food: hearty soups, grilled fish, steak tartare, chops, meatloaf, pies, burgers. Also old-fashioned cocktails and down-to-earth prices. Hot off the launch pad this year are **Joe's Bar & Grill**, 142 W 10th St ☎ (212) 727 1785 (recommended by CAROLINE HUNT), **The TriBeCa Grill**, 375 Greenwich St ☎ (212) 334 3220, owned by Robert De Niro and Drew Nieporent (of Montrachet) and based in their new TriBeCa Film Center, and **la Cité and Grill de la Cité**, 120 W 51st St ☎ (212) 956 7100, two-thirds Parisian brasserie and one-third *grill*.

THE QUILTED GIRAFFE, AT&T Arcade, 550 Madison Ave, NY 10022 ☎ (212) 593 1221
One of the old guard – revered, renowned and rip-roaringly expensive. Sensational New American cuisine that can be *"wonderfully surprising"* – LORD LICHFIELD.

ROSA MEXICANO, 1063 1st Ave, NY 10022 ☎ (212) 753 7407
One of the best Mexican restaurants in New York, despite its location far from the border. Highbrow Mex mix – from red snapper in cilantro (coriander) to the best guacamole in town.

RUSSIAN TEA ROOM, 150 W 57th St, NY 10019 ☎ (212) 265 0947
Pre-glasnost extravaganza where café society sip Russian tea, swig vodka and dine on traditional dishes. *"Exotic and plush, with some specialities unmatched anywhere else"* – LORD LICHFIELD. *"Consistent, full of celebrities. The blinis, caviare and sour cream are to die for"* – HELEN GURLEY BROWN. ANDRE PREVIN is partial.

SAN DOMENICO, 240 Central Park S, NY 10019 ☎ (212) 265 5959
A newish (arguably overrated) addition to the New York Italian menu. Bolognese dishes in chic wraps attract KENNETH LANE (*"wonderful Italian specialities"*), BARBARA KAFKA (*"wonderful red bean soup"*) and GAEL GREENE (for their foie gras, *"the ultimate liver and onions"*).

SERYNA, 11 E 53rd St, NY 10022 ☎ (212) 980 9393
The smart stop-off for sushi. RAYMOND BLANC was knocked out by the raw fish, *"so good and melting and clear. It was so pure, nothing was overdone. It was more than excellent."*

SHUN LEE PALACE, 155 E 55th St, NY 10022 ☎ (212) 371 8844
Considered by many to be the best Chinese. Highly orchestrated feasting on specialities from all over China. Its spin-off **Shun Lee Café** at 43 W 65th St is a similar style but cheaper.

SPARKS STEAKHOUSE, 210 E 46th St, NY 10017 ☎ (212) 687 4855
For the best cuts of beef in town. *"My new favourite restaurant. They couldn't be nicer – it could be the best in the world, wonderful service, wonderful wine list, marvellous meat…by far the best steak I've ever had"* – KENNETH LANE. *"For their steaks and the best Italian wines I've ever drunk"* – MICHAEL BROADBENT. DON HEWITSON says aye.

21 CLUB, 21 W 52nd St, NY 10019 ☎ (212) 582 7200
This gentlemen's clubbish restaurant is *"a New York institution, but you have to know someone who belongs and then hope to be seated at one of the 'in' tables"* – ELISE PASCOE. *"21 will always be 21, a club, a New York happening. The chicken hash and sunset salad are as good as ever"* – HELEN GURLEY BROWN. *"Chicken hash,"* confirms LORD LICHFIELD, *"is the best in the world – at a price."*

🐟 UNION SQUARE CAFE, 21 E 16th St, NY 10003 ☎ (212) 243 4020
Union kids are oh so hip – Danny Meyer's diner is a-bustle with publishing and advertising types

🐟 **Buzzz** JULIAN LLOYD WEBBER finds **McSorley's**, 15 E 7th St, *"a wondrous establishment…an Irish bar where, extraordinarily for New York, they brew their own ale."* 🐟......Sunday munch for the pious: go see **Lola**, 30 W 22nd St ☎ (212) 675 6700, for her high-spicy, Afro-Caribbean **Gospel Brunch** – *"you OD on muffins so you can't move and are rooted to your chair, and singers go round and put the microphone in your face and make you sing things like 'I believe in the Lord'"* – SEBASTIAN SCOTT 🐟......For simple, correct Japanese cuisine, **Hatsuhana**, 17 E 48th St ☎ (212) 355 3345, gets JOSHUA WESSON's vote: *"Their squid feet are the best in New York"* (that's tentacles to you and me)......................🐟

New York Delis

"Balducci's, Zabar's and Dean & Deluca are some of the best food shops in the world. Balducci's is like dying and going to heaven – my idea of bliss. I just ate so much. I tried everything from hot dogs to fresh papaya juice...and knishes...and bagels...and lox...it was heavenly. Every time my friends couldn't find me they went hunting in Zabar's" – SOPHIE GRIGSON. The family deli-grocer **Balducci's**, 424 Ave of the Americas ☎ (212) 673 2600, stocks fresh local and exotic produce with an Italian accent. **Zabar's**, 2245 Broadway ☎ (212) 787 2000, is the foodie's deli, an institution in which you can barely move for the crowds. Each week at least 30,000 customers get through 30,000 croissants, 10,000 lb of coffee and 2,000 lb of smoked salmon. Some feel the vast new **Dean & Deluca**, 560 Broadway ☎ (212) 431 1691, has capped Balducci's, if not Zabar's. Not only prime produce but kitchen ware, cook books, a pastry shop, and a cappuccino/espresso bar at the front of the store. **Eat**, 867 and 1064 Madison Ave ☎ (212) 879 4017, owned by Eli Zabar, brother of Saul and Stanley of Zabar's, is the place for *"cappuccino and the most marvellous brownies"* – ELISE PASCOE. **Carnegie Deli**, 854 7th Ave ☎ (212) 757 2245, is the archetypal Jewish deli, open 6am-4am; long queues form on Sunday morning for a fix of matzo ball soup and sandwiches.

who work in the fast-developing, ultra-fash Flatiron District. *"My other fave rave of New York. Fabulous Italian influence. It has amazing things like fresh garlic potato crisps, wonderful bruschetta. A great, great restaurant"* – LOYD GROSSMAN.

Shopping

See also Fashion designers.

Fifth and **Madison Avenues** are still the glossy home to designer boutiques and the biggest and best stores imaginable. Fifth and 57th is aglitter with jewellers – Harry Winston, Tiffany, Van Cleef & Arpels, Bulgari, Cartier. **Lower Fifth Avenue**, **SoHo** and **Greenwich Village** (particularly **Bleecker Street**) are the best for offbeat original clothes and for street life. The pumped-up **Columbus Avenue** is simply the centre of yuppieville with West Side versions of East Side stores plus some cute little shops.

ABERCROMBIE & FITCH, South St Seaport, 199 Water St, NY 10038 ☎ (212) 809 9000
The place to be kitted out for your Hemingwayesque safari. Bush jackets and other cool garb for hot climes, custom-made in their own cloth. Also sporting books, prints and desk accessories.

AMY DOWN HATS, 103 Stanton St, NY 10002 ☎ (212) 473 0237
"A young woman who makes beautiful, fun hats. She has a really cute shop" – TAMA JANOWITZ. Open Wed to Sat.

ARMY & NAVY, 221 E 59th St, NY 10011 ☎ (212) 755 1855; 328 Bleecker St; 110 8th Ave
A 57-year-old family biz that is *"the best place in the world to buy jeans and socks and T-shirts. It's cheap and has the best selection. The whole Levi's range that you can't get anywhere else, 3-packs of Hanes or Klein T-shirts, Dexter's loafers, good underwear and flying jackets. That's where most of my money goes"* – ROBERT ELMS.

🍴 BARNEYS, 106 7th Ave, NY 10014 ☎ (212) 929 9000
The store for the image-conscious. Art/design/music/film types flock in, attracted by a different kind of buying, a superb sense of taste. Stacked with designer labels for men and women and their sassy homes. *"One of my favourites for looking around"* – JOAN BURSTEIN. ROBERT ELMS, Lauren Hutton, Cindy Crawford and Lucy Ferry are fans too. Barneys is now breeding – first in Beverly Hills, then across the States.

BARRY KIESELSTEIN-CORD at Bergdorf-Goodman, Neiman Marcus
For precious jewellery and belts. It was he who cultivated the chunky Western unpolished gold belt buckle. Illustrious clients include the Reagans, Frank Sinatra, Jack Nicholson, Mick Jagger, Eddie Murphy, Diana Ross.... JOAN BURSTEIN's fave for costume jewellery.

🍴 BERGDORF-GOODMAN, 754 5th Ave, NY 10019 ☎ (212) 753 7300
"Probably the single best store in America today" – STANLEY MARCUS. Still a sizzling supremo, this fashion-conscious department store is switched on to all the hottest designers. Brilliant, eclectic buying; goods are beautifully

Hijinks in the Lower Fifth

Known as the 'Flatiron District' (after the famous building at 23rd and 5th), Lower Fifth Avenue is the new rising star, for shops, diners (**Sofi** [South of Flatiron], **Union Square Café**, **Live Bait** bar), clubs (**Tramps**), billiard parlours (**Chelsea Billiards**, **Society Billiards**) and even **Putters Paradise**, an indoor mini golf course. Your whistle-stop shoppers' tour starts from the east side of 5th Ave at 23rd, moving south: **Dot Zero**, the International Design Center of New York's store, for housewares, toys, stationery, etc; **Otto-Tootsi Plohound** shoes; **Daffy's** designer discount store;

Barnes & Noble for books, with cheapo reads and records at their Sale Annex across the street; **Kenneth Cole** shoes; **Folklorica** – great for presents by folk artists; **B Shackman** for toys. We're down to 15th St now; cross to the west side of 5th and walk north: **Alain Mikli** for not only the widest and wildest array of specs but a ceiling that is *"painted midnight blue with Corinthian gold accents. It is very stark and very cool"* – TYLER BRULE; **Paul Smith**, **Emporio Armani** and **Matsuda** – all for the designer man (and woman); and finally **Tropica** – for knick-knackery on a tropical theme.

displayed – in the windows and in the store. *"Remains the uptown store that is most appealing"* – BILL BLASS. JOAN BURSTEIN agrees.

BIJAN, 699 5th Ave, NY 10022
☎ (212) 758 7500
This whirling dervish designs the whole package for men bar underwear. *"Whatever I wear is my own line,"* quoth he. *"Shoes – I do it myself. Jewellery – I do it myself..."* Ties, suits, shirts, he does it himself. What he does are classics with an innovative Middle Eastern twist, plus perfume that's an international bestseller from Neiman Marcus to Harrods. Clients include King Hussein II, King Juan Carlos, Julio Iglesias and Jack Nicholson. *"Flourishing – a unique personality,"* enthuses ELEANOR LAMBERT. Back to BIJAN: *"I am honoured that I have the most important, obviously difficult, powerful customers from all over the world – a king, a president, a captain of industry – I love them and I respect them. I am in heaven after I have done my job for an embassy or a palace and I see them wearing my clothes...."*

BLOOMINGDALE'S, 59th St and
Lexington Ave, NY 10022 ☎ (212) 705 2000
A New York institution and landmark, taking up almost a whole block. All the top labels are there for adorning self and home. One of the best food halls in the Big Apple – an amazing array of munchables, excellent bakery, the cream of European produce and speciality imports. Kitchen equipment, too.

BROOKS BROTHERS, 346 Madison Ave, NY 10017 ☎ (212) 682 8800
The trad place for men's classics, where preps grow up to be smart financial boys. The classic pale blue button-down Oxford shirt remains their bestseller, but they do the full kit (for preppy girls too) – cricket jerseys, cotton knits, ties, off-the-peg suits, plaid skirts, shoes and separates. *"I have 15-year-old shirts from Brooks Brothers. They last forever"* – PETER YORK.

CHARIVARI, 18 W 57th St, NY 10019
☎ (212) 333 4040; branches at 2307 and 2339
Broadway, 257 and 441 Columbus Ave
Up-to-the-second stash of fashion. Exclusive, well-edited batch of mainly European designers for men (Armani, Versace, Montana, Byblos, Casely-Hayford, Matsuda, Dominguez) and women (Gigli, Sybilla, Alaïa, Gaultier).

DE VECCHI at Bergdorf-Goodman,
I Magnin, Neiman Marcus
Pioneering bags and belts by Hamilton Hodge (ex-Ferragamo and Donna Karan). Skins and leathers – Louisiana alligator, lizard, kid – are hand-woven around wooden forms so that there are no seams. *"For experimental new shapes in the classic mode. Innovative forms using precious skins"* – ANIKO GAAL.

ERIC BEAMON at Barneys
Wild, wacky, weighty jewellery. After bead curtain belts for Jasper Conran and jangly charm bracelets, he's doing miles of multi-strand gilt medallion necklaces and the longest gilt filigree drop earrings you've seen in your life.

FRANK OLIVE, 9th Fl, 134 W 37th St, NY
10018 ☎ (212) 947 6655
Classy custom-made hats from an enduring headmaster. Kentucky Derby numbers of lacquered straw and linen. Ready-to-wear at Saks.

FRED LEIGHTON, 773 Madison Ave, NY
10021 ☎ (212) 288 1872
The best period jewellers in the world for late 19C and 20C well-wrought blockbuster rocks.

Lots of estate jewellery. The exclusive on René Boivin of Paris; using his original moulds, they have re-created old designs such as animal jewellery studded in canary diamonds.

GO SILK at Neiman Marcus, Bergdorf-Goodman, Charivari
Clothes in a new pre-washed and shrunk silk that is wowing all wearers. Developed in Hong Kong, with a New York designer. *"I'm a Go Silk person at the moment. It feels fabulous to wear and they do a huge range of very basic shapes. The director said that once I put it on I would be hooked, and I am. I've got a red suit, a white suit, a blue suit, a coat and trousers"* – DUGGIE FIELDS. *"The hottest new fabric...wonderful clothes. They have a genuine indigo dye and their shirt with brass studs looks just like a denim shirt until you take a step nearer. It's the best joke in clothes I've seen"* – GLYNN CHRISTIAN.

> **❝People ask me why I do not design for women, but I say I do. I make her husband, her boyfriend, her father look good. That's what I do for women❞**
>
> BIJAN

HAMMACHER SCHLEMMER, 147 E 57th St, NY 10022 ☎ (212) 421 9000
No 1 cult home of high-class gadgetry (they were the first ever to stock the pop-up toaster and the electric shaver). Full of expensive little somethings for the person who has everything...a $6,500 full-size fibre-optic Christmas tree that changes colour; a desk-top weather station. DUDLEY MOORE is a fan of the Beverly Hills branch.

HARRY WINSTON, 718 5th Ave, NY 10019 ☎ (212) 245 2000; at Trump Tower
Knockout jewels. You come to the Grand Salon more for stupendous stones and classic styles than for innovative design. The Petit Salon in Trump Tower has more practical pieces.

HENRI BENDEL, 10 W 57th St, NY 10019 ☎ (212) 247 1100
The first department store to present itself as a chi-chi set of boutiques on a cobbled street. Intimate and inviting, it's LORD LICHFIELD's first stop for the best pot-pourri, Agraria.

JAMES ROBINSON, 15 E 57th St, NY 10022 ☎ (212) 752 6166
Venerable East Side jewellers, more like a mini department store. The very best period pieces from all over the globe.

JAY FEINBERG, 42 W 39th St, NY 10018 ☎ (212) 575 8474 and at stores
Decorative jewellery, some faux, some semi-precious, some the real McCoy. *"Still very good with multi-coloured stones – amethyst, topaz, sapphire, emerald – in lovely Arabian-influenced necklaces. With the new spare fashion shapes, all you need is one fabulous pair of earrings or a necklace"* – ANIKO GAAL.

JOAN & DAVID, 816 Madison Ave, NY 10021 ☎ (212) 772 3970; in major stores
Wife/hubby team producing hand-crafted footwear with a Western lilt (lots of lace-ups and mixed skins), belts, luggage and sportswear.

JOHNNY FARAH, 41 Wooster St, NY 10013 ☎ (212) 777 7711
Still setting the style for belts and bags. One of the first to use exotic skins, they're now strutting their Western stuff: new buck baby-smooth suede, dyed earthy hues and ornamented with sterling silver itsy bits (cowboy boots, bulls' heads); braided leather belts with tiny bags.

JUDITH LEIBER, 20 W 33rd St, NY 10001 ☎ (212) 736 4244; at Saks Fifth Avenue
Handsome handbags – chic little crocs; lightweight canvas holdalls with initials and a crest; animal-shaped bags. *"Her bags are the best!"* – HELEN GURLEY BROWN.

KENNETH COLE, 95 5th Ave, NY 10003 ☎ (212) 675 2550; 353 Columbus Ave
Cole keeps in step with fashion, not only with his Italian-made shoes for men, women, children and trendy toddlers but also with witty, socially conscious ads.

KENNETH JAY LANE, Trump Tower, 725 5th Ave, NY 10018 ☎ (212) 868 1780; 250A Columbus Ave
King of costume jewellery and a sparkling society figure himself, he provides the pearls that dress the neck of the First Lady Barbara Bush. Other famous falsies used to adorn style doyenne Diana Vreeland.

LACRASIA, 389 5th Ave, NY 10016 ☎ (212) 545 9210
Handsome hand couture by Donna Williams: Egyptian cotton gloves with chains of coins and tassels, gauntlets with whip-stitching, Indian-style beaded ethnicities, bridal gloves with pearls and lace.

LINDA DRESNER, 484 Park Ave, NY 10022 ☎ (212) 308 3177
A shop that suits JOAN BURSTEIN: *"I don't like to see a lot of clothes together. Linda Dresner is one of the most selective for ladies' clothing."* So edited down that there used to be nothing at all in the window; now you see a few accessories. Inside are Mugler, Montana, Alaïa, Gigli, Muir.

LUC BENOIT, 315 5th Ave, NY 10016 ☎ (212) 239 0043
"Beautiful alligator, crocodile and ostrich bags and belts. Beautiful new shapes and re-creations of classics" – ANIKO GAAL.

MACY'S, 151 W 34th St, NY 10001
☎ (212) 695 4400
'Macy's, the world's largest store' pipes the telephonist when you call this 2 million-sq ft whopper. Not quite in the style ranks of the big Bs (Bergdorf's, Barney's, Bendel's), it has its fair share of chi-chi designer boutiques (Klein, Armani, Mizrahi, Lempicka, Pomodoro). One of the best Christmas stores, with floors given over to Santaland, Puppetland, and present-strewn Holiday Lane.

MAEVE CARR, 35 W 36th St, NY 10018
☎ (212) 714 9140
Whimsical witty hatter, who also designs in different mode for Donna Karan.

MARTHA, 475 Park Ave, NY 10022
☎ (212) 753 1511
Selectively swanky couture style for women, a pantheon of top establishment names – Bill Blass, Christian Lacroix, Carolina Herrera, Valentino, Galanos. Now the daughters of Martha's clientele can wet their heads (and whet their appetites) at the new **Martha International** next door at No 473. This showcase of contemporary ready-to-wear designers affords a 'global vision' of fashion for a 'vibrant new generation' of young women. The result is a discerning, non-run-of-the-mill, polished collection for the wardrobe, by designers like Christian Francis Roth, Charlotte Neuville, Carmelo Pomodoro, Rebecca Moses, Marion Lesage, Albert Capraro and Fernando Sanchez. Personal service is still a Martha's watchword.

ORA FEDER, 171 Madison Ave, NY 10016
☎ (212) 532 9236
The most exclusive lingerie in the USA. Exquisite silken smoothies, bias cuts and sensational fabrics. Very Jean Harlow.

OTTO-TOOTSI PLOHOUND, 137 5th Ave, NY 10010 ☎ (212) 460 8650
"Younger shoes with huge bows on them – a lot of wit" – ANIKO GAAL. The best contemporary tootsies come for style-setting footwear marched in from Europe – Robert Clergerie, Sybilla, Stephane Kélian, Montana. Also branches in Prince St and the Village at Nos 110 (women) and 124 (men).

PATRICIA UNDERWOOD, 265 W 40th St, NY 10018 ☎ (212) 840 6934
Hats with style and bravado that elicit admiration but never outrage. She's designed for Calvin Klein and Rifat Ozbek. *"My favourite. She designs just the right hats for the sort of clothes I wear. I enjoy seeing people in her hats"* – JOAN BURSTEIN.

PAUL STUART, 350 Madison Ave at 45th St, NY 10022 ☎ (212) 682 0320
Upbeat, fashion-conscious American classics for men. Top-to-toe gear and the best braces. For the true New Yorker.

🍎 POLO/RALPH LAUREN, 867 Madison Ave, NY 10021 ☎ (212) 606 2100
"The best shop in the world. I don't think there is a better shopping experience" – BOB PAYTON. As a design and marketing phenomenon, Lauren wins hands down. He gives you a lifestyle and then keeps on nourishing it so that you keep on buying and never get bored. BRUCE OLDFIELD is not the only one to admire him for his business acumen. Lauren does the whole caboodle for the whole family. At his Madison Ave 'French' mansion, he presents the prêt-à-porter English country-house look, home decorations and clothes for him, her and the kids. *"Still caters to a romantic lifestyle, and whether you have that lifestyle or you don't, you <u>want</u> it. He consistently creates items that you must have because they will perk up your wardrobe"* – ANIKO GAAL. There's low-key daywear, there's glam evening wear, and there's Polo, his runaway-success casual menswear line – find a chap who *hasn't* got that little polo player emblazoned on his chest. One of PATRICIA HODGE's faves. *"It's been his decade"* – ELEANOR LAMBERT. At this rate the 90s will be his too.

ROBERT LEE MORRIS GALLERY, 409 W Broadway, NY 10013 ☎ (212) 431 9405;
ARTWEAR GALLERIES, 456 W Broadway, NY 10012 ☎ (212) 673 2000
Sleekly understated, rather organic, jewellery designed by RLM and other artists. KEN LANE and TAMA JANOWITZ are admirers.

SAKS FIFTH AVENUE, 611 5th Ave, NY 10022 ☎ (212) 753 4000
A big store (and g-r-o-wing) with the view of a speciality boutique. The best-dressed bunch teeter in for really smart clothes by famous European and American designers (the exclusive on Adolfo; Armani, Saint Laurent, Ungaro, Blass, Karan and the 2 Kleins – Calvin, Anne). 1990 sees the opening of a new beauty salon and spa.

STEPHEN DWECK JEWELERS, 21 W 38th St, NY 10018 ☎ (212) 764 3030
A designer who puts *"semi-precious stones into romantic settings. It's like having treasures from your grandmother handed down, very nostalgic. I think he's terrific"* – ANIKO GAAL.

SUSAN BENNIS WARREN EDWARDS, 440 Park Ave, NY 10022 ☎ (212) 755 4197
Billed the most extravagant shoe store in the world, this is their only outlet. For handmade satin-lined shoes, swanlike evening slippers, summer mules, kid courts. Wizard with lizard – or any other skin, left natural or dyed every colour under the sun (don't you step on my hot pink alligator pumps).

TIFFANY, 727 5th Ave, NY 10022
☎ (212) 755 8000
A name that starts a little tremor in the hearts of New Yorkers. Anything with the Tiffany

stamp or stashed in Tiffany blue box is a status symbol. Jewels, trinkets, expensive little presents (silver straw, silver toothpaste key), and a new accessories line that keeps ELEANOR LAMBERT keen: *"It's taking off like a house on fire – scarves, handbags – only in a small corner at the moment, but people go because the designs are so interesting."* The exclusive on Elsa Peretti (for silver abstracts) and Paloma Picasso (for chunky gold and silver pieces with socking rocks). *"My favourite place in New York. You never go wrong there. It just isn't the same anywhere else"* – JOAN BURSTEIN.

TOM BINNS at Barneys and Bergdorf-Goodman

Young British jewellery designer who describes his work as 'almost poetry, using glass that looks like it has been washed up on the beach. I wouldn't even call it jewellery.' STEPHEN JONES is convinced: *"He is a very superior designer. Whatever he turned his hand to would be extremely good as he has total taste. His jewellery has an intelligence which is awe-inspiring, and just happens to be very, very beautiful."*

WIFE MISTRESS, 1042 Lexington Ave, NY 10021 ☎ (212) 570 9529

Luxy lingerie and cruise wear: cashmere and silk kaftans, chemises, swimwear, bustiers in silk brocade or velvet, silk tuxedo pyjamas. Which for wife? Which for mistress?

WILLIAM FIORAVANTI, 45 W 57th St, NY 10019 ☎ (212) 355 1540

The best tailor in America, where craftsmen handmake suits for US captains of industry, athletes, presidents, religious leaders even. Anthony Quinn, Paul Anka and lofty basketballer Walt Fraser have a Fioravanti.

Theatre

BROADWAY

Broadway is still in the unhappy situation of only being able to back winners. Productions cost so much to stage that it only dares to put on musicals and conventional theatre that is a tried-and-tested guaranteed sell-out. Not only are most of the shows imported from Britain but they often get premièred elsewhere in the States to ensure their American appeal. New York audiences are tough and opinionated, the critics are avidly read; shows can close in a matter of days. You can't knock Broadway's cachet, though, and if a show makes it that far, it will play to packed houses. However, with tickets so expensive (from $40), many punters prefer to dish out their greenbacks Off-Broadway – or Off Off-Broadway. (NB Some of Broadway's major theatres are not actually *on* Broadway.) **Off-Broadway** refers to theatres with under 400 seats. Based in SoHo, the Village and other locations off Broadway, these theatres are still staging tomorrow's hits – serious dramas, comedies, new and avant-garde plays, unconventional productions of classics. This is the cutting edge of American theatre – and cheaper than Broadway. **Off Off-Broadway** is a more extreme, more experimental version of Off-Broadway.

NEW YORK SHAKESPEARE FESTIVAL, 425 Lafayette St, NY 10003 ☎ (212) 598 7100

A summer series of excellent free Shakespeare plays (mostly directed by founder and president Joseph Papp), at the Delacorte Theater in Central Park. Top actors have starred – William Hurt, Kevin Kline, Martin Sheen, Meryl Streep, Christopher Walken. First-come first-served seating unless you're a sponsor.

Palm Springs

Palm Springs and nearby Palm Desert are where Los Angelinos go at weekends to do what they already do (tennis, golf, swimming, getting fit, beautifying) in less smoggy surroundings. Ever springing up are new resorts and spas, blending a taste of old Mehico with the biggest and best pool, spa bath, golf course, computerow, treadmill, rebounder, Lifecycle, shopping arcade, etc, etc. Mosey on down to **Marriott's Rancho Las Palmas**, Rancho Mirage ☎ (619) 568 2727 or their **Desert Springs Resort**, Palm Desert ☎ (619) 341 2211 with its 'Venetian-inspired' network of lakes and waterways that flows right through the 8-storey atrium lobby. The oldest resort hotel is **La Quinta**, 49-499 Eisenhower Drive, La Quinta ☎ (619) 564 4111, where stars of the golden era would swing a 9-iron and brush up their lob. *"It's designer Western with Indian rugs and Mexican paintings"* – WILLIAM DAVIES. Another old Hollywood haunt is the **Palm Springs Racquet Club**, with *"the best pool on the West Coast – a great big slab of unbelievably blue water, like a wonderful ice-bath"* – WILLIAM D. The best spa for complete rejuvenation is **Two Bunch Palms**, Desert Hot Springs ☎ (619) 329 8791 with its geothermal soaking pools and clay cabana mud baths. When you're Mexicana'd out, taste life at the new **Ritz-Carlton Rancho Mirage**, 68-900 Frank Sinatra Drive, Rancho Mirage ☎ (619) 321 8282, which, for all the world, looks like ...a European country home.

PALM BEACH

—— Art and museums ——

**HENRY MORRISON FLAGLER
MUSEUM (WHITEHALL), Cocoanut Row,
PO Box 969, FL 33480 ☎ (407) 655 2833**
Whitehall is Henry Flagler's ravishingly restored private residence, built in 1901. Behind
the colonial façade lies a marble hall with double
staircase and frescoed ceiling, a Louis XIV music
room, Italian Renaissance library, Louis XV
ballroom and an Elizabethan breakfast room –
all of which must have led to an identity crisis.

**NORTON GALLERY & SCHOOL OF ART,
1451 S Olive Ave, W Palm Beach, FL 22401
☎ (407) 832 5194**
Mainly modern European and American works
of art. Also Chinese jades; ceramics, bronzes and
sculpture. Concerts, films and lectures, plus the
annual Bal des Arts, one of the highlights of the
Palm Beach season.

PHILADELPHIA

—— Art and museums ——

**🐟 PHILADELPHIA MUSEUM OF ART,
26th St and Benjamin Franklin Parkway,
PO Box 7646, PA 19101 ☎ (215) 763 8100**
The neo-classical building is one of the greatest
art institutions in the world, housing over
500,000 works from classical to modern times.
Chinese antiquities, reconstructed period rooms,
European masters, antique furniture, American
painting and decorative arts, and international
modern art (including a *Bathers* by Cézanne and
a *Sunflowers* by Van Gogh). The **Rodin
Museum**, 22nd St and Benjamin Franklin Pky
☎ (215) 787 5431, has casts of most of his great
sculptures, plus drawings and memorabilia.

**WINTERTHUR MUSEUM & GARDENS,
Winterthur, DE 19735 ☎ (302) 888 4600**
Some 30 mins from Philadelphia is Henry F du
Pont's country estate, housing his collection of
mid-17C to mid-19C American decorative arts.
Delightful garden.

—— Hotels ——

**FOUR SEASONS, 1 Logan Square, PA
19103 ☎ (215) 963 1500**
*"Very stylish and very personal, with instant
service. Fantastic location looking out on the
Square (which is in fact a circle), wonderful
views, a nice terrace. Really comfortable rooms
and beds, and probably the best-equipped bathrooms of any hotel"* – JEFFERY TOLMAN.

Florida Seafood
🐟

"I like going to **Apalachicola**, *Florida,
enormously. It's a teeny-weeny wooden
seaside town on the Gulf of Mexico – very,
very pretty. It used to be an important port
and I don't think anything has changed
since about 1890. It has golden beaches,
lots of birds, a jetty and people fishing,
and Apalachicola oysters, which are very
small, very soft, very sweet and don't
travel"* – JAMES BURKE. For DAVID LITCH-
FIELD, **Snack Jacks**, Ormond Beach, in
northern Florida, is memorable: *"There
are very few restaurant/bars on the beach
in that part of the world. It's beautiful, a
cross between* American Graffiti *and something Steinbeck would have written. Just
wonderful, oysters and fish and beer. Most
of the people who work there look like
Golden Gloves contenders – bent noses and
handy baseball bats."* **Joe's Stone
Crabs**, 227 Biscayne St, Miami ☎ (305)
673 0365, is, for LARRY KING, *"one of the
great restaurants of the world. The best
potatoes, the best vegetables, the best variety of food. It's noisy but enjoyably
noisy."* *"Legendary,"* adds BOB PAYTON.
The crabs are boiled, then served cold with
mustard sauce or drawn butter.

—— Restaurants ——

**LE BEC-FIN, 1523 Walnut St, PA 19102
☎ (215) 567 1000**
Grandiose French restaurant run by chef-owner
Georges Perrier. Gorgeous Louis XV décor
(chandeliers, damask, mirrored walls), modern-
classic cuisine and faultless service.

**OLD ORIGINAL BOOKBINDER'S, 125
Walnut St, PA 19106 ☎ (215) 925 7027**
Based in an 1865 building, Bookbinder's is renowned for its seafood, flown in daily. Dip into
their snapper soup and celebrated bouillabaisse
(this on Fridays only, when the retired chef
returns to re-create his inimitable secret recipe).
"Spectacular restaurant with very good wines"
– TERRY HOLMES.

**RESTAURANT ODEON, 114 S 12th St, PA
19107 ☎ (215) 922 4399**
A winner for innovative French regional cuisine
– sautéed crab cakes with lemon butter sauce,
fresh foie gras with purée of lentils, grilled duck
breast with Sichuan peppercorn crust.

SAN FRANCISCO

Ballet

SAN FRANCISCO BALLET, 455 Franklin St, CA 94102 ☎ (415) 861 5600
Founded in 1933, this classical-based company is the oldest in the States. Directed by Helgi Tomasson, ex-New York City Ballet, they also perform new works. *"An important company"* – EDWARD THORPE.

Bars and cafés

TOSCA CAFE, 242 Columbus Ave, CA 94133 ☎ (415) 986 9651
"Still one of the places to hang out after dinner if you want to see the movie, music and artistic crowd, from Russian dancers to rock and roll stars" – JEREMIAH TOWER.

TRADER VIC'S, 20 Cosmo Place, CA 94109 ☎ (415) 775 6300
The original, and part of the fabric of San Fran drinkeries (in the Captain's Cabin). The new management may just give it the shot it needs.

Clubs

DNA LOUNGE, 375 11th St, CA 94103 ☎ (415) 626 1409
The best new wave dance club, run by Brian Raffi, ex-DJ extraordinaire. Live music and the latest contemporary hits play to a thronging art school set.

KIMBALLS, 300 Grove St, CA 94102 ☎ (415) 861 5555
Terrific little jazz club with top acts every week. Across the Bay Bridge in East Bay is Kimball East, his bigger, more elegant jazz club.

MASON'S, Fairmont Hotel, 950 Mason St, CA 94108 ☎ (415) 772 5000
The Fairmont's elegant bar on Nob Hill pulls a smart crowd to hear Peter Mintun tinkling the ivories in vintage 40s and 50s style.

SESAR'S LATIN PALACE, 3140 Mission St, CA 94110 ☎ (415) 648 6611
An authentic Latin ballroom in the heart of the South American district, where all ages converge to salsa the night away to Sesar's Latin All-Stars live sets. Occasional after-hours shows (2-6am) on weekends.

SLIM'S, 333 11th St, CA 94103 ☎ (415) 621 3330
With Boz Scaggs as co-owner, this 300-seat rock club is the hot, happening place for American roots music (R&B, blues, jazz). Dance, drink and dine too.

"It would be hard to beat San Francisco for every reason. It's got everything – the climate, the sea, universities. It's remarkably free of the decimation that's gone on elsewhere in the States"

 JAMES BURKE

THE STONE, 412 Broadway, CA 94113 ☎ (415) 391 8284; 391 8282
Taken over by John Nady, this is *the* place for heavy metal, hard rock and punk bands, with bags of street cred. Open till 6am.

SWEETWATER, 153 Throckmorton St, CA 94941 ☎ (415) 388 2820
Across the Golden Gate in Mill Valley is this secret little dive, the fave hang-out of Marin County rock stars. John Lee Hooker, Huey Lewis, Sammy Hagar of Van Halen, Ry Cooder and Carlos Santana drop by and may even play. Folk, blues and rock.

Hotels

CAMPTON PLACE, 340 Stockton St, CA 94108 ☎ (415) 781 5555
Under the new management of Jim Nassikas (who *made* Stanford Court), this promises to be better than ever. Impeccably decorated in cosy/contemporary mode, behind an older façade. Rooms can be small, but service and style more than compensate. Popular with Brits and Australians, it's No 1 for GEOFFREY ROBERTS and ELISE PASCOE: *"Beautifully decorated rooms and fabulous breakfasts in the prettiest dining room."* Still a fine restaurant (though it has lost its former chef to the Lark Creek Inn).

THE DONATELLO, Pacific Plaza Hotel, 501 Post St, CA 94102 ☎ (415) 441 7100
Highly individual, personal hotel. The gleaming lobby blends antique furniture and contemporary art. Marble hauled in from the very same quarries as Michelangelo's *David*, Fortuny fabrics, hand-painted arabesque panels, Salviati glass. The northern Italian **Ristorante Donatello**, with its crystal wall lamps and arched mirrors, is one of San F's supremos.

FOUR SEASONS CLIFT, 495 Geary St, CA 94102 ☎ (415) 775 4700
A top rater in the States, a distinguished affair with acres of wood panelling, art deco cocktail lounge, top-notch French dining room, and caring staff that know your name. Good for families, with thoughtful extras for children. *"I love it, just fantastic"* – LARRY KING. *"Nice, and great staff"* – BOB PAYTON. *"It gets my vote – it's the best in San Francisco"* – EDWARD CARTER.

HUNTINGTON HOTEL, 1075 California St, CA 94108 ☎ (415) 474 5400
At the top of Nob Hill, a quiet hotel in a 1920s block with fab views. Its classy accoutrements include Irish linens thru' Ming treasures to a Rolls-Royce Silver Shadow courtesy car. Classy, old-fashioned, restaurant, **L'Etoile** ☎ (415) 771 1529, for classic French cuisine. LORD MONTAGU OF BEAULIEU, Luciano Pavarotti, Robert Redford and Paloma Picasso are all Nob Hillbillies.

⚑ MANDARIN ORIENTAL, 222 Sansome St, CA 94104 ☎ (415) 885 0999
As suspected, this stunning twin-tower high rise (joined by a glass bridge) has risen to one of the top slots in the city. Faultless on every count – rooms, service, atmosphere, view. *"Do not miss the service in the Mandarin suites. The bathtubs have the best sweeping view of the Golden Gate Bridge in the whole area"* – JEREMIAH TOWER. Dining is tops too, at the swish **Silks**, for French-Californian fare that continues to wow international foodies. Impeccable, if slightly intimidating, service.

⚑ PORTMAN HOTEL, 500 Post St, CA 94102 ☎ (415) 771 8600
A starry super-luxe addition to the SF fold. STANLEY MARCUS is impressed: *"It has a quality of service that reminds me very much of the Peninsula in Hong Kong or the Oriental, Bangkok."* Not surprising, since they're affiliated to the Peninsula group; each room has its own 24-hour personal valet who comes running at the touch of a button. Top-notch restaurant, **Portman Grill**, with exquisite presentation.

STANFORD COURT, 905 California St, CA 94108 ☎ (415) 989 3500
Taken over last year by Stouffer Hotels, it remains to be seen whether it can maintain its hitherto fine reputation. Standing resplendent on 'Snob' Hill in Governor Leland Stanford's former mansion, it now has a complimentary limo service in a sapphire blue Rolls-Royce Phantom VI. **Fournou's Ovens** ☎ (415) 989 1910 is as charming and romantic as ever, though cuisine has been inconsistent (a change of chefs).

––––––––– *Music* –––––––––

OPERA IN THE PARK, Music Concourse, Golden Gate Park
A free concert featuring the San Francisco Opera Orchestra and stars from the opening night production, held on the Sunday after the opening of the fall season.

⚑ SAN FRANCISCO OPERA, War Memorial Opera House, 301 Van Ness Ave, CA 94102 ☎ (415) 565 6431
Very highly regarded company, one of the top 3 in the States, under the directorship of Lotfi Mansouri. Many of the world's great artists made their début here – Francis Ford Coppola, Sir Geraint Evans, Elisabeth Schwarzkopf, Sir Georg Solti. Operas are sung in their original language with English surtitles. Also recitals, concerts and visiting ballet. *"Very old-established, and a very fine opera house. They bring in famous singers for their fall season"* – RODNEY MILNES. *"Very well run, well lit, good acoustics"* – VISCOUNT HAMBLEDEN. The opera is at the apex of high society in San Francisco, strongly supported by Ann and Gordon Getty. The Sept opening of the 3-month fall season is the West Coast event of the year – a grand dinner, gala performance and a ball.

⚑ THE SAN FRANCISCO SYMPHONY, Davies Symphony Hall, Van Ness Ave, CA 94102 ☎ (415) 552 8011
One of the best orchestras in the States, under the baton of Herbert Blomstedt. A forward-thinking company, they champion young up-and-coming artists and commission important new works (eg Sir Michael Tippett's *New Year Suite*). Also hot on gala benefits, they hold a biennial Black and White Ball and one-off extravaganzas.

––––––––– *Restaurants* –––––––––

See also Hotels.

CHINA MOON CAFE, 639 Post St, CA 94109 ☎ (415) 775 4789
Barbara Tropp's eatery is a love-it or hate-it experience. Some worship her and her spicy Occident-meets-Orient cuisine (*"a must for any adventurous foodie. I eat there every time I visit San Francisco, and never tire of it"* – ELISE PASCOE. *"People are more sensitive to comfort and aware of value, which is why I mention the China Moon. It's rather innovative, very elegant and very good value"* – BARBARA KAFKA. Others are not over the China Moon about it ('small portions', 'uncomfortable', 'expensive', would you believe?).

> **“The whole Californian gastronomic scene is, at the moment, heavily influenced by northern Italian food ”**
>
>  SERENA SUTCLIFFE

FLEUR DE LYS, 777 Sutter St, CA 94109 ☎ (415) 673 7779
One of the few truly classic French restaurants in town, under the helm of Hubert Keller (who trained at Auberge de l'Ill). JEREMIAH TOWER votes it tops for French food in SF (*"still wonderful"*). Diners bask under red silk tenting.

FOG CITY DINER, 1300 Battery St, CA 94111 ☎ (415) 982 2000
A homage to architecture, this brill diner feels

like an old-time train with individual compartments and studded leather upholstery. It fair steams along after theatre and at lunch; good oyster bar and pou pou platter (the Oriental answer to tapas – baby satays, spring rolls, ribs).

JACKSON FILLMORE TRATTORIA, 2506 Fillmore St, CA 94115 ☎ (415) 346 5288
Boisterous trat, packed with yuppies. *"One of my all-time favourite restaurants. Superb no-nonsense Italian food. The aromas draw you from off the street. You can sit at the counter for homy pastas and linger over biscotto (home-made by Jack's wife) with Vin Santo"* – BEVERLEY ZBITNOFF.

THE MANDARIN, Ghirardelli Square, 900 N Point St, CA 94109 ☎ (415) 673 8812
The best-known Chinesery in San F – and you pay for it. Sichuan and Hunan cuisine under the deft touch of Madame Chiang. ROBERT MONDAVI loves the smoked tea duck.

POSTRIO, 545 Post St, CA 94102 ☎ (415) 776 7825
A first for Wolfgang Puck in SF, it's Spago all over again, crowded, rowdy and unmissable. So named because it's at Post Street with a trio of chefs – Annie and David Gingrass, and (occasionally) Puck himself. *"The most exciting restaurant design I've ever seen...but the staff were so hip and cool..."* – BOB PAYTON. *"The hottest restaurant – elegant, interestingly designed and pretty smart. Very exciting Californian food and a good wine list"* – GEOFFREY ROBERTS. The small herb-filled pizzas are like a poem.

SOUTH PARK CAFE, 108 South Park, CA 94107 ☎ (415) 495 7275
"Not for tourists expecting a blockbuster San Francisco evening, but, if tired and foot-weary and in need of a change of pace with very simple good food, this is it. On a square that's unique in San Francisco" – JEREMIAH TOWER.

🦐 **SPEEDOS 690, 690 Van Ness Ave, CA 94102 ☎ (415) 255 6900**
Jeremiah Tower's second string is tropicana meets Americana (Caribbean, Indian, Thai and Californian flavours converge), with no red meat

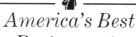

America's Best Restaurants

1	LE BERNARDIN · New York
2	LAFAYETTE · New York
3	STARS · San Francisco
4	BOULEY · New York
5	ZUNI CAFE · San Franciso
6	CHEZ PANISSE · Berkeley
7	CHINOIS ON MAIN · Los Angeles
8	LE CIRQUE · New York
9	FOUR SEASONS · New York
10	JEAN-LOUIS AT WATERGATE · Washington, DC

or pork. It's Stars for the kids (guys in ponytails, girls in bike shorts). Based in an old car workshop called Speedos (hence the nickname), it has an open kitchen and counter, and staff wear baseball caps. *"The hot new restaurant if you're young and trendy. Great fun, huge, very relaxed. The food is less formal than at Stars, more spicy, more innovative"* – GEOFFREY ROBERTS. Smoked chicken salad comes in cashew cream with black bean purée and edible flowers. Tropical trifle is laced with rum and coconut cream, layered with fruit and doused with mango sauce. However, BOB PAYTON isn't taken in: *"It's like the Hard Rock Café of California cuisine – I think it's Jeremiah's joke."*

SQUARE ONE, 190 Pacific St, CA 94111 ☎ (415) 788 1110
Lofty, spacious restaurant for eclectic/Mediterranean cuisine with a West Coast thrill. *"Joyce Goldstein serves terrific up-to-date food. It's always delicious and very interesting. Her son Evan is responsible for the fabulous wine list"* – ELISE PASCOE.

🦐 **Buzzz** China meets California at **Monsoon**, 601 Van Ness Ave ☎ (415) 441 3232. No cheaper than China Moon, but heaps more satisfying (and a menu that changes every 2 weeks)🦐......Best modern Mexican is **Casa Aguila**, 1240 Noriega St ☎ (415) 661 5593, for genuine 'fresh Mex' – seafood, vegetables, cheviche (marinated fish in lime juice and chillis), guacamole served in a stone mortar. Hearty platefuls, and not a bank-breaker🦐.....**Yank Sing**, 427 Battery St ☎ (415) 362 1640, is yum yum for dim sum🦐......The elegant **Manora's**, 1600 Folsom St ☎ (415) 861 6224, has superb, creative Thai food (run by daughter, it has the edge on mother's branch at 3226 Mission St ☎ (415) 550 0856)................🦐

The Importance of Being Antique

If you're wondering where the most important antiques of Europe and the Orient are, look no further than America's hotels. Their multi-million dollar refits are spent largely on English, French, Italian and Chinese furniture, decorative objects and works of art. Consider the **Madison**, Washington DC, whose '...objets d'art are symbols of our dedication to our greatest treasure – the world's most discriminating clientele...'. The blurb continues more like a Christie's catalogue than a hotel brochure: 'A rare antique Chinese Imperial altar table... a Louis XVI palace commode with ormolu mounts... a Louis XVI gold leaf girandole mirror with Sèvres plaques ... a fine example of antique kingwood and marquetry writing table.' Or, at the **Donatello**, San Francisco: an Italian Empire settee flanked by Italian Empire columns, and an 18C Austrian applewood secretaire. At the **Windsor Court**, New Orleans: portraits by Reynolds, Gainsborough, Van Dyck and Kneller. At the **Ritz-Carlton**, Chicago: a rococo console table, a French neo-classical marquetry commode. NB If they don't extol its antique virtues, you can bet your bottom dollar it's *repro*.

STARS, 150 Redwood St, CA 94102
☎ **(415) 861 7827**
Jeremiah Tower's high-energy diner continues to be one of the brightest stars on the West Coast, a leading light of Californian cuisine – mesquite grilling; lobster, wild mushrooms and brioche with roast chilli butter; spit roast pheasant breast with foie gras and potato galette. *"A special place for great 1990s food and good wines. I get a great buzz from being there. Jeremiah's such an accomplished restaurateur"* – ELISE PASCOE. *"One of my favourite restaurants. There's always something new and exciting there as far as Jeremiah's food is concerned...absolutely wonderful"* – KEN HOM. *"I had a great meal there, it's still good"* – BOB PAYTON. *"Still great"* echoes DON HEWITSON. A favourite of WOLFGANG PUCK and BARBARA KAFKA. The attached **Stars Café** is great for breakfast.

YUJEAN'S, 843 San Pablo Ave, Albany, CA 94706 ☎ **(415) 525 8557**
Modern Chinese cuisine, charmingly served. *"The best Chinese meal I had last year was at this wonderful restaurant. The Taiwanese chef-owner, Yujean, is an absolute genius. He is the only Chinese restaurateur I've ever met who is passionate about wine, so he's got a super wine list and, even more amazing, wonderful glasses"* – SERENA SUTCLIFFE. A pet haunt of Berkeley University gastronomes.

ZUNI CAFE, 1658 Market St, CA 94102
☎ **(415) 552 2522**
Everyone's loony about Zuni, a breezy diner with stark white décor, open kitchen, and a long copper bar. *"A place I love, it's marvellous, very California, very North Italian, with a terrific woman chef-owner, Judy Rodgers. She has a lot of followers and is making a big name for herself"* – SERENA SUTCLIFFE. *"What a great place! I asked what I should have for a starter and they told me the arugula and croûton salad. I said I am a carnivore, I do not eat cheese and lettuce. But it was the best salad I have ever had – wonderful"* – BOB PAYTON. *"Really terrific, the kind of food that you can absolutely digest, which is extremely important"* – KEN HOM. *"Wonderful wood-oven fired pizzas"* – ELISE PASCOE. Buzzy piano bar scene and oyster bar, too.

Shopping

Union Square is the best shopping area, with new department stores springing up all the time. One of the best Chinatowns in the world centred around **Grant Ave** – check out Shanghai Bazaar (Chinese bargains, antique and new) and Long Boat Enterprises Co (for Rosita Young's jewellery, a jangle with Oriental curios).

GUMPS, 250 Post St, CA 94108
☎ **(415) 982 1616**
A smart old favourite store, for antiques, home furnishings, presents, quality clothes, the lot.

HEMISPHERE, 1 Harrison St, CA 94105
☎ **(415) 896 5700**
Part of The Gap empire, along with Banana Republic. *"A lot of private labels, Michael Kors, wonderful suede shirts. Andrée Putman designed the store with remarkable taste and wonderful lighting"* – TYLER BRULE.

I MAGNIN, 135 Stockton St, CA 94108
☎ **(415) 362 2100**
The original branch, for a broad sweep of top designer clothes and sportswear. Exclusive Chanel boutique, Ungaro, Valentino, Saint Laurent, Dior. A phalanx of 'personal shoppers' can organize your wardrobe for you, sometimes bringing entire collections to your house.

MACY'S, 170 O'Farrell St, CA 94102
☎ (415) 397 3333
One of the best Macy's in the US, known especially for the men's department – probably the largest in the country, stacked on 4 floors. Top designer farrago: wade through Armani, Perry Ellis, Polo, swimwear and night-time dappery.

NORDSTROM'S, 865 Market St, CA 94103
☎ (415) 243 8500
The best Nordstrom's in the States, with the best buyers, and all the top Euro and US designers. *"Fantastic department store. It occupies the top floors of an 8-storey vertical mall, with a spiral escalator to take you up to the store"* – TYLER BRULE. *"The best department store in America, maybe the world. Best socks, best underwear, best service – you have never seen staff in your life like at Nordstrom's. It's ace"* – BOB PAYTON.

WILKES BASHFORD, 375 Sutter St, CA 94108 ☎ (415) 986 4380
Tops for men's garb – beautiful, expensive suits and a funkier dept showing Gaultier, Basile, Matsuda, Brioni and Alexander Julian. The women's dept is big on evening wear. A bar on every floor for inter-cheque-signing sustenance.

· REST OF ·

CALIFORNIA

Hotels

LE MERIDIEN, 2000 2nd St, Coronado, San Diego, CA 92118 ☎ (619) 435 3000
New French-owned resort hotel with spa, right on the bay. *"I was very impressed. It's unusually high quality for San Diego. A small, beautifully designed hotel; everything is nice – it's cool and the service is excellent"* – JAMES BURKE.

MEADOWOOD RESORT & COUNTRY CLUB, 900 Meadowood Lane, St Helena, CA 94574 ☎ (707) 963 3646
The best country resort in the Napa Valley, north of SF, with its own wine school, croquet lawns, golf, tennis, swimming pool and two restaurants. Book in for the Napa Valley Wine Auction in June. High praise from ELISE PASCOE.

❝I'm absolutely minimalist when I travel. You can only be that way if you can depend on your hotel having good-quality toiletries. That builds great loyalty❞

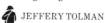 JEFFERY TOLMAN

VENTANA INN, Highway 1, Big Sur
☎ (408) 624 4812
"Our favourite hotel in the world. We love it… you're in a wood facing the ocean. The hotel consists of small chalets where you feel at home and everything is perfect…" – FENDI SISTERS. BARRY HUMPHRIES pronounces lunch on the terrace *"exquisite"*.

Restaurants

AUBERGE DU SOLEIL, 180 Rutherford Hill Rd, Rutherford, CA 94573
☎ (707) 963 1211
Grand Napa Valley dining (with bedrooms, too) in a spectacular country setting. Sophisticated Californian-French cuisine, using local ingredients (ROBERT MONDAVI prizes the *"fresh garden vegetables and fresh fish"*).

🐟 CHEZ PANISSE, 1517 Shattuck Ave, Berkeley, CA 94709 ☎ (415) 548 5525
Foodie pioneer Alice Waters's famous restaurant saw the genesis of Californian cuisine and begat some remarkable young chefs. It is still a temple of cooking, where the likes of WOLFGANG PUCK, KEN HOM and Sally Clarke pay homage. Downstairs, there is a different one-off, 5-course, fixed-price menu *every* night (a tough standard to maintain… and some feel inspiration is waning). Join the queue to eat upstairs at her trattoria-cum-bistro, **Café Chez Panisse**, for beautifully fresh salads, pasta, etc. ELISE PASCOE has a soft spot for the calzone [folded pizza], *"the best I have ever eaten – filled with Sonoma goat's cheese, shallots and other wondrous things"*.

DOMAINE CHANDON, California Drive, Yountville, CA 94599 ☎ (707) 944 2892
This Napa winery restaurant serves exceptional French food by Philippe Jeanty, in a stunning setting. *"Lakes…beautiful lawns, winding paths and overhanging trees with lovely Japanese lanterns, all lit up like fairyland"* – ELISE PASCOE.

🐟 LARK CREEK INN, 234 Magnolia Ave, Larkspur, CA 94939 ☎ (415) 924 7766
In Marin County, north of the city, a *"fabulous new place opened by the former chef at Campton Place, Bradley Ogden. Serves some of the most wonderful American food, very simple, really well cooked and well prepared. Delightful. Ogden is really one of America's best chefs. I love his meatloaf. He doesn't over-embellish his food"* – KEN HOM. WOLFGANG PUCK tucks in.

MUSTARD'S GRILL, 7399 St Helena Highway, Yountville, CA 94558
☎ (707) 944 2424
Still a top trendspot in the Napa Valley, with a loyal local clientele – the butcher, the baker and all the winemakers. Californian cooking, especially good seafood. Recommended highly by DON HEWITSON and ROBERT MONDAVI.

🦃 **Buzzz** DON HEWITSON raves about **Raymond Vineyards**, *"a superb, but relatively unknown, winery in St Helena. Their* **Reserve Cabernet Sauvignon** *is a delicious mouthful of beautifully structured fruit – beg, steal or borrow (and drink!) the 1978 vintage; there are still a few bottles around"* 🦃......**Dominus**, made in California by Christian Moueix of Pétrus fame) continues to make waves. SERENA SUTCLIFFE (not to mention Moueix himself) thinks the 1985, the third vintage, the best so far🦃......**California sparkle**: Of the French or joint French-Californian sparkling wines, the new **Roederer Estate** from the northerly Anderson Valley is a stunner (*"more finesse and class than the others"* – SERENA S). **Domaine Chandon**, **Deutz**, **Piper-Sonoma** and **Mumm** bubble along nicely... Of the native Californians, **Schramsberg** is on top form, while Sonoma's **Iron Horse Vineyards** is a front runner for GEOFFREY ROBERTS and STEVEN SPURRIER..........🦃

TRA VIGNE, 1050 Charter Oak St, St Helena, CA 94574 ☎ (707) 963 4444
Under the same ownership as Mustard's, this Puck clone is one of the most popular eateries in Napa Valley. Californianized northern Italian cuisine, imaginative pizzas, risotto, pasta and dreamlike breads. Lovely outdoor dining.

Wine

Although the great winemakers such as André Tchelistcheff got there first, it was Robert Mondavi who, in building his Napa Valley winery in 1966, uncorked the torrent. Today, California wineries are producing better wines every year, as GEOFFREY ROBERTS testifies: *"They are the best-made wines in the world ... they combine the best of European techniques, yet maintain a consistency of style that is the envy of the Europeans."*

This young industry is ever-experimenting. *"A number of California winemakers are using varietals other than Cabernet Sauvignon and Chardonnay. There is interest in wines we associate with the Rhône Valley – Syrah, Grenache, Viognier – and also Sangiovese from Italy. They may seem obscure at the moment, but it could be the beginning of a trend.*

"Another new development is the **Meritage** *wines – those made from a blend of grapes rather than a single varietal. Before, if a wine wasn't a Cabernet or a Chardonnay, nobody knew where to put it on the wine list. Now it has its own category. Of course, a number of wines already fall under the Meritage heading, notably Opus 1 and Dominus"* – GEOFFREY ROBERTS.

Carneros

Southern extension of Napa that is now very fashionable in its own right. *"The place for Pinot Noir.* **SAINTSBURY** *make alarmingly good wine: don't miss their Chardonnay"* – SERENA SUTCLIFFE.

Napa Valley

ANDRE TCHELISTCHEFF
Dean of Napa, worshipped by fellow winemakers. The **Georges de Latour Private Reserve Cabernets** (Beaulieu vineyard) of the 50s and 60s are thought to be his masterpieces. MICHAEL BROADBENT singles out the 1946 **Beaulieu Pinot Noir** as *"the best Californian version of this grape I've ever tasted".*

DUNN VINEYARD
A small vineyard, esteemed among the California cognoscenti. *"I had never even heard of Dunn and it came as a complete surprise to find I had marked* **Dunn's Cabernet Sauvignon** *top in a blind tasting of 1982s among all the first-growth Bordeaux, including Pétrus and the finest California Cabernets"* – MICHAEL BROADBENT.

JOE HEITZ
Heists accolades too. He buys his grapes from friends, and the ones Martha May sells him go to make the famous **Martha's Vineyard Cabernet Sauvignon**.

JOSEPH PHELPS
"The late-harvest Riesling is unforgettable, and the red **Insignia** *Cabernet Sauvignon is a whopper of a wine"* – SERENA SUTCLIFFE. GEOFFREY ROBERTS says aye to that.

ROBERT MONDAVI
The perennial high-profile house of Napa. Top quality on an industrial scale. His best wines are from the grape variety the Napa Valley is chiefly famous for: Cabernet Sauvignon. His **Reserve** wine is one to lay down (SERENA SUTCLIFFE says the 1982 is superb now), while his pièce de résistance is **Opus 1**, a joint venture with Baron Philippe de Rothschild. It's STEVEN SPURRIER's best California wine. On the white side, both GEOFFREY ROBERTS and LORD GOWRIE think Mondavi's **Fumé Blanc** a great wine.

TREFETHEN

For beautifully long-lived, well-balanced Chardonnay (praised by GEOFFREY ROBERTS), one of the best Rieslings in Napa Valley, and a marvellous winery building.

Other Napa wineries that are rarely caught napping on the Cabernet front are Bernard Portet's **CLOS DU VAL** (Bernard was brought up at Lafite, where his father was manager); **CHAPPELLET**; **FREEMARK ABBEY**; **STAG'S LEAP WINE CELLARS** (a hit with SERENA SUTCLIFFE) and **GROTH VINEYARD** (another SS hit: *"their Cabernet Sauvignon comes out very well indeed in blind tastings, as it has balance to match the power"*).

For Chardonnay, **ACACIA** earns acclaim from SERENA S.

Santa Clara

RIDGE

Paul Draper is, according to SIMON LOFTUS, *"one of the great winemakers of the world"*. Draper has said, 'We are really trying to make the finest wine not just in California but in the world', and his **Montebello** Cabernet Sauvignon is his trump card (at a blind tasting, some couldn't tell it from Latour). Ridge's **York Creek** is nearly as good, and their red **Zinfandel**s are winners.

Sonoma Valley

CHATEAU ST JEAN

Owned by Suntory, it still has a great name. White wine specialists whose Chardonnay is one of California's leaders. A fine winery to visit.

SONOMA-CUTRER VINEYARDS

The best winery, for Chardonnay only. **Les Pierres** is its answer to Montrachet.

Of the rest, **JORDAN**, Sonoma, is California's answer to Eden, for one of the greatest Cabernet Sauvignons; **KALIN CELLARS**, in Marin County, produce a range of fabulous wines, particularly Pinot Noir; **CALERA**, Monterey, is another force in Pinot Noir.

SANTA FE

Music

🐟 **SANTA FE OPERA, Box 2408, NM 87504 ☎ (505) 982 3851**
No 1 music festival in the US, of high international regard, held in June-Aug, with some 40 performances of 5 operas. In the foothills of the Sangre de Cristo mountains, this is *"a real mindblower. An open-air opera house in amazingly spectacular landscape. The summer season attracts international connoisseurs"* – RODNEY MILNES. ANDREW LLOYD WEBBER agrees, *"you'd have to go far to find something as visually stunning."*

Hotels and spas

ELDORADO, 309 W San Francisco St, NM 87501 ☎ (505) 988 4455
The best in New Mexico, a modern Pueblo Revival-style hotel in the desert highlands at 7,000 ft. Whitewashed walls, hand-painted friezes, local works of art, and courtyards where musicians play under the stars. It's convincing enough for the Spanish royal family, not to mention James Garner, Judge Reinhold and the De Vito/Schwarznegger twins.

10,000 WAVES, PO Box 6138, NM 87502 ☎ (505) 982 9304
A Japanese-style spa carved into a mountain, where you sit in your hot tub under the stars, then don kimono and slippers and shuffle inside for massage (Swedish, deep tissue, shiatsu), body wrap (herbal, salt glow) and a sauna.

Restaurants

COYOTE CAFE, 132 W Water St, NM 87501 ☎ (505) 983 1615
Mark Miller's ace place, serving some of the most interesting southwestern cuisine in the country, enjoyed by WOLFGANG PUCK and BARBARA KAFKA.

🐟 **Buzzz** Wax lyrical in vino lingo: learn winespeak, how to discern an expensive Cabernet from a cheap one, and how to taste/evaluate/buy/store and serve wine at **Meadowood's Wine School** (see Meadowood Resort, Hotels)🐟......Log-cabin luxe: **Timberhill Ranch**, 35755 Hauser Bridge Rd, Cazadero, CA 95421 ☎ (707) 847 3258 has 10 rustic cabins dotted in 80 acres, *"run by two golden parachutist couples from San Francisco who opted out of the corporate world and provide delicious serenity and delightful food"* – EDWARD CARTER🐟......**Spa trek**: At **Cal-a-Vie**, 2249 Somerset Rd Vista, San Diego ☎ (619) 945 2055, you start the morning with a 3-mile hill hike under crystalline blue skies. Invigorating and blubber-dissolving... 🐟

TOMASITA'S, Old Railroad Station, 500 S Guadalupe, NM 87501 ☎ (505) 988 3614
The hottest restaurant in town, at the end of the Denver and Rio Grande railway line. Genuine northern New Mexican cuisine, based on the food of the Pueblo Indians. They have ways with blue, yellow and white corn...try their burritos, tamales made with corn husks, white corn pisole, and sopaipilla (Indian puffy fried bread).

WASHINGTON, DC

Art and museums

HIRSHHORN MUSEUM & SCULPTURE GARDEN, Independence Ave at 8th St SW, DC 20560 ☎ (202) 357 2700
The Smithsonian's extensive collection of modern and contemporary art; best known for sculpture – a garden and plazaful of Rodin, Moore (including his *King and Queen*), Arp, Giacometti and co. Inside are Matisse, Degas and Daumier, plus Cubists, Nihilists and contemporary American, European and Latin masters.

🦃 NATIONAL GALLERY OF ART, 4th St and Constitution Ave NW, DC 20565 ☎ (202) 737 4215
Under the direction of J Carter Brown, this is one of the best art galleries in the States. A fine collection of European and American art from the 13C onwards, plus some outstanding special exhibitions. The sleek modern East Building, designed by I M Pei, houses the permanent collection of 20C art. MARGAUX HEMINGWAY, ANIKO GAAL and SERENA FASS rave about it.

PHILLIPS COLLECTION, 1600 21st St NW, DC 20009 ☎ (202) 387 2151
With its new Goh Annex, the Phillips is one of the eminent small museums in the USA. Mainly American and European paintings from the Impressionists to present day: Bonnard, Braque, Cézanne, Daumier, Renoir (his celebrated *Luncheon of the Boating Party*); Rothko, Avery, Dove, Marin, O'Keeffe, Prendergast. Excellent concerts and lectures put paintings in context.

SMITHSONIAN INSTITUTION, 1000 Jefferson Drive SW, DC 20560 ☎ (202) 357 2700
A mammoth concern, with 14 museums and a zoo under its umbrella, sheltering over 78 million works (though you'll only ever get to see about 1%). At various addresses around town are the **National Museums of American Art** and **American History, National Portrait Gallery, Renwick Gallery** (American crafts and decorative arts), the **Freer Gallery** (19C-20C American art; Oriental art) and the **National Air and Space Museum**, 6th St and Independence Ave: *"One of the great museums of the world, with original artefacts from space, a*

planetarium, great IMAX films and a beautiful building" – LARRY KING. Such aircraft as the 1903 Wright Flyer, Lindbergh's *Spirit of St Louis* and Neil Armstrong's little runabout, the Apollo 11 Command Module, are displayed in 23 thematic galleries (eg planets and stars, World War II).

Arts centres

THE JOHN F KENNEDY CENTER, 2700 F St NW, DC 20566 ☎ (202) 416 8000
Second only to the Lincoln in New York. The wood-panelled Eisenhower Theater stages major shows, the Terrace stages music, the American Film Institute Theater new films and retros; the small Theater Lab shows cabaret, comedy, etc; the Opera House is base to the Washington Opera, and the Concert Hall is proud home of the National Symphony Orchestra. International companies visit, from La Scala to the Bolshoi. John Gielgud, Katharine Hepburn, Ella Fitzgerald and Frank Sinatra have taken the stage. Scene of the Kennedy Center Honors.

Clubs

ANTOINE'S 1201 CLUB, 1201 Pennsylvania Ave NW, DC 20004 ☎ (202) 783 1201
New 40s-style supper club that attracts America's top entertainers.

BAYOU CLUB, 31-35 K St NW, DC 20007
☎ **(202) 333 2897**
Club and concert hall mainly for established groups, plus comedy acts. Strict marine-cadet waiters. University hang-out.

BLUES ALLEY, 1073 Wisconsin Ave NW, DC 20007 ☎ **(202) 337 4141**
Smart jazz club/wine bar. Small in area, big in reputation – Ella Fitzgerald, Bradford and Wynton Marsalis and Dizzy Gillespie have played.

FIFTH COLUMN, 915 F St NW, DC 20004
☎ **(202) 393 3632**
Snazzy club-cum-art gallery with progressive dance music. Still the diplomatic brat set.

9.30 CLUB, 930 F St NW, DC 20004
☎ **(20) 393 0930**
A London-style new-wave club where English bands play to a downbeat punky crowd. Lots of new acts and flicks.

PISCES, 3040 M St NW, Georgetown, DC 20007 ☎ **(202) 333 4530**
Still the Annabel's of Washington, for politicians, diplomats and social factotums. Good dining room and disco.

RIVER CLUB, 3223 K St NW, DC 20007
☎ **(202) 333 8118**
Smart dinner-dancing club for smart oldies, with nostalgic music. Renowned for its cuisine. *"Creative dining – it doesn't matter if you order 4 appetizers – they really do cater to your needs. A fun, relaxed place to go"* – ANIKO GAAL.

TRACKS, 1111 1st St SE, DC 20003
☎ **(202) 488 3320**
The liveliest danceteria in town – a gay bar (straight on Saturday nights) with 2 large dance floors for disco, New Age and pop. Volley ball court and pool tables too.

—— *Fashion designers* ——

ANNA WEATHERLEY at Garfinckel's
A Hungarian designer who has always followed her own nose. Her métier is silk chiffon, combined with delicate antique Russian and Byzantine fabrics. *"She dresses women who dress for men. Very sensuous, fragile, vulnerable clothes in beautiful burgundy and spice colours. She adds a new dimension to fashion – if you can't afford Gigli, get Weatherley"* – ANIKO GAAL. A chiffon-swathed Pamela Harriman, Baroness di Portanova and Elizabeth Taylor say aye.

—— *Hotels* ——

🏆 **FOUR SEASONS HOTEL, 2800 Pennsylvania Ave NW, DC 20007**
☎ **(202) 342 0444**
Now under General Manager Stan Bromley (for-
merly of the Four Seasons Clift, San Francisco), this one is thriving. Lovely red-brick building with a clock tower and a lobby full of foliage and flowers. Top stop-off for afternoon tea.

HAY ADAMS, 1 Lafayette Sq, DC 20006
☎ **(202) 638 6600**
The restoration on this hotel whisks you back in time to the lofty-arched Italian Renaissance lobby and the Tudor-style John Hay Room, all wood-panelled and tapestried. Bedrooms are very English country house. Such comfort – and service – under watchful management attracts film stars, diplomats and politicians, who can keep an eye on the White House from their rooms. The sunny yellow **Adams Room** is the place for biz breakfasting.

THE MADISON, 15th and M Sts NW, DC 20005 ☎ **(202) 862 1600**
"Enter the Madison and you enter an old world. It's run by a great hotelier, Marshall Coyne, who is a perfectionist and antique-lover. He flavours the hotel with his personal selections. An exquisite reputation and excellent dining" – ANIKO GAAL. It's LARRY KING's No 1 in town.

🏆 **RITZ-CARLTON, 2100 Massachusetts Ave NW, DC 20008** ☎ **(202) 293 2100**
A chintzy, European-style hotel, with restrained elegance. The **Fairfax Bar** is reminiscent of Annabel's in London, with animal portraits and private little nooks. Once you've stayed, you'll never stray. Dining is taken seriously at the renowned **Jockey Club** restaurant, for American nouvellerie. A who's who of Washington can be spotted at lunchtime, while dinner is more a family treat.

WESTIN HOTEL, 2401 M St NW, DC 20037
☎ **(202) 429 2400**
Gleaming marble blends with antique tapestries and carpets, but its main draw is its impressive fitness centre, with the best equipment and trainers in Washington. Select membership keeps it uncrowded. Guests get an entrée. LARRY KING is keen.

🏆 **THE WILLARD INTER-CONTINENTAL, 1401 Pennsylvania Ave, DC 20004** ☎ **(202) 628 9100**
Built in 1816 one block down from the White House, this is *"the best in Washington. Even though it is so large, it provides the special service of smaller hotels. You feel someone is looking after you"* – ANIKO GAAL. *"The nicest hotel in the USA"* – JEFFREY ARCHER. The famous **Round Robin** bar thrives, as does the **Willard Room**, for American/French cuisine with regional specialities and wines from 39 wine-producing states in the USA as well as France and Italy. ANIKO commends *"excellent food and service and a selection of wines that I don't think can be beaten in the city. The tables are far enough apart to have a really good business lunch."*

Restaurants

See also Hotels.

AMERICA, 50 Massachusetts Ave NE, Union Station, DC 20002 ☎ (202) 682 9555
God bless America, lamb that I love – everything from grilled lamb chops thru' hot dogs and burgers to a dressed-up PBJ (peanut butter and jelly sandwich). High-tech, chromy surroundings; bar downstairs.

BELMONT KITCHEN, 2400 18th St NW, DC 20009 ☎ (202) 667 1200
Lively diner for contemporary cuisine with American flair. Seasonal menu, great Sunday brunch, wonderful home-made puddings. Famous for their upside-down pizza. Azzip.

CHRISFIELDS, 8012 Georgia Ave, Silver Springs, MD 20910 ☎ (301) 589 1306
Downscale simplicity – yet sophisticated townies put on their dungarees and venture into the unknown in order to savour the best seafood of their lives. There's even a photo of Ron and Nance up there, smiling in appreciation.

DUKE ZEIBERTS, 1050 Connecticut Ave NW, DC 20036 ☎ (202) 466 3730
"One of my favourite eating places in Washington. A great gathering place with good old-fashioned American food – ribs, steaks and fish. The atmosphere is 5-star and the owner is a character. It's a hang-out" – LARRY KING.

GALILEO, 2014 P St NW, DC 20036 ☎ (202) 293 7191
"Gives Italian cuisine a new dimension. I have grilled porcini mushrooms when they're in season – out of this world. They have wonderful pasta dishes, risotto with truffles, excellent meat and fish dishes. Their zabaglione sauce over fruit is the just end to a perfect meal" – ANIKO GAAL.

⚓ THE INN AT LITTLE WASHINGTON, PO Box 300, Washington, VA 22747 ☎ (703) 675 3800
At the foot of the Blue Ridge Mountains is *"the best inn in America, no question. The best food and fabulous accommodation, designed by an English interior designer"* – EDWARD CARTER. *"Exquisite surroundings. The décor is reminiscent of Thomas Jefferson's America, romantic*

> **❝ *I don't go through barbed wire for food. I like it when it is very good and I hate it when it is very bad. I'm not one of those people who discuss sauces with the chef . . . it's not very important to me* ❞**
> ANDRE PREVIN

and charming. Truly the best dinner I have ever had. The food is consistently excellent" – ANIKO GAAL. That food has won the highest awards America can bestow. Washington political élite, Europeans and Japanese flock along. But with only 8 rooms and 2 suites, you'll have to wait about 3 months to get a look-in. King of inns for LARRY KING.

I RICCHI, 1220 19th St, DC 20036 ☎ (202) 835 0459
A terrific trattoria where you can munch Tuscan specialities in company with George Bush. *"A great northern Italian restaurant. Just delicious, great"* – LARRY KING. Try their herb-scented wood-grilled meats.

⚓ JEAN-LOUIS AT WATERGATE, Watergate Hotel, 2650 Virginia Ave, DC 20037 ☎ (202) 298 4488
The most elegant diner in the capital. Renowned for its French chef, Jean-Louis Palladin (one of the best in the country), and its multi-course, prix-fixé meals (though they are fixed pretty high). Scintillating flavours that really taste different, based on super-select raw ingredients.

OCCIDENTAL, 1475 Pennsylvania Ave NW, DC 20014 ☎ (202) 783 1475
The great 19C restaurant where statesmen from Roosevelt to Churchill have dined, re-created with the same mahogany bar and vintage elevator car. The meeting place of literati, politicos and stars (from the President to Baryshnikov).

RED HOT & BLUE, 1600 Wilson Blvd, Arlington, VA 22209 ☎ (202) 276 7427
Memphis pit barbecue restaurant specializing in ribs, smoked pork roast, chicken and brisket. Mouth-watering stuff, great atmos and old blues music (early Elvis, BB King). Bush's right-hand man Lee Atwater is a co-owner, and the big man himself drops in from time to time.

⚓ TWENTY-ONE FEDERAL, 1736 L St NW, DC 20036 ☎ (202) 331 9771
For haute French/American cuisine that continues to send ANIKO GAAL into raptures: *"Robert Kinkead cooks with spirit and passion. He is constantly experimenting and he creates extraordinary dishes. I especially love the seafood dishes like swordfish gazpacho, grilled tuna or lobster and crab cakes, or crayfish and artichoke salad. I always think of Europeans as better chefs, but he proves me wrong."* ELISE PASCOE applauds *"terrific up-to-date food in a sparse setting. Also a great bar."*

Shopping

GARFINCKEL'S, 1401 F St, DC 20004 ☎ (202) 628 7730 and branches
Still the most prestigious store in town, for the chic traditionalist. Women can bask among all the top Americans and Europeans (Versace,

Ferré, Lagerfeld, Mugler, Chanel, Fendi, Beene, Roehm, de la Renta, Karan), 2 Anna Weatherley boutiques, plus own-label wear. Men have their own set of élites – Valentino, Ungaro, Armani, Charvet. Terrific accessories, cosmetics, scent and high-class ornamental and table ware from Baccarat, Lalique, Cartier, Herend. New corporate gift service means CEOs can palm off their obligations on Garfinckels, who will ship the perfect prezzie worldwide.

HELGA O, 1455 Pennsylvania Ave NW, DC 20004 ☎ (202) 783 0204
Helga Orfila has left town, but her tiny jewellery shop remains in the Willard plaza. "*Almost like a jewellery box itself. A great selection of faux jewels – more and more people are substituting faux jewels for real*" – ANIKO GAAL.

SAKS JANDEL, 5510 Wisconsin Ave, Chevy Chase, MD 20815 ☎ (301) 652 2250; SAKS AT WATERGATE, 2522 Virginia Ave, DC 20037 ☎ (202) 337 4200
Owned by Ernest Marx, pioneer in bringing ready-to-wear designerdom to Washington. Fine furs, the exclusive on Saint Laurent, Valentino, Lagerfeld, plus Montana, Ungaro, Chanel et al. Their boutique **The Right Stuff** has fast fashions for the young, from Isaac Mizrahi on.

SHARPER IMAGE, 529 14th St NW, DC 20045 ☎ (202) 626 6340 and branches
Gadgetry galore. They often beat rivals to the draw. New waves in health, music, electronics and avant-garde designer and kids' stuff.

SUTTON PLACE GOURMET, 3201 New Mexico Ave NW, DC 20016 ☎ (202) 363 5800
Gourmet food store of the Balducci's kind, "*with a little more space and a little more grace ... it's a calmer environment. Local and international produce, a terrific variety of meats and fish – the smoked fish and caviare are wonderful*" – ANIKO GAAL. At the branch on 600 Franklin St, Alexandria, Virginia ☎ (703) 549 6611, is an unpretentious little restaurant, the **Sutton Place Café**, for great salads and pastas.

Theatre

ARENA STAGE, 6th St and Maine Ave SW, DC 20024 ☎ (202) 554 9066
America's most highly regarded regional theatre company. A complex of 3 theatres that puts on a variety of works, from classics to new plays by American writers. Occasional tours by the resident Arena Company (they were the first American company to tour Moscow).

NATIONAL THEATER, 1321 Pennsylvania Ave NW, DC 20004 ☎ (202) 628 6161
The oldest cultural institution in DC, established in 1835. DC's other top theatre, for mainly pre-Broadway shows – musicals, comedy and drama.

· REST OF ·
AMERICA
Festivals

🔱 **SPOLETO FESTIVAL USA, PO Box 157, Charleston, SC 29402 ☎ (803) 722 2764**
An offshoot of the original (see Italy), under the same direction of Gian Carlo Menotti. 17 warm southern days in May-June are packed with over 100 performances of opera, concerts, theatre and dance. Many new or rarely performed works. This year's festival honoured Charleston's survival of Hurricane Hugo (the festival office lost its roof and some venues were damaged). Always a festive spirit throughout the town, with black-tie dinners, dances, champagne bashes, a floating fiesta and fireworks on the harbour.

Music

PLYMOUTH MUSIC SERIES OF MINNESOTA, 1900 Nicollet Ave, Minneapolis, MN 55403 ☎ (612) 870 0943
A choral and orchestral performing society, under founder and conductor Philip Brunelle, who has "*really done remarkable things there, with very unusual programmes*" – JULIAN LLOYD WEBBER. On the map since making the only recording of Benjamin Britten's *Paul Bunyan*, they play little-known works by major musicians and commission new works. Fall to spring season, and touring the rest of the year.

Shopping

LL BEAN, Casco St, Freeport, ME 04033 ☎ (207) 865 4761; mail order ☎ (207) 865 3111
Retail home of the preppy look. Everything you need for the great outdoors, from waders to docksiders, silk turtlenecks to Alpine trail knickers (that's knicker*bockers* to you non-Yanks), chinos to chamois cloth shirts (their original 1927 design). Also sporty macho accessories such as the Swiss Army Knife or Heuer's Formula 1 Watch. A hit with LOYD GROSSMAN and BOB PAYTON: "*I guess the LL Bean catalogue is still the best, far and away.*"

Ski resorts

"*I prefer skiing in America to Europe because it's much more friendly, you don't have to queue and the mountains are much more beautifully landscaped. You have a pretty tree line going up to 10,000 feet. A much more attractive type of skiing*" – VISCOUNT HAMBLEDEN.

ASPEN
This old mining town is now the most social ski resort in the States. Powder-hound John

Denver, Jack Nicholson, Don Johnson, Goldie Hawn, Robert Wagner, Christie Brinkley, Billy Joel, Rupert Murdoch and countless others own chalets or visit each season. Check out the new **Ritz-Carlton**, at the base of Aspen mountain – ice skating, cross-country skiing, swimming, Jacuzzis, saunas and steam rooms galore. *"Aspen is fun for a week, though it's a bit tinselly now. I love* **Telluride**, *south-west of Aspen. It's tucked right up in the mountains... it's one street. The actual town (apart from the condominiums and a little airport that's opened) hasn't changed since 1890. Magnificently difficult skiing, and wonderful walking in summer"* – VISCOUNT HAMBLEDEN.

SUN VALLEY
Top ski resort in Idaho for expert skiers. Despite its isolation, Californians and powder skiers from all over the USA swoop in to test their mettle. Favourite resort of Brooke Shields and MARGAUX HEMINGWAY. *"Enormous charm, good skiing"* – VISCOUNT HAMBLEDEN.

VAIL
Colorado resort fashioned after an Alpine village – known as 'Instant Tyrol'. The 1989 World Championships here saw new ski developments. Centralized and slickly run, Vail has the fastest ski lifts in the USA (maximum uplift is a prime concern) which means no Alpinesque queues. *"Beautifully prepared pistes, unlike anything in Europe. They believe in 200% service to the skier"* – JANE LINDQUIST. A pile-up of names from the Social Register attend – Gerald Ford, the Texas clans of Bass, Murchison and Wyatt, and Denver doyennes. Best hotel, after a multi-million-dollar facelift: the Orient-Express-run **Lodge**. Best spa: **Cordillera**.

—————— *Wine* ——————

See also Rest of California.

In their fight against the sweeping anti-alcohol trend in the States, winemakers and consumers are trying to encourage a more Latin approach to wine-drinking – with meals (in moderation) rather than in bars (heavily). Two wine-producing areas have proved their worth – the Pacific North-West and, to a lesser extent, New York State.

New York State

Winemaking is old-established in this area; the shock of the new here is the invasion of European grape varieties. **GOLD SEAL** are persistent innovators: their Chardonnay and Riesling show the way.

The smartest wines in New York restaurants are from Long Island – look out for the **BRIDGEHAMPTON** whites and **HARGRAVE VINEYARD**'s Chardonnay and Pinot Noir.

Pacific North-West

The major forces are the states of Oregon, Washington and Idaho, where **STE CHAPELLE** produces a great Chardonnay.

ANTHONY HANSON recognizes the importance of Oregon as *"potentially the best source of Pinot Noir in the USA"*. So did **ROBERT DROUHIN** of Burgundy, who is now making wine there in his new winery. Try also the **EYRIE VINEYARDS** and **KNUDSEN ERATH** Pinot Noirs.

ARGENTINA

BUENOS AIRES

"Buenos Aires is absolutely super, without a doubt the Paris of South America. Beside it, Rio is a most awful tourist trap, whereas Buenos is a beautifully laid-out city, with tree-lined avenues and wonderful restaurants where you sit outside. **Gato Dumas** *is a restaurant I particularly liked, in the lovely Ricolita district. You eat outside under huge parasols and the food is new Californian. It is very sophisticated, one of the most exciting places I've been to lately"* – SERENA SUTCLIFFE.

—————— *Hotels* ——————

GRAN HOTEL DORA, Calle Maipú 963
☎ **(01) 312 7391**
An old-fashioned hotel frequented by people up from the country. *"Very comfortable with good service"* – QUENTIN CREWE.

—————— *Music* ——————

TEATRO COLON, Avenida 9 de Julio
☎ **(01) 355414**
The most famous opera house in South America. Sumptuous in red plush and gilt, with a stage of gargantuan proportions and grand banqueting rooms. It was on the circuit of Caruso and co, and is still an important centre for music. No ticket problems here: just go along 3 days before the performance – *and* you'll get change from a 10-dollar bill.

❝Argentina has the best beef and the most elegant women in the world ❞

 ELISABETH LAMBERT ORTIZ

AUSTRALIA

ADELAIDE

—— *Art and museums* ——

**ART GALLERY OF SOUTH AUSTRALIA,
North Terrace, SA 2000 ☎ (08) 223 7200**
Australian and European art, plus the gen on
SA's history. *"The best art gallery in Australia.
Marvellous British pictures, particularly won-
derful works by Edward Lear..."* – BARRY
HUMPHRIES.

—— *Arts centres* ——

**ADELAIDE FESTIVAL CENTRE,
King William St, SA 5000 ☎ (08) 213 4788**
Superb performing-arts complex with regular
concerts, ballet and theatrical performances.
Rated by ANDREW LLOYD WEBBER as *"the finest
modern building for music theatre in the world
– wonderful acoustics and sight lines."*

—— *Festivals* ——

**ADELAIDE FESTIVAL, GPO Box 1269, SA
5001 ☎ (08) 216 8600**
A major international festival held biennially in
Feb-March of even years. A blend of cultures,
of classical and of contemporary works – theatre,
dance, art exhibitions and classical music – with
eminent conductors such as Sir Georg Solti,
Michael Tilson Thomas and Pierre Boulez wield-
ing the baton. A massive outdoor stage allows
50,000 to drink in the opening-night music spectacular. Writers' Week is one of Adelaide's
features – a gathering of over 60 international
writers, who read, debate and perform. State-
of-the-art cuisine at **Lyrics** restaurant: special
festival menus are created by visiting chefs.

—— *Hotels* ——

**HILTON INTERNATIONAL, Victoria
Square, SA 5000 ☎ (08) 217 0711**
Was tops till the advent of the Hyatt partly

because it was the *only* place in town – to stay,
dine, drink and dance. Still popular (despite
décor of the stylized flower-power era), and the
Grange remains one of the best restaurants in
Oz. Dig into kangaroo or buffalo meat over a
bottle from a cellar that boasts 400 Australian
and foreign wines. *"Still very good"* – DON
HEWITSON.

**🏆 HYATT REGENCY, North Terrace, SA
5000 ☎ (08) 231 1234**
This impressive new hotel, with not 1 but 4
soaring atriums and acres of polished granite and
marble, has ousted the Hilton out of top place in
the city. *"Excellent rooms, top suites and very
good Regency Club on the upper floors"* – LEN
EVANS. Part of the Adelaide Plaza, which also
houses the first casino in SA and the Festival
Centre, it's also tops for dining: at **Fleurieu** (see
Restaurants) and at the fab Japanese **Shiki**.

—— *Restaurants* ——

*"Adelaide restaurants have tended to be inno-
vative, despite Adelaide's small-town parochial-
ity. Attention to freshness and variety of produce
is improving, along with a greater sense of
regionality. The Australiasian style of cooking
is still strong, with Thai, Japanese, Chinese and
Indonesian influences dominating. But now,
not just fresh coriander, soy or chilli with everything, but signs that chefs are starting to understand and respect the integrity of these styles of
cooking"* – NIGEL HOPKINS.

**THE BRIDGEWATER MILL, Mount
Barker Rd, Bridgewater, SA 5155
☎ (08) 339 4227**
Owned by Brian Croser, Petaluma winemaker
extraordinaire. The building, a revamped flour
mill, is not as romantic as it sounds (pre-fab
cement walls), but the food is exquisite and
inventive. Catherine Kerry does raw tuna with
tiny potato-and-chive cakes and sour cream,
mallard duck pie with Madeira glaze, kangaroo
fillet with anchovy butter. And, of course, Petaluma wines. *"Fantastic"* – DON HEWITSON.

**CHLOES, 36 College Rd, Kent Town, SA
5067 ☎ (08) 422574**
Based in a finely restored old villa, this high-
class dinery is run by well-known restaurateur
Nick Papazahariakis. He bones his own

🏆 Buzzz NIGEL HOPKINS rounds up a taste
of Adelaide's best: **Beijing**, 72 Angas St ☎ (08) 232 1388 provides *"the best northern
Chinese cooking in town"*🏆...... **Star of Siam**, 67 Gouger St ☎ (08) 231 3527 is *"a
rapidly upward-mobile little restaurant with the best Thai food in the city"*🏆......
For what LEN EVANS has described as the best fish and chips in Oz, check out **Paul's
Seafood Restaurant**, 79 Gouger St ☎ (08) 231 9778. *"He might even be right,"* chips
in NIGEL HOPKINS... 🏆

The Best Advice

What is the best advice you have ever been given? This is what our contributors revealed: *"To live my life for myself and not for the world. Shakespeare said it better in Hamlet: 'To thine own self be true'. And always to have goals, something to strive for – my mother always said to me, 'reach for the stars'"* – BARBARA TAYLOR BRADFORD. *"The best advice ever given to me was to say 'no'. If there is any shadow of a doubt, so many people say 'yes', but if there is any shadow of a doubt, you should say 'no'. Also 'to thine own self be true', which was an old maxim of my dad's that I hold very dear, and the family motto of 'Never let the sun go down upon your wrath'"* – SIMON WILLIAMS. *"To be oneself – and if you upset people, too bad!"* – NICO

LADENIS. *"Don't get married again (I have never taken this advice). 'She who does not learn from her mistakes is doomed to failure'"* – JOAN COLLINS. *"Do not argue with fools – that's when two fools argue"* – BENNY ONG. *"First I must tell you some things so that you understand what I want to say. I am a very rich man, we are talking about a very rich man. I have the best cars, the best aircraft, the best wife, best homes, best clothes and the most beautiful income a man could have. OK …my advice from my father was, 'never, never believe, Bijan, that you are there'. Don't believe in your publicity and become a snob"* – BIJAN. *"Do what you truly want to do – then you will do it with true enthusiasm and passion"* – DUDLEY MOORE.

pheasant, quail and chicken, makes great crustacean creations and a mean abalone mousseline. Impressive, trendy, with masterly presentation. Splendid wine selection.

🦐 **FLEURIEU, Hyatt Regency, see Hotels**
Sophisticated dining in French/Australian mode. *"The usual compromises of hotel restaurants are not found here. A rather calm, low-key dining room; an excellent cellar with one of the best ranges of SA wines. Service and trappings are first-class. Swiss chef Urs Inauen's menu is not the hot, steamy stuff of a gastronomic thriller, but calm and refined like his cooking. In terms of freshness, dedication and technical detail, hard to beat anywhere in Australia"* – NIGEL HOPKINS.

GLO-BO'S, 125 Gillies St, SA 5000
☎ (08) 223 6271
An 'in' restaurant with bags of panache. The menu hops from kangaroo to more trad meats wrapped up in inventive ways. Mainly modern Frenchified dishes. Excellent service.

JASMINE, 31 Hindmarsh Square, SA 5000
☎ (08) 223 7837
Some like it hot…if you do, speed along to this brilliant Indian restaurant run by the Singhs, who grind up their own spices. Trendy, Westernized atmosphere.

MEZES, 287 Rundle St, SA 5000
☎ (08) 223 7384
If you think Greek cooking stopped with souvlaki and dolmades, test this, for the sort of innovative cooking which leaves anything you'd find in Greece for dead.

🦐 **MISTRESS AUGUSTINE'S, 145 O'Connell St, N Adelaide, SA 5006**
☎ (08) 267 4479
A marvellous, maverick eatery. *"Owner-chef Ann Oliver has picked up Phillip Searle's creative mantle with innovative and challenging cooking. Like Searle, she has at times stunned her clients with sledge-hammer boldness, but she's learnt a little restraint, gained a great deal more skill, sought out new techniques and ingredients, and has had the nerve to go more for simplicity and honesty in her cooking – all without losing her considerable passion. Her restaurant is, by contrast, austere in style, modern and elegant, which throws the focus on what's on the plate. Seasonal menus, gutsy flavours, lots of colour and character. A trademark dish is the dessert Chocolate Slut"* – NIGEL HOPKINS.

🦐 **NEDIZ TU, 170 Hutt St, SA 5000**
☎ (08) 223 2618
Kate Sparrow and chef Le Tu Thai continue to create masterly cuisine in the Oriental-Occidental-antipodean vein. *"Le's Vietnamese-Chinese background melds nicely with Kate's Anglo-French training to provide some of the best and most consistently good food. The menu oozes character and interest…millefeuille of scallops with coriander butter sauce; venison with a crisp crêpe filled with parsnip purée and served with a lemon ginger glaze. His mother is also in the kitchen in charge of soups. Clientele includes touring and local foodies, smart professionals, anyone with the brains to recognize terrific tucker at give-away prices"* – NIGEL HOPKINS. Dinner only.

· REST OF ·

SOUTH AUSTRALIA

Hotels

PADTHAWAY ESTATE, Padthaway, SA 5271 ☎ (087) 655039
A colonial refuge in the wilderness, with lace-work verandahs and 6 comfortable rooms. Remarkable for the superb food served at polished tables with crystal and silver. Sip Padthaway sparkly on the verandah as the sun sets over the estate's vineyards.

Restaurants

THE BARN, Main Rd, McLarenvale, SA 5171 ☎ (08) 323 8618
This restaurant, based in a 140-year-old former horse-changing station, is some 25 miles out of Adelaide in a premier wine-producing area. Pick a wine from 300 mostly local varieties. Casual dining at wooden tables; in summer you can sit in the grapevine-filled courtyard. "*A touch of the New World*" – DON HEWITSON.

🐦 PHEASANT FARM, Samuel Rd, Nuriootpa, SA 5355 ☎ (085) 621286
The best restaurant in South Australia, jammed with local winemakers, businessmen playing hookey and city refugees. "*Wine areas tend to have good food and the Barossa Valley is no exception. Maggie Beer and her husband, Colin, rear their own pheasants and ducks and buy in local rabbits and kangaroos to produce the best game dishes in the country. The atmosphere is friendly and the view over the dam is wonderful*" – ANNE WILLAN. An echo from NIGEL HOPKINS: "*Marvellously bucolic surroundings overlooking a large dam filled with ducks and geese, comfortable service, terrific wine list (heavily Barossa-biased) and, above all, Maggie Beer's stunning cooking. This is regional country cooking at its best, with Maggie drawing on local butchers and bakers, as well as many small local suppliers. Pheasant is reared on the premises; her salad of smoked kangaroo with keta caviare has become famous. Lunches here have been known to last more than 24 hours.*"

VINTNERS, Nuriootpa Rd, Angaston, SA 5353 ☎ (085) 642488
What Vintners lacks in country atmos, it makes up in the kitchens and cellars. Run by Marjorie and Don Coats (she in the kitchen, he at front of house). "*This is a totally regional restaurant. Everything from bread to ice cream is made on the premises, and local produce includes trout and fresh rabbit, olive oil, and the Shiraz used in the spiced claret jelly served with a Peter Lehmann Semillon Sauternes ice cream. A trademark dish is superb consommé*" – NIGEL HOPKINS. On target with local winemakers.

BRISBANE

Art and museums

MUSEUM OF CONTEMPORARY ART, 164 Melbourne St, Qld 4101 ☎ (07) 846 2255
Brisbane's own MOCA is a relatively new gallery based in a stylish 1930s building. Large private modern collection plus visiting exhibitions.

Arts centres

QUEENSLAND CULTURAL CENTRE, South Bank, Qld 4000 ☎ (07) 840 7229
A slick modern complex housing the Queensland Museum, Queensland Art Gallery and the **Brisbane Performing Arts Complex** ☎ (07) 846 4444, which includes the Lyric Theatre and 2,000-seat Concert Hall, judged by JULIAN LLOYD WEBBER to be "*wonderful, one of the best I've played in.*"

Hotels

🐦 SHERATON BRISBANE HOTEL & TOWERS, 249 Turbot St, Qld 4000 ☎ (07) 835 3535
The hotel is memorable, but it seems the name ain't: the 'Brisbane Hilton', mentioned one contributor, the 'Brisbane Hyatt' said another – but it was the Sheraton they had in mind. One of Australia's best, it's superbly decorated – JULIAN LLOYD WEBBER notes the "*quite extraordinary entrance hall*". Glass-panelled lifts shoot up the 30-storey building to the rooftop restaurant. Also the extra-exclusive Sheraton Towers, a small hotel within a hotel, on the skyline floors.

Restaurants

🐦 BAGUETTE, 150 Racecourse Rd, Ascot, Qld 4007 ☎ (07) 268 6168
"*Very French. He has 2 chefs, one of whom is Thai and refuses to cook Thai food but does French-style instead. The result is an amazing mixture of styles and flavours. Fantastic*" – DAVID BRAY.

FOUNTAIN ROOM, Queensland Cultural Centre, South Bank, Qld 4000 ☎ (07) 840 7111
An excellent riverside restaurant built on 3 levels within this cultural complex. Menus make use of the best local produce – mud crabs, fish, tropical fruits and nuts.

MICHAEL'S, Riverside Centre, 123 Eagle St, Qld 4000 ☎ (07) 832 5522
Classic continental seafood, spectacular views, magnificent wine cellar. So popular with businessmen that it's virtually a club.

PIER 9, Waterfront Place, Eagle St, Qld 4000 ☎ (07) 221 1300
1,000 ways with shellfish, in a gorgeous glassy restaurant with a gorgeous, classy clientele. *"Seafood like you have never seen prepared and served before, in all sorts of tempting styles. Particularly brilliant on the Cajun side; the oysters in vodka are notably good. Ideal place to spend an afternoon in the sun, gazing at the view, with a good bottle of white burgundy within reach"* – DAVID BRAY.

RUMPOLES, Cnr of North Quay and Turbot Sts, Qld 4000 ☎ (07) 236 2877
"Modern in style, modern in cuisine, modern in the kind of people who go there. Specializes in designer food...lots of little courses. Designer pizzas are particularly good" – DAVID BRAY. Nibblers love to pick at a starter or 2 (no full-size main courses) from the adventurous, ever-changing menu. Try croc-meat with wasabi cream sauce.

🐟 SIGGI'S, Cnr Edward and Margaret Sts, Qld 4000 ☎ (07) 221 4555
This chic Europeanesque dinery is the most upmarket restaurant in Brisbane. Traditional Continental cuisine.

· REST OF ·

QUEENSLAND

—— *Hotels and resorts* ——

BEDARRA ISLAND, c/o Australian Airlines, see Tours & Charters
Two separate resorts, Hideaway and Bedarra Bay, with 16 villas apiece – and that's it, like a private club. Units are built *around* trees, so you're likely to have a palm shooting up through your bedroom. No entertainment, just rainforest

to explore, catamaran sailing, snorkelling, fishing, tennis, a spread of tropical food and a beach to yourself. All-in price includes all the French champagne you can swallow. Once on the island it's a cashless society.

CAPE WILDERNESS LODGE, c/o Air Queensland Resorts, 62 Abbott St, Cairns, Qld 4870 ☎ (070) 504305
The best mainland getaway, at the tip of northern Queensland on Cape York. Tropical waters, deep-sea fishing and d-e-e-p relaxation.

🐟 HAYMAN, N Qld 4801 ☎ (079) 469100
The best Whitsunday Island resort, owned by Ansett, who have poured millions into the luxury hotel accommodation and grounds. Man-made lagoon the size of 5 Olympic pools with freshwater pool in the centre. Diversions include helicopter tours, game fishing, a health club complete with flotation tanks, floodlit tennis and diving. Fine cuisine at **La Fontaine**, though some find it incongruous not to say irksome to trek to the tropics only to find a posh French restaurant where collar and tie are required. *"It has vast expanses of lobby. They brought in 1,200 yards of marble a day for a year. Not only is it extraordinary to behold in its own right, but the fact that it's on this island in the middle of nowhere makes it even more extraordinary"* – EDWARD CARTER.

HOTEL CONRAD AND JUPITERS CASINO, Gold Coast Highway, Broadbeach, Qld 4218 ☎ (075) 921133
Fans feel it beats the Vegas hotels into a cocked hat. An amazing pool in tropical setting with palms and fountains, colonnades of Queensland sandstone, and beautiful rooms with enormous beds. Hit venue for the Queensland charity mob. The **casino** complex, open 24 hours, houses 2 gargantuan gaming rooms lined with over 100 tables and blackjack machines for which the jackpot is over A$100,000. Also a new glam gaming room, **Club Conrad**, with a flavour of Monte in the 30s.

🐟 Buzzz Scuba scoop: Ever-more Qld resorts means ever-more ways to reach the divers' dream, the **Great Barrier Reef**, a 1,200-mile semi-submerged causeway of live coral, home to 1,900 varieties of tropical fish. Best diving is off Heron Island. Best time to visit is after the sea wasps have gone, March to Sept🐟...... ELISE PASCOE has Surfers sussed: A walkway away from Sheraton Mirage Gold Coast, at 74 Seaworld Drive, Main Beach, is **Le Beach Club** ☎ (075) 916770, run by the Staleys (of Fanny's and Chez Oz fame). *"Fabulous food, mainly seafood – it's the place to dine north of Surfers...Next door, **Café Aroma** is open from mid-morning to the early hours, serving an eclectic menu. Right on the Broadwater, it is the new eatery on the Gold Coast"*... If you're hangin' loose in **Noosa**, *"for great food, dine at **Palmers at Ocean Breeze** ☎ (071) 475666. A nice Mediterranean feel and far more glamorous than the old one"* – EP ....🐟

Australia's Best Resorts

1	SHERATON MIRAGE · Port Douglas
2	CABLE BEACH CLUB · Broome
3	HYATT REGENCY · Coolum
4	SHERATON MIRAGE · Gold Coast
5	HAYMAN ISLAND · Queensland

HYATT REGENCY, Warran Rd, Coolum Beach, Qld 4573 ☎ (071) 461234
Low-level resort and spa aimed at reviving the body and soul. There's tennis, golf, 8 swimming pools and the beach (20 mins from Noosa); therapeutic spa baths, treatments, fitness programmes, courses such as Tai Chi, and a Creative Arts Centre. Variety of al fresco eateries plus the smart **Petries**.

LIZARD ISLAND, c/o Australian Airlines (see Tours and charters)
The most northerly island in Queensland, on the fringe of the Outer Reef, with powdery white sand and clear waters. Stay in the Lodge or a private suite, dine on fresh fish, seafood and tropical fruit, go game fishing for the prized Black Marlin, scuba dive, snorkel and sunbake. In the visitors' book at Cook's Look you'll find Bob Hawke, Earl Spencer (Diana's pa) and Prince Charles. *"Wonderful – there are 24 little private beaches"* – CAROLINE HUNT.

NETANYA NOOSA, 75 Hastings St, Noosa Heads, Qld 4567 ☎ (071) 474722
Modern luxe on a fabulous long, sandy, surfy beach. Suites-only hotel in the most upmarket resort on this part of the coast, surrounded by National Parkland.

ORPHEUS ISLAND RESORT, Qld 4850 ☎ (077) 777377
A chic blend of tropics and Mediterranean, with wicker furniture, ceiling fans (somewhat hazardously low-slung) and muslin drapes. Only 50 guests, who stay in a serviced studio, bungalow or villa, with a choice of 7 beaches. Swim, sail or snorkel against a National Park backdrop. Bob Hawke and the Duke and Duchess of Westminster have stayed.

SHERATON MIRAGE, Port Douglas Rd, Port Douglas, Qld 4871 ☎ (070) 985888
Striking low-rise hotel and condo complex, surrounded by 5 acres of salt-water lagoons with walkways and islands. Bundles on offer – it's a stone's throw from Four Mile Beach and Marina Mirage, starting point for the Great Barrier Reef, Daintree Rainforest and Mossman Gorge. Sports for sea salts and landlubbers.

SHERATON MIRAGE GOLD COAST, Seaworld Drive, Main Beach, Surfers Paradise, Qld 4217 ☎ (075) 911488
Beautifully designed lagoon-locked resort complex, similar to its Darwin twin (only it's that bit closer to home for Sydneysiders). *"I have been there 3 times in one year and I love it. Their butler service is second to none. There's no need to go into town...a choice of 2 pools and the beach, a sports centre, and the Marina Mirage complex with restaurants and shopping. Lovely ocean suites or lagoon-side rooms are the pick"* – ELISE PASCOE. Private condominiums, too.

CANBERRA

—— Art and museums ——

AUSTRALIAN NATIONAL GALLERY, Parkes Place, ACT 2600 ☎ (062) 712501
The leading art gallery in the country for contemporary Australian and Aboriginal works. Also the best examples of leading overseas artists in Australia. Over 70,000 pieces in total. Eerily silent lakeside terrace with modern sculpture.

—————— Hotels ——————

PARK HYATT HOTEL, Commonwealth Ave, Yarralumla, ACT 2600 ☎ (062) 701234
A badly needed top-class hotel for the capital, a complete rethink for the old 1924 Hotel Canberra, applying chic modern structuralism to the original art deco style. *"Excellent in every way. Unquestionably tops. It's now the adopted pub for all politicians"* – DORIAN WILD. *"Canberra's No 1"* agrees LEN EVANS. The **Oak Room** is one of the classiest dining rooms in town, with delicate, complex cuisine; the **Promenade Café** is the place for Sunday brunch (slap-up smorgasbord), plus beautifully presented seafood.

———— Restaurants ————

FRINGE BENEFITS BRASSERIE, 54 Marcus Clarke St, ACT 2600 ☎ (062) 474042
The most fashionable hang-out in town – lots of politicians, including the very Minister for Finance who taxed expense-account lunching. Modish food of the char-grilling, pasta, pizzas and innovative salad variety – char-grilled liver with potato roesti, warm salad of quail and spinach, and pig-out puds.

HILL STATION RESTAURANT, Shepard St, Hume, ACT 2620 ☎ (062) 601393
Classical French cuisine cooked up by Steve Muscat for a typically political clientele. Dine in the Garden Room.

TONG REN, Mort St, ACT 2600
☎ **(062) 474448**
Arguably the best Chinese, where ministers tuck
in to light cuisine. Fun dim sum on Sun.

DARWIN

---------- *Hotels* ----------

**BEAUFORT HOTEL, The Esplanade, NT
5790** ☎ **(089) 829911**
A new 4-star super-luxe hotel for the far north
– a sure sign that international tourism has
arrived. *"A lovely hotel in every way: relaxed
yet gracious and charming"* – LESLEY WILD.

---------- · REST OF · ----------

NORTHERN TERRITORY

**SHERATON AYERS ROCK, Yulara Drive,
PO Box 21, Yulara, NT 0872** ☎ **(089) 562200**
Still can't fail to impress, with its windsurfer-
like sails masking the low-level complex from the
scorching sun, and Ayers Rock brooding beyond.
Top business facilities, superb pool, and dining
on kangaroo tail soup, should you so desire.

MELBOURNE

---------- *Art and museums* ----------

**NATIONAL GALLERY OF VICTORIA,
180 St Kilda Rd, Vic 3000** ☎ **(03) 618 0222**
Arguably the best art gallery in Australia.
Government-funded and highly patronized by
Melbourne's merchant princes, it houses the
finest, most comprehensive collection of Australian art – particularly of the Heidelberg School

(Australian Impressionism). The lofty Great Hall
has a dramatic stained-glass roof.

---------- *Arts centres* ----------

**VICTORIAN ARTS CENTRE, 100 St Kilda
Rd, Vic 3004** ☎ **(03) 617 8211**
Perhaps the largest visual and performing arts
centre in the world. It houses the National
Gallery, the Museum of Victoria, a 2,600-seat
concert hall, 3 theatres (including the Playhouse
– tops for drama, and the State Theatre – tops
for opera), a Performing Arts Museum, Children's Museum and a vast outdoor entertainment
area. Acoustically and architecturally innovative, the building extends 6 floors underground,
into the old bed of the Yarra River.

---------- *Ballet* ----------

🏇 **AUSTRALIAN BALLET, 11 Mount
Alexander Rd, Flemington, Vic 3031**
☎ **(03) 376 1400**
Under the artistic directorship of Sir John Gielgud's niece, Maina Gielgud, this company performs both full-length classical ballets and
shorter modern works, at home and abroad.

---------- *Bars and cafés* ----------

**CAFE DI STASIO, 31 Fitzroy St, St Kilda,
Vic 3182** ☎ **(03) 525 3999**
*"It would be difficult to find a more Italian bar
in Italy. The wine list covers some wonderful
wines from Tuscany and further north. The
carpaccio is superb and the al dente spaghetti
has no peer in Melbourne. This is a chic, mad,
intimate place with a wonderfully mad, ebul-
lient owner in Ronnie di Stasio"* – ANNE WILLAN.

**SODA SISTERS, 382 Chapel St, S Yarra,
Vic 3181** ☎ **(03) 241 4795**
A 50s-style soda fountain with rollerskating
waiters and waitresses, crooning Andrews Sisters and mountainous ices. Open late.

🏇 **Buzzz** Spiritual home of Crocodile
Dundee, **Kakadu National Park** in the Northern Territory is revered by all but the
most business-minded Aussies. So much so, that the Federal Government refused a
A$600 million gold development there – to the disgust of the biz boys, who saw it as
a Hawke ploy to win the green vote. See Kakadu for yourself on a Wild Goose Tour
by Mick Alderson, an Aboriginal elder with an English grandfather. Info from Croc 2:
the **crocodile-shaped Four Seasons Kakadu**, Flinders St, Jabiru, NT 5796 ☎ (089)
792800. Owned by local aborigines and fashioned on their totem, this beast has yellow
eyes that light up at night. Enter through gaping jaws; crunch crocodile terrine and
sip croctails🏇 ...... Crocodile 3: clock the real thing on a **Yellow Waters** cruise along
the billabong in Kakadu. Book via **Four Seasons Cooinda** ☎ (089) 790145 .... 🏇

Clubs

THE CLUB, 132 Smith St, Collingwood, Vic 3066 ☎ (03) 417 4425
Run by ex-Skyhooks musician Bob Stakey, this is still the best nightly venue for prominent local rock 'n' roll bands.

THE HIPPODROME, 14 King St, Vic 3000 ☎ (03) 614 5022
Smart club in an 18C building with original stained-glass windows and an art deco bar. 3 floors a-jumpin' with 3 types of music.

Australia's Best Clubs

1	ROGUES · Sydney
2	THE METRO · Melbourne
3	THE IVY · Melbourne
4	UNDERGROUND · Melbourne
5	KLUB KAKADU · Sydney
6	INFLATION · Melbourne

🏆 INFLATION, 60 King St, Vic 3000 ☎ (03) 614 6122
One of the best clubs in town, like one of the old New York-style blockbusters, built on 3 levels. Giant video screens and electronic razzmatazz attract a hip crowd, on weekdays more than weekends. Upstairs is a cocktail/dance/video bar, downstairs a huge dance floor.

🏆 THE IVY, 145 Flinders Lane, Vic 3000 ☎ (03) 650 5377
With a A$5 million investment from entertainment entrepreneur Glen Wheatley, this is Melbourne's newest hotspot, rapidly established as *the* place for the local glittocracy. On any night social voyeurs can OD on local TV and radio stars, rock musicians and the pampered offspring of Melbourne plutocrats. Slick disco with lots of cosy corners for intimate tête-à-têtes.

🏆 MELBOURNE UNDERGROUND, 22-24 King St, Vic 3000 ☎ (03) 614 7677
Comfortable club in a renovated bluestone warehouse. Masses of room, good food, and screening at the door – the place to show visiting celebs where it's at. Very young set.

🏆 THE METRO, 20 Bourke St, Vic 3000 ☎ (03) 663 4288
Still the trendiest nitery in town, though The Ivy's creeping up on it. Former cinema with 5 layers to dance and drink on, and the latest technology in lighting and videos.

Fashion designers

ADELE PALMER, 671 Chapel St, S Yarra, Vic 3141 ☎ (03) 240 0611
Palmer's keynote is an insouciant style. Casual printed cottons, sportswear with an energetic twist, and the best jeans in Australia, Jag. All the American film-star tough guys 'n' gals (Redford, Newman, Cher) wear Jag.

JANE LAMERTON, 55 Moore St, Fitzroy, Vic 3065 ☎ (03) 417 1366
A young 'un who goes from strength to strength with her intriguing mix of funky new garb and unashamed classics.

JENNY BANNISTER, c/o 80 Wellington St, St Kilda, Vic 3182 ☎ (03) 518932
A young designer who is *"wild, irreverent, unique – bravo for her energy and enthusiasm!"* – KIRSTIE CLEMENTS. Stocked at Perruche, 437 Chapel St, S Yarra ☎ (03) 824 1848.

🏆 PRUE ACTON, Shop 10, 12 Bridge Rd, Richmond, Vic 3121 ☎ (03) 429 4122
An original Australian motivator in the field of fashion, Prue Acton has been awarded an OBE. Designer basics for day and evening: unstructured summer suits with long gauzy skirts; plentiful monochrome appliqués and 'cornelli' work – a form of buttonhole edging. *"Fashion would not be here today without her"* – KIRSTIE CLEMENTS.

SCANLAN AND THEODORE, 539 Chapel St, S Yarra, Vic 3141 ☎ (03) 241 2449
The hippest designers in Melbourne. Full of inspiration and surprise. *"If you are young and want something absolutely unique, this is the place to go"* – JANE ROARTY.

Festivals

SPOLETO FESTIVAL, 6th Level, 1 City Rd, S Melbourne, Vic 3205 ☎ (03) 614 4484
A branch of Menotti's Italian festival, held in 2 weeks of Sept. Expect contemporary and classical dance, drama and musicals as well as classical music. A truly international event. Held mainly at the Victorian Arts Centre, plus churches and other venues.

Gardens

ROYAL BOTANIC GARDENS, Domain Rd, S Yarra, Vic 3141 ☎ (03) 639424
Victoria is regarded as Australia's Garden State and nowhere is this better seen than in this manicured feat of Antipodean horticulture. Modelled on the great landscaped gardens of Europe, the gardens provide a year-round splash of colour. Melburnians love them, as does tree-lover LORD LICHFIELD.

———————— *Hotels* ————————

**HILTON INTERNATIONAL
MELBOURNE ON THE PARK, 192
Wellington Parade, E Melbourne, Vic 3002**
☎ **(03) 419 3311**
This is the cricketers' haunt, overlooking Melbourne Cricket Ground and Fitzroy Gardens. Good business facilities and dining at the oak-panelled Cliveden Room. Imran Khan, Prince Philip and Margaret Thatcher have stayed. *"A very good hotel; it's large but doesn't feel that way because of the service"* – TERRY HOLMES.

🏃 **HYATT ON COLLINS, 123 Collins St,
Vic 3000** ☎ **(03) 657 1234**
Undoubtedly the swishest hotel in Australia, beautifully styled with over 89,700 sq ft of gleaming Veronese marble – *"a world of total opulence"* – DORIAN WILD. Here in lifestyle city, there's a dramatic skylit galleried space, Collins Chase, with carriage-trade shops and 9 bars and cafés, **Max's** seafood restaurant, **Monsoon's** membership nightclub, and the **Regency Club** hotel-within-a-hotel on the top 4 floors. The cost of all that? Over A$200 million. ELISE PASCOE declares: *"I haven't stayed anywhere else in 2 years. Max's is one of the loveliest hotel restaurants in the world, beautiful accoutrements and very good food."* BETTY KENWARD finds *"very good service, good food, good locality, everything good, except lack of cupboard room".*

**MENZIES AT RIALTO, 495 Collins St, Vic
3000** ☎ **(03) 620 9111**
A successful blend of ancient (well, Victorian) and modern, this hotel links two 10-storey neo-Gothic buildings with an atrium, though with all that red brick and red carpets and red light fittings, it's all a bit *red* in there.

🏃 **THE REGENT, 25 Collins St, Vic 3000**
☎ **(03) 653 0000**
Based on the top 15 floors of a 50-storey atrium skyscraper, it's not for those with vertigo. The top-floor suites are a blast, with windows from floor to ceiling, but common-or-garden rooms are rather small. Superb business facilities, with

———————— 🏃 ————————
Australia's Best Hotels

1	HYATT ON COLLINS · Melbourne
2	THE REGENT · Sydney
3	SHERATON BRISBANE HOTEL & TOWERS · Brisbane
4	INTER-CONTINENTAL · Sydney
5	HYATT REGENCY · Adelaide
6	PERTH INTERNATIONAL · Perth
7	PARK HYATT HOTEL · Canberra
8	THE REGENT · Melbourne
9	SEBEL TOWN HOUSE · Sydney
10	ROCKMAN'S REGENCY · Melbourne

huge auditorium. Guests include Rupert Murdoch, Jackie Collins, and top tennis stars. *"The best hotel I've stayed in in Australia. Truly stunning. You have to be very secure of stomach to eat in the restaurant during the day because of this amazing sheer drop. I had the best room service ever – fabulous food delivered one course after the other"* – GLYNN CHRISTIAN.

🏃 **ROCKMAN'S REGENCY HOTEL, Cnr
Exhibition and Lonsdale Sts, Vic 3000**
☎ **(03) 662 3900**
As Morgans is to New York, this is to Melbourne, a zazzy boutique hotel with a friendly approach that attracts celebs – Whitney Houston, Bob Hope, John McEnroe, Sean Connery, Rex Harrison.... Videos in all rooms, Jacuzzis in suites; pool and spa. Superb **Ritz** restaurant.

WINDSOR, 103 Spring St, Vic 3000
☎ **(03) 653 0653**
An impressive Victorian hotel, built on the truly grand scale and restored by the Oberoi group. The penthouse, for years the private home of

🏃 **Buzzz** At the City Club health and fitness centre at the **Hyatt on Collins**, the space-age Powercise equipment talks you through your paces. Choose your **humanoid coach** (Chester, Wally, Pierre, Curly – there's a type for everyone) and wait for its 'humorous comments' as you go into a taxing leg curl🏃......The **best blossoms, possums**, are artily arranged by **Kevin O'Neill**, 123 Toorak Rd, S Yarra ☎ (03) 266 5776, who's sent truckloads of gladdies (etc) to Bond, Packer and Potter events🏃......Party 2: Planning and catering supremo **Peter Rowland**, 3 Tivoli Rd, S Yarra ☎ (03) 240 1353 has the **monopoly** on Melbourne society hooleys and *"is now prominent in Sydney. In fact he is everywhere,"* declares ELISE PASCOE: *"no one comes close to his flair and standards"* ....🏃

roué Peter Jansen, is on hire once more. One for traditionalists, this is the preferred pub of Lady (Primrose) Potter and Malcolm Fraser.

Restaurants

See also Hotels.

"The more innovative of Australian chefs are using Asian influences in their cooking, the lighter flavours, the variety of spices.... Other restaurants are getting nostalgic for home cooking: big, hearty meals" – CLAUDE FORELL.

CAFE FLORENTINO, 80 Bourke St, Vic 3000 ☎ (03) 662 1811
Florentino's reincarnate after a complete overhaul. Old faithfuls were worried, but ROBERT SANGSTER assures that *"it is back to No 1."*

FANNY'S, 243 Lonsdale St, Vic 3000 ☎ (03) 663 3017
One of the best-loved restaurants in the country, and part of the Staley stable. Upstairs is smart with flawless service, downstairs is a bistro with an open kitchen and cheaper food. Cuisine is constantly updated, with seasonal specialities. Bacall and Dietrich have dined here.

FLOWER DRUM, 17 Market Lane, Vic 3000 ☎ (03) 662 3655
One of the best Chinese restaurants in Australia. Upmarket and expensive with a spacious main dining room plus smaller, more private rooms. Chef-owner Gilbert Lau does masterful egg noodles according to an ancient recipe, lobster rolls, drunken squab. *"Fantastic"* – DON HEWITSON. A hit with BARRY HUMPHRIES.

🐟 JACQUES REYMOND'S RESTAURANT, 259 Lennox St, Richmond, Vic 3121 ☎ (03) 427 9177
Hot from his acclaimed kitchens at Mietta's, Reymond continues to wow Melbourne with sensational menus. *"Superb French food, served in a modern manner. The restaurant itself doesn't have a great deal of charm, a bit kitschy, but the food is wonderful"* – CLAUDE FORELL.

JEAN JACQUES BY THE SEA, 40 Jacka Blvd, St Kilda, Vic 3182 ☎ (03) 534 8221
Despite inconsistencies in service and food, JJs is still a winner, not least for its beachside setting. *"Seafood for serious diners. Not a fashionable restaurant but a great place to dine and entertain people. Also, no finer place in Melbourne to see the sun go down over Port Phillip Bay"* – CLAUDE FORELL.

KENZAN, Lower Gr Fl, Collins Place, 45 Collins St, Vic 3000 ☎ (03) 654 8933
A Japanese restaurant beneath the Regent Hotel, with food you'd commit harakiri for. Go for kaiseki (traditional banquet), nabe ryori (cooking in the pot) or sushi.

THE LAST AUSSIE FISHCAF, 256 Park St, S Melbourne, Vic 3205 ☎ (03) 699 1942
The 50s start here: milk-bar décor complete with lino floor, chrome-edged tables, loud jukebox. This fab fishery is stuffed to the gills with ad and film types. Fish dishes smack of creole and Oriental cuisines – or simply of home. Everything from blackened fish fillets through boudin of char-grilled seafoods or prawn tempura to good ol' fish and chips. The best part of the evening is when co-owner John Flower mimes to golden oldies, leaping from bar stool to bar stool. *"Very loud, very noisy, very trendy, full of fun. A place where you can be entertained while you eat: the staff impersonate Elvis and co. Also limbo dancers and magicians. Great fun"* – CLAUDE FORELL. Branches in Sydney and Brisbane.

LYNCH'S, 133 Domain Rd, S Yarra, Vic 3141 ☎ (03) 266 5627
Owner Paul Lynch sets a distinctive style – an air of Parisian Bohemia, faded elegance, and the feeling that you are a guest. Tables are packed in to the 3 little dining rooms and the covered 'winter garden'. Original French-based dishes.

MASK OF CHINA, 115-117 Little Bourke St, Vic 3000 ☎ (03) 662 2116
A great Chinatown BYO, with cool modern décor and finely balanced MSG-free Chiu Chow cuisine (similar to Cantonese, from a seaboard region in Guangdong Province). *"Specialities are shark fin soup (the best in Australia), abalone, soyed goose and live lobster and mud crab"* – ANNE WILLAN.

🐟 MIETTA'S, 7 Alfred Place, Vic 3000 ☎ (03) 654 2366
A perennial best for Melbourne, in a grand setting in a former gentlemen's club, with plenty of waiters hovering. Elegant seasonal epicure plus particularly heavenly pastry, petits fours and cheeses. Renowned, too, for its fabulous, rare wines. *"Situated in an old Victorian building, this is the most European of all Melbourne's restaurants. Excellent food"* – CLAUDE FORELL. *"With its period décor, breathtaking floral arrangements and formal service, Mietta's looks and feels like an elegant Parisian restaurant. Chef Pierre Stinzy is a worthy successor to Jacques Reymond and the wine list contains the best choice of burgundies in Australia"* – ANNE WILLAN. Downstairs is an informal lounge for drinks, snacks and entertainment – take tea while listening to readings and singers.

PIERONI'S, 172 Toorak Rd, S Yarra, Vic 3141 ☎ (03) 241 7833
Airy, echoey place, combining Italian railway station and old palazzo – lots of shiny black marble, walls with trompe-l'oeil faded frescoes. Row upon row of tables, seating the most fashionable types in town for day-long dining or simply sipping coffee.

Pukka Tucker

ANNE WILLAN sniffs out the best food shops in town: *"Like a mini-Peck's of Milan, the* **Lygon Street Food Store**, *Lygon St, Carlton, is an Aladdin's cave of parmigiano, prosciutto, luscious home-made quince jellies and jar upon jar of marinated antipasti. Try* **David Jones Food Hall** *in Bourke St Mall for another adventure in high-quality, fresh foods."* Sweet tooths will already know that **Fleischer's**, 586 Chapel St, S Yarra, is the best continental cake shop in Melbourne, while **Haigh's**, 521 Toorak Rd, Toorak, provides the best chocolates. A speciality is segments of orange, lemon or grapefruit dipped in chocolate. At **Victoria Market**, Cnr of Elizabeth and Victoria Sts, browse around the exotic open-air mélange of stalls and stallholders – Turkish, Greek, Italian, Chinese, Indian.

SHARK FIN INN, 50 Little Bourke St, Vic 3000 ☎ (03) 662 2552
Brill authentic Chinese restaurant, always packed, with the best yum cha (dim sum) in town. **Shark Fin House** is the newer, grown-up version at 131 Little Bourke St ☎ (03) 663 1555, on 3 levels and equally packed. 8 chefs fresh out of Hong Kong *don't* spoil the broth.

🦐 STEPHANIE'S, 405 Tooronga Rd, Hawthorn East, Vic 3123 ☎ (03) 822 8944
International foodies continue to shower accolades upon Stephanie Alexander, one of the most innovative chefs in Australia. *"The top of the tree. The most individual and creative chef in Melbourne. Creates the closest thing to Australian cuisine, a sort of modern Australian with provincial French overtones. Definitely a place for people who take their food seriously"* – CLAUDE FORELL. *"At the forefront of the search for the true Australian cuisine. She buys much of her produce from small local suppliers and effortlessly incorporates Asian and indigenous ingredients in her dishes. The Victorian mansion that houses the restaurant has been lovingly restored, and Sri Lankan-born Dur-é Dara heads up an immaculate floor staff"* – ANNE WILLAN. The restaurant has recently been extended; menus are now more diverse and change only twice a year.

🦐 TANSY'S, 555 Nicholson St, Carlton N, Vic 3054 ☎ (03) 380 5555
A delightful Victorian terrace with iron fretting and fresh, unpretentious interior. Post-nouvelle cuisine – deliciously frail mousses, warm salads; duck, quail and hare. *"It's a BYO and one of the best. Modern French food, served in a light, informal setting. Very popular among a young, trendy crowd"* – CLAUDE FORELL.

VLADO'S, 61 Bridge Rd, Richmond, Vic 3121 ☎ (03) 428 5833
Chef-owner Vlado Gregurek is the hero of the meat-mad. *"Not so much a restaurant as a carnivore's castle. Specializes exclusively in meat dishes...some of the finest cuts of meat imaginable. Great technique. Great restaurant"* – CLAUDE FORELL. Start with a mini-kebab, home-made sausage or a snippet of fillet – then move on to the serious stuff.

Shopping

CASTALLIA ANTIQUES, 1 Murphy St, S Yarra, Vic 3141 ☎ (03) 266 8053
For antique and costume jewellery. *"A favourite – they have an uncanny eye for picking the best"* – KIRSTIE CLEMENTS.

COUNTRY ROAD, 45 Collins St, Vic 3000 ☎ (03) 650 3829; 332 Collins St ☎ (03) 670 2113
The definitive Oz country style – dateless polished tailored daywear, plus designer ideas on how to be the belle of the bush.

EVELYN MILES, Shop 1, Tok-H Centre, 459 Toorak Rd, Toorak, Vic 3142 ☎ (03) 241 5844
The best women's designer footwear, from Gianni Barbato, Tokio Kumagai, Robert Clergerie, Versace, Stephane Kélian, Dior, Pancaldi, Charles Jourdan, Valentino – all the smartypants labels for real tarting-up occasion shoes. Also accessories by Chantal Thomass.

GEORGES, 162 Collins St, Vic 3000 ☎ (03) 630411
This genteel establishment is part of the fabric of Melbourne, and a supreme fashion treat (Valentino, Saint Laurent, Ungaro, Genny, Montana, Kenzo, Rykiel, Laurel, plus Liberty scarves). Long-standing staff and customers of old-style elegance. The loos are a paradisal vision with free telephones, old sofas, magazines, flowers, tinkling chandeliers.

HENRY BUCK'S, 320 Collins St, Vic 3000 ☎ (03) 670 9951 and branches
Tops for menswear. A distinguished environment of Persian carpets, polished timber and sniffy staff, Buck's is where young – and old – bucks go for a strictly classical, off-the-peg wardrobe. The Mecca for bow ties.

LE LOUVRE, 74 Collins St, Vic 3000 ☎ (03) 650 1300
A salon steeped in leopard skin, where formid-

able Melbourne matrons hoover up the best in European fashion – imports only. Glitterbug evening wear and lavish wedding gowns.

MAKERS MARK, 85 Collins St, Vic 3000 ☎ (03) 654 8737
Jewellery by innovative designers such as Sandy Kilpatrick, whose exquisite gold designs are much-coveted.

MASON'S, 111 Toorak Rd, S Yarra, Vic 3141 ☎ (03) 266 5106
For the most desirable and directional imports – such as Romeo Gigli and Norma Kamali. Always a stampede at the beginning of each season. *"Sleek and wonderful"* – JANE ROARTY.

McCLOUD'S, 120 Queen St, Vic 3000 ☎ (03) 673386
This men's shoe shop is a stomping ground for English, Italian and German shoes in kid and hand-tooled leather for the footwise gourmet.

MISS LOUISE, 471 Toorak Rd, Toorak, Vic 3142 ☎ (03) 240 1984; at the Hyatt on Collins ☎ (03) 654 7730
Fabulous range of Australia's best shoes and the pick of imports such as Walter Steiger, Maud Frizon and Robert Clergerie.

SABA, 131 Bourke St, Vic 3004 ☎ (03) 654 6176
Amid on-line visual input from fash videos of the European shows, you can sort through supercool selections from Yohji Yamamoto, Comme des Garçons and Saba himself (who produces wonderful tailored wear).

TAMASINE DALE, Shop 1, 94 Flinders St, Vic 3000 ☎ (03) 650 7122
"Without doubt the most wonderful young milliner in Melbourne. Her hats are creations. As good as the French, maybe better" – JANE ROARTY.

WENDY MEAD HATS, Shop 11, 521 Toorak Rd, Toorak, Vic 3142 ☎ (03) 240 9093
Romantic, extravagant headgear, always one step ahead of fashion. Ready-to-wear and custom-made one-offs. She makes about 300 hats for the Melbourne Cup, to adorn heads such as the Baillieus, Myers, Lady Stephen, and Tamie Fraser, wife of ex-PM Malcolm.

─────── *Theatre* ───────

MELBOURNE THEATRE COMPANY, 19 Russell St, Vic 3000 ☎ (03) 654 4000
Melbourne's leading theatrical company, ranging from classics to new Australian plays. Directors are also quick to seize upon box-office hits from London and New York for local productions. Though a tad starchy, the MTC maintains a high repertory standard envied by the rest of Oz.

· REST OF ·
VICTORIA
─────── *Hotels* ───────

BURNHAM BEECHES COUNTRY HOUSE, Sherbrooke Rd, Sherbrooke, Vic 3789 ☎ (03) 755 1903
First-rate hotel near the Dandenong Hills. The white art deco mansion with its sweeping sun decks was built by a ship-mad family. Gorgeous leafy garden and renowned cuisine – it feels like you're dining on the Captain's table every night, as – KEITH FLOYD will testify – it's one of his 2 fave eateries in the world.

🏄 DELGANY COUNTRY HOUSE HOTEL, Delgany Ave, Portsea, Vic 3944 ☎ (059) 844000
From the Schneiders, who ran the famous restaurant Two Faces in Melbourne, a converted 1920s limestone castle with 35 rooms. Lovely views over Port Phillip Bay, and magnificent dining experiences reminiscent of the old days.

HOWQUA DALE GOURMET RETREAT, Howqua River Rd, PO Box 379, Mansfield, Vic 3722 ☎ (057) 773503
The best country-house weekends in Australia, set in the lush region seen in *The Man from Snowy River*. Only 12 guests, who dine on delectable home-made dishes using local seasonal produce. Tennis, riding, fishing and swimming. Weekend and 5-day cooking schools with occasional guest chefs.

🏄 THE QUEENSCLIFF HOTEL, 16 Gellibrand St, Queenscliff, Vic 3225 ☎ (052) 521982
Refined, classic seaside Victoriana, with white lacework verandahs, stained glass, tessellated floor tiles, dark wood furniture, bunches of violets, and lavender bags under the pillow. Run by Patricia O'Donnell, sister of Mietta (see Restaurants), who caters to gastronomes with equal gusto: beef fillet with ginger, spinach and wild mushrooms; saffron pasta with local fish and dill.

PERTH
─────── *Hotels* ───────

🏄 HYATT REGENCY, 99 Adelaide Terrace, WA 6000 ☎ (09) 225 1234
The old Merlin, still a winner, entering to the same futuristic lobby with pink Italian granite floor and atrium that soars 13 storeys to a domed, tubular steel and glass roof. As in Melbourne and Adelaide, the Regency Club offers extra exclusivity. **Jessica's** is one of the trendiest and

finest eateries in town, with views over the Swan River. Alan Bond goes, as does LORD LICHFIELD, for superlative fish and seafood – try grilled dhufish (unique to the west), shark, whole Western Rock lobster and chowder.

OBSERVATION CITY RESORT HOTEL, PO Box 202, The Esplanade, Scarborough Beach, WA 6019 ☎ (09) 245 1000
The newest addition to Perth's hotel élite (actually 5 miles north of the centre). Marvellous sense of light and space, with an original Henry Moore in the lobby, and the best ocean views. Décor rather Habitat modern.

PARMELIA HILTON, Mill St, WA 6000 ☎ (09) 322 3622
Still an old favourite for many, who appreciate consistent, individual service and an olde worlde atmos. *"The rooms are very good, large and spacious, and it's in a good position"* – JULIAN LLOYD WEBBER. All the top America's Cup crews stay here; others feel it's a little out of the action ...The **Garden** restaurant is tops for bizmen and ladies who lunch. Flawless international cuisine.

🐟 PERTH INTERNATIONAL, 10 Irwin St, WA 6000 ☎ (09) 325 0481
Modern and first-class, decorated in the colours of the Bush. Views over the Governor's garden and the best hotel restaurant in town, the **Irwin**, for haute French gastronomy in a small, soft pink dining room. Delicious seafood dishes such as fresh crab, scrambled eggs and caviare in a sea urchin; interesting game.

SHERATON PERTH HOTEL, 207 Adelaide Terrace, WA 6000 ☎ (09) 325 0501
Another swanky modern hotel, where *"VIPs get an astonishing butler, Brook, who is English, ex-theatre. Unbelievable – I've never had clothes looked after quite so well"* – LORD LICHFIELD.

—— *Music* ——

PERTH ENTERTAINMENT CENTRE, Wellington St, WA 6000 ☎ (09) 322 4766
The main auditorium is the largest in Australia, and the best pop concert venue. The smaller, more intimate Concert Hall is a winner with JULIAN LLOYD WEBBER: *"One of those places where you can walk on stage, click your fingers, and the sound will resonate around yet remain very clear. It has one of the 'livest' acoustics that I've ever known. I always think these things are pure chance...somehow it's worked."*

—— *Restaurants* ——

"Australia has really grown up in recent years. The best of our restaurants are really very good indeed. They have lifted their standards enormously. Our chefs have started to cook in a way

which is, at last, relevant to Australia. They are cooking the kind of things we like to eat...We are now opting for a lighter style of food, simply cooked; lots of char-grilling and steaming" – JOAN CAMPBELL.

MEDITERRANEAN GARDEN RESTAURANT, 414 Rokeby Rd, Subiaco, WA 6008 ☎ (09) 381 2188
Despite the falling stocks of Perth's high rollers, the Med continues to set the pace for trendy lunching and dining – big deals and Bolly all the way. Practically a private club. Californianesque menu with daily specials – but once you're in with the staff, they'll prepare just about any dish you wish.

ORD STREET CAFE, 27 Ord St, W Perth, WA 6005 ☎ (09) 321 6021
Light modern cuisine is served in the drawing room or on the verandah of this old house which trebles up as a cosy, romantic evening dinery, smart business lunchery and a cool place for power or leisure breakfasts.

SAN LORENZO, 23 Victoria Ave, Claremont, WA 6010 ☎ (09) 384 0870
Started 2 years ago by Eileen Bond, who named it after her fave fooderie in London, it's now under the same ownership as Ord Street Café. Swish, trendy and relaxed; innovative menu big on seafood, veal and pasta.

—— *Shopping* ——

ELLE, 56 Weld St, Nedlands, WA 6009 ☎ (09) 386 6868
Takes fashion in a broad stride from classy conservatism à la YSL through to the avant-garde beatitudes of the Japs via Katharine Hamnett, Saint Laurent, Giorgio Armani and Lagerfeld. Hats, shoes, bags and costume jewellery. *"Easily the best shop in Perth"* – SKYE MACLEOD. *"The best of the best – no one in Australia has a collection like Elle's"* – KIRSTIE CLEMENTS.

R M WILLIAMS, Shop 38, Carillon Centre, Hay St Mall, WA 6000 ☎ (09) 321 7786
'The Original Bushman's Outfitters', pride of Australia, producer of some of the nation's most coveted exports. Drovers' moleskin trousers (moleys), graziers' and stockmen's shirts, kangaroo-hide plaited belts, Crocodile Dundee-style Akubra hats (hanging corks not included), and the famous Aussie oilskin Drizabone (equivalent of the Barbour). For bushboys and townies with outback swagger. About 50 stores across the continent; mail order.

SCARPERS, Shop 13, City Arcade, WA 6000 ☎ (09) 321 6941
The most eclectic imported feet in Perth – Robert Clergerie, Christian Dior, Rayne, Sonja Bettine, Charles Jourdan, Sergio Rossi and further Italian-crafted showy shoes.

· REST OF ·
WESTERN AUSTRALIA

🏨 **CABLE BEACH CLUB, Cable Beach Rd, Broome, WA 6725 ☎ (091) 922505**
Lord McAlpine's getaway resort is a synthesis of old and new, of natural and created: Oriental antiques, modern Australian art (Arthur Boyd, Sidney Nolan, Elizabeth Durak), one of the best white sand beaches in the world, landscaped tropical gardens with pagodas and Eastern ornaments, health club, scuba school, and cuisine in consultation with Albert Roux. Based in an old pearling port, it's *"luxury on the simple scale. The best of everything without being pretentious and without the ubiquitous marble and brass. The best accommodation is in the old pearlers' bungalows, done up with lots of lattice and fly-wire ... to provide maximum privacy while allowing a natural flow of fresh air"* – MARION VON ADLERSTEIN. Don't miss the Lord's pet love – his Pearl Coast Zoo and bird park.

──── *Restaurants* ────

LEEUWIN ESTATE RESTAURANT, Leeuwin Estate, Witchcliffe, WA 6286 ☎ (097) 576253
The best country restaurant in the west, on Denis Horgan's blooming wine estate, half a day's drive south of Perth. Table tops are slabs of Karri tree from the estate. The glassed-in restaurant has a verandah and sloping lawns leading to acre upon acre of vines. Superb wine list, natch.

──── *Music* ────

LEEUWIN CONCERTS, Leeuwin Estate, Gnarawary Rd, Margaret River. Tickets: Barrack House, 262 St George's Terrace, Perth, WA 6000 ☎ (09) 322 2288
A highlight of the WA cultural calendar, when over 6,000 people flock to these al fresco classical concerts in Feb/Mar. A magical evening held on multi-millionaire Denis Horgan's magnificent estate, some 175 miles from Perth, where guests picnic in casual or evening wear à la Glyndebourne. Top international orchestras perform to the accompaniment of cackling kookaburras.

SYDNEY

──── *Art and museums* ────

ART GALLERY OF NEW SOUTH WALES, Art Gallery Rd, NSW 2000 ☎ (02) 225 1700
Under the dynamic directorship of flamboyant

"Anyone coming to Sydney has to take a ferry ride on the harbour, even if only to the zoo. Sydney is a city and a resort all in one: a wonderful, glitzy, sophisticated city and yet surrounded by so much natural beauty "

 MARION VON ADLERSTEIN

Edmund Capon, the gallery has captured the hearts and minds of Sydneysiders. While the collection is strongest on Australian art, exhibitions are world-class – works from the Hermitage, Leningrad; German Impressionists; French Impressionists; Gold of the Pharaohs; Chinese Warriors. *"They're so good that even the philistines come along"* – LESLEY WILD. *"Capon has transformed it from dusty provincialism into a gallery which plays an important role in the cultural life of Sydney"* – LEO SCHOFIELD. Well supported too as a social venue.

AUSTRALIAN MUSEUM, 6 College St, NSW 2000 ☎ (02) 339 8111
The best representation of Australian natural history and Aboriginal artifacts, with ever-changing displays. Management that is anything but prehistoric keeps the place highly regarded.

POWERHOUSE MUSEUM, Harris St, Ultimo, NSW 2007 ☎ (02) 217 0111
Housed in an old power station, this born-again Museum of Applied Arts and Sciences is the buzziest in Oz. *"It has widened the meaning of the word museum – exhibits include 6 light planes suspended from the ceiling, whole trains to explore, traction engines and steam engines in full working order. No wonder kids go ape!"* – LESLEY WILD. Art and design students flock in for constant and changing exhibitions of Australian fashions, donated by leading designers and VIPs. Former PM's wife Lady (Sonia) McMahon bestowed the scandalous slit-to-the-thigh frock she wore to meet Nixon at the White House.

TUSCULUM, 3 Manning St, Potts Point, NSW 2011 ☎ (02) 356 2955
The first architectural and design gallery in Australia. Its main base is the 2-storey double-verandah villa, Tusculum, designed in 1832 by John Verge, who designed Elizabeth Bay House.

──── *Ballet* ────

SYDNEY DANCE COMPANY, Pier 4, Hickson Rd, Walsh Bay, NSW 2000 ☎ (02) 221 4811
Easily the most exciting modern dance company in Australia, led by Grahame Murphy and Janet Vernon. Local performances meet with rap-

Cockatoo Island

'Where has it taken 3 million years to finish landscaping?' asks the blurb. *'Where can you follow in nobody's footsteps? Where is the world's largest, freshest supply of free oysters?'* The answer to all these posers and more is: on the latest patch of exclusivity, an old mining island 124 miles north of Broome in Western Australia. Owned by Alan Bond's company Dallhold, Cockatoo is a hilly island of rocky bluffs, small sandy coves, rich red earth and lush foliage. The miners' cottages have been luxuriously souped up by Eileen Bond in her favourite colour, pink – and that's the outside. Inside it's colonial gone troppo. The island is home to a kaleidoscope of bird life (butcher bird, honey eater, sea eagle, the eponymous white sulphur crested cockatoo), turtles, oysters – and salt-water crocodiles. It's also paradise for anyone who likes catching – and eating – fish; the daily catch at the spectacular seafood restaurant may include red emperor, barramundi and oysters. There's tennis, squash, bushwalking trails, open-air movies and a cinematically blue pool that looks as if it drifts right into the sea – yet it's 328 ft above sea level. Cockatoo Island, Yampi Sound, WA ☎ (09) 321 2794 or c/o Ansett Holidays ☎ (09) 325 0201.

turous write-ups and play to packed houses. Frequent tours overseas – to New York, Tokyo, Europe, even China – earn further praise.

—— *Bars and cafés* ——

See also Hotels.

BAR COLUZZI, 322 Victoria St, Darlinghurst, NSW 2011 ☎ (02) 357 5420
An ultra-fash café-society haunt that does the best espresso in Sydney. So packed that latecomers have to quaff on the pavement.

DEAN'S VERANDAH, 13-15 Kellett St, Kings Cross, NSW 2011 ☎ (02) 358 4177
New-look Dean's, across the road from the old one. Still great as a late-night café, but not for dining. Best hot chocolates in town – tall, with a dollop of cream and a sprinkling of cinnamon.

HARD ROCK CAFE, 121-129 Crown St, Darlinghurst, NSW 2010 ☎ (02) 331 1116
The latest in Peter Moreton's globe-spanning Hard Rock chain opened last year with a A$100,000 party which had Sydney socialites fighting for invitations – Susan Renouf and Rene Rivkin made it. Great drinks, fast food and the best rock music. A 1960 Cadillac hangs from the ceiling and the back half of a Ford Thunderbird is engineered as having crashed into the front wall. Crash in yourself after midnight (on Fri/Sat – otherwise closes at 11.30), or meet up and tank up before hitting the town.

JO-JO IVORY'S NEW ORLEANS RESTAURANT, 40 Macleay St, Potts Point, NSW 2011 ☎ (02) 358 1955
Late-night cocktail and piano bar, with a robotic black man tinkling the ivories.

LAMROCK CAFE, 72 Campbell Parade, Bondi, NSW 2026 ☎ (02) 306313
Very casual café, with a glassed-in section for people-gazing, as close to the beach as you can be. Great Bloody Marys. Trendies like fashion designer Stuart Membery and the Double Bay Ferrari set come here for breakfast on Sunday – fabulous eggs benedict.

🦜 **Buzzz Fly like the wind** – Qantas knocked spots off all previous records when it flew London-Sydney (11,179 miles) in 20 hrs 9 mins, **non-stop**, at 45,000 ft and 571 mph. Following the Kangaroo Route, that was a helluva hop compared with the 1935 service which stopped 42 times to refuel and took 12 to 14 days. Loaded with passengers, the new Boeing 747-400s can manage London-Melbourne, one-stop at Singapore, in a speedy 22 hrs 25 mins🦜......Look out for the new **Ritz-Carlton** opening in **Double Bay**🦜......*"Two of the greatest influences on European cuisine are the Australian magazines* **Australian Gourmet Traveller** *and* **Vogue Entertaining**. *They are regularly thought to be the best food magazines in the world"* – GLYNN CHRISTIAN... 🦜

**TROPICANA COFFEE LOUNGE, 110
Darlinghurst Rd, Kings Cross, NSW 2011
☎ (02) 331 6486**
For high-fashion lounging. *"Is this the Via Veneto or what? The vespa outside is still humming, the focaccia [bread] is fresh and crusty and the espresso is so good you just have to have another"* – ANNE WILLAN.

Clubs

**BENNY'S BAR-RESTAURANT, 12 Challis
Ave, Potts Points, NSW 2011 ☎ (02) 358 2454**
Still the place for ragers with stamina to wind up – a smoky dive beloved of the rock industry.

**THE CAULDRON, 207 Darlinghurst Rd,
Darlinghurst, NSW 2010 ☎ (02) 331 1523**
Small, steamy disco, still a-bubble with girls in mini skirts. It may be a bit of a meat-market, but it's brilliant fun.

**🐾 KLUB KAKADU, 163-169 Oxford St,
Darlinghurst, NSW 2010 ☎ (02) 331 4001**
Big trendy disco with live music too. Theme nights attract a good-looking young bunch.

**METROPOLIS, 99 Walker St, N Sydney,
NSW 2060 ☎ (02) 954 3599**
Heavily influenced by Fritz Lang's movie of the same name, the 1920s lines of this very elegant nitery attract Sydney's ultra-fickle socialites and the local have-money-what's-new flash cash ad/media set. Boogie to great music on the small dance floor (set apart from the main club), lounge in the piano bar, or simply gaze through the windows over Sydney.

**🐾 ROGUES, 16 Oxford Square, Oxford St,
Darlinghurst, NSW 2010 ☎ (02) 336924**
Still Australia's No 1. Since elevating their award-winning restaurant to an elegant street-front setting· and renaming it **Rogues Streetons**, this club is enjoying a financial and social renaissance. Dine on zippy Italian/Californian fare in palazzoesque surroundings. *"Excellent restaurant food and a great spot for late-night partying, or simply a snack or drink on the way home"* – ELISE PASCOE. It's the nearest Oz gets to Annabel's (though the crowd smacks more of Stringfellow's and the tone can sink pretty low on occasion). Still, there's moderately strict membership, a high-profile dance floor, 3 bars and glamorous waitresses. Joan Collins boogies there till dawn, Michael Parkinson, Bernie Leser (President of Condé Nast Publications) and DORIAN WILD are keen.

**🐾 ROUND MIDNIGHT, 2 Rosslyn St,
King's Cross, NSW 2011 ☎ (02) 356 4045**
One of the coolest joints in town, frequented by an upmarket Hoorayish gang plus a flash of fashion types. Lots to do on different levels. When you're not right by the dance floor, you could be in a gentlemen's club with all the sofas and glossy mags.

Fashion designers

**CARLA ZAMPATTI, 435A Kent St, NSW
2000 ☎ (02) 264 8244**
Squillionaire society dame Zampatti has the Australian fashion scene wrapped up with her draped silk evening dresses and breezy day clothes. Olivia Newton-John's fave.

**🐾 GEORGE GROSS & HARRY WHO, c/o
Viva, 19-27 Cross St Plaza, Double Bay,
NSW 2028 ☎ (02) 322485**
George is still master of designs to make a woman feel female – sexy and sensuous evening wear, a shade OTT. By day he is more classic and tailored, using natural fibres. The look stretches to silk jersey body suits and a lavish amount of leather and suede. Australians are just wild about Harry. A younger clientele than his partner – sculptural linens and silks for women, plus casual, stylish menswear with an easy beachboy-goes-big-city feel.

**JENNY KEE, Flamingo Park, Suite 102, 2F,
Strand Arcade, George St, NSW 2000
☎ (02) 231 3027**
Aussies may stifle their yawns, but internationally Jenny Kee is an icon of originality (and much copied) for dynamic knitwear. Bold, rhythmic patterns in vibrant colours. Some knits are the ready-to-wear equivalent of a Ken Done painting, abounding with multicoloured squiggles of Australian images. Also cotton and silk prints.

🐾 **Buzzz** Water-divining: the *most* divine, says ELISE PASCOE, is **Hepburn Spa**, *"the best Australian mineral water with gas"*, and **Pureau**, *"the best still water. It's so pure, say the makers, that even your pets can drink it"* (why not buy enough to fill your aquarium while you're about it)🐾 ......Groovers must keep eyes skinned for Richard Weiss's **Dance Deliriums** and **Dance Bacchanalians** – outsize warehouse parties that float from venue to venue (Hordern Pavilion, Pier 4, Darling Harbour). Real happening stuff – but only word-of-mouth will tell you *where* and *when* it's happening .... 🐾

🐧 **JILL FITZSIMON, 3 Little Collins St, Surry Hills, NSW 2010 ☎ (02) 212 5366**
The First Lady of Australian fashion. Season after season, she blazes a trail of high feminine style that leaves others floundering in her wake (a striking ash blonde herself, she's not unused to this effect). Evening wear is her forte – glorious one-of-a-kind appliquéd silk numbers. Also tailored suits for the executive woman. *"She's in a class of her own"* – DORIAN WILD.

LINDA JACKSON, 22 Glenmore Rd, Paddington, NSW 2021 ☎ (02) 360 6949
Arty-smarty bush couture using that key Aussie talent for moody painting on fabric. Best-dressed Alexandra Joel loves her things. *"The most unique individual spectacular clothes that reflect her passion and exuberant sense of life"* – KIRSTIE CLEMENTS.

🐧 **MARCUS TUSCH, 51-63 O'Connor St, Chippendale, NSW 2008 ☎ (02) 318 0477**
Modern classics for the modern woman with just a *tusch* of avant-garde. Styles heavily influenced by his hero Giorgio Armani. *"I'm a classicist,"* says Tusch, *"because at the bottom line that's what all art and all design comes down to."* SKYE MACLEOD finds him *"without doubt the best of Sydney's New Wave designers. He's simply got it. He's also an absolute dish...."*

🐧
Australia's Best Designers

1	WEISS
2	ROBERT BURTON
3	TRENT NATHAN
4	JILL FITZSIMON
5	MARCUS TUSCH

PETER MORRISSEY & LEONA EDMISTON, 74 Strand Arcade, NSW 2000 ☎ (02) 232 7606
Leading the new wave of young Australian design talent, this pair are *"quirky, upbeat and to the minute"* – KIRSTIE CLEMENTS. Kylie Minogue is just one fan.

🐧 **ROBERT BURTON, 104 Bathurst St, NSW 2000 ☎ (02) 267 2877**
Australia's answer to couture, with all the attendant pampering service one would expect. Jodhpur-clad Burton produces expensive, one-off designs for day and evening; good fabrics, impeccable cuts. Ready-to-wear and great accessories too.

Tusch truths
🐧
The new order of Australian design is uncompromising and unfrivolous. It seems that being a woman in Sydney is as serious a business as in New York or Milan. MARCUS TUSCH tells it like it is: *"I only target one kind of woman. She is, above all things, intelligent. She is in the workplace and I want her to look good in the workplace. My woman is totally independent. She stands on her own and doesn't rely on men for survival. I really can't relate to women who just sit at home and do nothing. My designs are very stylish, very feminine, very classical, but I don't have any time for frills or pretty things."*

STEPHEN GALLOWAY, 217 Glenmore Rd, Paddington, NSW 2021 ☎ (02) 336005
A young designer known for sensational evening wear with a superb colour sense. *"His embroidery is incredible. Quite beautiful"* – JANE ROARTY.

🐧 **TRENT NATHAN, 220 Henderson Rd, Alexandria, NSW 2015 ☎ (02) 550 3355**
One of the fash Establishment. Sophisticated exec wear – great tweeds and easy-to-wear fabrics, dolled up with an Aussie sexiness.

🐧 **WEISS, c/o Weiss Pringle, Shop G12 Gallery Level, Centrepoint, NSW 2000 ☎ (02) 232 7894**
Peter and Adele Weiss are international hits for their top-quality, minimal-styling knitwear and separates, served up in a multitude of colours. Their fashion aims to be relevant to Oz, not a rehash of overseas styles. 'Sown in Australia', their new label, focuses on a younger market. Shops all over Australia.

------ *Festivals* ------

FESTIVAL OF SYDNEY, 175 Castlereagh St, NSW 2000 ☎ (02) 267 2311
Sydney lets its hair down each January for this hurdy-gurdy of performing arts. Hyde Park is given over to a fun-fair with rides, games and family concerts; sporting events and processions fill the streets, stadiums and harbour; and theatres and performing spaces take on an international fervour that would have Thespes cheering in his shroud. Highlight is the free Opera in the Park in the Domain, when more than 100,000 punters pack in with champagne picnics, to hear stars of the Australian Opera. Conceived by Dame Joan 'Wonderlungs' Sutherland, her per-

formances in *La Traviata* and *Lucia di Lammermoor* were masterpieces. *"A wonderful idea which has been outstandingly successful. The performances are first rate"* – LEO SCHOFIELD.

Gardens

ROYAL BOTANIC GARDENS, Macquarie St, NSW 2000 ☎ (02) 231 8119
57 acres of lawns rolling down to the harbourside, with flower beds, exotic and Australian trees and a hothouse of ferns and orchids. A LORD LICHFIELD favourite: *"The place to take people who think botanical gardens are all science, just to see how wonderfully well they can be landscaped."* And for LESLEY WILD, *"there's no finer way to savour Sydney than by drinking the perfumed air of these splendid gardens. The harbour setting is simply breathtaking – and you can get a good lunch at the secluded restaurant."* Don't miss the famous view from Mrs Macquarie's Chair.

Hotels

♠ INTER-CONTINENTAL, 117 Macquarie St, NSW 2000 ☎ (02) 230 0200
The first choice for many Sydney regulars. *"I always look forward to going there. Very good service and, from the rooms at the top, a lovely view over Sydney Harbour"* – JEFFREY ARCHER. CAROLINE HUNT seconds that: *"one of the best hotels in the world...the best views."* Former HQ of the NSW Government Treasury, the original arcaded Victorian-Romanesque building is preserved as part of the inner atrium, topped with a skyscraperful of bedrooms. *"Suites are lovely with different Australian fabrics, and the beauty salon is as good as any in the world"* – ELISE PASCOE. Not just for biz whizzes: U2 stayed when last in town. **The Treasury** means *"grand dining in a grand setting"* – EP.

RAMADA RENAISSANCE, 30 Pitt St, NSW 2000 ☎ (02) 259 7000
Swish new hotel in the central business district – lots of high-roller appeal. The Renaissance Club, on the top 4 floors, offers extra-special attention.

♠ THE REGENT, 199 George St, NSW 2000 ☎ (02) 238 0000
No resting on any laurels here: Sydney's No 1 had a A\$12 million facelift last year. Still loved for its spectacular location overlooking the Opera House and harbour, but even more so for the service under General Manager Ted Wright: *"I have been there at least 4 times and I think it's not only the best Australian hotel, but one of the best in the world, because they are so attentive – to me the hallmark of a good hotel. They really care about service and doing things properly. Ted Wright is really a terrific guy with a keen sense of style"* – KEN HOM. *"The Regent has always been special. It never changes in the talented hands of Ted Wright"*, agrees ELISE PASCOE. *"Lovely"* – CAROLINE HUNT. Other guests include Michael Jackson, Dan Quayle, Tom Cruise, Pavarotti, Sophia Loren, the Aga Khan, Mel Gibson, Jodie Foster, Cher, LEN EVANS. GLYNN CHRISTIAN points out there are *"poky rooms"*, so go for a harbour-view suite with telescope (and avoid rooms facing the motorway). **Don Burrow's Supper Club** is *"the best jazz club in Sydney"* – LORD LICHFIELD and the excellent **Kable's** (see Restaurants) is the staff canteen for *Vogue*.

Best Beaches

Sun, sand, surf and s-s-s-sewage. Sydneysiders now think twice about diving into the ocean, since an exposé last year in the *Sydney Morning Herald* confirmed what they had long known – that sewage treatment plants using the outfall pipes at North Head (near Manly) and Maroubra (near Bondi) were hopelessly inefficient. Raw, untreated sewage and industrial chemicals have frequently been dumped into the sea. A brown sewage slick 100 yards wide and far more menacing than Jaws has been spotted lurking off the famous Manly and Bondi beaches. The Sydney Water Board was found to be issuing false figures on its summer Surfline, declaring beaches safe when in fact pollution exceeded legal levels. Surf life-savers threatened to desert any beach where they felt pollution was unacceptable (effectively closing it to the public). While POOO (People Opposing Ocean Outfalls) are busy rallying against all this, the best advice is to avoid dodgy beaches. **Bronte**, though not guaranteed sewage-free, has such a beautiful park behind it that as a total environment (barbies, cricket, football, sunbaking...paddling?) it gets the thumbs up. Pretty much out of the firing line are **Palm** and **Whale** Beach, **Dee Why** and **Narrabeen**, all good northern beaches for surfing and preening. **Balmoral** is still the best harbour beach, with a distinct Californian free 'n' easy flavour.

**RITZ-CARLTON, 93 Macquarie St, NSW
2000 ☎ (02) 252 3755**
Smart new 5-star hotel to rival the Inter-
Continental, with its own version of the view
over the Royal Botanic Gardens and Sydney
Harbour. Small enough (106 rooms) for truly
personal service.

**THE RUSSELL, 143A George St, Circular
Quay, NSW 2000 ☎ (02) 241 3543**
Sweet little private hotel that's very low key,
like staying with friends in an English country
home – stripped pine, Laura Ashley. Have a nice
cuppa at the **Café Russell**.

**🏊 SEBEL TOWN HOUSE, 23 Elizabeth
Bay Rd, Elizabeth Bay, NSW 2011
☎ (02) 358 3244**
Still the place to go if you're from the trendy
world of rock and showbiz. Intimate and som-
brely plushy, it knows how to treat its stars. The
legendary bar got *so* popular that partying took
up most of the lobby too; now popsters find all
they need at the new **Ricky May Bar** (named
after the Australian jazz singer). *"Still one of
Sydney's favourite hotels – a great place to see
and be seen. The barman knows your drink, you
don't even need to order"* – ELISE PASCOE. *"Bohemian people and vaguely relaxed rules, so you
do have astonishingly interesting happenings
going on which would never happen at Claridge's"* – LORD LICHFIELD. MAUREEN LIPMAN,
JOAN COLLINS, Dire Straits, Elton John, Tina
Turner, Paul Simon and Bob Dylan are regular
Sebel ravers.

**SHERATON WENTWORTH, 61-101 Phillip
St, NSW 2000 ☎ (02) 230 0700**
In the process of a A$14 million revamp, bringing
the sheen of granite and marble to the entrance
and lobby, and upgrading the rooms. A
thoroughly well-run hotel with many loyal
guests, particularly in the diplomatic set, who
like its clubbish atmosphere and long-standing
staff. Venetian concierge Tony Facciolo remains
one of the most highly thought-of in the world.
Garden Court is one of the best hotel restaurants in town.

———— *Music* ————

**AUSTRALIAN OPERA, 480 Elizabeth St,
Surry Hills, NSW 2010 ☎ (02) 699 1099**
Despite the enormous logistical and financial
problems of staging opera in such a large and
thinly populated country, the AO treats en-
thusiastic patrons to an exuberant annual
programme, Jan-Feb and June-Oct at the Opera
House. Verdi, Mozart, Wagner, Puccini *and*
Gilbert & Sullivan are seat-fillers; so are more
adventurous avant-garde productions. *"Maintains a good provincial standard, at its best when
performing as an ensemble and not when trying
to rival some of the world's major companies"* –
LEO SCHOFIELD.

**SYDNEY OPERA HOUSE, Bennelong
Point, Circular Quay, NSW 2000
☎ (02) 250 7111**
This famous landmark and arts centre (for opera,
ballet, theatre, music and film) continues to
excite controversy. From the sea or air, the
spectacular spinnakered building dazzles and
gleams, its sails mimicking the yachts on the
harbour. Close up, those off-white tiles are a bit
of a let-down. The inside story is even less
hopeful: *"An interesting building which is hope-
less for opera. The stage is too small and so is
backstage for anything except Mozart and Doni-
zetti. Sydney simply needs another venue where
opera can be performed properly"* – LEO SCHO-
FIELD. Till then, it's still home to the best
companies in town.

———— *Restaurants* ————

See also Clubs and Hotels.

*"Australian cuisine has never been in better
shape. Although Sydney and Melbourne continue to lead the way in terms of trends and
innovations, there are signs that other parts of
the country are fast catching up, especially
Queensland. What Australia offers the imaginative, innovative chef above all is quality, freshness, and a wide choice of materials . . . outstanding Australian cheeses, superb vegetables and
amazing seafood, which are available all year
round"* – LEO SCHOFIELD.

**🏊 ARMSTRONG'S, 1 Napier St, N
Sydney, NSW 2060 ☎ (02) 955 2066**
The latest from Mark Armstrong (ex-Pegrum's
and Macleay Street Bistro) and another sure-fire
hit. *"Like so many of Sydney's most talented
chefs, he has gone downmarket from the days of
nouvelle cuisine to a situation where he now
provides quality food for all in a lively, fun
atmosphere"* – LEO SCHOFIELD. *"A new rather
large brasserie with a great open kitchen that
lets you view the goings on. The food is excellent
as you would expect from this talented chef. An
asset to the 'other side' of the bridge"* – ELISE
PASCOE.

**THE BALKAN, 209 Oxford St,
Darlinghurst, NSW 2010 ☎ (02) 360 4970;
BALKAN II, 215 Oxford St ☎ (02) 331 7670**
Simple, cheapie haunt for barbecued hunks of
meat and sausages, delicious thick bean soup,
and, at the slightly more elegant **Balkan II**,
brilliant char-grilled seafood specials. MAX LAKE
likes it to the max.

**BAYSWATER BRASSERIE, 32 Bayswater
Rd, Kings Cross, NSW 2011 ☎ (02) 357 2177**
As fashionable as ever, a livewire haunt for
media types. Subtle, consistently good food. No
booking, just diners with clout. *"One of the
happening places. Opened 7 years ago and is
still wonderful. Good food, economically priced,*

helpful waiters, all in a big brasserie atmosphere. Very relaxed, very informal, sums up Sydney" – LEO SCHOFIELD.

BEPPI'S, Cnr Stanley and Yurong Sts, E Sydney, NSW 2000 ☎ (02) 360 4558
Brill Italian joint, run by Beppi Polese for over 30 years. Lauded by LEN EVANS and MAX LAKE, it offers the best of trad and modern cuisine, and a superb wine list.

CHEZ OZ, 23 Craigend St, Darlinghurst, NSW 2010 ☎ (02) 332 4866
This bright, breezy, noisy Spago-alike is still thriving. *"Crowds left in droves when the original chef [Andrew Blake] returned to Melbourne. But now it is back in favour and doing a roaring trade both at lunch and dinner"* – ELISE PASCOE. Char-grilled fresh fish and meat, and fancy pizzas.

CHOYS JIN JIANG, 2nd Fl, Queen Victoria Bldg, Cnr Market and George Sts, NSW 2000 ☎ (02) 261 3388
Tip-top chop-chop Chinese dinery, in an unrivalled setting (1930s-cum-Ming dynasty). *"An elegant restaurant, serving delicious food; an excellent wine list and brilliant service. Not cheap but special"* – ELISE PASCOE. Sichuan and Shanghai head the menu. Try yin yang prawns in two sauces, red pepper oil and sesame chicken. Spot on for LEN EVANS.

♠ CLAUDE'S, 10 Oxford St, Woollahra, NSW 2025 ☎ (02) 331 2325
Intimate, unlicensed restaurant with exemplary standards of classic French cuisine and service. Damien Pignolet has a loyal following, which keeps the place booked solid. Devotees particularly love the traditional bouillabaisse evening on the first Friday of the month and the grand set dinner on the first Saturday.

DARCY'S, 92 Hargrave St, Paddington, NSW 2021 ☎ (02) 323706
Nothing changes at Darcy's, a terrifically popular Paddo haunt with an air of true-blue Brit (despite traditional Italianate fare). A sea of media faces attend – Rupert Murdoch, Sam Chisholm, Jana Wendt, Mike Gibson, and Tony Greig – it's the Channel 9 canteen. *"Excellent Italian food and a very good wine list"* – ROBERT SANGSTER.

DOYLE'S ON THE BEACH, 11 Marine Parade, Watsons Bay, NSW 2030 ☎ (02) 337 2007
At worst an overrun fish 'n' chippy, Doyle's is nonetheless an institution, beautifully placed in a grand old waterfront house with tables overlooking the sea. Dig in to mud crabs, seafood chowder, and massive platefuls of exotic fish – barramundi, red snapper, John Dory – uniformly battered. Now Doyle's also offers an alternative view, at **Doyle's At the Quay**, Circular Quay W ☎ (02) 252 3400.

EDOSEI, 22 Rockwell Crescent, Potts Point, NSW 2011 ☎ (02) 357 3407
In swanky new premises, Edosei is now one of the highest-ranking Japanese (high prices, too). Unbeatably fresh sushi and sashimi – watching the sushi chefs do their magic with prawn, sea urchin, squid and fish is a delight. *"Wonderful Japanese food with the best sushi bar in town. Beautifully decorated and furnished, it's a special-occasion restaurant"* – ELISE PASCOE. Jenny Kee and Linda Jackson love it.

HOUSE OF GUANGZHOU, 76 Ultimo Rd, Ultimo, NSW 2007 ☎ (02) 281 2205
Opened by the Imperial Peking's former hostess, this is a LEN EVANS favourite for mainly Cantonese cuisine. Sensational seafood and Peking duck.

♠ IMPERIAL PEKING HARBOURSIDE, 13-17 Circular Quay W, The Rocks, NSW 2000 ☎ (02) 223 1128
A grand Chinese affair, expensive and superb, as LEN EVANS and Michael Parkinson will vouch. *"Dominates the quality end of Chinese dining, with an unmatched view of Sydney Harbour"* – LEO SCHOFIELD.

♠ KABLE'S, The Regent, 199 George St, NSW 2000 ☎ (02) 238 0000
The Regent's lavish, grown-up, elegant dining room is the recognized best hotel restaurant in town. Don't expect a variation on a truffle or foie gras here – this is true, modern all-Australian cuisine, backed by a superb wine list. LEN EVANS relishes it, as does ELISE PASCOE: *"Kable's is better than ever. Executive chef Serge Dansereau is undoubtedly the best of his kind in Australia. His food is always good whether it's for 500 in the ballroom or a table of 2 at Kable's. He is cooking with Australia's best produce, pointing the way for Australian food in the new decade."*

LAST AUSSIE FISHCAF, 24 Bayswater Rd, Kings Cross, NSW 2011 ☎ (02) 356 2911
A spin-off from the Melbourne original, where a raucous crew head for innovative fish, seafood and oysters galore. Bags of fun, with a nickelodeon and dancing.

LA STRADA, 95 Macleay St, Potts Point, NSW 2011 ☎ (02) 358 1160
Run by the Italian Toppi family, this swish, busy restaurant is full of starry faces – George Michael, Julian Lennon, BRUCE OLDFIELD and BARRY HUMPHRIES: *"A wonderful restaurant – the best steak Diane in the world and very good home-made pasta, especially the boscaiolo."*

MACHIAVELLI RISTORANTE, 123 Clarence St, NSW 2000 ☎ (02) 262 4816
Run by Giovanna Toppi (whose daughters now run La Strada), this vies with Rogues Streetons for top celeb-spotting lunch-spot. Politicians, radio stars, real estate moguls and barristers cram in for wonderful antipasti and spaghetti at paltry prices.

**MACLEAY STREET BISTRO, 73A
Macleay St, Potts Point, NSW 2011
☎ (02) 358 4891**
Ravy bistro with no bookings and a chalked-up
menu offering, say, goat's cheese and aubergine
tart, scrummy seafood, char-grills, and wicked
puddings to follow.

**MARIGOLD, 299 Sussex St, NSW 2000
☎ (02) 264 6744**
Highly popular Chinese restaurant in Sydney's
compact Chinatown. For the best yum cha in
town, as LORD LICHFIELD notes and weekend
queues testify.

Australia's Best Restaurants

I	STEPHANIE'S · Melbourne
2	BEROWRA WATERS INN · NSW
3	OASIS SEROS · Sydney
4	NEDIZ TU · Adelaide
5	JACQUES REYMOND'S RESTAURANT · Melbourne
6	KABLE'S · The Regent, Sydney
7	ROCKPOOL · Sydney
8	MIETTA'S · Melbourne
9	BAGUETTE · Brisbane
10	FLEURIEU · Adelaide

**MARIO'S, 73 Stanley St, Darlinghurst,
NSW 2021 ☎ (02) 331 4945**
Wonderful Italiano teeming with life. *"The haunt
of models, moguls, magazine people and
discerning journalists. Here the food never dis-
appoints. Pioneered the trend towards minimalism (bare white walls, bare white-topped tables)
but what it lacks in architectural grandness is
more than made up with zappo food and atmosphere"* – LEO SCHOFIELD. Carla Zampatti, Maggie
Tabberer and June McCallum join the mêlée.

**🐧 OASIS SEROS, 495 Oxford St,
Paddington, NSW 2021 ☎ (02) 361 3377**
Seros stuff... pioneering, too. Phillip Searle is a
leading light in the new wave of inventive
Australian cooking. *"Simply magnificent. Excellent food, excellent service and a chef with
flair. Classic, fresh cuisine with a pan-Asia
flavour. One of the very best. Never fails"* – LEO
SCHOFIELD. Now celebrated are his daredevilish
desserts – eg the chequerboard of pineapple
sorbet, anise ice cream and liquorice.

**PEGRUM'S, 36 Gurner St, Paddington,
NSW 2021 ☎ (02) 357 4776**
Despite Mark Armstrong's departure, this re-
mains confident, cosy, eclectic, expensive *and*
delicious, thanks to Ralph Potter's sure hand.
Cuisine of the nouvelle kind. Excellent wine list.

**🐧 ROCKPOOL, 109 George St, The
Rocks, NSW 2000 ☎ (02) 252 1888**
The pooled talents of Neil Perry (ex-Bluewater
Grill), his wife Nicole, and Greg Frazer (former
sommelier at Berowra Waters) have rocked the
Sydney dining scene. *"Until Neil Perry opened
this glossy New York-style restaurant, there was
nowhere in Australia that could do justice to the
local seafood. But Perry's delightful belon-type
oysters opened to order, his whole deep-fried fish
and his Queensland mud crab, steamed with just
a little black bean, has changed that overnight"*
– ANNE WILLAN. *"High-style designer restaurant
...the rage in Sydney. The best place for seafood.
Brilliant"* – LEO SCHOFIELD. *"It's pricy but marvellous. There's also an oyster bar upstairs with
good views of the Opera House sails and the
quay"* – ELISE PASCOE. *"Deliciously fresh seafood by a young, go-ahead chef. A real find"* –
LORD LICHFIELD.

**SALA THAI, 778 Military Rd, Mosman,
NSW 2088 ☎ (02) 969 9379**
*"One of the rare Thai restaurants in Australia
that hasn't modified its food for Australian
tastes. The mixed entrée platter is a breathtaking
feast for the eyes and palate"* – LEN EVANS.
Breathtaking is the word – no stinting on spices.

**SOMI'S JITTRA THAI RESTAURANT, 14
South Steyne St at Victoria Parade, Manly,
NSW 2062 ☎ (02) 977 7220**
Another high Thai on the North Shore, with a
magnificent view of the Pacific from upstairs. Go
for seafood specialities on the endless menu.

**SUNTORY, 529 Kent St, NSW 2000
☎ (02) 267 2900**
Further testament to the Suntory chain's supremacy. High-class Japanese, with individual
rooms for tempura, teppanyaki and shabu shabu,
and a knockout kaiseki. Savoured by LEN EVANS.

**TAYLOR'S, 203-205 Albion St, Surry Hills,
NSW 2010 ☎ (02) 361 5100**
Classy restaurant based in a pair of colonial
houses with a pretty garden where you can dine.
No longer fully fledged Italian (the Italian maître
d' has departed), it still has a strong suit in
antipasti and Med-meets-mod seafood.

**THAI POTHONG, 294 King St, Newtown,
NSW 2042 ☎ (02) 550 6277**
*"Regarded by people who know their Oriental
spices as the best Thai restaurant in Sydney.
Situated in a highly unfashionable area, this
big, noisy, fun-filled restaurant is also one of
the best-value places. Attracts a trendy crowd"*
– LEO SCHOFIELD. Great regional cuisine. BYO.

TRE SCALINI, 174 Liverpool St, E Sydney, NSW 2000 ☎ (02) 331 4358
3 steps to success – good fodder, chipper service and a great atmosphere. *"The main rival to Mario's. Attracts a similar crowd as well as the high rollers of the real estate game. A wide range of simple Italian fare. Most people choose from the specials which are usually delicious. Impossible to get a table"* – LEO SCHOFIELD.

LE TRIANON, 29 Challis Ave, Potts Point, NSW 2011 ☎ (02) 358 1353
Master of meat and game, and a magician with puds, Peter Doyle (nothing to do with fishy Doyle's) updates classic French cuisine with skill and ingenuity. Swish, flower-filled dining room.

THE WHARF, Pier 4, Hickson Rd, Walsh Bay, NSW 2000 ☎ (02) 250 1761
Great, go-ahead restaurant, perfect pre-theatre (Pier 4 is home to the Sydney Theatre Co). Pleases one and all, with Anders Ousback as food consultant, an all-NSW wine list, and non-trad harbour views.

Shopping

Double Bay – Cross St, Bay St, Knox St in particular – is still Sydney's Rodeo Drive, a low-rise area providing a glassy showcase for international designerdom. Lots of outdoor eating and little arcades. The **Queen Victoria Building** in George St is not only the best shopping centre but an architectural treat. A vast and lofty structure with galleried levels, wrought-iron railings, original tiled floor and arched glass roof, its chi-chi shoplets house Adele Palmer, Country Road, Benetton, Zanolli jewellery and more. **Castlereagh Street** promises to be the Rodeo Drive of Sydney with the likes of Vuitton, Gucci, Cartier, Hermès and Chanel. **Strand Arcade** has the trad Strand Hatters and sleek international/young trendy designer boutiques. **Oxford Street**, from Woollahra to Darlinghurst, is the equivalent of London's King's Road of the 1960s, a buzzy roam-around area for the best contemporary fashion, plus cafés and restaurants. On Saturdays, **Paddington Market** provides extra shopping focus – arty-crafty oddments, jewellery, clothes. **Sydney Fish Markets**, Gipps St, Pyrmont, is fabulous for the best fish and seafood in Sydney (best stall is **De Costi's**).

ANNABEL INGALL, 24 Oxford St, Woollahra, NSW 2025 ☎ (03) 331 2626
Annabel was a leading force in the resurgence of millinery Down Under. *"Witty, wonderful hats for the young"* – JANE ROARTY. Now youthful swimwear and resort gear too.

ANNE LEWIN at David Jones, see Shopping
Australia's No 1 lingerie designer, for luxurious little snippets of silk.

ANNE SCHOFIELD ANTIQUES, 36 Queen St, Woollahra, NSW 2025 ☎ (02) 321326
Far and away the best collection of antique jewellery in Sydney – at a price. Worth it for her remarkable eye for quality.

THE CHEESE SHOP, 797 Military Rd, Mosman, NSW 2088 ☎ (02) 969 4469
"The best cheese shop in Sydney due to owner Rick Newman's knowledge and care. Sells pasta dishes and pasta sauces which his wife Debbie makes" – ELISE PASCOE.

CHRIS HAND MADE SHIRTS, 4A Tank Stream Arcade, 175 Pitt St, NSW 2000 ☎ (02) 231 6094
For just what it says. They're well known and well worth wearing.

DAVID JONES, Elizabeth St, NSW 2000 ☎ (02) 266 5544, and branches
Sydney's best store, the Harrods of Australia. An edited and wide-ranging collection of home-grown and foreign-label designs – the exclusive on Rykiel, Versace and Missoni, plus Ungaro, Lacroix, Armani and Valentino. *"One of the few department stores that actually has a real tailor on staff, and not just someone who measures and makes alterations. Value for money in every way. The best business suits"* – DORIAN WILD. Also a fab menswear department in the Market St/corner of Castlereagh St branch, for the exec/sportif/preppy man – Louis Féraud suits, Country Road casuals. The Food Hall is *the* place for stocking up on goodies. *"The finest upmarket supermarket in Australia. The best selection of everything, beautifully displayed and very tempting. I lunch at the oyster bar as often as I can. It's all very civilized"* – ELISE PASCOE.

DINOSAUR DESIGNS, 73 Strand Arcade, NSW 2000 ☎ (02) 223 2953
Offbeat jewellery designers – affordable Australiana using resin and perspex, plus classic creations. Oodles of flair.

DORIAN SCOTT'S AUSTRALIAN FASHION DESIGNERS, 105 George St, The Rocks, NSW 2000 ☎ (02) 274090
Dorian herself knits up fine merino classics but is even better known as the forcing-house for young Aussie talent. Her current stock of about 30 embryonics includes Susie Cooks, Amy Hamilton, Jennifer Layther, Libby Peacock and Christine Wilkie – all specialists in one-offs.

EUROPA EPIC CURE, 17 Kellett St, Kings Cross, NSW 2011 ☎ (02) 358 6266
For Tasmanian smoked trout, from the Tasmanian Smoke House, and smoked salmon.

FIVE WAY FUSION, 205 Glenmore Rd, Paddington, NSW 2021 ☎ (02) 331 2828
European upbeat dressing for men: beautiful imports from Montana, Armani, Miyake and more. LEO SCHOFIELD blows dollars on hankies here.

Darling Harbour

Ranking alongside Sydney's Historic Rocks is Darling Harbour – darling of the tourist beat. Although the much-vaunted hotel-casino complex still hasn't got off the ground and the monorail ('no-no-rail') continues to lose money, the Convention Centre, Exhibition Centre, Festival Market Place and Harbourside, with their vast array of shops and eateries, are flourishing. If you can't live without *Le Figaro*, the *Washington Post* or *The Independent*, head for Harbourside (international papers within 48 hours at the World News Centre). Ditto if you need to swap a mark, a yen, a buck or a pound (30 currencies offered at up-to-the-second exchange rates at Westpac, hooked into the international money market). Darling Harbour is also jam-packed with novelty shops (Ken Done, Canned in Australia, Desert Designs, Cuddly Colonials...), fashion boutiques (Sportsgirl, Linda Jackson Bush Couture, Surf Dive 'n' Ski, Country Road, The Irish Shop), fast-food stalls and relaxed harbourfront restaurants. Trendy munching at **Jordon's** for seafood and sushi, and the more downmarket but ever-popular **Bobby McGee's** bar/diner, where you are served by infantrymen and women in 18C colonial working dress).

GEORGE'S DELICATESSEN, 2 Hopetoun St, Paddington, NSW 2021 ☎ (02) 332 3395
"Now reverted back to its original owners Nita and Joe Bonaventura. It's now better than when they first owned it. They have the best prosciutto" – ELISE PASCOE.

GRACE BROS, 436 George St, NSW 2000 ☎ (02) 238 9111 (and branches countrywide)
A great old department store with the best set of women's shoes around – Clergerie, Steiger, Kélian, Myma, Espace, Freelance, Hope, Frizon – all the young bloods are here, alongside the footy Establishment.

HUNT LEATHER, MLC Centre, King St, NSW 2000 ☎ (02) 233 1681; 141 George St, The Rocks, NSW 2000 ☎ (02) 241 2918
The best leather goods in Sydney at amazingly competitive prices. Strongly favoured by the A team as one of the few stockists of genuine Filofaxes and all Filo accessories.

I M DESIGNS, 18 Prince Alfred Walk, Queen Victoria Bldg, NSW 2000 ☎ (02) 261 2180
Divine Australian lingerie plus the best from France and Italy. *"Naughty but nice"*, quips JANE ROARTY. PS Caters for men, too.

J H CUTLER, Level 3, 33 Bligh St, NSW 2000 ☎ (02) 232 7351
Old-fashioned English-style tailoring. John Cutler is fourth generation in the biz, and doing a suit that equals Savile Row in a land bereft of men of the cloth. *"This is what bespoke tailoring is all about"* – DORIAN WILD. LEO SCHOFIELD has forsworn Turnbull & Asser for Cutler's shirts. *"The bespoke tailor in Sydney. Women are just as welcome as men"* – ELISE PASCOE.

JOHN SERAFINO, 20 Bay St, Double Bay, NSW 2028 ☎ (02) 329884
One of the best menswear shops in Australia and one of the most innovative tailor-designers. Specializes in Italian fabrics and styles. Launched a new range of fully washable suitings in Oct 1989 by donning a suit and aqualung and walking along the bottom of the harbour at Sydney Aquarium; he then hosed down the suit and hung it up to dry. Showbizoid clientele includes TV star Graham Kennedy.

LA PATISSIER, 121 Military Rd, Neutral Bay, NSW 2089 ☎ (02) 953 8550
For a small but stunning selection of pastries. Open 7 days a week.

MARC'S, Shop P, Mid City Centre, 197 Pitt St, NSW 2000 ☎ (02) 232 2948; 430 Oxford St, Paddington, NSW 2021 ☎ (02) 332 4591
Top place for men's casual clothes of the Brooks Bros persuasion, plus women's wear.

MARIA FINLAY, 30 Bay St, Double Bay, NSW 2028 ☎ (02) 328 7001
Doyenne of the ultra-stylish thirtysomething-plus set. Maria Finlay has been around for yonks, dressing local ladies in unlocal fashions – designers like Louis Féraud.

MASON'S BOUTIQUE, 45A Bay St, Double Bay, NSW 2028 ☎ (02) 329894
Darlings of the fashion industry, for the most switched-on selection of European designers. JANE ROARTY and ANNE LEWIN are fans.

MIDAS SHOES, Imperial Arcade, Pitt St, NSW 2000 ☎ (02) 233 3612, and branches
Best for the younger buyer who doesn't want to pay an arm and a leg for a shoe. Truckloads of imagination (and no relation to English Midas).

MORAY MILLINERY, 306 Strand Arcade, George St, NSW 2000 ☎ (02) 233 1591
The best milliner in Sydney and one of the best in Australia. All styles of made-to-measure headgear for ladies and gents.

THE NORTHERN ITALIAN FOOD SHOP, 15 Penshurst St, Willoughby, NSW 2068 ☎ (02) 958 3621
"An Italian alimentari serving good ingredients similar to the Bonaventuras' of George's Deli" – ELISE PASCOE.

PAPOUCCI, Shop 20, Cosmopolitan Centre, Knox St, Double Bay, NSW 2028 ☎ (02) 327 4167; 20 Bay St, Double Bay ☎ (02) 328 7722
One of the best shoe shops in town for imports (Dior, Jourdan and top Italian lines) and Australian makes.

PASSELLO, 27 Bronte Rd, Bondi Junction, NSW 2022 ☎ (02) 389 3304
The best home-made pasta in Sydney, savoured by LEO SCHOFIELD. Wonderful sauces, too, plus imported goodies.

PHILIP GRAVES, 49 Bay St, Double Bay, NSW 2028 ☎ (02) 328 6880
Arguably the best in Sydney, a delectable shop for classic and fancy footwork.

RAYMOND CASTLE SHOES, 21 Bay St, Double Bay, NSW 2028 ☎ (02) 327 3864
Fab shoe store, chocker with international designer toelines. Their own range too, which are carefree designer copies, just as nice and half the price.

ROBIN GARLAND, 15 Bay St, Double Bay, NSW 2028 ☎ (02) 329971
One of the best clothing and accessory shops in Sydney. Exclusively her own designs.

ROX JEWELLERY, 31 Strand Arcade, Pitt St, NSW 2000 ☎ (02) 232 7828
The place for spectacular costume counterfeit, Jezebel jewels and other outrageous ornament, all the way up to real gold and diamonds. The most contemporary designs from New York appear here. Tina Turner, Boy George, David Bowie and Olivia Newton-John have all been bejewelled at Rox.

SPEEDO KNITTING MILLS, 54 Chandos St, St Leonards, NSW 2065 ☎ (02) 438 5211
The world's best sporting second skin, solid-gold Olympic-medal swimwear that now has serious fashion status. Beautiful straightforward but shape-conscious maillots and two-piece cossies. Australia's top model Elle 'The Body' McPherson struts her stuff in a Speedo.

STUDIO NOKO, 2 Bay St, Double Bay, NSW 2028 ☎ (02) 326 2087
A showroom for owner Philip Noakes's superb modern jewellery using precious metals, plus work by some of Australia's leading designers. *"The pieces are akin to mini art works"* – KIRSTIE CLEMENTS.

SURF, DIVE 'N' SKI, 466 George St, NSW 2000 ☎ (02) 267 3408
Where surfers get their beach-cred together: Billabong, Quicksilver and 100% Mambo board shorts, T-shirts and Rip Curl wet suits. Other splashy brands are Hot Tuna and Lightning Bolt.

TRELLINI MENS WEAR, 139 Elizabeth St, NSW 2000 ☎ (02) 264 6498
The trendspot for imported designer fandango for men and women – Comme des Garçons, Katharine Hamnett, Jean-Paul Gaultier, Panchetti, Romeo Gigli. Shirts are made to measure under their own label. An equally wide range of clients – Billy Connolly, Sting, Gough Whitlam, and Judy Davis.

Theatre

SYDNEY THEATRE COMPANY, Pier 4, Hickson Rd, Walsh Bay, NSW 2000 ☎ (02) 250 1700
Sydney's leading showcase for classical theatre, new Australian plays, plus the best of Broadway

Theatre Threat

For a city of 3 million people, Sydney is starved of theatre space. Former best venue The Regent is being redeveloped into offices despite well-orchestrated opposition from actors and theatre-lovers. The Theatre Royal usually hosts long-running box-office bonanzas such as *Cats* and *Les Miserables*, which play for up to 2 years at a time, putting enormous pressure on other major venues. Nevertheless, theatre in Sydney is marked by enormous energy. Among producers there's an air of catch-as-you-can in claiming space at Her Majesty's, the Seymour Centre and the Footbridge Theatre. Even the grand old cinema, The State, in Market Street, has been nabbed for musicals and revues despite being fundamentally unsuitable. For the best productions, head for **Ensemble Theatre** in Kirribilli ☎ (02) 929 8877; **Belvoir Street Theatre** in Surry Hills ☎ (02) 699 3257 and the Sydney Theatre Company's 2 venues, **The Wharf** and **Opera House Drama Theatre**.

and the West End. 10 productions a year, at its own in-the-round theatre here at the Wharf, and the Drama Theatre of the Opera House. One new Australian play, *Harold in Italy*, attracted mega media hostility... if controversy is the lifeblood of theatre, the STC will run and run.

· REST OF ·

NEW SOUTH WALES

– Hotels and restaurants –

BELLTREES, Scone, NSW 2337
☎ (065) 461119
Self-contained guest house on the historic and thoroughly well-connected Belltrees Estate, in the White family for 5 generations. Michael White is No 1 stop-off on the Old Etonian network. Rustic isn't in it – you share the great outdoors here with 5,000 Merino sheep.

🐦 BEROWRA WATERS INN, Berowra Waters, NSW 2082 ☎ (02) 456 1027
Still regarded universally as one of Australia's greatest, Berowra never fails to delight and excite the senses. What's more, with current exchange rates, A$80-plus a head seems quite a bargain for such haute cuisine, service and surroundings (not to mention the welcoming dram of champagne). Reached by light aircraft or boat, this is *"simply the best food in Australia served in the best-located restaurant in Australia"* – LEO SCHOFIELD. *"The tripe lyonnaise, the bone marrow en brioche and the crème brûlée will usually be on the menu. If they're not, don't worry. Whatever Gay Bilson and Janni Kyritsis decide to cook will be full of flavour and character. And there's always that beautiful view of the Hawkesbury River"* – ANNE WILLAN. Open weekends only.

CARRINGTON HOUSE, 130 Young St, Carrington, NSW 2294 ☎ (049) 613564
This guest house is a sleek operation, providing stunning modern Australian cuisine such as confit of goose legs, fillet of buffalo. Best Hunter Valley produce and wines.

CASUARINA, Hermitage Rd, Pokolbin, NSW 2321 ☎ (049) 987562
A rival to Peppers with only 8 suites decorated on a theme (French bordello / Federation / nautical) and a splendid menu. *"Very good flambé, stir-fry food with Thai influence"* – LEN EVANS.

🐦 CLEOPATRA, Cleopatra St, Blackheath, NSW 2785 ☎ (047) 878456
The best restaurant in this neck of the mountains, a tiny place in pretty floral surroundings. Dani Chouet dreams up a compact menu of superb, unpretentious French country food. Bring your own vin. A handful of guests can stay en pension; ELISE PASCOE and Jenny Kee adore being pampered here.

MILTON PARK, PO Box 676, Hordern's Rd, Bowral, NSW 2576 ☎ (048) 611522
This country-house hotel is an even more splendoured thing under new ownership – set in floral gardens and copses, it boasts fine art and antique collections, a vast conservatory, indoor swimming pool, serious equestrian centre and (soon) a championship golf course. Lovely rooms, fine cuisine. No wonder ELISE PASCOE loves it.

PEPPERS GUEST HOUSE, Ekerts Rd, Pokolbin, NSW 2321 ☎ (049) 987596
This modern country-house affair doesn't exactly live up to its preferred image of old colonialism (spanking new pine with nary a hint of patina, etc), but nonetheless pleases its guests by award-winning cuisine, a swimming pool, tennis court, sauna, spa and vineyard vistas. *"Great getaway retreat"* – ELISE PASCOE. *"Good food, French chef. Easy-going atmosphere and pleasant gardens"* – LEN EVANS.

POKOLBIN CELLAR RESTAURANT, Hungerford Hill Wine Village, Broke Rd, Pokolbin, NSW 2321 ☎ (049) 987584
"A lovely place with a really laid-back country atmosphere. It's like being in a big greenhouse with fresh flowers. Food depends on what's in season – game pies in the autumn, wonderful soufflés in winter, sitting around a roaring log fire" – ELISE PASCOE. *"Very innovative; very fresh ingredients"* – LEN EVANS.

Resorts

LORD HOWE ISLAND, c/o 20 Loftus St, Sydney, NSW 2000 ☎ (02) 272867
Only one hour's flight from Sydney, here you get Pacific island solitude without the oppressive heat and humidity of the Barrier Reef islands. Informal atmos with tennis, great bush walks and fishing. Best accommodation: the unpretentious **Pinetrees Lodge** ☎ (02) 387 2305 – good food and wine list. Favoured bolthole of stressed politicians and business high-rollers who are loath to sever the umbilical with Sydney.

THREDBO
Premier ski resort in Oz, where Aussie surfers and European skiers head from June to end-Sept. Varied pistes from beginner to expert level. Millions of dollars have been poured into the development recently; it now has the most modern snow-making facilities in the southern hemisphere – when autumn drags on, you ski on man-made snow. Best hotel: **Bernti's Alpine Lodge** (smaller and superior to the Thredbo Alpine, run by the resort). Best glühwein: from the **Keller**. Nearby **Falls Creek**, over the border into Victoria, is the next best ski area.

TASMANIA

DEAR FRIENDS, 8 Brooke St, Hobart, TAS 7000 ☎ (002) 232646
Upmarket restaurant in a cleverly converted warehouse. French-influenced cuisine with local and European wines.

MURE'S FISH CENTRE, Victoria Dock, Hobart, TAS 7000 ☎ (002) 311999 (Upper Deck); ☎ (002) 312121 (Lower Deck)
If fish is your favourite dish, Mure's your cure. *"Wonderful fish, especially the curried scallops"* – BARRY HUMPHRIES. The Upper Deck is smarter, the Lower Deck a bistro/sushi bar.

PROSPECT HOUSE, Richmond, Tas 7025 ☎ (002) 622207
Georgian house with a small house-party's worth of rooms and one of the best game restaurants.

PROSSER'S ON THE BEACH, Sandy Bay Regatta Pavilion, Beach Rd, Sandy Bay, Tas 7005 ☎ (002) 252276
Informal, fun diner for seafood cooked contemporary-style.

WREST POINT CASINO, 410 Sandy Bay Rd, Hobart, Tas 7000 ☎ (002) 250112
Tassie is the top holiday spot for Aussies, and this hotel/casino, though not super-luxe, is an old favourite. Big rooms with 7ft beds in a circular building. Views of Derwent River.

· REST OF ·
AUSTRALIA

— Tours and charters —

AUSTRALIAN AIRLINES, 50 Franklin St, Melbourne, Vic 3000 ☎ (03) 665 1333
Holidays in Bedarra, Lizard, Orpheus, Daydream, Great Keppel, Heron and other islands. Bases in all Australian capitals.

AUSTRALIAN AIR TOUR AND CHARTER, 247 Pennant Hills Rd, Carlingford, NSW 2118 ☎ (02) 684 9721
Exclusive light-aircraft charter from David Le Claire. Mostly business clientele (first-class air fares can be slashed), but can take trippers anywhere, no worries.

EASTSAIL, New Beach Rd, Rushcutters Bay, NSW 2027 ☎ (02) 327 1166
Sleek fleet of 30-ft to 37-ft Beneteau yachts for charter by the day in Sydney Harbour (until 8pm in summer to allow for twilight tipples). Billy Joel, Johnny Cougar and Michael Hutchence of INXS have sallied forth. Sailing school, too.

QUICKSILVER CONNECTION, Marina Mirage, PO Box 171, Port Douglas, Qld 4871 ☎ (070) 995455; bookings: (070) 995500
For the quickest, smoothest ride to the Reef, in new Wavepiercer catamarans. Daily cruises to the Low Isles (a coral cay) and the Outer Reef; trips by helijet, semi-submersible and glass-bottomed boats; scuba and snorkelling.

SEAIR PACIFIC, Whitsunday Airport, Air Whitsunday Rd, Whitsunday, N Qld 4802 ☎ (079) 469133
Seaplane charter and scheduled air services to island resorts; scenic flights; flying boat and 'submareef' trips to the Great Barrier Reef.

SYDNEY IN STYLE, 1 Wharf Rd, Longueville, NSW 2066 ☎ (02) 427 5471; 427 0213
Exclusive tour service for visitors. Individually planned tours to unusual parts, with personal guides. Gourmet lunches in private homes, special views of art galleries, collections and private houses. All fed and cultured, you can then follow stockmen's cattle trails through mountain river country. Travel by chauffeured limo, light plane, helicopter. Interpreter available (fair dinkum).

— *Wine* —

Australian vineyards are peppered (grapeshot, of course) across the bottom of the continent. There are a few wine-growing areas in Western Australia and Tasmania, but South Australia, NSW and Victoria pouch the kangaroo's share. Aussie connoisseurs know their grapes.

Cabernet Sauvignon

Bordeaux, with a heavy Australian accent. The best Cabernets have emerged since tiny wineries such as **IDYLL** and **MOUNT MARY**, near Melbourne, started producing delicate French-

---

A Crate of Greats

Our man Down Under, LEN EVANS, advises what to look out for in Antipodean wines: *"Rich, flavoursome, fat Chardonnay from Cowra and Hunter Valley in NSW. Fine, rich Pinot Noirs from Yarra Valley, Victoria. 'Cool climate' Pinot Noir and Chardonnay from Adelaide Hills, SA (ideal base material for elegant new sparkling wines). Sauvignon Blanc crisp dry whites from Blenheim district, South Island, New Zealand. All are world-class and doing very well internationally."*

Grapies' Best Wineries

The following wineries come out tops: **CHATEAU TAHBILK**, Victoria ("*The best Australian wine. The Sauvignon in particular – lay it down for a while, it's magic*" – DON HEWITSON). **LINDEMAN**, Hunter Valley ("*terrific*" – LEO SCHOFIELD). **PETALUMA**, SA ("*Outstanding whites. Stunning Chardonnays and Rieslings*" – SERENA SUTCLIFFE. Their **Croser** sparkling wine, in conjunction with Bollinger, beats others into a cocked hat). **PENFOLD'S**, SA, for their **Grange Hermitage** and Cabernet. **TALTARNI**, Victoria (a fine pedigree – set up by Dominique Portet, brother of Bernard of Clos du Val, Napa, and son of André of Château Lafite. "*Dominique has the best of everything. Lovely soil, his French knowledge, daily contact with his brother in Napa…*" – ELISE PASCOE. His sparkling wines reach fizzy heights for MAX LAKE and LEN EVANS). **LEEUWIN ESTATE**, WA ("*I consulted for them from 1970 to 1982 and they are making far superior wines today – richer, fuller, more elegant*" – ROBERT MONDAVI). **COLDSTREAM HILLS VINEYARDS**, Victoria (SERENA SUTCLIFFE eulogizes about their Chardonnay and particularly their Pinot Noir – "*for me the best in Australia by leagues*").

style Cabernets. At Clare and Coonawarra, SA, **WYNNS'S, ROUGE HOMME, PENFOLD'S, HILL-SMITH, BRAND'S LAIRA** and **WOLF BLASS** fight for the crown. Grapies give Brand's Laira the Golden Mouton award: Wolf, too, likes to be seen in Mouton's clothing. In the Hunter, the biggest wines come from small barrels used by MAX LAKE for his LAKES FOLLY wines. LAKE thinks 1969, 1972, 1978, 1980, 1981 and 1985 his best vintages.

Chardonnay

The great white wonder. It's done for Australian wine what waltzing did for Matilda. The Hunter Valley, New South Wales, is one of the finest producers of Chardonnay. Particularly good are **ROSEMOUNT**'s, **TYRRELL**'s ("*their Vat 47 is never a disappointment*" – MICHAEL BROADBENT) and **LINDEMAN**'s. Many back Brian Croser at **PETALUMA**, SA. Meanwhile, the rest of the best's in the west. Chardonnay from the **LEEUWIN ESTATE**, Margaret River, WA, sends grapies into ecstasies – enough aroma, liveliness, richness and grip to outdo all Australia and most of California. It's one of SERENA SUTCLIFFE's 2 best Aussie wines ("*but it's terribly expensive*"). Denis Horgan, the brains (and wallet) behind Leeuwin, chose the site on Robert Mondavi's recommendation. **TISDALL's Mount Helen** is also a SERENA S supremo.

Muscat

Comes in two styles: light and aromatic, and thick and sticky. MAX LAKE eulogizes: "*I don't think there is a better drink than the Muscats from North Victoria which are equal to the best ports.* **MORRIS, BAILEY'S, CHAMBERS' ROSEWOOD, BROWN BROS** and **STANTON & KILLEEN** *are the best.*" MICHAEL BROADBENT qualifies that: "*I think* **CHAMBERS' ROSEWOOD** *Muscats are the most delightful; of the 3 qualities, I admire their* **Old Liquer** *but prefer to drink the less heavy, more elegant* **Special Liquer Muscat.**"

Rhine Riesling

Its relatively undemanding flavour has always pleased punters. The best are excitingly flowery, just off dry, satisfying acid and well worth several years' ageing. True Riesling does best when there's a nip in the air and where the grass stays green all summer: Tasmania's **PIPER'S BROOK** and **MOORILLA ESTATE** are tipped and tippled by the best money. **PETALUMA's Rhine Riesling** (trucked home to the Adelaide Hills by Brian Croser) is "*outstanding*" thinks SERENA SUTCLIFFE.

Semillon

A white grape variety the French use for Sauternes and Graves. Australia turns it into a triumphant wine, light, dry and soft, Chablisgreen when young, ageing superbly for up to 20 years. The best area is the Hunter Valley; the catch is that Semillon still sometimes gets called Riesling there. **TYRRELL's Vat 1** is the one to drown in. If you get pulled out, make for **LINDEMAN's Ben Ean.** SERENA SUTCLIFFE finds the Sauvignon/Semillon blend of both **TISDALL** and **CAPE MENTELLE** "*really intriguing. Aged* **ROTHBURY ESTATE** *Semillons are also fabulous.*"

Shiraz (Hermitage)

The same red grapes that are used in the Rhône (where they are called Syrah). The Rambo of the wine world: finds muscles in your mouth you never knew were there. Much admired by the best palates. The magnificent **PENFOLD'S Grange Hermitage** is described by AUBERON WAUGH as *"Australia's equivalent of Château Latour"*. It is one of the finest Australian wines MICHAEL BROADBENT has ever tasted (he pines for the 1955 vintage). Sparring partners include those from **ROTHBURY ESTATE, TALTARNI** and **SEPPELT**. DON HEWITSON raves about **MILDARA's Jamiesons Run** 1986, a Shiraz/Cabernet/Merlot blend: *"It is difficult to get hold of, but has won virtually every award in the business."*

AUSTRIA

SALZBURG

—— *Festivals* ——

🐾 **SALZBURG FESTIVAL, Postfach 140, Hofstallgasse 1, A-5010 ☎ (06222) 8045**
Perhaps the most famous festival in the world, held end-July to end-Aug. *"It needs no explanation: Salzburg has been the top festival in the world since the 30s"* – ANDRE PREVIN. Home of Mozart (who always heads the menu), Salzburg sees a gathering of the musical clans, the most revered performers and conductors, both on and off stage. Expect opera, orchestral concerts, recitals, theatre and open-air candlelit concerts. Evenings are sophisticated, with dressy and bejewelled audiences; days are more of a scrum, with droves of twee lederhosen- and dirndl-clad locals. *"It's a big treat, except for the loathsome traffic. Once you get to the concert hall it's wonderful, but on the way you can suddenly think 'maybe I would be better off in Grimsby'"* – AP. Praises are sung verily by ANDREW LLOYD WEBBER, MARCHESA BONA FRESCOBALDI, GIORGIO ARMANI, LYNN WYATT and MARIUCCIA MANDELLI (*"the best cultural festival"*). Tickets: first stab must be made by Jan; try again for left-overs in Mar-Apr. If you fail, sniff out a black-market ticket from a hotel doorman.

—— *Hotels* ——

HOTEL OSTERREICHISCHER HOF, Schwarzstrasse 5, A-5024 ☎ (0662) 72541
The best hotel in the centre of town, on the banks of the Salzach with picture-book views over Old Salzburg.

SCHLOSS FUSCHL, A-5322 Hof-bei-Salzburg ☎ (06229) 22530
Former hunting lodge of the Prince-Archbishops

of Salzburg, an enchanting lakeside hotel in lush green parkland. *"One of the most romantic hotels in the world with delicious Austrian food and charming service…and beautiful* Sound of Music *country to walk in"* – ELISE PASCOE.

VIENNA

—— *Art and museums* ——

ALBERTINA, Augustine Strasse 1, A-1010 ☎ (01) 534830
The best representation of graphic art in the world, with about 1 million works. One of the 3 art galleries in the world that ANDRE PREVIN (*"I'm very much a museum-goer"*) most enjoys visiting. For the greatest collection of Dürer, plus Raphael, Rubens, Poussin….

🐾 **KUNSTHISTORISCHES MUSEUM, Burgring 5, A-1010 Vienna ☎ (01) 934 5410**
One of the most prodigious collections on earth, amassed over the centuries by the powerful Hapsburgs. Spanning antiquity to Post-Impressionism, a tremendous diversity of paintings (hot on court portraiture), sculpture and the decorative arts. All the major masters are here – Raphael, Titian (who was state artist to Emperor Charles V), Caravaggio, Velázquez, Bruegel, Hals. Also the famous Cellini salt cellar. The **Neue Galerie** at Stallburg palace houses works of the 19C and early 20C.

—— *Bars and cafés* ——

DEMEL, Kohlmarkt 14, A-1010 ☎ (01) 533 5516
Magnificent coffee house and tea salon, the old favourite of Emperor Franz Josef. Savour Sacher Torte and Dobostorte. *"The best pastry shop of all. Also great for lunch if you can get in"* – ELISE PASCOE. *"Severity, style and formality of waitressing to open the eyes. Make sure you look up to the ceilings and mirrors…"* – CLARE FERGUSON.

—— *Hotels* ——

HOTEL ASTORIA, Kärntner Strasse 32, A-1015 ☎ (01) 515770
"Grand, faded, with bedcovers like giant white clouds and bathtubs you can get lost in. Brilliant balconies. Breakfasts fit for an Empress" – CLARE FERGUSON.

IMPERIAL, Kärntner Ring 16, A-1015 ☎ (01) 50110
The sort of palatial surroundings that can't be imitated. This magnificent building was opened by Emperor Franz Josef in 1873. Waltzing down marble-clad corridors, past crystal chandeliers,

rococo furniture and portraits of Winterhalter, you'll feel like a queen... speaking of which, HM Elizabeth II von England has this to say: 'This hotel is by far the most beautiful I have ever stayed in. It cannot be compared to any other.' BARBARA TAYLOR BRADFORD and ANDRE PREVIN second and third that.

HOTEL SACHER WIEN, Philharmonikerstrasse 4, A-1015 ☎ (01) 51456

A slice of old Vienna along with your slice of world-famous, tortuously scrummy Sacher Torte ("*one winter I went on a Sacher Torte-tasting through Vienna. The Sacher's is the best*" – ELISE PASCOE). It's a café, it's a pâtisserie, it's a charming, old-style hotel where well-mannered service is inherent. That and the white-painted, pink-upholstered rococo furniture goes down a treat with BARBARA CARTLAND, while ANDRE PREVIN likes the Red Bar. For NICHOLAS VILLIERS, it "*continues to be one of the best. Privately owned and privately run...thoroughly old-fashioned in the best sense of the word.*"

—— Music ——

MUSIKVEREIN, Bösendorfer Strasse 12, A-1010 ☎ (01) 505 8681

Home of the great Vienna Philharmonic, and venue for top touring musicians, this "*is the great hall in the world. The best*" – ANDRE PREVIN.

VIENNA FESTIVAL, Wiener Festwochen, Lehargasstrasse 11, A-1060 ☎ (01) 586 1676

A major festival of old and modern classical music, promenade concerts, jazz, theatre, ballet,

> **❝The arts are supported more in Vienna than anywhere, but it is not necessarily the most <u>exciting</u> place musically because they tend to be very, very safe in their thinking❞**
>
> ANDRE PREVIN

puppet shows and exhibitions, mid-May to end-June. The whole city enters into festive mood.

VIENNA STATE OPERA, Opernring 2, A-1010 ☎ (01) 514440

A lavish opera house with a tremendous tradition of opera, under the directorship of Claudio Abbado. "*The one that everyone thinks of as being the greatest in Europe*" – RODNEY MILNES. "*One of the best opera houses*" – BARBARA CARTLAND. "*I love to go to the opera in Vienna*" – BARBARA TAYLOR BRADFORD. "*For me, Vienna is the home of opera*" – NICHOLAS VILLIERS. The central pit offers the best standing room in the world.

—— Restaurants ——

STEIRERECK, Rasumofskygasse 2, A-1030 ☎ (01) 713 3168

Mooted by many to be the best in Austria, this snazzy restaurant offers creative variations on a Viennese theme – duck timbale with goose liver and mushrooms, saddle of young wild boar with black nut sauce and crêpes, capped by iced

🕵 Buzzz Viennese whirl: dive in and waddle out of the old artsy coffee houses, **Hotel Sacher Wein**, **Demel**, **Café Sperl**, Gumpendorfstrasse 11 ☎ (01) 564158 and **Café Hawelka**, Dorotheergasse 6 ☎ (01) 512 8230 – a sea of marble-topped tables, newspapers, chess and rich cream-encased coffees and cakes: "*The most famous and loved in all Vienna*" – CLARE FERGUSON 🕵...... Swan in to **Schönbrunn Palace**, 13 Schönbrunner Schloss Strasse ☎ (01) 839 0982, summer residence of the Austrian rulers and a not-so-poor man's Versailles, redecorated à la rococo in 1765. It was Emperor Franz Josef's favourite palace, and one of Napoleon's pads. Don't miss *their* rooms, nor the garden room, the Chinese porcelain room or the Millionzimmer (it cost a million), with its panelled marquetry walls set with 260 Indian miniatures 🕵...... Waltz along to the **Vienna Imperial Ball**, c/o Vienna State Opera, a splendid trad affair held on New Year's Eve in the state rooms of the Hofburg Palace. Grand dinner, much clinking of crystal at midnight, followed by formal dancing to the VSO orchestra in the grand ballroom 🕵. ..... Nip to the Naschmarkt, Wienzeile 6, recommended by CLARE FERGUSON for food during the week (cheese, herbs, game, sausages), and antiques on Saturday: seek out De Stijl and Secessionist decorative works... 🕵

eggnog timbale with fresh berries, or apple and cinnamon ravioli. Fine wines and flawless service.

ZU DEN DREI HUSAREN, Weihburggasse 4, A-1010 ☎ (01) 512 1092
One of the most internationally glamorous restaurants in the country. Candlelight, antiques, a piano tinkling away…and expensive haute cuisine. Top Austrian and French wines.

· REST OF ·
AUSTRIA
Hotels

SCHLOSS DURNSTEIN, A-3601 Dürnstein an der Donau, Wachau ☎ (02711) 212
Real Austria. An old hotel on the banks of the Danube, with a liltingly beautiful view from the leafy terrace. Renowned cuisine and wine cellar. Wonderfully out-of-control rococo churches in the region to visit.

Music

BREGENZER FESTSPIELE, Festspiel-und-Kongresshaus, Platz der Wiener Symphoniker, A-6900 Bregenz ☎ (05574) 22811
This medieval town hosts a spirited festival (July-Aug) on Lake Constance. Performances take place on an elaborate floating stage against dramatic evening skies and fireworks. Also an indoor theatre. Opera and symphony concerts.

BRUCKNERFEST, Brucknerhaus, Postfach 57, Untere Donaulände 7, A-4010 Linz ☎ (0732) 275225
A week of predominantly Anton Bruckner recitals and concerts. Special open-air 'Cloud of Sound' performances envelop the audience from all sides.

MORBISCH LAKE FESTIVAL, c/o Femdenverkehrsbüro der Gemeinde, A-7072 Mörbisch ☎ (02685) 8430
Another summer festival where operetta is staged on the lake. "*You sit in tiers on one side of the lake, looking across at Hungary on the far side. It's very beautiful to see an opera at night, floating on the water, lit by flaming torches. At the end they have a fireworks display*" – BARBARA TAYLOR BRADFORD.

SCHUBERTIADE HOHENEMS, Postfach 100, Schweizer Strasse 1, A-6845 Hohenems ☎ (05576) 2091
A June festival devoted to the works of Schubert. Performances are held in the courtyard or inside the Palasthof, a Renaissance castle that opens only at festival time.

Ski resorts

KITZBUHEL
Rather stiff weekend resort for Munich café society (worth the trip for **Praxmair**'s hot chocolate). Pretty medieval walled city with casino and swish sports centre. Low altitude means unreliable snow (skiers are used to walking the last bit) but expert off-piste skiing can be found.

LECH
Chic neighbour to St Anton – a short drive up through Zürs, down 2 rocky passes and through a tunnel, leads to the wide valley of Lech, the end of the road. Buzzy little town with sparkling river and toytown church, expensive hotels and clientele to match. On a clear day, you can hear bands playing on hotel roof terraces. Best hotel: **Kristberg**, where PATRICIA HODGE stays.

ST ANTON
Serious skiing and serious queues. Top spot to descend from is Valluga Mountain. Expect raucous Brits back in town. Best hotel: **The Post**. Best nightclub: **Krazy Kanguruh**.

BELGIUM
BRUSSELS
Hotels

HOTEL AMIGO, 1-3 rue de l'Amigo, 1000 ☎ (02) 511 5910
For VIPs and VVIPs, "*the senior hotel in the city, worth visiting because of its Brusselian charm. Rooms are a bit stark by modern standards, but it's very quaint with perfect manners*" – JEFFERY TOLMAN.

HILTON INTERNATIONAL, 38 Blvd de Waterloo, 1000 ☎ (02) 513 8877
In a league apart from most Hiltons. "*Tremendous executive rooms which are fantastically equipped, with proper bars and personal computers*" – JEFFERY TOLMAN. Fabulous views across the whole city and a stylish restaurant.

Restaurants

🍴 COMME CHEZ SOI, 23 place Rouppe, 1000 ☎ (02) 512 2921
A grand 19C auberge of world renown, where Pierre Wynants contends for the title of best chef outside France. Despite the splendour of the setting, the welcome and service is warm and

unintimidating. Exquisite cuisine... *"it's so nice when they offer you seconds out of their copper pots – a really nice touch, all of that"* – BOB PAYTON. 'All of that' could include a light, inventive mousse of Ardennes ham, perfectly cooked game or fish, and a perfectly wicked dessert.

BOTSWANA

The safari destination of the 90s. Divided into desert and delta (the Kalahari and the Okavango), the latter provides a 5,800-sq mile oasis of tranquillity. Weave your way by boat along a network of narrow channels, past small wooded islands, viewing hippos, elephants, buffaloes and birds. Or fly from camp to camp (mostly delightfully small – about 16 guests is the norm).

CHOBE GAME LODGE, PO Box 32, Kasane ☎ 250340
High-level luxe on the banks of the Chobe River. Cool rooms with baths and verandahs; suites have their own swimming pools. Boat hire for bird-watching and fishing.

TSARO, Moremi, c/o Okavango Tours and Safaris, 28 Bisham Gdns, London N6, England ☎ (01) 341 9442
Luxury camp with swimming pool. *"Glorious, very comfortable, with thatched bungalows and huge oval sunken baths – in the bush that's something – and marble fireplaces, except you don't actually use the fires because birds nest in the chimneys. Decorated with local fabrics and crafts, so it looks natural. Really beautiful setting"* – CAROL WRIGHT. They also organize game viewing in the Moremi Wildlife Reserve.

BRAZIL

OURO PRETO

POUSO DO CHICO REY, Rua Brigadeiro Musqueira 90 ☎ (031) 551 1274
Travellers clamour to stay in this perfect old colonial house with authentic furniture. Since they don't accept bookings, just plead.

Borneo Days

"Borneo is the best island in the world. They are immensely sophisticated, polite people who will give you hospitality which you repay in kind – a bottle of whisky, a bag of sugar.... Longhouse life is the best organized communal existence. There is no discomfort. Don't believe everything in *Into the Heart of Borneo* – Redmond O'Hanlon will be uncomfortable wherever he goes – he barks his shins in our house! Comfort is a matter of contrast. You can be more comfortable in a longhouse than in the Mandarin in Hong Kong because outside the Mandarin it's just shops, but outside the longhouse it's jungle. The contrast is greater, the purity of comfort is total" – ROBIN HANBURY-TENISON.

PARATI

The lush Costa Verde between Rio and São Paulo is the Riviera of Brazil – without the towns and the people. Parati doesn't even have a beach. But it is one of the most important and beautifully preserved colonial towns in the world. Sparkling white architecture is crisply contrasted against blue skies, bright paintwork and fine iron latticework. Fashionable weekend getaway for fraught arty types.

POUSADA PARDIEIRO, Rua Tenente Francisco Antonio 74 ☎ (0243) 711370
A small but stylish, low, rambly, red-tiled hotel in lovely gardens. Rooms blend colonial Brazil (hammocks as well as beds), with such swish ideas as foie gras and champagne in your fridge.

RIO DE JANEIRO

Film

RIO FILM FESTIVAL, c/o Hotel Nacional Rio, Ave Niemeyer 769, Sao Conardo CEP 22450 ☎ (021) 322 2860
A maverick festival. The poverty and chaos of

Buzzz Hot chocs in Brussels: **Maison Leonidas**, 46 Blvd Anspach ☎ (02) 720 5980 (with **Godiva Chocolatier**, Grand Place ☎ (02) 511 2537 not far behind) is the one that keeps globetrotting chocoholics coming back for more... and more... and more ....

the city have driven Rio festival out to the resort of Fortaleza. A big international festival with goodies laid on – trips to the best samba school, football matches – all under armed guard. Tickets are fiercely in demand. DEREK MALCOLM and IAIN JOHNSTONE view it through similarly glazed eyes: "*Along with Moscow, the most disorganized festival in the world. In its way, great fun ... you have to know where to drink*" – DM. "*Ineffective in starting a film on time or at all or the right one when it eventually does start. They get around this by a thing called caipirinha, a drink of white rum and sugar that induces amnesia and paralysis*" – IJ.

Hotels

COPACABANA PALACE, Av Atlantica 1702 ☎ (021) 255 7070
Splendid white Riviera-style palace looking over the famous anything-goes beach. In the old days, Dietrich, George V and de Gaulle would conga in... and it's still the hot spot at carnival time.

HOTEL INTER-CONTINENTAL, Av Prefeito Mendes de Morais, 222 Sao Conrado, PO Box 33011 ☎ (021) 322 2200
Large-scale modern international hotel with choice of restaurants, swimming pools and tennis courts. LORD LICHFIELD and ANIKO GAAL are impressed.

RIO PALACE HOTEL, Av Atlantica 4240, Copacabana ☎ (021) 521 3232
Landmark hotel in a superb beachfront position, with 2 pools, fitness centre and excellent dining. Execs enjoy the 8th floor Imperial Club – not least for the view.

Tours

TURISMO CLASSICO, Ave N S Copacabana 1059, Office 805 ☎ (021) 287 3390
Made-to-measure holidays anywhere within Brazil – eg, to Manaus, 1,000 miles up the Amazon and the starting point for the heart of the jungle; then you take a boat along the river to the island of Marajo. Hotel reservations, transfers, tours.

BRITAIN

BATH

Bath Festival in May/June is hot on music and fringe events. The **Theatre Royal** is a favourite for touring productions.

Art and museums

John Wood père et fils revolutionized town planning in Britain with their 18C scheme for Bath. The town is now littered with museums that reflect life in Roman and Regency Britain. Wallow in the **Roman Baths** and **Roman Museum**, housing the gilded bronze head of *Minerva*, found on the site. See life as it was when Beau Nash was dandying around town at: the **Pump Room**, social centre of the spa; the authentically furnished Georgian house at **No 1 Royal Crescent**; and the **Carriage Museum** (the finest in the country). Dedicated followers of fashion can pursue their love from the 17C to the present day at the **Museum of Costume** in the Assembly Rooms. Don't miss the charming **American Museum** at Claverton Manor, with its collection of folk art, furniture and handmade patchwork quilts.

HOLBURNE MUSEUM, Great Pulteney St ☎ (0225) 66669
Beautifully proportioned Regency building containing the Holburne family's collection of 17C-18C decorative and fine art, plus an excellent art library and works by contemporary craftsmen. "*Really rather charming and nice*" – JOHN BROOKE-LITTLE.

Hotels

ROYAL CRESCENT HOTEL, Royal Crescent ☎ (0225) 319090
Superb building in the centre of the famous John Wood the Younger crescent, with more rooms in a Palladian villa at the back. Lavish Regency suites – the Sir Percy Blakeney, the Beau Nash – have 4-posters, swagged curtains and spa baths filled from the hot springs.

CAMBRIDGE

This small historic city is home to the famous university, rival to Oxford. Only some 40 years its junior (dating back to 1209), among its notable colleges are **Peterhouse** (the oldest, founded c. 1280 – the original hall survives), **St John's** (spectacular Tudor gateway and its own Bridge of Sighs), **Corpus Christi** (whose Old Court is in fact the oldest in town), **Trinity** (the largest court and the prized Wren Library). Unmissable is **King's**, for the Chapel, a high point of Gothic architecture with spectacular fan-vaulting: "*One of the most written-up places in the world and it does live up to it. The first court of King's is terrific*" – JOHN BROOKE-LITTLE. JBL also advocates **Emmanuel** ("*a very nice college with an absolutely beautiful garden*") and **Magdalene** (with the celebrated Pepys Library – he was an undergrad – including his diary). One of the loveliest walks in Britain is along the **Backs**, where the college lawns meet the River Cam. The jewel of Cambridge's gardens is the stone-walled **Fellow's Garden of Clare College**. The **Cambridge Festival** (July) makes use of the most beautiful buildings in the town.

Art and museums

See prints of colleges and town at the **Bene't Gallery**.

FITZWILLIAM MUSEUM, Trumpington St ☎ (0223) 332900
A lovely museum for Old Masters (important Renaissance, Dutch, English and other paintings), medieval illuminated manuscripts, antiquities, arms and armour, and, in the revamped Lower Marlay Gallery, European and Oriental porcelain. *"A wonderful all-round collection, probably the best unsung museum in England today"* – JEFFREY ARCHER. *"Quite one of the best -- it doesn't just plonk pictures or furniture down, it marries them all together in beautiful rooms with bowls of flowers"* – SERENA FASS.

LONDON

Art and museums

Some of the most spectacular shows (Frans Hals, Monet) are staged at the **Royal Academy of Arts**, Burlington House, Piccadilly, W1 ☎ (071) 439 7438. Their annual Summer Exhibition (mid-June to mid-Aug) of about 1,000 contemporary works is a much-loved if dyed-in-the-wool institution. In other respects, the RA is sharpening its image with a flurry of younger, more avant-garde activities. Major contemporary exhibitions and modern retrospectives are staged by the **Hayward Gallery**, South Bank Centre, Belvedere Rd, SE1 ☎ (071) 928 3144.

🔖 BRITISH MUSEUM, Great Russell St, WC1 ☎ (071) 636 1555
Renowned for its impressive collection of antiquities. It was to the BM that the Greeks lost their marbles... the Elgin Marbles, that is. Roll along if only to see these – and the awesome Egyptian mummies. Also prehistoric, medieval and Renaissance works, engravings, English watercolours and beautifully mounted shows. The new Japanese galleries present the most comprehensive collection in Europe. *"A really good, wide choice of things that will surprise you – a totem pole, something Celtic or Roman... it's like a world tour"* – ROBERT ELMS.

🔖 COURTAULD INSTITUTE GALLERIES, Somerset House, Strand, WC2 ☎ (071) 872 0220
In its splendid new home in William Chambers's 1775-80 building by the Thames. Now you can

Britain's Best Galleries and Museums

1	NATIONAL GALLERY · London
2	BRITISH MUSEUM · London
3	TATE GALLERY · London
4	WALLACE COLLECTION · London
5	COURTAULD INSTITUTE GALLERIES · London
6	VICTORIA AND ALBERT MUSEUM · London

see 80% (as against 35%) of the collection – one of the finest in existence of Impressionist and Post-Impressionist paintings, including Renoir's *La Loge*, Van Gogh's *Man with Bandaged Ear*, and famous works by Manet, Gauguin, Seurat, Degas, Pissarro and Cézanne. Also Flemish, Dutch and Italian Old Masters. New custom-built prints and drawings room. BARRY HUMPHRIES is keen.

DULWICH PICTURE GALLERY, College Rd, SE21 ☎ (081) 693 5254
Designed by Sir John Soane, a manageable-sized gallery with a fine collection of Poussins, Claudes, Rembrandts and others. LOYD GROSSMAN and LORD GOWRIE are fans. Note Soane's mausoleum (for 3 buddies) with its eerie amber light cast through coloured glass.

IMPERIAL WAR MUSEUM, Lambeth Rd, SE1 ☎ (071) 735 8922
Reopened on the 50th anniversary of the outbreak of WW2, the IWM offers 4 new floors of displays; a large exhibition hall – see a Sopwith Camel, Spitfire, Italian human torpedo and the smallest Dunkirk evacuation craft; the Blitz Experience – re-created through sound, smell and sight; the latest in interactive audio-visuals, plus photographs and paintings of the war years. *"It's stunning now that they've opened the new rooms. Also a jolly good shop and cafeteria"* – SERENA FASS. More support from KEITH FLOYD and military specialist LEO COOPER: *"It's gone through a fantastic transformation. It's there to remind you not to do it again."*

🔖 NATIONAL GALLERY, Trafalgar Square, WC2 ☎ (071) 839 3321
No 1 on the tourist circuit, a supremely fine, extensive and balanced collection of masterpieces from the Italian, Dutch and other European schools up to 1900. Due to open in 1991 is the handsome Sainsbury Wing, a new home for the Early Renaissance collection plus swish temporary exhibition space, an auditorium for events, a new shop and restaurant. Meanwhile

flit from Van Eyck's *Arnolfini and his Wife* to Titian's *Bacchus and Ariadne* to Velázquez's *Rokeby Venus* to Gainsborough's *Morning Walk* to Constable's *Hay Wain* to Turner's *Fighting Temeraire*...the list of golden greats is inexhaustible. "*Everyone loves it because one can't help it*" – LOYD GROSSMAN. BARBARA TAYLOR BRADFORD subscribes to that.

NATIONAL PORTRAIT GALLERY, Trafalgar Square, WC2 ☎ (071) 930 1552
Britain's history depicted through portraits of its leading figures (Kings and Queens, politicians, writers, actors...). Reynolds, Gainsborough, Lawrence and co are represented. The NPG constantly commissions new works of current notabilities. "*An enormous improvement in the presentation – more imaginative*" – LEO COOPER. It remains dear to LORD MONTAGU OF BEAULIEU, PATRICIA HODGE, MAUREEN LIPMAN and VICTOR EDELSTEIN. 1993 will see the unveiling of a new Research Centre, housing drawings, prints and photos. The expansion will enable far more paintings to be displayed (currently only 25% of the collection is on show).

SIR JOHN SOANE'S MUSEUM, 13 Lincoln's Inn Fields, WC2 ☎ (071) 405 2107
An innovative and eclectic 1813 house designed and lived in by Sir John Soane. His ideas and attention to detailing are remarkable, as is his squirrel-like hoard of noteworthy antiques, archaeological relics and paintings (Turner, Lawrence, Canaletto, and the famous Hogarth series, *The Rake's Progress*). "*My favourite museum by a long way. Whenever you're in there, you think no-one else knows about it. It's one of those nice arcane London things*" – ROBERT ELMS. Tops too for VICTOR EDELSTEIN, BARRY HUMPHRIES and SOPHIE GRIGSON.

🐓 TATE GALLERY, Millbank, SW1 ☎ (071) 821 1313
The national collection of British and modern European art, now more logically and spaciously

Auction Houses

The household names of **Christie's**, 8 King St, SW1 ☎ (071) 839 9060, and **Sotheby's**, 34 New Bond St, W1 ☎ (071) 493 8080, are still writ largest in the auctioneering world. There's an old adage that says Christie's are gentlemen pretending to be auctioneers, while Sotheby's are auctioneers pretending to be gentlemen. If record-breaking sales are any measure, Christie's now has the business edge (their *Portrait of Dr Gachet* – £49,100,000 – plays Sotheby's *Irises* – £31,800,000). In reality, both monopolize the international market place for the grandest (down to quite homely) furniture, fine art, sculpture, antiquities, porcelain, glass, silver, jewellery, books, sporting guns, vintage and veteran cars, wine – virtually anything of value. Best saleroom secret: without ever dipping your hand in your pocket (or waving it in the air), you can view great works of art in what amounts to a vast and ever-changing exhibition space. In Jan-Feb, Christie's even mount special exhibitions (Japanese porcelain, the history of silver...).

presented after the much-vaunted rehang. A superb store of Stubbs, Blake, Constable, Pre-Raphaelites and all the key moderns and contemporaries. Turners are housed under one roof (in accordance with the painter's will) in the Clore Gallery. "*A spectacularly user-unfriendly gallery...but my God it's got wonderful pictures*" – LOYD GROSSMAN. Also a flourishing new outpost in Liverpool (see Rest of England). PS The restaurant is renowned for its wine list.

🐓 **Buzzz** After 5 years under restoration, Inigo Jones's startlingly pared-down 1630s **Queen's House**, Greenwich ☎ (081) 858 4422, has reopened to 17C-style celebrations, complete with minstrels and Jonesian masque🐓......A century later Jones's one-man classical revival developed into full-blown Palladianism: check it out at Lord Burlington's geometric pleasure villa, **Chiswick House**, Burlington Lane, W4 ☎ (081) 995 0508🐓......Lordly retreats 2: inspired by Moorish palaces, Victorian artist Lord Leighton built the exotic **Leighton House**, 12 Holland Park Rd, W14 ☎ (071) 602 3316, with its gold and turquoise Arab Hall and paintings by Alma-Tadema and the Pre-Raphaelites🐓......If you can beg a pass, the best place to read a book in the world is the **Reading Room of the British Library**, thinks ROBERT ELMS – "*so magnificent*" (not bad for writing either – Karl Marx whipped off *Das Kapital* here).. 🐓

🦆 **VICTORIA AND ALBERT MUSEUM, South Kensington, SW7** ☎ **(071) 589 6371**
Glaringly in the public eye since Elizabeth Esteve-Coll took over directorship and many of the old, scholarly guard departed. However, as LOYD GROSSMAN acknowledges, *"In spite of becoming like the Sock Shop it has in fact improved the level of service it offers to the public."* It's easy to criticize display; galleries are often infuriatingly shut. However, the collection is unsurpassable: knockout arrays of ceramics (endless Meissen, Sèvres, Chelsea), glass, silver, furniture, textiles, costume, sculpture (Rodin, Bernini), prints, drawings, photographs, a Far East gallery, a new Indian gallery due in 1992, the prized Raphael Cartoons, the largest collection of Constable (some 400 works). Excellent temporary exhibitions, a very good shop and restaurant. What's more a sparkling clean façade will soon emerge from under the wraps.

🦆 **WALLACE COLLECTION, Hertford House, Manchester Square, W1** ☎ **(071) 935 0687**
A celebrated collection of French furniture, porcelain and 18C paintings, in a Georgian house setting. See Oeben and Riesener's opulent desk made for King Stanislas of Poland, plus other elaborate ormolu-encrusted pieces. Masses of paintings by Watteau, Boucher and Fragonard – including the latter's *The Swing*. Other fine European works include Frans Hals's *Laughing Cavalier*. A winner with LORD GOWRIE, JOHN BROOKE-LITTLE, VISCOUNT HAMBLEDEN, LORD LICHFIELD, SERENA FASS and BOB PAYTON: *"The best because it is manageable, not too big."*

————— *Arts centres* —————

BARBICAN, Barbican Centre, EC2 ☎ **(071) 638 8891**
This modern complex is certainly complex to negotiate, but worthy of bestdom for being London home of the **Royal Shakespeare Company** (hallowed by STANLEY MARCUS, DOUGLAS FAIRBANKS JR and MICHAEL GRADE) and the **London Symphony Orchestra**. *"I go to concerts nearly every week and I think everyone is wrong about the Barbican. The acoustics are very warm and lively, and inside it's actually a very attractive place to be. The concerts there are the best in London. Michael Tilson Thomas is the most exciting conductor in Europe – he really has charisma"* – LORD DONOUGHUE. Also some fine art exhibitions. NB The RSC theatres may close for winter 1990/91 because of lack of funds.

————— *Ballet* —————

🦆 **ROYAL BALLET COMPANY, Royal Opera House, Covent Garden, WC2** ☎ **(071) 240 1066**
The company that has had the most influence on international ballet, founded by the pioneering Dame Ninette de Valois. The brilliant founder choreographer Frederick Ashton established the lyrical English style – more dramatic, less athletic. Sensational productions of Ashton's work, that of principal choreographer Kenneth MacMillan and resident choreographer David Bintley – plus, of course, the classics – under the directorship of Anthony Dowell. Dancers are drawn almost exclusively from their ballet school. The former Sadler's Wells Royal Ballet has moved to Birmingham (see Rest of England).

————— *Bars and cafés* —————

MILDRED'S, 58 Greek St, W1 ☎ **(071) 494 1634**
Excellent café for vegetarian whole food (and occasionally fish), full of arty Soho types like Derek Jarman and Boy George. *"One of my*

🐧 **Buzzz Caatchi the Saatchi Collection**, 98A Boundary Rd, NW8 ☎ (071) 624 8299, on Fri-Sat, noon-6pm, for an ad-man-and-his-wife's eye view of the last 30 years of British, European and American painting and sculpture🦆...... For retrospectives of major international contemporary artists, the **Whitechapel Gallery**, Whitechapel High St, E1 ☎ (071) 377 0107, *"does an excellent job"* – LOYD GROSSMAN🦆...... **MOMI, how I love ya**: explore the wonderful world of cinema and telly (extracts, laser vision, 3-D projection, a cast of actors) at the **Museum of the Moving Image**, South Bank Centre, SE1 ☎ (071) 401 2636: *"My favourite museum, because it keeps children happiest longest"* – CLARE FRANCIS 🦆......**Soane clone**: see the scholarly reproduction of Sir J's **Stock Office of the Bank of England** (entrance Bartholomew Lane, EC2). While you're in the museum, check out the bank's history from 1694 ☎ (071) 601 5793🦆......**Soane zone**: immerse yourself in the designer's designer pad of 1803, **Pitshanger Manor**, Mattock Lane, Ealing, W5 ☎ (081) 567 1227..🦆

favourites. Based on the Joan Crawford movie Mildred Pierce. It's extremely cheap and unpretentious, with style in a simple way" – DUGGIE FIELDS. No licence, no smoking.

PORTOBELLO CAFE, 305 Portobello Rd, W11 ☎ (081) 969 1996
One of the best in this trendy-shabby area. *"You can sit outside and see all the people passing by, which is quite wonderful. Healthy-ish food"* – DUGGIE FIELDS.

———— Clubs ————

🐚 ANNABEL'S, 44 Berkeley Square, W1 ☎ (071) 629 3558
Annabel's remains, without question, the world's No 1 private nightclub. Established and conventional, it offers to members of all ages the ultimate in comfort (thanks to owner Mark Birley's perfectionist taste), faultless service (the invisible ashtray swop and glass top-up) and discretion (door staff must be the best liars in London: 'Joan Collins? Sorry, haven't seen her tonight', as La Collins bops away inside). *"Still the most exclusive nightclub in London. You really do see the Prince and Princess of Wales and Princess Caroline of Monaco and the odd Duke or Earl dancing away. Very good food and very good drink, champagne particularly"* – RICHARD COMPTON-MILLER. Strict membership (wannabees must be proposed and seconded for the £500-a-year membership). *"The doorman is the nicest I've ever met. The club is immaculately run; incredibly clean, good crowd"* – SEAN MACAULAY. Tops for HELEN GURLEY BROWN (who'd *"almost take a trip to London just to go to Annabel's"*), ROSS BENSON (*"if you just want to sit around, have a drink and talk"*), JOAN COLLINS, LORD DONOUGHUE, JEFFREY ARCHER, SHAKIRA CAINE, LORD LICHFIELD and ANDREW LLOYD WEBBER.

> **❝ There are only 3 nightclubs that count in London: Annabel's, Tramp and Stringfellow's. Each has an owner who understands his market and knows everybody within it; so it's more like a 6-days-of-the-week party ❞**
>
> RICHARD COMPTON-MILLER

CAFE DE PARIS, 2 Coventry St, WC1 ☎ (071) 437 2036
Word regularly has it that the Café de Paris is finished, yet queues for the ravy Wednesday night (jazz, blues, cha-cha) live on. Red flock and gilt jaded elegance; old-time dance music the rest of the week.

CHELSEA ARTS CLUB, 143 Old Church St, SW3 ☎ (071) 376 3311
A ramshackle country rectory and rambling garden in the heart of Chelsea – home from shabby home for local Bohemians. Not for *them* the Perrier luncheon. Pubbish bar with pool table; cosy restaurant, art everywhere. *"The problem is it's very difficult to become a member, so you have to rely on someone you know getting you in. But once you're in, you're in"* – SEAN MACAULAY. ROY ACKERMAN enjoys the monthly art exhibitions.

COMEDY STORE, 28A Leicester Square, WC2 ☎ (071) 839 6665; 839 6642
Brilliant, packed-out little comedy club with 2 bars and minimal décor. Expect to see the Comedy Store players / guest acts with a compère/improv nights/music/audience participation – your turn. Where the Comic Strip started out, with Ric Mayall, Adrian Edmondson, Dawn French, Jennifer Saunders, excompère Alexi Sayle. Wed-Sun, no booking.

DAISY CHAIN, at The Fridge, Town Hall Parade, Brixton Hill, SW2 ☎ (071) 326 5100
Tuesday-night high-energy bop in the spirit of the old Taboo. *"I still think my favourite club would have to be the Daisy Chain. It's a big, big club. I just like the idea of wandering around"* – STEPHEN JONES. DUGGIE FIELDS wanders along, too.

FRED'S, 4 Carlisle St, W1 ☎ (071) 439 4284
A compact private boîte for young media/arty types. Drink in the narrow bar, pick at tapas at the U-shaped counter, dance in the minuscule basement. A favourite of ROBERT ELMS and STEPHEN JONES: *"I love Fred's. My friend Dick is the head barman there...it's just so great, when I go in he asks me what kind of day I've had, and I say 'happy' or 'rows with the bank' and he will make me a cocktail to fit in with my mood. An intuitive barman. The best bourbon sours in the world – I've never had better. Perfect club food too...quite small and it doesn't get in the way."*

GAZ'S ROCKIN' BLUES, at Gossips, 69 Dean St, W1 ☎ (071) 434 4480
The only one-night wonder (Thursdays) that's stood its ground – for 10 years. Gary (Gaz) Mayall plays ska, R & B, reggae and rockabilly, and a rollicking good time is had by all. Complete mix-up of ages and styles of bopper, from quiff-heads through rastas to chic rag-traders. *"Its strength is that it remains the same. The emphasis is less on fashion and looking good and more on genuine music lovers"* – SEAN MACAULAY.

THE GROUCHO CLUB, 45 Dean St, W1 ☎ (071) 439 4685
The media drinking and dining club. Civilized and unflashily glamorous, it attracts an upbeat liter-arty set – publishers, agents, major bylines, media and music kids, plus a tad too many telly

One Night in London...

One-nightism continues to dominate hip London, and the dogged rhythm of 'house' continues to dominate the style of music. *"The one-off party thing is absolutely it. It's not about a place, it's about who's doing it – it can be at any place on any night. The music has all been house...not all acid house, but deep house and garage and all sorts"* – ROBERT ELMS. *"Everything at the moment is house music, just every-thing in terms of trendy nightclubs"* echoes SEAN MACAULAY: *"They're all one-nighters that move around, so you do 3 to 6 months in one place, then change the name and start again at another venue."* Here's where to catch the beat (but check first in *Time Out* to see what's on and what's in each week):

Mon.... **Kinky Gerlinky** at Legends (second Mon of the month)
Tues.... **Daisy Chain** at the Fridge
Wed.... **Café de Paris**
Thurs.. **Gaz's Rockin' Blues** Gossip's; **Ascension** at Maximus (first Thurs of the month); **Reflex** at Legends
Fri..... **Club MFI** at Legends
Sat..... **FAT** at the Wag
Last word to DAVID LITCHFIELD, acting for the prosecution: *"I think one-nighters should be discouraged – they are the death of nightclubs. They have no responsibility, here one week and gone the next. The only clubs left are Tramp and Annabel's at the top end of the market, and Stringfellow's – that's all."*

and admen. Spacious lounge-around bar, 3 top-class restaurants, plus 11 bedrooms upstairs for those members who find it all too much.... *"I've stuck with it. A lot of people have migrated, saying it's too full of pony-tailed video tech-nicians and less of the original writing/ publishing crowd. But I think the upstairs res-taurant is still really nice, calm, peaceful, tasteful...with the hushed, reverent atmosphere of sealing big deals. Downstairs the brasserie is more see-and-be-seen. The influx of the TV crowd is a plus and a minus. It's nice because it buzzes, but you feel these alien urbans should be at Fred's. If you are going to wear a leather jacket you really should go to Fred's"* – SEAN MACAULAY. *"I'm plugging the Groucho because it's great. Of the new rooms, No 400 is terrific, at the very top, the only suite...We're moving and I'm going to have to stay somewhere in London, so I'll stay in a room at the Groucho"* – ED VICTOR.

HEAVEN, Under the Arches, Craven St, Charing Cross, WC2 ☎ (071) 839 3852
The gayest nightspot in town, and the vastest gayspot in Europe. **Delirium** on Thursday is straights' night – stars go to hear live music plus hip-hop, rap, scratch, garage, house and deep house.

JONGLEURS AT THE CORNET, 49-51 Lavender Gardens, SW11 ☎ (081) 780 1151
A groovy cabaret of singers, tap-dancers, jug-glers and young comedians on Fri, Sat and Sun. Some of the best comic acts in town – Joan Collins Fan Club, Arthur Smith, Brighton Bottle Orchestra, Dennis and Punt – and, on occasion (unannounced), the likes of Lenny Henry.

🏃 LEGENDS, 29 Old Burlington St, W1 ☎ (071) 437 9933
"A venue that has really come back. The real fashion there is transsexual" – SEAN MACAULAY. Sure is at **Kinky Gerlinky**, on the second Monday of the month. *"The best once-a-month. It's one of the most mixed environments I've ever been into. It's all these men in dresses who really ought to know better. There are regular trans-vestites, a few well-known fashion designers, some who are so chic, and some who look like suburban aunts. Music is mixed, with 3 disc jockeys. A very good atmosphere but very bizarre"* – DUGGIE FIELDS. On Thursdays it's **Reflex** with DJ Colin Hudd (open house and garage). If you're after a change of house and garage, go down to MFI – **Club MFI**, that is, on Fridays. A terrific hop, with a fashion-orientated crowd. ROBERT ELMS is a fan, but SEBASTIAN SCOTT regrets it *"never has a sale like its namesake."*

LIMELIGHT, 136 Shaftesbury Ave, W1 ☎ (071) 434 0572
The most luxurious of London's trendy clubs, with all the cool trappings – selective doorper-son, lots of one-nighters and special events, VIP room for £500-a-year gold card members (non-VIPs pay £150 a year or by the night). Once you're past the door it's positively welcoming, with warm dragged/mottled walls, antiques, etc. Based in an old Welsh Presbyterian church, the lofty, leathery, loungy, galleried Dome Bar dominates (open to non-members/payers for lunch and early-evening drinks). The Study (VIPs only) is got up in ye olde English hunt fabric (with barmen to match). In the basement is the high-energy dance floor. Go for live music (Sun) or jazz, comedy and jamming (Wed).

MOSCOW CLUB, 62 Frith St, W1
☎ (071) 437 0062
A narrow, spartan little drinking club out of the
Groucho's/Fred's mould, with a more creative/
pop video/advertising leaning; actors and pop
stars rock up after their shows (it's open till 1am).

🔳 RONNIE SCOTT'S, 47 Frith St, W1
☎ (071) 439 0747
The best live jazz venue in town, and the oldest
at over 30 years. Archetypally dark and smoky,
with tight-skirted waitresses wiggling their way
round tightly packed tables. Big-name stars
perform – it's easier to mention who *hasn't*
played than who has (Duke Ellington is their one
regret). GEORGE MELLY and John Dankworth
have very warm feelings for it. Audience of
enthusiasts who forget the outside world (you
may even see MPs John Prescott (Lab) and
Kenneth Clarke (Con) the same evening).

Britain's Best Clubs

1	ANNABEL'S · London
2	HACIENDA · Manchester
3	WAG CLUB · London
4	RONNIE SCOTT'S · London
5	TRAMP · London

**STRINGFELLOW'S, 16-19 Upper St
Martin's Lane, WC2 ☎ (071) 240 5534**
A perennial for showbizzos, with great nightclub
food. *"Peter Stringfellow is like Mark Birley of
Annabel's and John Gold of Tramp – brilliant
at understanding his market. There are lots of
Flash Harrys, but he also gets actors and act-
resses and models and it is always packed"* –
RICHARD COMPTON-MILLER. According to SEAN
MACAULAY it has *"kitsch appeal. If you want to
go famous footballer and Page 3 spotting,
then Stringfellow's and the Hippodrome are
definitely the hunting grounds."*

SUBTERANIA, 12 Acklam Rd, W10
☎ (081) 960 4590
The best in the west – a newish club under the

Westway, with post-industrial design, under-
floor lighting and thick pipes, giving a certain
submarinesque quality. Curving gallery above
so you (along with the DJ) can look down on the
dancers. Great sound system, theme nights, live
bands, serious dancing.

🔳 TRAMP, 40 Jermyn St, W1
☎ (071) 734 0565
A long-established membership nightclub out of
the Annabel's mould, only less refined and less
expensive (£200 a year). Part-owned by Oscar
Lerman, hubby of Jackie Collins, and John Gold.
Good-looking, starry clientele – Imran Khan,
Michael and Shakira Caine, Rod Stewart, Dudley Moore, Lady Sarah Armstrong-Jones,
George Best, Pamela Stephenson, Mick Jagger,
Sting, Lady Helen Windsor.... *"Tramp is still
tops of the slightly lower end of the market. It's
the sort of place that Tom Jones or Tony Black-
burn or Roger Moore might go to"* – RICHARD
COMPTON-MILLER. *"Really good, the only place
I go to dance ... but never at weekends"* – ALISON
DOODY. For ROSS BENSON, *"there are only 2 clubs
in London, Tramp and Annabel's. People keep
trying other clubs, but they never seem to work."*

2 BRYDGES PLACE, WC2 ☎ (071) 836 1436
Hidden in a narrow alley is this comfy, laid-back
little club in a Georgian house. Drawing-room
ambience, open fire, wood-panelled walls, a
mishmash of furniture and an even greater
mishmash of members. Low-profile local artsy/
publishing types, members of the English
National Opera (a stage's length away), Simon
Callow, Lucian Freud.... *"One of the genuine
places to drink"* – ROBERT ELMS. *"A really nice
one, really low-key. The food is really cheap, so
you can use it as a regular dine"* – SEAN
MACAULAY. TYLER BRULE is keen.

🔳 WAG CLUB, 35 Wardour St, W1
☎ (071) 437 5534
The music biz barometer, one of the coolest
regular clubs in town. Monday is still jazz (live
and DJs). The rest of the week it's a packed house
for house music – at Milky Bar Kids (Thurs),
Love (Fri) with DJs Dave Dorrell and Paul
Anderson, and FAT (Sat) with Fat Tony and
Tim Simenon. *"Still the best full-time venue...
though the best nightlife is more by word-of-
mouth so that people can't look it up in a book.*

🔳 Buzzz Viva España: *"Anything
Spanish has been very fashionable recently. House music was also known as the
Balearic beat, there's that whole Ibizan nightclub scene. It's all about trying to pretend
you're still on holiday"* – ROBERT ELMS🔳...... Hispanic 2? The hottest nightspot in
Britain is **Hacienda**, 11-13 Whitworth St W, Manchester ☎ (061) 236 5051. Owned
by New Order and Factory Records, it packs 1,200 in to its severe post-modernist
environs (no carpet, no velour, no bar lamps). Disco nights Wed to Sat, live bands/
events Mon and Tues. PS *Every* Mancunian taxi driver knows it...................... 🔳

Right of Passage

Getting in to trendoid clubs ain't easy. Let us count the ways: 1. Know the owner/doorman; 2. Go with someone else who does; 3. Look extraordinary/like a fashion victim (with *confidence*); 4. Approach the doorman 'in the right way' (even hardened club-goers DUGGIE FIELDS and TAMA JANOWITZ are at a loss to describe quite what this means, since they stick to methods 1, 2 and 3... try conviction and *a lot of bluff*).

But if you have to have a nightclub then the Wag is the best in Britain" – ROBERT ELMS. *"A reliable old fave. Its strength is that it remains the same. For the best up-and-coming bands" –* SEAN MACAULAY.

WALL STREET, 14 Bruton Place, W1
☎ (071) 493 0630
Fun club that *"has taken over from Café de Paris a bit. More of that ornate décor, gold-painted banisters and purple wallpaper...a sort of brothelly look. People come and run their own night. Most nights are very good value – for fashion victim types" –* SEAN MACAULAY.

WESTWORLD
The best club-without-a-home, a bumper affair held a handful of times a year (find it through *Time Out*). *"The roving club that has been going the longest and looks like it will keep on going. They go big-scale, with fun park stuff, dodgems, ghost rides, stage acts, etc. You just have to pick up on the grapevine which venue they'll be at" –* SEAN MACAULAY. Their offshoot **Wetworld** sees cool-cossied swimsters making waves at a public swimming pool.

—— *Fashion designers* ——

ALLY CAPELLINO, 95 Wardour St, W1
☎ (071) 494 0768
The quintessential English look with a contemporary interpretation. Easy separates, coats, accessories, even toiletries, for women and men. *"Wonderful British classics that are modern, revamped and very relevant. Every detail is thought out" –* ANGELA KENNEDY.

ANOUSKA HEMPEL, 2 Pond Place, SW3
☎ (071) 589 4191
A magnificent midnight-blue showcase for this perfectionist's demi-couture collection, accessories and interior furnishings – from brocade cushions to a Biedermeier sofa. Structured garments for the salon or an English occasion (Ascot, a wedding, a ball), minimal shoes, maxi hats. Highly groomed ladies like Princess Michael of Kent, SHAKIRA CAINE and Aliai (Mrs Rocco) Forte adorn her couture shows.

ANTONY PRICE, 34 Brook St, W1
☎ (071) 629 5262; at A La Mode
Glamour Designer of the Year, 1989/90, he has a cult rockstar/showbiz following for his sexy couture wear. Ballgowns are constructed with

The English Season

The English season kicks off with the débutantes' Berkeley Dress Show at the Savoy in April. After that, it's a matter of following in the wake of the royal family. For 3 muddy days in April, county clans gather at **Badminton Horse Trials**, all clad in tree green from head to toe. A bevy of coming-out balls follows in May, headed by the **Rose Ball**, where blossom the latest generation of bright young things. In June, **The Derby** and **Royal Ascot** bring out the morning suits and toppers, and outrageous headwear for women (the crown must be covered in the Royal Enclosure at Ascot). *"June is the best month in Britain for open-air events...I love Wimbledon"* – PATRICIA HODGE. For, although **Wimbledon** has turned into one of the most corporate occasions, it remains dear to English hearts, including JEFFREY ARCHER's. Equally dear are **Goodwood**, a delightful week of Pimm's-swilling and racing in July, and **Henley Royal Regatta**, a blissful long weekend by the river, characterized by boaters, blazers, bunting, bands and blades. Last fling before the hols is **Cowes Week**, the first week in August. *"Great fun, even if you're not interested in sailing. The hospitality is fantastic – everything from the swank and élitism of the Royal Yacht Squadron and the royal presence right through to local bars that stay open 18 hours a day"* – DAVID LITCHFIELD. *"I go to Cowes every year and stay with friends on the harbourfront. As for the actual event itself, I know nothing about sailing, but it's still a fun weekend"* – ROSS BENSON.

architectural precision – no way are these casual little numbers. He did the whole look for Bryan Ferry and co and he's a top fave of Jerry Hall and MARIE HELVIN, *"for the sexiest clothes in the world"*. Also daywear and suits for biz-men.

 ARABELLA POLLEN at Harvey Nichols, Harrods
Young but mainstream designer who is *"really very big – she has influenced fashion, bringing back the slightly older, more elegant look"* – ANGELA KENNEDY. Inspired by the sun, she takes hot colours and Inca emblems through to winter. Tailored daywear of tweed and crêpe; swingy summer dresses with polka dots or gypsy flounces; slim cigarette pants; skittish evening wear in opulent fabrics; the perfect little black dress.

BENNY ONG, 3 Bentinck Mews, W1
☎ (071) 487 5954
Charming Singapore-born designer with a sensuous sense of colour. Pampering luscious evening wear and daywear with a glamorous edge.

BETTY JACKSON at Harrods, Liberty, Harvey Nichols
A consistent winner for unstructured, baggy clothes for the modern woman. Lots of linen and cotton in natural and spicy colours and exciting prints. Beautiful loose suedes. Also menswear.

 BRUCE OLDFIELD, 27 Beauchamp Place, SW3 ☎ (071) 584 1363; **at Harvey Nichols**
Known for a punch packed with glamour and pzazz, Oldfield has mellowed out of late. His look is softer, but he still makes you feel like a woman. *"He knows what suits the client and it's always beautifully made"* – ROBERT SANGSTER. Sophisticated day and evening wear with embroidery, appliqué and other couture detail. MARIE HELVIN still votes him *"the best for drop-dead glamour"*; JOAN COLLINS, CHARLOTTE RAMPLING, SHAKIRA CAINE, TESSA DAHL and other international stars love to dress up here. His Diffusion range is prêt-à-porter day and occasion wear, more palatable to the pocket. LADY ELIZABETH ANSON recommends Bruce to brides (and their mothers).

 CATHERINE WALKER, Chelsea Design Company, 65 Sydney St, SW3
☎ (071) 352 4626
The Princess of Wales's favourite designer – this French couturier's unfussy, long lean looks are perfect on the Diana brand of figure. Dressy day ensembles and structured ballgowns emanate good taste and an inherent sense of chic. Painstakingly made clothes, reliant on cut, proportion and lovely fabrics rather than excess frills. *"My clothes from Catherine Walker have lasted and lasted and lasted..."* – TESSA DAHL. *"She's just so fabulous, the best here. I could wear her clothes forever, they are dateless"* – SHAKIRA CAINE. Also a bridal shop at 46 Fulham Road, SW3 ☎ (071) 581 8811, for the complete entourage.

Britain's Best Designers and Couturiers

1	RIFAT OZBEK
2	JOHN GALLIANO
3	KATHARINE HAMNETT
4	JASPER CONRAN
5	WORKERS FOR FREEDOM
6	BRUCE OLDFIELD
7	CATHERINE WALKER
8	JEAN MUIR
9	VIVIENNE WESTWOOD
10	ARABELLA POLLEN

EDINA RONAY, 141 King's Rd, SW3
☎ (071) 352 1085; **42 Burlington Arcade, W1**
☎ (071) 495 3034
Ronay is synonymous with sharp fashion-forward tailoring. Her serious clothes line takes in tailored linens, little flared skirts, wool and gabardine suits – those expensive-looking ensembles that so suit the Duchess of York. Also wool and cashmere separates, brocade hooded coats and evening wear in brilliant fabrics – velvet and gold lamé. PATRICIA HODGE and TESSA DAHL are fans.

GEORGINA GODLEY at Whistles
A small intellectual collection, combining aesthetics, sociology and philosophy: Godleyness carries a message. Avant-garde in extremis, her look is minimal, Op Arty, futuristic. Innovative fabrics – woven pleated silk, hand-rolled felt that looks like a mossy bank. Arty, fringe clientele.

HARDY AMIES, 14 Savile Row, W1
☎ (071) 734 2436
The Queen's couturier. The collection is designed by Ken Fleetwood and Jon Moore, who still do the upper-crust English thing to a nicety, from little tweed suits to elegant evening wear, ball gowns, the works. Their *grande dame* clientele includes BETTY KENWARD and LADY ELIZABETH ANSON, who recommends him for the whole wedding party.

 JASPER CONRAN, 303 Brompton Rd, SW3 ☎ (071) 823 9134
Jasper always turns out wearable, polished collections, though fashion-watchers have noticed more than a passing resemblance to Galliano and Yamamoto when he departs from his more classical norm. At his best in high colour – scarlet and lime, white and orange – on soft tailoring. His 90s look traces the body with fluid A-line day

dresses, stretch velvet blousons and leggings. Also hooded bathrobe coats. Men's and women's wear for folk like Lenny Henry, MARGAUX HEM-INGWAY, Paula Yates, Nell Campbell.

🏃 JEAN MUIR, 59-61 Farringdon Rd, EC1 ☎ (071) 831 0691

The saucer-eyed, black-bobbed queen of mini-malism continues her enduring, puritanically pared-down look. Her following are stuck on her sleek classics – silk jersey cut on the bias with perfectionism, waterfall-frill jackets, little knits with blocked colour. Mark the mistress's words: "*As every painter knows it is the tone that matters most. There are many different kinds of red, blue and yellow, but my red, blue or yellow must be exactly the right tone*" – JEAN MUIR. One of PATRICIA HODGE's top designers. Jean Muir Studio is the successful cheaper line (lambswool rather than cashmere).

> **❝Every designer should work in his or her own time and never try to imitate the past. The basic craft of the métier – cut and fit – is timeless❞**
>
> 🏃 JEAN MUIR

JOE CASELY-HAYFORD at Harvey Nichols, Harrods, Joseph

The 'urban taylor' is known for men's and women's wear with meticulous detailing and bizarre twists (trousers with a fly at front *and* back). This summer he went elemental – from fiery colours, flame-hemmed skirts and sun-ray collars to airy flocked chiffon, goddess and wind dresses. Michael Jackson, Annie Lennox and Rick Astley step out in his gear, BRUCE OLDFIELD votes him best up-and-coming designer. Also doing a sportier look for Piero Panchetti.

🏃 JOHN GALLIANO at Harrods, Joseph

Less radical than he was, Galliano is still Britain's great innovator and master of the asymmetric cut. Never short on inspiration, he's doing everything from the African Queen to the Sicilian widow to the jockey in racing satins, via 40s and 50s short crêpe bias-cut dress, layered chiffon (even chiffon leggings), bold black and white contrasts. As a rule (rules are made to be broken), expect fluid fabrics, swinging free, hitched up or draped; and elemental colouring, from mist through mud and sludge. Fans include Madonna, Diana Ross, Helena Bonham-Carter and Susannah Constantine.

🏃 KATHARINE HAMNETT, 20 Sloane St, SW1 ☎ (071) 823 1002; at Browns

A leading force in street-cred separates for both genders, Hamnett is a designer that her peers respect – and wear. She continues to blend the highly wearable with the outrageously spirited. Easy, sexy gear in cotton drill, lycra, poplin, parachute silk; tailored wools, cottons and linens; velvet *everything* this winter, and a diffusion line of denim and active wear. You'd be forgiven for thinking her boutique was a pet shop, its window display consisting of stacked aquariums. Designed by surrealist architect Nigel Coates, the idea is you're under water. Get the drift?

New Age Nineties

The New Age is dawning. The message is 'We care' – about the planet, world peace, fellow man, the family. Sounds like born-again hippydom? A last gasp by fortysome-things? A bandwagon for spry young things in the media? Perhaps ... but fashion reflects the times and this is what our fashion-watchers had to say: "*The years of aggressive power looks and sexy sensuous looks are over. I've worn my Ungaros and really enjoyed them, but do you know what? Every time I put one on now, I take it off again, because it doesn't feel right any more. It's relieving to be in simple clothes with great style. Puritanical simplicity and restrained shapes will be absolutely crucial. Accessories, colour, or just the fabric will give the newness. Gigli, Mizrahi, the Dutch designer Dries Van Noten, Sybilla, Klein, Karan – all these are right on target*" – ANIKO GAAL. "*People want clothes that are clean, modern, easy and comfortable. European designers are taking a leaf out of the American sportswear designer's book. Yes, there is glamour, but it's not putting on an act, it's not over the top; it's believable, it's human-scale. Fashion can make you feel more together and happier and contented*" – STEPHEN JONES. Taking a broader view, a sage ELEANOR LAMBERT says: "*We are in a dead-water period. At the end of a century there is a lack of novelty and adventure. But, as the 90s draw to a close, there will be a burst of luxury and decadence, a flaunting of the body, a final fling, as in the 1790s and 1890s. People are drawn along by history.*"

Young Designerdom

The new showcase for contemporary British fashion and art is **Fusion**, Trocadero Centre, 13 Coventry St, Piccadilly Circus, W1 ☎ (071) 287 8828, with snack bars and catwalk (occasional shows) to boot. Track down the newest, youngest and wackiest British designers at **Hyper Hyper**, 26-40 Kensington High St, W8 ☎ (071) 938 4343 (about 70 designer stalls, from Boy to Lek Thunderpussy) and the more downbeat **Garage**, 350 King's Rd, SW3 ☎ (071) 351 3505 (baseball gear, rubber wear, badges, belts and so on), based in the marvellous white 30s building where Bluebird was made (see the bluebird tiles on the gateposts), with American chevies parked outside. At Hyper Hyper, look for PAM HOGG (also 5 Newburgh St, W1 ☎ (071) 287 2185) – her Warrior Queen theme sees skirts with castles cut out of the hem. Lycra, studs, bright colours, leather. Next door to the Garage are daft dressers RED OR DEAD, 350 King's Rd ☎ (071) 352 1519 (also 61 Neal St, WC2; 22 Rupert St, W1) for Heidi outfits and clubland clothes in extraordinary fabrics... see-through plastic suits, shiny macs, huge lapels, black holes, futuristic fantasies.

MARGARET HOWELL, 29 Beauchamp Place, SW3 ☎ (071) 584 2462
True British classics with a fashion twist – a hacking jacket in Harris tweed with a variation in the stitching, gabardine baggy trousers, jodhpurs in butter-nut cotton twill, a silk shawl blouse. Menswear too (poplin shirts with detachable collars, waistcoats) and accessories (hats, gloves, silk scarves, small leather goods). PATRICIA HODGE is a fan.

MARION FOALE, 13-14 Hinde St, W1 ☎ (071) 486 0239
Quality hand-knits in dreamy-hued silk, cotton and wool yarns. A touch of gentlewoman golfer, a hint of matelote. Also accessories by various designers, and a limited amount of tailoring – soft tweeds and gabardines. Tasteful shop in the English-country mould.

NICOLAS GEORGIOU at The Beauchamp Place Shop
A mere fledgling at 25, Georgiou is nonetheless a big new name in the tailor-designer field for women. Trained under Ozbek, his collections are clearly thought-out, produced and marketed. Suits and separates with modern, curvy cuts and a smouldering palette of olive, moss and bordeaux. Dark, sophisticated evening wear in satin-backed crêpe and stretch sequinned lace with embroidery and beading.

NICOLE FARHI, 193 Sloane St, SW1 ☎ (071) 235 0877; at Harvey Nichols; menswear 27 Hampstead High St, NW3
Recent award winner in the British Classics category, Farhi has put the pared-down exec look to the back of the wardrobe, and gone into more relaxed mode for the 90s. Expect more knitwear and evening wear, mixed colours and textures (washed silk, tweeds, suedes, lurex and flannel – all mixed up). Still the perfect slim black pants, too. MAUREEN LIPMAN is a fan. Her casual menswear collection introduces 'new but unthreatening' colours for men... aubergine and bottle green shouldn't rock the boat too much.

PAUL COSTELLOE at Harrods, Liberty, Harvey Nichols
This Irish designer displays a strong suit in tailoring and special-occasion wear in beautiful Irish linens, hand-loomed tweeds and fine silks. Dressage, the little sister range, has a soft, faded floral, country garden image – the British answer to Ralph Lauren's answer to Britain.

RICHARD JAMES at Browns, Joseph
A young designer for men's classics in not-so-classic colours – canary, bright pink and orange.

🐦 RIFAT OZBEK at Browns, Joseph, Harvey Nichols
In the past you could spot an Ozbek by its brilliant, exotic detail – tassels, gold embellishment, embroidery, a sense of couture militaire, a touch of Turkish, a hint of Mexicana. Then last summer he went white, white, white, relaxed, relaxed, relaxed. Heralding the New Age, his look was hippy meets hip hop: hooded bomber boleros, shorts and waistcoats with the word Nirvana in diamanté studs, a smidgen of sequins and fringing. Clients include the Princess of Wales, Madonna, Soul II Soul, MARIE HELVIN ("*for sexy ethnic wear*"), Whitney Houston, Daryl Hannah and Jerry Hall. O for Ozbek, the cheaper line, is strong on lycra, jersey, denim.

🐦 VICTOR EDELSTEIN, 3 Stanhope Mews W, SW7 ☎ (071) 244 7481
Tall, elegant and soigné, he is master of the society ball gown. Wonderful daytime and cocktail couture; lavish, classy evening dresses in sensuous, jewel-tinted fabrics; heavenly wedding frocks. Princesses Diana and Michael, Ladies Dashwood, Harlech and Sieff, Lucy Ferry and Lucy Snowdon are among his coterie.

🏃 VIVIENNE WESTWOOD, 430 King's Rd, SW10 ☎ (071) 352 6551; 6 Davis St, W1 ☎ (071) 629 3757
Mother of street fashion and a true original, Westwood always has immense influence on fashion. Her lopsided shop at World's End saw the birth of Punk, New Romanticism, the mini-crini and the puffball. Now she's got 2 floors full of way-out wackiness in Soho, too. She did porcelain prints this summer ('the half-dressed city gent finds himself in an arcadia of 18C porcelain shepherdesses...') with a smattering of nuclear fallout; for winter, trad English tweeds with a few wicked twists. A TV-friendly outfit for Westwood means flesh-coloured tights with fig leaf topped by a mis-buttoned cardigan. Admirers include Michael Clark, Nell Campbell, Madonna, Cyndi Lauper and Donatella Getty.

🏃 WORKERS FOR FREEDOM, 4A Lower John St, W1 ☎ (071) 734 3766
Designers of the Year 1989/90, WFF are an intriguing law unto themselves. Swimming against the tide (or with it, depending which way the rest of fashion swings that season), they produce a diverse range of designer collectables with a hint of Africa and Spain, and bags of Green appeal. Comfortable, roomy gear – full skirts, outsize shirts and shorts – in natural fabrics, neutral and monochrome hues (white is right). Beautiful detailing – self-coloured embroidery, braiding, appliqués on swirly skirts.

Film

LONDON FILM FESTIVAL, National Film Theatre, South Bank, SE1 ☎ (071) 928 3232
More of an arts event for the movie-goer in the street than Cannes and co. 150 films – British and foreign premières, the best of the new international films, multi-million-dollar movies, low-budget Third World films, archive flicks, and the Junior Film Fest for young 'uns.

Gardens and parks

CHELSEA PHYSIC GARDEN, 66 Royal Hospital Rd, SW3 ☎ (071) 352 5646
An idyllic walled garden founded in 1673 by the Society of Apothecaries. Blissfully solitary, since it's open only to Friends (from £16 a year) except on Wed and Sun afternoons, mid-Apr to Oct. A vote from SERENA FASS.

PARLIAMENT HILL, Hampstead Heath, NW3
A chunk of old countryside rather than urban parkland, with marvellous views of the city. "Absolutely the outstanding best" – LORD DONOUGHUE. JOSETTE SIMONS agrees.

RICHMOND PARK, Richmond, Surrey
The deer park is as rural and rugged as you get so close to town. See DUGGIE FIELDS's discovery,

the Isabella Plantation, "a breathtaking place". Go in May/June when the rhododendrons bloom.

ROYAL BOTANIC GARDENS, Kew, Surrey ☎ (081) 940 1171
300 acres of lovely gardens, with over 50,000 types of plant. Everyone has their own vision of Kew – the bluebells and daffodils, the russet autumn, the tropical glasshouses, the pagoda. For LORD LICHFIELD, it's mid-winter, when the gardens are quiet and a few shrubs in bloom. Also 2 art galleries, plus a new exhibition hall.

Hotels

THE BEAUFORT, 33 Beaufort Gdns, SW3 ☎ (071) 584 5252
Chintzy country-home appeal set in 2 early Victorian houses a hop and a skip from Harrods. Nice flowers, soaps, chocs, books, and an all-in rate that includes drinks, health club, room service food and a large breakfast tray (no restaurant).

🏃 THE BERKELEY, Wilton Place, SW1 ☎ (071) 235 6000
Although the building is modern, it takes on the established air of its sister hotels (the big 3 – Connaught, Claridge's and Savoy), with the discreet atmosphere of a gentlemen's club. "It's extremely well run and they are very nice people" – VISCOUNT HAMBLEDEN. Appeals to Americans such as DOUGLAS FAIRBANKS JR, BIJAN and LYNN WYATT. Many think the head porter is the best in London. Rooftop swimming pool.

BLAKES, 33 Roland Gdns, SW7 ☎ (071) 370 6701
The Morgans of London (only Blakes got there first), with high popster and fashion appeal. Anouska Hempel's swanky hotel is exotically decorated with lavish silks, Oriental lacquer screens, carved and gilded beds, artistic dried flower arrangements – all put together with her usual perfectionist eye for detail. Ultra-stylish, expensive bar and restaurant. "One of the most beautiful hotels in the world. It has the type of interior that no international hotel would ever dare put together. It hasn't been done to please everybody, just to please Anouska Hempel" – DAVID LITCHFIELD. "It's amazing. Anouska has done it wonderfully. The most delicious English breakfast" – ALISON DOODY. Restaurant-wise, JULIAN LLOYD WEBBER gulps, "It's certainly a place to go for a special occasion, exceptionally good food and extremely unusual, but the portions are absolutely enormous. There are starters that would finish most people off for the evening."

CAPITAL HOTEL, 22 Basil St, SW3 ☎ (071) 589 5171
A cosy town house where the likes of DOUGLAS FAIRBANKS JR feel at home. Rooms are either floral and pretty or sombre and masculine, using Ralph Lauren furnishings. Nina Campbell dec-

orated the warm peachy **restaurant**, where Philip Britten (ex-Chez Nico) is the much-hallowed culinary king. KEN HOM is a fan; LEN EVANS considers it *"the best small hotel in London"*.

🏆 CLARIDGE'S, Brook St, W1
☎ (071) 629 8860

The best in London and one of the best in the world. The grande dame of the great London hotels, she's been in operation since 1812, though the interior is largely art deco, with fabulous mirrors, gleaming black and white tiled floors, glam ballrooms and enormous bedrooms. *"Simply total world-class class. They remember you whenever you come back, put newspapers by the door before you wake up, do everything soundlessly but enthusiastically"* – HELEN GURLEY BROWN. *"Still has a style that is almost unrivalled worldwide"* – DAVID LITCHFIELD. *"For me it's like a second home. Friendly, personal service, regular staff. To go there on a busy day and sit in that wonderful foyer and have somebody terribly nice ask you whether you'd like something to drink, with the music playing... you think 'aaah'"* – LADY ELIZABETH ANSON. *"Ron Jones, one of the few British General Managers, is top-flight, as good as any of his Swiss or German counterparts"* – LORD LICHFIELD. *"Still the best. Ron Jones was not Hotelier of the Year for nothing,"* echoes PRUE LEITH. *"Completely non-commercial. Of all the hotels I like, I get the most satisfaction from Claridge's"* – STANLEY MARCUS. *"The Tartan Suite is quite mad, with tartan carpets, thistle stencils and sporrans, lots of Scottish pictures and an open fire. It's quite bizarre but very effective and cosy"* – CAROL WRIGHT. *"The nicest place for a drink. Very civilized... if you want to feel grown-up"* – BOB PAYTON. Further devotion from BARBARA CARTLAND, BETTY KENWARD, CAROLINE HUNT, DOUGLAS FAIRBANKS JR, FRANK BOWLING, JANE SEYMOUR and LORD MONTAGU OF BEAULIEU. See also Restaurants.

Secret Service

"Undoubtedly Claridge's and the Connaught have the most outstanding room service. People will think I wouldn't say anything else, but I really do believe it because we do our room service in a slightly different way. Each floor has its own kitchen rather than a central depart-ment, so on one floor you see your own waiters. They become known to you and that gives you a better feeling, like you have your own staff looking after you... much more personal" – GILES SHEPARD.

🏆 THE CONNAUGHT, Carlos Place, W1
☎ (071) 499 7070

Of the Connaught's many qualities, discretion and personal service by long-standing staff are its most treasured. Distinguished and old-fashioned (to the point of not wanting to admit they have a fax – they like business to be done by letter or telephone). Set in residential Mayfair, it's No 1 for those members of its charmed circle. *"The reason why I like it is because it's like home, and they treat you as if it's your home... so I wouldn't mind living there permanently"* – KEN HOM. *"Still in a class of its own,"* agrees HILARY RUBINSTEIN. *"The most exclusive hotel in London and there's nothing new about that. If you were really rich and had taste, you'd book in here"* – RICHARD COMPTON MILLER. *"Pretty nice,"* ventures STIRLING MOSS. *"One of the hotels I like best in England. Of course it has delicious food and they're sweet people"* – VISCOUNT HAMBLEDEN. More support from DOUGLAS FAIRBANKS JR, BARBARA KAFKA and FRANK BOWLING. See also Restaurants.

🏆 **Buzzz** Live like an English gent or lady at one of these quiet, discreet establishments: the 24-room **Draycott Hotel**, 24-26 Cadogan Gdns, SW3 ☎ (071) 730 6466, where Michelle Pfeiffer stays: *"We [The Good Hotel Guide 1990] gave it our César as best newcomer of the year. It has really become known to the hotel-watchers. It's tucked away and hellish to find. Quiet, very nicely furnished, lovely rooms"* – HILARY RUBINSTEIN. PATRICIA HODGE and TESSA DAHL agree 🏆......**11 Cadogan Gardens**, Sloane Square, SW3 ☎ (071) 730 3426: *"I like it because it is small. I always stay there"* – MARIO BUATTA🏆......**Number Sixteen**, 16 Sumner Place, SW7 ☎ (071) 589 5232: *"luxury bed and breakfast home away from home, good pictures, fine décor, restful garden, obliging staff – a wonderful combination"* – LADY ELIZABETH ANSON🏆......Just opened, from the same designers as Emporio Armani, is the **Halkin Hotel**, 4 Halkin St, SW1 ☎ (071) 823 1033, boasting ex-Inigo Jones chef Paul Gayler, whose cuisine and wine list are tipped for the top.....🏆

Britain's Best Hotels

1	CLARIDGE'S · London
2	THE CONNAUGHT · London
3	THE SAVOY · London
4	STON EASTON PARK · Chewton Mendip
5	CHEWTON GLEN · New Milton
6	THE BERKELEY · London
7	INVERLOCHY CASTLE · Fort William
8	THE RITZ · London
9	STAPLEFORD PARK · Melton Mowbray
10	HUNSTRETE HOUSE · Hunstrete

DUKES HOTEL, 35 St James's Place, SW1
☎ (071) 491 4840
More *rus in urbes*, with dignified, masculine rooms downstairs, suites just like country drawing-rooms. Good but extortionate restaurant. *"Has its own exclusive club-like charm and gives a lot of satisfaction"* – HILARY RUBIN-STEIN; KEITH FLOYD's best bar in London.

FOUR SEASONS INN ON THE PARK, Hamilton Place, Park Lane, W1
☎ (071) 499 0888
A smooth-running hotel of typical Four Seasons professionalism, it's reckoned by some to be a smart alternative to the stuffier London hotels, and by LEO COOPER, *"probably the best hotel in London at the moment"*. *"The service is a combination of the hospitality of the British without the snobbery. It's a combination I like very much"* – BIJAN. *"Still one of my favourite hotels. I love it – it's fabulous"* – ROBERT RAMSAY. See also Restaurants.

HALCYON, 81 Holland Park, W11
☎ (071) 727 7288
Another little home from home, with fanciful décor and lots of trompe-l'oeil and paint effects. The Desert Room has murals and a colonial mosquito net, one suite has a parasol-filled conservatory. Lauren Bacall, Bryan Ferry, Tina Turner and Richard Harris have stayed. Fine **Kingfisher** restaurant. It's impressed LADY ELIZABETH ANSON and LORD LICHFIELD.

HAZLITT'S, 6 Frith St, W1 ☎ (071) 434 1771
A secret corner of civilization in Soho, one of the cheapest hotels at about £75 a double, no restaurant. *"The best in London by a long way. It's Hazlitt the writer's old house – in fact three 1718 houses knocked together. You're given a key. The rooms are full of antiques and they are named after people who stayed in them. The idea is that*

Soho is your restaurant" – ROBERT ELMS. Tops for TYLER BRULE.

THE MAY FAIR, Stratton St, W1
☎ (071) 629 7777
A business hotel also loved by big-name celebs for its discretion and concern for personal tastes. Michael Jackson, Prince, Madonna, Dustin Hoffman, Stevie Wonder and Sammy Davis Jr are but a few.... The French restaurant, beauty parlour and health club keep them in shape.

THE PORTOBELLO HOTEL, 22 Stanley Gdns, W11 ☎ (071) 727 2777
A Victorian terrace, the secret haunt of models and rock stars (Eric Clapton; U2 and Simple Minds before they hit May Fair status). Always a fight for the rooms with the 4-posters and for Suite 16 (round bed, outsize Victorian bath).

THE RITZ, Piccadilly, W1
☎ (071) 493 8181
A name that still spells glamour and sophistication, a realm of belle époque gaiety. The nightingale sang in Berkeley Square and there were angels dining at the Ritz...follow the angels into the glittering gilded and candlelit dining room, the most beautiful in London, with one of the best wine lists. Whether a tourist trap or not, tea at the Ritz is an *event*, partaken in Palm Court around the sculptured fountain. Between the hotel and Green Park is the best secret garden in town. Revamped rooms may have lost their old style, but guests such as BARBARA TAYLOR BRADFORD still flock in.

THE SAVOY, The Strand, WC2
☎ (071) 836 4343
One of the old grandees, a lovely luxe hotel with superb service, unruffled since management passed from the hands of the great Willi Bauer to Austrian Herbert Striessnig. With striking views over Embankment Gardens and the Thames, a river suite is unsurpassable, reckon MICHAEL GRADE, FREDERIC RAPHAEL and DOUGLAS FAIRBANKS JR. The glossy American [piano] Bar is a great post-work meeting-place. At the famous yew-panelled **Grill** and the **Upstairs Bar**, food goes from strength to strength (see Restaurants). *"A style that is unique"* – HILARY RUBINSTEIN.

THE STAFFORD, St James's Place, SW1
☎ (071) 493 0111
Under the same Cunard umbrella as the Ritz, this quiet little clubby hotel has been going since 1912, and is prized for its many loyal staff. Charming terrace bar in the cobbled mews.

Music

ENGLISH NATIONAL OPERA, London Coliseum, St Martin's Lane, WC2
☎ (071) 836 3161
The one opera buffs puff. As adventurous, stimu-

How does the Garden Grow

It just ain't Godunov, complained the Royal Opera House. If we are to flourish in Covent Garden, we must be allowed to grow and improve. After much toing and froing, a £175 million expansion programme is to go ahead. The resident companies will battle on from 1990-1993, and then find an alternative venue until completion in 1996. Jeremy Dixon and Ed Jones's bold scheme will enable all elements of the Royal Ballet and Royal Opera to be housed under one roof. There will be space for scenery storage, backdrop-painting and ballet rehearsal studios; in the 1858 Barry auditorium, sightlines will be improved and air conditioning installed. An additional 30 performances each year are planned, plus smaller-scale productions in the underground orchestra rehearsal room and experimental ballet in rooftop studios. The stunning new foyer, occupying the new-look Floral Hall should certainly be something to make a song and dance about.

lating and polished as ever, though its wings are being clipped because of lack of funding. Trad and 20C opera plus some music theatre, with as strong an emphasis on dramatic staging as music. The only full-time repertory company in Britain, with bags of team spirit. More casual than Covent Garden – and more penetrable. *"For music alone there is no better in London. Their production in the main is brilliant"* – LEO COOPER. *"I still think it's a fabulous operation but it would be even better if they could get really great English translations"* – ANDREW LLOYD WEBBER.

HENRY WOOD PROMENADE CONCERTS, Royal Albert Hall, Kensington Gore, SW7 ☎ (071) 589 8212
The Proms are a season (July-Sept) of superb classical concerts with cheap standing room. *"They make serious music accessible to everyone"* – MICHAEL GRADE. The Last Night, a beloved British tradition, sees a mass of swaying bodies roused in patriotic frenzy to the strains of *Rule Britannia* and *Land of Hope and Glory*.

ROYAL FESTIVAL HALL, South Bank Centre, SE1 ☎ (071) 928 3002
The best concert hall in Britain, where all the top dogs play. Together with the smaller Queen Elizabeth Hall and Purcell Room, it presents more live music than anywhere else in the world. Home to the London Philharmonic.

🦃 ROYAL OPERA HOUSE, Covent Garden, WC2 ☎ (071) 240 1066
The grand opera house, due to close for renovations in 1991, is home to the Royal Opera and Royal Ballet. The new regime under Jeremy Isaacs, John Sainsbury and Bernard Haitink is still being watched, but views are optimistic. *"There have been some adventurous new productions and the standard of revivals has risen sharply. There is a feeling of buzz about the place which there hasn't always been"* – RODNEY MILNES. *"In the season I go once a week – my most important recreation"* – CLARE FRANCIS. *"Obviously Covent Garden... it's a nice romantic spot"* – VISCOUNT HAMBLEDEN.

—— *Restaurants* ——

See also Hotels.

🦃 ALASTAIR LITTLE, 49 Frith St, W1 ☎ (071) 734 5183
Small, spare eatery where Alastair's much-praised modern Anglo-eclectic cuisine is served to an image-conscious crowd. *"Alastair Little, I think, has some of the best food in London. It's really terrific"* – KEN HOM. *"One of the restaurant stars..."* – STEPHEN JONES. *"Serious food, informally served"* – PRUE LEITH. *"Great"* – DREW SMITH. *"I do recommend Alastair Little"* – YAN-KIT SO, and so does GEOFFREY ROBERTS.

AU JARDIN DES GOURMETS, 5 Greek St, W1 ☎ (071) 437 1816
In spacious, grown-up surroundings with forest-green upholstery, Joseph Berkmann's restaurant is gaining an appreciative following. The wine list is outstanding; cuisine is rich and delicious, by an imaginative young chef from Lyons, who trained under Bocuse and Troisgros – feuilleté of fresh asparagus with beurre blanc and chives, pan-cooked sea bass in sauce vierge, divine nougat glacé with raspberry coulis. *"Old-fashioned plush of a bygone age"* – PRUE LEITH. Strikes a chord with GEORGE MELLY.

🦃 BIBENDUM, Michelin House, 81 Fulham Rd, SW3 ☎ (071) 581 5817
Fashionable dinery based in the famous art deco former Michelin garage (M Bibendum is the bubbly Michelin man), with tuned-in design by owner Sir Terence Conran. Through Bristol-blue stained-glass windows (M Bibendum with cigar and M Bibendum on a bicycle) a glorious dappled light falls on lunchers. As to Simon Hopkinson's food, opinions fly: *"I really love Bibendum, it's*

🎩
Britain's Best Restaurants

a place where you can really eat, the food's delicious and it's not too heavy. Everything is carefully prepared, it looks easy, but that's because the chef's so skilled" – KEN HOM. *"One of the best. I think it is iniquitous that he hasn't got a Michelin star"* – JOHN TOVEY. *"An extraordinary restaurant. Simon reworks French bourgeois classics which he takes to a standard that was never achieved in their original state. It's the sort of food you dream about having in France but don't ever get"* – ALASTAIR LITTLE. *"Delicious, very comfortable. Good caramel ice cream"* – BARRY HUMPHRIES. *"Extraordinarily uneven. We had one dinner there which I thought was one of the best I'd ever had in London, absolutely first class, then I went for lunch 2 or 3 times and it was all swimming in butter"* – FREDERIC RAPHAEL. *"I would very much endorse Bibendum, which I had high expectations of, and it really did live up to them"* – JULIAN LLOYD WEBBER. *"Still fantastic. They have a super wine list and super food, but I feel their wine list is too greedily marked up. It discourages you from choosing another bottle"* – SERENA SUTCLIFFE. *"Places like Bibendum produce tremendously good food but aren't aiming at an elevated level of experience. It's high-quality food of a more basic, less sophisticated, nature"* – MATTHEW FORT. *"Great for mashed potatoes"* – DAVID SHILLING. *"Still great"* – DREW SMITH. *"Going great guns"* – ROY ACKERMAN. BENNY ONG, GEOFFREY ROBERTS and BRUCE OLDFIELD agree. BOB PAYTON doesn't: *"I think the service is atrocious."*

BLUE ELEPHANT, 4-5 Fulham Broadway, SW6 ☎ (071) 385 6595
Gourmets may scoff, but punters love the total Thai experience. *"Wonderful Thai food in a garden setting and a fun atmosphere"* – MARIE

HELVIN. *"For Thai food it is still hard to beat"* – BARRY HUMPHRIES. *"Décor-wise it's spectacular and I think the service and staff are well worth mentioning"* – TERRY HOLMES.

BOMBAY BRASSERIE, Bailey's Hotel, Courtfield Close, Courtfield Rd, SW7 ☎ (071) 370 4040
Upmarket Indian restaurant, a slice of the Raj with ceiling fans and a conservatory. Despite some unfavourable reports, our contribs remain true: *"Good for a leisurely lunch"* – VICTOR EDELSTEIN. *"Very good Indian food"* – JOHN GOLD. *"Best for ethnic food"* – RAYMOND BLANC. *"Still good"* – DREW SMITH. MARK MCCORMACK agrees.

BURT'S, 42 Dean St, W1 ☎ (071) 734 3339
Hyper-modern stuff – predominantly fish and vegetarian haute cuisine in a cool blue/grey dining room. *"The style of the 90s – essentially light ingredients cooked in such an entertaining and interesting way that they still make a satisfying meal. The cassoulet of fish, a mix of fish and beans, shows a profound understanding of affinities. Nutritious and fun to look at"* – GLYNN CHRISTIAN. Try also aubergine sausages, fennel soufflé, wild rice and asparagus risotto and sigh-worthy sorbets. *"It's frightfully chic,*

Tapas on Tap
🎩

Trend-watchers ROY ACKERMAN, RICHARD COMPTON-MILLER and ROBERT ELMS note the craze for tapas (*"gone barmy"* – ROY A; *"very fashionable"* – RICHARD CM. *"Really trendy, maybe not ultra-trendy but they're about to go mass. What wine bars were 10 years ago"* – ROBERT E). Nibble España-style on itsy-bitsy portions of tortilla (Spanish omelette), garlic chicken, salads, meatballs in tomato sauce, calamari, garlic prawns, grilled marinated peppers. Check out **Meson Don Felipe**, 53 The Cut, SE1 ☎ (071) 928 3237 (*"where all the media folk go, very near the Daily Express and London Weekend TV. Delicious, delicious little tapas and good Spanish wines and sherries obviously"* – RICHARD CM), and **Meson Doña Ana**, 37 Kensington Park Rd, W11 ☎ (071) 243 0666 (both *"authentic-style bars"* – ROY A). Tap in to the best of the rest: **El Parador**, 245 Eversholt St, NW1; **Escoba Tapas Bar**, 102 Old Brompton Rd, SW7; **Bar Gansa**, 2 Inverness St, NW1; and late-nighters **Costa Dorada**, 47 Hanway St, W1, and **Bar Madrid**, 4 Winsley St, W1.

Table d'Hotel

"The best underrated pleasure in London is dining in hotel restaurants. They have made a tremendous change. I'm passionate that they offer best value for money because they have big kitchens and enough space to have the full brigade supporting the restaurant" – GLYNN CHRISTIAN. On top of the trad trio (see Savoy Fare), 2 young bloods have carved their names in the annals of culinary excellence. The **Four Seasons** (**Inn on the Park**, see Hotels) is, sighs ANDREW LLOYD WEBBER, *"the best restaurant in London. I just couldn't believe it – it was the best meal I've ever had. Really great, incredibly together"*; and for GLYNN C, *"the best-kept secret of hotel restaurant dining. The chef is Bruno Loubet, a disciple of Raymond Blanc. He's doing absolutely spectacular cooking."* RAYMOND BLANC himself tips Loubet as a man to watch; DREW SMITH qualifies that: *"I think it's the wrong setting for him, but I've great respect for his cooking."* Over at the lavish oak-panelled, gilded and mirrored **Oak Room** at **Le Meridien**, Piccadilly, W1 ☎ (071) 734 8000, praise is unanimous: *"Terribly good – spectacular and majestic room; wonderfully light, absolutely delicious food. Outstanding"* – LORD LICHFIELD. *"A magnificent dining place. I think the food is really exceptionally good"* – MATTHEW FORT. *"The best value at lunchtime"* – JOHN TOVEY. *"The service and the food is consistently excellent"* – TERRY HOLMES. *"Still turning out consistently good food,"* echoes LOYD GROSSMAN. *"Now has a Michelin star – terribly well deserved"* – GLYNN C. The cuisine is modern French, from consultant chef Michel Lorain (from La Côte Saint-Jacques in Burgundy) and resident chef David Chambers. At the elegant **Chelsea Room** of the **Hyatt Carlton Tower**, Cadogan Place, SW1 ☎ (071) 235 5411, Bernard Gaume's cuisine and presentation are *"terribly good"* – LORD LICHFIELD.

simply wonderful" – NED SHERRIN. DREW SMITH adds a tempering note – one *"awful"* meal, one *"good"*, and a rather empty restaurant.

🦐 CHEZ NICO, 35 Great Portland St, W1 ☎ (071) 436 8846

This is positively the final move, says Nico... and a triumphant one it appears. *"Currently the best restaurant in London. Absolutely, tremendously sophisticated and well run. I think he's cooking better than ever. His whole pace has stepped up. He seems to be more flexible, the influence of North Africa is an obvious example and some of the herbs that he's using seem to speak of a livelier, more eclectic approach. Still tremendous sauces, good quality of ingredients and tremendously direct and powerful flavours. The smoothness of the whole machinery is such that you feel soothed and coddled"* – MATTHEW FORT. *"The best restaurant in Britain and the best cook"* – BOB PAYTON. *"Undoubtedly the best chef in England"* – BARBARA CARTLAND. *"The one I recommend for a European restaurant"* – YAN-KIT SO. One of the tops for RAYMOND BLANC. *"His cooking is still developing, pretty powerful"* – DREW SMITH. As to whether the chef has simmered down, the consensus says yes; you *could* be out on your ear if you ask for your meat well done (one critic remarks, *"Nico's got more ex-customers than customers"*), but LORD LICHFIELD feels *"it's the right kind of intimidation – you learn about food"*.

CIBOURE, 21 Eccleston St, SW1 ☎ (071) 730 2505

"A gigantically underrated, extremely elegant little restaurant with an extremely elegant owner and food. Never had a bad meal there. The service is impeccable and the food beautifully done... it's 'evolved nouvelle', designed carefully like nouvelle but you get enough to keep you alive. A very nice little place, unpretentious and always full" – JAMES BURKE.

🦐 CLARKE'S, 124 Kensington Church St, W8 ☎ (071) 221 9225

Sally Clarke's a smart kid – everyone will tell you. The concept is a no-choice evening menu that makes for a dinner-party atmosphere, and a small-choice lunch. *"Continues to do exceedingly, excruciatingly wonderful business. I told Sally it would never work to serve 100 people a fixed menu, but she's done it and you can't get near the place. It's a phenomenon – she's not just getting away with it – she has the great confidence to make it work. It's an absolutely barn-burning success"* – BOB PAYTON. *"Much loved and highly rated. I'm not entirely convinced about the evening menu. It's a restaurateur's dream isn't it? No wastage, control of your overheads. Lunch is much more enjoyable. People tend to label the food Californian, but it's more interesting, more personal to Sally than that"* – MATTHEW FORT. An Alice Waters disciple, trained in Paris and California, Sally uses prime market produce and bakes unforgettable herb and fruit breads (loaves and dishes are also sold at her shop next door). *"Pretty place, pretty food and not-so-pretty prices"* – PRUE LEITH. Pretty praise from LADY ELIZABETH ANSON, GEOFFREY ROBERTS, LOYD GROSSMAN, YAN-KIT SO and DREW SMITH.

DRAGON'S NEST, 58/60 Shaftesbury Ave, W1 ☎ (071) 437 3119

"A wonderful new Chinese restaurant, one of the best that has opened in London for a long, long time. Excellent food, very well prepared and very authentic. Their steamed dumplings are a must – I'd die for them right now, I'll start drooling" – KEN HOM. *"Very good...excellent dumplings. The cooking is Taiwanese, with spicy hot dishes. Their specialities are tripe dishes and blood and guts"* – YAN-KIT SO.

GAY HUSSAR, 2 Greek St, W1 ☎ (071) 437 0973

Still a Soho institution, frequented by Lefties and literati, who cram in for gossip accompanied by large platefuls of traditional Hungarian-based nosh. Former owner Victor Sassie may have sold up, but his name is still on every customer's lips. *"Everybody misses Victor but, I must say, the new regime has done it's best to maintain the old standards, it's still good value. The atmosphere at lunchtime is still good"* – LORD DONOUGHUE. *"An old favourite of mine. My feeling is that while the food remains true to Victor Sassie's grand design, it has lost some of the heart and edge that he gave to it"* – MATTHEW FORT. *"Just as good as it was under Victor Sassie"* – PRUE LEITH.

GREEN'S, 36 Duke St, SW1 ☎ (071) 930 4566

Solid English restaurant/champagne bar with clubbish snob appeal and a good St James's address. *"A reincarnation of what London used to be like...rather Edwardian"* – DREW SMITH. *"The place that the young royals go to – Fergie, Diana, Charles and Lady Helen Windsor. The food is excellent, good champagne"* – RICHARD COMPTON-MILLER. *"Has displaced Wilton's as the best English restaurant in town"* – ALAN CROMPTON-BATT. *"For traditional English food, I love it. Particularly for Sunday lunch, it's great"* – JOSEPH. *"Good fizz and wonderful fish cakes"* – PRUE LEITH. At the stove is Beth Coventry (sister of food critic Fay Maschler), whose ice cream has been voted best in London. JEFFREY ARCHER and GEORGE MELLY recommend, but there are also reports of the food being mediocre and overpriced. *"Green's is wonderful for what it serves, but they need to start taking the cooking a little further"* – ANDREW LLOYD WEBBER.

> **❝During the revolutionary time in nouvelle cuisine, many radical and outlandish things were tried as a reaction against the old order, and there were some very unfortunate results. Chefs had begun to cook in much the same way that Salvador Dali painted... and food really should not strain the mind!❞**
>
> RAYMOND BLANC

❦ HARVEY'S, 2 Bellevue Rd, Wandsworth, SW18 ☎ (071) 672 0114

'The customer is always right' went out with Nico; the maxim has been torn to shreds by wild boy Marco Pierre White. His cooking is sensational, no one can deny. But the atmosphere set by this, the John McEnroe of restaurateurs, is tense. Food critics are of one voice: *"He is an incredibly talented cook, a lot of people rave about him, but he lives on a knife edge. When I go out for a meal I don't want to sit on the edge*

Ethnic Round-up 1

Lucky Londoners can skip from cuisine to cuisine, keeping their tastebuds stirred. The Lebanese **Al Hamra**, 31-33 Shepherd Market, W1 ☎ (071) 493 6934, remains *"lovely, one of the best in London,"* for DREW SMITH and LORD LICHFIELD. **Cheun Cheng Ku**, 17 Wardour St, W1 ☎ (071) 437 1398, is still great for Sunday dim sum, an ANTON MOSIMANN fave. **Fung Shing**, 15 Lisle St, W1 ☎ (071) 437 1539, is *"very much in the forefront"* – YAN-KIT SO. The Chinese **New Diamond**, 23 Lisle St, WC2 ☎ (071) 437 2517, is *"still a favourite haunt"* says ROY ACKERMAN, who reckons **The Village Taverna**, 198 Fulham Rd, SW10 ☎ (071) 351 3799, for Greek-Cypriot food, *"takes a lot of beating. The best kleftika in London."* For mainly Swedish food, **Anna's Place**, 90 Mildmay Park, N1 ☎ (071) 249 9379, is *"chic, glorious. I adore it. The most delicious bread I have ever tasted, just beyond belief"* – STEPHEN JONES. **Wodka**, 12 St Albans Grove, W8 ☎ (071) 937 6513, is *"a very trendy, friendly, rather youthful and casual Polish restaurant, where the jeunesse dorée drink flavoured vodka and eat sautéed goose breast. Really good fun"* – LOYD GROSSMAN. To be continued...

of my seat thinking that someone is going to throw a strop" – ROY ACKERMAN. *"A restaurant in the process of development. I think Marco is a phenomenal chef and he's unquestionably brilliantly talented but... Harvey's is not a comfortable restaurant to be in"* – MATTHEW FORT. *"He is the first genuine genius that English cooking has produced. He and his staff are all in their 20s, it's a bunch a kids running the place – what do you expect? But on a plate nobody touches him except Blanc"* – DREW SMITH. Note the less troubled experiences of non-critics: *"Still ace"* – NED SHERRIN. *"Wonderful"* – LADY ELIZABETH ANSON. *"Very good, no problem with it... but they can be a bit snooty there"* – ANDREW LLOYD WEBBER.

IKEDA, 30 Brook St, W1 ☎ (071) 499 7145
"The best sushi bar in London" – MARIE HELVIN. *"My pick of the Japanese, a sushi restaurant par excellence. Also the most wonderful grilled sesame aubergine"* – LOYD GROSSMAN. And *all* sorts of Jap nosh.

KALAMARAS, 76-78 Inverness Mews, W2 ☎ (071) 727 9122
"Remains the great Greek restaurant of London, even though the famous owner, Stelios Platonos, is less in evidence. It's less charming when he's not there" – LOYD GROSSMAN. *"The only place for proper Greek food"* – DREW SMITH. *"Genuine food – everything tastes and that's very important"* – LORD LICHFIELD. Still a winner with ROY ACKERMAN for simple, fresh food.

🐟 KENSINGTON PLACE, 201 Kensington Church St, W8 ☎ (071) 727 3184
Fashionable and cacophonous, this glassily shop-fronted designer space is as lively as ever. *"Very good. I find it too noisy but that may be the testament to its own success. Dishes vary between the good and the really exceptionally good. In the same league as Bibendum"* – MATTHEW FORT. An original, eclectic repertoire from Rowley Leigh, often using extraordinary food combinations. Favourites include foie gras with sweetcorn pancake, baked tamarillo with passion fruit sauce. *"A large, busy, fun restaurant with good food and reasonable prices – and there aren't many of those in London"* – ALASTAIR LITTLE. *"Similar to Le Caprice, not quite as smart, but the food is very good and the people are interesting"* – DUGGIE FIELDS. *"Great fun for taking teenagers to. They love it because it's a tremendously bustling brasserie of the kind you get much more in Paris. A nice mix of ethnic food – some Moroccan, a little Italian – they mix it. It works as a permanently full, very-long-hours brasserie... London should have more of them"* – SERENA SUTCLIFFE. LADY ELIZABETH ANSON and DREW SMITH add approval.

LA FAMIGLIA, 7 Langton St, SW10 ☎ (071) 351 0761
Chelsea-ites' favourite local, for modern Italian cooking and a warm, where-it's-at atmosphere.

"Probably the most fashionable Italian restaurant. It is always packed and it has a good cross-section of people from the royal family and aristocrats to actors, models and media folk" – RICHARD COMPTON-MILLER. *"My absolute canteen"* – NED SHERRIN. A fave of TESSA DAHL'S.

LANGAN'S BRASSERIE, Stratton St, W1 ☎ (071) 493 6437
Langan's is still Langan's, magnet for the rich and glitzy. *"People thought Richard Shepherd might lose his edge when Peter Langan died, but he hasn't, it just keeps improving. It's the most consistently busy restaurant I ever go to"* – TERRY HOLMES. *"It's such a stage. If you want to take people out and say 'this is London and it's a groove', it's still Langan's"* – BOB PAYTON. A *face* is bound to be there; paparazzo Richard Young checks in most evenings for gossip-column fodder. Clock proprietor Michael and SHAKIRA CAINE, Mick Jagger, Jerry Hall, David Bowie, Bryan Ferry, GEORGE MELLY, NED SHERRIN – often supplemented by a brassy sub-pop star set. *"The evergreen Langan's suits me – it's a fun scene"* – PETER STRINGFELLOW. *"I still enjoy it"* – JOHN GOLD. While the spinach soufflé with anchovy sauce and crème brûlée are legendary, food does not always delight. *"Trading on old friends, trends and reputation. Variable"* – MATTHEW FORT.

🐟 L'ARLEQUIN, 123 Queenstown Rd, SW8 ☎ (071) 622 0555
Christian Delteil's fearsomely French restaurant has a charming terraced-house setting and high standing in foodie circles. *"Very good,"* say MATTHEW FORT and ALAN CROMPTON-BATT. Proven dishes (from scallops with mushroom and fennel ravioli to divine sorbets) of supreme quality. *"It lay in the shadow of Nico [once based opposite] but has burgeoned on its own"* – LORD LICHFIELD.

🐟 LA TANTE CLAIRE, 68 Royal Hospital Rd, SW3 ☎ (071) 352 6045
Top of the serious food-lover's list, this is the best French restaurant in London, run with dedication by revered chef Pierre Koffmann. RAYMOND BLANC and DREW SMITH love it. So does ROY ACKERMAN *"...for simple elegance, food which is quite rustic in its background, served in modern style, in sleek surroundings."* GILES SHEPARD raves: *"Absolutely marvellous, absolutely sensational."* MATTHEW FORT recognizes that *"places like La Tante Claire, L'Arlequin and Chez Nico are serious gastronomic experiences"*. Kitted out in cool blue with bird's-eye maple, and filled with an almost all-male business-suited clientele at lunchtime (tucking into the £20 set lunch).

🐟 LE CAPRICE, Arlington House, Arlington St, SW1 ☎ (071) 629 2239
The most consummate dinery in town – glamorous grey/black décor, fine modern food, and a glittering international crew of film, fashion,

Ethnic Round-up II

...Continuing the ethnic quest, **Chiang Mai**, 48 Frith St, W1 ☎ (071) 437 7444, is *"very, very good. I love it. Talk to the waiters because they can guide you. The food is authentic Thai and excellent"* – KEN HOM. **Busabong Too**, 1A Langton St, SW10 ☎ (071) 352 7414, *"has an upstairs where you take your shoes off and eat Thai-style, it's great"* – ALISON DOODY. Gets LORD LICHFIELD's vote. **Hiroko**, Kensington Hilton, 179 Holland Park, W11 ☎ (071) 603 5003, is a top Jap for LORD L and STEPHEN J, but **Suntory**, 72 St James's St, SW1 ☎ (071) 409 0201, is *"without doubt the best – and most expensive – Japanese"* for LORD L and RAYMOND BLANC. BARRY HUMPHRIES thinks **Kitchen Yakitori**, 12 Lancashire Court, W1 ☎ (071) 629 9984, is *"the best Japanese in town. Very good value, unpretentious."* **Mao Tai**, 58 New King's Rd, SW6 (071) 731 2520, is, for MICHAEL BROADBENT, *"the best Chinese in London,"* while the family-run Thai, **Benjarong**, 95 Fulham Palace Rd, W6 (071) 741 5808 is *"my regular – excellent and incredibly cheap"* – MB. **Poons**, at 4 Leicester St, W1 ☎ (071) 437 1528, is a fave Chinese of SIMON HOPKINSON; go to the tiny original in 27 Lisle St, WC2 ☎ (071) 437 4549, for gritty authenticity.

media stars and young royals – Diana, Fergie, Helen Windsor and Sarah Armstrong-Jones. Crudités, fresh fish, salmon fish cakes and chips are hot favourites; bullshots and spritzers take precedence over great vintages. *"I think it is total drop-dead glamour and get a great thrill every time I go in there. I just love it"* – STEPHEN JONES. *"Still my favourite restaurant"* – CLARE FRANCIS. *"Stylish and the food is consistent"* – BRUCE OLDFIELD. *"I like it very much"* – VICTOR EDELSTEIN. *"Still a favourite. They are always very friendly, very hospitable, so one goes there habitually. I like the fish cakes"* – BARRY HUMPHRIES. *"One of my favourites – the Caesar salad is out of this world. The menu changes constantly and everything is delicious. A good mix of different types of cuisine"* – MARIE HELVIN. *"It's an idiom rather than cooking... but an important place in London"* – DREW SMITH. *"My quieter version of Langan's"* – PETER STRINGFELLOW. NED SHERRIN, GEORGE MELLY

❝I like, more and more, absolutely traditional restaurants and, less and less, gimmicky ones. I particularly don't like those which are determined to make you uncomfortable with barbed-wire furniture and tables the wrong height and octagonal plates. I really find more comfort as I get older in old red plush ones with ancient waiters trembling slightly ❞

GEORGE MELLY

and JEFFREY ARCHER enjoy it. *"It's very highly rated amongst fellow restaurateurs. A brilliantly run restaurant, it fulfils its ambitions ..."* – MATTHEW FORT.

🍴 LE GAVROCHE, 43 Upper Brook St, W1 ☎ (071) 408 0881
Leader of the old guard of super-haute French restaurants, a gentlemen's clubby affair run by Albert Roux with his son Michel. There are those who remain strictly anti-Roux, but most bow to authority. Steep prices make you savour every precious mouthful, though the set lunch still allows a few bargain swallows. *"I still rate Le Gavroche very highly at £21 for a 3-course set menu. I think it is remarkably good value and a very competent standard of cooking in luxury surroundings"* – ROY ACKERMAN. *"Wonderful machine, classic stuff"* – MATTHEW FORT.

LEITH'S, 92 Kensington Park Rd, W11 ☎ (071) 229 4481
Prue Leith's restaurant remains on top for solid English/international fare, including a gourmet vegetarian menu and an eye-popping hors d'oeuvre trolley. *"Personifies splendid middle-class virtues. It's zapped up its menus recently"* – MATTHEW FORT. *"She's a pillar of culinary excellence in this country"* – LORD LICHFIELD.

L'INCONTRO, 87 Pimlico Rd, SW1 ☎ (071) 730 6327
The more fashionable, chi-chi little sister of **Santini**, 29 Ebury St, SW1 ☎ (071) 730 4094. *"An excellent Italian restaurant"* – ROY ACKERMAN. *"Very sophisticated. The food is brilliant and it's very relaxing to be there. It feels like you are really going out"* – JOSEPH.

MIYAMA, 38 Clarges St, W1 ☎ (071) 499 2443
This calm Japanesery has *"wonderful set lunches*

and a fabulous à la carte menu with everything from freshly roasted gingo nuts to deep-fried soft-shell crab. Try the razor-thin hirame (raw turbot) with ponzu sauce" – MARIE HELVIN. *"Lovely"* – DREW SMITH. *"Good at lunchtime"* – LORD DONOUGHUE. Branch at 17 Godliman St, EC4 ☎ (071) 489 1937 for financial whizzes.

ONE NINETY QUEEN'S GATE, 190 Queen's Gate, SW7 ☎ (071) 581 5666
The latest from Antony Worrall-Thompson (ex-Ménage à Trois). Contemporary cuisine (highlights include the lobster rockpool) or ask for the chef's menu (good old English bubble and squeak, broth, shepherd's pie . . .). *"A very good selection of Australian and Californian wines"* – GEOFFREY ROBERTS. After last orders you'll find yourself in esoteric company, when Roy Ackerman's Chef's Club starts up (private bar, but the restaurant stays public).

⚑ ORSO, 27 Wellington St, WC2 ☎ (071) 240 5269
Orso is now Londoners' favourite Italian eatery, less expensive and pretentious than Santini and co and always buzzing at lunch and dinner. *"It's the best – the best balance of fun people, food, service and value in London"* – DAVID SHILLING. *"Marvellous. Delicious, not too expensive – and very handy for my theatres"* – BARRY HUMPHRIES. *"Excellent North Italian cuisine"* – PATRICIA HODGE. *"Great"* – STEPHEN JONES. *"Noisy and crowded especially after the theatre, excellent Italian food – the menu changes regularly. Fun atmosphere"* – MARIE HELVIN. *"I love it – Italian fast food. Terrific, I rate it very highly"* – MATTHEW FORT. So do BRUCE OLDFIELD, MAUREEN LIPMAN and NED SHERRIN.

The Ageing Process

Cognac, as against brandy, is subject to strictly defined ageing periods. Each year, the equivalent of 21 million bottles evaporates. What is lost – the 'Angels' Share' – is essential to the quality of what is left. As Tom Stevenson wrote in *Vogue*: 'A full-strength cognac will take a good 50 years to reduce naturally to 40% . . . which is why the very best cognacs are rare and expensive. Courvoisier XO is a fabulous blend containing cognacs matured in cask for more than 50 years.' But is age everything? DAVID MOLYNEUX-BERRY thinks not: *"The skill is in the blend. Each cognac is carefully selected to provide consistency, and the final product is beautifully sculpted."*

A vintage cognac (rarely ever produced) is an altogether different matter. DAVID M-B elucidates: *"A vintage is valuable for its rarity, exclusivity and history – it's a complete experience, not just a glass of spirit. The date puts it in perspective and enhances its value."* Yet even he was not prepared for the £5,500 fetched at Sotheby's for a bottle of 1789 Courvoisier Curlier: *"A mighty price. To see an 18C bottle, in such good condition and with the house's name is very rare."*

⚑ Buzzz Late-night dining: a few break London's wimpy curfew – Le Caprice, Orso, Langan's (last orders midnight), Village Taverna (last orders 1am), Costa Dorada, Bar Madrid (open till 3am)⚑ . . . . . . The restaurant 116 Knightsbridge came and went, but SERENA SUTCLIFFE thinks chef **Ian McAndrew** is *"a major talent. He was once at the Dorchester and I rate his food easily up to Mosimann himself or La Tante Claire. Definitely one to watch"*⚑ . . . . . . Best **Reuben** (a hot open sandwich of pastrami, sauerkraut and Swiss cheese on rye) comes from **Mitchell & O'Brien**, 2 St Anne's Court, W1. Order by phone ☎ (071) 734 1630 or fax ☎ (071) 287 7150⚑ . . . . . . STEPHEN JONES has carried out his own survey of diet dinners and finds **"Weight Watchers** *frozen dinners are the best, the most tasty"*⚑ . . . . . . **Best burgers**: the purest and meatiest are turfed out at the best 50s throwbacks in town, **The Rock Island Diner**, London Pavilion, Piccadilly Circus, W1, and **Ed's Diner**, 12 Moor St, W1 and 362 King's Rd, SW10, *"an incredibly, beautifully, real honest pastiche of 50s American culture. Great burger and chips"* – LOYD GROSSMAN ⚑ . . . . . . Americana 2: the setting is Martha's Vineyard, the food eclectic and fast, the restaurant is **Deals**, Chelsea Harbour, SW10 ☎ (071) 352 5887; wheeler dealers include ALISON DOODY, RICHARD COMPTON-MILLER and JOHN GOLD. . . . . ⚑

🐟 RIVER CAFE, Thames Wharf, Rainville Rd, W6 ☎ (071) 381 8824
From the illustrious team of Richard and Ruth Rogers and Rose Gray, this high-tech space is one of the trendiest outposts of London dining. *"When it appeared it was unique. Nowhere else could you get Italian food like that. Good plain food, char-grilled squid, langoustine, sardines, imaginative vegetables...you feel you're eating healthily"* – LORD LICHFIELD. *"Has given me the greatest pleasure. It's got a wonderful informality about it. It's basically a very smart café by the river, a sort of canteen for Richard Rogers's architectural practice. The most wonderful invigorating Italian food which is prepared virtually before your eyes. Really good-quality regional cooking of the sort we haven't seen very much of in England"* – SIMON LOFTUS. *"Among my personal favourites"* – MATTHEW FORT. *"I love it"* – JOSEPH. Echoes from DREW SMITH and ROY ACKERMAN.

SAN LORENZO, 22 Beauchamp Place, SW3 ☎ (071) 584 1074
This glossy greenhousy Italian joint is a perennial haunt of the international fash. JOHN GOLD, BRUCE OLDFIELD and ROSS BENSON love lunching there. So do the Princess of Wales, Duchess of York, Princess Margaret, Lady Helen Windsor, Tina Turner, Jack Nicholson, Maggie Smith, Viscount Linley, Susannah Constantine, Rifat Ozbek, SHAKIRA CAINE, PATRICIA HODGE (*"the ultimate in Italian cuisine"*) and MARIE HELVIN: *"a home away from home, especially if you know the owners well (Mara and Lorenzo Berni). Cosy*

food and atmosphere with basic Italian home-style cooking."* TWIGGY LAWSON agrees: *"I've known Mara and Lorenzo since I was 16 and have seen the restaurant grow from one tiny room to the wonderful, beautiful restaurant it is today. For Leigh and me it's very special and the food is always fantastic. It's got a really nice atmosphere and you must have crêpe San Lorenzo!"*

STEPHEN BULL, 5-7 Blandford St, W1 ☎ (071) 486 9696
Airy new trendspot for inventive contemporary cuisine at remarkably reasonable prices. *"Very good with interesting ingredients. It doesn't cost an arm and a leg. All the foodies are going there, we should have more restaurants like it. Often these places are a lot of hype but this one's a stayer, really good"* – SERENA SUTCLIFFE. *"Love it. It's nice, it's state-of-the-art British cooking, not top-flight but very good second-flight"* – DREW SMITH. *"I like it because it's a 90s revival of luxury as against minimalism ... post-nouvelle"* – LORD LICHFIELD.

TURNER'S, 87-89 Walton St, SW3 ☎ (071) 584 6711
A quality act. Subtlety is a key factor – subtle flavours, subtle service. *"I think that Brian Turner is interesting and doing very good food. There is a kind of inverse snobbery because he is successful and gets rich clientele ... he's almost looked on with suspicion by the food establishment in London. But it really is superb and consistent"* – BARBARA KAFKA.

Savoy Fare

If hotel dining is London's 'best underrated pleasure', start redressing the balance right here, at the hotels in the Savoy Group. ROY ACKERMAN considers the **Connaught** *"No 1 for visiting Americans or a power lunch"*; BARBARA TAYLOR BRADFORD recommends it *"for a really nice English meal"*. ED VICTOR thinks it's *"the best restaurant in London. I'm afraid I do, I really love it. Everything adds up – the room (both rooms – the Grill too); the service (wonderful) and the food (excellent)."* For LORD LICHFIELD, it's *"still the best hotel restaurant, with Bourdin as the least flamboyant hotel chef"*. DREW SMITH asserts: *"It is what it is and it does it pretty well. In style it's unparalleled."* The **Savoy** is *"greatly underrated. People who know are beginning to go back to the bars and the restaurants"* – GLYNN CHRISTIAN.

At the **Grill**, spot the Duke of Devonshire, Sir Alastair Burnet, Denis Thatcher, Norman Tebbit, David Frost, Nigel Lawson. ... *"Anton Edelmann has really picked the Savoy up. The best catering for large numbers in the world"* – LORD L. He finds the **Upstairs Bar** (open till midnight) *"perfect post-theatre...and they don't mind what you wear. Top-quality plain fare."* Great breakfasts in the **River Restaurant** (porridge, kippers, kedgeree). At **Claridge's**, *"the best possible treat for someone interested in food is to see the new kitchens. It's just the most amazing sight"* – GLYNN C (as is *"the gorgeous period pink restaurant where the food has improved even further"*). LORD L highly prizes the **Causerie**'s smorgasbord (as well as the **Buttery**'s at the **Berkeley**) – *"full of well-heeled thirtysomething ladies"*.

Dining Clubs

Paying twice to get a good meal is no deterrent for a select and soigné few. Firstly there's Mark's and Harry's, both run by Mark Birley, king of clubs: "*Nobody else in the world has his style,*" says LORD LICHFIELD in admiration. **Mark's Club** appeals to JEFFREY ARCHER and BARBARA TAYLOR BRADFORD, but doesn't hold a candle to **Harry's Bar**, 26 South Audley St, W1 ☎ (071) 408 0844, with its idolatrous clientele – Di, Fergie, Princess Michael, Sean Connery, Dustin Hoffman, Sly Stallone, MICHAEL GRADE, MARK MCCORMACK, SHAKIRA CAINE, BARBARA TB again. "*My favourite restaurant in London, always*" – JOAN BURSTEIN. "*Elegant and sophisticated with absolutely delicious Italian food. I die for the granita-caffè with cream*" – MARIE HELVIN. "*Very exclusive, with the young royals always popping in*" – RICHARD COMPTON-MILLER.

Over at Anton **Mosimann's**, 11B W Halkin St, SW1 ☎ (071) 235 9625, things are "*rather special*" – ROY ACKERMAN. "*Elegant and cosy. The most exquisite food prepared by my favourite chef*" – MARIE H. "*I had experiences there on my palate that I never had before. Absolutely wonderful*" – SIMON WILLIAMS. "*Very good. I used to go there for lunch but it is rather expensive. When I last went, it seemed to be all men speaking throat-clearing languages*" – ROSS BENSON. "*Really a great chef but he doesn't change the menu very often. It's a really fantastic place...*" – DREW SMITH. "*I don't have to tell you about his bread and butter pudding....Anton's new cooking is astounding. He is the best marketing man in the business. Talk about the Roux Bros, Raymond Blanc, myself at the popular end – we all pale in comparison! He's a good guy*" – BOB PAYTON.

ZEN CENTRAL, 20 Queen St, W1 ☎ (071) 629 8103; Zen W3, 83 Hampstead High St, NW3 ☎ (071) 794 7863; Zen Chelsea Cloisters, Sloane Ave, SW3 ☎ (071) 589 1781
Designer Chinese at a hefty price. Zen Central gets most votes: "*The indisputable top of the league for me. I don't think it's a purist's restaurant – it's perhaps rather too clean, too Westernized – but I think it's just wonderful. Minced oysters wrapped in lettuce is just sensational...their chicken and coriander rolls... everything in that place is great except for the bill, which is a nightmare!*" – LOYD GROSSMAN. "*Still very popular, very good. It is now a Mecca for people visiting London*" – ROY ACKERMAN. STEPHEN JONES goes for Zen W3 (despite reports of increasing tattiness): "*I love it...it's supposedly unfashionable to make somebody necessarily comfortable in a restaurant, but Zen has a very nice interior and is always relaxing and the people are always polite. Simple things like if you ask for a glass of water, it arrives in 10 seconds. That is as important as how well cooked your meat is*" – STEPHEN JONES.

Shopping

Establishment international designers live in and around **New Bond Street** and **Sloane Street**. **Knightsbridge** has the top stores and classy high-street shops, giving way to bastions of old-fashioned boutiquery towards Hyde Park Corner. Young trendy fashion areas are **Floral Street, Beauchamp Place** and **'Brompton Cross'**, where Fulham Rd turns into Brompton Rd. **King's Road** is still a major stomping ground on Saturday afternoon – Whistles, Hobbs, Midas and co at the Sloane Square end, second-hand chic at World's End, with a lot of over-priced designer boutiques for the boys in the middle. **Soho** remains the hotbed of new street fashion. The 'West Soho' bunch are centred on **Newburgh Street** (Academy Soho, Helen Storey, John Richmond, Duomo, Junior Gaultier, Pam Hogg, Tessa James jewellery, and nearby, Beau Monde, Ben de Lisi). **St Christopher's Place** and **Covent Garden Market** are part-trendy, part-touristy, part-chi-chi. VICTOR EDELSTEIN, CANDIDA CREWE and GLYNN CHRISTIAN are **Portobello Road** junkies – for food, antique prezzies, junk. Best bargains (second-hand clothes, bric-à-brac) are to be had under the flyover, early on Fri and Sat. **Brick Lane** market (Sun, dawn) is for even more earnest scrabblers; **Greenwich** (Sun) yields a few incredible finds among the junk; **Bermondsey** (Fri, daybreak) is the best source of antiques (where all the trade go). Hit **Camden Passage**, Islington, at weekends, for antiques, second-hand lace, clothes and jewellery; and trendsville **Camden Lock** for new arty-crafty wares.

A LA MODE, 36 Hans Crescent, SW1 ☎ (071) 584 2133
Switched-on source of high fashion by Gaultier, Isaac Mizrahi, Antony Price, Rifat Ozbek, Helmut Lang, Callaghan and Sybilla; plus Liza Bruce swimwear, hats by Philippe Model and

Stephen Jones, an exclusive line of jewellery by Dinny Hall, and more jingle-jangle jewels by ex-Chanel model Mercedes Robirosa.

ASPREY, 165 New Bond St, W1
☎ (071) 493 6767
A dignified establishment for high-class (and high-cost) present-buying – jewellery, silver, leather, china, tableware, clocks, watches, luggage and antiques. JOSEPH loves a wander round, RICHARD COMPTON MILLER recommends it for *the* signet ring, *the* attaché case, *the* watch – and for gifts.

THE BEAUCHAMP PLACE SHOP, 55 Beauchamp Place, SW3 ☎ (071) 589 4155
The perfect wardrobe, edited by Patsy Blair, featuring the best of British with a supporting cast of Europeans – Betty Jackson, Ally Capellino, Marion Foale, Edina Ronay, Ventilo and Cerruti, and accessories by J&M Davidson and Mulberry. Liza Minnelli and the Duchesses of Westminster and Kent drop in.

BROWNS, 23-27 S Molton St, W1
☎ (071) 491 7833
The exclusive showcase for many leading international designers, run by Joan Burstein and husband ("*I think if you like one thing you'll like it all. We really do edit collections*" – JB). Purist fashion for women and men by thoroughbreds like Azzedine Alaïa, Sonia Rykiel, Donna Karan, Romeo Gigli, Comme des Garçons, Byblos, Missoni. *"The best shopping area is South Molton St, and Browns is the best shop. A big selection...great for quality clothes"* – ALISON DOODY. The starry clientele also includes Barbra Streisand, Liza Minnelli, JOAN COLLINS, BRUCE OLDFIELD, Faye Dunaway, Twiggy, MARIE HELVIN, Lee Remick and Jacqueline Bisset.

BURLINGTON ARCADE, Piccadilly, W1
A beautiful pink and aquamarine covered arcade lined with deliciously British shops (the best cashmeres, table and bed linen, antique jewels and objects....) Well-heeled visitors flock here to stock up on jerseys. **N Peal** is the undisputed best for fash cashmere in gorgeous jewel-bright or muted colours. **Lord's**, the oldest inhabitant in the arcade (est 1774), is great for classic knitwear, Valerie Louthan cashmeres and exclusive silks, menswear, leather and silk goods. At **Pickett** are Georgina von Etzdorf's handprinted silk accessories. **S Fisher** has a good British stock of bright-coloured woollens – Shetlands, cashmeres, Arans – plus sea island cotton polo-necks, nice ties and socks.

BUTLER & WILSON, 189 Fulham Rd, SW3 ☎ (071) 352 3045; 20 S Molton St, W1 (071) 409 2955
Still No 1 for fashion-conscious costume jewellery, they help set the season's look for ears, wrists, necks and lapels. From flying-saucer gilt or silver bangles, through diamanté lizards and hands, dangling gilt and coloured glass, to ropes

of twisted pearl and jet. Also original Celtic and art deco items. *"Very nice for presents, for sparklies"* – BARRY HUMPHRIES. Gilt-diggers include Lauren Bacall, Faye Dunaway, Jerry Hall, SHAKIRA CAINE, Dame Edna Everage and MARIE HELVIN.

CHARBONNEL ET WALKER, 28 Old Bond St, W1 ☎ (071) 491 0939
Royal chocolatiers, established in 1875 and patronized originally by Edward VII. Top-quality dark chocs in floral boxes or the famous boîte blanche, which is filled to the brim at your whim.

CHRISTINE AHRENS at Jones, 71 King's Rd, SW3 ☎ (071) 352 6899
Young shoe designer who does buckled/strapped/laced boots and shoes, with round or chisel toes. Has designed for Jasper Conran and fash films.

COBRA & BELLAMY, 149 Sloane St, SW1 ☎ (071) 730 2823; also at Liberty
Tania Hunter and Veronica Manussis have a tiny trove of covetable fashion jewellery – antique and one-off designs in gold and silver with gemstones, by Barbara Bertagnoli and Christophe Blum. Also objets d'art, silver tableware and little trinkets for the lads (silver speedboats...).

COLLINGWOOD, 171 New Bond St, W1 ☎ (071) 499 5613
Antique and modern jewellery, specializing in Edwardian and Victorian pieces. Royal warrants from the Queen, the Queen Mother and the Prince of Wales (shelling out on his wife).

THE CONRAN SHOP, 81 Fulham Rd, SW3 ☎ (071) 589 7401
Based in the sleekly renovated art deco Michelin garage, its spacious interior is full of designer, ethnic and eatable temptations for house and person.

CRABTREE & EVELYN, 134 King's Rd, SW3 ☎ (071) 589 6263 and branches
For scented and foodie goodies, packaged to perfection.

CZECH & SPEAKE, 39C Jermyn St, SW1 ☎ (071) 439 0216
"The best shop for men? A sports shop or a fragrance shop rather than a fashion shop. Czech & Speake – that's the best men's shop – really good modern fragrances to go with your Scotch House basic cashmere jumper" – STEPHEN JONES. It's where VICTOR EDELSTEIN heads for the eau de toilette.

DAVID MORRIS, 25 Conduit St, W1 ☎ (071) 734 5215
Some of the best modern glossy jewellery. High-fashion, high-quality, continental-style glamour. A winner with BARBARA TAYLOR BRADFORD *"for superb jewels"*.

The Savile Row Suit

Do you judge a man by the cut of his jib? You can certainly tell an Englishman by the cut of his suit, and the Savile Row style is still revered the world over. **HUNTSMAN**, 11 Savile Row, W1 ☎ (071) 734 7441, has the cutting edge over the others. Expect to pay a good £1,500 for an everlasting suit in fine cloth made for them in Scotland. MICHAEL BROADBENT votes them No 1 *"for understated perfection"*. **HENRY POOLE**, 15 Savile Row, W1 ☎ (071) 734 5985, is the oldest bespoke establishment on the Row. Livery for the Queen's footmen, suits for noblemen, the best field coats and jackets. **ANDERSON & SHEPPARD**, 30 Savile Row, W1 ☎ (071) 734 1420, were tailors to Fred Astaire and Gary Cooper. Nowadays Calvin Klein will fly over specially for fittings. **DOUG HAYWARD**, 95 Mount St, W1 ☎ (071) 499 5574, is tops for LORD LICHFIELD, Viscount Linley, Michael Parkinson, Michael Caine, Roger Moore, Jackie Stewart, Frank Muir and James Coburn. Meanwhile, military tailors **GIEVES & HAWKES**, 1 Savile Row, W1 ☎ (071) 434 2001, have progressed from uniforms for Nelson and Wellington to the diverse requirements of the Duke of Edinburgh, Gorbachev and Geldof. **JOHN KENT**, 11 Old Burlington St, W1 ☎ (071) 734 2687, is official tailor to the Dukes of Edinburgh (in mufti) and York and Prince Edward. **STOVEL & MASON**, 32 Old Burlington St, W1 ☎ (071) 629 6924, is trusted tailor to DOUGLAS FAIRBANKS JR. Dandies' eyes light up at **TOMMY NUTTER**, 19 Savile Row, W1 ☎ (071) 734 0831, for classics turned up swaggeringly loud – brocade waistcoats and other finery. LORD LICHFIELD goes for *"anything really special or ornate"*. It was Nutter who designed The Joker's suit for Jack Nicholson in *Batman*.

DAVID SHILLING, 44 Chiltern St, W1
☎ (071) 487 3179
Born-again picture hats and flirty couture extravaganzas adorn many noble heads. Romantic ribbons-and-bows showroom.

DINNY HALL at Browns, Harvey Nichols
Beautifully crafted jewellery that graces chic lobes and wrists. Winner of the British Accessory Designer award last year, she combines intricately wrought silver with amethysts, garnets, ebony or sand-blasted resin (similar to frosted glass). Lacquer-work bangles, beaded necklaces. Also designs in more outrageous mood for Rifat Ozbek and Bruce Oldfield. *"Her jewellery is perfectly feminine and perfectly flattering …it actually makes a woman look good. Balanced and carefully made, never flashy but interesting. She's very clever"* – STEPHEN JONES.

DUFFER OF ST GEORGE, 27 D'Arblay St, W11 ☎ (071) 439 0996
The Duffers do street fashion for boys – the *GQ* set. From ultra-casual sporty stuff to tailored suits; shoes, hats, belts, too. *"Streety, kind of funky, sort of ethnicky, good stuff. A lot of kids like to dress like middle-aged West Indian rude boys – it's the latest look"* – ROBERT ELMS.

ELIZABETH STUART-SMITH, c/o The Shoe Shop, Burlington Arcade, W1
☎ (071) 225 2329
Young shoe designer for simply cut footwear that is tight-fitting to the foot; extravagant evening shoes using silk and beads. *"Delicate but not too fabricky, nor too clunky or macho – just a good balance"* – STEPHEN JONES.

EMMA HOPE, 33 Amwell St, EC1
☎ (071) 833 2367
Extravagant shoes with Klimt-style embroidery, dainty cocktail kickers, sculpted shapes, high vamps, interesting heels. Collections for Nicole Farhi and Betty Jackson, bridal shoes and a new range for men – from classics (with the proverbial twist) to pané velvets with golden baroque embellishment.

FLORIS, 89 Jermyn St, SW1
☎ (071) 930 2885
A heavenly scented institution, for soaps, bath oils and LORD LICHFIELD's favourite shaving soap (in a king-size dish that lasts aeons).

🍴 FORTNUM & MASON, 181 Piccadilly, W1 ☎ (071) 734 8040
Known first and foremost for its hushed, carpeted food hall, with liveried doorman and black morning-coated attendants. Traditional English foods; mustards, preserves and chocolate under their own suave wraps. *"I love to go in. You pay a bit over the odds but it's extremely elegant"* – SIMON WILLIAMS. SOPHIE GRIGSON, ANTON MOSIMANN, GIORGIO ARMANI and BARBARA TAYLOR BRADFORD hotfoot it here. Such gourmet pilgrims can also stock up on surprisingly tasty fashion – by Jean Muir, MaxMara, Edina Ronay, Lindka Cierach and Tomasz Starzewski

(glamour ball gowns). Suede gloves, jewellery and other accessories. STANLEY MARCUS drops in whenever he's in town.

GABRIELLA LIGENZA, 1 Mere Close, SW15 ☎ (081) 788 4499
This dynamic flame-haired Pole makes modern, feminine hats using great block shapes. Also in Bath and Cirencester.

GARRARD'S, 112 Regent St, W1 ☎ (071) 734 7020
Terrifically smart royal jewellers in a magnificent shop. Many a Garrard's gold cuff-link has graced a princely cuff.

GENERAL TRADING CO, 144 Sloane St, SW1 (071) 730 0411
Heartland of the Sloane Ranger, the GTC is one of the best presents stores in town, where the Prince and Princess of Wales had no hesitation in having their wedding list. Ultra-tasteful selection of things for the home (china, ornaments, sofas, linen, cushions, garden furniture, dried flowers), plus toys, books, stationery and an Oriental department.

GEORGINA VON ETZDORF, 149 Sloane St, SW1 ☎ (071) 823 5638; at Burlington Arcade
Garments of divine slippery silk, plush velvet and finest wafty chiffon, hand-printed in Georgina's swirly fantasyland designs. The ultimate pyjamas, dressing-gowns, gloves, cummerbunds, ties, scarves, braces and waistcoats.

GILLY FORGE, 14 Addison Ave, W11 ☎ (071) 603 3833
Couture millinery, beautifully made and detailed. Straw hats with enormous brims and full-blown silk flowers; black and white target-striped picture hats, classic 50s Audrey Hepburn lampshades. Also collections for Anouska Hempel, Jean Muir and Arabella Pollen.

GRAHAM SMITH, 2 Welbeck Way, W1 ☎ (071) 487 4888
Beautiful couture hats with the Parisian touch – by appointment only. Has hatted Princesses Di and Margaret, Elizabeth Taylor and Barbra Streisand.

HACKETT, 27 King St, WC2 ☎ (071) 497 9383 and branches
England's answer to Ralph Lauren (which was the American answer to the English Country Gentleman). A whole lifestyle catered for in an ever-expanding empire (London, Paris, Madrid, Boston and...*Tokyo*). It all began in '84 with a better second-hand rail than the rest – old grandees' cast-off shooting garb, silk dressing-gowns and other young fogey fodder. At 117 Harwood Rd, SW6 you'll find trad formal clothes (new and second-hand) – DJs, morning suits, loud accessories. At 65B New King's Rd, SW6, daywear – cords, moleskins, shirts, tweed jack-

Buy'n'Fly

Airport shopping doesn't just mean a chunky novel and a toothbrush. Heathrow Terminal 4 is now the exclusive home to some vital venues for shopoholics. In Departures, **Caviar House** of Geneva serve not only Sevruga, Oscietre and Beluga, but Imperial (previously reserved exclusively for the Shah of Iran's family) and Royal Black (from a 20- to 40-year-old Iranian Oscietre sturgeon). Cosmetics company **Danièle Ryman** has opened the world's first jetlag shop, where you can blow your left-over currency on an In-flight Comfort Kit (rehydration gel, exercise rub, mouth rinse, eye compress, nasal freshener... mmmm) or an After-flight Regulator (2 aroma baths, one to wake you up, one to send you to sleep). At Check-In, **The Leading Edge** (...of design and innovation, that is) purvey such indispensables as a personal mini-shredder, a duck-shaped telephone that quacks instead of rings, a personal stereo in the guise of a washing machine or fridge.

ets, City boy flannels and blazers; at 65A, off-the-peg and made-to-measure suits cut on trad lines. No 1 Broxholme House, New King's Rd, is the shirt/accessories shop; No 6 is for the gentleman traveller – Phileas Fogg leather suitcases, razors, brushes, toiletries, and a barber shop.

HARRODS, Knightsbridge, SW1 ☎ (071) 730 1234
Where does one begin with the world's most famous store whose motto is 'Omnia, omnibus, ubique' (Everyone, everything, everywhere)? Acres of the right stuff – all the bright Brits (Galliano, Pollen, Oldfield), Lacroix, DKNY, Dior, Fendi, Krizia, de la Renta, Ferragamo, Lagerfeld, plus Byblos, Armani, Cerruti and Ballantyne for men. Also children's wear, presents, accessories, furniture, fabric, books, hi-fi, scent, make-up...just as the motto says. The only thing you won't find is furs – Harrods led the way in closing their fur department. If VICTOR EDELSTEIN shops at all, he shops at Harrods. STANLEY MARCUS calls in. NED SHERRIN is *a great Harrods user*. So is BRUCE OLDFIELD – for socks. *"Getting better and better..."* – BARRY HUMPHRIES. STEPHEN JONES likes their tie department – *"you know why? They've got everything, everything. If you want navy blue with purple spots, they've got it."* The food halls still earn accolades as the most beautiful and comprehensive ever. *"The prepared food section has*

everything from Indian to Japanese, Lebanese to Indonesian. I like the Mexican burritos and salsa. Beautifully prepared Japanese sushi" – MARIE HELVIN. NICO LADENIS, WOLFGANG PUCK, SHAKIRA CAINE, MARK MCCORMACK and BARBARA TAYLOR BRADFORD heap on praise.

HARVEY NICHOLS, 109-125 Knightsbridge, SW1 ☎ (071) 235 5000
The most directional store, fashion-wise, discriminately bought and well displayed (with the best windows in town). Oldfield, Cerruti, Complice, Dolce & Gabbana, Conran, Muir, Byblos, Gaultier, Krizia, Montana, Kors, Mizrahi, Paul Costelloe, Ozbek, Rykiel, Armani, Lauren, the exclusive on Calvin Klein... plus the new men's basement for fashion-conscious chaps. Great for costume jewellery, hosiery, scarves, cashmere stoles, gloves, bags – all the kit for the London sophisticate.

HARVIE & HUDSON, 77 Jermyn Street, SW1 ☎ (071) 930 3949
Menswear – shirts that cost an arm and a leg (over 100 for silk); own-design stripes and matching ties for City camouflage. ROSS BENSON gets his socks here.

HERBERT JOHNSON, 13 New Bond St, W1 ☎ (071) 408 1174
Traditional hatter to the Englishman – and woman. Jam-on trilbies and caps plus more feminine head-hugs. The rarely hatless GEORGE MELLY knows a good hat when he sees one; BARRY HUMPHRIES goes in for gangsterish guise. Accessories too.

H R HIGGINS, 79 Duke St, W1 ☎ (071) 629 3913
The best coffee suppliers in London, full of beans from around the world; roast-to-measure and mail-order services. Tea, too.

I CAMISA & SON, 61 Old Compton St, W1 ☎ (071) 437 4686
The best Italian deli in London – a ceiling full of salamis and Parma hams, cheeses, fresh pasta and seasonal sauces. *"I love to go in here, I love the smell of it. Dried foods and parmesan... beautiful smell"* – SIMON WILLIAMS.

JANE SMITH STRAW HATS, 131 St Philip St, SW8 ☎ (071) 627 2414
Not just straw picture hats, but all manner of natty headgear, using good blocks. Spot Jane's titfers on TV and the flicks.

JEROBOAMS, 24 Bute St, SW7 ☎ (071) 225 2232; 51 Elizabeth St, SW1 ☎ (071) 823 5624
Supreme cheese shop, specializing in unpasteurized French and English farmhouse cheeses (up to 120 varieties). Wines, too. Run by New Zealander Juliet Harbutt, Master of Cheese. *"Exceptionally good. The cheeses are kept in very good condition"* – JULIAN LLOYD WEBBER.

JIGSAW, 21 Long Acre, WC2 ☎ (071) 240 3855 and branches
Recent Young Contemporary Designer award winner. The pre-Whistles youth goes here for sporty co-ordinates, neat little jackets, skirts, linen blouses, etc. *"I only ever go to one shop and that's Jigsaw. All my friends go there, so we all wind up wearing the same clothes"* – CANDIDA CREWE.

JOHN LOBB BOOTMAKERS, 9 St James's St, SW1 ☎ (071) 930 3664
The best traditional shoes in the world, hand-made on the premises by wrinkly craftsmen. Royal bootmakers to Princes Charles and Philip and the Queen, not to mention JEFFREY ARCHER, DOUGLAS FAIRBANKS JR and LEO SCHOFIELD. LORD LICHFIELD and GIORGIO ARMANI add votes.

JOHNNY MOKE, 396 King's Rd, SW10 ☎ (071) 351 2232
Funny feet trot in for toe-wraps of ornamented velvet, duchesse satin, reptile skins, patent and plain leather, and strong-coloured fabrics for summer. Moke designs his own lasts and heel shapes, plus a collection for Arabella Pollen. Moke folk include the Duchess of York, Jean-Paul Gaultier and Romeo Gigli.

JOSEPH, 26 Sloane St, SW1 ☎ (071) 235 5470; 77 Fulham Rd, SW3, and branches
The Joseph Ettedgui designer lifestyle is spread evermore thickly across fashionable London, culminating in his 2 ultra-sleek flagship stores. So spacious and unrushed is the environment, so enticing the displays, that you want *every*thing. *"I love Joseph at Sloane St. It's huge, a really nice place to shop"* – ALISON DOODY. A flairful modern collection of well-proportioned suits, little dresses and separates for women and men. Joseph takes the cream of young British design (Galliano, Ozbek) and adds a dash of foreign blood (Montana, Alaïa) – nothing too mind-bending, all things that last. Joseph Tricot (16 Sloane St, etc) is his knitwear line – huge homespun jumpers, leggings, tube skirts, in greys and neutrals, plus a more colourful seasonal range. Joseph cleverly spans all ages and figures – if not pockets. TESSA DAHL, MARIE HELVIN and JOAN COLLINS have been Tricoted. Also a cluster of Josephs in South Molton St (Nos 13, 14, 16); and cheaper bend-and-stretch gear at 130 Draycott Ave, SW3; jeans and accessories at Le Joseph, 53 King's Rd, SW3. And don't forget the Joseph eateries – **Joe's Café** at 126 Draycott Ave; **L'Express** at 16 Sloane St.

KIRSTEN WOODWARD, Unit 26, Portobello Green Arcade, 281 Portobello Rd, W10 ☎ (081) 960 0090
Inspirational pie-in-the-sky millinery to order, plus a cheap 'n' cheery range for heads that want to walk out hatted. Bags too in such surreal guises as vases and urns. Still doing Lagerfeld's witty whimsies, she goes down a wow in Paris.

LA PICENA, 5 Walton St, SW3
☎ **(071) 584 6573**
A deli *"for absolutely the best freshly prepared Italian food in London"* – MARIE HELVIN. BRUCE OLDFIELD agrees.

LES 2 ZEBRES, 38 Tavistock St, WC2
☎ **(071) 836 2855**
"The best little clothing store for men in London. Wonderful shirts, sweaters, gorgeous suits... everything beautifully chosen. You feel you have a great choice because everything they stock is something you want" – ED VICTOR. *"Terrific for ties, beautiful ties. Very unusual things – they buy wonderful designs from Italy"* – BARRY HUMPHRIES.

LES SPECIALITES ST QUENTIN, 256 Brompton Rd, SW3 ☎ **(071) 225 1664**
French pâtisserie selling exquisite tartlets, flans and demi-baguettes stuffed with ripe brie and jambon blanc. *"It's brilliant and a good place for cheese"* – CANDIDA CREWE. Also the **Charcuterie St Quentin** at 215 Brompton Rd, *"for made-up dishes... they are wonderful at doing instant dinner-party meals"* – RICHARD COMPTON-MILLER.

♠ LIBERTY, Regent St, W1
☎ **(071) 734 1234**
One of the most delectable shops in town. An immense store best known for the wonderful wood-panelled, galleried hall of silk scarves (over 13 miles' worth sold daily at sale time) and dainty Liberty-print granny gifts (lavender bags, covered frames and books). Gorgeous leather goods, super-duper young designer jewellery, bags, tights, stockings. Sumptuous fabrics – their own printed tana lawn, handkerchief-fine linen, zingy Oriental silks, crewelwork. Fashion is excellent in places – cashmeres, coats, menswear, etc – but a little incoherent. Own-label goods are your best buy.

LOCK & CO, 6 St James's St, SW1
☎ **(071) 930 8874**
As Lobb's is to gent's feet, so Lock's is to their heads. Now doing titfers for ladies too – country style.

♠ MANOLO BLAHNIK, 49-51 Old Church St, SW3 ☎ **(071) 352 3863**
The modern authority on shoe design, the maestro of fancy footwork, Manolo is No 1 in the world. Once your feet have been cosseted by these whispers of lusciously concocted kid, suede, satin, brocade, velvet it's hard to consign them to mere shoes. Displayed in his Roman villa-esque shop, these oh-so-sexy shoes are the irresistible complement to the couture body. Tina Chow, Arianna Stassinopoulos, MARIE HELVIN, Bianca Jagger, the Duchess of York, Sarah Brightman, JOAN BURSTEIN, GIORGIO ARMANI, MARIUCCIA MANDELLI and Katharine Hamnett are among those who know the meaning of well-heeled.

MARINA KILLERY, W11 ☎ **(071) 727 3121**
Hats by appointment only. From elegant classics to innovative, experimental confections such as a strawberry pâtisserie. She appealed to the Duchess of York's humour with her Christmas pudding hat and a curled-up snoozing cat beret.

♠ MARKS & SPENCER, Marble Arch, 458 Oxford St, W1 ☎ **(071) 935 7954 and branches**
Where everyone shops for *some*thing, though they may be reluctant to admit it. Great for lingerie and underwear, jerseys, and men's classics. *"They have a new range of menswear that is like semi-underwear – T-shirts and so on. The seams on the inside are absolutely flat... the ribbed neck of the T-shirt looks as through it is constructed from one piece of fabric. Things like that are great"* – STEPHEN JONES. Another top sock stock for BRUCE OLDFIELD. *"Leads for precooked meals and the best smoked salmon, from Pinney's of Scotland. Marvellous fresh-squeezed mandarin juice and very good chilli – you can't make it as good at home"* – LORD LICHFIELD. Foodwise, LADY ELIZABETH ANSON, MAUREEN LIPMAN and JILLY COOPER are devoted. CANDIDA CREWE sums up: *"Obviously it's brilliant – completely bloody brilliant."*

McAFEE SHOES, 100 New Bond St, W1
☎ **(071) 629 7975; women at 35 Brompton Rd, SW3** ☎ **(071) 584 5439**
New-fashioned vintage classic shoes. Good leather brogues, Oxfords, monogrammed velvet slippers. *"I still think they are the best of the English shoemakers. What's nice is that they combine the traditional stuff with things that are a bit more quirky"* – ROBERT ELMS. BARRY HUMPHRIES has shoes made here, BRUCE OLDFIELD and ROSS BENSON slip on a ready-to-wear pair.

MIDAS, 27A Sloane Sq, SW1
☎ **(071) 730 7329; 22 Carnaby St, W1**
☎ **(071) 439 8134; Way In at Harrods**
The best source of fashion footwear from the young British and French designers – Carlos Suarez, Robert Clergerie, Martine Sitbon and Charles Kammer. Small, exclusive collections from each. Also own-label shoes, plus a rail or two of select high-fash clothing.

NEW & LINGWOOD, 53 Jermyn St, SW1
☎ **(071) 493 9621; 155 Fenchurch St, EC3**
☎ **(071) 929 1582**
Shirtmakers second only to Turnbull & Asser in quality, with perhaps the best collars of all. Also sleek, expensive, men's shoes in glorious woody and crème caramel tones (KENNETH LANE gets all his here). *"The best shoe store in London, with the best shoeshiner in town – he does a great job. In 'The Bonfire of the Vanities', poor Sherman McCoy is always talking about his New & Lingwood brogues and it brought an influx of Americans into N&L. I knew I wasn't the only American to wear them, but there are certainly*

more now" – ED VICTOR. By far the best velvet slippers with hand-embroidered crests, monograms, motifs. Branches in Eton and Cambridge as well, to see a man through life.

PANZER'S, 13-19 Circus Rd, St John's Wood, NW1 ☎ (071) 722 8162
"*Full of love for food, like a New York delicatessen. Half a dozen sorts of herring, a constant supply of bagels and a great selection of imported American food*" – LOYD GROSSMAN. "*Great smoked salmon. I always take it to America with me*" – JOAN BURSTEIN.

PARKES, 18 S Molton St, W1
☎ (071) 629 9195; Unit 13, Covent Garden, WC2 ☎ (071) 836 0497
Men's garb, all made in England – shirts and jumpers (coarse knits, Guernsey shapes), plus well-cut tweedy suits, jackets, and accessories.

PAUL SMITH, 41-44 Floral St, WC2
☎ (071) 379 7133; 23 Avery Row, WC2 ☎ (071) 493 1287; at Harrods
One of the top names in menswear with branches worldwide (they love him in Japan). The Paul Smith look is classic, updated with a shot of colour and pzazz. Zany print ties, well-cut suits and beautifully made shirts in snappy colours. No 41-42 is his mini designer dept store.

PAXTON & WHITFIELD, 93 Jermyn St, SW1 ☎ (071) 930 9892
200-year-old purveyors of choice cheeses, the cream of English and Continental varieties. "*The best cheese in town*" – BENNY ONG.

RIGBY & PELLER, 2 Hans Rd, SW3
☎ (071) 589 9293
Serious undergarments. These old stalwarts, corset-makers to the Queen, re-rose to fame during the fashion for a) the bustier and b) the exacting silhouette needed to fill an Alaïa in the right places. Made-to-measure boned satin corsets, bras in sizes you never knew existed.

SAINSBURY'S at branches countrywide
Leading the food field in different ways from

M&S, it's an excellent all-rounder (acres of top-quality produce, from vegetables and wines to a great deli and bakery), plus it's "*very good for breakfast – exotic fruits – and has a marvellous fresh wet fish counter*" – LORD LICHFIELD.

S J PHILLIPS, 139 New Bond St, W1
☎ (071) 629 6261
Probably the best antique jewellery shop in the world, stocked with fantastically important pieces. Only the rich and brave stride through the portals. Once inside, you are privy to a powerhouse of Renaissance treasures and exquisite 18C-20C jewels.

STEPHEN JONES, 29-31 Heddon St, W1
☎ (071) 734 9666
Eccentric and inventive as ever, a sense of irony, glamour and, of late, nature can be seen in his hats. He recently took the rock formations and natural forms of the American desert as his well-spring. Everyone loves his headpieces – the Princess of Wales, Azzedine Alaïa, MARGAUX HEMINGWAY. Collections for Enrico Coveri, Rifat Ozbek, Katharine Hamnett, Claude Montana and Hermès.

THOMAS PINK, 2 Donovan Court, Drayton Gdns, SW10 ☎ (071) 373 5795; 16 Cullum St, EC3; 35 Dover St, W1
Jermyn Street style only cheaper, with a nice Chelsea/City/Mayfair clientele that pops in for a poplin shirt (spottable by the pink cotton inset between the shirt-tails). In Bath and Edinburgh, and by mail order too.

TURNBULL & ASSER, 71 Jermyn St, SW1
☎ (071) 930 0502
Still voted the best bespoke shirts in London – if not the world. "*The best neck-ties, I guess (though their designs have become too strange for me lately) and still the best shirts*" – BOB PAYTON. JOHN GALLIANO lives in his T&A cream silk scarf. LORD LICHFIELD, STANLEY MARCUS, BARRY HUMPHRIES, ROSS BENSON, HELEN GURLEY BROWN, BRUCE OLDFIELD and DOUGLAS FAIRBANKS JR rate them highly. GEORGE MELLY goes for their hats.

Buzzz The best place to buy the **latest dance hit** is **Black Market Records**, 25 D'Arblay St, W1. You'll have to queue up with all the DJs...... For **jazz**, follow the hip, beret-clad jazz kids into **Rays Jazz Shop**, 180 Shaftesbury Ave, WC2, with **Mole Jazz**, 291 Pentonville Rd, N1, hot on their heels...... The **best haircut** for Bryan Ferry and ROBERT ELMS is at **Atlas Associates**, 4 Northington St, WC1 ☎ (071) 405 6011, a "*lovely, lovely place, very discreet, on the 4th floor of a 30s building. You have to ring the bell and they come down and get you in the lift*" – R ELMS...... While we're on the subject, for him, the ultimate **English shave** is from **George F Trumper**, 9 Curzon St, W1 ☎ (071) 499 1850, who also do a fine line in gentlemen's preparations, such as West Indian extract of lime after shave, eau de toilette, etc.............

**VAN PETERSON, 117A-119 Walton St,
SW3 ☎ (071) 589 2155**
Dead stylish jewellery: striking fashion pieces
and more serious wear – chunky bangles and
earrings of sterling silver or coppery gold,
sheeny pearls, and chic designs from the 20s and
30s. Also ashtrays, cigarette cases and cuff-links.

**WARTSKI, 14 Grafton Street, W1
☎ (071) 493 1141**
Fabulous Fabergé. Run by A Kenneth Snow-
man, grandson of the original Wartski and world
specialist on Fabergé, with Geoffrey Munn at his
right hand to advise on the best in 19C jewels.

**WHISTLES, 12 St Christopher's Place, W1
☎ (071) 487 4484 and branches**
An excellent young designer showcase with a
strong identity. Lucille Lewin buys not only safe
bets but also more avant-garde designs – Lolita
Lempicka, Georgina Godley, Myrène de
Prémonville and Junior Gaultier. Also her own
eclectic Whistles label.

**ZANZIS, 84 Heath St, Hampstead, NW3
☎ (071) 431 0639**
A pretty Georgian house converted into the
smartest shop in this neck of the woods, selling
razzle-dazzle ball gowns and slick daywear to
local Jewish American Princesses. Designers
include Pollen, Ozbek, Moschino, Antony Price,
Nicolas Georgiou, Eric Beamon for accessories
and Tommy Nutter and Conran for men.

Wine merchants

MICHAEL BROADBENT recommends **Berry Bros
& Rudd**, 8 St James's St, SW1 (071) 839 9033,
"for old-fashioned service and faultless service"
and **Winecellars**, 153-155 Wandsworth High St,
SW18 (081) 871 3979, *"for the best selection of
the new, superb and still-good-value Italian
wines."* For ED VICTOR, **John Armit**, 190
Kensington Park Rd, W11 ☎ (071) 727 6846 is
*"wonderful, a brilliant selection of wines. The
catalogue itself is a great art object"*; and for
SERENA FASS, *"terribly good, discerning, extremely good wine at reasonable prices. They provide a very good service and can get anything
you want to anybody you want within 24 hours."*
Haynes Hanson & Clark, 17 Lettice St, SW6
☎ (071) 736 7878, for fine affordable wines;
specialists in Bordeaux and burgundy. **La
Vigneronne**, 105 Old Brompton Rd, SW7 ☎
(071) 589 6113, run by Liz Berry, MW; a treasure
trove of fine old wines. **O W Loeb & Co**, 15
Jermyn St, SW1 ☎ (071) 734 5878 – top-quality
stuff, AUBERON WAUGH's choice for German and
Alsatian wine. **Corney & Barrow**, 118 Moor-
gate, EC2 ☎ (071) 638 3125 (and branches) –
expensive, but *the* place for clarets from St-
Emilion or Pomerol. *"A very nice wine shop. I
don't even drink but they have the most beautiful
black and gold labels"* – CANDIDA CREWE. **Les
Amis du Vin**, 51 Chiltern St, W1 ☎ (071) 487

3419 – the best source of California wines, a wine
club too. They own **The Winery**, 4 Clifton Rd,
W9 ☎ (071) 286 6475, which has an impressive
range of American and Australian wines. As for
the chains, **Oddbins** is adventurous but reliable
with a well-trained staff and *"terrific for champagnes"* – SERENA S, while she votes **Waitrose**
"the wine connoisseur's supermarket". **Majestic Wine Warehouses** are *"absolutely brilliant
in offering a huge variety of moderately priced
wines – interesting bottles from California,
Chile, Australia, New Zealand – but not serious
wines"* – AUBERON WAUGH. See also Rest of
England.

Theatre

**ALDWYCH, Aldwych, WC2
☎ (071) 836 6404**
*"I love it. I've had very few bad evenings in the
audience there and I had a very happy time there
as an actor"* – SIMON WILLIAMS. Other happy
actors include Dame Judi Dench.

**CRITERION, Piccadilly Circus, W1
☎ (071) 930 3216**
Resplendent from its recent restoration, this is
one of London's prettiest theatres, a bijou
Victorian affair built underground.

**DRURY LANE THEATRE ROYAL,
Catherine St, WC2 ☎ (071) 836 8108**
Perhaps the oldest theatre site in London – 4
theatres have existed there since Restoration
days. Now one of the best venues for musical
extravaganzas such as *Miss Saigon* – and for
ghosts (look out for the man in grey...). A
PATRICIA HODGE fave.

**HAYMARKET THEATRE ROYAL,
Haymarket, SW1 ☎ (071) 930 9832**
A gracious Regency building, it's one of the
oldest, most prestigious and beautiful theatres
in London. Superior plays (Shaw, Wilde, the best
contemporaries) and actors (Derek Jacobi,
Denholm Elliott, Alan Bates, Maggie Smith).
One of the most beautiful theatres in London for
JEFFREY ARCHER and VICTOR EDELSTEIN.

**HER MAJESTY'S THEATRE, Haymarket,
SW1 ☎ (071) 839 2244**
A prestigious theatre, still playing the almost
unstoppable *Phantom*, with daily queues as long
as those outside the Hard Rock Café.

**OPEN-AIR THEATRE, Regent's Park,
NW1 ☎ (071) 486 2431 end-May to mid-
Sept); ☎ (071) 935 5884 (all year)**
Pretty (and often pretty chilly) stage moulded
into the grassy garden, an evocative setting for
plays such as *A Midsummer Night's Dream*. The
New Shakespeare Company perform 2 Shakes-
peares each summer season plus one other trad
play and a children's play. Bring cushions and
blankets; buy mulled wine and hot food there.

"I love to go to the opera, but I first have to cross off everything I want to see in the theatre, which I just love. The theatre is my main idea of a real treat. They are the most wonderful buildings after churches "

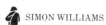 SIMON WILLIAMS

PALACE THEATRE, Shaftesbury Ave, W1
☎ (071) 434 0909
An opulent Victorian theatre, built as an opera house by Richard D'Oyly Carte. Now owned by Andrew Lloyd Webber's Really Useful Group, and sporting another long-runner, known in the trade as *Les Mis* or The Glums.

THE ROYAL COURT, Sloane Square, SW1
☎ (071) 730 1745
Off the main drag is this fine, often controversial, theatre which specializes in new writing. Many leading dramatists cut their teeth at this nucleus of creativity. Also the **Theatre Upstairs** ☎ (071) 730 2554 for more new works.

ROYAL NATIONAL THEATRE, South Bank, SE1 ☎ (071) 928 2252
Now under the patronage of HM The Queen (but still known as the National), this is still considered, in tandem with the RSC, the best large-scale theatre company in the world. A key part of the South Bank Centre, the complex has 3 theatres, the Olivier, Lyttelton and the baby Cottesloe. Always a buzz of excitement; close contact between audience and cast. *"I love it, they always have a good production on"* – ALISON DOODY.

WYNDHAM'S, Charing Cross Rd, WC2
☎ (071) 867 1116
One you can rely on for quality drama. Sir Charles Wyndham's theatre, with its gorgeous gilt swagged ceiling, is still run by the same family. One the actors – such as SIMON WILLIAMS – like. So does JOHN BROOKE-LITTLE.

Fringe theatre

A fuzzy term that can refer to the type of production (new/experimental), the location (miles away from the West End) or the budget (low). Venues vary from pubs to small theatres, but the calibre of production can be extremely high. The best are the barely-fringe-at-all **Young Vic**, 66 The Cut, SE1 ☎ (071) 928 6363 (tight productions, in-the-round, from *A Christmas Carol* to *Coriolanus*, Arthur Miller to Molière, with stars such as Helen Mirren, Timothy Dalton and Vanessa Redgrave) and **Riverside Studios**, Crisp Rd, Hammersmith,

W6 ☎ (081) 748 3354 (more alternative, more new writing, an annual black season, children's theatre). More fine fringe at: the **Man in the Moon**, 392 King's Rd, SW3 ☎ (071) 351 2876, whose illustrious patrons Ben Kingsley and Geraldine James have performed there; **Almeida Theatre**, Almeida St, N1 ☎ (071) 359 4404; **Hampstead Theatre**, Avenue Rd, Swiss Cottage, NW3 ☎ (071) 722 9301; **King's Head**, 115 Upper St, N1 ☎ (071) 226 1916; **Gate Notting Hill**, above Prince Albert pub, 11 Pembridge Rd, W11 ☎ (071) 229 0706; **Tricycle Theatre**, 269 Kilburn High Rd, NW6 ☎ (071) 328 1000; **Battersea Arts Centre**, Old Town Hall, Lavender Hill, SW11 ☎ (071) 223 2223.

OXFORD

The city of dreaming spires/aspiring dreams/ steaming mires, Oxford is synonymous with the oldest and most famous university in Britain (founded c. 1167). Of the glorious golden-stone colleges, see **Merton** (whose Mob Quad and library are the oldest in Oxford), the majestic **Christ Church** (Wren's Tom Tower), **New College** (enchanting cloisters and *"many things that are curious and beautiful, such as Epstein's Lazarus, which caused so much of a stir in the ante-chapel, and the magnificent hall"* – JOHN BROOKE-LITTLE); and **Magdalen** (cloisters, deer park and the landmark bell tower). Don't miss the 15C **Divinity School** in Broad St, the oldest lecture room in the city.

Art and museums

The **Museum of the History of Science** has the finest collection of early astrological, mathematical and optical instruments in the world. **Christ Church Picture Gallery** is rich in Italian Renaissance drawings (Lippi, Mantegna, Leonardo, Raphael) as well as Old Master paintings and portraits of eminent erstwhile members of college.

ASHMOLEAN MUSEUM, Beaumont St
☎ (0865) 27800
Superb collection of prints and drawings – some by Michelangelo and Raphael, Old Master paintings, Eastern art and decorative works, archaeology, and the Alfred Jewel, believed to have belonged to King Alfred (of burnt cakes notoriety).

Gardens

BOTANIC GARDENS, Rose Lane
☎ (0865) 276920
These peaceful riverside botanic gardens are thought to be the oldest in Britain. LORD LICHFIELD and JOHN BROOKE-LITTLE are both enchanted.

· REST OF ·
ENGLAND

—— Art and museums ——

TATE GALLERY LIVERPOOL, Albert Dock, Liverpool ☎ (051) 709 3223
The new dockside structure by Liverpudlian James Stirling houses 3 floors of exhibition space plus a warehouse gallery for contemporary works, space for performances, artists' studios and a restaurant. Frequently changing exhibitions of 20C works from the London Tate and other galleries.

—— Ballet ——

BIRMINGHAM ROYAL BALLET, Birmingham Hippodrome, Hurst St, Birmingham ☎ (021) 622 7486
The Royal Ballet of the north. An exciting move for the formerly London-based Sadler's Wells RB (the RB's second string), now set to expand and become established in their own right. Their first 2 years (1990-92) will see premières of newly created ballets and several full-length productions. Annual season back in the Sadler's Wells Theatre in London, plus regional visits.

—— Festivals ——

The best arts fests are: **Chichester** (July), which revolves around the cathedral; **Three Choirs Festival** (Aug), the oldest music festival in Britain, alternating between the cathedrals of Worcester, Gloucester and Hereford; the highly respected musical feast at **Aldeburgh**, Suffolk (June), founded by Benjamin Britten – *"they have kept the programme very interesting and lively. It is still a fascinating festival"* – JULIAN LLOYD WEBBER; **Lichfield**, Staffordshire (July), for choral and orchestral works and a good fringe; **Cheltenham** (July) for largely contemporary music; **Salisbury** (Sept), for music mainly at the cathedral, and theatre at the Playhouse; and **Brighton** (May), the largest in England. **Henley**'s 4-day festival (July), after the rowing regatta, is a rather different affair: it's Regatta meets May Ball meets Last Night of the Proms. Dining, cabaret, dancing, and concerts on a floating stage, culminating in fireworks over the river. Tickets: 27 Hart St, Henley ☎ (0491) 575751. *"I know it's mine, but truthfully I just love it"* – ROY ACKERMAN.

—— Historic buildings and gardens ——

Most country houses are open to the public from around Easter to the end of October. Do check opening hours. The **National Trust**, 36 Queen Anne's Gate, London SW1 ☎ (071) 222 9251, owns over 300 properties and gardens of historic interest or natural beauty. *"They make it a real pleasure to visit their houses, the guides are absolutely charming, the restaurants are always excellent and the shops are an aggro-free place to do your gift-buying"* – SERENA FASS. **English Heritage**, Fortress House, 23 Savile Row, W1 ☎ (071) 973 3000, is a similar but government-sponsored body that has saved some 350 monuments, and restored them *"with loving care and attention. I think they are jolly impressive these days"* – SF. Join both and get their handbooks and free entry to their properties.

BLENHEIM PALACE, Woodstock, Oxfordshire ☎ (0993) 811325
Architect and playwright Sir John Vanbrugh's magnificent baroque palace and grounds, a money-no-object commission in 1705 to reward the Duke of Marlborough for battle victories.

> **"***English cathedrals and their shops and restaurants are absolutely smashing. Gloucester is wonderfully organized, so is Durham – one of the finest cathedrals in the country. Norwich and Salisbury are terribly well done. Visitors wouldn't know they could have a really good lunch in Gloucester Cathedral***"**
>
> SERENA FASS

BURGHLEY HOUSE, Stamford, Lincolnshire ☎ (0780) 52451
The largest Elizabethan house in existence in the UK, built by William Cecil, set in Capability Brown deer parks.

CASTLE HOWARD, York, N Yorkshire ☎ (065384) 333
Sir John Vanbrugh's heroic building starred as Brideshead in the TV series of Waugh's novel. Still owned by the Howard family, whose ancestral portraits – by Gainsborough, Romney and Reynolds – cover the walls. Fine sculpture collection, tapestries and furniture.

CHARLESTON FARM HOUSE, Nr Firle, Lewes, E Sussex ☎ (032183) 265
No stately, but the cottagey former home of Charles and Vanessa Bell, decorated from head to toe by Vanessa, Duncan Grant and other pals and relations. No fireplace, screen, table, door or wall is left untouched by the free Bloomsbury hand and muted paint palette.

CHASTLETON, Nr Moreton-in-Marsh, Gloucestershire ☎ (060874) 355
"A country house that isn't – instead of being famous, it's just romantic. Simply an old, rather run-down house that is very charming, with lots of atmosphere. It's right in the middle of over-grown gardens. I always take people there and they love it" – JOHN BROOKE-LITTLE.

CHATSWORTH, Bakewell, Derbyshire ☎ (024688) 2204
One of the grandest and most important houses in England, sensational for the architecture (late 17C), the Capability Brown grounds, and the interiors (including many fine Old Master drawings and paintings). Seat of the Duke and Duchess of Devonshire. JOHN BROOKE-LITTLE, LORD GOWRIE and LORD MONTAGU OF BEAULIEU swell with admiration.

HAREWOOD HOUSE, Harewood, Leeds, W Yorkshire ☎ (0532) 886225
Standing in one of Capability's largest and most beautiful parks is this marvellous 18C house. Interiors by Robert Adam, with Chippendale furniture, Chinese and Sèvres porcelain, Italian and English Old Masters. Also a bird garden, with a tropical house containing rare species.

LEEDS CASTLE, Maidstone, Kent ☎ (0622) 765400
Surely the most picturesque castle in the land, surrounded by a moat and gorgeous baize-green hills. Built in 1119 (but dating back to 857), it's also one of the most ancient and well preserved.

LONGLEAT HOUSE, Warminster, Wiltshire ☎ (09853) 551
Longleat, seat of the Marquis of Bath, is probably best known for its lions – part of the 11,000-acre grounds forms a spectacular safari park (☎ 328) with around 50 lions, tigers and other wild animals. Capability Brown's landscaping includes a chain of lakes. The house, built in 1580, is one of the earliest to show the influence of the Italian Renaissance.

NEWBY HALL, Nr Ripon, Yorkshire ☎ (0423) 322583
Renowned for its outstanding gardens. For Yorkshire lass BARBARA TAYLOR BRADFORD, it's *"a place I love . . . very beautiful."*

PENSHURST PLACE, Penshurst, Tonbridge, Kent ☎ (0892) 870307
Viscount de L'Isle's country house has, apart from one of the finest medieval halls in the country (the house dates back to 1340), a magnificent 10-acre Tudor walled garden, subdivided by yew hedges.

ROUSHAM PARK, Rousham, Steeple Aston, Oxfordshire ☎ (0869) 47100
The 1635 house is set in William Kent gardens: *"They are not show gardens, but they are lovely, with little streams and waterfalls, peacocks galore, dovecots and a nice church. I love going there"* – JOHN BROOKE-LITTLE.

SHUGBOROUGH, Milford, Nr Stafford ☎ (0889) 881388
Lord Lichfield's 18C Palladian mansion is all the more remarkable for its Grade I gardens, boasting perhaps the greatest collection of neo-classical monuments and follies in the country, with some fine examples by James 'Athenian' Stuart.

SISSINGHURST CASTLE GARDENS, Cranbrook, Kent ☎ (0580) 712850
A great – and ultra-popular – English garden, created by Vita Sackville-West in the 1930s, designed and planted with inspiration. Her famous White Garden has white pansies, white peonies, white irises, white lilies. . . . The house is open, too.

STOURHEAD HOUSE, Stourton, Warminster, Wiltshire ☎ (0747) 840348
A Palladian country house with Arcadian classical grounds: rolling parkland landscaped by Henry Hoare II, flowering shrubs, follies, grottoes, temples and a lake. *"Absolutely breath-taking in the spring when the camellias and rhododendrons are all out, and in autumn when the leaves are changing colour"* – SERENA FASS.

—————— *Hotels* ——————

🏠 CHEWTON GLEN, New Milton, Hampshire ☎ (0425) 275341
In the New Forest, it's reckoned by many, including BOB PAYTON, to be: *"The most professionally run and slickest country-house hotel."* *"The best country hotel"* – LEN EVANS. *"Absolutely fabulous"* – ROSEMARY SEXTON. Luxurious in a stylized way, with attentive service and exemplary cuisine that has earned toques, turrets and rosettes galore.

CLIVEDEN, Taplow, Berkshire ☎ (06286) 68561
Former seat of the Astors and scene of the Profumo/Keeler scandal, this famous Thames-side stately home is now a flourishing 25-room hotel. Liveried footmen, valets and maids unpack your luggage, press your frock, and bow or curtsey. Décor is eclectic and grand. The new Pavilion, styled after Barry's classical mansion, houses an indoor pool, Jacuzzi, saunas, gym, massage and beauty therapy room. *"John Sinclair runs the hotel almost as though it were his home. Very few people can carry that off. Consistently good food"* – TERRY HOLMES.

THE FEATHERS HOTEL, Market St, Woodstock, Oxfordshire ☎ (0993) 812291
Small hotel near Blenheim Palace, occupying several 17C terraced town houses. *"Extremely good and very English. Country house-style décor. Food is cosmopolitan and always good –*

The English Country-House Hotel

The English country-house hotel *was* a peculiarly English phenomenon. Now you see them everywhere from New England to New South Wales – *including* the cities. But the genuine article is the only one for BOB PAYTON: *"I don't think anyone does country-house hotels like the English. In America they have country inns, but they don't compare. What the English did better than anyone else was perfect their country lifestyle."* Which is why he set up this side of the Atlantic – see **Stapleford Park**. **Chewton Glen** is recognized by the co-ho cognoscenti as the spearhead. *"There's been an enormous explosion of country-house hotels, but Chewton Glen was first and, in most people's view, they and* **Ston Easton** *still lead the pack"* – LORD LICHFIELD; *"Martin Skan was well ahead of the field and I think still is in many respects,"* agrees GILES SHEPARD. Apart from those listed, you can't lick **Lucknam Park**, Colerne, Wiltshire ☎ (0225) 742777 (a 1720 house, with leisure spa, *"newly opened and very nice"* – ROY ACKERMAN); **Summer Lodge**, Evershot, Dorset ☎ (093583) 424 (a HILARY RUBINSTEIN recommendation); **The Manor**, Chadlington, Oxfordshire ☎ (0608) 76711 (strongly tipped by HILARY RUBINSTEIN); or the Duke and Duchess of Devonshire's **Cavendish Hotel**, Baslow, Derbyshire ☎ (024688) 2311.

---

the maître-chef Sonia Kenny does this superb toffee pudding... it is definitely delicious. Run in a friendly way" – JOHN BROOKE-LITTLE. "I had a wonderful Christmas holiday there. The food was excellent and we had this horn band serenade us" – MAUREEN LIPMAN. More praise from GILES SHEPARD: "I prefer those country hotels which are part of town life."

🛉 GIDLEIGH PARK, Chagford, Devon
☎ (06473) 2367

Alone in a tree-lined valley, this small 14-roomer is *"the nicest country-house hotel in England, the one I want to go back to more than any place else. Here's a tip: 2 couples should book the Pavilion, a 2-bedroom thatched cottage – it's really nice. Gidleigh is as good as they get"* – BOB PAYTON. Renowned for Shaun Hill's brilliant modern British cuisine with Oriental tinges. Innovative handling of the freshest of ingredients, from pasta with fresh white truffles to ragout of wild mushrooms and baby vegetables. Wonderful breads and cream teas too. *"Outstanding for its wine list – a huge section of New World wines that is absolutely fascinating, especially as you can get many old vintages there which are almost unobtainable elsewhere"* – SIMON LOFTUS. Foodwise, a vote from MATTHEW FORT; ALAN CROMPTON-BATT's joint No 2 (with L'Ortolan) out of London.

GRAVETYE MANOR, Nr East Grinstead, W Sussex ☎ (0342) 810567

A 16C manor, *"rather swish, wonderfully organized and in a beautiful situation. Peter Herbert really understands every detail of the rooms, the gardens, everything. Probably the best hotel just outside London, to use as a base"* – RICHARD COMPTON-MILLER. *"I always love it"* – ROSEMARY SEXTON. JULIAN LLOYD WEBBER thinks: *"To stay is very comfortable, and very convenient for people who come in to Gatwick."* But as to its highly reputed restaurant, he found it *"a little daunting. Not a place to relax in"*.

GREAT FOSTERS, Egham, Surrey
☎ (0784) 433822

"Exciting because it's so old. It really is Elizabethan built in the shape of an E. Beautifully kept up, and the gardens are gorgeous. There is a stream running through with the biggest fish I've ever seen – they're supposed to be fancy goldfish but they're monsters" – ELIZABETH LAMBERT ORTIZ.

HAMBLETON HALL, Hambleton, Oakham, Rutland, Leicestershire
☎ (0572) 56991

Overlooking Rutland Water, this Victorian hunting lodge is still the perfect place for outdoor pursuits. Fine fresh fish and game cooked by acclaimed chef Brian Baker, savoured by BARBARA CARTLAND; accompanying wines from an *"outstanding list, very interesting and strongly personal"* – SIMON LOFTUS.

HARTWELL HOUSE, Oxford Rd, Aylesbury, Buckinghamshire
☎ (0296) 747444

Making up the trio of Historic House Hotels, this is the latest object of Richard Broyd and his team's faithful restorations. *"Architecturally and staff-wise, it really is a very spectacular country hotel. The feeling is very welcoming"* – TERRY HOLMES. HILARY RUBINSTEIN concurs.

🛉 HUNSTRETE HOUSE, Hunstrete, Chelwood, Nr Bristol, Avon ☎ (07618) 578

Thea and John Dupays's hotel epitomizes the English country house – Georgian, antique-filled, with walled garden, croquet lawn, tennis court and heated swimming pool. Small enough for you to feel like a private guest, and warmly approved by ROY ACKERMAN, JEFFREY ARCHER and GILES SHEPARD.

🐾 MIDDLETHORPE HALL,
Bishopthorpe, York, Yorkshire
☎ **(0904) 641241**
This elegant William and Mary house overlooking York racecourse is still a front runner in the country-house hotel stakes. "*A lovely house. They do it absolutely beautifully, as does their sister, Bodysgallen*" – SERENA FASS. "*Very special,*" agree TERRY HOLMES, ROY ACKERMAN and GILES SHEPARD.

MILLER HOWE, Rayrigg Rd,
Windermere, Cumbria ☎ **(09662) 5236**
John Tovey's lakeland hotel has many loyal guests such as RICHARD COMPTON-MILLER, who enjoys "*wonderful views overlooking Lake Windermere and the mountains*". JULIAN LLOYD WEBBER loves the cuisine: "*It holds its place absolutely. There is no choice, but it's a beautifully balanced menu and I felt able to eat the whole lot.*" However, others find the much-trumpeted 5-course dinner experience slightly overwhelming.

SHARROW BAY, Lake Ullswater, Penrith,
Cumbria ☎ **(07684) 86301**
The grande dame of country-house hotels, still much loved by guests for her big-hearted generosity. Furnishings look a little dated (brown dralon sofas...) compared with dashingly done-up younger hotels, but king-sized feasts and a fabulous lakeside setting win the day for HILARY RUBINSTEIN, TESSA DAHL, BARBARA CARTLAND and ROY ACKERMAN.

🐾 STAPLEFORD PARK, Nr Melton
Mowbray, Leicestershire ☎ **(057284) 522**
Carved on this lovely 16C/17C stately is the legend: 'And Bob Payton Esq Did His Bit, Anno Domini 1988.' "*I set out to make it the best of its kind – the best showers, the biggest bathtubs, the best beds, the easiest-to-use TV remote controls,*

the finest stables in the country. I didn't want to let you guys down. People really appreciate all that." They certainly do. "*A lot of people think he is a hustling type of American and actually he and Wendy are delightful hosts, the rooms are wonderful, the food is simple and unpretentious*" – EDWARD CARTER. "*He has done it as only Bob Payton could, completely over the top! It's very, very good and works well*" – ROY ACKERMAN. Nominated by Bob himself for the best Kosher hot dogs and joint-best crème brûlée with Langan's, the 23-room hotel seems more like a house-party. TERRY HOLMES sums up: "*It is both luxurious and relaxing.... He keeps asking, 'are you enjoying yourselves?' I think the answer is probably 'yes'*".

🐾 STON EASTON PARK, Chewton
Mendip, Bath, Avon ☎ **(076121) 631**
A grand-scale Palladian stately boasting a magnificent saloon with original white stucco and carved wood decoration, and a rare Georgian print room. "*I thoroughly recommend it*" – SERENA FASS. The leader of the country pack, along with Chewton Glen, according to LORD LICHFIELD – "*the yardstick of how a country-house hotel should be*". "*Has made great strides forward foodwise*" – ROY ACKERMAN.

THORNBURY CASTLE, Thornbury,
Bristol ☎ **(0454) 412647**
The only Tudor-castle hotel in the land, with its own vineyard and walled garden. JEFFREY ARCHER is a fan, while ROY ACKERMAN is still impressed by the food – all British produce.

——————— *Music* ———————

Opera North in Leeds is an independent, international opera company of high repute, ranking alongside Scottish Opera and a close second to the Royal Opera and ENO.

🐾 GLYNDEBOURNE FESTIVAL
OPERA, Lewes, E Sussex ☎ **(0273) 812321**
Top of the ops and No 1 on the social-cultural calendar in Britain, in an Elizabethan country

🐾 **Buzzz** The Jacobean **Hunters Lodge**, High St, Broadway, Oxfordshire ☎ (0386) 853247, provided JULIAN LLOYD WEBBER with "*one of the best meals I've ever had – traditional English food, Regency syllabub which was absolutely delicious, highly calorific*"🐾...... Invitingly warm, dark and shabby, the real **McCoy's**, The Tontine, Staddlebridge, N Yorks ☎ (060982) 671, is a high-rating restaurant/bistro (plus half a dozen bedrooms) for divine and bounteous dining🐾...... Wanna **live like a Lord?** The Earl and Countess of Normanton open the doors of their stately **Somerley**, Ringwood, Hampshire BH24 3PL ☎ (0425) 473621, to groups of 16 at a time – eg shooting parties, or for their courses on fine arts (spring/autumn) or gardening (summer). "*They do it absolutely beautifully, in the most lovely house*" – SERENA FASS... 🐾

Miles Kington on The Great British Hype

"It is reasonable to say that food in Britain advertised as 'The Great British something' should be avoided as being the worst in the world. The British sausage is sometimes advertised as The Great British Sausage. It is actually full of bread or rusk and nearly devoid of meat. The British mushroom has been advertised as The Great British Mushroom. It is actually a nearly flavourless button mushroom. The British must be the only nation in the world who do not realize there is more than one kind of mushroom. Fish and chips are sometimes trumpeted as The Great British Dish, the British breakfast is often touted as The Great British Breakfast...but you get the idea. Just avoid anything The or Great or British and you will be safe."

estate setting. High standard of opera – Sir Peter Hall is artistic director, the London Philharmonic is the resident orchestra, top artists are creamed from all over the world. 5 or 6 operas are presented from end-May to mid-Aug. Old hands arrive well before the 5pm-ish start and bag a hot spot in the garden for their interval picnic (rugs are de rigueur, tables are out). The faint-hearted can dine indoors – book dinner (2 restaurants) along with the tickets. Ah yes, tickets...the only way to guarantee one of the 830 seats is to be or know a member of the Festival Society (though the public can try – get a form in March; booking starts Mar/Apr). Praise is unanimous: "Marvellous, of course – it hasn't altered" – ANDREW LLOYD WEBBER. "Pretty spectacular" – ROY ACKERMAN. And from JAMES BURKE: "You can't beat Glyndebourne. I like the way they are putting on 20C opera more and more. We had cows, rabbits, ducks and Stravinsky."

PAVILION OPERA, Thorpe Tilney Hall, Nr Lincoln, Lincolnshire ☎ (05267) 231
The creation of Freddie Stockdale, whose troupe tours the drawing rooms of English country houses, performing 18C and 19C operas in the round (eg *La Traviata* at Blenheim). The room itself is the scenery; you are a fly on the wall watching a real drama. "The best opera experience you can have in England. We hired them for my 50th birthday – amazing" – ED VICTOR. However, Our Man in Opera sniffs: "It's purely social".

——— Restaurants ———

CARVED ANGEL, 2 South Embankment, Dartmouth, Devon ☎ (08043) 2465
In a lovely position by the estuary, this expensive little restaurant is legendary for the best of British ingredients prepared with Mediterranean flair. Garlicky provençale fish soup, Dart salmon with rhubarb, aubergine salad with sour cream and herbs. Strong wine list. "My ideal meal is boiled beef and carrots cooked by Joyce Molyneux" – KEITH FLOYD.

COCO'S, 18 Fountain St, Manchester ☎ (061) 832 6176
"A very good Italian restaurant with a marvellous atmosphere. If ever I'm in Manchester, I'm at Coco's almost permanently. Very good Roman dishes, good veal..." – BARRY HUMPHRIES.

🕯 LE MANOIR AUX QUAT' SAISONS, Church Rd, Great Milton, Oxfordshire ☎ (08446) 8881
This 15C manor keeps its status as one of the best in the world, with the brilliant Raymond Blanc at the helm (as Robert Carrier has said, Raymond can do no wrong). His invention is startling – from the little layer-cake of shredded potato and confit de canard to his baby cup and saucer made of chocolate and topped with ice cream and sabayon. "Blanc is probably the best cook in England" – PRUE LEITH. "Nico is a great cook but Blanc is a great chef, the best in Britain. His table, his setting, his linen, his china, his cutlery, all of that, is the finest in Britain" – BOB PAYTON. "Still supreme" – ROY ACKERMAN. "The only one you need to know about – he's miles ahead of the others" – DREW SMITH. ANDREW LLOYD WEBBER, MATTHEW FORT, LADY ELIZABETH ANSON and ELIZABETH LAMBERT ORTIZ love it. Le Manoir is also a small hotel, so that punters can make a weekend of it.

🕯 L'ORTOLAN, The Old Vicarage, Church Lane, Shinfield, Berkshire ☎ (0734) 883783
One of the most exquisite culinary experiences to be had in Britain, from the amuse-gueules through to the petits fours. John Burton-Race creates breathtakingly complex dishes of finely tuned flavour. "It lives up to everything it is recommended to be" – ANDREW LLOYD WEBBER. One of the top 3 in Britain for RAYMOND BLANC, joint No 2 outside London for ALAN CROMPTON-BATT. "Absolutely stunning food" – MATTHEW FORT. "A pretty nice place" – STIRLING MOSS. "Le Manoir and L'Ortolan just get better and better. And in this world we're not supposed to have perfection.... What I like is that Raymond is so generous in his praise of Burton-Race and they like each other and it's wonderful. I keep going

to *L'Ortolan – I'm so dotty about the place, I'll go broke. They'd grace any nation, those two"* – ELIZABETH LAMBERT-ORTIZ.

THE OLD WOOLHOUSE, Northleach, Gloucestershire ☎ (04516) 366
A minuscule restaurant (seats 18) run by Jacques and Jenny Astic. *"Excellent, I still think it is one of the best – the food is brilliant, he's very French and a talented cook"* – ROY ACKERMAN.

SEAFOOD RESTAURANT, Riverside, Padstow, Cornwall ☎ (0841) 532485
Richard Stein's seaside restaurant is light and modern to match his eclectic cuisine. Super-fresh fish and seafood is served as tempura, ravioli or simply beautifully grilled with herbs. Packed out night after night. LEN EVANS is a fan.

WATERSIDE INN, Ferry Rd, Bray, Berkshire ☎ (0628) 20691
Michel Roux's famous production number is one of the most expensive restaurants in Britain.

Pet Pubs

If an Englishman's home is his castle, his second home is *The* Castle, down the road, where they serve a great pint. SIMON WILLIAMS, like many of his compatriots, says: *"I'm a great pub man. I like proper pubs with shove ha'penny boards and people playing cribbage...."* Our (male, natch) contributors round up their country faves: **The Stirrup Cup** at Bisley, Gloucestershire, *"known locally as The Stomach Pump. Superb reputation – it's one of the best pubs I've been to in my entire life. Good, good food"* – LEO COOPER. For KEITH FLOYD, it's **Maltsters Arms**, Bow Creek, Tuckenhay, Devon (his pet beer is Murphy's stout, made in Cork). JEFFREY ARCHER checks out **Chequers**, Fowlmere, and **The Three Horseshoes**, Maddingley, both in Cambridgeshire. ROSS BENSON likes **The Mayfly**, Wherwell, Hampshire, *"right on the River Test. Decent ales and good food. Also the* **King William IV**, *Hailey, Oxfordshire, a very nice pub with beer from the wood... really olde-worlde."* JULIAN LLOYD WEBBER sighs: *"If I had to name one country pub, there's* **The Plough** *at Ford, Gloucestershire. They have a local beer from a small brewery called Donnington. Marvellous home cooking and a wonderful atmosphere."*

Food and clientele continue to be on the nouvelle side. As ROY ACKERMAN notes, it's *"really unsung at the moment but is of a tremendous standard"*.

WELL HOUSE, St Keyne, Liskeard, Cornwall ☎ (0579) 42001
Small hotel whose interior is as contemporary as the cuisine. David Pope (ex-Gidleigh Park) cooks seasonal game, salads and vegetables and delicious home-made rosemary and walnut bread. Exemplary wine list.

Shopping

MINOLA SMOKED PRODUCTS, Kencot Hill Farmhouse, Filkins, Lechlade, Gloucestershire ☎ (036786) 391
Oak-smoked wild Scottish salmon with an almost buttery consistency. Smoke pots made from whole English oak logs give the salmon its delicate smoky flavour. Other smoked foods too.

THE TOFFEE SHOP, 7 Brunswick Rd, Penrith, Cumbria ☎ (0768) 62008
The best fudge in England, still savoured by LORD LICHFIELD. Chocolate, vanilla, mint or choc-mint fudge, treacle or butter toffee. *"Worth a detour. My wife has a monthly standing order for their vanilla fudge, which is irresistible"* – MICHAEL BROADBENT. Mail-order too.

WELLS STORES, Bull Corner, Reading Rd, Streatley-on-Thames, Berkshire ☎ (0491) 872367
Hugh Rance (son of the famous Patrick of the famous finely tuned nose) continues to purvey a brilliant and expansive range of superb cheeses. Also the best (French) olive oil.

Wine merchants

Adnams, The Crown, High St, Southwold, Suffolk ☎ (0502) 724222, has a wide range of interesting wines from the Old and New Worlds, selected by Simon Loftus. Mail-order service. The other half of the East Anglia wine mafia is **Lay & Wheeler**, 6 Culver St W, Colchester, Essex ☎ (0206) 67261, for probably the greatest all-round list according to SERENA SUTCLIFFE. **Yapp Brothers**, The Old Brewery, Mere, Wiltshire ☎ (0747) 860423, are Rhône and Loire specialists. **Averys of Bristol**, 7 Park St, Bristol, Avon ☎ (0272) 214141 is good for old burgundies (where lover of heavy-style burgundies AUBERON WAUGH would go for his tipple); also Spanish, German and Australian wines.

Theatre

A quick trip round the provincials reveals the best to be: **Royal Shakespeare Theatre, Stratford-upon-Avon** ☎ (0789) 295623 (under

Ferrari for Hire

Diana Ross rented a Range Rover, Twiggy a Jaguar XJS, Meg Ryan a BMW 730, Mick Jagger a Porsche 928. Avis and Hertz eat your hertz out. If you want more than a runaround or a family hatchback, go to **Guy Salmon**, 7-23, Bryanston St, W1 ☎ (071) 408 1255. Think of a car, any car, and you can rent it here. A Porsche 911 will knock you back around £280 a day, a Ferrari Testarossa £1,115, but what the hell... they deliver the car to your door or chauffeur-drive you to it, and, being New Age-aware, they'll even fit baby seats. Other rent-a-Salmon-status-symbol sorts are Bros, Whitney Houston, George Michael and Dustin Hoffman. Alternatively, if, like Audrey Hepburn, Sir John Mills, Martina Navratilova and Stephen Fry, you would rather be driven, go for the swanky chauffeur service with driver in full livery.

the new directorship of Adrian Noble) – absolute tops, HQ of the RSC and the best place to take in the Bard. The **Theatre Royal, Bristol**, whose resident company, the Bristol Old Vic, can be relied upon·for quality theatre, old and modern. The **Citizens Theatre, Glasgow** – the 'Cits': lots of bold, European theatre. The **Leicester Haymarket** – highly reputed for classical works and musicals. **Crucible Theatre, Sheffield** – adventurous open-stage theatre, great musicals. **Chichester Festival Theatre** – established works, respected rep company (but murderous seats for Mr Longshanks); SIMON WILLIAMS views it from the other side: *"Lovely, with a nice open stage. Have a picnic before going."* For him, the **Royal Exchange Theatre, Manchester** is *"one of my favourites – it really works in the round"*. Indeed, it's one of the most exciting modern theatres in the country, set incongruously in the enormous Victorian cotton exchange.

— Tours and properties —

COUNTRY HOMES AND CASTLES, 118 Cromwell Rd, London SW7 ☎ (071) 370 4445 Private stays in some of the finest stately homes and castles of Great Britain, plus organization of unlimited extras – limos, private planes, golf, ballooning, racing (horses or Go-Karts).

THE LANDMARK TRUST, Shottesbrooke, Maidenhead, Berkshire ☎ (062882) 5925 For *the* smart short British break. Architectural conservation is the Trust's objective, and their

properties range from the sublime to the ridiculous – from a medieval Scottish castle to a stone pineapple for 4; a railway station to a Gothic fowl house (part of a model farm); the island of Lundy (21 properties) to a Victorian water tower (where you sleep beneath a cast-iron tank).

WORTHY INTERNATIONAL TRAVEL, The Power House, Alpha Place, London SW3 ☎ (01) 351 3373 Susie Worthy has a wealth of British aristocratic homes and country estates at her fingertips, where you can stay as a personal guest. Guided heritage tours, too, and she'll take the mystery and misery out of getting in to Ascot et al.

SCOTLAND

— Art and museums —

BURRELL COLLECTION, 2060 Pollokshaws Rd, Pollok Country Park, Glasgow ☎ (041) 649 7151 Ship-owner William Burrell amassed over 800 items – antiquities, Oriental art, stained glass, Dutch and French paintings, and his famous decorative arts collection of tapestries, silver and ceramics. *"The most beautiful gallery"* – MAUREEN LIPMAN. *"Absolutely superb. Everything you can think of is there, all beautifully arranged"* – CAROL WRIGHT. SERENA FASS agrees: *"You don't get indigestion – a dream to walk around."*

NATIONAL GALLERIES OF SCOTLAND, The Mound, Edinburgh ☎ (031) 556 8921 3 galleries – the recently restored **National** (fine paintings by the great masters – Raphael, Titian, Rembrandt, Van Dyck, Constable et al, and works by Scottish artists); the **Portrait Gallery**, Queen St (enter to the magnificent neo-Gothic hall; see great Scots on canvas, sculpture, photos), and the **Gallery of Modern Art**, Belford Rd (most major European and American 20C artists – Matisse to Moore, Picasso to Paolozzi). At the National, don't miss Raeburn's *Rev Robert Walker skating on Duddingston Loch* and Sargent's *Lady Agnew of Lochnaw*. A pleasing and balanced collection enjoyed by JEFFREY ARCHER. All galleries have frequent, acclaimed exhibitions.

— Festivals —

EDINBURGH INTERNATIONAL FESTIVAL, 21 Market St ☎ (031) 225 5756 *The* all-encompassing arts festival, held in August. Opera, theatre, dance, music and theatre draw in performers from far and wide – Houston, Seville, Krakow, Moscow, Tokyo.... Running concurrently are the famous **Fringe**, 180 High St ☎ (031) 226 5257 (endless low-budge shows of a serious/comic/loony/musical nature by some 500 individuals and companies from all over the world), the **Assembly Rooms**, 50 George St ☎ (031) 226 5992 (sharp shows that bridge Fringe and Fest), the distinguished **Film Festival** (*"an identity of its own – it's the best British festival"* – IAIN JOHNSTONE), **TV Festival**, **Jazz Festival** and to remind you where you are – the **Military Tattoo**. *"An amazing all-purpose festival . . . the range is enormous"* – DEREK MALCOLM. Your feet won't touch the ground. However, despite general acclaim and merriment by festival-goers, the quality end of the programme is still not as good as it could be. Hark at the LLOYD WEBBER bros: *"Musically it is pretty much off the boil. It is basically what happens to be passing through Britain at the time"* – JULIAN LW; *"It's worth going for the city, isn't it?"* – ANDREW LW.

Hotels

ALTNAHARRIE INN, Ullapool, Highland ☎ (085483) 230
A tiny inn by Loch Broom (slightly less tiny after recent alterations), run by Fred and Gunn Brown. With only 7 bedrooms, you are all treated as house-guests, with no choice of menu – but it's *all* delicious. LADY MACDONALD OF MACDONALD and HILARY RUBINSTEIN recommend.

GREYWALLS, Muirfield, Gullane, Lothian ☎ (0620) 842144
A lovely retreat not too far from Edinburgh, set in a privately owned Lutyens house. Cosy wood-panelled library with plumped-up sofas, wall-to-wall collectors' editions of books and the proverbial roaring log fire. Golf at Muirfield and windswept walks to the sea.

♠ INVERLOCHY CASTLE, Fort William, Highland ☎ (0397) 2177
Still No 1 in Scotland, set in gorgeous rhododendron-filled grounds by Loch Lochy, in the shadow of Ben Nevis. It found favour with Queen Victoria, and continues to do so with ROY ACKERMAN, LADY MACDONALD OF MACDONALD, BARBARA CARTLAND and STIRLING MOSS: *"We're very partial to it – very nice."* *"Greta Hobbs does a great job. Very superior hotel food rather than great food"* – LORD LICHFIELD.

ISLE OF ERISKA HOTEL, Ledaig, Connel, Strathclyde ☎ (063172) 371
Robin and Sheena Buchanan-Smith's hotel lies on a tiny but wild private island near Oban. *"It's quirky and eccentric. You certainly don't go for grande luxe, but you do go for home cooking and good malt whisky and a bit of Highland feel without pipers being marched in and people being forced into kilts. The Buchanan-Smiths really know about country living. I examined their vegetable garden and that convinced me"* – LORD LICHFIELD.

KNOCKINAAM LODGE HOTEL, Portpatrick, Dumfries & Galloway ☎ (077681) 471
"I gave it my best country-house hotel award. It's easy, comfy, there is a no-choice menu by a terrific young chef who is ex-Gavroche. The kind of place where you don't have to worry where to put your drink down and you can put your feet on the sofas. It's right on a deserted beach looking across the Irish Sea, so hidden away that Churchill used it as a secret meeting place with Eisenhower during the War" – EDWARD CARTER.

KINLOCH LODGE, Sleat, Isle of Skye, Highland ☎ (04713) 214
Quiet, comfy little hotel run by Lord and LADY MACDONALD OF MACDONALD. Wonderful seasonal food cooked by Lady M, and wild, craggy scenes in which to walk it off.

♠ ONE DEVONSHIRE GARDENS, 1 Devonshire Gdns, Glasgow ☎ (041) 339 2001
A chic conversion of a Victorian house, now *"a wonderful hotel, keeping all the original stained glass, with four-posters and all that. Really rather special"* – CAROL WRIGHT. *"A butler greets you at the door and the staff are dressed like Edwardian maids. The service is excellent and the food is superb"* – PATRICIA HODGE.

Music

Scottish Opera is one to be reckoned with under musical director John Mauceri, late of the New York Met.

🐓 **Buzzz** Dine and sleep your way around Scotland in the wake of LADY MACDONALD OF MACDONALD who's sussed out the best Scots hospitality: chez Nick and Alison Parsons at **Polmaily House Hotel**, Drumnadrochit ☎ (04562) 343, near Loch Ness; the 18C **Ardsheal House**, Kentallen of Appin ☎ (063174) 227, run by Americans Bob and Jane Taylor; and at Eric and Betty Allen's old ferry inn, **Airds Hotel**, Port Appin ☎ (063173) 236, also voted *"the best itty bitty country inn"* by BOB PAYTON🐓......Back in the capital, the **Caledonian Hotel**, Princes St ☎ (0620) 842144, is still *"the best in Edinburgh. Although it is huge it manages to be personal"* – LADY M OF M..................................... 🐓

USHER HALL, Lothian Rd, Edinburgh
☎ **(031) 228 1155**
"Still an exceptionally good hall. It's one of the few that you feel influences your performance. They were going to pull it down and it deserves every support" – JULIAN LLOYD WEBBER.

Restaurants

See also Hotels.

CHAMPANY INN, Champany Corner, Linlithgow, Lothian ☎ **(050683) 4532**
The best steak and beef in Britain. Clive Davidson upholds an entire philosophy of meat – cut, breed, thickness and cooking. Also wonderful salmon and lobster and the very best Stilton. Simplicity rules.

🐓 **THE PEAT INN, Peat Inn, Cupar, Fife**
☎ **(033484) 206**
This whitewashed inn is the sum of the cross-roads village. Chef-owner David Wilson serves real Scots food fashioned seductively à la française – 6 courses of it at dinner (4 at lunch). Scallops or lobster poached in Barsac, venison liver, wild duck with blueberries, grouse, pigeon and superb fish. An enviable wine list. *"It's fantastic"* – LADY MACDONALD OF MACDONALD. *"Really on form at the moment"* – ROY ACKERMAN. Also scores a hit with BARBARA CARTLAND.

LA POTINIERE, Main St, Gullane, Lothian
☎ **(0620) 843214**
Grapple to get a booking at David and Hilary Brown's restaurant (dinner on Saturday only, one sitting for each meal and a set, no-choice, menu). It's worth it – sensational cuisine is concocted with care and unswerving intuition using best Scottish produce with Oriental accents. Interesting wine list, compiled with a collector's fanaticism; amazingly good value. SIMON HOPKINSON was knocked out.

Shopping

JENNERS, 48 Princes St, Edinburgh
☎ **(031) 725 2442**
The Harrods of Edinburgh. Marvellous food halls displaying Speyside smoked salmon, smoked trout from Mull, 70 different honeys, 68 cheeses, 112 teas, and bread baked on the premises.

PINNEY'S OF SCOTLAND, Brydekirk, Annan, Dumfries & Galloway ☎ **(05763) 401**
Superb salmon go through a subtle smoking process and are finely carved by hand. No colouring or preservatives, *naturally*. Suppliers to all the best shops – Harrods, Fortnum's, Marks & Spencer – and a mail-order service. LORD LICHFIELD is impressed. Also a fishy line in gravadlax, smoked trout, mackerel, eel, fish pâté....

WALES

Hotels

🐓 **BODYSGALLEN HALL, Llandudno, Gwynedd** ☎ **(0492) 84466**
Remains the best in Wales, an imposing 17C grey stone mansion in the hills above Conway. Grounds, including a rare knot garden, contain a sprinkling of self-contained cottages for shy guests. Sumptuous bedrooms, bathrooms with fine brass fittings and wraparound towels. *"A wonderful hotel...the walks around there are quite something"* – TESSA DAHL. Support from ROY ACKERMAN, SERENA FASS and GILES SHEPARD.

Music

BRECON JAZZ FESTIVAL, Watton Chambers, Brecon, Powys ☎ **(0874) 5557**
Variously described as 'New Orleans beneath the Beacons' and 'The Jazzers' Glyndebourne', this fizzy little August festival is in Humphrey Lyttelton's European top 10 and gets a warm recommendation from GEORGE MELLY.

> **❝Powys Castle has the most wonderful grounds. It's built on a hill and has terraces and formal parterres and a 'wilderness'. Absolutely magic. There is a tunnel of immaculately clipped hedge that you walk through❞**
>
> DUGGIE FIELDS

🐓 **WELSH NATIONAL OPERA, John St, Cardiff** ☎ **(0222) 464666**
Arguably the best in Britain. Heartfelt, exciting, sometimes shoestring productions. Tremendous team spirit and a great Welsh chorus. Regional tours.

Restaurants

WALNUT TREE INN, Llandewi Skirrid, Nr Abergavenny, Gwent ☎ **(0873) 2797**
French-trained Italian chef-owner Franco Taruschio has made this bustly little pub a gourmet's country retreat. Local produce is imbued with Italian and Eastern highlights. Home-made pasta, superb seafood and fish, bresaola, Thai pork and wild game, washed down with a rare Italian or French wine. *"I like it very much"* – GEORGE MELLY. So do SIMON HOPKINSON and ALASTAIR LITTLE, whose chefs' eyes fix on the white Piedmontese truffles, olive oil, wind-dried beef and gravadlax.

Shopping

VIN SULLIVAN, 11 High St, Abergavenny, Gwent ☎ (0873) 2331
A special fishmonger, gamery and grocer (very fine fruit and veg) that supplies fish to many top-class restaurants in Britain. Isle of Man scallops, baby crayfish, Kenyan and Turkish écrevisse, Cornish and Canadian lobster, wild Wye salmon, and live sea urchins (collected at their peak, during a full moon).

CANADA

MONTREAL

Bars and cafés

LUX, 5220 St Laurent Blvd, H2T 151 ☎ (514) 271 9272
At 3am, any francophone worth his salt is sipping steamy coffee, tucking into a delicious breakfast, and flipping through the latest European mags at this 24-hour bookstore-cum-café-bar. *"In Montreal everything happens after midnight. It's a wonderful concept that no other city in the world has been able to replicate. You can read, eat, and dance till dawn"* – TYLER BRULE. MICHEL ROBICHAUD pops in for lunch.

Clubs

LE BELMONT, 4483 St Laurent Blvd, H2W 2Z8 ☎ (514) 845 8443
If you're 'in', in fashion, and in Montreal, you'll be boogieing down at Le Belmont.

L'ESPRIT, 1234 Mountain St, H3G 1Z1 ☎ (514) 397 1711
Still a top dance club, based in a century-old building with cathedral ceilings and multi-levels. 1,200 groovers crowd in and bop to international high-energy hits.

LOLA'S PARADISE, 3604 St Laurent Blvd, H2X 2V4 ☎ (514) 282 9944
A late-night restaurant-bar-café-nightclub of the plush velvet boudoir variety. Piano, jazz, blues and classical music. People-watching *starts* at 3am.

METROPOLIS CLUB, 59 St Catherine St E, H2X 3P5 ☎ (514) 288 5559
The largest dance club in Canada – space for 2,000 – set in an old art deco cinema. 6 bars, high-tech lighting, zappy disco music.

Fashion designers

JEAN CLAUDE POITRAS, 4200 St Laurent Blvd, Suite 800, H2W 2R2 ☎ (514) 844 0885
A designer of faultless taste, who calls the tune in Montreal. He dresses Mila Mulroney. *"Still very much an important part of Canadian fashion"* – BONNIE BROOKS.

MICHEL ROBICHAUD, 5253 Avenue du Parc, #525, H2V 4P2 ☎ (514) 273 1567
Wonderful classy clothes that mean business – every fashionable Montreal madame has a Robichaud. Also cosmetics and a new kid's line.

SERGE ET REAL, 1359 Ave Greene, Westmount, H3Z 2A5 ☎ (514) 933 3600
Serge Senéchal and Réal Bastien do custom-made clothes for wealthy women – Canadian couture. Réal started out as a theatrical costumier, now he brings a sense of theatre to chi-chi Montreal. A small prêt-à-porter line too.

Film

MONTREAL WORLD FILM FESTIVAL, 1455 blvd de Maisonneuve Est, H3G 1M8 ☎ (514) 933 9699
A festival of increasing importance, held annually in Sept, just before Toronto. Over 200 movies are screened. *"Fiercely competitive for films. Being a French city means there is perhaps a better nexus with Cannes"* – IAIN JOHNSTONE. Certainly the celebs pile in – Clint Eastwood, Jane Fonda, Sergio Leone.

Hotels

HOTEL DE LA MONTAGNE, 1430 de la Montagne St, H3G 1Z5 ☎ (514) 288 5656
Intimate old French hotel in the Arts district. Its 5-star restaurant **Lutitia** is a gourmet's dream.

LE QUATRE SAISONS, 1050 Sherbrooke St W, H3A 2R6 ☎ (514) 284 1110
Typical Four Seasons attentiveness in an elegant hotel with one of Montreal's great dining rooms, **Le Restaurant**. *"My favourite – not too big, very warm, beautiful, and I always feel welcome"* – MICHEL ROBICHAUD.

❝Four Seasons is the best hotel group. Many hotels claim they offer a high level of personal service, but the Four Seasons takes it to incredible levels❞

 ROBERT RAMSAY

🦑 **RITZ-CARLTON, 1228 Sherbrooke St W, H3G 1H6 ☎ (514) 842 4212**
European-style turn-of-the-century hotel near all the best boutiques and galleries. *"It is a very warm hotel, with class, a good location and quality of service. You are addressed by name and made to feel welcome"* – LISE WATIER. MADELEINE POULIN concurs: *"I adore it because it is small and the personal attention is warm and cordial. I love the bar, and* **Bar Maritime***,"* which is also tops for MICHEL ROBICHAUD – *"excellent fish – a bit of a tradition for my wife and myself".* The **Garden** is BONNIE BROOKS'S No 1 in Montreal (*"The place is exquisite and so is the food"*).

Music

FESTIVAL DE JAZZ DE MONTREAL, 355 St Catherine St W, Room 301, H3B 1A5 ☎ (514) 871 1881
For 10 days in June/July, all varieties of international jazz musicians swarm in to perform in clubs and on the street. *"I like it because it's out on the streets. There is a lot of respect from the crowd"* – MICHEL ROBICHAUD.

MONTREAL SYMPHONY ORCHESTRA, 85 St Catherine St W, Suite 900, H2X 3P4 ☎ (514) 842 3402
Housed in the beautiful Place des Arts, the Symphony is the best in Canada, led by world-renowned conductor Charles Dutoit.

Restaurants

BEAVER CLUB, Queen Elizabeth Hotel, 900 Blvd Rene Levesque W, H3B 4A5 ☎ (514) 861 3511
A political and business who's who can be seen power-lunching here. *"I very much like it at lunchtime. A place where business people meet for the impeccable service, excellent food and its businesslike atmosphere"* – LISE WATIER.

🦑 **LA MAREE, 404 Place Jacques Cartier, H2Y 3B2 ☎ (514) 861 8126**
Brilliant, old-established seafood restaurant that BONNIE BROOKS enjoys.

LE PARIS RESTAURANT, 1812 St Catherine W, H3H 1M1 ☎ (514) 927 4898
An old favourite, in business some 40 years – menu, owner and clientele have remained the same. *"A restaurant que j'adore. It is the most authentic restaurant in Montreal, where clients are truly loyal. There is nothing else like it"* – MADELEINE POULIN.

🦑 **LES HALLES, 1450 Crescent St, H3G 2B6 ☎ (514) 844 2328**
A Montreal institution, très français, and a hive of activity at night. Chef Crevoisier Dominique has been here from the beginning (some 16 years

ago), turning out delicious gourmet cuisine to the well heeled. *"I still love it. I go there every time I'm in the city"* – ROBERT RAMSAY.

LES MIGNARDISES, 2035 Rue St Denis, H2X 3K8 ☎ (514) 842 1151
The service is immaculate, the food spectacular and the linen luxurious. Bring beaucoup d'argent. Co-owner Jean Pierre Monnet is an alumnus of Les Halles's kitchens.

MILOS RESTAURANT, 5357 Ave du Parc, H2V 4G9 ☎ (514) 272 3522
A great Greek restaurant. *"My favourite for dinner – for quality food, service, freshness – the way the food is prepared and seasoned, and a very relaxed atmosphere. It's my restaurant!"* – LISE WATIER.

🦑 **PREGO, 5142 St Laurent Blvd, H2T 1RB ☎ (514) 271 3234**
A superb Italian restaurant. Zebra-striped chairs, beautifully set dining tables, jump-to service and imaginative pastas. *"One of my favourites. The cuisine is 'belle' and the restaurant has beautiful art deco décor. When things are going well and I want them to go better, I go to Prego"* – MICHEL ROBICHAUD.

RESTAURANT LALOUX, 250 Ave des Pins E, H2W 1B3 ☎ (514) 287 9127
"Even better than ever. The food is cooked with extreme care, décor is very simple and clean. Laloux can be compared to any of the great restaurants in Paris" – MADELEINE POULIN.

Shopping

In what were once the stately homes of rich colonials on **Sherbrooke Street**, high fashion jostles with smart art galleries and fancy antique joints.

GREGE, 2130 Crescent St, H3G 2B8 ☎ (514) 843 6228
Nicole and Patrick Loth stock the more avant-garde designers – Yamamoto, Comme des Garçons, Dolce & Gabbana, Kenzo, selling to a star-studded clientele, including Tina Turner.

HENRY BIRKS & SONS, 1240 Phillips Square, H3B 3H4 ☎ (514) 397 2511
A jewellery store run by the Birks family for more than 100 years. A wonderful Canadian tradition of fine jewellery and glamorous gifts.

HOLT RENFREW, 1300 Sherbrooke St, H3G 1P7 ☎ (514) 842 5111
The most beautiful shop in Canada. Upmarket, classy fashion store with a crisp, wised-up designer selection. Young French designers like Myrène de Prémonville are here alongside well-established names – Ferré, Lagerfeld, Byblos, Montana, Donna Karan, Armani (MADELEINE POULIN is sold on his boutique here), plus

Canadians Alfred Sung and Jean Claude Poitras. *"Still the only store to shop in. The service and selection are fantastic and always on the leading edge of fashion"* – TYLER BRULE.

LES COURS MONT ROYAL, 1455 rue Peel, H3A 1X6 ☎ (514) 842 7777
Swish new shopping complex in a beautifully renovated building, where a huge chandelier dominates the main lobby. Boutiques include Parachute, Bijan and the smart foodie paradise Hédiard. Also a see-and-be-seen Harry's Bar.

LES CREATEURS, 1444 Sherbrooke St W, H3G 1K4 ☎ (514) 284 2102
A characterful wonderland of wit, tops for the younger Parisian and Japanese lights – Jean-Paul Gaultier, Azzedine Alaïa, Junko Koshino, Jean Charles de Castelbajac.

LILY SIMON, 1320 Beaubian St E, H2G 1K8 ☎ (514) 273 1771
For chic traditionalists it's *the* place to shop, for all the die-for designers that spell established elegance – Givenchy, Scherrer, Rykiel, Biagiotti.

OGILVY'S, 1307 St Catherine St W, H3G 1P7 ☎ (514) 842 7711
The grande dame of department stores, still upholding the tradition of a bagpiper wailing through its halls at noon. Exclusive boutiques for Valentino, Joan & David, Escada and Perry Ellis. *"I go from floor to floor with great pleasure. I like the variety of choice, and the décor is wonderful"* – MADELEINE POULIN.

L'UOMO, 1452 Peel St, H3R 1S8 ☎ (514) 844 1008
Terrific menswear, lots of Italian imports – Basile, Byblos, Armani, Gaultier, Valentino, Cerruti, Gigli – the whole gang.

TORONTO

—— *Ballet* ——

🐦 **NATIONAL BALLET OF CANADA, 157 King St E, M5C 1G9 ☎ (416) 362 1041**
A fine company under director Reid Anderson, who brings the Royal Ballet tradition to Canada (via his days as principal at Stuttgart under Cranko). Dancers such as Karen Kain and Evelyn Hart match the best in the world. At Christmas it's a great Toronto tradition to turn out for *The Nutcracker*.

—— *Bars and cafés* ——

AMSTERDAM Brasserie & Brewpub, 133 John St, M5B 2E4 ☎ (416) 595 8201
Bright, airy, stand-up bar in a loft-style warehouse with industrial windows, beams and sky-

❝Toronto is a very fine metropolitan, cosmopolitan city – and a fine theatrical city ❞

 DOUGLAS FAIRBANKS JR

lights. Packed with young execs and *faces* (go early to avoid the queue). Home-brewed special ale and lager; great brasserie food.

BELLAIR CAFE, 100 Cumberland St, Yorkville, M5R 1A6 ☎ (416) 964 2222
Chic restaurant-bar, haunt of the beautiful people – models and pop stars inside, Ferraris and Lamborghinis double-parked outside.

—— *Clubs* ——

BAMBOO, 312 Queen St W, M5V 2A2 ☎ (416) 593 5771
Wild reggae club owned by Toronto socialite Patty Habib. Bags of atmos, not too big, an outdoor terrace and spicy Thai food. *"Still a happening place. The entrance is half the fun – you go down this interesting alleyway.... A real great time"* – STEVE PODBORSKI.

DIAMOND CLUB, 410 Sherbourne St, M4X 1K2 ☎ (416) 927 0910
Part of the Toronto establishment. Huge dance floor with new music. Androgynous coat-check/cigarette girl/guy.

LA CAGE, 2nd Fl, 279 Yonge St, M5P 1P4 ☎ (416) 364 5200
Zany cabaret/dinner club with drag shows, impersonations of some of the brassier broads of showbiz, plus impromptu performances.

THE SQUEEZE CLUB, 817 Queen St W, M6J 1G1 ☎ (416) 365 9020
Cool pool club – the cue-barging craze continues to sweep North America. *"Students, execs and artsy types play pool in a very urban, smoky, dark interior. Calming atmosphere, lazy and loud music"* – TYLER BRULE. Matt Dillon and a handful of Rolling Stones pitched up recently.

STILIFE, 217 Richmond St W, M5V 1W2 ☎ (416) 593 6116
Entered on Duncan St, this dance club is a hangout for models, pop stars and other fash 'n' flash types. Rod Stewart and George Michael checked it out when they hit town.

—— *Fashion designers* ——

ALFRED SUNG, 55 Avenue Rd, M5V 2T3 ☎ (416) 968 8688
The best Canadian designer for easy, go-ahead, sexy separates in pared-away style, and for sensational tailored suits. There's an echo of

Armani, with a loosened sense of cut and a good eye for colour. Beautiful cocktail numbers, accessories and jewellery.

BENT BOYS, 110 Spadina Ave, M5V 2K4 ☎ (416) 368 7409
Young avant-garde design team comprising two *girls*. Trendy, wild, sporty wear. *"I love them – they're really fun"* – BONNIE BROOKS.

COMRAGS, 410 Adelaide St W, M5V 158 ☎ (416) 360 0056
Trendy, bendy, sporty gear of the Gaultier kind. *"On the leading edge, quite innovative and upscale"* – BONNIE BROOKS.

MAGGY REEVES, 108 Cumberland St, M5R 1A6 ☎ (416) 921 9697
An institution for Canadian couture. Romantic, swish tailoring, sophisticated evening and cocktail wear in rich fabrics. Society clientele. KAREN KAIN deems her clothes *"works of art"*.

ROGER EDWARDS, 150 Bloor St W, M5S 2X9 ☎ (416) 923 9333
The finest leather creations in North America. Eddie Murphy, Linda Evans and other movie stars have been donning his leatherwear for years. It even scored a hit with the Duchess of York. *"One of these fabulous Canadian designers who has more of a following outside Canada. The place for the perfect leather jacket"* – TYLER BRULE.

WAYNE CLARK, Suite 500A, 49 Spadina Ave, M5V 2J1 ☎ (416) 591 6991
The best designer for magnificent high-society get-ups – seriously sexy lavishments of lace and velvet. A distinct look, feminine and alluring. He's the man for BONNIE BROOKS.

WINSTON KONG, 158 Cumberland St, M5R 1A8 ☎ (416) 924 8837
The master of haute couture, which he's been producing for haute Canada for over 20 years. Special occasion outfits with a sense of the theatrical; queenly gala and wedding numbers.

Film

TORONTO FESTIVAL OF FESTIVALS, Suite 205, 69 Yorkville Ave, M4Y 2TI ☎ (416) 364 5924
10 days in Sept animated with documentaries, silent movies, international films. *"Of all the festivals at this time, it's probably the best of the bunch. Extremely well run...a combination of the best films from Europe, an original category of films from Central and Latin America, and a degree of commercial popularity. Film festivals are full of freeloaders and Toronto can accommodate them better than most!"* – IAIN JOHNSTONE. Not to mention *more* of them than most – some 300,000 attend, including many stars who flock in for premières and face-the-

Reach for the Sky

Toronto is one of the most technologically go-ahead cities in the world. It was here that **Imax** (360° screen) originated. It boasts the world's highest free-standing structure, **CN Tower**, which shoots up to 1,814 ft. The **Toronto Skydome**, 300 The Esplanade West ☎ (416) 341 3663, is the only stadium in North America with a retractable roof (which closes when the clouds open). This is the 50,000-seat home to the Toronto Blue Jays baseball team, Toronto Argonauts football team and host to rock concerts, festivals and spectacles such as *Aida*, staged with live elephants. *"Everyone is so blown away by this – it's top-dollar, a great addition to the skyline"* – TYLER BRULE. Get versed in the art of science at **The Ontario Science Centre**, 770 Don Mills Rd ☎ (416) 429 0193, *"a great hands-on museum where you get to work a lot of the exhibits. It really is extraordinary"* – TONY ASPLER. Interactive displays demonstrate the use of science in everything from food and communications to transport and space.

audience sessions: Warren Beatty, Jane Fonda, Richard Gere, Bruce Willis, Julie Christie, Paul Newman and Joanne Woodward.

Hotels

♣ FOUR SEASONS, 21 Avenue Rd, Yorkville, M5R 2GI ☎ (416) 964 0411
Arguably the best hotel in Canada. Chic and smooth-running, with ever-smiling staff. *"The best. Everything is first class. It's very opulent, and well run. An excellent cellar, too"* – TONY ASPLER. *"Still one of the best in Toronto – as they are worldwide"* – BONNIE BROOKS. Indoor and outdoor swimming pools, health-giving breakfasts, and the exquisite renovated **Truffles**, for award-winning 5-star French cuisine.

L'HOTEL, 225 Front St W, M5V 2X3 ☎ (416) 597 1400
"I stayed for a whole month. Lovely views over Lake Ontario, pretty suites and fabulous staff. The pool with its small outdoor terrace is one of the cleanest I have encountered" – ELISE PASCOE.

SUTTON PLACE HOTEL, 955 Bay St, M5S 2A2 ☎ (416) 924 9221
Swanky home to visiting stars – Kathleen Turner, Robert Redford, Ted Danson, Tom

Canada's Best Hotels

1	FOUR SEASONS · Toronto
2	RITZ-CARLTON · Montreal
3	PAN PACIFIC HOTEL · Vancouver
4	CHATEAU WHISTLER · Whistler
5	BANFF SPRINGS HOTEL · Banff
6	CHATEAU LAKE LOUISE · Lake Louise

Selleck.... Frequent visitors get their own bathrobe with embroidered initials. The restaurant **Sanssouci** boasts Canada's only Master Sommelier. *"For terrific breakfasts and a great bar"* – ELISE PASCOE.

WINDSOR ARMS HOTEL, 22 St Thomas St, M5S 2B9 ☎ (416) 979 2341
Charming old-fashioned old favourite, with a loyal clientele. The **Courtyard Café** plays host to power lunches. *"The place to be seen in Toronto and parade yourself. It's where all the film stars go"* – TONY ASPLER. So does MICHEL ROBICHAUD. The **Twenty-Two** bar in the lobby is the happening place for pre-prandials.

Restaurants

See also Hotels.

CENTRO, 2472 Yonge St, M4P 2H5 ☎ (416) 483 2211
Large, lofty Californian-style restaurant with warm décor and lotsa noise. *"The owner has* captured all the trends and packaged them all in to a great restaurant. Perfect Italian cuisine with wonderful presentation"* – ROBERT RAMSAY. *"The hottest restaurant with an Italian/Californian concept"* – TONY ASPLER.

CIBO RISTORANTE, 1055 Yonge St, M4W 2L2 ☎ (416) 921 2166
Buzzy Italian restaurant – always busy and always delicious. Open kitchens (more of the Californian concept) mean you can see what the chef's doing to your pasta (whatever he does, he gets it dead right).

FENTON'S, 2 Gloucester St, M4Y 1L5 ☎ (416) 961 8485
One of the prettiest restaurants in town, based in an old converted house. The garden room, a glass-roofed conservatory, is filled with fresh flowers and frondy trees all year and fairy-lit at night. In the drawing room, with its crackling fire in winter, you sit on small Chesterfield sofas rather than straight-backed chairs. The basement is slightly cheaper, but with the same soigné service and cuisine. *"An old favourite of mine. It is always wonderful. The food is consistent and the surroundings are beautiful"* – ROBERT RAMSAY. *"Still a great place, the presentation is wonderful"* – ROSEMARY SEXTON.

IL POSTO, York Square, 148 Yorkville Ave, M4W 1L2 ☎ (416) 968 0469
Arguably the best and most imaginative Italian food in Toronto – dishes such as sautéed fresh sardines stuffed with parmesan, spinach, eggs, garlic and parsley. Clubby atmosphere, a favourite of PETER USTINOV.

LE BISTINGO, 349 Queen St W, M5V 2A4 ☎ (416) 598 3490
One of the best and most fashionable eateries. It's sooo cool to dine here, on country French

Buzzz Tipple tattle: Next door to a working distillery is the **Seagram Museum**, 57 Erb St W, Waterloo, Ontario ☎ (519) 885 1857, a historic insight into the wine and spirits industry. *"One of the great museums which is very little sung. It is a cathedral to booze. A converted old whisky warehouse, most spectacular: you look up and see floors and floors of barrels"* – TONY ASPLER ...... Follow man through the ages at the **Museum of Men and Civilization**, 100 Laurier St, Hull, Quebec ☎ (819) 994 0840 – exhibits from Roman, Chinese and Inuit Indian cultures ...... An eye for an eye: in Vancouver, **Eyes on Burrard**, 3 Bentall Centre Mall ☎ (604) 688 9521, and **Eyes on Twelfth**, 1493 W 12th Ave ☎ (604) 732 8812, have the best Euro-style specs – Armani, Missoni, Gaultier and Alain Manoukian ...... Best **theatre festivals**: punters flock to the countryside outside Toronto for the **Stratford Shakespearean Festival**, PO Box 520, Stratford ☎ (416) 363 4471 (not just Shakespeare but Chekhov, Brecht, new plays... May-Nov), and **Shaw Festival**, PO Box 774, Niagara-on-the-Lake ☎ (416) 361 1544 (for Shaw and other 20C classics... Apr-Oct)...

Canada's Best Restaurants

1	LOTUS · Toronto
2	UMBERTO IL GIARDINO · Vancouver
3	LE BISTINGO · Toronto
4	LES HALLES · Montreal
5	THE LANDING · Vancouver

cuisine, amid slick, modern design. *"A real Toronto tradition. Always fabulous"* – TYLER BRULE. ROBERT RAMSAY is a fan.

LOTUS, 96 Tecumseth St, M6J 2H1
☎ (416) 368 7620
The best in Canada. Tiny, beautifully elegant dining room where every dish is a masterpiece. The French/Californian/Asian designer cuisine appeals to a suave designer set. *"If I have clients from out of town I always take them here. Definitely the best, all of the food is beautiful, a wonderful creation"* – BONNIE BROOKS.

MASANIELLO, 647 College St, M6G 1B7
☎ (416) 533 7046
An authentic trattoria in the heart of little Italy. They dish up healthy portions of country Italian cooking at its finest. A simple seafood risotto or pasta dish or mozzarella salad with fresh basil is perfection.

PRONTO, 692 Mount Pleasant Ave, M4S 2N3 ☎ (416) 486 1111
Hip hang-out for northern Italian cuisine. *"Always wonderful. They also have a great bar to sit at while you wait. It's always hopping and always crowded"* – ROSEMARY SEXTON. *"My favourite Toronto restaurant. A long way to go if staying downtown, but well worth the trek. Top-class food with affable owners and staff. Good fun too"* – ELISE PASCOE.

SCARAMOUCHE, 1 Benvenuto Place, M4V 2L1 ☎ (416) 961 8011
Elegant, expensive French restaurant where locals like KAREN KAIN go when they have something to celebrate. *"Very good French food and memorable overall"* – TONY ASPLER. Also a more affordable pasta bar – warm, cosy, good lighting, good nosh.

SENATOR, 249 Victoria St, M5B 1T8
☎ (416) 364 7517
A jizzed-up diner with one of the best California wine selections in the city and an unassailable bread pudding. Everyone from the nearby Pantages Theatre piles in after shows. TONY ASPLER admires Senator's cellar.

—— Shopping ——

Yorkville, with **Hazelton Lanes, Avenue Road** and **Cumberland Street**, is the chi-chi pseudo-villagey smart area to shop, eat, drink and promenade in your furs. Nearby, glossy big-time **Bloor Street** boasts the best stores (including the first free-standing Genny boutique at No 110 and Chanel boutique at No 131). **Queen Street** is the grooviest drag in town – street vendors selling artistic jewellery and bags, wild Bohemian boutiques, great cafés (*"the best place to cruise down in the evening"* – STEVE PODBORSKI). Miles more shopping underground.

ALAN CHERRY, 711 Yonge St, M4Y 2B4
☎ (416) 967 1115
From designer furs to couture ensembles to designer wedding gowns (all discerning brides head here). Elaborate organza, lace, sequinned creations. The most beautiful window displays.

CHEZ CATHERINE, 55 Avenue Rd, M5R 3L2 ☎ (416) 967 5666
Owner Catherine Hill is a walking advertisement for the gorgeous day and evening gowns stocked in her boutique. Top international designer stuff (some of it exclusive to her in Toronto) – Basile, Ferré, Carolyne Roehm, Bill Blass, Valentino.

CLASSICA UOMO, 150 Bloor St W, M5S 2X9 ☎ (416) 961 0683
European chic for men. From Armani to Byblos, *"the very best Italian clothes, and now wonderful Belgian designers"* – TYLER BRULE.

CLUB MONACO, 403 Queen St W, M5V 2A5
☎ (416) 979 5633, and branches nationwide
Alfred Sung's cult, preppy, sportswear line – the famous khaki chinos and jodhpurs, jeans, bomber jackets, cotton and wool jumpers and socks. No teeny can be without a Club Monaco label.

CREEDS, 45 Bloor St W, M4W 1A4
☎ (416) 923 1000
A Canadian institution, family-owned for 3 generations. Creeds started as a furrier and still do marvellous plushy furs that fans flock from all over North America for. Designer-wise they have slinks to go with the minks: Claude Montana, Sonia Rykiel, exclusive boutiques for Ungaro, Krizia and Joan & David shoes; Scene International for trendy young designers such as Marithe and François Girbaud.

DAVIDS, 66 Bloor St W, M5S 1L9
☎ (416) 920 1000
A step in the right direction: a large shop with the best, most elegant shoes in Canada, for men and women. Bags and accessories too.

FAB, 274 Queen St W, M5V 2A1
☎ (416) 979 7813
Trendy shop for the best jeans in town – C17 and Chevignon are all the rage from gay Paree.

Also Girbaud, Maggie Callaghan and other young designers. Covetable cowboy boots, too.

FETOUN'S, 97 Scollard St, M5R 1G4
☎ (416) 923 3434
Owner Fetoun 'Fifi' Yousif is the glamorous socialite wife of Saudi millionaire Bahnam Yousif. This boutique is *the* place for Christian Lacroix and everyone else who is haute couture and in the news. The raspberry-coloured boutique contains an ornate bedroom for clients who are overwhelmed with the strain of buying.

HARRIDGE'S, 55 Bloor St W, M4W 1A5
☎ (416) 968 3323
A stock of appealing apparel from Anne Klein, Liz Claiborne, N Peal (divine cashmeres) and a host of other designers, plus fab fabrics.

HARRY ROSEN, 82 Bloor St W, M5S 1L9
☎ (416) 972 0556
The largest store for men in the city, finished in sleek green marble and glass. Every size, every style, every executive look for him; the executive look for her, too. *"By far the best men's store. It has every size from the largest and tallest man to the smallest and shortest"* – ROBERT RAMSAY.

HAZELTON LANES, 55 Avenue Rd, M5R 3L2 ☎ (416) 968 8600
This chic, glassy, walk-around complex has been expanded and zipped-up to include yet more European and North American designer shoplets. Browse from Saint Laurent to Alfred Sung to Polo, plus Roots, Chez Catherine, Joan & David shoes and Sharon Batten – each in their own mini hall of fame. *"A great place to shop and be seen"* – ROSEMARY SEXTON.

HOLT RENFREW, 50 Bloor St W, M4W 1A1
☎ (416) 922 2333
Beautiful glossy store blazoned with glass and marble, a contemporary encore to the art deco palace in Montreal. The first exclusive Armani boutique in Canada and the first Mulberry in North America. Also Saint Laurent, Calvin Klein, Ralph Lauren and Gucci boutiques. Brilliant Birger Christiansen fur salon, plus all the other fashion greats bought with a discerning eye – Donna Karan, Polo, Liz Claiborne, Callaghan and Ghost. *"The only real fashion department store in Toronto"* – TYLER BRULE.

IRA BERG, 1510 Yonge St, M4T 1Z6
☎ (416) 922 9100
An old favourite that's been around for aeons, but keeps its fashion up to the mark. Glamour gowns under designer labels like Genny, Ungaro, Valentino, Art Wear, Byblos and Complice; fancy footwork too from Fratelli Rossetti.

MAREK, 110 Bloor St W, M5S 2W7
☎ (416) 923 5100
Subtitled 'The Best of Europe', this is the place for wonderfully original European ties and shoes designed by their own team.

ROOTS, 195 Avenue Rd, M5R 2J3
☎ (416) 927 8585
Don Green and Michael Budman started a great tradition when they went back to their Roots. Earthy leather shoes and coats, plus athletic shoes and other teenage dream gear. Roots are now dug in all over the world.

SPORTING LIFE, 2665 Yonge St, M4P 2J6
☎ (416) 485 1611
The only sports store that has its own policeman controlling the parking lot because of the eager crowds. What's more the salespersons can inform you intelligently about high-performance tennis racquets and ski equipment. Serious equipment and serious up-to-the-mark sportscred gear (designer sunglasses and sportswear by Bogner, Steinebronn, Sun Ice, Descente, Head, Rossignol, etc etc). *"Still one of the best stores in the world"* – STEVE PODBORSKI.

———— *Theatre* ————

PANTAGES THEATRE, 244 Victoria St, M5B 1V8 ☎ (416) 362 3218
A magnificent theatre with a superb lobby, reopened last year after renovations. Big hit productions such as *Phantom*. *"Really gorgeous. A wonderful renovated theatre; the sound is exquisite and the building is beautiful"* – ROBERT RAMSAY.

ROYAL ALEXANDRA THEATRE, 260 King St W, M5V 1J2 ☎ (416) 593 4211
An elegant old Victorian theatre owned by Ed Mirvish, who recently renovated the Old Vic in London. *"One of the finest theatres in North America. Everyone wants to play there, and I've broken in plays there"* – DOUGLAS FAIRBANKS JR.

VANCOUVER
———— *Bars and cafés* ————

MILIEU, 1145 Robson St, V6E 1B5
☎ (604) 684 4600
Cool café in European mode. Nouvelle cuisine is counteracted by a bakery on the premises that ruins good intentions.

PACIFIC PALISADES HOTEL, 1277 Robson St, V6E 1C4 ☎ (604) 688 0461
This hotel bar is one for the stars – Mel Gibson and Goldie Hawn have been seen a-sipping there.

🏊 PAN PACIFIC HOTEL, see Hotels
The lounge bar on the back terrace is *"a good place to meet for drinks at the start of an evening. One of the best views in the world over the whole Vancouver skyline – seaplanes, cruise liners, snow-capped mountains – an achingly amazing place"* – WILLIAM DAVIES.

PELICAN BAY, 1253 Johnston St, Granville Island, V6H 3R9 ☎ (604) 683 7373
The Granville Island Hotel bar is a regular yuppie haunt. Wonderful views at night – one entire wall of glass looks out over the city. Also a restaurant (French/seafood) and nightclub.

Clubs

GRACELAND, 1250 Richards St, V6B 3G2 ☎ (604) 688 2648
The largest dance club in Vancouver, based in a converted warehouse with 1,600 sq ft dance floor. *"Like an acid-house nightclub with the friendliest people on earth. Gorgeous people in psychedelic gear and cycling shorts, dancing on the bars and speakers"* – WILLIAM DAVIES. Music is brought in from top New York and London discos; tarot card readings too.

RICHARDS ON RICHARDS, 1036 Richards St, V6B 3E1 ☎ (604) 687 6794
Arguably the best nightclub in the city, still the in place to be, with endless queues on Fri and Sat to hear live bands.

Film

OMNIMAX AND SCIENCE WORLD, 1455 Quebec St, V6A 3Z7 ☎ (604) 687 8414
Built for Expo '86, Omnimax is *"like Imax but better. An unbelievable cinematic experience, with a dome, 7 screens high, wrapped round you. The seats lean backwards and you feel like you're in the picture"* – WILLIAM DAVIES. Expect travel and nature movies such as *Beavers* – 'the biggest dam movie you've ever seen', ho ho. Attached is Science World, ranging from robotic exhibits to live bee hives.

Gardens and parks

STANLEY PARK
1,000 acres of park in the heart of Vancouver, plus a zoo, 3 beaches, the famous aquarium, outdoor theatres and 3 restaurants – **Beachhouse**, **Teahouse** and **Prospect Point Café**. For WILLIAM DAVIES, a bike ride along the beautiful 6-mile path around the park, surrounded by water, is *"brilliant"*, while for BEVERLEY ZBITNOFF, *"the best tonic for a stressful day at the office or over-indulgent partying is a run or walk along the seawall"*. $5 to hire a mountain bike, free on foot.

Hotels

FOUR SEASONS, 791 W Georgia St, V6C 2T4 ☎ (604) 689 9333
Suavely appointed with fine antiques and mountains of fresh flowers. Dependable on every count, as expected.

PAN PACIFIC HOTEL, Suite 300, 999 Canada Place, V6C 3B5 ☎ (604) 662 3223
Based in the huge, futuristic, oceanside Canada Place, this slick hotel looks out on the spectacular Rocky Mountains and the Pacific. **Five Sails** restaurant is one of the best in town.

WEDGEWOOD HOTEL, 845 Hornby St, V6Z 1V1 ☎ (604) 689 7777
Intimate Euro-style hotel with only 90 rooms, where movie stars can remain inconspicuous. *"The suites are elegant and luxurious. Small, great service and a very good restaurant"* – ROSEMARY SEXTON.

Music

DU MAURIER INTERNATIONAL JAZZ FESTIVAL, c/o Coastal Jazz & Blues Society, 203/1206 Hamilton St, V6B 259 ☎ (604) 682 0706
June and July see a gathering of the world's finest jazz and blues artists plus plenty of unknown talent. Over 400 musicians turn up to play trad, contemporary and ethnic sounds at venues all over town.

Restaurants

THE BEIJING, 865 Hornby St, V6Z 2G3 ☎ (604) 688 7788
"There are some very good new Chinese restaurants in Vancouver, because of all the people coming in from Hong Kong. This is a marvellous restaurant" – ANDREW LLOYD WEBBER.

BRIDGES, 1696 Duranleau, Granville Island, V6H 3S4 ☎ (604) 669 2422
Romantic setting on the docks; superb seafood straight (almost) from the ocean. *"A consistently great restaurant and the hottest spot for summer evenings. It has a pub and bistro on a huge deck right on the Granville Island Marina and an elegant dining room upstairs. Fresh fish, an incredible wine list, and the best place for people-watching"* – BEVERLEY ZBITNOFF.

🔥 THE LANDING, 375 Water St, V6B 5C6 ☎ (604) 688 4800
Beautiful newish restaurant on the shores of Burrard Inlet, with breathtaking view over the sea and Rocky Mountains. *"The best of West Coast seafood and grain-fed Alberta beef prepared in traditional European ways. The décor is soothing and beautifully lit in a renovated turn-of-the-century heritage building in the Gastown district. All of the desserts are beautiful, but my favourite is the fragrant rum-saturated savarin with fresh fruits"* – BEVERLEY ZBITNOFF.

SANTA FE CAFE, 1688 W 4th Ave, V6J 1L9 ☎ (604) 738 8777
Tiny whitewashed restaurant for southwestern flavours. The house speciality is home-made

Yucatán sausages, loaded with anise and fennel. Service is chummy and unpretentious and it's packed every night.

THE TEAHOUSE, Ferguson Point, Stanley Park ☎ (604) 669 3281
Overlooking the ocean with mountains in the background, this restaurant is perfect for imbibing romantic sunsets in between nibbles of the best West Coast salmon dish.

♣ UMBERTO IL GIARDINO, 1382 Hornby St, V6Z 1W5 ☎ (604) 669 2422
The best of foodie king Umberto's restaurants (**Umberto's** at 1380 is the original, for northern Italian cuisine; **La Cantina di Umberto** at 1376 serves fresh local seafood). This one dishes up delicious Italian cuisine, specializing in wild game. *"Still the best Italian restaurant in the city and the best place to spot the stars. My favourite pasta is the sweet squash-stuffed cappelletti in prawn sauce. The grilled funghi assortiti is the starter"* – BEVERLEY ZBITNOFF. STEVE PODBORSKI loves all his restaurants.

Shopping

South Granville (especially from 9th to 14th Ave) is the best shopping street by a long chalk – lined with boutiques like Bacci, Byblos, Bratz and Boboli. The hungry head for **Granville Island Market**, *"beautifully laid out, easy to park, right on the water and selling absolutely everything a foodie heart desires. Particularly impressive is the Stock Market – a stall selling vacuum-packed bags of well-flavoured home-made stock"* – ELISE PASCOE.

BACCI, 2788 Granville St, V64 3J3 ☎ (604) 732 7317
Fashophiles vote it the best shop in Vancouver. A hip boutique with Memphis furniture and trompe-l'oeil fitting rooms. Riffle through Genny, Romeo Gigli, Complice and Montana and swanky shoes from Fratelli Rossetti, Romeo Gigli and Robert Clergerie. Jewellery too. Next door at 2790 ☎ (416) 737 0368, Bacci has opened Canada's first Byblos boutique, whose quiet interior is a mirror image of its Milano counterpart. The entire Byblos line – women's, men's and accessories.

BOBOLI, 2776 Granville St, V6H 3J3 ☎ (604) 736 3458
The poshest nook in town, owned by stylemongers Catherine Guadagnuolo and Margaret Ross. Super-cool with its black façade and huge windows – and the very best wrapping, in glossy black boxes with gold bows. Top Euro lines for men and women.

BRATZ, 2828 Granville St, V6H 3J5 ☎ (604) 734 4344
For the best-dressed bambino – a children's store with the cream of European imports.

GEORGE STRAITH'S, 900 W Georgia St, V6C 2W6 ☎ (604) 685 3301
Classy home of European classics – Liberty prints, Bally shoes, Burberry, Ballantyne, Hermès, Valentino, plus fine French lingerie. A branch of the main store in Victoria, at 921 Government St.

IMA:GO, 2756 Granville St, V6H 3J3 ☎ (604) 737 8800
"A great boutique. Quite unpretentious, with such fashion-forward stuff as Katharine Hamnett and Yamamoto" – BEVERLEY ZBITNOFF.

LEONE'S, 757 W Hastings St, V6C 1A1 ☎ (604) 683 1133
Italy comes to Vancouver. *"A wonderful concept for a store. They brought in everything Italian, from Valentino and Versace to Italian music, a cappuccino bar and amazing shoe store. Clients fly in from San Francisco"* – TYLER BRULE. Armani, Ferretti and Mondrian are there too.

MARK JAMES, 2941 W Broadway, V6K 2G6 ☎ (604) 734 2381
Più d'Italia: after flipping through the Armanis and Versaces (who rub shoulders gracefully with younger flibbertigibbets Girbaud, Marcel Dachet and C17) you can slink through to the Italian restaurant, **Fiasco**, the minimalist magnet for fashionable Vancouverites.

· REST OF ·
CANADA
Art and museums

NATIONAL GALLERY OF CANADA, 380 Sussex Drive, Ottawa, K1N 9N4 ☎ (613) 990 1985
Canada's first national art gallery. Designed by Moshe Safdie, this is one of the most breathtaking buildings in the capital, covering more than 500,000 sq ft. The most extensive collection of Canadian Art, including the Group of Seven, plus European and American artists. *"A great statement for the capital city. The architecture is very striking"* – TYLER BRULE. *"I like the special room devoted to Henry Moore – it's the best collection of Moore in the world"* – TONY ASPLER. *"It takes 2 trips, the first to see the building, the second to see the art. Absolutely out of this world...Moshe Safdie is brilliant. A home worthy of being our national showcase for art"* – ROBERT RAMSAY.

Hotels

HASTINGS HOUSE, PO Box 1110, Ganges, BC V0S 1E0 ☎ (604) 537 2362
"An English Tudor-style hotel on Salt Spring

Island. Each room is decorated differently and uniquely with antiques and chintz" – ROSEMARY SEXTON.

MILLCROFT INN, Box 89, John St, Alton, Ontario L0N 1A0 ☎ (416) 791 4422
Small country hotel managed by the Windsor Arms in Toronto, noted for its cuisine (lobster and scallop ragout with honey-saffron sauce, roast veal loin with chanterelles) and extensive wine cellar. Based in a former knitting mill and next-door Manor House, set in rural woodland. Be sure to nab a table overlooking the waterfall.

SOOKE HARBOUR HOUSE, 1528 Whiffenspit Road, RR #4, Sooke, BC V0S 1N0 ☎ (604) 642 3421
"A beautiful inn on Vancouver Island, with rooms in Californian West Coast style with big picture windows, Indian blankets and huge round wooden bathing tubs. Splendid, innovative food, well-known across Canada and America. They tend to use beautiful flowers in the cooking which is a treat, and they grow all the food in an organic garden" – ROSEMARY SEXTON.

Ski resorts

BANFF
"The most scenic drive I've ever done was between Vancouver and Banff. It was stunning country, absolutely beautiful" – STIRLING MOSS. This Canadian Rockies ski resort is "a blue-blooded, even more olde-worldier version of Whistler" – WILLIAM DAVIES. **Mount Norquay** is famed for its steep runs; **Lone Pine** is one of the meanest masses of snow and you can ski across the Great Divide into BC. The nearby resort town of Lake Louise has two mountains with long runs. Best hotels, both standing like majestic castles in the middle of mountain ranges: 🍂 **Banff Springs Hotel**, PO Box 960, Spray Ave, Banff, T0L 0C0 ☎ (403) 762 2211 ("stay in a suite overlooking the Bow River and the golf course. A marvellous old building with a bygone-era air in an idyllic setting" – ELISE PASCOE) and 🍂 **Château Lake Louise**, Lake Louise, T0L 1E0 ☎ (403) 522 3511 ("plan to stay during the poppy season and book into the new wing facing the lake and the spectacular Victoria Glacier. The Edelweiss dining room has a top European menu. Book a table in the window and watch dusk descend on one of the world's most beholding scenes" – ELISE P.). Best dining: the old **Post Hotel**, Lake Louise; **Giorgio's**, Banff Ave, "serving some of the best food in Canada. Downstairs (at **La Pasta**), sit at the bar. Great fun and the best pizzas and salads. Upstairs (**La Casa**) has a more formal menu and elegant décor. Not to be missed" – ELISE P.

WHISTLER MOUNTAIN
Whistler and nearby Blackcomb Mountain offer the best skiing in Canada with the longest vertical drop in North America (4,278 ft). "It's

a brilliant drive from Vancouver through the mountains and snow to get there. Then you can ski, windsurf and sunbathe" – WILLIAM DAVIES. That's only the half of it: also tennis, swimming, heli-skiing, paragliding, glacier flightseeing, and plenty of customized après ski. Luxury condos, hotel, or Alpinesque pensions. **Whistler Resort**, PO Box 1400, Whistler, BC V0N 1B0 ☎ (604) 932 3928. Best hotel: the castle-like **Château Whistler**, PO Box 100, Whistler, BC V0N 1B0 ☎ (604) 938 8000, at the base of Blackcomb, latest from the group that brought you Château Lake Louise and Banff Springs.

Tours

See also Travel Directory.

CANADIAN MOUNTAIN HOLIDAYS, PO Box 1660, Banff, Alberta T0L 0C0 ☎ (403) 762 4531
Top heli-skiing tours to top spots – the Bugaboos, Cariboos, Monashees and Bobbie Burns. "The best. I go every year, each time to somewhere different in the Rockies... it is breathtaking" – STEVE PODBORSKI. Expert guides, introductory weeks for first-timers. Luxury lodges have saunas, Jacuzzis and massage therapists to soothe the muscle-shocked. Up to C$4,000 a week.

CANADIAN OUTWARD BOUND WILDERNESS, PO Box 116 Station S, Toronto, Ontario M5M 4L6 ☎ (416) 787 1721
Wilderness survival trips for executives who wish to face the challenge of a lifetime. "The most amazing experience. There are 2 schools in Canada and the Duke of Edinburgh is the royal patron. Outward Bound is open to all. It is physically tough and demanding, but it is the most fun you can have! You are faced with elements and experiences that you would never encounter on any other trip. You learn how to get along with everyone, what your limitations are, and what experiences you can survive" – ROBERT RAMSAY.

WAYFARER HOLIDAYS, 235 Yorkland Blvd, Suite 610, Willowdale, Ontario M2J 4W9 ☎ (416) 498 5566
Adventure tours around Canada and the Arctic, from whale-watching in British Columbia to the Anne of Green Gables tour around Prince Edward Island. Also holidays to the Caribbean and Mexico.

WHITEWATER ADVENTURES, 1616 Duranleau St, Vancouver, BC V6H 3S4 ☎ (604) 669 1110
White-water rafting adventures of up to 3 days down the Chilco and Nahani rivers of British Columbia. A 6-day tour down the Tatshenshini River whooshes you through glaciers, mountain streams and forests galore. Great for wildlife viewing.

CARIBBEAN

ANGUILLA

**CAP JULUCA, Maunday's Bay
☎ (809) 497 6666**
Challenging the Malliouhana for exclusivity, with only 18 suites set in Moorish-style villas. *"The rooms are absolutely glorious. The bathrooms must be some of the best in the world – double baths with padded headrests and shelves around for your champagne. Each one has its own patio garden. A place to spend the day rather than just have a wash. They light lovely candles around the property in the evening. Very lush and tranquil"* – CAROL WRIGHT.

COVECASTLES, PO Box 248, Shoal Bay West ☎ (809) 497 6801
A private compound that is *"startling, quite out of Caribbean character, very Cubist. It's stuck out on some salt flats and at first you think 'what an extraordinary, hideous building', but inside everything is in white and cane and terracotta and it's amazingly effective. There are complete walls of windows looking out over the sea, so you can lie in your cane bed and watch the sea pounding in. Very romantic"* – CAROL WRIGHT.

MALLIOUHANA HOTEL, PO Box 173, Maids Bay ☎ (809) 497 6111
One of the most exclusive hotels in the Caribbean, with 2 miles of white beaches and 3 freshwater pools. Spectacular marble building perched on a cliff, each room with a sea view.

ANTIGUA

BLUE WATERS, Soldiers Bay, PO Box 256, St John's ☎ (809) 462 0290
A relaxed, discreet resort hotel with snorkelling, sunfish sailing, Hobie Cats, canoes and paragliding. Nearby golf course.

COPPER & LUMBER STORE, PO Box 184, St John's ☎ (809) 463 1058
A different kettle of fish from the norm: this warehouse in Nelson's Dockyard, English Harbour, is restored to 18C style with bare brick walls, exposed beams, Persian rugs and Georgian antiques. Great for yacht spotting and day chartering.

CURTAIN BLUFF, PO Box 288, Old Rd, Curtain Bluff Peninsula, St John's ☎ (809) 463 1115
Standing on a golden-sanded peninsula, between both surf and calm waters, it has *"some glorious new suites with little private patio gardens with hammocks slung, which are absolutely blissful. Probably the best wine cellar in the Caribbean. And a wonderful tennis complex as well"* – CAROL WRIGHT. Complimentary sunfish sailing, windsurfing, waterskiing and diving.

JUMBY BAY, PO Box 243, Long Island ☎ (809) 462 6000
A 300-acre slice of paradise on a private island 2 miles north of Antigua. Luxurious villas hidden among oleander and bougainvillaea, first-rate cuisine at the Estate House, all sorts of sports.

MILL REEF CLUB, PO Box 133, St John's ☎ (809) 463 2081
Namesake of the racehorse *Mill Reef*, owned by chief club member Paul Mellon. Punters stay well hidden from the rest of Antigua – this club is exclusive, and intent on keeping it that way.

BARBADOS

Those who have been Barbados-way include Paul McCartney, Mick Jagger (who rents a villa at Bathsheba on the east coast), Elton John, Princess Margaret, Omar Sharif and Bryan Ferry (who stays at the **COLONY CLUB**, St James

Buzzz The wreck of the 19C clipper HMS *Rhône*, off Fallen Jerusalem in the British Virgin Islands, makes for startling diving......Liveliest yachting centre: Antigua – check out **Antigua Sailing Week** at the end of April (gorgeous scenes on the water, less so on the land ...)...... Don't miss the **green flash**: from Shirley Heights, Antigua, at dusk, when the sinking sun hits a calm sea, the keen-eyed see a momentary, magical green flash. Sundays are party nights, with reggae and steel bands, barbecue and rum punch......Strange but true too: in a little cove between the Pitons (2 tall, conical mountains) on St Lucia lives an **elephant** who loves to bathe......**Barbadian stopover**? Stay at **Ocean View**, Hastings ☎ (809) 427 7821, near the airport, LORD LICHFIELD's recommendation for *"people who want a real feel of the West Indies. It's charmingly run, very relaxed"*...

☎ (809) 422 2335. **Raffles** and **Reids** are the 2 best restaurants on the island, says ROBERT SANGSTER.

CORAL REEF CLUB, St James
☎ (809) 422 2372
An established favourite, with cottages set in tropical gardens. Barbecues with steel bands, flaming limbo and calypso dancing; endless water sports, tennis, golf, riding and even polo. Formal dress is decreed on occasion.

GLITTER BAY, St James ☎ (809) 422 4111
The Great House was built in the 1930s by Sir Edward Cunard (nephew of Emerald), and now the Glitterati are returning en force. *"English-man Mike Pemberton has injected a tremendous amount of verve into it. I think this, and his Royal Pavilion, will take over as the luxe hotels on the island"* – LORD LICHFIELD. The estate is dotted with Andalusian-style whitewashed villas with clay-red roof tiles. Dine in style at the white-domed **Piperade**.

ROYAL PAVILION, St James
☎ (809) 422 4444
The latest and snazziest resort on the island, a sister for Glitter Bay. The main building is a lavish re-creation of colonial classicism, in beautifully kept tropical gardens. Beach-front accommodation, complimentary water sports and an excellent restaurant, **Palm Terrace**.

SETTLERS BEACH HOTEL, St James
☎ (809) 422 3052
Landing spot of the first settlers in Barbados. 22 self-catering villas amid coconut palms.

BARBUDA

According to CAROL WRIGHT, *"the best beach is in Barbuda, the tiny undeveloped sister island of Antigua. The beach at Cedar Point looks pink – not just Bermuda pink, but a rich pink. It's actually not sand but minute pink shells. There are miles of beach, running down into really clear water."* Barbuda is also MARIUCCIA MANDELLI's favourite holiday destination, with *"the best beach in the world"*. She loves the **K CLUB** ☎ (809) 460 0300, a new resort 'conceived to give total bliss to a special few', owned, surprise surprise, by Krizia.

BERMUDA

CAMBRIDGE BEACHES, Mangrove Bay, Sandy's Parish ☎ (809) 294 0331
The original cottage colony, dating back to the 17C, and spawning hundreds of similar resorts in the West Indies. Set on a peninsula with glorious ocean beaches and its own bay.

GRENADA

At the southern end of the Grenadines (St Vincent is at the northern), *"a wonderfully beautiful island, hoping now for an assault of the tourist rather than the military kind"* – LORD LICHFIELD. A few decades behind some of its ritzier neighbours, it boasts original 18C architecture in the capital town of St George's. Fertile land means top-quality food in the restaurants. Stay at the **CALABASH**, L'Anse aux Epins, Box 382, St George's ☎ (809) 444 4234, a small hotel with pretty rooms and high-rating cuisine or **SPICE ISLAND INN**, St George's ☎ (809) 444 4528, which is bang on the superb Grand Anse Beach.

GRENADINES

MUSTIQUE
A private island and playground of royals and super-rich, who own colonial-style houses designed by Oliver Messel or Japanesque pads (all little bridges, paper screens and Futons). The only locals you're likely to see here are those wearing white bonnets and pinnies, sweeping the verandahs. The best way to visit is to know or be related to Princess Margaret/Lords Glenconner or Lichfield/Prince Rupert Löwenstein/ Lynn Wyatt/Mick Jagger/David Bowie, etc. Otherwise it's book way ahead for the **COTTON HOUSE** ☎ (809) 458 4621, a former cotton storehouse made of stone and coral. Plans are still afoot for a new restaurant on the island.

PALM ISLAND
John and Mary Caldwell sailed round the world to find this little Garden of Eden. Sloop for sailing parties. Local Creole cooking. **PALM ISLAND BEACH CLUB** ☎ (809) 458 4804.

🏊 PETIT ST VINCENT
One of the most idyllic Caribbean caches, a tiny island of tufty grass and palms, entirely occupied by the resort. Hide away here and you might never be found. Privately owned and traffic-free, except for Mini-mokes that scoot round tending to guests' every whim. As none of the 22 cottages has a phone, guests hoist a yellow flag to summon room service or a red flag to keep the mokes at bay. **PETIT ST VINCENT RESORT** ☎ (809) 458 8801.

HAITI

LE RELAIS DE L'EMPEREUR, Petit Goave ☎ (509) 240318; reservations ☎ (212) 980 5140
The place to stay in Haiti. Private, palatial,

Scuba Scoop

Belize is the new buzz diving spot, tipped by LORD LICHFIELD. It boasts the second-longest reef in the world (after the Great Barrier Reef), which runs almost the length of the country, in the Caribbean Sea. Swim amid coral splendours, psychedelic fish and the odd shark or barracuda. Stay on the island of Ambergris Caye, at **Ramon's Reef Resort** ☎ (026) 2071, which will arrange diving and courses. Take a boat trip to the spectacular Blue Hole, a 400 ft-deep sinkhole; get marooned on one of myriad islands; or simply gaze at some of the 425 species of bird. (If you get bored with birds and fish, check in to **Chan Chich Lodge**, c/o Reef and Rainforest Tours [see Travel Directory], a luxury camp amid tropical forest, ancient Mayan ruins and wildlife.)

The **Turks** and **Caicos Islands** comprise some 40 islands and cays to the east of the Bahamas, surrounded by a magnificently conserved reef. Turtles, manta rays and a zillion marine creatures can be spotted around the reef, and beyond it tuna, marlin, barracuda, even migrating humpback whales (Nov-Dec). Send off for the *Divers, Snorkellers and Visitors Guide to the Turks and Caicos Islands*, from Palm Publications, PO Box 101, Grand Turk. For **Red Sea** diving, plunge in to *Twickers World Diving Dossier* ☎ (081) 892 7606, which has trips to Hurghada and Taba in Egypt, Eilat in Israel, and Jordan. For more about the astonishing **Great Barrier Reef**, see Australia.

exotic, it is run by the flamboyant Olivier Coquelin with the help of his Burmese leopard Sheba. The aim is to materialize the whims of guests before they are expressed. Olympic pool, deserted beach and lovely gardens.

JAMAICA

THE HALF MOON CLUB, PO Box 80, Montego Bay ☎ (809) 953 2211
Well established and superbly run, this vast estate of over 400 acres has a mile of private beach, an 18-hole Robert Trent Jones golf course, 13 tennis and 4 squash courts.

JAMAICA INN, Ocho Rios ☎ (809) 974 2514
Down the road from swinging Ocho Rios, home of reggae, is this small, elegant resort. One of the loveliest stretches of beach, private cove, freshwater pool.

ROUND HILL, PO Box 64, Montego Bay ☎ (809) 952 5150
Vernacular whitewashed villas with high ceilings and verandahs, set in lush greenery by a rocky and sandy coast. Cosmopolitan cuisine with mountains of fresh fish. The piano has been played by Noel Coward and Leonard Bernstein.

SANS SOUCI, PO Box 103, Ocho Rios ☎ (809) 974 2353
Seafront resort and health spa with gazebos and grottoes, all hidden among burgeoning trees and shrubs. Tennis club, swimming pool and a natural spring-fed mineral spa.

TRYALL GOLF, TENNIS & BEACH CLUB, PO Box 1206, Montego Bay ☎ (809) 952 5110
Zazzy 2,200-acre resort centred around the 1834 Great House. Roomy sea- or hillside villas, each with private cook, chambermaid, laundress, gardener and swimming pool. Tennis and an 18-hole golf course, of course.

ST KITTS & NEVIS

Separated by a 3-mile channel, The Narrows.

GOLDEN LEMON, Dieppe Bay, St Kitts ☎ (809) 465 7260
This is one of the most elegant jewels of the Caribbean, based around an 18C house with open verandah and gallery. Where Kennedys and other faces hide away.

MONTPELIER PLANTATION INN, PO Box 474 Nevis ☎ (809) 469 5462
Small English-owned inn with an informal, house-party atmosphere. Set on the slopes of Mount Nevis are 16 cottages around an old sugar mill. Fruit and veg are grown in the grounds, bread and marmalade are home-made. *"Very English and very elegant, a quiet place to stay that is beautiful"* – ROBERT RAMSAY.

ST LUCIA

Remarkable for the Pitons, twin volcanic mountains that shoot steeply out of the sea. The nearby volcano La Soufrière is surrounded by health-giving hot sulphur springs. On Thursday nights the main town of Castries erupts into a wild jamboree, with dancing in the streets.

LA TOC HOTEL, PO Box 399, Castries ☎ (809) 455 3081
One of the smartest in the West Indies, with the best suites – individual hillside units with plunge pools outside the bedrooms. *"You can roll straight out of bed into the pool. The trick is to roll back into bed! If you can do that you win a free trip on the QE2"* – TERRY HOLMES.

ST MARTIN/MAARTEN

Half-French, half-Dutch – and vive la différence. The Dutch half is more built up, with resorts, nightclubs, casinos, duty-free shops and flower-filled streets; the French more breezy and buzzy, colourful and congenial, with old colonial architecture, street markets and culinary flair.

LA SAMANNA, Baie Longue, PO Box 159, Marigot 97150 ☎ (590) 875122
Renowned resort, styled as a Moorish village, with loyal following (though some feel it could do with a facelift). French and Creole cuisine.

"There's a lovely market in Curaçao, along the side of a canal, where they cover the stalls with sails from old ships, so it looks like a floating arcade"

 CAROL WRIGHT

TOBAGO

MOUNT IRVINE BAY HOTEL & GOLF CLUB, PO Box 222 ☎ (809) 639 8871
Manicured resort with its own golf course and a 200-year-old converted sugar mill restaurant. Excellent scuba and snorkelling.

VIRGIN ISLANDS

"The British Virgin Islands are very underrated, totally different to the US Virgin Islands, so much nicer. People are pleased to see you, there are beautiful beaches..." – ROY ACKERMAN.

⚓ PETER ISLAND, BVI
Virtually the entire island belongs to the **PETER ISLAND HOTEL & YACHT**

HARBOR, PO Box 211, Tortola ☎ (809) 494 2561, one of the ritziest resorts in the Caribbean. The marina and big game fishing attract seafaring sorts. Best villa: the hilltop **Crow's Nest**. Best bay: Deadman's Bay.

"One of the best sights in the world is in Trinidad when the scarlet ibises come in to roost in the Caroni Swamp Bird Sanctuary. As they land, the island gradually turns red, like a rhododendron in full bloom. It's incredible when the full moon rises behind the island, and these stains of scarlet streak across..."

 ROBIN HANBURY-TENISON

ST JOHN, USVI
A quiet, classy island of National Parkland, with wonderful scuba diving – flip along the underwater trail of flora and coral formations at Trunk Bay. Luxuriate on one of the 7 squeaky clean white beaches at **CANEEL BAY**, PO Box 120 ☎ (809) 776 6111; 7 tennis courts too, and an old sugar mill to dine in.

Galapagos Islands

The ultimate Green destination. Some 60 volcanic islands uninhabited by man but crawling with unique flora and fauna. From the days when Darwin landed in 1835 and developed the *Origin of Species*, little has changed. You'll still see penguins, fur seals, marine iguanas, pelicans, ancient tortoises some 4 ft across, blue-footed boobies, red-footed boobies and a zillion other species. You can go by air or sea to the main island, Isabela, and hire a boat with guide and cook (who fetches your dinner fresh from the sea). Or travel with companies such as **Abercrombie & Kent** or **Twickers World** (see Travel Directory), which arrange smart cruises around the islands with naturalist guides. You go ashore by rubber raft and wander among the birds and beasties. For lazy luxe-lovers, Twickers World can combine days at the islands with nights at the **Hotel Delfin**, Puerto Ayora, Santa Cruz Islands.

TORTOLA, BVI

The largest in the BVI, yet still only some 18 x 5 miles. The Atlantic rolls in on one side (great surfing) and the Caribbean laps at the other. Scuba around brilliant-coloured coral, whisk to neighbouring islands a mere 20 minute-tack away; ramble in the rainforest, cavort at the summer carnival. **PROSPECT REEF**, PO Box 104, Road Town ☎ (809) 494 3311, is the smartest resort; **SEBASTIAN'S ON THE BEACH**, Little Apple Bay, is rougher, readier and younger, but a great place for catching waves – and the best-looking surfers in the BVI.

VIRGIN GORDA, BVI

The 'Fat Virgin', second largest of the BVI. The sparkling **LITTLE DIX BAY**, PO Box 70 ☎ (809) 495 5555, is the sister resort to Caneel Bay. 300-acre paradise with stilted thatched cottages, marina, open-air dining room and activities such as scuba, cruises and picnics.

CHINA

BEIJING

—— *Hotels* ——

JIANGUO, Jianguomenwai Rd
☎ (1) 500 2233

Part of the Peninsula group. Not in the best shape, but the one travellers in the know choose for its clubbiness, service and good location. **Charlie's Bar** is a great expat hang-out.

PALACE HOTEL, Wang Fujing St
☎ (1) 512 8899

Large hotel of rather sparse grandeur, based in the Wangfujing shopping district, not far from the Forbidden City and Tiananmen Square. Cuisines for every palate, health club, disco, piano bar, the works.

SHANGRI-LA, 29 Zizhuyuan Rd
☎ (1) 831 2211

One of the best in China, and the most reliable in Beijing – still new, and therefore shipshape,

and under strong management. A vast 24-storey, 786-room deluxe affair with health club, business centre, antique and craft shops, Bank of China facility and tennis courts.

—— *Restaurants* ——

FENGZE YUAN, Zhushikou, No 83
☎ 332828

Expensive, prestigious place for fine seafood.

SHAGUO JU, Xisi Kaijie, No 60 ☎ 663206

This 300-year-old restaurant is the oldest in Beijing. Its Manchurian specialities centre around pork.

SICHUAN FANDIAN, Rongxian Hutong, No 51 ☎ 336356

A 9-courtyard old mansion with beautiful décor (rare in China). Excellent hot Sichuan dishes.

TINGLI GUAN, Summer Palace ☎ 281276

Formerly the private theatre of the Dowager Empress Ci Xi. Set on the north shore near the Marble Boat, it's a stunning place to eat Imperial dishes.

· REST OF ·

CHINA

—— *Hotels* ——

GOLDEN FLOWER HOTEL, 8 W Changle Rd, Xian, Shaanxi Province ☎ 32981

The one, when you visit the great archaeological site of the Terracotta Army. In China's top echelon of hotels (though it suffers, along with the others, from problems with labour). Two top restaurants for those who want to eat indigenously (a contender for the best Sichuan in China) and those who prefer everything but.

🦆 SHANGHAI HILTON INTERNATIONAL, 250 Huashan Rd
☎ (8621) 550000

One that makes guests forget they're in China. Only those who have battled against Chinese bureaucracy appreciate the huge efforts made to achieve 24-hour room service, immaculately groomed staff that speak perfect English, zippy

🕵 **Buzzz** The main attraction of **Maxim's Peking** is the **ashtrays** (emblazoned with the restaurant name), which are surreptitiously filched by foreign devils🕵...... Filch 2: word has it that **Beijing's best chefs** have been purloined by the government for State functions🕵......YAN-KIT SO recommends the daily **market** in **Shanghai**, at the Wuyuan Road/Urumchi intersection, about 10 minutes walk from the Shanghai Hilton. *"It's an open market with provisions from vegetables to live eels, and flower stalls"*............................🕵

sports and exercise facilities, and a selection of superb restaurants (**Sichuan Court** beats any in Hong Kong, **Suiyuan** is tops for Cantonese cuisine, **Shanghai Express** offers good, clean regional food). Great Sunday brunch with jazz band playing.

"Guangzhou is not like the rest of China. It's bustling with street life, like a Mediterranean city"

 SERENA SUTCLIFFE

WHITE SWAN HOTEL, Shamian Island, Guangzhou ☎ (20) 886968

Part of the Fok empire and one of the first Western-style hotels in China. *"An absolute oasis, stunning by any standards. It's on a little island joined to the mainland by bridge, with the Pearl River flowing around it, the most beautiful gardens, 2 pools..."* – SERENA SUTCLIFFE. The central skylit atrium hall contains an indoor water garden with waterfall. Good bar, too (*"It's fantastic to have these wonderful barmen make you bourbon sours and margaritas while watching Hong Kong television on a huge screen"* – SS).

DENMARK

Ballet

🩰 ROYAL DANISH BALLET, The Royal Theatre, Kongens Nytorv, PO Box 2185, DK-1017 Copenhagen ☎ 3314 1002

Director Frank 'We are the highest leapers in the world' Andersen has led the Danish Ballet back to the first league, alongside the greats in Paris, Russia, New York and London. As well as new works, they continue to perform the dances of the great Danish choreographer August Bournonville. The ballet school (training begins at the age of 5) has turned out such luminaries as Peter Schaufuss and Peter Martins. Annual Copenhagen Festival of Ballet and Opera in May.

Hotels

HOTEL D'ANGLETERRE, Kongens Nytorv 34, DK-1050 Copenhagen ☎ 3312 0095

This Danish institution, opened in 1755, has all the hallmarks of a first-class hotel. A lovely setting, near the harbour, royal palace and theatre; beautiful antique décor, top-grade restaurant and individual service.

Restaurants

SAISON, Skoys Hoyed Hotel, 267 Strand Vegen, 2920 Charlottenlund ☎ 3164 0028

Installed in his new restaurant 5 miles north of Copenhagen, Irwin Lauterbach is something of a culinary celebrity. *"The éminence grise of Danish cooking. It's not nouvelle cuisine...he is redefining Danish cooking. Lots of lovely obscure wild mushrooms, delicious fish. And the restaurant is not stuffy, nor are prices enormously high"* – ALASTAIR LITTLE.

DUBAI

HATTA FORT HOTEL, PO Box 9277, UAE ☎ (4) 660311

Small hotel with little wood-roofed chalets, at the foot of the Hajar mountains. *"There are beautiful lush gardens and colourful shrubs. Lovely balconies in local stone. Superb service. Built out over the swimming pool is a little coffee shop with sides of white muslin, like an enormous, sophisticated Arab tent. You have the impression of water all round you. Very cool, idyllic and peaceful, and exquisite pastries. They'll arrange for you to go camel racing or hire a 4-wheel drive and go belting off into the desert"* – CAROL WRIGHT.

INTER-CONTINENTAL, PO Box 476, Bin Yass St, UAE ☎ (4) 227171

Swanky modern hotel that boasts the knockout **Fish Market** restaurant: *"Remarkable, run in the Thai style with nothing but fresh fish which you choose yourself and then have it fried, boiled, steamed, grilled or whatever. Absolutely the best fish I've ever had. People are queuing to get in"* – LORD LICHFIELD.

To Dine by the Bullet

🩰

"The only restaurant still open in West Beirut is a spaghetti house, right on the front overlooking the Corniche. There you don't get candlelight, you get chaser bullets. Seriously you do. There's no glass in the windows in case they hit the glass and shatter on to your spaghetti. So you sit there with elegant white-coated waiters offering wine, etc, while chasers flash up and down the Corniche" – ROSS BENSON.

The Sultanate of Oman

Only just opening its doors to tourism, the ancient land of Oman is somewhat jumpy about Westerners and their ways. It is difficult for individuals to get a permit, and nigh on impossible for single female travellers. Persevere. The legendary home of Sinbad the Sailor is a real Arabian Nights wonderland of little villages cut into rock, magnificent mosques (men only), forts, souqs, old harbours and glistening seas. In Muscat, the rich man's home really is his castle (newly built), while his holiday venue is Salalah ('shining city'). The most gobsmackingly OTT hotel is the octagonal **Al Bustan Palace Hotel**, PO Box 8998,

Muscat, Oman ☎ 799666, with *"the most impressive lobby. It's like going into an absolutely enormous mosque. The ceiling looks like the night sky with stars, great domes, and turquoises and golds everywhere. It's 9 storeys high, very opulent, with huge sofas and cushions, and galleries looking down from different levels"* – CAROL WRIGHT. The top floor is reserved for kings and sultans – the poor old POW of England, a mere prince, didn't make the grade. It has its own theatre, a lavish banqueting room reminiscent of a royal court, and belly dancing. Best tours: **Twickers World** (see Travel Directory).

EGYPT

Hotels

MENA HOUSE OBEROI, Pyramid Rd, Giza, Cairo ☎ (02) 855444
The old colonial weekend palace where Army and diplomatic bigwigs would meet, now run in great style by the Oberoi group. Marvellous views directly on to the Pyramids.

SALAMLEK, Kasr El-Montazah, Alexandria ☎ (03) 860585
A converted wing of Al-Montazah Palace, summer residence of the former Egyptian Royal family. High above an exquisite beach on the eastern tip of Alexandria, surrounded by colossal gardens and woods.

Art and museums

EGYPTIAN MUSEUM OF ANTIQUITIES, Eltahrir Sq, Cairo
The greatest collection of antiquities in the world. The treasures of Tutankhamen (provided rumours that the originals were long ago sold to Russia are unfounded), plus a wealth of other artefacts from the ancient civilization, dating back to 4000 BC. The best museum catalogue.

Tours

A cruise down the 40 million-year-old Nile is the best way to take in the sights: the Temple of Karnak at Luxor and the Valley of the Kings at Thebes (with the tombs of Tutankhamen and Rameses VI) and Aswan. (From here, take a dawn flight to Abu Simbel to see the Temples of

Rameses II and Queen Nefertiti, which were moved lock, stock and column when the Aswan dam was built.) Best trips: **Abercrombie & Kent** (their own offices and small luxury cruiser, MS *Sunboat*, in Egypt, balloon trips), **Bales Tours** (Egypt specialists, the greatest variety of tours, including a cruise on the brand new luxury MS *Ra*), **Serenissima** and **Renaissance** (upmarket, small, arty groups accompanied by a lecturer), **Voyages Jules Verne, Kuoni, Silk Cut Travel, Tempo Travel**. See Travel Directory.

HELIOTOURS EGYPT, 105 Higgaz St, Heliopolis☎ (02) 224 3124
Cruises arranged locally on MS *Helio*, one of the best boats on the river.

FIJI ISLANDS

THE REGENT OF FIJI, PO Box 9081, Nadi ☎ 70700
Gorgeous complex on the lines of a Fijian village. A central lofty lobby opens on to restaurants, bars and shops, set in a lush palm-fronded Garden of Eden dotted with villas. Humorous, friendly staff with bushy bushy hairdos; don't overlook the barman/beach boy Sam Meat Pie. Pacific, Oriental and French cuisine, singers, fire-walkers and tropical feasts. Take a picnic lunch off to the island of Akuilau (deserted – save for Regent guests), practise golf, or brush up your tennis at John Newcombe's neighbouring South Pacific Tennis Ranch.

TAVEUNI
On the 180° longitude line – where (in theory)

you can stand with one leg in today and one in tomorrow. Scuba addicts stay with **DIVE TAVEUNI**, c/o Matei Post Office ☎ 406M, a house party for 10 run by two New Zealanders.

TOBERUA ISLAND, PO Box 567, Suva ☎ 26356 (office); 49177 (island)
A microdot undetected by rainclouds and mosquitoes. Stay in serious peace in one of only 14 private thatched bures (cottages). Eye-boggling tropical feasts; their own boat (nicknamed the Love Boat) for honeymoon escapes.

TURTLE ISLAND, PO Box 9317, Nadi ☎ 72921
Private island reached by seaplane, where couples cast off their cares in this cash-free, informal atmosphere. Only 12 bures – and 12 beaches.

FRANCE

PARIS

—— *Art and museums* ——

The best international touring exhibitions – as queues testify – are staged at the **Grand Palais**, ave du Général Eisenhower, 75008 ☎ (1) 4289 5410. The **Petit Palais**, opposite, at ave Winston-Churchill ☎ (1) 4265 1273, holds 2 major exhibitions each year, on top of its permanent collection of antiquities through to 19C art.

CENTRE GEORGES POMPIDOU, place Beaubourg, 75004 ☎ (1) 4277 1233
The famous Richard Rogers/Renzo Piano landmark building, a young, living, cultural centre. It houses the Musée National d'Art Moderne – the national collection of art from Matisse and the Post-Impressionists up to c. 1945. Frequent visiting exhibitions of contemporary art and photography. Excellent library; great source of postcards and posters. In the courtyard outside, buskers, mime artists and students galore don't deter Pompidou fan STANLEY MARCUS.

LE PALAIS DE TOKYO, ave du Président-Wilson, 75016 ☎ (1) 4723 3653
Following a FF180 million restyle, this 1930s building is one of the buzziest arty meeting-places in Paris. The right wing is the Musée d'Art Moderne de la Ville de Paris ☎ (1) 4723 6127, the left wing the Palais – the national centre for photography (the largest exhibition/archive space in the world) and for cinema (4 projection rooms with the latest in technical wizardry, a vast archive, and a training school). At the Musée, see Raoul Dufy's *La Fée Electricité*, the biggest painting in the world, and (when it's on show) Nam Jun Paik's 1980s video art answer to it. Add the library, brasserie, bookshop and views over the Seine, and you just might never leave.

MUSEE CARNAVALET, 23 rue de Sévigné, 75003 ☎ (1) 4272 2113
Recently expanded and beautifully restored, the delightful museum of the history of Paris now occupies the 17C Hôtel Carnavalet and its neighbour Hôtel Le Peletier de Saint-Fargeau. Reconstructions of rooms from the ages of Louis XIV and XV, of 18C rooms filled with boiseries (panelled decoration) by Ledoux, and of the art nouveau shop, Fouquet, by Mucha. The greatest collection of art and memorabilia of the Revolution. Further renovations will allow works from antiquity and the Middle Ages to be displayed. KARL LAGERFELD is a devotee.

Institut du Monde Arabe

The new Institut du Monde Arabe, 23 Quai St Bernard, 75005 ☎ (1) 4051 3838, is a *"unique centre for the enhancement of the Arabic culture. The Arabs are so divided that they couldn't agree in which of their countries to build it, so it's in Paris. A very strong artistic centre with a very good restaurant at the top"* – ALEXANDRE LAZAREFF. Never mind the wealth of wonders inside (video lab, cinema, art, antiquities, etc)... what leaves the architectural world awestruck is Jean Nouvel's building (1987), which takes in all the references of modern architecture, Europe, America and the Arab world. One of the 2 sections comes to a sharp point like a dagger or a ship's prow; the south façade has Moorish geometric-patterned apertures that control sunlight like the eye of a camera; inside, the fluctuating play of light is all part of the complex design. The library is built on a continuous spiral curve, like the Guggenheim in New York. You travel in glass lifts through the guts of the building, and you move across space from one section to the other in a glass-enclosed bridge. The result: an urban oasis of mirages and reflections.

🐚 **MUSEE DU LOUVRE, 34 quai du Louvre, 75001 ☎ (1) 4260 3926**
One of the greatest collections of art in the world, housed in the former palace of the French monarchy, and entered by that love-it-or-hate-it glass pyramid of I M Pei's. Though pertinent both to the Nile-faring Napoleon and the antiquities beneath it, the structure sits incongruously in the historic palace, and blocks the old vista from the Cour Carrée as far as the Arc de Triomphe. No matter for STANLEY MARCUS: *"I always try to see the Louvre, particularly as Pei designed the new pyramid."* Escalators lead from this skylight to an underground plaza with arteries to 200-plus galleries. The awesome collection covers Egyptian, Greek (*Venus de Milo*, etc), Roman and Oriental antiquities; objects and furniture; and sculpture and paintings of the European schools – including the *Mona Lisa* (behind grubby bullet-proof glass after the uncharitable attempts to wipe that smile off her face). It's one of the 3 galleries HELEN GURLEY BROWN *"could spend a year at".*

🐚 **MUSEE D'ORSAY, 62 rue de Lille, 75007 ☎ (1) 4549 4814**
Despite Gae Aulenti's controversial restructuring within the soaring fin-de-siècle steel and glass framework of the Gare d'Orsay, this museum is universally admired. The Mecca for lovers of 19C French art, it's crammed with Courbets and Corots and crowned with the Impressionists and Post-Impressionists, absorbed from their old home at the Jeu de Paume. See Manet's scandalous *Déjeuner sur l'Herbe* and *Olympia*, Degas's dancers, Monet's garden, works by Rodin and Redon, Cézanne and Sisley, Renoir and Pissarro, Gauguin and Van Gogh. Also the newly fashionable 'Art Pompier' masters (the art Establishment at the time of the Impressionists). Add to this sculpture and dec arts (superb art nouveau section), a swanky restaurant and a café behind the glass clockface. *"It's a brilliant place because it makes use of the building as a period frame for its contents"* – FRANCOISE VERNY.

MUSEE PICASSO, Hôtel de Salé, 5 rue de Thorigny, 75003 ☎ (1) 4271 2521
One of the most attractive museums in town, based in a lovely 17C hôtel with fine stone carving. An airy space with lighting by Diego Giacometti, brother of the sculptor. Follow Picasso's life through his work: paintings, statues, ceramics, book illustrations and manuscripts; even little owls by Picasso peek at you over doorways. Also displayed is Picasso's collection of paintings by other artists such as Cézanne.

MUSEE RODIN, Hôtel Biron, 77 rue de Varenne, 75007 ☎ (1) 4705 0134
The Kiss, The Thinker, they're all represented, amid the calm of Rodin's pretty 18C house and garden, as the sculptor intended. Also working drawings and sketches.

—— *Arts centres* ——

THEATRE DES CHAMPS-ELYSEES, 15 ave Montaigne, 75008 ☎ (1) 4720 3637
Chic centre for opera, ballet, music and mime. Also home to Paris's second auction house (after Drouot), where big-name, big-bucks sales (such as the US$49 million Picasso) take place.

—— *Ballet* ——

🐚 **L'OPERA BALLET, Palais Garnier, 8 rue Scribe, 75009 ☎ (1) 4266 5022**
The oldest ballet company in the world, developed from the Académie Royale de Musique, founded in 1669 by Louis XIV. Even though mega-étoile Rudolf Nureyev left his post as director last year, the company continues to impress the dance world. There is an ever-brimming fount of new dancers from the excellent ballet school. Sylvie Guillem and Elisabeth Platel sprang from this source. 10-12 productions each year. Based in the grandiose Second Empire opera house, the largest in the world with room for 450 artists on stage. (The Paris Opéra has meanwhile moved to the Opéra de la Bastille, to loud boos from critics, who say the acoustics here were superb...)

—— *Bars and cafés* ——

AUX DEUX MAGOTS, 170 blvd St Germain, 75006 ☎ (1) 4548 5525
Very obviously on the tourist beat, but it's a fabulous place to sit and watch the world strut by, near the little cobbled Place St Germain des Prés. A haunt of the Left Bank literati. *"The place to have breakfast. After that le tout Paris arrives"* – ALEXANDRE LAZAREFF.

BEDFORD ARMS, 17 rue Princesse, 75006 ☎ (1) 4633 2560
An English-style pub filled with Victoriana – the last place an English visitor would wish to find himself in Paris, but high on the BCBG social list. DOMINIQUE PIOT recommends.

BLUE FOX, Cité Berryer, 25 rue Royale, 75008 ☎ 4265 0847
Steven Spurrier's wine bar is packed with Paris-based pin-stripers. Good selection of wines, and a great fruit crumble.

CAFE DE FLORE, 172 blvd St Germain, 75006 ☎ (1) 4548 5526
La même chose as Aux Deux Magots, next door; former lair of Picasso, Sartre, Simone de Beauvoir and Albert Camus. *"Fabulous scrambled eggs"* – ALEXANDRE LAZAREFF.

HOTEL RAPHAEL, 17 ave Kléber, 75116 ☎ (1) 4502 1600
English-style bar where Isabella Rossellini – plus a wider circle of Italian and French movie

types – goes. Don't overlook the real Turner painting by the bar.

L'ECLUSE, 15 Quai des Grands-Augustins, 75006, and branches
The best chain of wine bars, according to CLARE FERGUSON: *"Blissful and minimal. Order assiette autour de l'oie ('round the goose'), drink a glass of Sauternes and bless your good luck."*

WILLI'S, 13 rue des Petits-Champs, 75001 ☎ 4261 0509
Another Brit-style wine bar, run by Mark Williamson, and perhaps the best in Paris, with fine French nosh. A similar catchment to the Blue Fox plus a dash of fash from the likes of Gaultier and Inès de la Fressange. *"Atmosphere, fabulous simple wine and good, simple food"* – JEREMIAH TOWER.

Clubs

⚑ CASTEL'S, 15 rue Princesse, 75006 ☎ (1) 4326 9022
Officially called Club de Saint-Germain des Prés, this is Paris's answer to Annabel's, a homy club with a warm ambience, run – as Mark Birley has observed – on a friends-of-Jean-Castel basis. Castel must have a pretty big address book. Here you'll find fathers and sons – each with his girlfriend; sportsmen, chefs, actors, film producers, people like JEAN-PAUL BELMONDO (*"I have spent some of my most memorable evenings there..."*), Roger Vadim, Christopher Lambert, FREDERIC BEIGBEDER. Nevertheless, if Castel doesn't want you, you don't get in. King Hassan got the order of the boot because JC disliked his bodyguards hanging around. *"There simply is no other place"* – MARQUIS DE LASTOURS. *"The best"* – ROLAND ESCAIG.

⚑ CHINA CLUB, 50 rue de Charenton, 75012 ☎ (1) 4343 8202
More than just a restaurant, this club was inspired by colonial Shanghai, this club-restaurant is good for late-evening drinking, talking and old-time music. There's a downstairs red-lacquered bar and an upstairs fumoir (smoking room) with sofas and chairs around a fireplace. Habitués sip cognac or mai-tais and play chess or mah-jong. A favourite with Mitterrand's adviser Régis Debray and CLEMENCE DE ROCH, *"because it's quiet and very atmospheric"*.

LA LOCOMOTIVE, 90 Blvd Clichy, 75018 ☎ (1) 4257 3737
Groovy dance club next door to the Moulin Rouge. *"2 floors of music make this the best place for Le Twisting the night away – especially Tuesday"* – DAVID SHILLING.

LA NOUVELLE EVE, 25 rue Fontaine, 75009 ☎ (1) 4526 7632
Friday-night club run by Albert and Serge. 1900s

vaudeville décor – OTT theatrical rococo – sets the stage for swing, cha-cha, rumba and modern music. Upper-class kids go to have more unbridled fun than at the season's balls. BEATRICE DALLE preferred it when it was rougher.

Paris's Best Clubs

1	CASTEL'S
2	LES BAINS
3	SHEHERAZADE
4	LE TANGO
5	LE BALAJO

LE BALAJO, 9 rue de Lappe, 75011 ☎ (1) 4700 0787
Fabulous old club with an orchestra playing old-time dance music. On Sunday afternoons, grannies go to thés dansants; on Monday nights, retro is forgotten and modern hippery is in, but ALEXANDRE LAZAREFF advises: *"Go for the Saturday ball – there you have some hairdressers with the moustaches, some workers with the T-shirts and some ladies who wear the wedding dress of their sister-in-law – and that's fun because these people go out to have fun. You must know it's for them and not for you... a very tender place, be discreet."*

LE KEUR SAMBA, 79 rue la Boëtie, 75008 ☎ (1) 4359 0310
This predominantly black club becomes more mixed as the evening goes on – after 4am, it's the hippest place in town, with such varied patrons as tennis player Yannick Noah, Mick Jagger (usually *sans* Jerry Hall), Rupert Everett and Rob Lowe.

LE PALACE 999, 8 rue du Faubourg Montmartre, 75009 ☎ (1) 4246 1087
Recently re-opened under new management, this club is set in a former theatre with cupola and balconies. Still an egalitarian scene with a glamorous edge – *les top-models*, film and pop stars (CHARLOTTE RAMPLING, Terence Trent D'Arby, Madonna) and jeunesse dorée.

LE ROSEBUD, 11 bis rue Delambre, 75014 ☎ (1) 4335 3854
One of the very first jazz clubs in Paris. It figured in Jean-Luc Godard's *A Bout de Souffle*, and the director still drops in when he's in town, as do American jazzmen. *"A very friendly, relaxing place where you can go alone just to talk"* – ALEXANDRE LAZAREFF.

⚑ LES BAINS, 7 rue du Bourg-l'Abbé, 75003 ☎ (1) 4887 0180
This branché boîte, based in the old public baths,

is where you go to see, be seen, but God forbid you dance or show you're having fun. That's the way Grace Jones, Harrison Ford, Michael Douglas, Paloma Picasso, FREDERIC BEIGBEDER and Iman like it. JEAN-PHILIPPE CHATRIER advises unknowns how to get in: don all-black Japanese garb with Alain Mikli sunspecs.

LES TROTTOIRS DE BUENOS AIRES, 37 rue des Lombards, 75001 ☎ (1) 4233 5837
Paradise for tangomaniacs – sensational live Argentinian music is your raison d'être for trotting along here. HECTOR SOLANAS is a fan because *"people take tango seriously"*.

🍴 LE TANGO, 13 rue au Maire, 75003 ☎ (1) 4272 1778
An Afro-Latin club that's jam-packed, sweaty, abandoned – dance for dance's sake. *"Fa-bulous! But a girl should wonder before accepting an invitation to this place – when people dance, they stick, really stick, to each other. If a man turns his head for a moment, the girl will immediately be asked to dance by one or two African dancers"* – ALEXANDRE LAZAREFF. The in place for private theme parties (the satirical group Jalous started the trend with their hop for the 30th anniversary of the Cuban Revolution). Keep your ear to the ground.

NEW MORNING, 7-9 rue des Petites-Ecuries, 75010 ☎ (1) 4523 5141
Dark, laid-back, rough 'n' ready hall for the best jazz in town. Top international performers such as Astrud Gilberto. *"The best jazz place and the best place for the general public – if you have blue grass, you'll have cowboys listening with hats on the nose and cowboy boots. If a Brazilian is playing, Brazilians go…"* – ALEXANDRE LAZAREFF.

REGINE'S, 49 rue de Ponthieu, 75008 ☎ (1) 4359 2160
Just as you think this disco-queen's club is passé, she reviews her members' list, shuffles names and décor, and comes up with another success. Anthony Delon is a regular; Prince Henri de France, Duke of Vendôme, drops in; Michael J Fox, Liza Minnelli and Julio Iglesias never stopped bopping here.

🍴 SHEHERAZADE, 3 rue de Liège, 75009 ☎ (1) 4874 4168
A 90s re-interpretation of a 40s Hollywood re-interpretation of the Arabian Nights. Le jetset groove to the pulsating rhythms of soul and rai. Intoxicating stuff. Très branché, très friqué (just take a fat wallet along).

—— *Fashion designers* ——

See also Italy – the Italian presence is ever-increasing in Paris (Valentino, Versace, Armani and Gigli show their collections here; Ferré is designing Dior and Tarlazzi is doing Laroche).

AGNES B, 6 rue du Jour, 75001 ☎ (1) 4508 5656; menswear at No 3, children's at No 2; and branches
Chic, easy, comfortable separates that every young person needs – the undemonstrative but essential short black skirt, leggings, wrap-over top, jacket, suit. Brian and Lucy Ferry, Nastassja Kinski, Philippe Starck and Kevin Kline are monster fans.

🍴 AZZEDINE ALAIA, 17 rue du Parc-Royal, 75003 ☎ (1) 4272 1919
Having well and truly shaken off the tag 'Has-been Alaïa', Azzedine holds a strong suit of making beautifully structured knits and impeccably cut jackets and skirts that sexily skim and caress the curves of the female form. Models and stars – Grace Jones, BEATRICE DALLE, Cher, Tina Turner – still adore his look. Tops *"for body-consciousness,"* confirms MARIE HELVIN. *"There is no one who cuts knitwear like him. At any time in my life I will always need something from Alaïa"* – PALOMA PICASSO. *"Continues to evolve. He is more separates-orientated than previously, but his designs are still sensuous and body-hugging. There is a new emphasis in fashion in the use of lycra and Alaïa really is the master of lycra"* – ANIKO GAAL. *"Definitely No 1 for modern style"* – JOAN BURSTEIN.

CERRUTI 1881, 24 rue Royale 75008 ☎ (1) 4261 1112 (men); 15 place de la Madeleine ☎ (1) 4742 1078 (women)
Classic but contemporary good looks for men and women, the epitome of Italian taste. Revered most for superb menswear – wonderful day and dinner suits, impeccably tailored; beautifully wide-cut trousers; the best blazers in the world; casual lounge-around togs. JAMES BURKE likes their *"very good new line of heavy cotton light-weight suits, beautifully designed"*.

🍴 CHANEL, 31 rue Cambon, 75001 ☎ (1) 4286 2800 (couture); 42 ave Montaigne, 75008 ☎ (1) 4723 7412 (boutique)
Karl Lagerfeld continues to re-interpret the Chanel look with wit, sophistication and youth. Each season he finds yet another way to redefine the little braided jacket – giving it new proportions, dividing it up like a Mondrian, cinching it at the waist, cutting it off-the-shoulder. The signature black bow, camellia, gilt buttons and chains are never far away.

However, Lagerfeld's support was rocked by a much-publicized dispute with his muse of 5 years, Inès de la Fressange. Some now feel he's weary of Chanel, others hailed his post-row couture collection as the best ever. Whatever the truth, the label, style and workmanship remain unassailable, adored by Princess Caroline, Jackie Onassis, No 5 girl Carole Bouquet, Queen Noor of Jordan and Ann Getty. BRUCE OLDFIELD still admires him *"for his acceptable wit and humour and glamour"*. BIJAN says: *"I love what Chanel does, but recently if my wife wears Chanel too much, I don't like it any more."* Ah well... go for accessories: costume jewels, belts, scarves, shoes, and who *hasn't* got a quilted leather bag on a chain? *"The best place for me is always the Chanel boutique in any city"* – HELEN GURLEY BROWN.

France's Best Designers

1	CLAUDE MONTANA
2	JEAN-PAUL GAULTIER
3	KARL LAGERFELD
4	AZZEDINE ALAIA
5	MARTINE SITBON

CHRISTIAN DIOR, 11 rue François 1er, 75008 ☎ (1) 4073 5444 (couture); 32 ave Montaigne, 75008 (boutique)

The 'in' house. For his very first collection, Gianfranco Ferré won the coveted Golden Thimble award as best couturier. Naturally, the changes at Dior did not pass without the usual heated Gallic controversy. How dare they sack Marc Bohan! And bring in an *Italian*! Princess Caroline stoically wore her 2-year-old Diors by Bohan to society galas. But the sheer quality and direction of Ferré's collection won over all critics. Breathing a contemporary air into the house style, he produced a spirited new New Look – clear-cut suits, cocktail and evening wear with nipped-in waists, plunge necklines, lace, fur and diamanté. Isabelle Adjani, PALOMA PICASSO, Grace Jones, Daryl Hannah and Ivana Trump lapped it up. Dior is still the place for mixed-pelt furs, lingerie and hosiery, and impeccable menswear by Dominique Morlotti.

CHRISTIAN LACROIX, 73 rue du Faubourg St Honoré, 75008 ☎ (1) 4265 7908

The sophisticate, the baby doll, the tart, the temptress – Lacroix caters to them all. His frivolity and originality are infectious, his influence far-reaching. Accredited with giving couture a new lease of life, he has brought in a new, younger clientele – Lucy Ferry, Madonna, Bond girl Maryam D'Abo, Bette Midler, Faye Dunaway – for whom FF50,000 is a mere bagatelle. 'Simplicity' and 'pared-down' mean nothing to Lacroix. Five fabrics at once and a dozen types of detail do ... imagine Duchesse satin plus damask plus velvet plus leopard print silk plus tulle, embellished with embroidery, beading, quilting, lace, tassels, fringing, arabesque swirls and a golden embossed Sun King. That type of thing. ANNE-ELISABETH MOUTET advises *"he uses texture and colours so subtly that you really have to see the clothes to appreciate them"*. PALOMA PICASSO does just that. His Luxe collection is semi-couture at half the price; also prêt-à-porter, accessories, a new perfume and licensing deals (all essential to regain the multi-million-franc losses on the couture). Fashion-hounds have thrown out their Chanel chains in favour of Lacroix's extravagant faux jewels – a huge cross that takes up half your breastbone, a neck-hugging encrustation of dulled gold and whopping rocks, enormous spangled earrings that brush the shoulders.

CLAUDE MONTANA, 31 rue de Grenelle, 75007 ☎ (1) 4549 1302

Very much in vogue for perfect tailoring (with a twist – pleated trousers, backless jackets, soft draped necklines, long shorts), marvellous colouring (ochre, lime...) and deft handling of leather. *"Very sophisticated tailoring, very sleek, very clean, which somehow seems applicable now....His evening biker things are good, with the right sense of humour and glamour"* – STEPHEN JONES. *"One of my favourites. Every time I go to Paris I run through his shops to see what they have. His clothes are cut in a way that makes Asian men look so good"* – KEN HOM.

EMANUEL UNGARO, 2 ave Montaigne, 75008 ☎ (1) 4723 6194 (couture); 58 rue du Faubourg St Honoré, 75008 ☎ (1) 4742 1606 (boutique)

For colour, cut and sophistication, this couturier can't be beat, although his brand of hyper-dressiness is temporarily out of synch with the current mood of fashion. Effervescent outfits in sugar-bright colours, zazzy print mixes and jewel-like brocades have the power to turn any woman into a ravishing beauty. JOAN COLLINS, Anouk Aimée (Emanuel's ex *and* ex-muse), Nastassja Kinski and Princess Ira von Fürstenberg need not fear: their Ungaros can soon come out of the wardrobe and go to the ball.

GIVENCHY, 3 ave Georges V, 75008 ☎ (1) 4723 8136; 8 ave Montaigne, 75008

Givenchy's look remains true to that which originally won the devotion of Audrey Hepburn (who has received a Fashion Oscar for 30 faithful years' dressing). Danielle Mitterrand too stands by Count Hubert de Givenchy, who, at 63, is still plying the pencil and scissors. Refined, restrained daywear and screen goddess evening wear that make you look a *lady*.

GUY LAROCHE, 29 ave Montaigne, 75008 ☎ (1) 4069 6800 (couture); 30 rue du Faubourg St Honoré, 75008 ☎ (1) 4265 6274 (boutique)

When Guy Laroche died, the new collection was entrusted to Italian Angelo Tarlazzi, whose past daring work could have shocked such staid habituées as Madame Pompidou, Bernadette Chirac and Marie-Hélène de Rothschild. But Tarlazzi shares with Laroche a flattering sense of proportion and a way with bright colours that has earnt much praise. *"Angelo Tarlazzi is a young couturier who I think is absolutely smashing"* – HELEN GURLEY BROWN. PS Boutique prices are a fraction of Chanel's for equal quality.

HELENE HAYES, 42 ave Montaigne, 75008
☎ **(1) 4720 4494**
This secret couturier has kitted out Mercedes
Kellogg, Mrs Oscar Hammerstein, Mrs John
Heinz and Mrs Rupert Murdoch in dazzling
evening gowns. A special recommendation from
BARBARA TAYLOR BRADFORD for *"beautiful hand-
made custom-designed couture clothes."*

**JEAN-LOUIS SCHERRER, 51 ave
Montaigne, 75008 ☎ (1) 4359 5539 (couture);
31 rue de Tournon, 75006 ☎ 4354 4907
(boutique)**
One of the couture establishment, renowned for
well-structured cocktail and evening wear with
crisp-cut necklines and dripping in detail –
embroidery, jewels, fringing, frogging, tassels,
epaulettes.... Dresses the crowned and coro-
neted heads of Europe, politicians' wives such
as Madame Giscard d'Estaing. Look out for last
season's numbers at half-price or less at 29 ave
Ledru Rollin, 75012 ☎ (1) 4628 3927.

🐦 **JEAN-PAUL GAULTIER, 6 rue
Vivienne, 75002 ☎ (1) 4286 0505**
The peroxide blond Boy Wonder has elevated
offbeat street fashion into mainstream French
dressing (though less successfully in France than
in Britain). 'Inventive', 'witty', 'irreverent' –
you've heard the epithets before, but never so
apt as when applied to Gaultier or his spectacular
shows (when his theme may range from Soviet
Expressionism of the 30s to ecclesiastical, with
trendy nuns arising from the earth). You'll see
shorts, jumpsuits, lycra ski pants, zingy bright
cropped trousers for men, murky-toned jersey
pants for women, but his bestseller is always
tailoring that fits like a dream – exquisite cut,
incredible seaming. Other designs are more slap-
stick than witty: from his famed conical bras to
stretch-satin Y-fronts with lycra or lace frontis-
pieces, teamed with braces lest the lycra should
wilt, and *matching gloves. "Fun and young...
he's my favourite"* – BEATRICE DALLE. He designed the costumes for Peter Greenaway's *The*

Cook, The Thief, His Wife and Her Lover. His
Junior line – less wacky, half the price – distils
his style, while retaining the sharpness of
design.

🐦 **KARL LAGERFELD, 17-19 rue du
Faubourg St Honoré, 75008 ☎ (1) 4266 6464**
Lagerfeld is still winning hearts and admiration,
for his own label as well as those of Chanel and
Fendi. *"The most brilliant of all designers. He
has such a keen eye for fashion and style. No
one seems to have such power of observation or
such enormous versatility. He is also a superb
photographer..."* – ANIKO GAAL. *"I think he's a
still-rising star. Now that Ferré is at Dior,
Lagerfeld is doing a far younger, pop-ier, more
casual look, showing his excellence as a designer. He still does immaculately tailored
suits, but the styling of his last show was more
believable, not such high-camp"* – STEPHEN
JONES. He even pleases BIJAN without qualifi-
cation: *"Best of all I like Lagerfeld. I like the
old-style management."* Old-style but shrewd –
KL's signature scent has been out for years; now
he is competing in the accessories line – beautifully shaped bags, shoes and jewellery, all
stamped with his trademark fan.

**KENZO, 3 place des Victoires, 75001
☎ (1) 4236 8141**
Japanese by birth, Parisian in spirit, Kenzo is
always independent in his outlook. Tops for
wearable, colourful, floral, patterned gear. Embroidered blouses, peasanty skirts, vivid knits,
fabulous scarves and shawls, a riot of ricrac and
appliqué, plus boyish tailored separates.

**LOLITA LEMPICKA, 2 rue des Rosiers,
75004 ☎ (1) 4277 4045**
This young designer has settled into the mainstream with her modern, feminine, youthful,
sophisticated look. She maintains a strong suit
in the sassy little wool crêpe suit and the coat-
dress, experimenting all the time with more
outré colour and shape.

🐦 **Buzzz Water lilies:** For Monet's late,
giant canvases, bite into the **Orangerie des Tuileries**, place de la Concorde, 75001
☎ (1) 4297 4816, purpose-designed by the artist soi-même🐦...... **Empire building:**
Napoleon and Josephine's home, **Château de Malmaison**, 92500 Rueil-Malmaison ☎
(1) 4749 2007, shows the stylish, witty décor of the early 1800s (see Napoleon's bedroom,
draped like a campaign tent)🐦...... Best **frame-maker** in Paris is **Christian de
Beaumont**, 21 rue Frédéric Sauton, 75005 ☎ (1) 4634 6306, who designs individual
frames for Old Masters and modern works alike🐦...... Medieval eye: **Musée de
Cluny**, 6 place Paul Painlevé, 75005, is a 15C monastic house containing superb
tapestries, jewellery, sculpture and Books of Hours🐦...... Done the Pyramid? Of
equal architectural standing is the gleaming **Arche de la Défense**, the modern
conclusion to the unswerving line that starts at the Arc de Triomphe du Carroussel (in
front of the Louvre) and travels through the Arc de Triomphe........................🐦

MADAME GRES, 17 rue du Faubourg St Honoré, 75008 ☎ (1) 4742 5218
This nonagenarian was the first to make silk jersey her medium, creating the fluid Grecian goddess look. Now semi-retired, she still oversees the collections, designed by the young Japanese, Takashi Sakaki (the house is now under Japanese ownership). JANIE SAMET loves the new-style Grés: "*It has retained the sense of almost austere purity that was the hallmark of Madame Grés.*"

MARITHE & FRANCOIS GIRBAUD, 38 rue Etienne Marcel, 75002 ☎ (1) 4233 5469
Hovering outside the establishment, this young design team produce casual, switched-on clothes for day and evening. Acquiring a following at home and abroad.

France's Best Couturiers

1	YVES SAINT LAURENT
2	KARL LAGERFELD at CHANEL
3	GIANFRANCO FERRE at DIOR
4	CHRISTIAN LACROIX
5	GIVENCHY

⚓ MARTINE SITBON, 161 rue St Honoré, 75001 ☎ (1) 4260 9474
Martine is queen of the 60s revival, with her body-hugging garb, catsuits, bare midriffs. Also a collection for Chloë – swing coats, wide trousers, halter-necks. "*If anyone can give Chloë the identity they lost when Lagerfeld left them it's Sitbon*" – CATHERINE ROUSSO.

MYRENE DE PREMONVILLE, 52 blvd Richard Lenoir, 75011 ☎ (1) 4807 2325
Echoes of the sophisticated 40s, structured outfits for the modish gamin in bright, mixed blocks of colours. "*That great, easy, relaxed, Katharine Hepburn type of tailoring*" – STEPHEN JONES.

SONIA RYKIEL, 175 Blvd St Germain, 75006 ☎ (1) 4954 6000
Understated, well co-ordinated, sleek, fluid knitwear in muted fudgy colours – pure Rykiel, and her following love it. But soft...there was a whisper that her spring collection was *dull*. (It was no use her trying to chivvy it up with rhinestones. It just wasn't her.) Just wait... and you'll see Rykiel rise again.

⚓ YVES SAINT LAURENT, 5 ave Marceau, 75016 ☎ (1) 4723 7271
The unimpeachable champion, the all-hallowed originator of modern fashion. Not only is each couture collection more stunning than the last, not only are his sleek-lined classics perennial bestsellers, but Saint Laurent is also one of the shrewdest men in French couture. When he and companion/business partner Pierre Bergé took the company public last year, it was 27 times oversubscribed on the Paris stock market; they now control a multi-million-dollar cosmetics and fashion empire. Beloved by the Mitterrands, Raisa Gorbachev, Catherine Deneuve, PALOMA PICASSO and the Duchess of York, Yves is master of the seductive little frock and lavishly embellished evening wear, in drop-dead black or vivid colour clashes. Hallmark designs – the beautiful V-necked navy suit, the short sharp skirt, Le Smoking – reappear seasonally in contemporary guise. A fave rave for SHAKIRA CAINE and BIJAN: "*I do love what he does for women. Obviously I hate what he does for men.*"

Hotels

⚓ HOTEL DE CRILLON, 10 place de la Concorde, 75008 ☎ (1) 4265 2424
The nearest you'll get to the Versailles standard of living. Stunning 18C palace behind Gabriel's famous façade, agleam with marble, mirrors and chandeliers. "*If money is no object, I think it is very difficult to beat the Crillon. The best location, best views, best rooms, softest towels. It is an exemplary grand hotel*" – LOYD GROSSMAN. **Les Ambassadeurs** is one of the most glittering dining rooms in Paris, not to mention one of the best, with Christian Constant heading the kitchen.

HOTEL DE L'ABBAYE SAINT-GERMAIN, 10 rue Cassette, 75006 ☎ (1) 4544 3811
Former monastery that's now a charming little hotel; only a short walk from the boulevard cafés, yet as quiet as a sleepy provincial town. Stay in a ground-floor bedroom which leads into the lovely bird-filled garden.

HOTEL LANCASTER, 7 rue de Berri, 75008 ☎ (1) 4359 9043
A discreet member of the Savoy group with the air of a private house. The antiques and works of art have been chosen with taste and restraint, and it works. Here, movie stars such as Michelle Pfeiffer can relax. "*A consistently good hotel. After some refurbishment it's back on top – although I think it's always been on top*" – TERRY HOLMES. Further votes from PATRICIA HODGE, NED SHERRIN, KEITH FLOYD and LADY ELIZABETH ANSON. Noted for inventive nouvelle cuisine; dine in the interior garden in summer.

HOTEL LE BRISTOL, 112 rue du Faubourg St Honoré, 75008 ☎ (1) 4266 9145
As glamorous as ever, filled with superb antiques and a plethora of marble and crystal. Exclusive and discreet, it's where prominent Americans and diplomats stay, plus a loyal VICTOR EDELSTEIN. Terrace, gardens and a fantasy

pool like an Edwardian yacht, with polished wooden 'deck'. *"I love the Bristol because of the swimming pool – it's absolutely lovely"* – JOSEPH. A restaurant of elegance and excellence.

HOTEL MEURICE, 228 rue de Rivoli, 75001 ☎ 4260 3860

Overlooking the Tuileries is this beautifully swish hotel, with gilded salons and ballrooms – all very Madame Pompadour. Dali made the Royal Suite his Paris pad for 30 years.

HOTEL PLAZA ATHENEE, 25 ave Montaigne, 75008 ☎ (1) 4723 7833

A glossy status symbol for the nouveaux, awash with lustrous silk couches, swept-back curtains, glittering chandeliers and marble fireplaces. Spot rock and film stars such as Michael J Fox, and older ladies lunching with toy boys.

HOTEL RITZ, 15 place Vendôme, 75001 ☎ (1) 4260 3830

Still the ritziest (and probably the most expensive) hotel in Paris, glistening from its multi-million revamp. Supreme setting, comfort, service and cuisine, and the wildest suite in town, the Impériale, with crested baroque bed. *"For complete over-the-top extravagance, the best place ever in the world. You don't have to phone for a maid – you press a bell and she arrives within a minute. It's your private château in the middle of Paris"* – ROSS BENSON. *"They have opened a new health club and nightclub. It's quite sensational"* – FRANK BOWLING. *"The health centre is very good. Service is better than ever, including an offer of packing and unpacking for guests"* – BETTY KENWARD. More votes for the health club from CAROL WRIGHT, SHAKIRA CAINE and JEREMIAH TOWER: *"The world's best cure for jet lag is sitting around the pool at the new spa, sipping champagne and nibbling on toasted chicken sandwiches. Not for the faint-hearted."* Romantics BARBARA TAYLOR BRAD-FORD, BARBARA CARTLAND, JOAN COLLINS and STANLEY MARCUS love it, while the STIRLING MOSSes are *"quite partial"*. BARRY HUMPHRIES lavishes praise on **L'Espadon**: *"Still the best place to eat in Paris and not excessively expensive. Exquisite. You must finish with the 'Napoleon'."* The famous **Hemingway Bar**, erstwhile haunt of Hemingway, natch, and Scott Fitzgerald, is where Isabelle Adjani and CHARLOTTE RAMPLING make their rendez-vous. Also at the Ritz are the **Cambon** and **Vendôme** bars.

HOTEL ST REGIS, 12 rue Jean Goujon, 75008 ☎ (1) 4359 4190

"Super little hotel with only 44 rooms, all individually styled. Privately owned and right in the heart of the couturier district, so the clientele is fashion-orientated. Tiny, discreet and very comfortable – the place I like most in Paris" – JEFFERY TOLMAN.

LA VILLA, 29 rue Jacob, 75006 ☎ (1) 4326 6000

The Morgans of Paris. *"A very brave and very well-done attempt at turning a little Left Bank hotel over to a young progressive French designer and giving him carte blanche. It's really quite remarkable"* – LOYD GROSSMAN. Rooms are sound-proofed and have satellite TV.

——— *Music* ———

CENTRE DE MUSIQUE BAROQUE, Versailles ☎ (1) 4396 4848

Concerts, opera and ballet staged in the château, the park and in town.

FEP FESTIVAL ESTIVAL DE PARIS, 20 rue Geoffroy-l'Asnier, 75004 ☎ (1) 4804 9801

A summer of classical music held at different churches and auditoria.

L'OPERA DE LA BASTILLE, 2 bis place de la Bastille, 75010 ☎ (1) 4001 1799

Buzzz Sophistication de la boudoir: taste 18C life via the perfect Louis XVI house and contents, **Musée Nissim de Camondo**, 63 rue de Monceau, 75008 ☎ (1) 4563 2632 . . . the Boucher and Fragonard-filled period rooms at **Musée Cognacq-Jay**, now transferred to their new home at Hôtel Donon, 8 rue Elzévir, 75003 ☎ 4272 2113 . . . the finest example of French rococo décor in situ, the oval salon in the Princesse de Soubise's apartments, **Hôtel de Soubise** (Archives Nationales), 60 rue des Francs-Bourgeois, 75003 ☎ (1) 4027 6000 . . . . . . More dec arts, from medieval to modern, at the **Musée des Arts Décoratifs**, 107 rue de Rivoli, 75001 ☎ (1) 4260 3214 – rooms from couturier Jeanne Lanvin's house, Louis XIV-XVI furniture, Lalique glass, art nouveau jewellery . . . . . . Next door at No 111 is the **Musée des Arts de la Mode** – the first national costume museum in France, displaying couture numeros donated by some of the world's great clothes-horses, and exhibitions of the fashion greats (Saint Laurent, Dior . . .) . . . .

Amid the typical furore that accompanies Paris's more avant-garde ventures in the arts world, Carlos Ott's ultra-modern, much-unloved building opened for the 14 July 1989 festivities and promptly shut again, the acoustics pronounced less than superior. Re-opened in spring this year, it is now home to the ♠ PARIS OPERA, a controversial move under the orders of Directeur des Opéras de Paris Pierre Bergé, who shocked the city by dropping erstwhile musical director Daniel Barenboim. The post is now held by the unknown 36-year-old Korean Myung-Whun Chung. Despite the hoo-ha, the Opéra remains one of the leading companies in the world.

THEATRE MUSICAL DE PARIS, 2 place de Chatelet, 75001 ☎ (1) 4261 1983

This hall for recitals, concerts, musicals and opera has regained its former high standing. It was the major opera venue for the 1989/90 season, post-Palais Garnier and pre-Bastille, and now Chirac has doubled its subsidies, enabling it to hire world-class conductors such as Leonard Bernstein and Simon Rattle.

VERSAILLES FESTIVAL OPERA, c/o Syndicat d'Initiative, 7 rue des Réservoirs, 78000 Versailles ☎ (1) 3950 3622

A programme of opera and concerts held for one week in May/June. The highlight is still the beautiful baroque opera staged at the Château de Versailles in the original setting and costumes. The lavish little opera house was built by Gabriel for the future Louis XVI's marriage to Marie-Antoinette. MARQUIS DE LASTOURS would never miss the event: *"Without the tourists and the postcard stands, it's as if the palace were miraculously restored to its splendid past."*

———— *Restaurants* ————

See also Hotels and Shopping.

AMPHYCLES, 78 ave des Ternes, 75017 ☎ (1) 4068 0101

"The most talked-about new place, another one named after an ancient Greek...Important because the chef is the best-known protégé of Robuchon. A big hit" – ROBERT NOAH. BARBARA KAFKA joins in the gastro-gabble.

APICIUS, 122 ave de Villiers, 75017 ☎ (1) 4380 1966

Image is all-important here, from the designer monochrome plates to the film-starrish looks of chef Jean-Pierre Vigato and his wife. *"Very few people don't like it"* – ROBERT NOAH. *"A good bistro and not too expensive"* – ROLAND ESCAIG. Proving that one man's meat is another man's poison, ALEXANDRE LAZAREFF finds it: *"Pretentious."*

BENOIT, 20 rue St Martin, 75004 ☎ (1) 4272 2576

The quintessential Parisian bistro. *"An old-fashioned French place that I particularly like"* – VISCOUNT HAMBLEDEN. *"A bistro with hearty food"* – BARBARA KAFKA. One of MICHEL ROBICHAUD's favourites.

♠ CARRE DES FEUILLANTS, 14 rue de Castiglione, 75001 ☎ (1) 4286 8282

The brilliant Alain Dutournier is inspired by cuisine of the south-west of France. Delicacies include ravioli stuffed with foie gras and truffles or with lobster; wild salmon with smoked bacon. Votes from MATTHEW FORT, JUDITH KRANTZ and ROBERT NOAH.

CAVIAR KASPIA, 17 place de la Madeleine, 75008 ☎ (1) 4265 3352

Above the caviare shop is a romantic wood-panelled restaurant with a glass cabinet displaying Tsarist silver and memorabilia. Sample an ounce of Beluga, Oscietra, etcetera, with a chilled glass of Sancerre, bubbly or vodka. *"Elegant but unfussy. You can eat at the bar and the management are easy about dress. Delicious blinis and caviare and fresh crab salad"* – MARIE HELVIN. *"Excellent, especially for lunch or a caviare tea-break"* – ROBERT NOAH. *"Take lemon tea and vodka, have a blini and some steely Beluga, and look out of the window at the flowers"* – CLARE FERGUSON. Expect *"movie stars, ministers who don't pay or queue, middle-aged lovers"* – ALEXANDRE LAZAREFF.

CHEZ EDGARD, 4 rue Marbeuf, 75006 ☎ (1) 4720 5115

Any night of the week you could form a new cabinet by walking into Paul Benmussa's red and black dining room. *"The place, the new Lipp, for the political and media world...Europe No 1 radio station and Antenne No 2 TV station"* – ALEXANDRE LAZAREFF. Everyone is treated with the same warmth: there are good tables for all. You might rub épaules with Liza Minnelli, Mick Jagger, Alain Delon or Anouk Aimée. The food is good too – try tartare de saumon or selle d'agneau aux petits légumes. And don't forget to save space for Paul B's delectable chocolates (see Shopping).

DODIN-BOUFFANT, 25 rue Frédéric Sauton, 75005 ☎ (1) 4325 2514

A grand bistro that has various toques and stars to its credit and an illustrious clientele. The best raspberry soufflé in town. *"Perfect. Mitterrand goes there without his bodyguards. Famous for hareng cru, first to have salade folle (with foie gras and haricots verts)"* – ALEXANDRE LAZAREFF.

DUQUESNOY, 6 ave Bosquet, 75007 ☎ (1) 4705 9678

A former provincial chef who has moved up to town. Quiet, bourgeois setting for upscale, bourgeois cuisine. Flavourful cooking – quail and foie gras pie, apple soufflé. *"Excellent"* – ROBERT NOAH; BARBARA CARTLAND agrees.

Unsung Bistros

3, 2 or even 1 lone Michelin star may not be the reason you prize a restaurant. Paris has plenty of characterful eateries that our contributors hold dear. *"Very few places make my heart give a little leap, but there are 2 in Paris – Le Voltaire, 27 quai Voltaire, and Louis XIV, Place des Victoires, which has Lyonnaise cuisine and is wonderful"* – VICTOR EDELSTEIN. JEREMIAH TOWER is wild about Louis too: *"What every city in the world should have – a simple bistro."* LOYD GROSSMAN says: *"For classic French bistro cooking, one of the best is Le Bistro de la Grille, 1 rue Guisarde, 75006 ☎ (1) 4354 1687. Another is Aux Charpentiers, 10 rue Mabillon, 75006 ☎ (1) 4326 3005. Their boeuf à la ficelle is the most orgasmic form of boiled beef imaginable."* For BARBARA TAYLOR BRADFORD, *"Chez André, 12 rue Marbeuf, 75008 ☎ (1) 4720 5957, is a lovely bistro"* (Roman Polanski agrees). JEAN-MICHEL JAUDEL remains true to Le

Berthoud, 1 rue Valette, 75005 ☎ (1) 4354 3881: *"It's a measure of its calibre that, even though that's where I had the fight with my wife that led to our divorce, I still go!"* JOSEPH loves Chez Georges, 1 rue du Mail, 75002 ☎ (1) 4260 0711: *"It's a very old, traditional restaurant, all the waitresses are old ladies and they remember everybody. It's like a little family place."* Local arties in the know hop over the road to the titchy Chez Pierrot, 4 rue du Mail ☎ (1) 4296 2436, for fantastic pot-au-feu and family French fare (roast chicken, tarte tatin); a MICHEL ROBICHAUD fave. DOMINIQUE PIOT goes for La Foux, 2 rue Clément, 75006 ☎ (1) 4325 7766: *"A rarity – a Lyonnaise restaurant that manages to keep the food light. Even their quenelles are almost as light as soufflé. Incredible cellar – one can still order Brouilly."* Check out Chirac's pal Pierre Vedel, 19 rue Duranton, 75015 ☎ (1) 4558 4317, for 2-star food at moderate prices.

FAUGERON, 52 rue Longchamp, 75016 ☎ (1) 4704 2453

Remains No 1 for PETER USTINOV: *"There are no other bests on this level, despite Michelin, Lichfield, Gault Millau et al. There simply aren't any better."* Tuck into Paris's most arty dish, pyramide de melon, created in homage to the Louvre pyramid.

FOUQUET'S, 99 ave des Champs-Elysées, 75008 ☎ (1) 4723 7060

The archetypal fashionable Paris brasserie, expensive, overrated, yet: *"The restaurant for movie people like Belmondo, all the dinner parties for the Césars (French Oscars), and premières for theatre shows. You have to be on La Veranda. Most famous pot-au-feu in Paris"* – ALEXANDRE LAZAREFF.

GUY SAVOY, 18 rue Troyon, 75017 ☎ (1) 4380 4061

The eponymous chef is still much toqued about for his fine combinations of poultry, fish, offal and vegetables, served in unusual ways. One of RAYMOND BLANC's top 3 in France. *"Really tremendous"* – MATTHEW FORT. *"A good bistro"* – ROLAND ESCAIG. Further confirmation from ROBERT NOAH and BARBARA CARTLAND. *"One of the current fashionable 2-star restaurants"* – STEVEN SPURRIER. Film execs are in their element at lunch, all swanky service with dishes under silver cloches.

JAMIN (ROBUCHON), 32 rue de Longchamp, 75116 ☎ (1) 4727 1227

Joël Robuchon is voted best chef in the world. A dictator in the kitchen, he is one of the few top chefs who personally checks every dish before it goes out. When he dishes up pig's head and heavenly mash his way, or truffle, foie gras and seafood masterpieces, foodies dish out accolades (and the Michelin men, 3 stars). What price ecstasy? Some FF600 a head, sans vin (and that's the cheaper set menu). MATTHEW FORT speaks for many when he says: *"The finest meal I have ever had in my life."* *"In terms of sheer dazzling cookery it is one of the handful of best restaurants in the world"* – LOYD GROSSMAN. *"Quite wonderful. It's the only really classy 3-star we-think-a-lot-of-ourselves restaurant where ...well, we took one of our sons there for his 21st and it wasn't just a meal, it was a parade, and they also sent over a bottle of Beaumes de Venise with their compliments, which I thought was handsome in a place which didn't have to do that ...those things do count"* – FREDERIC RAPHAEL. *"Still one of the best in the world"* – BARBARA KAFKA. *"The best restaurant in Paris"* – ROLAND ESCAIG. *"Of course"* – DREW SMITH. More applause from KEN HOM, ROY ACKERMAN, LEO SCHOFIELD and ALEXANDRE LAZAREFF, who sighs: *"The best. I only go once a year, so as not to spoil the pleasure, because as a food critic if I went more often I couldn't taste the others. It is perfect."*

LA CAGOUILLE, 10 place Brancusi, 75014
☎ (1) 4322 0901
Fresh-as-fresh fish and seafood in Gérard
Allemandou's seasidy bistro. *"Fantastic, the best
fish restaurant in Paris with the best list of
cognacs"* – STEVEN SPURRIER.

France's Best
Restaurants

1	JAMIN · Paris	
2	GUY SAVOY · Paris	
3	ESPERANCE · St Père, Vézelay	
4	TAILLEVENT · Paris	
5	LOUIS XIV · Monte Carlo	
6	LES PRES ET LES SOURCES D'EUGENIE · Eugénie-les-Bains	
7	L'AUBERGADE · Puymirol	
8	BOYER · Reims	
9	LOU MAZUC · Laguiole	
10	L'ARPEGE · Paris	

**LA MANUFACTURE, 30 rue Ernest
Renan, Issy-les-Mouleneaux**
☎ (1) 4093 0898
Jean-Pierre Vigato's new venture, based just
beyond the Porte de Versailles. *"The most in-
teresting of the wave of second restaurants.
Instead of being a pseudo-bistro like the others
(Michel Rostang, Guy Savoy), his is a sort of
dégriffé – a mark-down version of the expensive
Apicius. Similar food at half the price"* – ROBERT
NOAH. *"Very impressive indeed"* – MATTHEW FORT.

LA MAREE, 1 rue Daru, 75008
☎ (1) 4227 5932
One of the best fish and seafood restaurants in
Paris, owned by mother-son team Babette and
Eric Trompier. Power lunching at a price – and
how! Gérard Rouillard knows how to pick the
freshest fish and concocts new recipes – belons
au champagne, suprême de turbot à la moutarde.
Arguably the best rougets grillés in France.

**LA ROTISSERIE DU BEAUJOLAIS, 17
quai de la Tournelle, 75005** ☎ (1) 4354 1747
Claude Terrail (of La Tour d'Argent) has opened
a bistro right next to La Tour. *"Very good value,
excellent products from the Lyonnaise region"* –
ROBERT NOAH.

🍴 **L'ARPEGE, 84 rue de Varenne, 75007**
☎ (1) 4551 2002
Alain Passard hasn't looked back since he took

over the premises of L'Archestrate (where he
worked under Senderens). 2 Michelin stars and
a delighted clientele, who love his original,
piquant flavours (lobster salad with sweet-sour
vinaigrette, savouries with a streak of caramel).
*"One of the best new restaurants that I've been
to. Very, very good, unpretentious…it's food
that has a great deal of flavour, intense flavour,
but not too much sauce, which is wonderful. You
can tell the chef has a passion for what he does.
He's just terrific"* – KEN HOM. *"The FF150 lunch
menu is the best in Paris. This chef is one of the
greatest French chefs. He serves as an amuse-
bouche, un chaud-froid d'oeuf au sirop d'érable
[maple syrup]"* – ALEXANDRE LAZAREFF. LISE
WATIER brings him Canadian maple syrup
whenever she's over: *"His cuisine is light, extremely elegant and refined. There is a
mysterious touch…maybe his secret is the
maple syrup!"* Further votes from STEVEN
SPURRIER and ROLAND ESCAIG.

**LA TOUR D'ARGENT, 15 quai de la
Tournelle, 75005** ☎ (1) 4354 2337
The famous, if hackneyed, Tour d'Argent suffers
from an attitude problem…as one contributor
puts it, *"they treat you with an air of 'aren't you
lucky to be here' and the answer is 'no I'm not'"*.
However, it has a string of bests to its credit:
the best view, over the Notre Dame; the best
wine cellar in Paris if not the world; the most
elegant setting – and a better-than-ever menu
under Manuel Martinez (Claude Terrail is proprietor). Walls are graffiti-stricken with auto-
graphs of the *right* sort of diner – Princes of
Wales past and present, Sir Winston Churchill,
de Gaulle, Roosevelt, Woody Allen, Robert De
Niro. *"My favourite place in Paris"* – DUC
D'ORLEANS. *"Pretty nice"* – STIRLING MOSS. A hit
with BARBARA TAYLOR BRADFORD *"for the view
and the duck"*. *"I love it – I know a lot of people
don't, but it's an experience"* – ROBERT NOAH.

**LE COCHON D'OR, 192 ave Jean-Jaurès,
75019** ☎ (1) 4208 3981
Some of the best steaks – and foie gras – in Paris.
Huge 4-inch wedges of meat, scorched on the
outside, red but warm inside. *"Go when you're
really hungry. Even though the local meat market has gone, this fabulous restaurant has main-
tained its standards"* – JEAN-MICHEL JAUDEL.

🍴 **LE GRAND VEFOUR, 17 rue
Beaujolais, 75001** ☎ (1) 4296 5627
Grand is the word. An 18C treasure by the
gardens of the Palais Royal. Light classical
cuisine under a chef who spent 5 years with Joël
Robuchon. *"At the most rarefied level I would
still go for Le Grand Véfour because it's probably
the most beautiful restaurant in the world, the
bitter chocolate soufflé should have been called
'death by chocolate', and it is so unbelievably
grown-up and special that you feel you are being
given an amazing treat"* – LOYD GROSSMAN. *"The
most evocative Paris restaurant"* – MICHAEL
BROADBENT.

Dining with Scott Roberts

Upscale and downbeat, haute and branché, FIONA SCOTT ROBERTS casts an alternative, unfoodie eye over the scoffing and quaffing scene in Paris. "**Le Bakonyi**, 5 rue du Cloître St Merri, 75004 ☎ (1) 4804 9050, is as yet undiscovered by guides and tourists, in spite of being in Les Halles. A conservative upper-class set mix with TV and film personalities. A lovely place to lunch is **La Ferme Saint-Simon**, 6 rue St-Simon, 75007 ☎ (1) 4548 3574, in company with people from the Breakfast TV News. Rather difficult to find is **Le Bistrot de Paris**, 33 rue de Lille, 75007 ☎ (1) 4261 1683, a very good French bistro that attracts politicos, actors, etc. **Le Muniche** ☎ (1) 4633 6209, and **Le Petit Zinc** ☎ (1) 4633 5166, at 27 and 25 rue de Buci, 75006, are both owned by M Layrac. Consistently good food with an emphasis on coquillages; both make enchanting places to eat outdoors in summer. **Pré Catelan**, route de Suresnes, Bois de Boulogne ☎ (1) 4524 5558, is another charming place in summer, with a wonderful garden and an immaculately dressed clientele. So many business people have to go out to La Défense; at least they can eat extremely well at **Le Monarch**, Place des Reflets, 92400 ☎ (1) 4778 8459."

LE JULES VERNE, Tour Eiffel, Champ de Mars, 75007 ☎ (1) 4555 6144
Putting the haute in cuisine... it may sound like a tourist trap but it ain't. You arrive by private glass lift and enter one of the most striking salles in Paris, renovated in dark steel tones in keeping with the Tower. Breathtaking view and imaginative nouvelle cuisine by Louis Grondard – and growing *"better and better"* – ROBERT NOAH. Françoise Dumas has given memorable parties here, and it's a high spot for BARRY HUMPHRIES.

🍴 LUCAS CARTON, 9 place de la Madeleine, 75008 ☎ (1) 4265 2290
Inspiration and ingenuity have been breathed into this restaurant by Alain Senderens. Exquisite light, modern cuisine – he goes from strength to strength and expense to expense. Praise from MICHEL GUERARD, ROY ACKERMAN and DREW SMITH. *"For really interesting eating, and a flashy, dressy setting. Either you love it or you don't, but everybody should go"* – ROBERT NOAH. ALEXANDRE LAZAREFF recommends you wangle your way in to the first-floor private club, le Cercle.

MAXIM'S, 3 rue Royale, 75008 ☎ (1) 4265 2794
Exorbitant prices and fair cooking, but, most importantly, the art nouveau elegance of one of the world's best dining rooms, blooming with flowers. The glitzy clientele sit in the front room at lunchtime and the back for dinner. *"I love it – one of those places you'd choose to have a birthday party"* – ROBERT NOAH. Jacqueline de Ribes, JOAN COLLINS and Claus von Bülow go.

PATRICK LENOTRE, 28 rue Duret, 75116 ☎ (1) 4500 1767
Son of *the* smart caterer Gaston Lenôtre, Patrick is earning rapturous praise at his début restaurant. Try tender semi-cooked salmon, partridge wrapped in cabbage leaves and stuffed with foie gras, bitter chocolate ice cream with daubs of fresh vanilla ice cream.

🍴 TAILLEVENT, 15 rue Lamennais, 75008 ☎ (1) 4561 1290
A consistent front-runner, led by Jean-Claude Vrinat, a man of taste and – some say – genius. *"Internationally known as the best in France, ie the world"* – STEVEN SPURRIER. *"Consistently superb – quietly elegant setting, excellent food, faultless wine selection and immaculate service"* – MICHAEL BROADBENT. *"The best all-round restaurant"* – ROBERT NOAH. *"Still a classic"* – SERENA SUTCLIFFE. Worse than trying to get in to the theatre – book 6 weeks in advance and reconfirm the day before; impulse diners can try ringing at 6pm for returns.

TSEYANG, 25 rue Pierre 1er de Serbie, 75116 ☎ (1) 4720 7022
"The best Chinese I've ever been to" – JUDITH KRANTZ. Wonderful Peking duck and steamed delicacies.

Shopping

See also Fashion designers.

In and around **rue du Faubourg St Honoré** and **avenue Montaigne** reside the holy chic – Lacroix, Lagerfeld, Saint Laurent, Chanel, Scherrer, Ungaro, Dior, Guy Laroche; **place des Victoires** and its environs house the more outlandish: Gaultier and the Japs. **Le Marais** is the branché area full of hideaway one-off shops in little back streets (whither JOSEPH loves to wander) – designers like Alaïa and Lempicka, costume and antique jewellery; it's CLARE FERGUSON's fave district: *"Wonderful teahouses, cafés, large and small museums, dress* *shops, Jewish delis, leather and fabric shops, and the best felafel with pitta."*

The **St Germain des Près** area buzzes with young boutiques – avoid the Boulevard itself and make forays into rue du Four, rue Bonaparte, rue de Tournon and the first 60 or so numbers of rue de Grenelle. **Place Vendôme** is dripping in diamonds. Paupers find solace at the **Puces** – flea market – at Porte de Clignancourt, for everything second-hand under the sun. Here also, at **Marché Biron**, you can buy (expensive) antique and 1920s couture from Madame Geneviève Autran. Get up early for other good markets at **Porte de Vanves** (surprising finds – one primitive art collector makes formative buys here), **Porte de Montreuil** and **Marché d'Aligre** in the 12e.

ANDROUET, 41 rue d'Amsterdam, 75008
☎ (1) 4874 2690
A fabulous fromagerie, run by Pierre Androuet (*"a delight, the best cheese and wine master in Paris"* – CLARE FERGUSON). Cheeses from all over the country are aged in cellars below the shop. About 4½ tons of 400 varieties are sold a month. Tuck into their 7-course fromage extravaganza.

BARTHELEMY, 51 rue de Grenelle, 75007
☎ (1) 4548 5675; 92 rue Grande,
Fontainebleau ☎ (1) 6422 2164
The grandest cheese shop in town serves the crème of Paris society, including the Palais d'Elysée. It's le meilleur, according to JUDITH KRANTZ, STEVEN SPURRIER and DON HEWITSON.

BERTHILLON, 31 rue St Louis en l'Ile, 75004 ☎ (1) 4354 3161
The ice creams are a dream, although the queues and offhandedness of the staff can make it a nightmare. Azzedine Alaïa and MICHEL GUERARD line up. If you can't bear the wait, snoop around the rest of the île – there are lots of other glaceries selling Berthillon's wares.

BOUCHERON, 26 place Vendôme, 75001
☎ (1) 4260 3282
Haute joaillerie, as ever. A glittering favourite

of JOAN COLLINS, MARGAUX HEMINGWAY and Queen Noor of Jordan.

CAMILLE UNGLIK, 21 rue Pavée, 75004; 66 rue des Saints-Pères, 75007
☎ (1) 4222 7877
For soft-shoe shuffles in 20s- and 30s-inspired designs; ankle boots with elegant contoured heels and a contemporary air. CATHERINE ROUSSO is a fan.

CHARLES JOURDAN, 86 ave des Champs-Elysées, 75008 ☎ (1) 4562 2928
High heels for the well-heeled. Chic and shiny shoes with a touch of tart and a slick of sophistication. Exclusive range with the couture touch by designers such as Karl Lagerfeld, and Enrico Coveri. A favourite of HELEN GURLEY BROWN and JOAN COLLINS.

CHARVET, 28 place Vendôme, 75001
☎ (1) 4260 3070
The Turnbull & Asser of France, No 1 for shirts (they stitched up those of Charles de Gaulle and Giscard d'Estaing), plus nightshirts, pyjamas and accessories. An incredible range of fabrics and a very particular style of collar. They own the rights to make up all the Dufy prints, which they do on huge silk scarves. JOSEPH loves Charvet.

FAUCHON, 26 place de la Madeleine, 75008
☎ (1) 4742 6011
Arguably the grandest and most famous food hall in Paris. Over 20,000 products from home and abroad – exotic groceries and staples, pastries, chocolates, spices and charcuterie. CLARE FERGUSON's joint No 1 with Hédiard: *"Both these great shops mean utter excellence."*

GALERIES LAFAYETTE, 40 blvd Haussmann, 75009 ☎ (1) 4282 3456
The best department store in Paris. A gracious art nouveau building with a stained-glass roof, encompassing designer shoplets with a Francophile viewpoint (couture/prêt-à-porter from Lacroix, Dior, Saint Laurent, Balenciaga, Alaïa, Gaultier, Chantal Thomass, with a little Ralph

🦺 **Buzzz** The travelling élite eschew fashionable luggage these days. Louis Vuitton's so stealable (and so copiable). For Mick Jagger chic comes wrapped up in a **battered Samsonite**; for BOB PAYTON it's **Tumi**; for dozens of Parisians it's **Delsey**🦺...... CLARE FERGUSON buzzes around the city: *"A La Mère de Famille, 35 rue du Faubourg Montmartre, 75009, is the best epicerie fine, an old-style grocery with odd and wonderful wines, liquors, cakes, teas and sweets ...the best wine shop is Le Petit Bacchus, 13 rue du Cherche-Midi, 75006, where you should sit up at the counter, look, sniff, sample, nibble and listen...the best-ever tea merchants is Mariage Frères, 30-32 rue du Bourg Tibourg, 75004 (but avoid the café) ...and the best kitchen tool shop is Dehillerin, 18 rue Coquillère, 75001 – no one speaks English and it's pandemonium, but fun"*................................... 🦺

Lauren and Yamamoto thrown in), plus cool own-label gear and everything else you'd ever need – all with bags of style.

🍴 HEDIARD, 21 place de la Madeleine, 75008 ☎ (1) 4266 4436 and branches

The food hall with the greatest snob value. It was Mme de Gaulle's favourite, and is now tops for DOMINIQUE PIOT, CLARE FERGUSON and LOYD GROSSMAN: "*At the highest level I would go for Hédiard, incomparably superior to and far less touristic than Fauchon.*" Tremendous array of goods, down to their own spices, oils and vinegars, and superb wines.

To Market, To Market...

🍴

The food market in the **Rue de Buci** appeals to SERENA SUTCLIFFE: "*Colourful, bustling and packed with fruit, veg, cheese and charcuterie.*" CLARE FERGUSON favours a trio of top markets: "**Rue Mouffetard**, *a long, winding street filled with fruit, vegetables, dairy produce, fish, shellfish, game and poultry. Also here are old-fashioned cutlery shops, health shops, cheapo fashion, zillions of Greek tavernas with moustachioed Greeks and Cypriots who charm and badger you to death.* **Rue Daguerre** *is smaller, but has superb produce, all bliss. Best on Sunday mornings, when artists, madmen and polemicists take the air. Stop at M Peret's bistro for a dégustation of Beaujolais and Loire wines and Poilâne bread sandwiches. Finally, the* **Marché St Honoré***, just off the rue St Honoré, is small, but a gem for fish, game and wine.*"

🍴 HERMES, 24 rue du Faubourg St Honoré, 75008 ☎ (1) 4017 4717

Synonymous with the luxurious silk square, snaffled and swagged, equally at home on your wall as your shoulders. Also divine leather luggage, belts and handbags – the famous Kelly bag (prospective buyers join a waiting list) and the more recent Jane Birkin bag designed for another faithful customer. The new design director, female journalist Claude Brouet (ex-*Marie-Claire*), follows Eric Bergère in the task to rejuvenate the old establishment image. Diehards may wallow in the museum of original designs, historic carriages and curiosities such as Napoleon's overnight case. "*I love shops like this...an institution*" – JOSEPH. STANLEY MARCUS does too.

JAR'S, 7 place Vendôme, 75001 ☎ (1) 4296 3366

Haute exclusivité. Original jewellery designer who works on commission, for top-drawer necks, wrists and fingers – such as Baroness Marie-Hélène de Rothschild's. Exquisite colouring using precious stones.

LA MAISON DE LA TRUFFE, 19 place de la Madeleine, 75008 ☎ (1) 4265 5322

Among other delicious delicacies (caviare, terrine de foie gras, brimming hampers), the best and most expensive truffles can be sniffed out here between Nov and March.

LA MAISON DU CHOCOLAT, 225 rue du Faubourg St Honoré, 75008 ☎ (1) 4227 3944; 52 rue François 1er, 75008 ☎ (1) 4723 3825

Robert Linxe has been first in his field for years. Golden platters piled high with sinful wafers, truffles and filled chocolates tempt MICHEL GUERARD. At rue François 1er, you can choc out on wickedly rich hot chocolate with mountains of cream.

LANVIN, 15 rue du Faubourg St Honoré, 75008 ☎ (1) 4265 1440

Classic menswear. Old-fashioned shirts in good fabrics, to last a fair chunk of a lifetime; suits and ties with French flair.

LAURENT MERCADAL, 26 ave de Champs-Elysées, 75008 ☎ (1) 4561 4617; 56 rue de Rennes, 75006 ☎ (1) 4548 4387

The shoes to fit the outfit – beautiful, elegant, classic, with an innovative but not outrageous twist.

LES CAVES TAILLEVENT, rue du 199 Faubourg St Honoré, 75008 ☎ (1) 4561 1409

"*The best wine shop in Paris*" – SERENA SUTCLIFFE. A stride away from the restaurant Taillevent, it's run by the owner Jean-Claude Vrinat's daughter Valérie.

🍴 LIONEL POILANE, 8 rue du Cherche-Midi, 75006 ☎ (1) 4548 4259

His handmade sourdough pain de campagne, baked in wood-fired ovens, is known and loved the whole world over. "*The best bakery – staggering breads*" – CLARE FERGUSON.

LOUIS VUITTON, 54 ave Montaigne, 75008 ☎ (1) 4561 9414 (boutique); 78B ave Marceau, 75008 ☎ (1) 4720 4700 (luggage)

LV monogrammed luggage isn't about to become obsolete, but it's certainly taking a back seat. Now part of Bernard Arnault's mammoth Louis Vuitton Moët-Hennessy concern, the company is on the move. Design director Françoise Jollant, ex-head of design at the Centre Pompidou, has the delicate balancing act to achieve of winning round those who now yawn at the sight of the LV logo, while maintaining the support of the LV-crazed Japanese. Modern architects, designers and artists have been drafted in to create new products. Apart from zingily modern scarves and travel furniture, check out the Philippe Starck bag and the Gae Aulenti watch and pen.

MADAME JOSETTE, Tête à Tête, 183 rue du Faubourg St Honoré, 75008
☎ (1) 4359 3989

Like an old cognac, this milliner *hors d'age* has been around for years, but is better than ever. From designing the hats for Cecil Beaton for *My Fair Lady*, she has re-emerged as the most stunning hatter in Paris for events like the Arc de Triomphe. *"Madame Josette is the best person I can work with in Paris. She can make the hat to go with any hairdo"* – JEAN-MICHEL HENRY.

MARCEL BUR, 138 rue du Faubourg St Honoré, 75008 ☎ (1) 4359 5153

M Bur is one of the last great men's tailors in Paris. He has been working from this small shop for almost 50 years, dressing most of the senior diplomats in the neighbouring embassies, as well as an admiring FREDERIC MITTERRAND: *"Even his 'demi-mesure' suits fit better than most other tailors' custom-made suits at 4 times the price."*

♠ MAUD FRIZON, 81-83 rue des Saints Pères, 75006 ☎ (1) 4222 0693

Exquisite shoes – buttery leathers, divine suedes, handmade soles – and they fit like a glove. *"Still my favourite shoe designer"* – JOAN BURSTEIN. JOAN COLLINS, JEAN MUIR, BARRY HUMPHRIES (or could it be Dame Edna?) and DAVID SHILLING are Frizon fans too. Bags at 7 rue de Grenelle, 75006.

PAUL B..., 4 rue Marbeuf, 75008
☎ (1) 4720 8626

Next door to his Chez Edgard, this ivory-panelled shop is the place for Paul Benmussa's super-fresh chocs. Addictive but no additives. The pralines are unsurpassable and the dark chocolate-coated *smoked* almonds are subtly sweet-savoury. M Paul even closes during the hottest months rather than see his chocolates spoil. The politicians' choice.

PETROSSIAN, 18 blvd Latour-Maubourg, 75007 ☎ (1) 4551 5973

Cult caviare of the very best quality, sold in picturesque tins. Also very fine smoked salmon, foie gras, truffles, fresh blinis and Russian pastries. *"WHAT an emporium! An education in all that is sublime, simple and magnificent. No fuss – just perfection"* – CLARE FERGUSON.

PHILIPPE MODEL, 33 place du Marché St Honoré, 75008 ☎ (1) 4296 8902

Not only the most inventive and polished hatter in town (with more than a whisper of whimsy), but elegant shoes, bags, gloves and belts for street-wise women about town. Princess Caroline of Monaco wears his hats, ANIKO GAAL his shoes: *"Wonderful shapes. Beautiful modern shoes."* He is the only tradesman to be invited

to mega-chic Chantilly racecourse, where he set up a tent full of surrealist hats for women to hire.

PORTHAULT, 18 ave Montaigne, 75008
☎ (1) 4720 7525

For beautiful household linen made to their own designs. *"Unique bedlinens...the best sheets in the world"* – BARBARA TAYLOR BRADFORD.

RAFFI, 60 ave Paul-Doumer, 75016
☎ (1) 4503 1090; 60 rue Lafayette, 75009
☎ (1) 4770 1292

The original branch of this Armenian grocer's is at rue Lafayette, but the seizième branch is smarter. Anything Middle Eastern – all sorts of olives, halva, sackfuls of Oriental spices and basketfuls of dried fruits. *"You gain weight just by smelling it"* – JEAN-MICHEL JAUDEL.

Say it with Flowers

🌷

For the best blooms in Paris, go to **Lachaume**, 10 rue Royale, 75008 ☎ (1) 4260 5726, *"a wonderful flower shop. The most extraordinary flowers you have ever seen"* – BARBARA TAYLOR BRADFORD. JEAN-MICHEL HENRY uses only Lachaume flowers for his elaborate evening chignons: *"They have the most delicate pastel flowers, the best orchids in town, and also the loveliest forget-me-nots. I use them to make anything from a dainty bridal crown to a tiara that will rival any exotic piece of jewellery. The flowers are so fresh that they last a long, long time."*

ROBERT CLERGERIE, 5 rue du Cherche-Midi, 75006 ☎ (1) 4548 7547

For the fashionable foot brigade, *"he is the most directional shoe designer. He started the change in shapes of heel...he simply makes good shoes"* – ANIKO GAAL. Courts with high, sculpted heels, exquisite suede lace-ups – modern, original but not wacky.

SOLEIL DU MIDI, 6 rue du Cherche-Midi, 75006 ☎ (1) 4548 1502

A delightful stash of *"mind-blowing oils, honeys, soaps and foods from Provence"* – CLARE FERGUSON.

VAN CLEEF & ARPELS, 22 place Vendôme, 75001 ☎ (1) 4261 5858

One of the snooty old guard of jewellers, a house held in high esteem the world over for quality work.

WALTER STEIGER, 83 rue du Faubourg St Honoré, 75008 ☎ (1) 4266 6508; 7 rue de Tournon, 75006 ☎ (1) 4633 0145
A classicist in the footwear line-up, who knows how to take a simple pump and pump it up to great heights. Fashionable, great-quality, everyday shoes.

RIVIERA

— Art and museums —

ATELIER CEZANNE, 9 ave Paul Cézanne, Aix-en-Provence ☎ 4221 0653
See the cherub statue and what appear to be the original (distinctly mouldy) apples that the artist so often painted, in his tiny studio and overgrown garden.

FONDATION MAEGHT, 06570 St-Paul-de-Vence ☎ 9332 8163
Just outside St-Paul, this pair of modern rose and white buildings houses a much-loved gallery of modern paintings and sculpture. Stained-glass windows by Ubac and Braque, a Braque mosaic, sculpture by Giacometti and works by Provençophiles Chagall, Miró, Matisse et al.

MUSEE PICASSO, Château Grimaldi, place du Château, 06600 Antibes ☎ 9334 9191
Picasso turned out an astonishing number of works when living in Antibes in the latter half of 1946. Here they are – large-scale paintings, ceramics, prints and drawings inspired by Riviera life.

MUSEE RENOIR, Les Collettes, Cagnes-sur-Mer ☎ 9320 6107
The house, studio and gardens where Renoir spent the last 12 years of his life, each room preserved in its original state. A few authentic works such as the bronze *Venus* remain. Actress Emmanuelle Béart (of *Jean de Florette* fame) visits regularly.

VILLA EPHRUSSI DE ROTHSCHILD, ave Denis Semeria, 06230 St-Jean-Cap-Ferrat ☎ 9301 3309
Housed in a turn-of-the-century Italianate villa is the eclectic 18C art collection formed by Baroness E de R. Furniture, Sèvres and Meissen porcelain, French rococo paintings, Savonnerie carpets, Oriental decorative arts. Magnificent gardens in Florentine, Spanish, Japanese and indigenous styles; sea views through the palms and statuary.

— Casinos —

MONTE CARLO CASINO, place du Casino, 98007 ☎ 9350 6931
The best and most famous casino in the world.

The most glamorous gamblers are lured into its beautiful (and newly revitalized) belle époque interior. The first salon (entrance FF50) is for European roulette, 30-40, and slot machines; the private salon (entrance FF100, no betting limit) is for British roulette, blackjack and craps. The public casino (free entrance) is now at the teeming, touristy **Café de Paris**, opposite. Best season: in spring, when true Monaco-lovers arrive for Le Bal de la Rose.

— Clubs —

BEACH CLUB, Monte Carlo Beach Hotel, route du Bord de Mer, 06190 Roquebrune-Cap-Martin ☎ 9378 2140
A daytime club where Monte Coolos languish, bronzed and expensively, around the swimming pool, with occasional forays to the sea to jetski, paraglide, waterski or swim out to the raft. The Grimaldis hold court by their green-and-white-striped tent, with 2 guards on standby; spy Mark Thatcher and a coiffed Lady Sieff there too. Fantastic lunchtime spreads that threaten to spread that waistline.

JIMMY'Z D'HIVER (winter), place du Casino, 98007 Monte Carlo ☎ 9350 8080; JIMMY'Z D'ETE (summer), Monte Carlo Sporting Club, ave Princesse Grace ☎ 9326 1414
The best nightclub in Monaco, for kids and wrinklies alike. The summer home has a motorized sliding roof that opens to reveal the sparkling night sky.

PARADY'Z, Monte Carlo Sporting Club, ave Princesse Grace, 98000 Monte Carlo ☎ 9330 6161
A young Jimmy'z, open only in July and Aug, for babes of the rich – a sea of fluorescents, minis, ripped jeans, sloppy joe shirts, bare legs and baseball boots with the laces undone.

— Festivals —

FESTIVAL MONDIAL DE JAZZ D'ANTIBES, Maison du Tourisme d'Antibes, place Charles-de-Gaulle, 06600 Antibes ☎ 9333 9564
This great jazz festival blossomed naturally from an ongoing mutual love affair between black American jazz players and France. Now Antibes and Juan les Pins swing even more than usual for 2 weeks in July, with top singers and players such as Ella Fitzgerald, Ray Charles and Fats Domino.

— Film —

🏆 CANNES INTERNATIONAL FILM FESTIVAL, c/o 71 rue du Faubourg St Honoré, 75008 Paris ☎ (1) 4266 9220
The world's No 1 film festival and market place,

where the global glitterati defect in May. *"The most important and prestigious festival in the world by a long way. For competition awards you think first of Cannes. No one would turn down Cannes. Every kind of film is shown from the most commercial to the most arty"* – DEREK MALCOLM. *"So far in advance of any film festival it's out on its own. The market leader in every respect"* – IAIN JOHNSTONE. Top-drawer actors – Meryl Streep, Jane Fonda, Robert Redford – adorn the event, a round-the-clock marathon from film to film, lunch to lunch, gala to gala, party to party – theme parties, yacht parties, villa parties. Hottest invitations are to the **Hotel du Cap-Eden-Roc** (to meet megastars such as Michael Douglas or Cher) and to Cannes President Pierre Viot's exclusive matchmaking dinners. Lunch at the **Majestic** or **La Palme d'Or** at the Hotel Martinez (preferably with actor Jean-Claude Brialy) or **La Plage Sportive**, *the* beach. Hip hang-out after midnight is café-bar **Le Petit Carlton**, rue d'Antibes (no relation to its *grand* namesake).

Hotels

CARLTON INTER-CONTINENTAL, 58 La Croisette, 06406 Cannes ☎ 9368 9168

Top producers and stars immerse themselves in the Carlton's belle époque luxury and hold power talks over cocktails on the terrace, and dinner. Revamps include a new 13-room suite with private lift, butler and limo, and a casino. *"The one – along with the Majestic – where you more or less have to bribe your way in at Film Festival time"* – DEREK MALCOLM.

CHATEAU DE LA CHEVRE D'OR, 06360 Eze Village ☎ 9341 1212

Perched at 1,200 ft, with 14 sea-facing rooms and a tiny swimming pool terrace with knockout views. Fine cuisine under Bruno Ingold.

HOTEL DE PARIS, place du Casino, BP 2309, 98007 Monte Carlo ☎ 9350 8080

Monte's lavish landmark hotel, still oozing gloss and glamour during the Grand Prix and Red Cross Ball weeks, when the jetset stay in harbourside suites. *"To me it is the best in Monaco, forever the best. Absolutely classic"* – DAVID SHILLING. Home of **Louis XIV** (see Restaurants).

🍴 HOTEL DU CAP-EDEN-ROC, blvd J F Kennedy, Cap d'Antibes, 06604 Antibes ☎ 9361 3901

Still rates as the most glamorous hotel in the world – sweeping up to the grand entrance of the creamy château is an instant flashback to the days when Scott and Zelda Fitzgerald and Noel Coward would stay. (Now you could see Cannes-goers Harrison Ford, Cher, Jane Fonda, Jacques Chirac or Madonna.) You go up the stone stairway into an immense, marble-floored lobby, open at the far side on to beautifully tended green gardens and the sea. No credit cards or cheques,

only lashings of cash – *"that's why there are so many lorries parked outside…! It's where big Hollywood stars stay for privacy, away from the reporters"* – DEREK MALCOLM. *"The grandest hotel in the world – wonderful, but grossly overpriced"* – ANDREW LLOYD WEBBER. *"So romantic and glamorous,"* sighs MARIE HELVIN, who loves the cliff-top restaurant that juts out over the water. *"One of the few true luxury hotels for an elegant summer vacation"* – WOLFGANG PUCK. For MARQUIS DE LASTOURS, JOAN COLLINS, FRANK BOWLING and MARIUCCIA MANDELLI, it caps 'em all.

HOTEL HERMITAGE, Square Beaumarchais, BP 277, 98005 Monte Carlo ☎ 9350 6731

A mix of belle époque and less enchanting 70s, but its wonderful established, old-fashioned air leads devotees to declare it their best in town.

HOTEL MAJESTIC, 14 La Croisette, 06407 Cannes ☎ 9368 9100

This is *the* one in Cannes, as DEREK MALCOLM vouches, but *"not only is it incredibly expensive, you have to pay vast key money even to book a room"*. Dead close to the Palais du Festival, this sparkling white hotel has a heated pool and palm-filled garden. *"They care, so you don't need to"* – DAVID SHILLING. Star-spot in the daytime (later the scene shifts to the Carlton) over the best lunch served by the nicest waiters (and make sure you're seen by TV host Henri Chappier). Sting, Carole Bouquet, Marisa Berenson and Catherine Deneuve are among those diners you could chalk up.

HOTEL NEGRESCO, 37 Promenade des Anglais, 06000 Nice ☎ 9388 3951

If you must stay in Nice, this is the only place to be. A grand, gilded, belle époque hotel with knockout cuisine at **Chantecler**. The departure of Maximin made way for Dominique le Stanc (late of Le Château Eza, where he was a runaway success). *"Still excellent"* – ROBERT NOAH.

LA COLOMBE D'OR, 06570 St-Paul-de-Vence ☎ 9332 8002

Still an utter delight, on the edge of a perfect medieval hill town, but absurdly booked up with regulars (Yves Montand, David Lean). FRANK LOWE reckons it's *"better now in winter than summer when you can't park in town"*. Indeed, so tourist-infested is St-Paul that the hotel's heavy wooden gate remains firmly shut to by-passers. Former guests Dufy, Matisse, Picasso, Miró, Utrillo, Braque et al would pay their bills in kind. Almost every inch of the simple white-washed interior bears testimony to their work – paintings, sculptures, painted glass, decorated cushions and lamps. *"I love it – it is my favourite spot. Everywhere your eye falls, it falls on beauty. It is just wonderful. The art on the walls is just the icing on the cake. If you go with a girlfriend or boyfriend, you'll end up married. One dinner on the terrace and that's it, kid"* –

JOHN GOLD. Nibblers Michael Winner and Jenny Seagrove haven't yet succumbed. One note of dissent from ANDREW LLOYD WEBBER (*"we've all seen it, and it's over"*). PS Don't miss Chagall's simple gravestone in the hilltop graveyard.

LA RESERVE DE BEAULIEU, 5 blvd Général Leclerc, 06310 Beaulieu-sur-Mer ☎ 9301 0001

One of the finest resort hotels on the Côte d'Azur, as BARBARA TAYLOR BRADFORD and ANDREW LLOYD WEBBER know. An elegant apricot-tinted building with small private harbour overlooked by pool and restaurant terrace.

LA VOILE D'OR, 06230 St-Jean-Cap-Ferrat ☎ 9301 1313

Harbourside haunt of visiting actors such as Nigel Havers. *"Wonderful. Make sure you get a room with a balcony overlooking the court. The food is so good you won't want to eat anywhere else. It has the fastest room service – you order breakfast and 10 minutes later a whole 3-course meal arrives"* – FRANK LOWE. *"Marvellous, really marvellous"* – JOAN BURSTEIN. A further echo from ANDREW LLOYD WEBBER (with *"one caveat – my friends who have stayed say the walls are paper-thin"*).

LE CAP ESTEL, 06360 Eze Bord de Mer ☎ 9301 5044

Set on a promontory with gardens, a tiny private beach and 2 swimming pools, one indoor and heated, one that juts over the sea. Loyal clients such as BARBARA CARTLAND love the ambience.

LE CHATEAU EZA, 06360 Eze Village ☎ 9341 1224

Rustic hilltop stone château with only 9 rooms, pseudo-medieval furnishings and fantastic views. Bruno Cirino, who trained with Vergé, Maximin and Ducasse, is king of the kitchens.

LE GRAND HOTEL DU CAP FERRAT, blvd de Général de Gaulle, 06290 St-Jean-Cap-Ferrat ☎ 9376 0021

Trad Riviera palace, snazzily done up to boast a 15-acre park, 2 tennis courts and a funicular down to the seaside Club Dauphin, where the shimmering pool falls away at one side to give the impression that there's nothing between you and the sea (the *other* 3 sides are surrounded by naked sun-worshippers).

—— *Restaurants* ——

See also Hotels.

LE SLOOP, Port de St Jean Cap Ferrat, 06290 ☎ 9301 4863

The Riviera clan are to be found at Alain Kherlicocq's delightful seafood eatery in the new port. *"The most amusing restaurant and the one everybody is going to...the food is serious and it's not expensive for the coast"* – ANDREW LLOYD WEBBER.

♠ LOUIS XIV, Hotel de Paris, place du Casino, 98007 Monte Carlo ☎ 9350 8080

The great Alain Ducasse presides over this ultra-grand dining room to stupendous effect. *"Must surely be the most luxurious restaurant in the whole of Europe. It is very opulent yet never vulgar. They have achieved a fantastic balance and harmony"* – RAYMOND BLANC. *"The inside looks like a very bad bonbon box, but it's got extraordinary food"* – BARBARA KAFKA. *"For me it is the third best in France"* – ROLAND ESCAIG.

MOULIN DE MOUGINS, Quartier Notre-Dame de Vie, 434 chemin de Moulin, 06250 Mougins ☎ (1) 9375 7824

Though it is starred and toqued to the hilt, Francofoodies are dismissing Roger Vergé's famous restaurant as an industry. Nevertheless, a rich, ritzy clientele continue to throng in from the coast. Defenders of the faith include BARBARA CARTLAND and ROBERT SANGSTER: *"Has the most style of all the Côte d'Azur restaurants."*

TETOU, Golfe Juan, 06220 ☎ 9363 7116

"Like a little shack at the side of the water, with the best bouillabaisse in the world...absurdly good...I've had it in many different places, but this is clearly the best. You must have it with langoustine. My wife says the greatest dish they have is the grilled lobster – perfection" – ED VICTOR.

· REST OF ·

FRANCE

—— *Art and museums* ——

MUSEE DU VIN ET DE LA VIGNE DANS L'ART, Château Mouton de Rothschild, 33250 Pauillac ☎ 9908 5800

Owned by Philippine de Rothschild, who inherited the château from her father Baron Philippe, this is a magnificent museum devoted to objets d'art of an oenological nature. Etruscan statues of winemakers, Roman and Greek gold cups, Egyptian sculptures, German wine glasses and wine presses, Babylonian glass, wine labels by famous artists. By appointment only.

—— *Châteaux* ——

The most glorious Loire châteaux were built around the decade up to 1525 during François I's exile from Paris. They show the first influence of the Italian Renaissance on France. One of the earliest is **CHATEAU D'AZAY-LE-RIDEAU**, 37190 Azay-le-Rideau ☎ 4745 4204, set in beautiful grounds by the Indre river, a tributary of the Loire. **CHATEAU DE BLOIS**, 41000 Blois ☎ 5478 0662, is a rich and varied architectural treat, spanning c. 1400-1800s. See the famous Italianate spiral staircase within an octagonal well, and Mansart's baroque wing with its impressive interior dome. **CHATEAU DE CHAMBORD**, 41250 Bracieux ☎ 5420 3132, was one of François I's grandest achievements, and certainly the largest in the region, with 440 rooms and a 13,600-acre estate. The king wanted the Loire diverted to pass by his front gate but had to settle for the smaller river Cosson. See the famous double spiral staircase. Picturesquely built *in* the Cher river, with a multi-arched bridge and gallery, **CHATEAU DE CHENONCEAU**, 37150 Bléré ☎ 5478 0662, is *"the most beautiful château in France. Although it no longer belongs to the original family, I feel happier that there are people living there and it is not just a museum"* – MARQUIS DE LASTOURS.

When François I returned from exile, he went to live at the **CHATEAU DE FONTAINEBLEAU**, 77300 Fontainebleau ☎ (1) 6422 2740. Rebuilt in 1527–8, and now a hotch-potch of styles, the château's chief claim to fame is the revolutionary scheme of decoration by the Italian Mannerists Rosso and Primaticcio, a complex blend of fresco and stucco (as seen in the Galerie François I).

In 1656, **VAUX-LE-VICOMTE**, 77950 Maincy ☎ (1) 6066 9709, was built by a proud Fouquet, financial secretary to Louis XIV, to show off his rank and fortune. He teamed the architect Le Vau, the artist and decorator Le Brun and the garden-designer Le Nôtre to splendid effect (and today, the château and grounds, kept intact, are a perfect jewel to visit). In 1661, however, poor Fouquet was clapped in irons by an upstaged Louis XIV.

The Sun King then went on to commission the very same design team to transform **VERSAILLES** ☎ (1) 3084 7568, into the biggest and best château in Europe. Despite many subsequent extravagant additions to the palace, Louis's baroque apartments remain the most important. The Galerie des Glaces and adjoining salons are a magnificent tribute to the power and supremacy of the absolute monarch. Don't miss also Gabriel's delightful opera house, the gardens and fountains, Louis XIV's Grand Trianon (a mini château of pink marble), Louis XV's Petit Trianon (an early example of neo-classical architecture), and Marie-Antoinette's quaint Hamlet.

—————— *Festivals* ——————

CHOREGIES, BP 180, 84105 Orange ☎ 9034 2424
A 3-week season in July of magnificent one-off opera productions in the Théâtre Antique, a Roman amphitheatre. Recitals and concerts too. Big international names, chic dressing.

FESTIVAL D'AVIGNON, Bureau de Festival, BP 92, 84006 Avignon ☎ 9082 6511
A vibrant festival of drama, created by Jean Vilar, France's answer to Laurence Olivier. Held July-Aug, it offers experimental, comic, all-night

and ethnic theatre, sketches, mime, the lot. Also dance, lectures and exhibitions. It retains a purist quality despite tourists. *"If you are French and in any way involved in theatre, you have to go. It is the place to be discovered and to meet your peers"* – JEAN-PHILIPPE CHATRIER.

FESTIVAL MUSICAL DU PERIGORD NOIR, 53 rue du Général Foy, 24290 Montignac ☎ 5351 9517
The largest music festival in the south-west of France, held in mid-July to end-Aug, in Romanesque churches. 2 themes, usually starting with a celebration of early music and culminating in chamber music. *"An important festival, the place to be seen"* – ALEXANDRE LAZAREFF.

FESTIVAL INTERNATIONAL D'ART LYRIQUE, Palais de l'Ancien Archevêché, 13100 Aix-en-Provence ☎ 4223 3781
The best festival in France, one of great tradition and charm, held in July. The whole medieval town comes alive, concerts and recitals resound from churches and courtyards, jazz and rock bands play impromptu gigs to people sitting in outdoor bars and restaurants. Highlight is the opera series staged in the al fresco Théâtre de l'Archevêché in the Archbishop's Palace. France's favourite divas Jessye Norman and Barbara Hendricks perform regularly.

—————— *Film* ——————

DEAUVILLE FESTIVAL DU CINEMA AMERICAIN, c/o Promo 2000, 33 ave MacMahon, 75017 Paris ☎ (1) 4267 7140; or **Office de Tourisme, Deauville** ☎ 3188 2143
Though a mini-affair compared with Cannes, mega-celebs (Liz Taylor, Robert De Niro, Shirley MacLaine) turn out to see American (plus James Bond) films. Best hang-outs: **Chez Mioque** for good food, street cred and the company of M Mioque; **Les Vapeurs** in nearby Trouville for similar cuisine Normande in more exalted company (Anouk Aimée, Sabine Azéma). After dinner, it's the hotel bars – the **Royal** (Americans: Kevin Kline, Scott Glenn, Rosanna Arquette) and the **Normandy** (French: Philippe Noiret, Anthony Delon, Mathilde May).

—————— *Hotels* ——————

HOSTELLERIE DU PRIEURE, 49350 Chenehutte-les-Tuffeaux ☎ 4167 9014
A priory in 60 acres of parkland, now *"a very smart hotel overlooking the Loire, where lots of rich Parisians go for the weekend. We were extremely impressed with the way it was run. The service was provided in a very, very acceptable fashion"* – HILARY RUBINSTEIN.

HOTEL DU PALAIS, 1 ave de l'Impératrice, 64200 Biarritz ☎ 5924 0940
A place of supreme grandeur, built under Napo-

leon III, when Empress Eugénie made Biarritz fashionable. Central, yet standing in splendid isolation with formal gardens enclosed by railings. Excellent restaurant and views of a white spumy océan sauvage.

HOTEL MIRAMAR, 13 rue Louison-Bobet, 64200 Biarritz ☎ 5941 3000
No beauty from the outside, but beautifying on the inside: it's where Jean-Paul Belmondo and Princesses Stéphanie and Ira von Fürstenberg take sea-water therapy at the Louison Bobet Spa and Fitness Centre. The 2-star Michelin chef André Gaüzère applies wizardry to a diet menu (making 400 calories taste like 1,500).

Boy Oh Boyer!

BOYER, 64 blvd Henry-Vasnier, 51100 Reims ☎ 2682 8080, is a splendiferous château in champagne-land with only 16 palatial rooms and superb 3-star Michelin cuisine. No hums or hahs about this one: praise comes by the ream. *"My favourite hotel in the world. Boyer is the Polignac family mansion – the original Madame was an American Singer and I don't mean music, I mean sewing machines, so there was tons of money. The house is phenomenal. Half the rooms are very fine French, half are international perfect – staggeringly beautiful detail. The bathrooms are the best I've ever seen. The food – well it's probably one of the 3 best restaurants in France"* – EDWARD CARTER. *"The one I would recommend without reservation... world-class. The hotel is comparable to the Crillon or the Plaza Athénée. The cuisine is adored by the champenois, and I have known people to drive out from Paris, which is an hour and a half, just to dine there. It's not only the food – yes, his food is imaginative and of superb quality – it is beyond that. It's the ambience, the service, the site, and a fantastic champagne cellar"* – IRVING SMITH KOGAN.

HOTEL ROYAL, blvd Cornuché, 14800 Deauville ☎ 3198 6633
The place to stay for the American Film Festival, when stars are snapped lounging round its kidney-shaped pool. Run impeccably by Lucien Barrière (also of the Majestic, Cannes), whose tiny Hungarian wife is a former circus performer – watch out she doesn't dive from a great height into your soup. Suites decorated to honour major Hollywood stars... Liz Taylor's is a symphony

in lavender. *"I go every year. It's wonderfully swish and has a fantasy atmosphere about it – you feel that it is being run just the way it was 100 years ago"* – RICHARD COMPTON-MILLER.

♠ LES PRES ET LES SOURCES D'EUGENIE, 40320 Eugénie-les-Bains ☎ 5851 1901
Star chef Michel Guérard's delightful country-house hotel, in the spa town made famous by Empress Eugénie. Go for the spring cure (it takes 3 weeks) or simply when your liver needs a holiday or you fancy rubbing slender shoulders with Catherine Deneuve, Isabelle Adjani and co. *"Heaven on earth. My wife and I make an annual pilgrimage and have got to know Christine and Michel Guérard. We even take the waters!" "What I like about Guérard is his personal modesty. His cuisine minceur is exquisite"* – MICHAEL BROADBENT. Indeed, the **restaurant** is a showpiece for his hallowed cuisine minceur and cuisine gourmande. None-too-slender recommendations from BARBARA KAFKA, ROBERT MONDAVI, ROBERT NOAH (*"he's my favourite..."*) and MARIUCCIA MANDELLI: *"The best restaurant for a romantic dinner."*

——— *Restaurants* ———

ALAIN CHAPEL, Mionnay, 01390 St-André-de-Corcy ☎ 7891 8202
Chapel is justly celebrated for his complex dishes based on the local cuisine Bressane – ragout of cocks' combs, kidneys with truffles. *"Very intellectual"* – ROBERT NOAH. *"Extraordinary and wonderful"* – BARBARA KAFKA. A vote from ROLAND ESCAIG. However, his restaurant has been described as being as attractive as a motel in Tucson, Arizona.

AUBERGE DE L'ILL, rue de Collonges, Illhaeusern, 68150 Ribeauvillé ☎ 8971 8323
Sadly the tour buses have started invading this restaurant by the river Ill, with its lovely flower garden full of willows. However, devotees still love the sophisticated combination of haute cuisine and Alsatian regional cooking. *"Superb"* – MICHAEL BROADBENT.

DIVONNE LES BAINS, Route de Gex, 01220 Les Bains ☎ 5020 0032
Earns the highest recommendation from ROLAND ESCAIG: *"a good restaurant, and the chef Guy Martin is a good, good one."*

♠ ESPERANCE, St Père, 89450 Vézelay ☎ 8633 2045
Tucked away in a small hotel is Meneau's orgasmic restaurant. Signature dishes from his 'sexual cuisine' repertoire are the cromesquis de foie gras that explodes in the mouth, and the fricassée de champignons des bois. *"One of the very very best"* – ROBERT NOAH. Rendered rapturously speechless are ROLAND ESCAIG (for whom it's No 2 in France) and RAYMOND BLANC (it's in his top 3).

GEORGES BLANC, 01540 Vonnas
☎ 7450 0010
This famous chef has earned the same criticism as some of his peers – of catering too much for tourists and Michelin men. However, as ROBERT NOAH notes, it's "*a 3-star industry, but very good*". "*I would speak very highly of Georges Blanc,*" confirms MATTHEW FORT. "*Very good restaurant, very romantic setting*" – STIRLING MOSS.

LA LICORNE, 31 rue Robert d'Arbrissel, 49590 Fontevraud l'Abbaye ☎ 4151 7249
The best rest in Saumur, frequented by the local cavalry school. "*A wonderful jewel of a restaurant. The owner bought an old private home, took a very good chef from Taillevent, and 4 cooks, and they serve 40 maximum – that's a lot of staff per customer. Excellent wine list, excellent produce, excellent restaurant*" – ROBERT NOAH.

🐟 **L'AUBERGADE, 52 rue Royale, 47270 Puymirol ☎ 5395 3146**
Michel Trama's red-hot restaurant is bowling gastronomes over. About an hour's drive from Bordeaux, in an old hill village. "*I was prepared for yet another French high-class 2-star, maybe 3-star meal with all the trappings such as endless successions of petits fours and little nibbles. But everything he served me (and it was a huge meal) made me sit bolt upright and say 'Gosh, how did you do that?' It really grabbed my attention*"– ALASTAIR LITTLE. One of RAYMOND BLANC's top 3 in France, while for SERENA SUTCLIFFE it was: "*One of the best meals of the entire year. Michel Trama is stunning. He did a lobster and black-truffle ravioli which I think was the most magic dish I have ever eaten in my life. It was absolutely memorable.*"

LEON DE LYON, 1 rue de Pleney, 69001 Lyons ☎ 7828 1133
Jean-Paul Lacombe's restaurant boasts Lyonnaise ambience, Lyonnaise specialities and – most telling – Lyonnaise customers. Sample his sole in black cuttlefish sauce, or Bresse chicken stuffed with foie gras. A hit with ROBERT NOAH.

The Blanc Maxim
🐟

To be highly favoured in RAYMOND BLANC's eyes requires certain qualities. He explains what his pet restaurants have in common: "*They have all created a brilliant environment which is totally relaxing and has the best food. The food has its roots in tradition, but is always creative and innovative, and moving away from the fads of nouvelle cuisine. They have created an atmosphere where the table becomes a place to celebrate life and friendship and where you don't have to think about the food – after all, food is not highbrow and intellectual, it is to be enjoyed.*"

LES ROCHES, 1 ave des Trois Dauphins, Aiguebelle, 83980 Le Lavandou
☎ 9471 0505
"*Geniale! Genius! The chef Laurent Taridec is so good, so good. He's young and he's wonderful*" – ROLAND ESCAIG.

🐟 **LOU MAZUC, 12210 Laguiole**
☎ 6544 3224
Peasant food made good. Chef Michel Bras is armed with a mass of new ideas that thrill the tastebuds of ROLAND ESCAIG and ROBERT NOAH: "*You must be willing to eat on his terms, but it's an exciting restaurant.*"

OUSTAU DE BAUMANIERE, Le Vallon, Les-Baux-de-Provence, 13520 Mausanne-les-Alpilles ☎ 9097 3307
Pretty hotel and restaurant with antique furniture, a flowery terrace and a fab view. Expansions have slightly spoilt the atmosphere and it's overcrowded in summer, so "*go off-season – then it's wonderful*" – ROBERT NOAH. Fans include TESSA DAHL and WOLFGANG PUCK.

🐟 **Buzzz** Le Train Bleu in the Gare de Lyon is "*the best railway restaurant in the world. Fabulous turn-of-the-century décor and murals and great views of the railway station*" – LOYD GROSSMAN 🐟 ...... **La Bonne Etape**, Chemin du Lac, 04160 Château Arnoux ☎ (1) 9264 0009, is the place "*for the best, authentic provençale cuisine*" – QUENTIN CREWE 🐟 ...... **Laborderie**, Tamniès, 24620 Les Eyzies-de-Tayac ☎ 5329 6859, is the one grapies pick for its wine list. Famous vintages almost given away (*almost*) 🐟 ...... For some of the best 1-star cuisine in the Dordogne, wind your way up to the knockout (if tourist-beset) hill town of Domme, to the "*very, very pretty little* **Hotel Esplanade**, *24250 Domme* ☎ *5328 3141. That I can recommend with a clear heart*" – FREDERIC RAPHAEL 🐟 ...... KEITH FLOYD's favourite food market is **L'Isle sur la Sorgue**, Vaucluse (where the **Café de la France** is a fave bar) 🐟 ...... MARIUCCIA MANDELLI's best antique market is in **Dijon**........ 🐟

🎣 **PAUL BOCUSE, 50 quai de la Plagne, 69660 Collonges-au-Mont-d'Or, Lyons** ☎ **7822 0140**

An inspired master of cuisine ancienne – home cooking exquisitely executed, followed by astounding arrays of cheese and desserts (as FREDERIC RAPHAEL notes, the Bocuse ethic is "*don't let them out still able to walk if they don't want to*"). "*I love it – I know it's overdone, but the food is <u>excellent</u>*" – ROBERT NOAH.

PIC, 285 ave Victor Hugo, 26000 Valence ☎ **7544 1532**

Always packed with local gastronomes, grapies and just plain locals, who come for superbly presented and flavourful food. BARBARA CARTLAND, ROLAND ESCAIG, ROBERT NOAH and QUENTIN CREWE pick Pic.

❝*There is no Champagne cuisine as such. All the chefs of the region are under a microscope because the place is inundated with visitors, and each tries to be outstanding in his own way. So one can have a ball going from restaurant to restaurant – and get gout as well*❞

 IRVING SMITH KOGAN

ST HUBERT, St Saturnin d'Apt, 84490 Vaucluse ☎ **9075 4202**

A winner with KEITH FLOYD: "*the chef draws heavily from regional sources. His roots are very much in Provence, but he cooks in his own very special modern way.*"

TROISGROS, place de la Gare, 42300 Roanne ☎ **7771 6697**

This family hotel-restaurant is an institution. Unpretentious, bourgeois cooking at its finest.

——— *Ski resorts* ———

CHAMONIX

Not just a resort, but a lively French town in the shadow of Mont Blanc. "*The best skiing in Europe. I'm permanently staggered by the place. The town is low and the mountains soar above – you feel quite overawed. If you really want to scare yourself, take the cable car to Aiguille du Midi and ski down the glacier through the most breathtaking scenery in Europe*" – JANE LINDQUIST. Or ski the famous off-piste Pas de Chèvre, a drop of some 6,500 ft. "*Nowhere else is so steep or rewarding. Imagine standing on the slope, put out your hand and you can touch it*"– JL. Her restaurant/champagne bar, **Restaurant Atmosphère**, happens to be one of the best in town, full of locals. The Lyonnaise chef specializes in fish, such as poisson au gros sel – cooked in sea salt. Go on Friday or Saturday, after the delivery from Lyons market, for a sea-fresh supper.

COURCHEVEL

Site of the 1992 Olympic ski jump and chic resort for young French and British – plus MARGAUX HEMINGWAY, Giscard d'Estaing, Roman Polanski, Roger Vadim and a host of French politicians, who have chalets on the pretty outskirts rather than the somewhat brutalist modern centre of town. Immaculately kept runs for all levels. Private jets wing into the Altiport. Best hotel: **Hotel des Neiges**. Best restaurant: **Chabichoud**. Best bar: **Jack's Bar**, aka La Saulire. Best clubs: **La Grange**; **Caves de la Loze** (mainly French); **St Nicolas** (mainly Brits).

MEGEVE

Very French, very chic, a charming resort set in a beautiful wide valley, ensuring longer daylight hours than most of its Alpine neighbours. Inès de la Fressange, tribes of Rossignols (*of the ski label*) and other ultra-smart natives go. Hotter on nightlife than skiing – it's too low to be sure of snow all season. Best hotel: **Chalet Mont d'Arbois** (best food, too).

🎿 **Buzzz** If you don't want to get **mown down by the Olympic entourage**, avoid Méribel, Val d'Isère and Courchevel not only in February 1992 but also Feb 1991, when they're testing out the runs🎿...... Good news for those who want to brave the aforementioned big 3: the swanky **new road system** should at last put an end to hair-tearingly long queues🎿......The famous **Haute Route**, from Chamonix to Zermatt, involves a week on skis with a pack on your back and a guide at your side. Info from the Bureau des Guides, Chamonix🎿......Immerse yourself in the landscapes paintings are made of at the **Hôtellerie du Bas-Bréau**, 22 rue Grande, 77630 Barbizon ☎ (1) 6066 4005🎿......Delusions of grandeur? Stay at the moated Renaissance **Château d'Esclimont**, 28700 St-Symphorien-le-Château ☎ 3731 1515, in beautiful parkland with a lake..............🎿

MERIBEL-LES-ALLUES

Attractive chalet resort, a venue for the women's events at the 1992 Winter Olympics, and the best base for off-piste skiing. Frequented by many smart, private British (such as the Dukes of Kent and Bedford). Extensive skiing at the hub of one of the major ski-lift systems of Europe. Small airport for private planes.

VAL D'ISERE

Hotting up for the 1992 Olympics, for which a new downhill run has been designed, this is the finest ski area in the world, thinks ex-ski champ Killy, who learnt here. Largely British and Swedish population (the Brits are the ones at the Members' Bar of **Dick's T-Bar** – a sophisticated nightclub with great light show and outdoor lasers shining on the mountains). Best hotel: **Hotel Savoyard**. Best wine bar/restaurant: **Au Bout de la Rue**, run by mustachioed José, for fine wines by the glass and tapas.

Wine

Alsace

Aromatic, spicy, light white wines combine French and German character. These are far and away the best wines to order in a restaurant when nothing else on the list beckons; the finest – like the **GEWURZTRAMINER** of **Théo Faller** – deserve ordering in their own right. Adventurous palates should seek out **Hugel's VENDANGE TARDIVE** and **SELECTIONS DE GRAINS NOBLES**: MICHAEL BROADBENT has *"only just realized how versatile the Tokay Pinot Gris can be, from minor and dry and good with food, to Hugel's glorious 1983 and 1976 Selections de Grains Nobles"*.

SERENA SUTCLIFFE considers the area's aristocrats to be the wines of **Domaine Zind-Humbrecht** and of **Trimbach**, especially the tiny jewel of **CLOS STE HUNE**.

Bordeaux

Would-be grapies, mark SERENA SUTCLIFFE's words: *"The 1989 vintage was picked earlier than it has been since 1893 and it looks a stunner. Early picking usually means something special."* MICHAEL BROADBENT surveys the past decade: *"Bordeaux has enjoyed a succession of marvellous vintages in the 1980s: 1981 good and undervalued; 82 rich and magnificent; 83 pretty good; 85 beautifully balanced; 86 firm, classic; 88 pretty good (excellent in Sauternes) and 89 probably an anno mirabilis."*

THE MEDOC

A small number of beautiful châteaux and a large number of valuable grapes redeem an otherwise dull landscape. The four *1er crus classés* dominate – **LAFITE-ROTHSCHILD** (owned by Baron Eric de R), **MOUTON-ROTHSCHILD**

(formerly Baron Philippe's, now his daughter Philippine's), **MARGAUX** (owned by Laura Mentzelopoulos) and the English-owned **LATOUR** (Allied Lyons). MICHAEL BROADBENT stands by his list of great vintages: the 1899 and 1953 Lafite, 1900 and 1961 Margaux, 1924 and 1949 Mouton, and 1929 and 1945 Latour. He also notes that the 1986 **Mouton-Rothschild** is *"brilliant"*. For JOSEPH BERKMANN, the 1949 Mouton *"remains supreme"*.

BERKMANN also admires the **Latour** 1955, noting that *"Latour does not always produce really enjoyable wine in great years... in fact some of the best wines are made in vintages of lesser renown. 1961, though famous and expensive, is rather patchy, with quite a few oxidized bottles. On the other hand, a relatively 'feminine' year like 1955 brings out the qualities of Latour – a depth of flavour (essentially cedar/cigar box) married to a soft and full body."* Latour is also tops with BRUCE OLDFIELD.

Château Margaux 1978 grabs BERKMANN, *"for its sheer stylishness. Not quite the 'great' wine everyone makes it out to be, because it lacks the depth, but it has style and elegance – an aristocrat of its kind"*. Margaux remains a best for STEVEN SPURRIER and DON HEWITSON (*"for serious occasions"*).

SERENA SUTCLIFFE offers a tip: *"The smart thing to do is buy the second wines of the top Bordeaux châteaux. For the 1er crus like Lafite and Latour, they select the absolute bees' knees; the remainder, which is still very good indeed, goes to make the second wine. Margaux's is* **Pavillon Rouge du Château Margaux***; Latour's is* **Les Forts de Latour***; Lafite's is* **Carruades***."*

Among the best 2ème-cru neighbours of the 1er crus are **CHATEAU LEOVILLE-BARTON**, (a winner with STEVEN SPURRIER), **COS-D'ESTOURNEL** (a *"super-second"* for ANTHONY HANSON) and **PICHON-LONGUE-VILLE, Comtesse de Lalande** (for SERENA SUTCLIFFE, *"a superlative château; their second wine,* **Reserve de la Comtesse***, gives you really top-flight Bordeaux at kinder prices"*).

Also snapping at the heels of the 1er crus are: the 1961 **CHATEAU PALMER**, a highlight for JOSEPH BERKMANN: *"tremendous finesse, marvellous flavour – everything a great claret should be."* For MICHAEL BROADBENT, **LEOVILLE-LAS CASES** *"consistently has an extra dimension"*; SERENA SUTCLIFFE recommends their almost-as-fine second wine, **Clos du Marquis**. She also tips **CHATEAU D'ISSAN** and **CHATEAU LAGRANGE**, while BROADBENT notes that *"the uncompromisingly classic* **GRAND-PUY-LACOSTE** *is undervalued"*.

THE GRAVES

Although surrounded by suburban Bordeaux, **HAUT-BRION** maintains its long-held dominance. MICHAEL BROADBENT continues to be haunted by the 1945 and 1961. SERENA SUTCLIFFE finds **HAUT-BRION BLANC** and **LAVILLE-**

HAUT-BRION (the white of **La Mission**), now both owned by H-B, among the best dry whites made anywhere.

ST-EMILION

"The most surprising value in the 1990s will come from Libourne, rather than the Médoc or Graves. The vineyards of St-Emilion, practically wiped out in the frost of 1956, are now coming of age and starting to produce the most glorious wines. **CHATEAU MAGDELAINE** *1982 is an early example, but there is a host of outstanding 1985s and 1989 promises unsurpassed greatness"* – JOSEPH BERKMANN.

The 2 titans of old are **CHEVAL BLANC** and **AUSONE**. Hugh Johnson has declared the Cheval Blanc 1947 one of the great classic vintages of all time, the marker for all claret-lovers, while MICHAEL BROADBENT has *"recently concluded that Cheval Blanc is the most consistently beautiful claret, from the exquisite 1899 and the perfect and best-of-all 1929, to the elegant 1966 and more recent vintages such as the 1982".* -

CANON and **PAVIE** have made superb wines in the 1980s, avers SERENA SUTCLIFFE.

POMEROL

"The tiny district of Pomerol is crowded with small top-quality châteaux. After **PETRUS** *come* **TROTANOY, LA FLEUR-PETRUS, LAFLEUR** *and* **LA CONSEILLANTE,** *all fleshy and superb"* – MICHAEL BROADBENT. *"The greatest bottles at present are* **Pétrus** *1971 (a great concentration to remind one almost of port) and* **Trotanoy** *1975, a more stylish wine"* – JOSEPH BERKMANN.

Pétrus, however, remains the pillar of Pomerol, one that costs double the price you first thought of and more. The 1961 is the finest wine AUBERON WAUGH has ever tasted, while simply any year is best for STANLEY MARCUS.

SAUTERNES/BARSAC

*"Sauternes has come up tremendously. People have started to buy the top Sauternes while they are still in cask. The 1988 vintage was marvel-*lous and everybody wanted to get in early and buy. Not just Yquem, but others like* **RIEUSSEC** *(by Lafite),* **CLIMENS** *and* **LAFAURIE-PEYRAGUEY"** – SERENA SUTCLIFFE.

CHATEAU D'YQUEM is the untoppled hero, definition and epiphany in one. Devotees include MICHAEL BROADBENT (*"The 1847 – just about the greatest wine ever"*), LORD LICHFIELD, DAVID SHILLING, DON HEWITSON, CHARLOTTE RAMPLING and LEO SCHOFIELD.

CLIMENS 1929, from Barsac, and **SUDUIRAUT** 1976 are alternative sweet-tooth soothers for BROADBENT.

Burgundy

Red burgundy is an unreasonable, irrational wine, but when it is good it is *very* very good. The climate in the Burgundy region is of almost British unpredictability and the grape (Pinot Noir) is a prima donna. The best red burgundies are wildly expensive. White burgundy is more reliable (though no less expensive), a sage queen to its mad red consort. MICHAEL BROADBENT pinpoints the vintages to look out for: 1983 and 1985 for red, 1986 for white.

RED BURGUNDY

The **Domaine de la Romanée-Conti** has the region very nearly stitched up, possessing the lion's share of the best vineyards (notably La Romanée Conti and La Tâche). The DRC is a partnership between vivacious Mme 'Lalou' Bize-Leroy and urbane Aubert de Villaine.

LA ROMANEE CONTI is the most celebrated red burgundy, with prices in the Pétrus league. QUENTIN CREWE would be *"very happy drinking that for the rest of my life"*, while for RAYMOND BLANC, *"it's really the very best burgundy, still made in the traditional way – bare feet, treading the grapes".* MICHAEL BROADBENT cites the 1937 vintage as the one to sell your house to buy. He also recalls the 1945 **LA**

Buzzz SERENA SUTCLIFFE keeps abreast of wine trends: *"The top cru bourgeois in Bordeaux (the category just under the crus classés) is* **Château Haut-Marbuzet**. *Stunning claret for people who are one step ahead"*...... **Wily winies** step in before their tipple gets as far as the bottle. *"They buy from the top châteaux while the wine is still in cask, then wait 2 years for delivery. It is a way of getting your hands on top wines early at a favourable price"*...... *Vin à la mode: "The most popular French brasserie wine is* **Madiran**, *from the southwest:* **Château Montus** *is the best"*...... *"It is fashionable at the moment to drink the new Beaujolais cru,* **Régnié**. *It got upgraded from plain Beaujolais-Villages for the splendid 1988 vintage"*......SS's inside-track champagne is **Bruno Paillard's Blanc de Blancs**......**Chablis**-lovers vote **Les Clos** the best of the 7 Grands Crus. **Domaine Moreau**'s Les Clos is delectable – greeny-gold and as clear as the day.....

TACHE with reverence; when JOSEPH BERKMANN tucked into a 1971 DRC magnum of the stuff, he found it *"enormously rich, soft, almost sweet"*. SERENA SUTCLIFFE says the 1985s are the ones to watch for the future.

Our experts lead the way through the rest of the minefield: BARBARA KAFKA goes for **Ponsot's CLOS DE LA ROCHE** and **Gouges's NUITS-ST-GEORGES**, while JOSEPH BERKMANN stands by the 1979 **Les Chaignots, Domaine Alain Michelot**, of Nuits-St-Georges, *"a glorious burgundy, rich in fruit, powerful stuff"*. The BERKMANN palate has had a good year. Here he shares a few tasting notes: *"CORTON BRESSANDES 1964, from an imperial bottled by the now legendary* **Michel Couvreur**, *had great depth, luxurious richness;* **CHAMBERTIN** *1985,* **Domaine Louis Trapet**, *is the best wine from that domaine for a decade, made by Jean Trapet but in the style of the great bottles produced by his father in the 60s.* **MUSIGNY Vieilles Vignes** *1978, from* **Le Comte de Vogüé** *is a memorable wine for its classic architecture. Surprisingly, a modest 1985* **SANTENAY Grand Clos Rousseau** *made by* **Bernard Morey** *turned out to be the most perfect expression of Pinot Noir, fresh fruit perfectly balanced, the best young red burgundy I have ever drunk."*

On Buying Burgundy

ANTHONY HANSON proffers advice to burgundians-in-the-making: *"It's a very good time to buy* **red burgundy**, *because there have been some excellent red burgundy vintages. 1988 is absolutely top quality in the same way that 1985 is . . . it could turn out to be one of the best vintages for the last 20 years. 1987 and 1986 are also yielding some healthy fruity wines, which are likely to mature more quickly than 1988, but are well worth buying.*

"The 1988 **white burgundy** *vintage is ripe, fruity and well balanced. 1989 has the makings of being a very good vintage. It was a very ripe year, so some of the wines may lack acidity, making them marvellous for early drinking but unsuitable for long ageing. When you have a plentiful harvest, as in 1989, the wines can lack the concentration and complexity of a year when there aren't very many grapes on the vine and when you get intense, rich character in the wines."*

The top-ranking *grands crus* for ANTHONY HANSON are **RICHEBOURG** (where *"rising stars of this great vineyard are* **Mongeard Mugneret**, **Jean Grivot** *and* **Méo-Camuzet"**), **CHAMBOLLE-MUSIGNY** (where *"Christopher Roumier has lifted* **Domaine Georges Roumier** *into the top league"*), **CHAMBERTIN-CLOS-DE-BEZE** (where **Domaine Louis Trapet, Joseph Drouhin, Joseph Faiveley** and Ets Leroy *"consistently field top examples"*) and **CLOS DE VOUGEOT** (*"choose from growers with their vines in the top section of the Clos touching the château.* **Domaine Jean Gros** *is one of the best"* – AH).

VOLNAY elicits votes from LORD MONTAGU OF BEAULIEU and ANTHONY HANSON (for whom the 1966 **Volnay Taillepieds, Domaine de Montille**, is *"an immaculately fine, earthy, elegant burgundy"*). For laying down, don't miss **Drouhin**'s 1988s, says SERENA SUTCLIFFE.

WHITE BURGUNDY

MONTRACHET and its satellites
LE MONTRACHET towers above all the others – just ask RAYMOND BLANC, LORD MONTAGU OF BEAULIEU, MICHEL GUERARD, ANNE WILLAN or MICHAEL BROADBENT (who thirsts after a 1978 **Laguiche** or a 1966 **DRC**). JOSEPH BERKMANN plumps for a **PULIGNY-MONTRACHET**: *"Etienne Sauzet's* **La Truffière** *remains unsurpassed, though we have to switch vintage from 1984 to 1985 (the 1986 is, alas, thinning out prematurely)."* ANTHONY HANSON votes for **CHEVALIER-MONTRACHET** (*"the greatest wine in the* **Domaine Leflaive** *stable – elegant, complex, silky, exquisite"*) and **BATARD-MONTRACHET** (*"Etienne Sauzet makes delicious wine, so does* **Joseph Drouhin"**). STEVEN SPURRIER finds the Bâtard by **Pierre Morey** a legitimate contender for best white burgundy. SERENA SUTCLIFFE lauds **Leflaive**'s and **Jean-Noël Gagnard**'s.

MEURSAULT
Topping, smooth, dry whites, tipped by LORD MONTAGU OF BEAULIEU and ANTHONY HANSON. Of **Meursault-Perrières**, HANSON says, *"***Comte Lafon** *has the deepest cellar in the village, and holdings in the best vineyards of Meursault."* For JOSEPH BERKMANN, the 1978 **Meursault-Perrières** from **Robert Ampeau** has *"added a new dimension to Meursault for me. Unfortunately the old man is a hoarder and hands it out like nuggets of gold – at about the same price. The sheer power of this wine can match anything produced in Côte d'Or."*

CORTON-CHARLEMAGNE
The C-C by **Bonneau de Martray**, is one of STEVEN SPURRIER's favourite white burgundies, while the 1986 by **François Coche-Dury**, is for JOSEPH BERKMANN, *"in a class of its own. No sheer power, but subtly backed up by a classic structure – Renaissance rather than modern"*.

Forever Amber

The top of the Cognac Courvoisier range has long been XO, a tawny amber blend aged in oak casks for 50 to 60 years. Can you produce a finer cognac than that? Yes, said Courvoisier, we can. Master-blender Jean Marc Olivier then spent 2 years creating a new supercognac that would prove them right. The result? **Initiale Extra**, a blend of hand-picked special reserve cognacs laid down at Château Courvoisier for an average of 75 years.

The amber nectar flows from a teardrop-shaped bottle with a silver stopper. Thane Prince described the Initiale experience in *The Daily Telegraph*: *"A rare and beautiful cognac ... it has the glowing colour and deep bouquet you would expect in a prestige product, and it tastes simply wonderful. M Olivier suggests that the bouquet has many sensations – mushroom, vanilla, coconut and passion fruit are a few, but to describe the taste is to describe 'a moment of pure happiness'."*

Champagne

BOLLINGER
Still the non-vintage favourite, for its majesty and balance. *"For luxury champagne, I think it takes a lot to beat **Bollinger RD**, particularly with caviare – it's the best champagne with caviare"* – SERENA SUTCLIFFE. The RD rates joint No 1 (with Pol Roger) for STEVEN SPURRIER.

DEUTZ & GELDERMANN
A small champagne house, whose luxury brand is **Cuvée William Deutz**, one that ED VICTOR puts above Roederer Cristal.

KRUG
The non-vintage **Grande Cuvée** is a match for anyone else's Cuvée de Prestige. ROBERT MONDAVI explains: *"The size of bubbles is very small and they almost seem to disappear as you taste – outstanding. Krug is harmonious and delicate, and has a beautiful after-taste."* More murmurs of rapture from LEO SCHOFIELD and MARGAUX HEMINGWAY, while SERENA SUTCLIFFE and DON HEWITSON vote for the *vintage* Krug (*"for drinking with food"* – DH).

LANSON
Both the **Black Label** and **Rosé** are continuing success stories. Watch out for their newly launched **Noble Cuvée 1981** – many grapies say it knocks spots off the Dom for style.

LAURENT-PERRIER
The non-vintage is admired for its floweriness, lightness and delicacy. AUBERON WAUGH and DON HEWITSON are fond of the **Cuvée Grand Siècle**, a brilliant blend of 3 vintages (except in the USA, which imports it as single vintage). LADY ELIZABETH ANSON chose the rosé as her house bubbly.

MOET & CHANDON
Dom Perignon is Moët & Chandon's flagship, and the Cuvée de Prestige with the highest profile. *"Very much the rich man's tipple. I nevertheless vote for the 1961 which, at its best, is the finest champagne I've tasted in the last 20 years"* – MICHAEL BROADBENT. Favoured too by LORD MONTAGU OF BEAULIEU.

PERRIER-JOUET
The luxury **Belle Epoque** comes in a floral painted bottle; together they please the eye and palate of ROBERT MONDAVI. SERENA SUTCLIFFE is stunned: *"They have just brought out the 1983, which I think is the best Belle Epoque ever made."* The insiders' bargain Cuvée de Prestige is **Blason de France**, a non-vintage blend that only connoisseurs know about.

Don Hewitson's Vintage Hints

*"The 1982 and 1983 vintages should be grabbed. It is rare to have 2 successive years of such quality. My best vintages at the moment are the **1982 Pol Roger** and the **1983 Moët & Chandon**. 1989 will be one of the best years of all time."*

POL ROGER
An aristocratic champagne, whose luxury cuvée, **Sir Winston Churchill**, holds STEVEN SPURRIER spellbound. Pol Roger has long been high in the affections of Hugh Johnson, LORD GOWRIE, SERENA SUTCLIFFE, LADY ELIZABETH ANSON and LORD MONTAGU OF BEAULIEU, while for MICHAEL BROADBENT: *"Their vintage is my consistently favourite champagne. I am still enjoying the 1976."*

ROEDERER
Roederer Cristal is the one that makes champagne-lovers go weak at the knees – before they've even had a sip. Cristal-gazers are MICHAEL GRADE, LORD LICHFIELD, SERENA SUTCLIFFE, QUENTIN CREWE, JEREMIAH TOWER, BARBARA KAFKA (*"I love it"*), LORD MONTAGU OF BEAULIEU and CHARLOTTE RAMPLING. MICHAEL BROADBENT thinks Roederer *"the most reliable and elegant of the non-vintage grandes marques"*.

SALON LE MESNIL
High snob value. The original Blanc de Blancs, it only appears about once every 5 years.

VEUVE CLICQUOT
Named after the widow ('veuve') Clicquot herself, this is "*a house that is bang on target at the moment – with their instantly recognizable Yellow Label non-vintage, and also with their vintage. They have just come out with a 1983. The 1982 was fabulous, and now the 1983 is impressive, a wonderful definite champagne*" – SERENA SUTCLIFFE. A fizzy hit with BRUCE OLDFIELD.

Loire Valley

Though best known for *dry* whites (a good **MUSCADET** is one of the best wines for seafood, while the sharp, smoky **POUILLY-FUME** is the perfect complement to smoked foods), the best Loire wines are the *sweetest*. **ANJOU RABLAY** 1928 is MICHAEL BROADBENT's best. SERENA SUTCLIFFE is mad about **Huet's VOUVRAY**s, which come in 3 versions – sec, demi-sec and moelleux: "*The king of the Loire. Very special – you can keep them for years.*"

> **❝ *Just as Italy was in the past few years, so the South of France is becoming the California of the Old World* ❞**
>
> SIMON LOFTUS

Rhône Valley

Red wines that are big and unbridled, smell of earth, animals and leather, and taste of fruit and spice. These are the top 3.

CHATEAUNEUF-DU-PAPE
The knave: at its worst, infernal and headsplitting; at it's best, rich, herby and headturning. MICHAEL BROADBENT's head is turned by the 1969 **Château Rayas** ("*the best Rhône I've ever tasted*"). ANTHONY HANSON recommends the 1978 and 1983 vintages from **Domaine du Vieux Télégraphe**.

COTE ROTIE
The queen: it has a delicacy foreign to Hermitage that makes it the finest of all Rhône wines. **La Mouline** is one of STEVEN SPURRIER's best French reds. **Etienne Guigal, Robert Jasmin** and **René Rostaing** are the best names.

HERMITAGE
The King. The best names are **Paul Jaboulet Aîné** (**HERMITAGE LA CHAPELLE**) and **Gérard Chave**. Impatient imbibers are warned away: no good Hermitage should even be approached before its 10th birthday, and the élite only begin to learn manners at 15.

Grapies-in-the-know buy up Hermitage's cheaper country cousin, **CORNAS**, especially **Jaboulet**'s or **Clape**'s.

CONDRIEU is *the* Rhône white wine – SERENA SUTCLIFFE recommends that of **Georges Vernay**, who pioneered the renaissance of the area.

FRENCH POLYNESIA

BORA BORA
Stunning island with a series of hotels and clubs boasting their own lush patch of greenery and idyllic beach. Best resorts: **CLUB MED**, whose lavish feasts are legendary; **HOTEL BORA BORA**, BP 1, Nunue, ☎ 482600, which has nabbed the best site on the island, on a promontory where the beach always looks magically picture-book white and palm-fringed (even though the adjacent shoreline is shabby). Thatched bures among the flowers or floating on stilts; outrigger canoes, sunset cruises, beach barbecues and lessons in essential Polynesian activities such as pareu-tying.

HUAHINE
Rapidly developing little island, with a few perfect beaches left with clear-as-clear turquoise waters. Best resort: **HOTEL BALI HAI HUAHINE**, BP 26, Tahiti ☎ 561352, with Polynesian bures set among canals, lily ponds and a tropical lagoon. Similar properties in Raiatea and Moorea run by the Bali Hai boys, a Californian triumvirate.

MOOREA
Another stunner as you sail in to Cook's Bay (though rather haphazardly cared for on land). Best spots: **CLUB BALI HAI** and the Polynesian-cum-Oriental-style **CLUB MED**, BP 575, Papeete, Tahiti, which occupies the most glorious corner of the island. Lavish feasts, their own private atoll to bask on, and all water sports on tap.

RANGIROA, Tuamotu Islands
An hour's flight from Tahiti, this flat atoll (the rim of an ancient volcano) is named Rangiroa, or 'boundless sky'. Unbeatable power boating and sailing to uninhabited isles, where you feast on freshly speared, grilled fish. Pure paradise. Stay in an individual thatched bungalow at the **KIA-ORA**, BP 706, Papeete, Tahiti ☎ 428672: "*A tiny hotel on a tiny island, built and designed in the traditional style. A perfect place to hide away in – run by 2 French couples who do all the fabulous food – you can go exploring on small atolls and never meet anyone except the Tahitian Lorry (a bird)*" – MARIE HELVIN.

GERMANY

BERLIN

— Film —

🐟 **BERLIN INTERNATIONAL FILM FESTIVAL, Budapester Strasse 50, D-1000 Berlin 30 ☎ (030) 25489**
No 2 in Europe after Cannes, held in Feb, this is "*a very good, very big festival, and the best-organized in the world with German efficiency*" – DEREK MALCOLM. The Golden Bear goes to the best film. "*A strange cold event in winter, where East has always met West – a lot of Soviet and Eastern bloc films have always been shown here, even before glasnost and the breaching of the Wall*" – IAIN JOHNSTONE. Also expect retrospective and children's films, and new German cinema. The 1990 festival saw *Steel Magnolias* stars Julia Roberts and Sally Field standing on the Wall. Blockbuster receptions are held on the first and final nights at the Hotels **Schweizerhof** and **Inter-Continental**. Cool types hang out at the **Paris Bar** and anything-goes **Café Einstein** (bare feet/designer clothes).

— Hotels —

BRISTOL HOTEL KEMPINSKI, Kurfürstendamm 27, D-1000 Berlin 15 ☎ (030) 884340
The best hotel in West Berlin, on the most famous street. A royal welcome, irreproachable service, and a grand old grill restaurant.

GRAND HOTEL, Friedrichstrasse 158-164, DDR-1080 Berlin ☎ (030) 20920
A magnificent hotel in East Berlin, built recently in classic retro style, with a truly grand galleried lobby. No stinting on swanky accoutrements or facilities – a swimming pool and spa, coffeehouse, and a plethora of salons and restaurants.

— Music —

Berlin boasts 2 opera companies of high repute – the 🐟 **Deutsche Oper** in the West (in RODNEY MILNES's world top 10) and the **Deutsche Staatsoper** in the East.

🐟 **PHILHARMONIE, Natthaikirch Strasse 1, D-1000 Berlin 30 ☎ (030) 254880**
Home of the top-ranking Berlin Philharmonic, under the new directorship of the great Claudio Abbado, this "*really is one of the best modern halls*" – JULIAN LLOYD WEBBER. YEHUDI MENUHIN goes one better than that – it's his favourite venue.

MUNICH

— Art and museums —

🐟 **ALTE PINAKOTHEK, Barer Strasse 27, D-8000 Munich 2 ☎ (089) 2380 5215**
This gallery, commissioned by Ludwig I, contains one of the best collections of Old Masters in the world – 65 Rubenses, a number of priceless Italians and all the German masters. Don't miss Dürer's *Four Apostles* and Rubens's *Self-portrait with his Wife*.

NEUE PINAKOTHEK, Barer Strasse 29, D-8000 Munich 40 ☎ (089) 2380 5195
A sensational modern building opposite the Alte Pinakothek, opened in 1981 to house 18C-19C European art, from the German Romantics to Realism.

STAATSGALERIE MODERNER KUNST, Prinzregentenstrasse 1 (Haus der Kunst), D-8000 Munich 22 ☎ (089) 292710
A leading museum of 20C art with some 400 paintings and sculptures. All major modern schools are covered – Cubism, Fauvism, Surrealism, Abstract Expressionism, Minimalism.... Good representation of Picasso, all the important German moderns (Klee, Marc, Beckmann and co) and Italians (Boccioni, de Chirico, Marini, Burri).

— Film —

MUNICH INTERNATIONAL FILM FESTIVAL, Türkenstrasse 93, D-8000 Munich 40 ☎ (089) 393011
A festival of increasing importance, held in June. Premières from 30 countries, new German films, unknown Russian films, highlights from Cannes. Expect galas, concerts and film buffs in their thousands.

— Hotels —

HOTEL VIER JAHRESZEITEN KEMPINSKI, Maximilianstrasse 17, D-8000 Munich 22 ☎ (089) 230390
Remains No 1 in the city, a bastion of Bavarian hospitality and one of STANLEY MARCUS's favourites. Open since 1858, it once hosted the King of Siam, with his 1,320 pieces of luggage. Muncheners are still munching in the top-notch **Walterspiel** restaurant.

— Music —

Munich's 🐟 **Bavarian State Opera** is the best in Germany and figures in RODNEY MILNES's world top 10.

MUNICH OPERA FESTIVAL,
Festspielkasse, Bayerische Staatsoper,
Maximilianstrasse 11, D-8000 Munich 22
☎ **(089) 221316**
A July festival of opera at the National theater
and Altes Residenz theater – plenty of Wagner,
plus Strauss, Mozart, Verdi et al.

——— *Restaurants* ———

🐟 **DIE AUBERGINE, Maximiliansplatz 5,**
D-8000 Munich 2 ☎ **(089) 598171**
The very best of the modern French-influenced
German cuisine. Inspirational and fastidious,
Eckart Witzigmann reworks national favourites
using seasonal delicacies... sautéed pigeon with
lentils, marvellous game and fish. *"One of the
best restaurants in Europe,"* enthuses BARRY
HUMPHRIES.

TANTRIS, Johann-Fichte-Strasse 7,
D-8000 Munich 40 ☎ **(089) 362061**
Heinz Winkler's luxy restaurant is one of the
best in the country. Dream terrines, mousses
and soufflés, unearthly fish dishes and one hell
of a cellar.

———————————————
· REST OF ·
GERMANY
———————————————

——— *Art and museums* ———

🐟 **STAATSGALERIE, Konrad-**
Adenauer-Strasse 32, D-7000 Stuttgart
☎ **(0711) 212 5108**
Based in James Stirling's seminal Post-
Modernist building, this is one of the most
impressive collections of 19C and 20C art, from
Impressionism to the present day. Strong on
Expressionism and other 20C Germans.

WALLRAF-RICHARTZ-MUSEUM/
MUSEUM LUDWIG,
Bischofsgartenstrasse 1, D-5000 Cologne
☎ **(0221) 221 2379**
The largest art gallery in the Rhineland, housing
2 fine collections – one of medieval, 16C-18C
European works and Impressionists, and one of
the 20C, good on Surrealism, Expressionism and
contemporary art.

——————— *Hotels* ———————

🐟 **BRENNER'S PARK, An der**
Lichtentaler Allee, Schillerstrasse 6,
D-7570 Baden-Baden ☎ **(07221) 3530**
*"The most astonishing hotel... it gives one as
good an idea as any of what it was like to be a
tsar because it is so impossibly palatial"* – LOYD
GROSSMAN. Ever since its Edwardian heyday,
people have been flocking to this tranquil spa to
take the waters and beautify themselves at the
Lancaster Beauty Farm. You can still trot along
in a coach and four, sip tea to the strains of a
string quartet, or swim in what BARBARA
CARTLAND votes one of the best baths in Europe.
Warm thoughts from EDWARD CARTER about
the heated marble floors.

BURGHOTEL TRENDELBURG, D-3526
Trendelburg ☎ **(05675) 1021**
Perched on a hill overlooking the Rhine is this
half-timbered castle that dates back to the 13C.
Enormous meaty pig-outs.

🐟 **HOTEL VIER JAHRESZEITEN,**
Neuer Jungfernstieg 9-14, D-2000
Hamburg 36 ☎ **(040) 34941**
Still the best in Germany and in the top league
for its impeccable service. A private hotel run
by Gert Prantner (unconnected with the Four
Seasons Group), it has a country-house atmo-
sphere with warm wood panelling, tapestries and
elegant antiques. A high standard of dining at the
Haerlin. PETER USTINOV remains loyal.

🐟 **Buzzz** Post-Post-Modern: Californian
Frank Gehry's **Vitra Design Museum**, Weil am Rhein (near Basel), is set to follow the
Centre Pompidou and Staatsgalerie in terms of influential architecture. **Deconstructivist**
is the nearest label for this unique museum of chairs (1850 onwards), an angular white
puzzle outside, and a brilliantly lit and linked sequence of spaces inside🐟......**Rococo
runs riot in Bavaria**: see sea shells, C-scrolls and Chinoiserie at the pleasure follies
of **Nymphenburg Palace**, Munich – the **Pagodenburg** (classical without, Chinese
within) and **Amalienburg**, a shooting pavilion by Cuvilliés, one of the earliest and
most triumphant masterpieces of the rococo🐟......**Cuvilliés 2**: at his eponymous
Theater, jubilant music and architecture fuse🐟......At such pilgrim churches as **Die
Wies**, Steingaden, and **Vierzehnheiligen**, Staffenstein, walls and ceilings merge in
a dizzying profusion of white and gold. Vierzehnheiligen's gallery resembles a row of
opera boxes and the altar **Cinderella's coach**......................................🐟

SCHLOSSHOTEL KRONBERG,
Hainstrasse 25, D-6242 Kronberg im
Taunus ☎ (06173) 7011
A castle set in parkland on the edge of a delightful
old town near Frankfurt. Lofty halls hung with
tapestries and a panelled dining room.

> **❝** *The best shopping street in the*
> *whole world is the Königstrasse in*
> *Düsseldorf. It's light years ahead*
> *of Bond Street or Fifth Avenue – I*
> *have never seen better-dressed,*
> *handsomer, more glamorous*
> *people in more exclusive shops.*
> *And the food displays . . . they took*
> *my breath away* **❞**
>
> BOB PAYTON

Music

🎵 **BAYREUTH FESTIVAL, Postfach**
100262, D-8580 Bayreuth 2 ☎ (0921) 20221
A temple to Wagner, still run by his descendants
and performed in the opera house he designed.
Notable on 5 counts: the gravity and prestige of
the event, the supremacy of the music, the
passion of the audience, the hardness of the
seats, and the impossibility of obtaining tickets.
Held from end-July to end-Aug, the official way
in is to get a programme by the end of Oct
and apply for tickets by mid-Nov. However,
marrying into an old festival-going family or
hiring a hit squad might produce better results.

Restaurants

GOLDENER PFLUG, Olpener Strasse 421,
Merheim, D-5000 Cologne 91
☎ (0221) 895509
Gold chairs, gold curtains, gold ceiling – it
couldn't be goldener (and your pockets need to
be lined with gold, too). A fine marriage of
German taste and French genius – sea bass with
truffles, lobster roulade, fresh goose liver.

LE CANARD, Martinistrasse 11,
Eppendorf, Hamburg 20 ☎ (040) 460 4830
Small, slightly strait-laced eatery for cuisine that
is unbound by any convention. Austrian chef
Josef Viehhauser conjures up superb seafood and
sweets, and stocks a wealth of vintage wines.

LE MARRON, Provinzialstrasse 35, D-5300
Bonn 1 ☎ (0228) 253261
In a suburb of the capital, this old chestnut
supplies adventurous German/French/Italian
dishes to off-duty politicians and diplomats.

Ski resorts

GARMISCH-PARTENKIRCHEN
Top ski resort only 1 hour from Munich that
attracts local military and home-based Americans. Wide valley with fabulous ski areas rising
impressively from the flat. Best hotel: **Eibsee**
Hotel, picturesquely set on a lake and run by
Anglophile Pieter Riepl.

Wine

German wines have been sniffed at for some time
(has anyone ever *drunk* a bottle of Blue Nun, or
is it just something you take to someone's
party?). But there is life after Liebfraumilch.
Connoisseurs are waking up to the great estate
wines of Germany. The best are always white,
made from the Riesling grape (and it will say so
on the label). Their charm lies in a combination
of fruit and acidity.

Mosel-Saar-Ruwer

DEINHARD is one of the best names in Germany, thanks initially to its 1900 acquisition of
a portion of the Mosel's best vineyard: **Doktor**
at **Bernkastel**. All its wines meet a very high
standard.
   EGON MULLER-SCHARZHOF is the best
name in the Saar: **Scharzhofberger** is a wine
of penetrating perfume, vitality and class.
SERENA SUTCLIFFE considers it *"akin to*
paradise", while the 1983 **Eiswein** and 1971
Auslese are *"like smoky honey"*. An estate to
watch for is **FRIEDRICH-WILHELM-**
GYMNASIUM, founded by the Jesuits – and
the wines continue to be heavenly. **DER**
BISCHOFLICHEN WEINGUTER may
sound like a mouthful, but a sip of any of its
elegant wines would be ample compensation for
attempting to pronounce it.
   MAXIMIN GRUNHAUS No 1 in the Ruwer
has a more musical ring: von Schubert is the
owner. Much loved for their fairytale label (more
Perrault than Grimm) and their magical wines.
   JJ PRUM's **Sonnenuhr** wines are among
the Mosel's most voluptuous. The **Wehlener**
Sonnenuhr Feinste Beerenauslese of 1949
was noted in golden ink by MICHAEL BROADBENT.
   The household name of the future, a rising
star, is **SCHLOSS SAASTEIN**.
   SERENA SUTCLIFFE suggests keeping all the
Mosel-Saar-Ruwer wines to see their full beauty.
"The 1971s are still wonderful, and 1983, 1985
and 1988 (this may be the best) should not be
missed."

Rheingau

SCHLOSS VOLLRADS is one of Germany's
greatest private estates (and their labels

Eastern Bloc-buster Wines

SIMON LOFTUS looks thirstily at **Hungary**'s answer to Château d'Yquem, **TOKAY ASZU ESSENCIA**: *"Without a doubt one of the great wines of the world. What is absolutely fabulous is that in the last few years the Hungarians have finally started releasing the single-vineyard wines rather than the blended wines, which are available only in tiny quantities and are extremely expensive. There are now some old vintages of top quality available, and they live up to the wine's fabled reputation.*

Most of the other Iron Curtain countries produce good value, inexpensive wines. **Bulgaria** *is improving its standards and beginning to produce wines that are closer to the class of French country wines."* TONY ASPLER agrees: *"The hottest trend is one of people looking to the Iron Curtain – Hungary, Yugoslavia and Romania – for cheaper wines."*

harbour, in smaller print, one of the wine world's best names: owner Graf Matuschka-Greiffenclau. From their cellars came MICHAEL BROADBENT's all-time Rhine wine: a 1947 **Trockenbeerenauslese** (TBA) – the sweetest and rarest grade of German wine. *"The great TBA is the best sweet wine in the world,"* echoes MAX LAKE.

Among the other great Rheingau estates are the **RHEINGAU STATE DOMAIN** at Eltville, **SCHLOSS SCHONBORN, VON SIMMERN** and **WEGELER-DEINHARD**.

Nahe

The best Nahe wines are often said to be between those of the Mosel and Rhine in character, while Hugh Johnson has noted a hint of Sancerre. Among the most delicate and hypnotic in Germany are the wines of **CRUSIUS, HANS** and **PETER**, and the **STATE DOMAIN OF NIEDERHAUSEN-SCHLOSS BOCKELHEIM**.

Rheinhessen

BALBACH is the dominant name of this area, making wines of enormous appeal.

Rheinpfalz

Germany's sunny back garden produces much wine, best drunk in sunny back gardens. The finest, though, are dining- or drawing-room affairs. The 3 Bs, **VON BUHL, BASSERMANN-JORDAN** and **BURKLIN-WOLF**, are among the names to go for.

GREECE

❝*I like the Greek Islands better than the Carribean to sail in. The islands are so close together, you can go from one to another on a long or a short trip. Why it took some of the ancient Greeks so long to get from place to place, I'll never know!***❞**

 DOUGLAS FAIRBANKS JR

Film

ATHENS FESTIVAL, 4 Stadiou St, Athens ☎ (01) 322 1459
One of the most spectacular festival settings in the world, at the foot of the Acropolis in the AD 161 Theatre of Herodus Atticus, beneath a flood-lit Parthenon. An international festival of classical Greek and modern drama, opera, ballet and concerts. Hard marble seats, heavy night air.

Hotels

AKTI MYRINA HOTEL, Myrina, 81400 Lemnos ☎ (0254) 22681. Outside May-Oct, c/o Athens office ☎ (01) 413 8001
Informal resort with stone villas clustered around a lovely beach. Delicious spreads laid out in the garden. Very watersportif.

ASTIR PALACE, Vouliagmeni, PO Box 1226, Athens ☎ (01) 896 0211
A short drive from Athens, a sophisticated if somewhat garish resort complex of 3 hotels and 77 bungalows on a pine-clad promontory. Every facility imaginable, in quadruplicate – 4 private beaches, 4 tennis courts, etc.

GRANDE BRETAGNE, Platia Syntagmatos, Athens ☎ (01) 323 0251
This recently restored landmark hotel is the oldest in town (open since 1872), and used to

serve as the Royal Palace's guest house for visiting heads of state and royalty. Palatial suites, gracious dining room. The cognoscenti – such as LORD LICHFIELD – remain faithful.

HOTEL ALIKI, Simi ☎ (0241) 71665
On the relatively unspoilt little island of Simi, near Rhodes, is this lovely seafront hotel, a restored neo-classical mansion with roof garden and tables on the waterfront.

HOTEL MIRANDA, Hydra ☎ (0298) 52230
Chic Athenians head for this exclusive little hotel, on one of the steep streets above the pretty port (take your walking shoes – Hydra is a car-free island). The elegant 18C house has hand-painted ceilings and Greek antiques.

—— *Tours and villas* ——

CV TRAVEL (see Travel Directory) have the best selection of villas in Corfu and Paxos – beautiful privately owned villas with maid, cook and swimming pool.

HONG KONG
—— *Arts centres* ——

HONG KONG CULTURAL CENTRE, 10 Salisbury Rd, Tsimshatsui ☎ 734 9011
Officially opened by the Prince and Princess of Wales last year, this new performance arts venue is meant to evoke images of the wings of a bird or a ship's sails. Sounds familiar? Well, it's nothing like the Sydney Opera House – more like a skateboard park. However, it does have an enviable harbourfront site (scuppering the

Clare Ferguson's Athens

"**Athinas Street Market** is a sight for all those people who thought Greece meant only moussaka and keftedes. Fish, game, meat, mushrooms, herbs, spices and zillions of other goodies. Anyone can bid and buy. Fish is exceptional! Go to **Monastiraki** [best on Sunday] to explore the stands of nut- and sweet-sellers, pastry-makers, antique clothes, shoes and bric-à-brac. Memorabilia (and tat) galore. The best museums are the **Benaki Museum**, 1 Koumbari, for embroidery freaks [with costumes, ceramics and furniture too] and, of course, the **Acropolis** and its museum [housing sculptures and friezes from the Acropolis] – go early or late, and walk up the hill."

poor old Pen's outlook). This is now one of the best spaces in Asia for concerts, theatre, opera and ballet, boasting a 2,100-seat high-tech Concert Hall, Grand Theatre, a more intimate Studio Theatre and exhibition space. The opening programme saw performances by Jessye Norman, Joan Sutherland, the Royal Danish Ballet and the Boston Symphony, plus Japanese classical court dance, Chinese opera.

—— *Bars and cafés* ——

BROWN'S WINE BAR, 1F, Tower Two, Exchange Square, Central ☎ 523 7003
Michael Parry's bubbly wine bar is stuffed to the

Anne Willan on Guatemala

"Guatemala is only 100 minutes' flight from Miami, yet you are transported to a different world. Go to the abandoned historic capital, Antigua. Destroyed again and again by earthquakes and volcanic activity, Antigua is Central America's Pompeii, except that it is still a colourful town with some most attractive hotels and restaurants – **Hotel Antigua**, **Posada de Don Rodrigo** and **Dona Luisa's Café**. Food is generally fun and interesting and many places have their own Marimba band. Continue to Lake Atitlán, set in perfect high altitude and tropical surroundings. For further magnificent scenery, drive on to the **Mayan Inn** in Chichicastenango for the Thursday or Sunday market – colour, colour everywhere and so many bargains (particularly hand-woven textiles) at unheard-of prices. A breathtaking tour...and if you have time to visit hotter, rougher areas in the lowlands, there are great Mayan sites like Tikal. Take US dollar traveller's cheques as, outside Guatemala city, banks are not authorized to convert other currencies."

gills at lunch time with Ex Sq brokers and at night with Honkers' young Turks.

THE CHAMPAGNE BAR, Grand Hyatt, 1 Harbour Rd, Wanchai ☎ 861 1234
Hong Kong's first champagne bar. Given that bubbly is yuppies' and chuppies' second favourite drink after cognac, it's on to a winner. 39 varieties to tipple amid the black lacquer and brass art decodom; requisite 20s-style singer and over-discreet, ie almost pitch black, lighting.

THE GODOWN, Admiralty Tower II, Harcourt Rd, Central ☎ 866 1166
In its new home (the old one was knocked down around it), this famous bar/restaurant has changed its image, but remains great for live jazz on Wednesdays and a disco the rest of the week. Joan Collins has dropped in.

GREEN'S, GF, East Tower, Bond Centre, Queensway, Central ☎ 845 4488
Formerly related to Brown's, this newish wine bar is rather glitzier and more Chinese-orientated, with a pianist most nights, live rock 'n' roll on Fridays and calypso by a Filipino band on Saturdays.

MANDARIN ORIENTAL, see Hotels
The **Captain's Bar** is *the* place to begin the evening during the week. Practically anyone who is anyone in the financial world hits it between 6 and 7.30. Meanwhile the signless **Chinnery Bar**, on the 1st floor, retains its gentlemen's clubbiness, with wood panelling, George Chinnery prints, beer served in pewter mugs and a cliquey clientele. Also the **Clipper Lounge** (the mezzanine lobby bar), where JEREMIAH TOWER *"cannot think of a better place to recoup on a searing hot or a bitterly cold day. It's like a huge private yacht"*; and the **Harlequin Bar** at the top (where the best whisky sours are whisked up).

NED KELLY'S LAST STAND, 11A Ashley Rd, Kowloon ☎ 366 0562
A whooping wild Aussie bar named after the bush ranger. Nightly jazz or rock bands. *"A bit of a madhouse!"* – CATHERINE GAYNOR.

Casinos

Money makes Macao go round, and hordes of Chinese speed over from HK (where the only legal form of gambling is on the horses) to wager serious bucks.

MACAO CASINO, Lisboa Hotel, Avenida da Amizade, Macao ☎ 77666
The best low-life casino in the Far East, with the best fung shui. *"Suspend all ideas of glamorous Monte Carlo or Las Vegas – it's absolute mayhem. No bow-ties or tiaras – all vests and shorts. It gives you an instant buzz...the amount of money won and lost is staggering. Roulette, pontoon and Japanese games the*

Chinese don't understand, not that it matters. Stanley Ho's Crazy Paris shows are still going, with European girls doing high kicks and extraordinary things with feather boas" – CATHERINE GAYNOR.

MANDARIN ORIENTAL CASINO, Avenida da Amizade, Macao ☎ 567888
Run by casino king Stanley Ho, this is the only dressy casino in Macao. Minimum stakes are HK$50 and HK$100 (as opposed to HK$10 elsewhere). *"More sedate, more dignified – but not as much fun"* – CATHERINE GAYNOR.

Rugby Sevens

There are two peaks (and one Peak) to Hong Kong life. One is New Year's Eve (when no end of Scottish-rooted traditions are aired willy-nilly). The other is the Sevens in April. *"A weekend of international rugby for which people magically find excuses to come to Hong Kong. As soon as the dates are announced, faxes go out and regional meetings are scheduled just before or after the weekend. Journalists find stories to do on Hong Kong. There's not a plane ticket left or a single seat"* – SAUL LOCKHART. Loyal supporters (ie expats on the Asian network who fancy a wild weekend with their old pals in Honkers) fly in from Tokyo, Taiwan, Singapore, Korea, etc, consume vast quantities of alcohol (they claim they hold the world record for the amount of beer drunk per capita in an afternoon), dig into lavish picnics, and arrive late for work on Monday (sometimes by a day or two).

Clubs

See also Bars and cafés.

CALIFORNIA BAR AND GRILL, 30-32 D'Aguilar St, Central ☎ 521 1345
Still the grooviest expat hang-out in town – start the evening here and go on to 97. *"One of the original magnets that started the nightlife area of Lan Kwai Fong. Roadhouse chic, with super hamburgers, a good discothèque and a good singles bar"* – SAUL LOCKHART. *"Great. Very yuppie – packed with portable telephones, and wall-to-wall videos"* – CATHERINE GAYNOR.

CANTON, 161-163 World Finance Centre, 19 Canton Rd, Harbour City, Tsimshatsui ☎ 721 0209

Sophisticated, funky, flamboyant, this disco has super-space-age videos and lighting, and the best sound system in HK. Packed with Chinese trendies with cool haircuts (10,000 have been known to squeeze into a space for 2,000). Good visiting bands 'play' there (well... *mime* there).

🐟 HOT GOSSIP, World Finance Centre, 19 Canton Rd, Tsimshatsui ☎ 721 6884
A disco that vies with its next-door neighbour Canton for the highest-tech equipment. Videos, lasers and imported technicians. Frequented by beautiful Cathay Pacific air hostesses (plus their groupies, who hang around on the off-chance that they might get a little off-flight service).

🐟 JJ's, Grand Hyatt, see Hotels
The most glamorous nightclub in HK. Packed with the sleek set, it's a multi-theme affair, with games room, bar, restaurant, disco and blues bar with live band from Chicago.

JOE BANANAS, 23 Luard Rd, Wanchai ☎ 529 1811
JB's is a buzzy bar-diner-disco of the rock 'n' roll era, with dancing to live music and discs (golden oldies and the latest US/UK hits). The usual uproarious expattish crowd, though the fishing fleet should watch it when the American and/or British ships are in – unless they want to reel in a drunken sailor.

NINETEEN 97, 9 Lan Kwai Fong, Central ☎ 810 0613
Singles bar/bistro/restaurant/disco. Spiritual home of the fishing fleet, where streams of single girls out to hook their man put in for a stint of waitressing. Excellent for Happy Hour champagne cocktails and late at night – 97 helps keep Lan Kwai Fong a-buzzing until 5am.

—— Fashion designers ——

DIANE FREIS, Shop 258, Ocean Terminal, Harbour City, Tsimshatsui ☎ 721 4342 and branches (Connaught Centre, Prince's Bldg)
Ubiquitous in Hong Kong and all over the South China Sea, Freis specializes in the one-size (gweilo-size), uncrushable, transatlantic, throw-on-throw-off, multi-patterned, much-copied, frou-frou georgette frock. Carol Thatcher, Diana Ross, Shirley MacLaine and Victoria Principal are Freis girls. Nighties and lingerie, too. Factory outlet at Chung Nam Centre, 414 Kwun Tong Rd, Kwun Tong, Kowloon ☎ 343 6275.

EDDIE LAU, Shop 6, GF, Central Bldg, Pedder St, Central ☎ 877 3100
The size-10 party crowd patronize him for extravagant ball dresses and more restrained day clothes. *"Still the darling of the cocktail set, very flamboyant bold shapes and colours, and lots of bows. Very 'look at me'"* – CATHERINE GAYNOR. Also *little* silk numbers sold through Chinese Arts & Crafts.

JENNY LEWIS, Shop 214, Ocean Centre, Canton Rd, Tsimshatsui ☎ 723 3071 and branches (The Peninsula, Swire House)
English designer who beads and embroiders in the antique Chinese style. Something of a Hong Kong institution, she holds more appeal for foreign big spenders (Victoria Principal, Zsa Zsa Gabor, Stephanie Powers) than locals.

Private Clubs

The club with the best service, the best food and the most kudos (theoretically) is the **Hong Kong Club**, Jackson Rd ☎ 525 8251, though its new premises ('airport lounge', 'high-rise car-park') leave a nasty taste. Would-be members are wait-listed so long that they've left HK before they get to the top. Thus only *belongers* belong. Dyed-in-the-wool gweilos can always be sure of the crusty **Shek O Country Club**, Shek O ☎ 809 4429, and the powerful **Royal Hong Kong Jockey Club**, Sports Rd, Happy Valley ☎ 583 7811, which controls the racing in HK (HK$34 *billion*-dollar turnover and bags of social cachet). According to CATHERINE GAYNOR, the **American Club**, 47F, Tower Two, Exchange Square ☎ 842 7400, *"really knocks* the other clubs for six, and proves to our North American cousins that HK is not the hardship posting they thought it was."* Featured in *Taipan* on telly; major plus point is its beautifully kept country club in Tai Tam on the south side of the island. **Foreign Correspondents' Club**, 2 Albert Rd ☎ 521 1511, remains the one with the most character, at the hub of it all, with a vast circular bar open day and night for gasping shift-workers. The ritziest, wealth-smacking outfit is the **Aberdeen Marina Club**, 8 Deepwater Bay Rd, Aberdeen ☎ 555 8321, with the best marina in Asia. On offer are billiards, bridge, a marvellous mah-jong room, swimming, tennis, room service out to yachts and packed champagne lunches.

RAGENCE, Shop 21, GF, Swire House, Central ☎ 521 4646
Ragence Lam is HK's hottest young contemporary designer, whose innovative designs are on the international fashion victim's list. Exclusive and expensive made-to-order evening and bridal wear.

Festivals

FESTIVAL OF ASIAN ARTS, c/o Urban Council Festivals Office ☎ 734 4290
Held biennially in Oct/Nov (catch the 1990 one quick), a feast of ethnic cultures – expect dancers from Bombay, horn-blowers from Nepal, ballet dancers from Japan, drummers from Sri Lanka.

HONG KONG ARTS FESTIVAL, c/o 13F, HK Arts Centre, 2 Harbour Rd, Wanchai ☎ 529 5555
The West wins out in Hong Kong. Held *annually* in Jan/Feb, this is *"an orgy of mostly Western culture – opera, dance, symphonic orchestras, mime, one-man bands, jazz"* – SAUL LOCKHART. Some Asian arts too, including Chinese theatre. DIANE FREIS is keen. PS Use your concierge as the box office.

HONG KONG FILM FESTIVAL, c/o Hong Kong Coliseum, Annex Bldg, Parking Deck Fl, KCR Kowloon Station, 8 Cheong Wan Rd, Kowloon ☎ 364 2217
Eagerly awaited by the movie-starved, this is very much a film-goer's festival, showing the latest and best films from Asia and worldwide. Held in March.

Hotels

🔱 GRAND HYATT, 1 Harbour Rd, Wanchai ☎ 861 1234
The Hyatt's new flagship, a sleek silhouette in silvered glass and polished marble, built on reclaimed land bang on the harbourfront. *"Really lovely, the mirror image of the Regent on the other side of the harbour, with similar views"* – CATHERINE GAYNOR. This no-holds-barred extravaganza leaves even blasé locals blasted. An unbelievably glossy galleried lobby with dome-lit ceiling and gleaming black marble floor (don't go in your high heels), a swimming pool that looks as if it flows into the harbour, and a ballroom that flabbergasts SAUL LOCKHART: *"It's unlike anything seen in Hong Kong before"*. A full hand of dining/drinking/night spots and the excellent Cantonese restaurant, **One Harbour Road**, modelled on a taipan's home on the Peak. Just don't expect to go strolling – the walkway system is worse than spaghetti junction.

HILTON, 2 Queen's Rd, Central ☎ 523 3111
In one of the older buildings of Hong Kong, the Hilton retains its loyal following, a great health

club and outdoor pool, the best cocktail bar, **Dragon Boat Bar**, and the excellent **Grill** (where financiers, journalists and Hollywood heroes like Mel Gibson dine). Also their own 100-ft brigantine for cocktail cruises and picnics.

Exodus
🔱

Post-Tiananmen Square and pre-1997 is a testy time for Hong Kong Chinese. A question mark hangs menacingly over their heads. The answer for many is to get a foreign passport as a safety catch, which means leaving the homeland to gain foreign residency. The result back in Hong Kong is a worrying shortage of skilled labour. As the maître d's and sommeliers pour out to Australia, Canada, Singapore and the like, young bell-hops and waiters are being promoted beyond their experience. Hotels are suffering. Their No 1 selling point – impeccable service – is under threat. On top of this, occupancy levels have been so erratic that new hotels have opened and shut, and even the Mandarin has been offering discounts. The original intention of these displaced nationals was to return ... but how many actually will?

🔱 MANDARIN ORIENTAL, 5 Connaught Rd, Central ☎ 522 0111
The Mandarin will always have the edge on its rivals for its assured atmosphere of being where it's at. Bang in the middle of Central, it's still the only one for the dark-suited high financiers, and still No 1 meeting-place in town (see Bars and cafés). Although businessmen tend not to notice, those with a discerning eye for décor prefer the taste of the Mandarin to the Regent ... the black marble lobby with gold temple carvings, the elegant Chinese bedrooms. As CATHERINE GAYNOR says, *"it's just got it – very stylish"*. Arguably the most comfortable bedding and, according to CAROL WRIGHT, the best down pillows in the world. LORD LICHFIELD can think of nowhere nicer to lay his head. JEREMIAH TOWER likes the pool – *"small, perfect, all rose marble and sublime"*. The hotel *is* suffering from the HK malaise of high staff turnover, and the lobby *is* somewhat frenetic. Nevertheless TERRY HOLMES still finds it: *"Lovely. It was the attention immediately on arrival that was very special."* *"I adore the Mandarin, it's special and so central"* – ELISE PASCOE. Still the best for LEN EVANS and MAUREEN LIPMAN. Superlative dining (see Restaurants).

🛉 THE PENINSULA, Salisbury Rd, Kowloon ☎ 366 6251

The grande dame of Honkers hotels, in operation since 1928, the revamped Pen is earning warm praise on all counts. "*Certainly one of the great hotels in the world. It has not only cachet but an old-world, discreet service almost impossible to find anywhere else. They really pay attention to you. And they really do pack your bags and draw your bath. The food is so good too. You arrive at the airport very tired, a Rolls-Royce [they have 8 Silver Spirits] is there to meet you, they ask you what you'd like to eat and telephone the hotel, so that when you get to your room, your breakfast is there*" – KEN HOM. LISE WATIER's sentiments exactly: "*A hotel that reflects the spirit of all great hotels of the era in all its splendour. The charm begins as their Rolls-Royce picks you up from the airport. The service is of a superior category and the cuisine is the very best.*" New rooms and spacious suites are to the English manor born, combined with space-age technology (suites have laser-disc videos, compact disc players, teletext and faxes); the national newspaper of your own country is delivered daily. The lobby remains *the* place to watch the world pass by during afternoon tea, and **Gaddi's** (see Restaurants) the most prestigious place to dine.

🛉 THE REGENT, Salisbury Rd, Kowloon ☎ 721 1211

The biggest and best. HK habitués feel that if it's humanly possible to top the service of the other supreme hotels in town, then the Regent's the one to do it. Your own butler introduces himself at check-in – it's that fraction more attentive without being pushy. On the other hand, it's less characterful and more modern than its chief rival, the Mandarin. One thing's for sure: guests (bags of rag-traders and showbizzos) cannot get over that 146 x 60 ft cinematic view from the lobby (it's even better from the outdoor spa pools). "*I think it's the best hotel in the world. Your every need is catered to. It has the most spectacular view of anywhere, and exceptional restaurants*" – TONY ASPLER. "*The best view in the world from one of the best bars. Also the best floor service in Hong Kong*" – JEREMIAH TOWER. "*I love their harbourside suites, very light and modern. The best way to soothe shopping feet is in your seductive Jacuzzi overlooking spectacular Hong Kong harbour*" – ELISE PASCOE. "*The only place that can come close to the Peninsula. What is remarkable is that it is much bigger and yet able to deliver the same type of incredible service. Really terrific. The view…it's literally like sitting in a boat. And they have great food*" – KEN HOM. "*The best in Hong Kong for its truly magnificent harbour views, superb lobby and elegant décor*" – DIANE FREIS (who also votes the Presidential Suite tops). Equally knocked out are MICHAEL GRADE and GLYNN CHRISTIAN.

🛉 SHANGRI-LA, 64 Mody Rd, Tsimshatsui E ☎ 721 2111

This glossy 719-room affair is yet another hotel to be placed No 1 in Hong Kong by its own devotees, who feel that *everyone* is treated like a celebrity here. Carrara marble lobby with Viennese crystal chandeliers; super-large rooms overlooking the harbour (bedside-controlled curtains mean you can gaze out each morning from your bed). See also Restaurants.

——— *Restaurants* ———

CAFE D'AMIGO, 79A Wong Nei Chong Rd, Happy Valley ☎ 577 2202

Sophisticated, formal, ultra-expensive, this classic French dinery is a match for the Western hotel restaurant monopoly. Frequented by Hong Kong high society, who like little touches such as matches inscribed with the host's name.

🛉 FOOK LAM MOON, 459 Lockhart Rd, Causeway Bay ☎ 891 2639

Remains the acid test of whether you have 'face' with the Chinese: you pass if you've been dined at Fook Lam Moon. Superb for fish-tank-fresh

🛉 **Buzzz** Can HK sustain yet more 5-star swanky hotels? Already open are the soothingly smart **Ramada Renaissance**, 8 Peking Rd, Tsimshatsui ☎ 311 3311 (see also Restaurants), and the **Hong Kong Marriott**, Pacific Place, 88 Queensway, Central ☎ 810 8366. About to be unveiled is the **Island Shangri-La**, also in Pacific Place, and due next year is the **Ritz-Carlton**, occupying the entire city block between the Furama and the Hong Kong Club, and aiming at the ambience of a private club🛉……Posterior problems: gweilos have discovered a new kind of **Chinese torture** – an evening at the Cultural Centre, where seats are designed for weeny indigènes and not **monster expats**🛉……Get Lost in Space: with its multi million dollar star projector, 13-channel sound system and over 100 special-effect projectors, the **Space Museum**, Kowloon ☎ 721 2361, is arguably the best planetarium in the world………………………………………………………………………🛉

fish and specialities such as abalone and shark's fin at humbling prices.

🐟 HUNAN GARDEN, The Forum, Exchange Square, Central ☎ 868 2880

Honkers expense-accounters eschew the Sichuan Garden and Guangzhou Garden in favour of this one. Hunanese cuisine is the new rage in Hong Kong, and this is the only place to get it. *"Very slick and very good"* – CATHERINE GAYNOR. *"The nicest of the Gardens"* – SAUL LOCKHART. And so says YAN-KIT SO. Try duck tongues in mustard sauce, braised mutton paw, freshwater eel and rather good pastries.

🐟 MANDARIN ORIENTAL, see Hotels

"Executive chef Jurg Munch is like Serge Dansereau at the Regent of Sydney – able to turn out the best-quality food in every area of the hotel. It's so rare to see, they should both be commended" – ELISE PASCOE. **Man Wah** is thought by locals to be a little ersatz – Cantonese dressed up for Mandarin-dwellers... Ingredients are wonderfully fresh, cooking is flawless, but there are few surprises. Nevertheless GLYNN CHRISTIAN votes it *"the best Chinese meal I have ever had"*. The French **Pierrot** is prestige stuff for bejewelled and fashionable Chinese and bizmen out to impress. Produce is flown in from France – sending the price sky-high. Refurbished to a more pastel, less masculine style, with large well-spaced tables. LORD LICHFIELD prizes **The Grill** *"for wonderful, fresh, clean-tasting food. Ingredients are flown in from all over the world."*

Dr Abalone

🐟

Q: Who can stop abalone tasting like rubber? A: The Abalone Doctor. Mr Yeung Koon-Yat is the recognized expert on how to cook abalone, for which he has earned himself an honorary doctorate. What *is* abalone? It's a delicacy, a mollusc, and it can cost £100 a portion. *"There is abalone and abalone. Mr Yat has a really special way of preparing abalone. He soaks it, then he boils it, then he braises it slowly with meat stock (chicken wings, ducks' wings, ham) so it gradually absorbs the flavour from the infusion. Then he prepares another sauce stock which is even richer. At the last moment he thickens the sauce with a tiny bit of tapioca flour and oyster sauce"* – YAN-KIT SO. So, after a successful day at Shatin races, blow your winnings on a plateful of the Doctor's best at his **Forum Restaurant**, 485 Lockhart Rd, Causeway Bay ☎ 891 2555.

NORTH SEA FISHING VILLAGE CO, Auto Plaza, Tsimshatsui E ☎ 723 6843; GF, 445 King's Rd, N Point ☎ 563 0187

At the centre of both these 2 restaurants is an authentic junk stacked with floodlit tanks of fishy victims (you choose your own). Excellent prawns, octopus, crab, shark's fin and dim sum.

PEAK CAFE, 121 Peak Rd, The Peak ☎ 849 7868

This famous old Cantonese greasy chopstick, based in one of the oldest houses left standing in HK, has been restored and reopened by hero-of-the-year Jeremiah Tower. Shunning modernity, he has kept the granite 2 walls and timber beams, added a fireplace, Chinese antiques, conservatory and garden. Trendy Honkers laps up the atmos and his 'Calasian' (Californian-Asian, geddit?) cuisine – freshest produce, lots of barbecuing, Chinese and Indian flavours. The cross-cultural approach spawns dishes such as Hawaiian tuna sashimi with lime and ginger, sweet and spicy tea, and smoked squab prepared à la West Coast, on the kitchen stage.

🐟 THE PENINSULA, see Hotels

Gaddi's remains the one for HK belongers and old Chinese families. The dining room encapsulates Edwardian England – white damask napery, sumptuous patterned carpet. Rolf Heiniger is the only maître d' that matters: when he greets you by name, you've arrived. *"For impeccable service, excellent food and an accommodating maître d'"* confirms DIANE FREIS. *"They have the most wonderful selection of vintage port. It was a surprise to find them there ..."* – SERENA SUTCLIFFE. It needn't be ruinously expensive (set lunch menu) and cuisine is not stuffy – guest chefs from all over the globe offer a breath of fresh air. Also **Spring Moon**, *"one of the most upmarket Cantonese restaurants with absolutely superb Peninsula service"* – SAUL LOCKHART.

RAMADA RENAISSANCE, 8 Peking Rd, Tsimshatsui ☎ 311 3311

Capriccio is based on Enoteca Pinchiorri in Florence, who stock their cellar (making it a contender for the best Italian wines outside Italy – some rare bottles go direct to Hong Kong) and supply them with a rotation of chefs. *"The maître d' is a great character called Mario d'Amico. He calls the cellar his church – he's an absolute wine fiend. I think it is one of the best hotel restaurants in town, except you don't feel as if you're in a hotel – you feel as if you could look out of the window on to a Florentine street instead of traffic jams and camera shops. The food is authentic, not heavy"* – CATHERINE GAYNOR. Also Cantonese dining at **T'ang Court**.

🐟 THE REGENT, see Hotels

In an artistic setting behind the prized picture windows, **Lai Ching Heen** is now considered to have *"the best Chinese food in Hong Kong. Absolutely the top, very creative and just utterly* *delightful*" – KEN HOM. "*Mind-boggling attention to detail. Modern Chinese cuisine – classics with a twist, immaculate dim sum. Guaranteed no MSG, very, very fresh ingredients. Place settings have ivory and silver chopsticks, jade plates. Beautifully presented*" – CATHERINE GAYNOR. "*Just so sophisticated and traditional at the same time. If you give them plenty of notice, they can give you snake's gall, disembowelled in your presence, in a private room. Tasty? We-e-ell, you'll never get rheumatism again*" – BARRY HUMPHRIES. DIANE FREIS loves **Plume** for the same reasons she loves Gaddi's. When the former chef left, Plume's feathers were ruffled. While HK waits for the cuisine to prove itself, some superlatives remain: the setting, natch; the shrine of a cellar, displayed in a glass-fronted room ("*the best wine cellar in South-East Asia*" – TONY ASPLER); their amuse-bouche of nan and chicken liver pâté ("*the hot nan is spectacular. They actually have an Indian cook and a tandoori oven*" – GLYNN CHRISTIAN).

Far East's Best Restaurants

1	LAI CHING HEEN · Hong Kong
2	LEMON GRASS · Bangkok
3	GADDI'S · Hong Kong
4	FUKUZUSHI · Tokyo
5	FOOK LAM MOON · Hong Kong
6	KISSO · Tokyo
7	HUNAN GARDEN · Hong Kong
8	LE RESTAURANT DE FRANCE · Singapore
9	LE BANYAN · Bangkok
10	KICCHO · Osaka

SATAY HUT, 144-148 Houston Centre, Tsimshatsui E ☎ 723 3681
Chef-proprietor Pearl Choo serves Nonya food from Singapore (all Singaporeans know it). Specialities include Hainan chicken rice; beef, chicken or pork satay; stir-fry quaytiew (ribbon-like) noodles, and, as YAN-KIT SO recommends, "*spicy crab with cellophane noodles – really delicious, curry-like, very spicy.*"

🐚 **SHANGRI LA, see Hotels**
For first-class nouvellish cuisine in super-luxe surroundings, **Margaux** gets top marks. Crystal glasses by the yard, the same deferential treatment for *all* diners, a fine cellar and an

exceptionally good female Chinese sommelière. If Hong Kong has left you spiced out, try the subtle Japanese restaurant, **Nadaman**, which, for RAYMOND BLANC, "*combines the unmatched splendour of the Far East with brilliant food*". Chinese dining at **Shang Palace**.

SUNNING UNICORN, 1 Sunning Rd, Causeway Bay ☎ 577 6620
The place for the Sichuan speciality, drunken prawns. Chinese yellow wine is poured over live prawns; when they are well and truly sozzled, they are dropped into a hotpot on the table and cooked. *Delicious* but not for the faint-hearted.

YUNG KEE, 32-40 Wellington St, Central ☎ 523 1562
This glittery Chinese emporium of a restaurant is the locals' fave, "*very famous for their unique roast goose. You have the 'one-dish meal' – roast goose and rice. They are terribly busy, it's really a wonder. All the Chinese go*" – YAN-KIT SO.

ZEN CHINESE CUISINE, LG/1 The Mall, Pacific Place, 88 Queensway, Central ☎ 845 4555
The ultimate coals-to-Newcastle restaurant, opened by Michael Leung of the London Zens. The same cool designer atmos, with lots of chuppie (Chinese yuppie) appeal and even fresher, more authentic cuisine. Excellent spare ribs and fish. "*Terrific. It's the current talk of Honkers*" – ELISE PASCOE.

Shopping

"*Hong Kong is the shopping mall of the world,*" declares DIANE FREIS. A tax-free port for just about everything, it's a shopper's seventh heaven for jade, pearls, gold, silk, linen, embroidery, designer and made-to-measure clothes, electronic goods, cameras and much more going cheap.

On HK Island, the zazzily refurbished **Mandarin** arcade has a select coterie of local bests (Kai-Yin Lo, A-Man Hing Cheong, David's Shirts, Mayer Shoes) and foreign glamour (Chaumet, Ferragamo – selling footwear like it's running out of fashion). A network of walkways leads to the ritziest, shiniest shopping complexes, **The Landmark** (best of the Euros – Buccellati, Bulgari, Chanel, Dior, Ungaro, Vuitton, Loewe, Hermès, Joyce Boutique, The Swank Shop), **Prince's Building** (second-rung Euros) and **Swire House** (the pick of the Japs). Kowloon is home to the swish arcades of the **Regent** (Diane Freis, Basile, Lanvin, Nina Ricci) and **Peninsula** (Joyce Boutique, Marguerite Lee, Hermès, Gucci), and impressive mega-centres like **Ocean Terminal**, **Harbour City** and **Ocean Centre**.

Choice Chinese goods can be found at **Chinese Arts & Crafts** or a department store such as **Chinese Merchandise Emporium**, **China Products** or **Yue Hwa Chinese Products**

Emporium. On HK Island, **Pedder Building** is a must for knock-down groovy designer wear (check out Boutique Bello, Boutique Tommi, Shopper's World, Due Trio, Shirt Stop and Piano). The stalls on **Wing On Lane** are excellent for fabric – silks, linen, shirting (do double-check that 'peeore siyook, madam' is genuine). The **Lanes** between Queen's Road Central and Des Voeux Road bristle with little stalls for all sorts of bargains and fakery. **Stanley Market** is still a ritual gweilo haunt on a Sunday (shop, lunch at Stanley's, shop), but requires energy and discrimination to cut through tourists and tat and find the real bargains (from Reeboks to jumbo jeans). On Kowloon, **Nathan Road** and all roads off to the east are bursting with jewellery, embroidery and electronic goods. The area for cheapo cheapo gear is **Kaiser Estate**, Phase I-III, Hung Hom, *"a rabbit warren of factory outlets for silk, linen, sportswear, etc – not necessarily high fashion, but dependable and cheap."* – CATHERINE GAYNOR. NB Bargain-hunters should check out prices back home before embarking, and only shop where the HKTA sticker is displayed. Take the HKTA's *Official Guide to Shopping* and Dana Goetz's *Complete Guide to Hong Kong Factory Bargains*.

A-MAN HING CHEONG, M4, Mandarin Oriental, Central ☎ 522 3336
One of the best and best-respected tailors, not a far cry from Savile Row, and a proficient copy-cat. High prices and a quick turnover (suits from about HK$3,000). He does shirts for NICHOLAS VILLIERS and LORD LICHFIELD, and suits for BARRY HUMPHRIES.

BOUTIQUE TOMMI, Pedder Bldg, 12 Pedder St, Central ☎ 845 1180
Trend gear at knockdown prices. The very best avant-garde and mainstream Brit designer labels for clothes and shoes – Bruce Oldfield, Katharine Hamnett, Jasper Conran, John Galliano.

CHINESE ARTS & CRAFTS, Star House, Kowloon ☎ 367 4061; Silvercord Bldg, 30 Canton Rd; Shell House, Wyndham St, Central; and branches

The best of China, all strictly government-controlled: bales of silk, guaranteed the real McCoy; jade, lapis and other precious and semi-precious jewellery; Kai-Yin Lo's beaded bags and belts; classic cashmeres; porcelain tableware and ornaments; exquisite embroidered and appliquéd linenware. Eddie Lau's slick little silk dresses are here, as are desirable undies.

Fur Facts

Furs are a fact of HK life: 1 in 6 women gets her paws on one. If you're unruffled by mass opinion, here's where to obtain bargains, copies and made-to-measure. **Siberian Fur Store**, 21 Chatham Rd ☎ 366 7039; 29 Des Voeux Rd ☎ 522 1380 are *"the very best, very expensive"* – CATHERINE GAYNOR. Have your faux Fendi run up to perfection here. The Korean company **Jindo Furs**, 308-309 World Finance Centre, Harbour City ☎ 369 9208, and in Kowloon Hotel, get their pelts made up ultra-cheap back home. Pick a pelt and they'll make it up in any style. *"It's like a fur supermarket – you whizz in there to get your fox"* – CG. **Christian Dior**, The Landmark ☎ 526 3647, attracts rich Chinese for real furs posing as fun furs – dyed wacky green and dark purple (the Dior colours). Other furriers to scurry to are **Singer Furs**, 136B Tai Shoh Gallery, Ocean Terminal, and **Stephen Fong**, Regent Arcade.

CLAIRE WADSWORTH, 1203 Central Bldg, Pedder St ☎ 522 3941
A European jewellery designer whom *"few people know about, but she has fabulous taste. She's a belonger – she's been in Hong Kong for*

🕵 **Buzzz** If you fancy a dainty pair of Chinese feet tippytoeing up and down your spine, trip along to the **Regent's Health Spa** (*"truly spectacular, it so impressed me. Instead of sharing your steam bath or sauna, you have a complete set to yourself: a huge green marble-lined room with sauna, whirlpool, steam bath, massage table and a series of people who lead you from one to the other. The best I've ever been looked-after"* – GLYNN CHRISTIAN)🕵......Home in on the **Hong Kong Museum of Science and Technology**, opening 1990/91 on Chatham Rd, Tsimshatsui🕵......Snaffled scarves are out, hats in for the prestigious **Hermès Cup**, held at the swanky Shatin racecourse in Dec. While not *forcing* ladies to wear hats, the Hermès hatter was flown in by way of *encouragement* – Melbourne or the Arc de Triomphe was what they had in mind, not **slap-Happy Valley**...........🕵

years" – CATHERINE GAYNOR. Specializes in black South Sea pearls and has the best connections for Colombian emeralds.

DAVID'S SHIRTS, M7, Mandarin Oriental, Central ☎ 524 2979; GF, 33 Kimberley Rd, Tsimshatsui ☎ 367 9556

The leading white-collar worker (not to mention blue collars, stripy collars, button-down collars …). Gweilos get a kick out of having their initials embroidered in Chinese on the pocket.

FASHIONS OF SEVENTH AVENUE, Kaiser Estate, Block M, Hok Yuen St, Hung Hom, Kowloon ☎ 365 9061; 12A Sing Pao Bldg, 8 Queens Rd, Central ☎ 868 4208

For your Karan drape-arounds at silly prices. Donna devotees ransack the place after each new shipment of silks and knits (labels are cut out, but fashoholics know they're for real).

 JOYCE BOUTIQUE, Shop 214, Gloucester Tower, The Landmark, Central ☎ 525 3655; The Peninsula

Fashion baroness Joyce Ma (of the powerful Shanghainese shipping/banking/Wing On department store family) not only runs her own boutiques, but is licensee for the leading lights of Italian and Japanese designerdom. Chez elle, she has snapped up Lacroix, Gaultier, Lagerfeld, Alaïa, Karan, Mary McFadden, Vicky Tiel, and accessories by Maud Frizon, Philippe Model and Butler & Wilson. Caters to the Chinese upper crust. **Joyce for Men & Women**, New World Tower, 16 Queen's Rd, Central ☎ 527 0002, carries contemporary chic by Comme, Sybilla, Galliano, Gigli, Moschino and co.

K S SZE & SONS, M6, Mandarin Oriental, Central ☎ 524 2803

Mr Sze now presides over the mezzanine floor, making anything you desire to any design. Exquisite inlaid work. *"The closest Hong Kong will ever get to a family jeweller. He's very much Establishment. I can't think of anyone better"* – CATHERINE GAYNOR.

KAI-YIN LO, M1, Mandarin Oriental, Central ☎ 524 8238; The Peninsula

Contemporary design from the woman whose name means 'dazzling revelation'. Very much a *look*, in semi-precious rocks and pearls, worked in with antique slivers of wrought bone or carved beads. Kai-Yin is dazzling 'em the world over – clients include Arianna Stassinopoulos, Natalia Makarova, Hanae Mori and British royals.

LEATHER CONCEPT, 11F, Union Hing Yip Bldg, 20 Hing Yip St, Kowloon ☎ 388 9338

The best leather factory outlet in HK. Jackets and separates by their own designer Hannah Pang plus international greats like Calvin Klein and Saint Laurent. A nightmare to find, so ask your concierge to write the address down in Chinese for the taxi driver.

"*The Japanese market is huge in Hong Kong. When Joyce Ma's new boutique opened, the whole shop was sold out in a morning***"**

 CATHERINE GAYNOR

MARGUERITE LEE, Shop 210-211, Gloucester Tower, The Landmark, Central ☎ 525 6565 and branches

Enticing lingerie by Anne Lewin, La Perla et al, plus swimwear and hosiery.

MAYER SHOES, M23, Mandarin Oriental, Central ☎ 524 3317

The best (though most expensive) made-to-measure shoes in the South China Sea. If it's got a skin, they can turn it into a shoe. Or a bag. Or a camera case, as ordered by LORD LICHFIELD. *"Brilliant. You can take a pair of Gucci loafers or Chanel shoes and they will copy them. This is the tops"* – CATHERINE GAYNOR.

ORANGE-ROOM, Shop 66, B1, New World Centre, Tsimshatsui ☎ 368 8051

Nifty shoes designed and produced in Japan, some a snip from $HK200 (to $HK800) a pair. Also ties and small leather goods.

PARIS SHOES AND LEATHERWEAR, Shop D5/6, BF, Sheraton Hotel, Kowloon ☎ 723 7170

The amazing 10-hour made-to-measure shoe, bag, briefcase – leather anything, including clothes. For the real jet-setter. But don't expect *too* much from a 10-hour shoe.

RONALD ABRAM, Shop 128, Prince's Bldg, Central ☎ 845 2279

Antique jewellery. Abram broke away from Siba to set up this shop, containing beautiful examples of old Cartier and Van Cleef & Arpels.

SAM'S TAILOR, Burlington Arcade, 92-94 Nathan Rd, Kowloon ☎ 367 9423

A tailor of world renown. Love him or knock him, there's no doubt that he's fast, cheap and pretty reliable. Huge variety of material and styles. Caters for everyone, from princes and politicos (shirts for Charles, suits for Denis Thatcher) to Jardine Johnnies (red satin boxers).

S P H DA SILVA, K226-227 Pacific Place, 88 Queensway, Central ☎ 522 5807

The best pearls in the Colony, by the river and rope. Reliable quality and prices for jade, diamonds and all kinds of glittering prizes. Will make up and copy special pieces.

TAK PAK, Room 301, Pedder Bldg, 12 Pedder St, Central ☎ 521 2547

For knock-down Anne Klein silk numbers (this is where garments are created and where they end up). Also Chantal Thomass.

INDIA

AGRA

MUGHAL SHERATON, Fatehabad Rd, 282001 ☎ (0562) 64701
Remains the No 1 hotel for those taking in the Taj Mahal, Fatehpur Sikri and Bharatpur Bird Sanctuary. Welcoming garlands of marigolds, exotic fruit and home-made biscuits in your room, charming service, and an ocean of blue swimming pool.

BOMBAY

THE OBEROI, Nariman Point, 400021 ☎ (022) 202 5757
The old Oberoi Towers is now flanked by this slick new atrium tower, with gleaming rust-coloured polished granite floors. Rooms and a rooftop pool look over the sweeping arc of sea-front. The Presidential Suite has pastel Shyam Ahuja furnishings and a black granite and white marble bathroom. The **Rôtisserie** has the best wine list in India; the **Bayview Bar** is where the Bombay élite meet. Bright, courteous staff.

TAJ MAHAL INTER-CONTINENTAL, Apollo Bunder, Colaba, 400039 ☎ (022) 202 3366
The head of the Taj hotel family, presiding regally beside the Gateway of India and looking out to the glittering Arabian Sea. Rooms vary, so stay in the refurbished old palatial part with its sweeping staircases. View the nightscape over cocktails in the 24th-floor **Apollo Bar**. BOB PAYTON, MADHUR JAFFREY, CHARLOTTE RAMPLING and QUENTIN CREWE are fans.

DELHI

HOTEL OBEROI MAIDENS, 7 Sham Nath Marg, Old Delhi 110054 ☎ (011) 252 5464
The place to relax in airy, colonial splendour. Enormous rooms and wide corridors, shady gardens and pool, out of central Delhi.

OBEROI NEW DELHI, Dr Zakir Hussain Marg, New Delhi 110003 ☎ (011) 699571
The best on the international traveller's map, with restrained décor of salmon or rose pink with mahogany fittings, and the usual thoughtful Oberoi service. **La Rochelle** serves fab French cuisine and the rooftop **Taipan** spicy Sichuan for a snip. SERENA FASS is a fan.

"Calcutta has the most cine-literate people in the world. Even the hotel waiters know what the films are and who directed them. The most cultured audience in the world"

 DEREK MALCOLM

GOA

FORT AGUADA BEACH RESORT, Sinquerim, Bardez, 403515 ☎ (0832) 7501; TAJ HOLIDAY VILLAGE ☎ (0832) 7515
Extensive resort set in fabulously lush, colourful terraced gardens overlooking a wild sweeping beach, in this laid-back Portuguese colony. The main area is a hotel complex spilling over into cottages. Above is the exclusive **AGUADA HERMITAGE** for self-contained villa luxury.

Richesse Oblige

The old measure of wealth used to be fatness. For bulging waistline you could read bulging wallet. Nowadays, Bombay's nouveaux riches would blend happily in Beverly Hills, with a new ostentatious display of thinness and money. Pamella Bordes is the type. Such immaculately turned-out women, accessorized with expensive fake European jewellery and dashing men, meet at the Taj and Oberoi hotels.

They belong to the **Dynasty Culture** Club, which presents cultural programmes (opera, film) expensively, and attend shop openings and seasonal previews. The leather boutique **Csango** sent out calfskin mementoes as invitations, while **Glitterati**, armed with an impressive hit list of 400 socialites, held a series of high-tea parties for 25 mutually acquainted clients. Each was collected by a chauffeur and ushered to a private entrance before being treated to a peep show of the new stock.

JAIPUR

Hotels

JAI MAHAL PALACE HOTEL, Jacob Rd, Civil Lines, 302006 ☎ (0141) 68381
Based in the first Jaipur observatory, this companion hotel to the Rambagh is similarly palatial, in equally beautiful surroundings. Fine Continental, Indian and Chinese cuisine.

HOTEL NARAIN NIWAS, Kanota Bagh, Narain Singh Rd, 302004 ☎ (0141) 65448
Don't expect grand luxe or great service, just enjoy this throwback to Raj days, a decaying ochre and pink villa built in 1881 with original decorative paintwork, four-posters, dhurries, portraits and weaponry. Breakfast on the verandah in peace, save the odd peacock screech. Under the same umbrella is **KANOTA CASTLE**, a 200-year-old fort 8 miles out of town with just 6 rooms.

🕊 RAMBAGH PALACE, Bhawani Singh Rd, 302005 ☎ (0141) 75141
The traditional best in town. Stunning palace with scalloped arcades, little domed turrets and verandahs, painted in buttermilks and creams. Lovely gardens and an indoor pool. Maharajahs and visiting society drink in the colonial **Polo Bar**. Prettiest suite is the Princess.

JODHPUR

UMAID GHAWAN PALACE, 342006 ☎ (0291) 22316
The most luxurious hotel in town, a fascinating, maze-like palace that OLIVIER COQUELIN finds *"positively breathtaking"*.

UDAIPUR

LAKE PALACE HOTEL, Pichola Lake, 313001 ☎ (0294) 23241
Floating resplendent on a shimmering lake like some Mississippi paddle steamer, this magical white marble palace is *"the most romantic hotel in the world"* according to BARBARA CARTLAND and a zillion others. Little formal flower and water gardens, courtyards with orange blossom and almond trees, follies with mirrored mosaics that glint in the sun. Rooms have been restored, but the exotic Khush Mahal and Udai Mahal suites are worth the extra. Service leaves a little to be desired.

SHIVNIWAS PALACE, 313001 ☎ (0294) 28239
On the mainland facing the Lake Palace, this wonderful historic palace is now a hotel/health spa. This is hand-crafted opulence like you have never seen – Belgian cut-glass armchairs and tables, carved ivory doors, glass inlay scenes of wildlife, a carved marble oval swimming pool. Knock-out suites, the best of which is the Imperial, with its wall-to-wall hand-cut glass and mirrors, circular bedroom, lounge and balcony where you can dine in private.

Tours

EXPLORASIA and **EQUINOX** are excellent for individual tours (see Travel Directory).

COX & KINGS, 404 Deepali, 92 Nehru Place, New Delhi 110019 ☎ (011) 641 4306
Veterans of Indian travel who once made the travel arrangements for the British Army in India. Tailor-made itineraries or set tours.

KASHMIR HIMALAYAN EXPEDITIONS, Boulevard Shopping Complex, Dal Gate, PO Box 168, Srinagar 190001 ☎ (0194) 78698; 17 Indian Oil Building, Janpath, New Delhi ☎ (011) 332 3829
Treks in Kashmir, Ladakh, India and Nepal, camel safaris in Rajasthan and Himalayan combination of trek, rafting and elephant-back jungle safari. Can also arrange the Palace on Wheels luxury train, and the best houseboat in Kashmir, *1002 Nights*, on Nagin Lake. Here, the number of guests is matched by staff: a cook, pantry-boy, houseboy, dust-boy, log-boy and 2 bearers.

TIGER TOPS MOUNTAIN TRAVEL, 1/1 Rani Jhansi Rd, New Delhi 110055 ☎ (011) 523057
The best Himalayan treks and camps, for the high-minded and sure-footed. Hike in Kashmir, Ladakh and Tibet with top-notch Sherpas and cooks. Also wildlife viewing at Bandhavgarh Jungle Camp in central India (best chance of spotting that tiger); and the Kabini River Lodge in Karnataka. See also Nepal.

INDONESIA

BALI

"The hotels, the capital and the airport are concentrated on the southern tip of the island. Avoid Kuta Beach, where all the Australians go, though it has a ghastly charm of its own. Hire a jeep and go off into the interior – that is the most rewarding experience. There is a non-

active volcano in the centre, with hot pools there. It's very jungly, with lots of little tracks that sometimes peter out into nothing. Continue over to the north coast, where there are quite deserted black sand beaches. But the very, very lovely part of the island is the east coast, which has white sands, is not very crowded and is cheap" – DAN TOPOLSKI.

AMANDARI, PO Box 33, Ubud ☎ (0361) 33333
The latest little sister in a curious family – the Hotel Bora Bora, Burnham Beeches, near Melbourne, and Amanpuri in Thailand. 30 stunning Balinese-style pavilion suites overlook the Ayung River gorge, with views of rice terraces, volcanoes and the distant ocean. *"One of the most exciting places ever to open. On the same lines as Amanpuri with the same respect for local material and design. A really chic marvellous place to go in that part of the world"* – EDWARD CARTER. *"This and the Amanpuri are the best getaways in the Far East. Unbelievable reward"* – JEREMIAH TOWER.

> **❝I know it comes a bit late to say it, but Bali is idyllic. Having done an awful lot of travelling in an awful lot of countries, I cannot think of anywhere in the world where people are nicer and more accommodating❞**
>
> DAN TOPOLSKI

BALI OBEROI, Legian Beach, PO Box 351, Denpasar ☎ (0361) 51061
Thatched lanai cottages amid unbelievably vibrant green foliage and technicolour tropical flowers, in a fabulous position way down the beach from the hubbub of Kuta (though you can still get fab massages on the beach – 2 ladies per body). Sunken baths opening on to private patios; lovely pool. Cinematic sunsets.

KUPU KUPU BARONG, Kedewatan, PO Box 7, Ubud ☎ (0361) 35663
Lush mountainside retreat with ultra-luxe

Pacific Basin

So we're heading for the Pacific Century, according to global economists. That means that the more politically stable Pacific Basin countries, such as Indonesia, Australia, Japan, Singapore, Thailand and Taiwan, are considered to have the greatest growth potential for the 21st century. Indonesia, with its large (and cheap) labour force, reckons it will forge ahead, particularly in the travel industry. So, if you want to know where you'll be lazing 10 years from now, it'll be by a sapphire pool in downtown Jakarta, under streaky violet skies in Lombok, or on a deserted beach on one of the thousands of micro-specks in the Indonesian sea.

---

bungalows, lantern-lit walkways and grotto pool, *"built into the side of a fantastic deep, deep green canyon. It is spectacular, absolutely astonishing"* – DAN TOPOLSKI. Bathrooms open to the elements.

TANDJUNG SARI, PO Box 25, Denpasar ☎ (0361) 88441
Delightful garden resort that feels like real Bali. Right on Sanur beach, it's dotted with thatched bamboo cottages (some privately owned or available for long rentals), stone temples, statues of gods and goddesses, parasols and lanterns, with works of art and antiques displayed in the interiors. *"Very, very beautiful on a small scale"* – SERENA SUTCLIFFE. *"One of the nicest hotels I've ever stayed at, in lovely grounds"* – DAN TOPOLSKI.

JAKARTA

HYATT ARYADUTA, Jalan Prapatan 44-48 ☎ (021) 376008
Expensively fitted-out new hotel containing only suites, plus the all-pampering Regency Club hotel-within-a-hotel.

Buzzz The best eateries in Kuta are **Made Warung** and **Poppies** ...... The interior of Bali, particularly the artist colony of **Ubud** (*"a bit of a hippy colony as well"* – DAN TOPOLSKI), is now more fashionable than the steamy coast. Cool nights and clear air keep cool people clear-headed .... ..The great new tourist development – *"the next Bali"* prophesies LORD LICHFIELD – will be neighbouring **Lombok**, *"a seriously beautiful island with the most wonderful beaches. It's unspoiled, like the interior of Bali"* ...... Watch out for the **Regent of Jakarta** and the **Grand Hyatt Jakarta**, both now destined for 1991. ....

JAKARTA HILTON INTERNATIONAL, Jalan Gatot Subroto, PO Box 3315 ☎ (021) 583051
Impressive and super-spacious. The vast lobby replicates the Sultan of Jogjakarta's palace in Java, with its carved and lacquered ceiling; a gamut of gardens and pools, bars and cafés, 9 tennis courts and the Executive fitness club.

MANDARIN ORIENTAL, Jalan M H Thamrin, PO Box 3392 ☎ (021) 321307
In the top league, natch. Recently refurbished, it's a refined environment, with outdoor pool, health centre and rooftop squash courts.

IRELAND

—— Art and museums ——

NATIONAL GALLERY OF IRELAND, Merrion Square W, Dublin ☎ (01) 615133
The splendidly restored gallery has a fine collection of European masters – Rubens, Rembrandt, Poussin, Claude, Velázquez and Gainsborough among them – as well as the national collection of Irish paintings. With an extension currently in construction, the gallery is on target for 1991, when Dublin is Cultural Capital of Europe.

——— Hotels ———

ADARE MANOR, Adare, Co Limerick ☎ (061) 86566
Former home of the Earls of Dunraven, this

"Anyone who doesn't like Ireland should be locked up. It is enchanting"

 DOUGLAS FAIRBANKS JR

monumental Tudoresque manor lies next to the River Maigue in 840 acres of Irish countryside. Hangar-sized bedrooms; banqueting in the Long Gallery, purportedly the second-longest room in Europe, with 15C Flemish choir stalls and glorious stained-glass windows. Huntin', fishin', shootin' and golfin' types will love it.

ASSOLAS HOUSE, Kanturk, Co Cork ☎ (029) 50795
Swans glide past on the river next to this peaceful 17C manor house. *"It is very homy, not like a hotel, much more personal. It has wonderful grounds and country walks. You have drinks by an open fire and then go in for dinner with incredible food"* – ALISON DOODY.

🕵 BALLYMALOE HOUSE, Shanagarry, Co Cork ☎ (021) 652531
In the midst of a 400-acre farm, this hotel is still a top favourite with foodie fans, who sigh for the locally fished and fresh farm produce. Run by Ivan and Myrtle Allen and numerous offspring and grand-children, it's *"a blissful piece of paradise and still going strong with very good reports coming in"* – HILARY RUBINSTEIN. *"I just love it,"* raves ROY ACKERMAN, with a chorus from KEITH FLOYD, who says *"It's one of my favourite hotels".* Daughter-in-law Darina Allen runs the cookery school ☎ (021) 646785. And drop in to Fern Allen's **Crawford Art Gallery Café** in Cork city for Ballymaloe food in arty surroundings.

🕵 Buzzz Take a Ulyssean trip around **Dublin**, then linger in the legendary, lofty, clattery café – **Bewley's**, Grafton St for a cafetière of Java🕵......With a theatre tradition of Wilde, Sheridan, Goldsmith and O'Casey you Shaw should catch the **Dublin Theatre Festival** in Sept/Oct🕵...... Down a few pints of GEORGE MELLY-recommended genuine Dublin-brewed Guinness at the **Shelbourne** or **Westbury** hotel bars, where the smart set sip🕵......Take a tip or two from BARRY HUMPHRIES and dine at **King Sitric**, East Pier, Howth: *"It's on the sea in a little fishing village – unpretentious, the best oysters I've had in my life."* And back in town, pop in to **Dobbins**, 15 Stephens Lane: *"Open late, lovely service, very good sole, beautiful lobster bisque and delicious puddings"*🕵......Moving on around the Emerald Isle, circle the **Ring of Kerry**, where wild fuchsia lines the hedgerows in a riot of red: *"I love the area round **Dingle**, a magical place, misty and yet vivid"* – ALISON DOODY🕵......Stop off at **Nick's Seafood Restaurant**, Main St, Kilorglin, for the best seafood platter you're likely to swallow🕵......Whizz around the Atlantic coast to **Galway** to catch the **Oyster Festival** in Sept and track down **Moran's on the Weir**, Kilcolgan, for unbeatable oysters and mussels............................🕵

BANTRY HOUSE, Bantry, Co Cork
☎ (027) 50047
Once the residence of the Earls of Bantry, now owned by a descendant, Egerton Shelswell-White and his wife, who have turned one wing into an 8-bedroom B&B. *"They have done wonders in restoring this 18C mansion and its romantic gardens. The converted wing is quite delightful, with wonderful views over Bantry Bay and the lush gardens. Breakfast is an elegant, civilized meal and the owners personally look after guests. It combines the comfort of the first-class hotel with the magic of an Irish country house"* – JOHN BROOKE-LITTLE. A snip at £30 a night.

> **❝The west of Ireland near Baltimore between Cork and Bantry is one of the loveliest places in Europe❞**
>
>  LORD DONOUGHUE

LONGUEVILLE HOUSE, Mallow, Co Cork ☎ (022) 47156
This Georgian mansion boasts its own salmon and trout waters, the only vineyard in Ireland, and some of the best food in the country. In summer, dine in the Victorian conservatory, *"my favourite restaurant"* – KEITH FLOYD.

MARLFIELD HOUSE, Gorey, Co Wexford
☎ (055) 21124
In Wexford, with its miles of golden deserted sands, sits this charming Regency house, former dower house of the Earls of Courtown. The award-winning restaurant has delicious seafood and wonderful Irish cheeses. It gets EDWARD CARTER's vote.

🏊 PARK HOTEL KENMARE, Kenmare, Co Kerry ☎ (064) 41200
One of Ireland's top foodie hotels. *"A lovely country-house hotel with the most amazing collection of antiques. The food is wonderful, Michelin-starred, using local produce, and the views over Kenmare Bay are absolutely amazing. They have wild end-of-season parties [they close in Nov and Dec] when they redecorate the hotel according to the theme of the party. Quite crazy!"* – CAROL WRIGHT.

SHELBOURNE HOTEL, 27 St Stephen's Green, Dublin ☎ (01) 766471
One of the few top-class old-fashioned hotels left in the heart of Joycean Dublin. Ideal location on the smart side of the green, on the smart side of the river. The recently refurbished Georgian bedrooms have fine views of the Dublin mountains (on a clear day). JEFFREY ARCHER is a fan.

TINAKILLY HOUSE HOTEL, Rathnew, Co Wicklow ☎ (0404) 69274
Take a trip through the magnificent mountains of Wicklow, and rest weary limbs here. *"It's a very nice country hotel, close to the sea. The food is a bit nouvelle cuisine [though you can have a vieille brandy-and-eggs breakfast], but the choice is tremendous. The rooms are absolutely lovely"* – LORD DONOUGHUE.

———— *Music* ————

GUINNESS JAZZ FESTIVAL, Cork.
Tickets: Cork Opera House, Emmet Place, Cork ☎ (021) 270022
A small, friendly festival in Oct, GEORGE MELLY's favourite (not least for the Guinness: *"There is absolutely no comparison between Irish and English Guinness"*).

WEXFORD FESTIVAL OPERA, Theatre Royal, High St, Wexford ☎ (053) 22240
The Glyndebourne of Ireland. A 3-week festival in Oct of 3 rare operas sung by young unknowns who often blossom into stars. Smarties descend from all corners of the Emerald Isle for the final long weekend, an occasion marked by formal dress and a devil-may-care atmosphere. Recitals, fringe events, bands playing in the street – and pubs open till 3am.

> **❝The best way to relax is to go to Ireland❞**
>
> KEITH FLOYD

ITALY

AMALFI COAST

———— *Hotels* ————

GRAND HOTEL QUISISANA, Via Camerelle 2, 80073 Capri ☎ (081) 837 0788
The best hotel on the hilly isle of Capri, a classical-style building with a stylish mix of modern and antique – marble floors and blackamoor candelabra, terracotta tiles and bamboo furniture. Individual terraces and a pool.

HOTEL PALUMBO, Via S Giovanni del Toro 28, 84010 Ravello ☎ (089) 857244
At the top of a hairy set of hairpin bends, way up in the mountainside above Amalfi, is this élite retreat, dating back to the 12C Palazzo

Confalone. A blend of Moorish and Med, it has a little tiled courtyard with pointed arches and a grapevine-covered terrace with a hazy view miles down the craggy coast. Fine cuisine.

🔥 SAN PIETRO, Via Laurito 2, 84017 Positano ☎ (089) 875455
One of Italy's very best, a secluded, romantic hotel chiselled into the cliff face, with terracotta-tiled terraces overhung by grapevines, lemon trees and bougainvillaea. Only 60 rooms, idiosyncratically shaped according to the prevailing rock formation and superbly decorated in the local style. Spellbinding views of the coast and an abundance of fresh seafood. A lift runs down through the cliff to a tiny private beach. *"One of the most beautiful hotels on the Amalfi coast. Very discreet and private with a magical atmosphere"* – MARIE HELVIN. BARBARA KAFKA and MARCHESA BONA FRESCOBALDI agree.

LE SIRENUSE, Via C Colombo 30, 84017 Positano ☎ (089) 875066
Charming, old-fashioned hotel right in town with a maze of rooms and terraces on 7 levels, and a swimming pool. *"I always stay here on holiday. A marvellous, small hotel run by a family who look after you impeccably. Very good food"* – GILES SHEPARD.

FLORENCE
—— Art and museums ——

🔥 GALLERIA DEGLI UFFIZI, Loggiato degli Uffizi 6 ☎ (055) 218341
The most important collection in the world of Florentine and Sienese art from the 13C to the Renaissance. Vasari's palazzo is crammed with drawings and prints, paintings and sculpture – by Giotto, Fra Angelico, Lippi, Bellini, Mantegna, Raphael et al. Highlights abound: Titian's glowing *Venus of Urbino*, the celebrated Botticelli *Birth of Venus* and *Primavera*, Leonardo's unfinished *Adoration of the Magi*, supposedly sketched in his own blood, and the famous classical *Medici Venus*.

MUSEO DEL BARGELLO, Via del Proconsolo 4 ☎ (055) 210801
The medieval palace is devoted to sculpture and arts and crafts – a beautiful, lofty space for works by Michelangelo, Donatello, Verocchio, Cellini, Giambologna.

PALAZZO PITTI, Piazza dei Pitti ☎ (055) 213440
A sturdy Renaissance/Mannerist palazzo housing several museums, including the Royal Apartments and Silver Museum for fine and decorative arts and the superb Palatine Gallery. Here, palatial rooms are filled with oils by Titian, Rubens, the Italian Mannerists, and Raphael (see two of his loveliest Madonnas, *del Granduca* and *della Sedia*).

—— Bars and cafés ——

DONEY'S, Piazza Strozzi 18r, 50123 ☎ (055) 298206
Smart café, in swish new premises just round the corner from its old home on Via Tornabuoni. Still bags of atmosphere.

GIACOSA, Via Tornabuoni 83, 50123 ☎ (055) 296226
Exclusive café-bar for the élite. Birthplace of the Campari-based Negroni, and source of melt-in-the-mouth handmade chocolates and pastries.

RIVOIRE, Via Vacchereccia 4r, 50123 ☎ (055) 214412
On the edge of the Piazza della Signoria, this slice of old-fashioned grandeur bustles in the splendid European café tradition. Delicious pastries, pralines and chocolates.

🔥 Buzzz Jewels in the town: **fruits of Florence** include the minuscule chapel of the **Palazzo Medici-Riccardi**, Via Cavour 1, vividly frescoed from top to toe in the fairytale International Gothic style by Benozzo Gozzoli🔥...... **Museo di Storia della Scienza**, Piazza dei Giudici 1, a fascinating collection of historic scientific instruments, many used by Galileo🔥...... the calm little **Casa Buonarotti**, Via Ghibellina 70, home to Michelangelo's earliest works, reliefs of the *Battle of the Centaurs* and *Madonna of the Stairs*🔥...... **Museo dell' Opera del Duomo**, Piazza del Duomo 9, for a close-up view of panels of the Baptistery Doors by Ghiberti, Michelangelo's unfinished *Pietà* and delightful *Cantorie* (choir-lofts) by Luca della Robbia and Donatello🔥...... **Santa Maria Novella** for Masaccio's famous *Trinità* fresco (and, at last revealed after restoration, his remarkable **Brancacci Chapel** frescos at Santa Maria del Carmine)🔥...... San Lorenzo for Michelangelo's **Medici Chapel**, an architectural and sculptural essay in Mannerism............... 🔥

Clubs

CENTRAL PARK/CAPITALE, Via del Fosso Macinato 2, Piazzale delle Cascine, 50100 ☎ (055) 356723
A hip disco in Cascine Park near the Arno. A young crowd bop along to a different style of music each night. The club changes its name to Capitale in winter.

SPACE ELECTRONIC, Via Palazzuolo 37, 50123 ☎ (055) 293082
Video disco with the most sophisticated sound and light system in town. Set on 2 floors, with aquarium bar and stainless steel dance floor. Live music too.

⚓ TENAX, Via Pretese 47, 50126 ☎ (055) 373050
The best club in Italy. A restored warehouse – vast (8,600 sq ft), sparse, on 2 floors. The upper floor has train seating and videos. New wave music and the most exciting live bands. Cool clientele. Open Thurs to Sat.

Hotels

HOTEL BRUNELLESCHI, Piazza S Elisabetta 2, 50123 ☎ (055) 562068
A small hotel that offers *"the charm of living in a 6th-century tower, furnished with the most modern comforts, all just steps away from the Duomo"* – MARCHESA BONA FRESCOBALDI.

⚓ HOTEL HELVETIA & BRISTOL, Via dei Pescioni 2, 50123 ☎ (055) 287814
Recently opened after renovations, this is a new contender for best city hotel in Italy. Swanky 5-star affair with exquisite antique furnishings, gilded mirrors, 17C oils, silk damask walls and curtains; marble bathrooms with flattering lighting and mirrors, Jacuzzi baths, and huge bath robes. *"This beautiful hotel has been completely refurbished but seems like an old and welcoming home"* – MARCHESA BONA FRESCOBALDI. **The Bristol** rose swiftly to the higher ranks of Florentine dining with elegant interpretations of trad Tuscan cuisine.

⚓ HOTEL REGENCY, Piazza M D'Azeglio 3, 50121 ☎ (055) 245247
One of the plushest hotels in Florence, set in two 19C villas in a quiet leafy square. Delightful, cosy drawing-room and library with plumped-up sofas and bowls brimming with sweets all help to give an air of the private house. Suave sense of style by designer Sturchio. Fine regional Italian and international cuisine at the **Relais le Jardin**.

LOGGIATO DEI SERVITI, Piazza SS Annunziata, 50122 ☎ (055) 298280
A different style of hotel: no five-star luxury or instant room service. Instead, a simple, tranquil hostelry that mirrors Brunelleschi's Ospedale degli Innocenti, opposite, one of the most important and early triumphs of the Renaissance. Lofty cross-vaulted rooms with pastel plaster walls and polished terracotta floors. Pretty yellow and white breakfast room with delicious hot croissants, bowls of home-made cherry or apricot jam, and – in season – fresh-squeezed blood-orange juice. Charming staff.

PENSIONE QUISISANA E PONTE VECCHIO, Lungarno Archibusiere 4, 50122 ☎ (055) 216692
The pensione made famous as the set of *A Room with a View* – and what a view, right on the Ponte Vecchio. Breakfast on the roof terrace.

Scenic Journeys

When travellers hit the road, which bit of tarmac would they most like to land on? *"It's a cliché, but I think State Highway 1 along the California coastline is just gorgeous"* – ED VICTOR. *"The Pacific Coast Highway from LA to San Francisco. It is recommended to drive from LA to SF, because you are driving along the cliffs, so you'd rather be on the inside track! That is just spectacular and you know that you're looking out over an ocean that goes on for one-third of the world..."* – SIMON WILLIAMS. *"Everybody says Big Sur is the best drive in the whole world and it's probably true. I don't know a better stretch of road"* – BOB PAYTON. MARIO BUATTA starts further south: *"The drive from Southern California to LA is just wonderful."* STANLEY MARCUS takes a broader sweep: *"From Santa Barbara to San Francisco; from Santa Fe to Taos in New Mexico; the Amalfi Coast in Italy."* 3 more Amalfites – TESSA DAHL, HELEN GURLEY BROWN and BARBARA KAFKA: *"One of the most spectacular if not the most dangerous drives is along the Amalfi Coast!"*

"The best drive is from Inverness over the moors to Golspie, on to Helmsdale, and on again to John O'Groats" – BARBARA CARTLAND. More support for the Scottish Highlands from STIRLING MOSS, ROSS BENSON and DOUGLAS FAIRBANKS JR.

🔥 VILLA SAN MICHELE, Via Doccia, 50014 Fiesole ☎ (055) 59451
Set amid cypresses and oleander, this former Franciscan monastery designed by Michelangelo has a private frescoed chapel, cells that have been sumptuously converted into bedrooms (all 28 have private Jacuzzi) and gorgeous misty views over the red-tiled roofs of Florence. *"As wonderful as ever"* – FRANK LOWE. The sort of supremacy you'd expect from an Orient-Express/Cipriani hotel.

—————— *Music* ——————

MAGGIO MUSICALE FIORENTINO, Teatro Comunale, Corso Italia 14, 50100 ☎ (055) 277 9236
The first and largest of the Italian festivals, held end-April to early July. Florentine music and opera.

—————— *Restaurants* ——————

NB Many Italian restaurants close in the summer and for about a month at New Year.

CANTINETTA ANTINORI, Piazza Antinori 3, 50123 ☎ (055) 292234
Behind heavy wooden doors, off a little palazzo courtyard is this wine bar/restaurant. The Antinori family produce their own fine wines; excellent cellars, with stacked bottles of wine forming the décor. JAMES BURKE approves.

🔥 **COCO LEZZONE, Via Parioncino 26r, 50123 ☎ (055) 287178**
Mooted by zealots to be the best trattoria in Italy. Hidden on a little corner with no sign outside, it teems with both blue and white collared workers, plus cool types from film,

Ferragamo Fancies
🔥

MARCHESA FIAMMA DI SAN GIULIANO FERRAGAMO discloses her latest discoveries in Florence: **Bottegone della Lana**, Via Trebbio 8r ☎ (055) 284726, a *"lovely little shop with everything for knitting. They can copy any design of cardigan in fabulous cashmere"*. **Lo Spillo**, Borgo San Iacopo 32 ☎ (055) 293126, a tiny shop which sells old and antique jewellery. The silversmiths **Pampaloni**, Borgo SS Apostoli 60 ☎ (055) 232 0523, for presents and objects for the house, old and new; and at No 58r, **Pratesi** ☎ (055) 287683, for small garden ornaments and antiques – all *"elegant things"*. **Michele et Catherine Finck**, Via della Vigna 15r ☎ (055) 213243, antique dealers specializing in 18C pieces.

finance and fashion (such as Giorgio Armani). The best bistecca fiorentina in town, and palate-piquing pappa al pomodoro.

DA NOI, Via Fiesolana 46r, 50125 ☎ (055) 242917
For 'cucina personale' – their own idiosyncratic, non-Tuscan, style of cooking, this is a *"very tiny, wonderful restaurant"* – FAITH WILLINGER.

ENOTECA PINCHIORRI, Via Ghibellina 87, 50122 ☎ (055) 242757
One of the suavest and most extortionate ristoranti in Italy. Formal, silver-service setting in a 15C palazzo. Superb cellars for Italian, French

🔥 **Buzzz Café society** oscillates between 3 greats on the Piazza della Repubblica: all in the grand, traditional style (wood panelling, pink tablecloths, black-tied waiters, lofty arches, the odd fresco), they are **Giubbe Rosse**, No 13-14r ☎ (055) 212280 (*the* turn-of-the-century literary hang-out); **Paszkowski**, No 6 ☎ (055) 210236 and **Gilli** ☎ (055) 296110🔥......**Ice cream dream**: arguably the best gelateria in the world is **Vivoli**, Via Isola delle Stinche 7 ☎ (055) 292334 – a zillion inventive flavours with dollops of panna on top; Flos in the know prefer **Perché No**, Via dei Tavolini 19r ☎ (055) 298969, for ices, yogurts and semifreddi, or **Baziani**, for their flavour 'buontalenti', named after Francesco di Medici's personal gelatier🔥......Best shop for home-made **fresh pasta** is **Pasta all' Uovo**, Via Nazionale 102 ☎ (055) 298806🔥......FAITH WILLINGER spreads her supping secrets: **Belle Donne**, Via delle Belle Donne 16r ☎ (055) 262609 is a *"casual place for lunch. You don't have to have a whole meal"*; **Omero**, Via Pian dei Giullari 11 ☎ (055) 220053 is *"one of the best trattorie for Tuscan cuisine"*; **Le Quattro Stagioni**, Via Maggio 61r ☎ (055) 218906 is *"the restaurant I wind up eating at most"*..............🔥

and California wines, as MARCELLA HAZAN and FAITH WILLINGER testify. However, nouvellish not to say pretentious French/Italian cuisine puts some foodies off.

🦞 IL CIBREO, via dei Macci 118r, 50100 ☎ (055) 234 1100

Superb little restaurant for soups, roast rabbit and other meats, artichokes, etc – but no pasta, which strikes a chord with ANDREW LLOYD WEBBER. Also **Cibrèo Trattoria** round the corner at Piazza Ghiberti 35 ('Poor Cibrèo' to locals) for the down-at-heel – same nosh, less dosh. *"Still very good"* – MARCELLA HAZAN.

Italy's Best Restaurants

1	DA FIORE · Venice
2	LA SCALETTA · Milan
3	IL CIBREO · Florence
4	PIPERNO · Rome
5	COCO LEZZONE · Florence

Shopping

Via Tornabuoni is the smartest street, replete with Gucci, Valentino, Fendi, Armani, Versace, Ferragamo and the other classics. The more avant-garde edge live on tinier medieval streets – **Via Porta Rossa, Via della Vigna Nuova, Via Roma, Via Condotta. Via Maggio** is tops for antiques shops, while the daily market at **Santa Croce** yields bargain finds (Murano beads that undercut Venetian prices...). **Mercato delle Cascine** near Ponte della Vittoria (Tues mornings) is the best for food, ceramics, shoes and clothes both new and second-hand.

BELTRAMI, Via Tornabuoni 48r ☎ (055) 287779

Beautifully groomed shop for beautifully groomed shoppers. Head-to-toe fetish leather – exquisite footwear, coats, bags – plus chic separates, slivers of silk and caches of cashmere to adorn the privileged body. Also at Via Calzaiuoli 31r and 44r.

CELLERINI, Via del Sole 37r, 50123 ☎ (055) 282533

The Florentine equivalent of Hermès for silk scarves and lush leather. Bags, belts, luggage and shoes for donna and uomo are all hand-stitched in their own workshops.

EMILIO PUCCI, Via de' Pucci 6, 50122 ☎ (055) 283061

No trace of modern shoppery from without, but resplendent within, the boutique occupies one of the most beautiful buildings in town, Palazzo Pucci. Marchese P is still bold-printing his draped and flowing silks – scarves, ties, wonderful women's clothing and men's tailoring. STEPHEN JONES is a tie fan.

FARAONE-SETTEPASSI, Via Tornabuoni 25r, 50123 ☎ (055) 215506

Jewellers that have decked out the Florentine nobility since 1860 in pomp and circumstance pieces. Classics plus plenty of modern, chunky gold settings.

FRATELLI PICCINI, Ponte Vecchio 23, 50125 ☎ (055) 294768

One of the oldest and most exquisite little jewellers on the Ponte Vecchio. Rivulets of rubies, emeralds, diamonds, sapphires – the very best stones – crafted to order.

GARBO, Borgo Ognissanti 2r, 50123 ☎ (055) 295338

Dainty silk, linen and lace foundation wear for women, embroidered and stitched by a team of ladies on the premises. Also blouses, ornamental wedding gowns, kitchen linen, and lacy little lovelies for the bambino.

LORETTA CAPONI, Borgo Ognissanti 12r, 20123 ☎ (055) 213668

Superior shop for beautiful lace and embroidered linenware, designed mainly for the chic house... *and* for you to drape yourself around the chic bedroom.

LUISA VIA ROMA, Via Roma 19-21r, 50100 ☎ (055) 217826

The best designer stash for the raffish and refined avant-garde. Clothes and shoes by Sybilla, Kamali, Kenzo, Gigli, Dolce & Gabbana, Yamamoto, Matsuda, Irie, Byblos, Gaultier, Moschino, Montana.... At **Luisa Il Corso**, Via del Corso 56, they sell their own designs in the same spirit.

MATUCCI, Via del Corso 46 (women) and 71 (men), 50100 ☎ (055) 212018

The snappy country in town look – outdoorsy skirts, jodhpurs, little leather jackets, sheepskin. Also **Beba Matucci** at No 36.

OSCAR PARISOTTO, Via Calimala 33-35r, 50123 ☎ (055) 214598

Young, trendy gear – velvet jeans and bombers, baseball jackets, cropped cowboy boots, loadsa denim – by Katharine Hamnett, Paul Smith, shoes by Patrick Cox, Free Lance. And they call it Il Look Parisotto.

SALVATORE FERRAGAMO, Via Tornabuoni 12-16r, 50100 ☎ (055) 292123

Salvatore's children continue along the well-trodden path of this famous shoe business, making impeccable footwear for the cognoscenti. The world's best narrow-fitting shoe. Also so-sleek clothes and zingily bright scarves to accessorize the shoes. The shop is set in a medieval palazzo, with monumental stone piers and acres of space.

MILAN

—— Art and museums ——

CASTELLO SFORZESCO, 20121
☎ (02) 870926
In this vast castle that dominates the city is the Municipal Museum of Art, containing Michelangelo's last work, the unfinished Rondanini *Pietà*. Also works by Lippi, Mantegna, Bellini and the Venetians.

🐾 MUSEO POLDI PEZZOLI, Via Manzoni, 20121 ☎ (02) 794889
A small but very charming collection of fine Renaissance paintings – by Piero della Francesca, Pollaiuolo, Bellini, the Lombard and Venetian schools, plus antique watches and clocks and armoury. It's MARIUCCIA MANDELLI's favourite small museum.

PINACOTECA DI BRERA, Via Brera 28, 20121 ☎ (02) 806969
Milan's major picture gallery, with works by Florentine, Lombard and Venetian painters – Lotto, Mantegna (see his *Dead Christ*), Piero della Francesca, Bellini, Veronese.

———— Clubs ————

NEPENTHA, Piazza Armando Diaz 1, 20123 ☎ (02) 873652
Open over 20 years, this is a straight and simple club, where smart middle-of-the-via Milanese feel safe.

PLASTIC, Viale Umbria 120, 20135
☎ (02) 733996
The trendiest club in Milan, teeming with young fashion designers. Modern, black and slick, apart from the incongruous Venetian glass chandeliers. Late late opening.

PREGO CLUB, Via Besenzanica 3, 20100
☎ (02) 407 5653
Labyrinthine disco with zappy dance floor, light shows and films, plus live concerts from local and foreign bands. Thurs is rock night, Fri and Sun general disco, Mon private TV shows and films.

—— Fashion designers ——

BYBLOS, Via Senato 35, 20121
☎ (02) 702959
Young international fash fans love this label – bags of versatility and vitality. Richly coloured and opulently textured or patterned clothes with a dash of English eccentricity provided by designers Alan Cleaver and Keith Varty. Velvet bombers, multi-coloured knits, lots of fun mix 'n' matching. A great men's collection too. Stocked also at Max Davoli, Via Marghera 45.

DOLCE & GABBANA at Marisa, Via Sant' Andrea 10A, 20121 ☎ (02) 780793
Italian rusticana. The Sicilian background of this young design team permeates their collections – long peasant dresses and country-boy trouser suits worn with flat caps.

🐾 GIANFRANCO FERRE, Via della Spiga 11-13, 20121 ☎ (02) 794864; menswear ☎ (02) 7600 0385
The man who's designing Dior continues on his own innovative way back in Italy. His architectural approach finds expression in sharp, to-the-point, city suits for the urban sophisticate, turning to luxurious ease at night. Status-symbol knitwear; great leather and suede gear. Classical menswear.

———— 🧥 ————

Italy's Best Designers

1	GIORGIO ARMANI
2	ROMEO GIGLI
3	GIANFRANCO FERRE
4	GIANNI VERSACE
5	VALENTINO

🐾 GIANNI VERSACE, Via della Spiga 4, 20121 ☎ (02) 7600 5451; menswear Via Montenapoleone 11, 20121 ☎ (02) 7600 8529
Impeccably cut dresses and chic suits by this master of creative cutting and sewing techniques. Uninhibited use of print and colour. Marisa Berenson, JOAN COLLINS and Grace Jones grace his Atelier couture shows in Paris and wear his clothes. Prêt-à-porter and the cheaper Versus range for uomo and donna (more *Elle* than *Vogue*). Menswear is exemplary, best in Europe for originally textured fabrics. KEN HOM is a Versace fan.

🐾 GIORGIO ARMANI, Via Sant' Andrea 9, 20121 ☎ (02) 792757; EMPORIO ARMANI, Via Durini 24, 20122 ☎ (02) 781094; MANI, Via Durini 23 ☎ (02) 790306; ARMANI BIMBO, Via Durini 27 ☎ (02) 794248
Remains No 1 in Italy and the bestselling Italian internationally. *"Still the master tailor of this world – for women and men. His use of fabrics, his texture and his simplicity of style are still the best"* – ANIKO GAAL. WOLFGANG PUCK agrees. His soft, gentle, de-structured tailoring and subtle, sensuous colouring are just perfect for the 90s. His sportier, more affordable range is **Emporio Armani**. Fab children's wear and, of course, menswear, where he started. He's the designer's designer – fans include JOHN GALLIANO, BRUCE OLDFIELD (*"for his moderness and comfort"*) and MARCUS TUSCH: *"Armani is my idol, beyond doubt. He's the master."*

KRIZIA, Via della Spiga 23, 20121
☎ **(02) 708429**
Mariuccia Mandelli designs Krizia, Krizia Uomo
and Krizia Baby – not to mention items for the
Krizia kitchen. Current fashion emphasis is on
soft, flowing fabrics; cashmere for the autumn,
plunging velvet and sequins for the evening.

> **❝Gigli's influence is very
> important. A whole softness and
> romanticism is coming in, the
> fluidity of the 30s and 40s – even
> tailoring is far far softer. Women
> have realized they don't have to
> emulate men to be taken
> seriously❞**
>
> STEPHEN JONES

MISSONI, Via Montenapoleone 1, 20121
☎ **(02) 700906**
Renowned worldwide for creative knitwear with
an artistic eye for colour and strong emphasis on
texture. Also Uomo and Baby lines, plus textiles,
tapestries and wall hangings. At **Vestor**, Via
Manzoni, you can stock up on Missoni goodies
for the house.

MOSCHINO, Via Sant' Andrea 12, 20122
☎ **(02) 7600 0832**
Milan's wild card has captured young Italian
hearts. While he doesn't see himself as a designer
(he's not above re-interpretation of others'
work), the result is like nothing you've seen
before. A crazy, irreverent, sexy mix-up of
styles, textures, detailing. Expect colour
clashes, nutty buttons, zips, crochet and appliquéd messages.

**🍴 ROMEO GIGLI, c/o Via della Spiga 46,
20121** ☎ **(02) 799978**
While Armani is the maestro, Gigli is the most
significant designer in Italy today. His look –
elemental, asymmetric, romantic – has caused
waves throughout the fashion world. Devotees
waft under waterfall pleating, chiffon petals,
twisted fabric wound round and draped. *"The
epitome of this new stylized simplicity in
fashion, with his cocoon coats and tapered
jackets, head-framing shirt collars and the way
he layers and mixes everything. He really has
brought a new dimension to wardrobes. He has
also made spiced brown a new desirable colour"*
– ANIKO GAAL. (She also loves his footwear. *"His
taffeta shoes look like you could wear them at
court."*) *"One of my all-time favourites"* –
BONNIE BROOKS. MARIE HELVIN's too *"for simplicity"*. Stocked at Cose, Via della Spiga 8 ☎
(02) 790703, and Pupi Solari, Piazza Tommogeo
2 ☎ (02) 463325.

**SYBILLA at Pupi Solari, Piazza
Tommogeo 2, 20145** ☎ **(02) 463325; Marisa,
Via Sant' Andrea 10A, 20121** ☎ **(02) 780793**
Swinging young Spanish designer based in
Milan, who is *"very directional for the 90s. She
reworks the classics beautifully. There is a
monastic quality to her clothes"* – ANIKO GAAL.
Simple, understated garb with a new sense of
volume and cut. Clothes, shoes, bags and hats
have a sculptural quality.

Hotels

**EXCELSIOR HOTEL GALLIA, Piazza
Duca d'Aosta 9, 20124** ☎ **(02) 650941**
Now part of Trusthouse Forte, the Gallia has
had a total refit and is setting its sights on No
1 spot in town. The rag trade stay for the Milan
collections, when the dining room smacks of a
private club. Light cuisine under Nicola Magnif-
ico; drinks at **Baboon** poured by barman of
nearly 30 years Francesco Frigerio.

**HOTEL PIERRE MILANO, Via dei Amici
32, 20123** ☎ **(02) 805 6221**
*"A new hotel. Quite small, so you get the kind
of service you don't necessarily get in the larger
ones"* – NICHOLAS VILLIERS.

**HOTEL PRINCIPE DI SAVOIA, Piazza
della Repubblica 17, 20124** ☎ **(02) 6230**
Milanese hotels are not establishments of great
international renown, but this one – grand,
expensive, good service – is reckoned by
JEFFERY TOLMAN to be the best in town.

Music

**🍴 LA SCALA, Teatro alla Scala, Via
Filodrammatici 2, 20121** ☎ **(02) 887 9211**
The famous opera house and a brilliant company
where all the greats sing – Pavarotti, Domingo
et al. *"This and Vienna are the 2 greats in
Europe. I'd go for La Scala"* – RODNEY MILNES.
So would MARIUCCIA MANDELLI and NICHOLAS
VILLIERS: *"There is something colourful about
the Italians that no one else can imitate."* Mostly
Italian opera, produced by the likes of Franco
Zeffirelli. The season runs from Dec to July,
opening on a spectacularly high note on 7 Dec,
the feast day of Sant' Ambrogio, patron saint of
Milan. The greatest social gaffe is to invite
someone out on the 7th.

Restaurants

🍴 AIMO E NADIA, Via Montecuccoli 6
☎ **(02) 416886**
Great ristoranti from little trattorie grow – a
lovely, warm environment for *"the best food in
all Milan. Tuscan, but very lightened up, not
too fancy. The restaurant is quite beautiful and
modern"* – FAITH WILLINGER. Try the courgette
flowers stuffed with seafood.

8

ANTICA TRATTORIA DELLA PESA, Viale Pasubio 10 ☎ (02) 655 5741
Small trat that's been in the same family for over 100 years. Trad Milanese dishes, such as risotto milanese, osso buco, cod with polenta, bollito misto. MARCHESA FIAMMA DI SAN GIULIANO FERRAGAMO is keen.

BAGUTTA, Via Bagutta 14, 20100 ☎ (02) 700902
"Old-fashioned, totally undesignery, very refreshing for Milan. Beautiful murals painted by a succession of Milanese artists – each paints a bit of the wall every year. A great hang-out of the literati and arty scene. The most unbelievable, fantastic, mind-boggling selection of hors-d'oeuvres, mostly fishy and garlicky. A great classic restaurant" – LOYD GROSSMAN.

BICE, Via Borgospesso 12, 20121 ☎ (02) 795528
Perennial chic eatery (open since the 30s), where all the Milanese fashion designers lunch. The smartest of the smart sit closest to the kitchen despite the smell and smoke – the owner keeps tables here for close friends who come in without a reservation. *"The best place for a simple dish of excellent pasta,"* chorus the FENDI sisters.

CASANOVA GRILL, Palace Hotel, Piazza della Repubblica 20, 20124 ☎ (02) 650803
"The food is quite exquisite. Sometimes it's a relief to eat in a hotel where you get really fabulous service" – FAITH WILLINGER. Regional specialities and Mediterranean cuisine.

FRANCA, PAOLA E LELE, Viale Certosa 235, 20151 ☎ (02) 305238
On the outskirts of Milan, a place for good, honest, country cooking. *"Rustic food, very simple, home-style. They make their own pasta"* – FAITH WILLINGER.

🍴 LA SCALETTA, Piazzale Stazione Genova 3 ☎ (02) 835 0290
The Milanese flock to this small, urbane restaurant, for top-quality food, artily presented. *"I have tried so many dishes there because the chef-owner comes from Emilia Romagna (as I do) and keeps sending me things to taste! Really I was surprised by the quality; all the food is very tasty and light"* – MARCELLA HAZAN.

LE IDEE DI GUALTIERO MARCHESI, Via Bonvesin della Riva 9, 20129 ☎ (02) 741246
One of the smartest in Milan, a temple of cucina nuova. Serious, expensive, foodie stuff with a seasonal menu. Sig Marchesi has imbued historical dishes and flavours with his own modern stamp and a high degree of decoration – try lobster gratin with peppers and baby marrows. Own classic liqueurs, vinegars and olive oils.

PECK, Via Spadari 9, 20123 ☎ (02) 871737
A restaurant that grew out of the best food shop in Italy. In the shop, superb displays of pasta, cheese, charcuterie, an amazing rôtisserie and tavola calda. KEN HOM is knocked out; so are MARCHESA BONA FRESCOBALDI and MARIUCCIA MANDELLI (*"the best fresh pasta"*). Dine on dishes that delve back to the roots of Italian cuisine.

SAVINI, Galleria Vittorio Emanuele II, 20121 ☎ (02) 805 8343
One of the oldest and most elegant ristorante in Italy (estab 1867). Giancarlo Guancioli serves daily-fresh home-made pasta and fine vegetable and fish specialities. Meeting point of international jetsetters, politicos and all-round VIPs such as Craxi, Agnelli, PETER USTINOV and MARCHESA FIAMMA DI SAN GIULIANO FERRAGAMO.

Shopping

Via della Spiga is the ritziest street for all levels of Italian fashion. **Via Montenapoleone** is the more established street for the major international names; **Via Sant' Andrea** is fashfull, too. The best markets for antiques and some clothes are **Via Madonnina** in the young trendy Brera district (third Saturday of the month) and the **Naviglio** along the canals of Porta Ticinese (last Sunday of the month). For new clothes try **Fiera di Senegallia**, around Via San Luca (Saturdays), and **Viale Papiniano**, for knock-down designer gear.

ARS ROSA, Via Montenapoleone 8, 20121 ☎ (02) 793822
Swoonworthy satin and silk dream lingerie. Feminine dainties in hand-embroidered silk, finely crafted wedding dresses and trousseau naughties. Dinky babes' and children's undies and nightwear, too.

BOMBINO at Mila Schön
Top-ranking tailor for made-to-measure suits, crafted with precision by Signor Bombino. BILL BLASS is an admirer.

CAFFE MODA DURINI, Via Durini 14, 20122 ☎ (02) 791188
The top fashion store in the city, for the latest prêt-à-porter from Ferré, Valentino, Krizia et al. Also a few imports of import.

🍴 CARACENI, Via Fatebenefratelli 16, 20121 ☎ (02) 655 1972
The first name in tailoring. Some of the most elegant men in the world trot along here for their made-to-measure suiting, Gianni Agnelli and Karl Lagerfeld among them. If you lean towards the Latin look, they're best in the world.

COIN, Corso Vercelli 30-32, 20122 ☎ (02) 469 7256
A department store run by an old Venetian family (with branches Italy-wide). In-store designer concessions for all your Italian and French faves, plus their own lines and the full complement of departmental goodies.

FRATELLI ROSSETTI, Via Montenapoleone 1, 20121 ☎ (02) 791650
The best shoes in Italy. Latin style using the finest leather. Globetrotting fashion-hounds follow slavishly in their footsteps.

LA BOTTEGA DEL MAGO, Via Bigli 7, 20121 ☎ (02) 791528
Gear for the preening palazzo: antique furniture, china, glass, mirrors, silver, ivory, table linen and lighting.

LA PERLA at Valentina, Via Manzoni 44, 20121 ☎ (02) 796028
The famous lingerie line – pleated, printed and plain silk camisoles, bras, basques, hosiery, swimwear and scent. Catherine Deneuve, Princess Stéphanie, Sophia Loren and Danielle Mitterrand are among those to go a Perla.

LA RINASCENTE, Via S Radegonda 3 (entrance on Piazza del Duomo), 20121 ☎ (02) 88521
The best store in Italy, with branches nationwide. An emporium of Italian goodies for the whole family. Signature designer stuff – Versace, Armani, Ferré and co – plus stylish own-label separates. Great accessories – whatever's new in jewels, belts, scarves.

L'ORO DEI FARLOCCHI, Via Madonnina 5, 20121 ☎ (02) 860589
The best present shop in Milan, for unusual objets d'art, say MARCHESA FIAMMA DI SAN GIULIANO FERRAGAMO and MARIUCCIA MANDELLI.

MILA SCHON, Via Montenapoleone 2, 20121 ☎ (02) 701803
The Jean Muir of Italy, a designer of Austro-Hungarian extraction, who presides at the classy end of the market. Elegant collection of wearables – little suits and separates for the well-heeled. Men's version at No 3 ☎ (02) 701333.

PRADA FRATELLI, Galleria Vittorio Emanuele II 63, 20121 ☎ (02) 876979
Swish stash of leather bags, luggage, jewel-encrusted pumps, mean boots. Still the place for dolly little quilted bags on gilt chains.

ROME

—— Art and museums ——

GALLERIA BORGHESE, Villa Borghese, Via Pinciana
Set in the largest park in Rome is the beautifully frescoed Palazzo Borghese, home to some of Bernini's most powerful sculptures – *David*, *Apollo and Daphne*, *Pluto and Proserpine*, etc – and paintings by Caravaggio. However, it could be years before restoration of the upper floor (with treasures by Raphael, Titian and Correggio) is complete. Open mornings only.

🏊 GALLERIA DORIA PAMPHILI, Piazza del Collegio Romano 1 ☎ (06) 679 4365
The 17C Palazzo Doria is still owned by the Doria family, who have one of the loveliest private collections in Italy. See Caravaggio, Claude, Carracci and Velázquez's portrait of the Pamphili pope, *Innocent X*.

MUSEO CAPITOLINO, Piazza dei Campidoglio, 00186 ☎ (06) 678 2862
Housed in 3 palaces on Michelangelo's oval piazza is this public collection of classical sculptures and mainly 17C paintings. See the bronze *Spinario* (Boy with a Thorn) and marble *Dying Gaul*.

🏊 MUSEI VATICANI, Viale Vaticano ☎ (06) 698 3333
The Vatican, palace of the popes, is a rich source

🏊 **Buzzz A beach for all regions**: unshowy northern Italians go to Portofino or Santa Margherita, where they have hidden villas; Florentines bask at Punta Ala and Forte dei Marmi; Romans race off to Monte Argentario, and razzy Neapolitans to Ischia or Positano🏊 . . . . . . For English style with Italian workmanship, go to NICHOLAS VILLIERS's tailor in Milan, **Pastore**, Via Andgari 18 ☎ (02) 7200 2298🏊 . . . . . . Best **views of Rome**, from the Penthouse or Villa Medici Suites of the **Hassler** (with their own terraces); suite No 840 of their neighbour in Via Sistina, **Hotel de la Ville**; and the top-floor restaurant of the **Eden** in Via Ludovisi 🏊 . . . . . . **Aroma of Roma**: the scent of pines? The redolence of ancient stone? Not if you're standing on the Spanish Steps. There, it's a **whiff of old McDonald's**🏊 . . . . . . For R&R take JAMES BURKE's advice and stay at **Hotel Verbano**, Isola dei Pescatori, 28049 Stresa ☎ (0323) 30408: *"On a tiny island in the middle of glassy Lake Maggiore. You have breakfast on a terrace, birds hop around the table and you can't hear anything except the water"* . . . . 🏊

of art – far more than a day's ogling (and a good deal of queuing). Home of the most gasp-making ceiling in the world, a 4-year labour of love (and hate) by Michelangelo, newly cleaned to reveal vivid, lively brushwork that has both art historians and first-timers rapt. Also in the **Sistine Chapel** is the artist's murky *Last Judgement* and many Renaissance works. Almost as astonishing are the frescos of **Raphael's Stanze**. A fine picture gallery, and the largest collection of antique art in the world – don't miss the famous *Apollo Belvedere* and *Laocoön*.

Italy's Best Galleries and Museums

1	GALLERIA DEGLI UFFIZI · Florence
2	MUSEI VATICANI · Rome
3	GALLERIA DELL'ACCADEMIA · Venice
4	PALAZZO PITTI · Florence
5	MUSEO POLDI PEZZOLI · Milan

Bars and cafés

ANTICO CAFFE GRECO, Via Condotti 86, 00187 ☎ (06) 679 1700
Founded in 1760, when British nobles were flocking down to Rome and classical civilization was the in thing, this café has long-standing intellectual and literary associations (it carries *"a lot of cultural references"* for the FENDI sisters). Under lofty arches, with oils covering the walls, latterday Grand Tourists join smart Romans to sip caffè or delicious hot chocolate and cream, served by tailcoated waiters.

BABINGTON TEA ROOMS, Piazza di Spagna 23, 00187 ☎ (06) 678 6027
Another hangover from Grand Touring days, set up by a Victorian Englishwoman who was gasping for a cuppa. Old-fashioned haunt of old ladies and young hipsters alike, for lunch and tea.

BARETTO DI VIA CONDOTTI, Via Condotti 55, 00187 ☎ (06) 678 4566
So exclusive that there's no sign to tell you this is Baretto. Trendies in the know go for mid-morning coffee.

HEMINGWAY, Piazza delle Coppelle 10, 00186 ☎ (06) 654 4135
Ultra-popular, plushy all-night bar where Romans lounge after dinner. 3 rooms – one in cosy red Victoriana, one in green marble with molto mirrors and one like a Greek taverna.

IL TARTARUGHINO, Via della Scrofa 2, 00186 ☎ (06) 678 6037
An elegant piano bar where smart older Romans and politicians gather. In summer, it follows its regulars to Porto Rotondo, Sardinia, where it is redubbed the Country Club.

SAN FILIPPO, Via di Villa San Filippo 8, 00197 ☎ (06) 879314
Known to Romans as 'Tre Froci', this café-bar is a smash hit for gelati. The cognoscenti dish up their ice-cream cakes for pudding. Worth a pilgrimage for their zabaglione.

Clubs

ALIEN, Via Velletri 13 ☎ (06) 841 2212
A spin-off from the Gilda clan. Rock 'n' roll looms large here, with 50s drawings in the rock room and a mix of ages getting on down. Closed Mon and Wed.

GILDA, Via Mario de' Fiori 97 ☎ (06) 678 4838
The club in Rome, where *everyone* winds up. Big, elegant disco/restaurant for all ages. The young gather round the bar, oldies sit near the stage. Décor incorporates a hint of classical ruins as is the Roman wont.

NOTORIOUS, Via S Nicola da Tolentino 22, 00187 ☎ (06) 474 6888
One of the hippest clubs, with a big celebrity following – it's always in the Roman papers. Grace Jones drops in, so do many Italian actors. Disco and cabaret. Last stop on the Roman

Buzzz Baroque brilliance: the style reached its zenith in 17C Roman churches. Unmissable masterpieces are the rhythmic, curvacious interiors of: Bernini's oval **Sant' Andrea al Quirinale**, Via del Quirinale, a dramatic fusion of architecture and sculpture; down the road, Borromini's tiny **San Carlino alle Quattro Fontane** with its dizzy-making dome of pink and white; and his joyous **Sant' Ivo alla Sapienza**, in the courtyard of Palazzo della Sapienza, Corso Rinascimento – like being inside a white jelly mould (the caretaker may require a little palm-greasing to let you in)......For **Caravaggio** at his dramatic best, see his paintings in situ at the churches of **Santa Maria del Popolo** and **San Luigi dei Francesi** (makes sense of those sharp perspectives and shafts of light)..............

nightbirds' 'Giro della morte' (circle of death), involving dinner-Hemingway-Gilda-Notorious, and ending in collapse at 4am.

—— Fashion designers ——

🏆 VALENTINO, Via Bocca di Leone 15-18, 00187 ☎ (06) 679 5862

Valentino is the couturier that brings out the seductive screen goddess in you. A technical wizard in the realms of stand-up ruffles, enormous bows and other glamour twists. Jewel-bright hues, magnificent fabrics and grandiose detailing. Prêt-à-porter, too. Fans include Marisa Berenson, Nan Kempner, SHAKIRA CAINE, Anouska Hempel, MARCHESA BONA FRESCOBALDI (who would walk miles for his shoes, designed by Rene Caovilla) and JOAN COLLINS (who wore black embellished with giant golden sea-horses to a recent show).

—— Hotels ——

🏆 HOTEL HASSLER, Trinità dei Monti 6, 00187 ☎ (06) 679 2651

"Still the best in Rome by a long way" – FRANK LOWE. A discreet, civilized establishment presiding majestically at the top of the Spanish Steps. Renovations mean rooms now glitter with Venetian mirrors, and bathrooms gleam with marble. Although common parts could do with a chivvy up too, the joy of this hotel lies in its faultless, friendly service and the perfect location. *"A jewel of a hotel, run with precision by Roberto Wirth"* – ANIKO GAAL. *"A very good hotel"* choruses GILES SHEPARD. The **Roof Restaurant** vista pans the famous domes of Rome.

🏆 HOTEL LORD BYRON, Via G de Notaris 5, 00197 ☎ (06) 322 0404

Intimate, high-class hotel in the small Ottaviani family chain. The same stylish comfort as its sister, the Regency in Florence, in the smart residential area, Parioli, beyond the Borghese gardens – prepare for many taxi rides. ANDREW LLOYD WEBBER and FAITH WILLINGER prize the first-rate restaurant, **Relais Le Jardin**.

HOTEL MAJESTIC, Via Veneto 50, 00196 Rome ☎ (06) 486841

Re-opened this year after a $20 million refit, the Majestic is aiming for No 1 slot in Rome. First opened in 1875, and the best until the 1930s, it certainly has the history and the location – and now the management (under Silvano Pinchetti, late of the Hassler). Fine restaurant with terrace.

LE GRAND, Via V E Orlando 3, 00185 ☎ (06) 4709

The *hotel* is undeniably grand, with all its gold leaf, hand-painted wallpaper, brocade, tapestries, mirrors and chandeliers ... but it's unfortunately in an area that is less and less grand, near the station.

Frescobaldi's Choice

♟

MARCHESA BONA FRESCOBALDI divulges some special Italian secrets: **Ilaria Miani**, Via degli Orti d'Alibert 13A, Rome ☎ (06) 686 1365, is the place for frames, *"custom-made and designed according to each individual painting and to the décor of the room"*. **Cartiere F Amatruda**, Via Fiume, Amalfi ☎ (089) 871315, for *"the most beautiful handmade stationery that one can imagine, created in one of the most charming locations"*. **Giannini**, 37r Piazza Pitti, Florence ☎ (055) 212621, where the Giannini family *"has practised the art of book-binding and hand-decorating stationery with extreme elegance for 5 generations"*. **Tirelli Costumi**, Via Pompeo Magno 11B, Rome ☎ (06) 321 2654, for opulent authentic antique costumes (1700 to the 1970s), which can be rented. They are costumiers to stars of opera and film (*Ludwig*, *Casanova*, *Amadeus*, etc). **Castel Viscardo di Ditta Sugheroni**, Via Europa 26, Orvieto ☎ (0763) 61370, where Signor Giuseppe will hand-make terracotta floor tiles in any dimension.

—— Restaurants ——

See also Hotels.

🏆 ALBERTO CIARLA, Piazza S Cosimato 40, 00183 ☎ (06) 581 6668

One of the finest fish restaurants in Italy, with soaring prices to match. *"Very creative, very elegant. He does a lot of research into older Italian recipes. A soup with a lobster base, and seafood and beans with pasta which is spectacular. Also some raw fish dishes. The nicest tables are outside"* – BARBARA KAFKA. Good for oysters and champagne. Dinner only.

CHECCHINO DAL 1887, Via di Monte Testaccio 30 ☎ 574 6318

Owned by the Mariani family, who have been cooking for generations, this is the place for Roman food at its roots, specializing in trad offal and meat dishes. Beautiful wine cellar excavated into the hills.

IL MATRICIANO, Via dei Gracchi 49-61, 00192 ☎ (06) 321 3040

Buzzy, unpretentious local restaurant in a smart

residential area, where you really do find your-self next to film bigwigs and actors such as Bernardo Bertolucci or Christopher Lambert. Delicious fried vegetables in a delicate batter (the Roman answer to Japanese tempura), superb pasta (especially the ravioli), moreish feather-light zabaglione with bitter chocolate sauce.

NINO, Via Borgognona 11, 00187
☎ (06) 679 5676
Lively trattoria with no sense of superiority as you might expect in this neighbourhood. Smarties go for hearty cooking – wonderful fagioli, penne all' arrabbiata, bistecca fiorentina. A winner with VICTOR EDELSTEIN and the FENDI sisters (*"one we love especially"*).

PATRIZIA E ROBERTO DEL PIANETA TERRA, Via del Arco del Monte 95, 00186
☎ (06) 656 9893
Small, trendy restaurant for the very best in new wave Roman food.

PIERLUIGI, 144 Piazza dei Ricci, 00186
☎ (06) 686 1302
Throngingly trendy haunt where Gilda disco-maniacs start the evening. Courtyard outside in summer, long waits for a table.

🍴 PIPERNO, Monte de' Cenci 9, 00186
☎ (06) 654 0629
A much-loved characterful eatery in a little square in the Jewish ghetto. Roman Jewish food – great gnocchi, exquisite light fried specialities. *"Very, very good, especially for the artichokes. They are deep-fried so they look like dry chrysan-themums, with the leaves like artichoke chips and the bottom creamy – lovely"* – MARCELLA HAZAN. PS Look like a tourist and you'll find they're booked up.

RISTORANTE PARIS, Piazza San Callisto 7,00153 ☎ (06) 585378
An old fave in Trastevere, for wonderful fish soup, clam dishes, and Jewish cuisine – carciofi alla Judea (light fried artichokes) and fritti veg-etale (mozzarella, artichokes, potatoes and courgette flowers). A hit with FAITH WILLINGER.

——— *Shopping* ———

Via Condotti, **Via Borgognona** and the little connecting streets are tops for fashion and jewel-lery. **Via del Corso** is the main, less exclusive, drag. Groovier little boutiques are dotted about **Trastevere**. Bargains can be sought out at the Sunday morning market at **Porta Portese**.

BORSALINO, Via IV Novembre 157B, 00187 ☎ (06) 679 4192
Classic hats for men and women in the best felts and velours. Also men's clothes. A vote from MARIUCCIA MANDELLI.

B70 SPORT, Salita San Sebastianello 7A, 00187 ☎ (06) 679 0843
A line in casual sportivi clothes – a look adopted by the FENDI sisters (when they're not in top-to-toe Fendi).

BULGARI, Via Condotti 10, 00187
☎ (06) 679 3876
Behind closed doors, the famous jewellery de-signers for important pieces with Renaissance, neo-classical and other historical influences. Chunky, geometric modern pieces, too.

CAMOMILLA, Piazza di Spagna 85, 00187
☎ (06) 679 3551
Trendy storehouse for stars of stage and screen

Roman Holiday

Summer in Italy sees a mass escape from city grime and grind, women and children first, to private villas dotted along the west coast, where the far more serious occu-pation of *acquiring a serious tan* begins. This is no exaggeration. Day upon day, week upon week, conversation upon con-versation is centred wholly and most sin-cerely on The Tan. In August there is a Roman exodus to Porto Ercole or Porto Santo Stefano on the bulbous little penin-sula of Monte Argentario. Smart residents (the Queen of the Netherlands, Vesteys, Borgheses, Corsinis...) have their own luxury villa, a yacht or two and use of the private beach at security-watched Sbarca-dello. For Argentarians, the boat is all-important. There's only one good public beach, Cannelle, so *everyone* is seafaring, even if it's only in a Zodiac. It's like Dunkirk as you grab your pizza in town, hop on your boat at Cala Galera and zip off to the islands of Giannutri, Giglio or Rossa. Eligible young machos belong to the self-styled GPA (Gruppo Playboy Argentario), an excuse for laddish gatherings. Best hotel: **Il Pellicano**, 58018 Porto Ercole ☎ (0564) 833801, hidden in the trees, with shady terraces. Lovely Italian style, loadsa lire. Best wine bar: **Kings Bar**. Best pasta: **Armando**. Best disco: **La Strega del Mare**.

and up-to-date yups. French and Jap designer clothes give them an edge over their all-Italian-buying rivals.

DAL CO, Via Vittoria 65, 00187
☎ (06) 678 6536
Superior shoes. Famed for their masterful handling of snakeskin, plus silk, embroidered and bejewelled evening shoes in a riot of colours.

🐾 FEDERICO BUCCELLATI, Via Condotti 31, 00187 ☎ (06) 679 0329
Arguably the best silversmiths in existence today. Elegant, intricate workmanship using tiny, flower-shaped diamonds with pearls, white gold and platinum. Exquisite silver-laminated seashells and snails; magnificently worked silver centrepieces and cigarette cases. Their jewels are a hit with JOAN COLLINS. Against Buccellati, the likes of Bulgari are frankly vulgari.

🐾 FENDI, Via Borgognona 39, 00187
☎ (06) 679 7641
The Italian woman adores her fur coat. There is nothing remotely controversial about wearing one here. A Fendi fur is the ultimate. The designer is, of course, that master of wit and inspiration Karl Lagerfeld. Sacrilegious slicing of fabulous pelts... hole-punched web-like capes, evening cloaks of fur petals, swing drama coats. A new process of treating pelts means the inside of the skin can be dyed instead of lined – rendering coats featherlight and reversible. Fendi has the street sewn up: apart from this sleek store, there's one for Fendissime, a line by the Fendis' daughters at 4L, accessories at 4E, 36A and 38, and clothes at 40.

GUCCI, Via Condotti 8, 00187
☎ (06) 678 9340
One of the world's most famous shops for knockout leather, feverishly branded with the notorious double G, snaffles and red and green striped ribbon. Also non-emblemed shoes, bags, wallets, belts, scarves, stoles, umbrellas and, at Via Condotti 77 ☎ (06) 679 6147, men's and women's clothes.

RADICONCINI, Via del Corso 139, 00186
☎ (06) 679 1807
The oldest milliners in Italy, for all sorts of topping hats. Also the best in shirts, handmade to measure with *hand-embroidered* monograms.

SUTRINI, Via Borgognona ☎ (06) 678 4168
The FENDI sisters' favourite jewellery shop.

VENICE
—— Art and museums ——

CA' D'ORO, Galleria Franchetti, Cannaregio ☎ (041) 523 8790
One of the Gothic palazzi on the Grand Canal, restored to its gilded glory. Venetian Renaissance works of art, plus ever-changing exhibitions.

CA' REZZONICO, Campo S Barnaba
☎ (041) 522 4543
A delightful baroque palazzo with original 18C decorations (fine frescos by Tiepolo padre e figlio), furniture and paintings.

COLLEZIONE D'ARTE MODERNA PEGGY GUGGENHEIM, S Gregorio 701, Dorsoduro ☎ (041) 520 6288
A breath of fresh air after the riches of old Venice: La Guggenheim's palazzo and garden (one of the largest in the city) houses her magnificent collection of modern art – Cubism (Picasso et al), Expressionism (she was once married to Max Ernst), abstract art and – her particular interest – Surrealism. Sculptures by Arp, Moore and a Marini horse and rider.

🐾 GALLERIA DELL' ACCADEMIA, Campo della Carità, Dorsoduro
☎ (041) 522 2247
The best in Venice, for a complete and brilliantly illustrated look at Venetian art. The masters are here en force: Bellini, Giorgione (including his

🐾 **Buzzz** In Venice, note the swift hand of **Tiepolo** at the magnificently frescoed **Palazzo Labia**, Campo S Geremia ☎ 781111 (ring first)🐾...... In the Veneto region, check out **Palladio**'s many and varied country villas (best: **Villa Barbaro**, Maser, with the Veronese frescos)🐾...... At Vicenza, see his marvellous little **Teatro Olimpico**, an indoor wood and stucco imitation of a Roman amphitheatre, with columns, statues, architectural vistas and painted sky 🐾...... In Mantua, Giuliano Romano's **Palazzo Te** is at last open again after restoration: a 16C Mannerist pleasure palace which cocked a snook at conventional classicism; don't miss the trompe-l'oeil Sala dei Giganti, intended to terrify those who entered🐾...... At Padua, visit the **Scrovegni Chapel**, whose wall-to-wall frescos by **Giotto** are an astonishing survival from 1306..................................... 🐾

famous and mysterious *Tempest*), Titian, Tintoretto, Veronese and Tiepolo.

PALAZZO DUCALE, Piazzetta S Marco
☎ (041) 522 4951
The spectacular pink and white Doge's Palace, former residence of the governors of the Republic of Venice, decorated by the major Venetian artists. You can't miss Tintoretto's immense canvas (70ft x 25ft), the weird and wild *Paradise*.

—— *Bars and cafés* ——

BAR AI SPECCHI, Hotel Antico Panada, Calle Specchieri, San Marco 646, 30123
☎ (041) 522 5824
The 'Mirror Bar' is so named because its walls are a glassy tapestry of antique mirrors. "*Still a very cute place, with very good grappa*" – MARCELLA HAZAN.

CAFFE FLORIAN, Piazza San Marco 56-59, 30125 ☎ (041) 528 5338
Established in 1720, the gilded and frescoed café-bar is at the hub of Venetian social life (if you can't get near Harry's). Frothy cappuccinos and scrumptious pastries. "*A very, very old café with the charm of Venice*" – MARCELLA HAZAN.

HARRY'S BAR, Calle Vallaresso 1323, 30124 ☎ (041) 523 6797
The most famous bar in the world. *Everyone* crams in to Arrigo's to say 'I'm in town' and to suss out who else is. Home of the bellini (champagne and fresh peach juice).

———— *Film* ————

VENICE INTERNATIONAL FILM FESTIVAL, Ca' Giustinian, S Marco, 30124
☎ (041) 520 0311
The oldest film festival, founded by Mussolini, it comes third in the traditional trilogy (after Cannes and Berlin). Held in late Aug-Sept, "*Venice has the pedigree but it's amateurish compared with Cannes*" – IAIN JOHNSTONE. Despite ailing direction, it's "*one of the nicest festivals, and still very prestigious*" – DEREK MALCOLM. Many international films are premièred here and vie for the Golden Lion. Social spots: **Harry's Bar** and **Des Bains** (scene of *Death in Venice*).

———— *Hotels* ————

🔱 CIPRIANI, Giudecca 10, 30100
☎ (041) 520 7744
This one always has our contributors in ecstasies. How could it fail, in that particular 3-acre plot, an island haven on the world's most beautiful lagoon? Service manages to remain flawless and personal, despite a fast turnover of Orient-Express trippers. "*Run by the remarkable hotelier Natale Rusconi, it is a home away from*

home. *A few days there and I can't tear myself away*" – ELISE PASCOE. "*Lunch at the pool is still one of the most pleasant ways of spending an afternoon that I know of. It is the best pool in the world*" – BARBARA KAFKA. Echoes are heard from yet more BARBARAS – TAYLOR BRADFORD and CARTLAND, plus BETTY KENWARD, JOAN BURSTEIN, LORD LICHFIELD, LEO SCHOFIELD and MARCELLA HAZAN ("*a very good kitchen*").

🔱
Italy's Best Hotels

I	CIPRIANI · Venice
2	VILLA SAN MICHELE · Fiesole
3	HOTEL HELVETIA & BRISTOL · Florence
4	HOTEL HASSLER · Rome
5	SAN PIETRO · Positano
6	VILLA D'ESTE · Como
7	HOTEL VILLA CIPRIANI · Asolo
8	GRITTI PALACE · Venice
9	HOTEL SPLENDIDO · Portofino
10	HOTEL LORD BYRON · Rome

🔱 GRITTI PALACE, Campo S M del Giglio 2467, 30124 ☎ (041) 794611
The Ciga-owned Gritti lords this bank of the Grand Canal with its own traghetto stop (for the cross-canal gondola), swish launches, and the cosy bar and **Club del Doge** dining-room (with maître d' Mr Bovo, late of the Connaught). "*Magnificent arrival by boat and the nicest place for a drink in Venice*" – BARBARA KAFKA. Regulars to the Serenissima are not so sure about the redecorated rooms (now a profusion of floral neo-rococo). Service can be high-handed, but once you're known, you're treated royally. "*Remarkable – slightly impersonal, but grand in the old-fashioned sense*" – RICHARD COMPTON-MILLER. Appreciated too by CLARE FRANCIS and MARIUCCIA MANDELLI.

PENSIONE ACCADEMIA, Dorsoduro 1058, 30123 ☎ (041) 521 0188
Delightful, cultivated family pensione that is everyone's first choice if they're not checking in to the Cip. An old villa with little garden and quiet canal frontage. Treatment can be typically brusque until you're in.

———— *Music* ————

CHIESA DI S MARIA DELLA PIETA
The Vivaldi church – for regular concerts of his and other baroque music.

TEATRO LA FENICE, Campo S Fantin, 30124 ☎ (041) 521 0161; 521 0336
One of Italy's oldest, most famous and glittering opera houses, under the new directorship of John Fisher. *"A theatre of astounding beauty"* – RODNEY MILNES. The season of opera, concerts, ballet and theatre starts with a mighty splash in Nov/Dec. *"I love it, it's tiny but it's beautiful"* – VISCOUNT HAMBLEDEN.

Restaurants

See also Hotels.

ALLA MADONNA, Calle della Madonna 594 ☎ (041) 522 3824
A brill trat, full of commotion, for the pick of the Adriatic. *"At lunch I really like this old-fashioned place for the best seafood in Venice"* – BARBARA KAFKA.

BARBACANI, Calle del Paradiso 5746, S Marco ☎ (041) 521 0234
Just 5 minutes from S Marco, this ristorante is, for MARCELLA HAZAN, *"one I like very much. They take very good care of the food they are cooking. Excellent spaghetti alla vongole, and a dessert made with fresh puréed fruit, lemon ice cream and prosecco wine all beaten up."*

🐓 DA FIORE, Calle del Scalater 2202, 30125 ☎ (041) 721308
Untouristy sanctuary for Venetian seafood and fish specialities, superb oysters, antipasti, vegetale and risotti. *"Hands-down the best restaurant in Venice. Really Venetian"* – BARBARA KAFKA. *"Still very, very good. Very simple food, but wonderful fresh fish – cappe lunghe, razor clams, coquilles St Jacques – for me it's one of the best fish restaurants"* – MARCELLA HAZAN. FAITH WILLINGER says aye.

PONTE DEL DIAVOLO, Torcello
Set on one of the Venetian islands, with a beautiful garden. MARCELLA HAZAN sings the praises of their *"delicious risotto with prawns, a lot of good fish dishes, good baccala (salt cod) and batacato (dried cod soaked, boiled in milk, then beaten with olive oil). When they do something new it tastes very good."*

RISTORANTE VINI AL COVO, Campiello della Pescaria, Castello 3968, 30122 ☎ 522 3812
"Pretty décor, with bare brick walls. They pay attention to wine, which is very rare in Venice. Mostly traditional Venetian food – a fabulous place" – FAITH WILLINGER.

· REST OF ·
ITALY
Festivals

BATIGNANO MUSICA NEL CHIOSTRO, S Croce, 58041 Batignano (Grosseto) ☎ (0564) 38096
Held in late July-Aug in the cloisters of a semi-ruined convent, Adam Pollock's enchanting festival offers rare and early opera.

🐓 FESTIVAL DEI DUE MONDI, Via del Duomo 7, Spoleto ☎ (0743) 28120; tickets also from Via Margutta 17, 00187 Rome ☎ (06) 361 4041
Founded by composer Gian Carlo Menotti, this is the best music, drama and ballet festival in Italy (late June-July), a definite date in the social/cultural diary. Opera, concerts, ballet and other arts events. The Spoleto set eat at **Il Tartufo**. The festival has spawned the Spoleto bambini in South Carolina and Melbourne.

🐓 ROSSINI OPERA FESTIVAL, Via Rossini 37, 61100 Pesaro ☎ (0721) 697360
A brilliant little opera festival in celebration of Rossini, held in Aug-Sept in his birthplace. Renowned for inventive, high-calibre productions, particularly of Rossini's rarer works.

🐓 **Buzzz** Gourmet checkpoint: new discoveries from MARCELLA HAZAN include **Escudo di Francia**, Vicenza (*"I had a kidney dish which was done very well – always a test for a restaurant"*); **Belvedere** in La Morra, Piemonte ☎ (0173) 50190 (*"in a tiny and beautiful village with a hilltop view. Quality traditional Piemontese food. Pasta with lots of egg yolks, a lot of cheese and eggs!"*); and **Diana**, Via Indipendeza 24, Bologna ☎ (051) 231302 (*"they have a lady upstairs who makes all their pasta by hand. Wonderful tortellini"*)🐓...... MARCHESA BONA FRESCOBALDI's foodie treats are: **Gambero Rosso**, Piazza Vittoria 72, S Vicenzo (Livorno) ☎ (0565) 701021, *"a must for whoever loves fish"*; **Ristorante Guido**, Costigliole d'Asti (Torino), for *"the best traditional dishes from the Piemonte region"*; and **Da Pietro**, Via Montanti 5A, Forte dei Marmi ☎ (0584) 82188, for *"the best pizzas and schiacciatine – Tuscan bread with oil and salt"*......................🐓

STRESA MUSICAL WEEKS, Settimane Musicale, Palazzo dei Congressi, Via R Bonghi 4, 28049 Stresa ☎ (0323) 31095
Gorgeous setting in the Lakes region for this 4-week festival (Aug-Sept) of classical music by international artists and young winners of prestigious music competitions. Some concerts take place in a baroque palace on Isola Bella, the largest island on Lake Maggiore. Stay along with many of the performers at **Hotel des Iles Borromées**, Lungolago Umberto I, 67 ☎ (0323) 30431.

Hotels

CERTOSA DI MAGGIANO, Via Certosa 82, 53100 Siena ☎ (0577) 288180
A mile out of town lies this tranquil hotel converted from a 14C monastery, set around the original cloisters. A quartet of lovely sitting rooms, decorated by Lorenzo Mongiardino, filled with fresh flowers, paintings and frescos. Here, civilized tea is served, with irresistible baby biscotti. Beautiful garden with swimming pool, vineyards, peach, apricot and olive trees. High-class nouvelle cuisine – at a prezzo.

HOTEL CALA DI VOLPE, 07020 Porto Cervo, Costa Smeralda, Sardinia ☎ (0789) 96083
The ritziest of the Aga Khan's Sardinian empire (his Ciga group owns all the hotels in exclusive Costa Smeralda and Porto Rotondo). A village-style resort rather like a film set: though relatively new, it blends into its rustic surroundings with chameleonic ease, from the irregular red-tiled roofs down to the little wooden jetty. *"An architectural masterpiece. It has its own bay and it's very well run"* – LORD LICHFIELD.

🏖 HOTEL SPLENDIDO, Salita Baratta 13, 16034 Portofino ☎ (0185) 269551
A holiday hotel on the Italian Riviera that sings with memories of Hollywood greats (Garbo, Bogart and co) and racy royals (Duke and Duchess of Windsor, Prince Rainier and Princess Grace). Rose-pink, green shuttered villa with sun-dappled terraces, swimming pool, tennis court, and traditional Ligurian cuisine.

🏖 HOTEL VILLA CIPRIANI, Via Canova 298, Asolo, 31011 Treviso ☎ (0423) 55444
A peaceful 16C villa, former home of Robert Browning, in the lush green Veneto – the perfect base camp for doing the Palladian villas. Lavish spreads using fresh vegetables from the garden. The Queen Mother stays. Reagan *wanted* to stay, but the hotel wasn't too happy about having to chop down all their trees to let the helicopter land. *"Beautiful views over the valley of olive groves and fruit trees. Fabulous service, great management"* – RICHARD COMPTON-MILLER. Pure bliss, say ROBIN HANBURY-TENISON, MARIUCCIA MANDELLI, GIORGIO ARMANI and MARCHESA BONA FRESCOBALDI.

"Siena is wonderful, absolutely fantastic. The Palio must be the only sporting event left on earth which isn't controlled by advertising"

 FRANK LOWE

LOCANDA DELL' AMOROSA, 53048 Sinalunga (Siena) ☎ (0577) 679497
Once a walled village, then a farm estate, now a heavenly country hotel set in rustic buildings around the old courtyard. Rooms have white-washed walls, tiled floors and beams; fab bathrooms with high-pressure showers. The stables form one of the best restaurants in the area (some 25 miles from Siena) for Tuscan specialities, with the Locanda's own wines, honey, herbs and delectable light, nutty olive oil.

🏖 VILLA D'ESTE, Via Regina 40, 22010 Cernobbio, Lake Como ☎ (031) 511471
At the fashionable end of Como, built in the 16C as a cardinal's palazzo, a serene hotel in manicured grounds with a pool that juts out into the lake. *"Get a room with a balcony by the water in what they call the new building, which is only a little newer than the old building. Very good waterskiing – it's one of the few places where you can rent a motor-boat and go off down the lake and have fun for the day. An absolute joy"* – FRANK LOWE. *"One of the last grand hotels. Extensive grounds with a fairy grotto and a pool, and very good food. Wonderful"* – RICHARD COMPTON-MILLER. MICHAEL GRADE and VICTOR EDELSTEIN are pleased punters.

Music

🏖 ARENA DI VERONA, Ente Arena, Piazza Bra 28, 37121 Verona ☎ (045) 590109. Tickets: Arch 6 of the Arena ☎ (045) 596517
A real *experience*. The ancient 1C AD arena hosts a festival season of opera and ballet in July-Aug. No-holds-barred productions (expect grand-scale operas such as *Aida*), virtuoso performances (Placido Domingo and Maria Callas made their débuts here), passionate listeners (who sing the highlights of the last act during intervals and give standing ovations to each aria) ... an all-round glittering spectacle (lit not only by stars but by candles held by the 25,000-strong audience). Something of an endurance test for the uninitiated – if you're seated on the stone tiers, bring a picnic, binoculars, extra cushions and blankets (for drinks follow the cries of 'Bibite, Coca-Cola, panini, sandweeech').

TEATRO DI SAN CARLO, Via San Carlo, 80132 Naples ☎ (081) 797 2111
One to attend purely for the *"fantastically beautiful 18C opera house. A wonderful place to*

go" – RODNEY MILNES. One of the grandest openings of the Italian season.

——— *Restaurants* ———

BECCHERIE, Piazza Ancillotto 11, Treviso ☎ (0422) 540871
Specialities from the Veneto region, with the accent on game and fowl – conjure with dishes such as pheasant liver with salsa pearada (a special pepper sauce).

BOSCHETTI, Piazza Mazzini 10, 33019 Tricesimo (Udine) ☎ (0432) 851230
A ristorante in the north-eastern Veneto for wholesome Italian fare such as pasta fagioli (beans), fish and lamb. MARCELLA HAZAN dreams of their minestre di fagioli e orzo (barley).

CA'MASIERI, 36070 Trissino (Vicenza) ☎ (0445) 962100
Little restaurant/inn in the Veneto region, with a handful of rooms and marvellous revamped regional cuisine.

GIAPPUN, Via Maonira 7, Vallecrosia (Imperia) ☎ (0184) 290970
On the Italian Riviera, a restaurant that still has ANDREW LLOYD WEBBER gobsmacked with admiration ("*9 kinds of olive oil ... infinite cellar of Italian wines ... the quality of the seafood and all they do is unlike anything I've experienced*").

RISTORANTE LA FATTORIA DI GRAZZI, Via del Cerro 11, Tavarnelle Val di Pesa ☎ (055) 807 0000
Superb family restaurant in the countryside between Florence and Siena. Light-fried courgette flowers and sage leaves with a film of anchovy are brought on arrival; fabulous pheasant, rabbit and bistecca fiorentina, cooked on olive wood; fagioli in fiasco (white beans with oil and garlic), cooked in the ashes of the fire.

ROMA, Piazza XX Settembre, 33028 Tolmezzo (Udine) ☎ (0433) 2081
"*Probably the best food in all Friuli and a very elegant little restaurant to boot*" – FAITH WILLINGER.

SAN GIORS ANTICO RISTORANTE TORINESE, Via Borgo Dora 3, Turin ☎ (011) 521 1256
"*The best bollito misto, a northern Italian dish – a mix of meats stewed together and served with a salsa verde (a spicy green herb sauce) and salsa rosso (red tomato-based sauce). That was pretty damn wonderful*" – SOPHIE GRIGSON.

STENDHAL, 43052 Sacca di Colorno (Parma) ☎ (0521) 815493
Marvellous local specialities and home-made pasta. "*They do tortelloni di zucca (pumpkin) very well; also that famous type of prosciutto, 'culatello' – they dismantle the ham to take just the pear-shaped muscle that's inside. It is air-dried and cured and has to have a damp atmosphere. Very hard to get it just right, and it's one of the most wonderful, expensive things on the menu*" – MARCELLA HAZAN.

TRATTORIA LA BUCA, Via Ghizzi 3, Zibello (Parma) ☎ (0524) 99214
A marvellous little trat for local, regional dishes – tortelli of marrow or ricotta, lingua in sugo di funghi (tongue in mushroom sauce). A recommendation from FAITH WILLINGER.

——— *Ski resorts* ———

CORTINA D'AMPEZZO
As Megève is to France, so Cortina is to Italy. Packed with immaculately turned-out Italians, who sip espressos at the Hotel de la Poste. Royals, film stars, the Pirellis, Buitonis, Cicognas and Colonnas go. Roger Moore's swansong as James Bond, *For Your Eyes Only*, was set here, in "*staggeringly beautiful scenery – the Dolomites are jagged and soaring and sometimes turn pink at sunset. Pretty main street with the warmth of old churches and gorgeous shopfronts ...*" – JANE LINDQUIST. Best hotels: **Miramonti Majestic**; **Cristallo**; **Hotel de la Poste**. Best restaurants: **El Toulà**, **El Camineto**, the tiny **Il Meloncino** and the lakeside **Meloncino al Lago**.

——— *Villas* ———

THE BEST IN ITALY, Count Momi and Countess Simonetta Brandolini d'Adda, Via Ugo Foscolo 72, 50124 Florence ☎ (055) 223064
Rentals of luxury private villas and palazzos with swimming pools, tennis courts and staff.

——— *Wine* ———

Italian wines have almost shaken off the old stigma of being the world's most maligned; the best are indeed as extraordinary as any work of art in Florence (take **GRECO DI GERACE CERATTI**, one of the world's best sweet aperitif wines). For SIMON LOFTUS, "*The developments in Italy are the ones which excite me most. There are a great many intriguing flavours and grape varieties which are still waiting to be discovered by the public at large.*

"*The best thing is that most Italian wines are not based on clones of French varieties, but on their own ancient grapes. One exciting development is that the grape Barbera, notoriously astringent, is now being vinified by one or two winemakers in the north-west of Italy to make absolutely magnificent wine.*" BARBARA KAFKA adds: "*Italian wine has shown the most incredible improvement of all wines in the world. There is a whole change of vinification ....*"

Piedmont

The great experimenters – no grape variety or wine style is left unturned. Piedmont's smash hits are the great reds, **BAROLO** and **BARBARESCO**, both rich in fruit and mysterious woodland smells, for long ageing.

In Barbaresco, one name dominates: **Gaja**. All of Gaja's wines are good: the best is the single-vineyard **Sori San Lorenzo**, and the 1961 was one of the best Italian wines MICHAEL BROADBENT has tasted. (JOHN TOVEY effuses about the Gaja Chardonnay: *"Wonderful, wonderful".*) SERENA SUTCLIFFE loves the wines of **Bruno Giacosa**.

Barolos to watch for, tips DAVID GLEAVE, are those of **Aldo Conterno, Giuseppe Mascarello** and **Elio Altare**. Then there's **Pio Cesare**'s all-conquering version. *"There are some frightfully good Barolos,"* confirms AUBERON WAUGH.

Tuscany

BRUNELLO DI MONTALCINO is a red that outprices any other wine in Italy (partly because, in poor years, the whole crop is declassified). The most expensive is **Case Basse**. **Castelgiocondo** is a Brunello di Montalcino to reckon with; **Talenti** and **Altesino** are *"very good and reasonably priced"* – DAVID GLEAVE.

The Cabernet Sauvignon **SASSICAIA**, could be the finest red wine in Italy, especially if aged, says SERENA SUTCLIFFE, when it becomes dramatic.

Piero Antinori, arguably the best winemaker in the country, has his own triumph: **TIGNANELLO**. STEVEN SPURRIER likes his **SOLAIA**.

Florence's fruity red, **CHIANTI**, gets a puff from MARCHESA BONA FRESCOBALDI for her family's **MONTESODI CHIANTI RUFINA** 1982 (only ever bottled in the best years). **Antinori**'s Chiantis are tops. The best producers of **CHIANTI CLASSICO**, says DAVID GLEAVE, are **Ama, Isole e Olena** and **Fontodi**. SERENA SUTCLIFFE goes for the bello **Castello di Volpaia**.

Many properties of **POMINO** are experimenting with Chardonnay and Sauvignon grapes with exciting results. **POMINO IL BENEFIZIO** is one of Italy's most prestigious white Chardonnays, from the aristocratic Frescobaldi fold. They also produce a fine red **Pomino**, a marriage of 4 noble grapes – Cabernet, Sangiovese, Pinot Noir and Merlot.

Umbria

LUNGAROTTI *is* Umbria, from the wine point of view. SERENA SUTCLIFFE is devoted to their magnificent reds – **SAN GIORGIO** and the classic **RUBESCO RISERVA VIGNA MONTICCHIO**.

Veneto

The best winemakers of the Veneto have big attics. In a good year, that's where they take their prize bunches of red grapes to have them wizen slowly in the warmth of the autumn. The resulting wines can be either very dry and very strong (**AMARONE**) or sweet and slightly less strong (**RECIOTODELLA VALPOLICELLA**). DAVID GLEAVE holds **Allegrini** in high esteem for their **AMARONE, RECIOTO** and **FIERAMONTE**. Other noteworthy bottles are **Tedeschi**'s **RECIOTO CAPITEL MONTE FONTANA** and **Giuseppe Quintarelli**'s **AMARONE MONTE CA' PALETTA**. SERENA SUTCLIFFE votes for **Masi**'s **SEREGO ALIGHIERI** (Dante's wine) and **CAMPO FIORIN**.

The best **SOAVE**s, says DAVID G, are **Pieropan** and **Anselmi**, while the best Italian fizz, opines SERENA S, is **CA' DEL BOSCO**.

JAPAN

KYOTO

The old capital (from 794 to 1868) is best hit at cherry-blossom or sakura time (for about 2 weeks in early to mid-April) when the country comes alive with ohana-mi – cherry-blossom-viewing picnics. *"You'd have to go a long way to beat the gardens in Kyoto. That place is nothing short of amazing"* – ANDRE PREVIN. *"Walking in Kyoto with some planning is very rewarding"* – BARBARA KAFKA.

——— *Hotels* ———

HIRAGIYA RYOKAN, Fuyacho-Aneyakoji-agaru, Nakagyo-ku
☎ (075) 221 1136
One of the best traditional Japanese inns (or ryokans), with superb rooms overlooking equally traditional gardens.

TAWARA-YA, Nakagyo-ku, Fuyacho, Oike-Sagaru ☎ (075) 211 5566
Small but perfectly formed ryokan that is *"awe-inspiring in its Zen-like simplicity. You leave your shoes and your ego at the door. What is extraordinary is, here you are in a typical, traditional room with tatamis [rush mats] and your own Zen garden outside, only to discover that there is a Western bathroom with a little red knob on the toilet seat so you can adjust the temperature for warming the seat. It's a scream"* – EDWARD CARTER. About 12 bedrooms, each with a garden. HELEN GURLEY BROWN is a fan.

Restaurants

AZAY LE RIDEAU, Kiyamachi at Takoyakushi ☎ (075) 223 0009
The best international restaurant in Kyoto, serving nouvelle cuisine with Japanese elements (the Japanese chef used to work at L'Orangerie in LA). Frequented by the local art and film set.

CHIHANA, Nawate-higashi-iru, Shijo-dori, Higashiyama-ku ☎ (075) 561 2741
Small kappo (top-grade restaurant for authentic Japanese cuisine) serving traditional Kyoto dishes. A hit with SHIZUO TSUJI.

— Temples and gardens —

ENRYAKU-JI TEMPLE, Mount Hiei
An ancient centre of Buddhism, a peaceful and haunting group of temples on a sacred mountain outside Kyoto. Here, the Inextinguishable Dharma Light has been glowing away for the past 1,200 years. Go by local bus to Shimeidake from Kyoto station.

HEIAN SHRINE
Renowned for its gardens of cherry blossom (confetti of the palest pink and white) and ponds.

KINKAKUJI TEMPLE
The Golden Pavilion, a replica of the c. 1400 original, is set in lovely water gardens. The nearby **Ryoanji Temple** garden displays the ultimate in precision raking: the tiny pebbles are coiffed daily.

KIYOMIZU TEMPLE
Perhaps the most beautiful temple, in the most serene and panoramic setting in the hills, offering just a glimpse of the city through the trees.

OSAKA

The city of the 21st century. The shift from crowded, earthquake-dogged Tokyo to this cosmopolitan city will become more apparent when **Kansai Airport**, Osaka Bay, opens in 1993.

— Hotels —

THE PLAZA, 2-2-49 Oyodo-Minami, Kita-ku ☎ (06) 453 1111
The Okura of Osaka, a large hotel with a mass of restaurants – Japanese, Chinese and French (in the style of Louis Outhier), an outdoor pool, beauty parlour, *and* personal service.

Restaurants

CHAMBORD, Royal Hotel, 5-3-68 Nakashima Kitaku, Osaka ☎ (06) 448 1121
The best European restaurant in Osaka, for mainly French cuisine by a French chef. The menu changes monthly; sensational seafood.

🏮 KICCHO, 3-23 Koraibashi, Higashiku, Osaka ☎ (06) 231 1937
The main branch and the most prestigious restaurant in Osaka. Family-run business that has been going for years. Dining here is aesthetically pleasing – nibble kaiseki ryori amid beautiful tableware and art treasures. *"Absolute perfection in all respects"* – SHIZUO TSUJI.

TOKYO

— Art and museums —

HARA MUSEUM, 4-7-25 Kitashinagawa, Shinagawa-ku ☎ (03) 445 0651
Toshio Hara is *the* authority on Japanese contemporary art. The first museum of its kind in Japan, it's the premier port of call for visiting experts.

IDEMITSU MUSEUM OF THE ARTS, International Bldg, 9F, 3-1-1 Marunouchi, Chiyoda-ku ☎(03) 3111
A private collection of traditional fine and decorative arts, including ukiyoe, the famous Japanese prints, and some of the finest Oriental porcelain in the world.

NIHON MINKA-EN, Muko Gaoka, Shinjuku-ku ☎ (044) 922 2181
Step back 200 years as you enter this museum of 'Important Cultural Properties' – ancient homes that were brought here to save them from ruin. See the former homes of merchants, village chieftains and horse-traders, as though the occupants were due back any minute.

SUNTORY MUSEUM OF ART, Suntory Bldg, 11F, 1-2-3 Moto-Akasaka, Minato-ku ☎ (03) 470 1073
Impressive collection of textiles, kimonos, lacquer objects, porcelain and painting. Regular changing exhibitions – but no English-language explanations.

TOKYO NATIONAL MUSEUM, 13-9 Ueno Koen, Taito-ku ☎ (03) 822 1111
The national collection of Japanese (and Asian) painting, sculpture, prints, porcelain and lacquer is the finest in the world. Spread among 4 buildings in Ueno Park, it includes the **Gallery of Horyuji Treasures**, open on Thursdays only, for a peek at the frail 6C-7C gems lent by the Horyuji Temple in Nara.

— Bars and cafés —

CAFE DE ROPE, 6-1-8 Jingumae, Shibuya-ku ☎ (03) 406 6845
The original gaijin-meets-Japan hot-spot, a see-

and-be-seen café on the fashion strip Omotesando, jammed with tall Western models.

RADIO BAR, 2-31-7 Jingumae, Shibuya-ku
☎ (03) 405 5490
Buzzing cocktail bar with a high-frequency turnout of gaijin and trendies. The ultimate – there is no concoction they can't make.

RED SHOES, B1, Azabu Palace, 2-25-18 Nishi Azabu, Minato-ku ☎ (03) 499 4319
Still on its toes after 10 years, Red Shoes is a venerable institution. The bar is a dark, moody red, with one wall covered by a large screen, showing an endless (and soundless) stream of music videos and films, while music plays out of synch in the background. A favourite haunt of musicians, including a handful of Rolling Stones when in Tokyo. Open 7pm to 7am.

TON TON, 2-1 Yurakucho, Chiyoda-ku
This movable underneath-the-railway-arches café has been going since 1946 (it only 'happens' from 5 to 11pm). Tables are made from stacked-up beer crates while overhead trains rumble. Fare is straight yakitori and sake.

Expat Bars

Much of Tokyo's expat nightlife goes on in tiny, fastidiously dressed-down bars. Start at *the* post-work expat rendezvous, **Frank Lloyd Wright Bar** at the Imperial Hotel, Tokyo's answer to the Captain's Bar in the Mandarin, Hong Kong. Go on to pre-prandials (or, better still, wait for late-late-night kick-off) at Roppongi's Gang of Four: **Charleston**, 3-8-11 Roppongi, a clubbish café-bar, jammed with Hoorayish expats and hopeful Japanese girls; the chic but rowdy little **Déja-vu**, Tohgensha Bldg, 1F, 3-15-24; **Henry Africa**, 3-15-23; and **Maggie's Revenge**, Takano Bldg, 3-8-12, where Aussie Maggie keeps the boisterous foreign contingent in order. Otherwise, it's a few snifters at the *in* watering hole, the **Jigger Bar**, Tohrikaku Bldg, 7-14-1: despite having nothing special to commend it (you stand around tree-trunk tables), *everyone* wants to be there.

—— Clubs ——

Roppongi, **Akasaka** and **Harajuku** are the trendy nightlife areas. The brassier **Shinjuku** and **Ginza** are packed, respectively, with gaudy gay and transvestite clubs and hostess bars.

GOLD, 3-1-6 Kaigan, Minato-ku
☎ (03) 453 3545
The place of the moment. Not in the least bit sparkly as the name suggests, this is in fact a gutted warehouse by the waterfront, installed with lights, deafening speakers, several podiums to display oneself upon and drinks machines which are operated by a special Gold card. The brainchild of Tokyo's most famous playboy, Sato-san, who stands suavely at the door with his walkie-talkie army, nodding in the Golden élite. Book to smooth your arrival.

INK STICK, Casa Grande Miwa Bldg, B1, 7-5-11 Roppongi, Minato-ku
☎ (03) 401 0429
The nightclub-bar that David Bowie and Ryuichi Sakamoto hit when in town. Occasional impromptu performances by visiting rock stars. Owner Isao Matsuyama also runs the warehouse-based club **Ink Stick Shibaura Factory** (live music, tango) and the café-brasserie **Tango**, both in Tokyo Bay.

JAVA JIVE, Roppongi Square Bldg, B2, 3-10-3 Roppongi, Minato-ku
☎ (03) 478 0087
A disco-bar with sand and sun-chairs on the dance floor, and a vibrant calypso/reggae beat drummed out by live bands. More trad disco rhythms in between sessions. Bankers, models and Roppongi ravers crowd in at weekends.

LEXINGTON QUEEN, 3rd Goto Bldg, B1, 3-13-14 Roppongi, Minato-ku
☎ (03) 401 1661
If there's a star in town, you can bet they'll wind up at this nightclub. Proprietor Bill Hersey has thrown brilliant beanos for Michael Jackson, Madonna, Bob Geldof, Eric Clapton, Whitney Houston, Tina Turner, Rod Stewart, David Bowie, et al. In attendance are sleek models, groupies and paparazzi.

LIVE HOUSE LOLLIPOP, Nittaku Bldg, 3-8-15 Roppongi, Minato-ku ☎ (03) 478 0028
A fun late-night bar with live music and a hairdressery clientele. On the 1st floor is the Beatles Live House, where look- and sound-alikes strum to the 60s beat.

SAMBA CLUB, 2F, 2-7-2 Nishi Shinjuku
☎ (03) 342 8877
If you want to avoid the endless crush of teeny-weenyboppers, try this plush nightclub – a more affluent, *mature* crowd.

—— Fashion designers ——

COMME DES GARCONS, 5-11-5 Minami-Aoyama, Minato-ku
☎ (03) 407 2480
The best, most respected designer from Japan, Rei Kawakubo is the matriarch of the Jap bag-lady look. While remaining purist, élitist and

avant-garde, she swings gently with the tide of fashion. She's also tops for unbalanced shoes, lingerie and hats. Homme Plus is cult among men, as STEPHEN JONES vouches. Rei designed her shop – small, with a minimal stock strewn carelessly on shelves and hangers (hours of fastidious arrangement go into creating this effect).

Japan's Best Designers

I	REI KAWAKUBO for COMME DES GARCONS
2	ISSEY MIYAKE
3	YOHJI YAMAMOTO
4	MATSUDA
5	HANAE MORI

HANAE MORI, Omotesando, 3-6-1 Kita-Aoyama, Minato-ku ☎ (03) 400 3301
'The Iron Butterfly' goes from strength to strength as a world fashion figure. Her métier is the little Ascot-style printed silk dress, but there's a whole lot more besides: couture and prêt-à-porter, tights, bedlinen, jewellery, handkerchiefs – all laid out in her own building.

ISSEY MIYAKE, Tessenkai Bldg, B1, 4-21-29 Minami-Aoyama, Minato-ku ☎ (03) 423 1408
Miyake sticks to his philosophy and loyal wearers stick to him. Hallmarks are organic origami cuts (stand-away leaf-pointed necks, armoured elbows), wrong-buttoning, unnerving colour mixes, inventive synthetics (metallic pleating), two outfits for the price of one (jackets turn into bags, bags back into fake-fur coats). But he ain't as weird as all that – KEN HOM likes him *"simply because he cuts clothes for the modern Asian man. Really nice and tailored-looking without being too strange and outlandish. You can walk into a business meeting wearing some of his classical things."* JOSETTE SIMON says: *"My favourite because I think absolutely anybody can wear his clothes – all ages, sizes, professions. Not only are they beautifully designed and cut, but they totally translate themselves to the wearer. You wear them, they don't wear you."* Less expensive lines are Plantation and Issey Sports. *"He has a natural, sympathetic approach to fashion. That is the way fashion will be going in the 90s"* – STEPHEN JONES.

JUNKO KOSHINO, 6-5-36 Minami-Aoyama, Minato-ku ☎ (03) 498 3404
Skiwear meets Star Trek. Sculptural lean and mean looks in black leather, jersey and rubberized fabrics, to show off every contour of the body. An increasing international presence.

MATSUDA for MADAME NICOLE, Nicole Bldg, 3-1-25 Jingumae, Shibuya-ku ☎ (03) 470 4821
Known as Matsuda overseas, he is head of the Nicole empire in Japan. Beautifully made suits, dresses, separates and menswear in luxury fabrics with superb detailing (insets of contrast fabric, intricate embroidery).

STUDIO-V by IRIE, Hanae Mori Bldg, Omotesando, 3-6-1 Kita-Aoyama, Minato-ku ☎ (03) 406 3177
A collective label for Hanae Mori's swinging young protégés, including Irie Sueo, a former designer for Kenzo.

TAKEO KIKUCHI, 6-6-22 Minami-Aoyama, Minato-ku ☎ (03) 486 6607
Witty, inventive menswear designer for guys with personality. His TK Building in Nishi Azabu is an extension of his tongue-in-cheek view of life – here his shop emulates a British prep-school bedsit.

TOKIO KUMAGAI, 3-15-10 Sendagaya, Shibuya-ku ☎ (03) 475 5317
Darling of Paris and Tokyo alike for his nutty couture-look shoes, he also does men's and women's wear, with the same irreverent spirit that possesses the Parisians. Frivolous feet find themselves encased in shoes half-chequered and half-leopard skin.

> **❝ Japan is successful because she copies well and improves what she copies . . . so much so that there's no one else left to copy, so she now copies herself! ❞**
>
> BENNY ONG

YOHJI YAMAMOTO, Maison Roppongi, 3F, 6-4-9 Roppongi, Minato-ku ☎ (03) 423 3200
Ringleader of the original gang of three, a masterful tailor and champion of origami asymmetrics. His clothes mould to your figure and feel like they were created for you alone. BEATRICE DALLE and Michèle Halberstadt adore their Yohjis.

YUKIKO HANAI for MADAME HANAI, Roi Bldg, 2F, 5-5-1 Roppongi, Minato-ku ☎ (03) 404 5791
A designer in the Hanae Mori mould – the up-market, conservative look for young Tokyo.

Hotels

CAPITOL TOKYU, 2-10-3 Nagata-cho, Chiyoda-ku ☎ (03) 581 4511
Still the favourite of Tokyoites in the know.

Best Bathrooms

"I think bathrooms are important...the ones in the **Regent**, *Hong Kong, are the most opulent. Frankly, I don't care about all these Jacuzzi things – you slide down and wind up ducking yourself. I like* any *bathroom, as long as it has an American adjustable shower rose, which goes from full spray to fine, and has high pressure"* – LORD LICHFIELD. EDWARD CARTER spouts forth: *"I think the Americans are the only people who really understand water. Americans get into a shower and they are there for 20 minutes, which would deplete most other people's supply of hot water.*

The most beautifully designed bathrooms are at **Boyer** *in Rheims. I don't know how many acres of marble slabs it took to make them...they are all grain-matched in every direction. They have fantastic custom-fitted cupboards, low-voltage lighting, magnifying mirrors, scales – terrific."* He also commends **Hotel Seiyo**, Tokyo (individual steam baths, humidity control, and heated mirrors that don't steam up), and **Brenners Park Hotel**, Baden Baden (heated marble floors). JEFFERY TOLMAN rates the bathrooms of the **Four Seasons**, Philadelphia, the best.

Rudolf Nureyev, Yehudi Menuhin, Phil Collins and other stars stay. Rooms are functional, décor garish – but that's par for the course.

HOTEL OKURA, 2-10-4 Toranomon, Minato-ku ☎ (03) 582 0111
Remains top of the pops, particularly with big-thinking Americans, despite being a hotel of the airport-lounge era – lurid décor, piped music. Like a mini-town, all you could ever want is there on tap: 8 restaurants, 4 bars, 41 shops, Japanese spa and massage, post office, photo studio, and flower arrangement and tea ceremony room. *"The most courteous and efficient hotel I've come across"* – MICHAEL BROADBENT. One of ANDRE PREVIN's top 3.

🏨 HOTEL SEIYO, 1-11-2 Ginza, Chuo-ku ☎ (03) 535 1111
One of a kind in this city of convention-orientated impersonal hotels. Only 80 luxury suites and supremely attentive service. The best of East and West philosophy means a 3:1 staff:guest ratio; proper American and English breakfasts; personal secretary and butler; a choice of 7 pillows; individual air-con and humidifier; a small

TV and radio in each sleek bathroom. Several top restaurants (including a branch of **Kiccho**) make it the top meeting place in town, like a club to dine or drink in. Liz Taylor goes. *"The best hotel in the world. Service is just staggering, down to getting your personal telephonist who deals with you and no one else. Food is wonderful and the rooms are just beautiful, the best"* – JEFFREY ARCHER. EDWARD CARTER adds his vote.

IMPERIAL HOTEL, 1-1-1 Uchisaiwaicho, Chiyoda-ku ☎ (03) 504 1111
A good location and an address that opens doors, this remains No 1 for foreign finance boys (particularly the younger, European set, who hang out at the Old Imperial Bar). Large and always chock-a-block. In common with ie tout Tokyo, it's screamingly expensive and lacks the personal touch; on the other hand, where else provides you with jogging togs for your 3-mile run round the Imperial Castle?

MEGURO GAJOEN, 1-8-1 Shimo Meguro, Meguro-ku ☎ (03) 491 0074
Real Japanese style in central Tokyo – an unusual ryokan with 'baroque' interior.

🏨 Buzzz STEPHEN JONES has the measure of massage in Tokyo. **Shiseido Beauty Parlour** is fab for a facial. *"Imagine you are a dolphin swimming along and you can feel the water rushing against your face... it's the most beyond experience"* – SJ. Tiny tiny **Tom Tom** salon *"does a hand massage that is the most extraordinary feeling in the world"* – SJ🏨......The best **designer sale** is at **Isetan** department store, 14-1-3 Shinjuku-ku ☎ (03) 352 1111, in Feb and Aug🏨...... Designer 2: a haven for the best of Japanese designer clothing under one roof is **From 1st**, 5-3-10 Minami-Aoyama, Minato-ku ☎ (03) 499 6786🏨......**The Dome**, Kanda, is the new hot concert venue for top visiting acts – Mick Jagger, Michael Jackson and Huey Lewis have stopped by. Just keep your ear to the ground for info... 🏨

The Great Escape

When muggy summers take their toll, Tokyo-dwellers clear off to **Karuizawa**, two hours north-west of the city, 3,200 ft above sea level, a cool, invigorating retreat for princes and artistic types alike. Gaijin nip off to the white sandy beaches of the **Izu** peninsula, some three hours from Tokyo, to the **PENSION SUNNY STEPS** ☎ (05582) 21999. Here you can lap up Pacific sunrises and dine on Mediterranean-style seafood. A room, bath, TV and 2 meals all for a paltry 13,000 yen.

Music

CASALS HALL, Ocanomizu Square 126, Kanda Surugadai, Chiyoda-ku ☎ (03) 294 1229
"*A very intimate concert hall, specifically designed for chamber music. There's a very, very good atmosphere there – it's one of those places where you really feel in touch with the audience*" – JULIAN LLOYD WEBBER.

SUNTORY MUSIC HALL, 1-13-1 Akasaka, Minato-ku ☎ (03) 505 1001
The Japanese beerage have sunk a fortune into making this the most advanced concert hall in the world, the apotheosis of Japanese technology. Leading conductors are itching to wave their batons here.

Restaurants

In Japan, it is usually advisable to dine at lunchtime from the set menu. Forget paying *double* à la carte – expect to *add a nought* to your bill.

A TANTOT, Axis Bldg, 3F, 5-17-1 Roppongi, Minato-ku ☎ (03) 586 4431
In the middle of the ultimate designer shopping arcade is the ultimate designer restaurant. Food is French/japonais.

BODAIJU, Bukkyo Dendo Center Bldg, 2F, 4-3-14 Shiba, Minato-ku ☎ (03) 456 3257
The official restaurant of the Buddhism Promotion foundation (the only place in Tokyo with ancient Chinese vegetarian cuisine). Excitingly different from the established Chinese cuisines.

CHIANTI, 3-1-7 Azabudai, Minato-ku: B1 ☎ (03) 583 7546; **2F** ☎ (03) 583 2240
Smart Italian that still plays to packed gaijin houses. Spaghetti alla vongole is a fave, followed by a sensational chocolate mousse and a mean espresso.

🎴 **FUKUZUSHI, 5-7-8 Roppongi, Minato-ku** ☎ (03) 402 4116
The ultimate Japanese restaurant for top-of-the-tree gaijin to entertain at (*heads* of broking houses). Marvellous traditional sushi bar and drinking bar. Also tops for chirashizushi, a platter of rice with raw fish laid out on top – roll-your-own sushi for DIY freaks.

🎴 **IL BOCCAIONE, Silk-Ebisu, 1F, 1-15-9 Ebisu, Shibuya-ku** ☎ (03) 449 1430
A new eatery for Italian country cuisine, cooked by Italians, who concoct hearty Tuscan dishes and occasionally burst into emotional discussions in their native tongue. "*Wonderful Italian restaurant, the nearest you'll get to the real thing in Tokyo. Recommended are the costoletta Boccaiona and the risotto served in a huge half-case of Parmesan cheese. The setting is 'paysan' and the only sleek thing you'll find here is Silvano, who runs the place*" – SARAH LONSDALE. Essential to book.

INAGIKU, 2-9-8 Nihonbashi Kayabacho, Chuo-ku ☎ (03) 669 5501
If you have a yen for tempura, this is the place – it has a list of 18 types. The height of luxury with hovering service.

> 🎴 ***One thing you must note is that Japan is breathtakingly expensive and the best places require an introduction by a Japanese***  BARBARA KAFKA

INAKAYA, 7-8-4 Roppongi, Minato-ku ☎ (03) 405 9866
The best true-Jap experience for visitors. *The* place for robatayaki (roast-buttered-grilled) amid a barrage of screaming and shouting. This noisy 'hello/welcome/sit down' is the norm, as is an elaborate clapping ceremony at each change of shifts. Food is served on long paddles. Apart from grilled prawns, fish, meat, etc, try nasu (aubergine) and jagaimo (potato).

KEIKA, 3-25-6 Shinjuku, Shinjuku-ku ☎ (03) 352 4836
Perhaps the very best ramen (robust, Chinese-style noodles) are those sold on street stalls under red lanterns. Such stalls are usually run by the yakuza (mafia) and it's not uncommon to find someone's little finger in your ramen. Beastly. However, if there is no red light in your district, Keika comes a close second for digit-free noodles.

🎴 **KISSO, Axis Bldg, B1, 5-17-1 Roppongi, Minato-ku** ☎ (03) 582 4191
This modern, fashionable, gaijin-friendly eatery

is the answer for those who are nervous of the formality of kaiseki ryori (it can be a tense experience).

⚓ LE CHINOIS, Bianca Bldg, 3-1-26 Jingumae, Shibuya-ku ☎ (03) 403 3929
Tokyo's most strangely glamorous restaurant, drawing late-night city sleekers. Décor is art deco (it inspired Wolfgang Puck's Chinois on Main in LA). The food is not wildly authentic Chinese, just clever-Zennish.

LES CHOUX, Central Toriizaka, 5-11-28 Roppongi, Minato-ku ☎ (03) 470 5511
The Sunday lunchery for gaijin, who grab the rare chance of sitting at outdoor tables. Chef Makino makes regular trips to France and concocts incredible desserts, the best lemon tart.

L'ORANGERIE, Hanae Mori Bldg, Omotesando, 3-6-1 Kita Aoyama ☎ (03) 407 7461
An elegant airy dining room, the place to be seen for brunch on Sunday. Fashion designers (including Madame Mori), architects, anyone who's in town, crowd in for the brill buffet.

♟ MAISON CAVIAR, Aoyama-dori, Shibuya-ku ☎ (03) 470 0063
Caviare, caviare and more caviare – Chinese, Russian and Iranian. Along the lines of Petrossian in Paris, it's the ultimate spot to see and be seen (Robert De Niro and Dolph Lundgren for starters). Next door to Daimaru Peacock store.

SELAN, Nakamiki-dori, Shibuya-ku ☎ (03) 478 2200
Surf 'n' turf's up at this crackling seafood and steak joint, sister to the hot-shot Chaya Brasserie in LA. Decorated à la Spago, it's one that Christopher Lambert gallops along to.

SPAGO, 5-7-8 Roppongi, Minato-ku ☎ (03) 423 4025
Though not quite as hip as it was, LA's sister pizza parlour still pulls a yuppie set for such culinary attractions as marinated raw tuna with red caviare, and capelli di angeli (angel hair pasta with goat's cheese and asparagus).

SUSHI BAR SAI, Dandling Core Andos Bldg, 2F, 1-7-5 Jinnan, Shibuya-ku ☎ (03) 496 6333
Sushi California-style. Combining the best of both sides of the Pacific, this is the real, fresh-as-fresh Japanese thing. Also tofu and vegetable sushi. Gaijin love it.

YOSHIWARA, 3-1-6 Kalgah, Minato-ku ☎ (03) 453 4235
An overkill of futuristic monochrome sleekness and steel in the capital has prompted a return to the serenity of Zen and to the basics of Japanese design. A couple of floors above the club Gold is this membership bar/restaurant that smacks of a Kyoto geisha house. Trad interior with tatami

mats, bamboo blinds and paper screens, plus the odd concession to the West – a long bar, and a Jacuzzi, of all things, with a view over Tokyo Bay. SARAH LONSDALE is impressed.

Shopping

Ginza has the major stores – Matsuya, Mitsukoshi, Takashimaya, Isetan, Kanebo, Hankyu and Seibu (avoid on Sunday when the whole of Tokyo tries to cram into the street). **Minami-Aoyama**, breeding ground for Yohji and the gang, is still a serious trend centre and forcing house for young designers; **Kita-Aoyama** and **Jingumae** are similarly trendoid. **Omotesando** is the sleek fashion boulevard, with the Hanae Mori Bldg, Spiral, Vivre 21, etc; it leads into Harajuku, with its boutiques and stalls.

AXIS, 5-17-1 Roppongi, Minato-ku ☎ (03) 587 2781
Designer building for design products (their slogan is 'living/design/concept'). The best in minimalist furniture, tableware, kitchen goods, crafts, fabrics and more.

BOUTIQUE YUYA, 3-10-12 Moto-Azabu, Minato-ku ☎ (03) 408 5749
The best place to find contemporary clothes made up in traditional, out-of-this-world Japanese kimono fabrics.

MATSUYA, 3-6-1 Ginza, Chuo-ku ☎ (03) 567 1211
A marvellous store displaying the whole gamut of fashion, plus, on the 7th floor, some of the world's best contemporary product design.

NUNO, Axis Bldg, B1, 5-17-1 Roppongi, Minato-ku ☎ (03) 582 7997
The best traditional fabrics. The place for beautiful hand-painted or printed silk kimono lengths.

ORIENTAL BAZAAR, Omotesando, 5-9-13 Jingumae, Shibuya-ku ☎ (03) 400 3933
For authentic, trad Japanese crafts and goods – little lacquer bowls and chopsticks, pearls, hand-blocked prints, paintings, china, furniture and ornate wedding kimonos of heavy silk brocade – to hang on the wall rather than your person.

PARCO, 15-1 Udagawa-cho, Shibuya-ku ☎ (03) 464 5111
Stylish Japanese shopping phenomenon, a store in the Seibu group. Divided into Parts 1 (general – for good, less extortionate shopping), 2 (the smallest – for one-stop Jap designer boutiques) and 3. A haven of customized shoplets where international designerdom vies for Tokyo's most taste-ridden customers. Its own exhibition space, cinema and theatre in Part 1.

SEED, 21-1 Udagawa-cho, Shibuya-ku ☎ (03) 462 0111
Tall, slim and grey, this is the chic-est part of

Seibu, home to all the trendsetters in fashion. On 2F ('The Express') are the young international crew – Hamnett, Betty Jackson, NO? YES!. 3F ('The Season') is for the last word in trendsetting accessories. Also cool menswear, the best of up-and-coming Jap fash as well as Miyake and the gang, fab jewellery and an English Tea House called Café Anglais.

SEIBU, (Ginza), 2-1 Yurakucho, Chiyoda-ku ☎ (03) 286 0111 and branches
The biggest and best store showing the cream of world fashion and design. A full spectrum of shoplets – Hermès, Vuitton, Rykiel, Lauren, Miyake, Comme des Garçons, Yamamoto and the young Japs – cover all fashion permutations, from indigenous futurist stretchy black to the English country look. Great for presents and Gaijin-sized tights. The foreign customer helpline is ☎ (03) 286 5482.

VIVRE 21, Omotesando, 5-10-1 Jingumae, Shibuya-ku ☎ (03) 498 2221
Slick, unusually spacious hall of fashion. Shin Hosokawa, Takeo Kikuchi, Nicole et al keep company with Jean-Paul Gaultier (in a replica of his steely Paris shop) and Koshin Satoh (in a sci-fi horror-movie theme cavern).

WAVE, 6-2-21 Roppongi, Minato-ku ☎ (03) 408 0111
The music store, tops for pop videos, compact discs, video laser discs and other state-of-the-art hi-fiery. Designer goods, too.

Theatre

Find out about performances of the traditional theatrical art forms of **kabuki, nō** and **bunraku** via the weekly *Tour Companion*. The best kabuki is at **Kabuki-za Theatre**, 4-12-5 Ginza, Chuo-ku ☎ (03) 541 3131 (in front of Higashi Ginza station). English-language programmes.

TAKARAZUKA, Takarazuka Theatre, 1-1-3 Yuracho, Chiyoda-ku ☎ (03) 580 1251
In answer to the all-male kabuki is this 500-strong all-girl revue, where women play the male roles. Eat your heart out, Ziegfeld.

· REST OF ·
JAPAN
Art and museums

HAKONE OPEN AIR MUSEUM, Kanagawa-ken ☎ (0460) 21161
A great collection of Japanese and Western sculpture set in gardens and galleries. Take the special open-top train, the Romance Car, from Shinjuku in Tokyo. Afterwards steam all intellectual thoughts away at the nearby hot springs.

Hotels

FUJIYA HOTEL, 359 Miyanoshita, Hakone ☎ (0460) 22211
The first Western-style hotel in Japan in a lovely position near Mount Fuji. Marvellously ramshackle yet scrupulously clean. The annexe, a former imperial villa, is run in the ryokan style. Former guests range from Douglas Fairbanks and Mary Pickford to Gandhi. Best time to visit is May when it's awash with azaleas.

MIYAJIMA LODGE, Miyajima ☎ (0829) 442233
A beautiful country inn on a little island outside Hiroshima, with the full bowing and scraping service/steaming bath/personally cooked dinner/tatami mat and futon treatment. Prince Charles has visited and the Emperor of Japan has a house nearby. *"An experience you never forget,"* sighs ANTON MOSIMANN.

Restaurants

ARAGAWA, 2-15-18 Nakayamate-dori, Chuo-ku, Kobe ☎ (078) 221 8547
Stupendous steakery, using beef from specially bred cattle. SHIZUO TSUJI holds it in high esteem.

SANKO-IN-TEMPLE, 3-1-36 Hon-machi, Koganei-chi ☎ (0423) 811116
Book a month in advance if you want to sample

Buzzz A thousand ways to indigestion: In Japan there are some 329 railway stations that sell **O-bento**, or boxed lunches, but some 2,872 different kinds of bento. You could spend an awayday just **guzzling**... .... Take a walk along the old **Tokaido road**, made famous by woodblock artists such as Hokusai and Hiroshige. Accessible from the Fujiya Hotel...... The Shogun era lives on at **Kanazawa**, a small neighbourhood of samurai houses. Set on the rugged Sea of Japan coast, it's also home of **Kenrokuen Park**, one of the 3 loveliest gardens in the country...... Clock the following English-speaking travel agents who make things tick: **STA Travel**, Sanden Bldg, 5F, 3-5-5 Kojimachi, Chiyoda-ku ☎ (03) 221 1043; **No 1** Travel, Shoritsu Bldg, 3F, 7-8-12 Nishi Shinjuku, Shinjuku-ku ☎ (03) 366 2429.......

Plain Tales from the Ryokan

"When you arrive at a ryokan, the mama-san snaps her fingers and points to one of the maids, who looks fairly shattered at the European hairy barbarians in front of her, but shuffles over in tiny steps, bows very low and tries to pick up all your bags. At one ryokan, the maid grabbed a carrier bag that contained a bottle of vodka and some sticky orange (we couldn't get any tonic). She wrenched it from us, carried it a couple of yards, then the handle broke. It fell on the marble floor and the orange smashed. We really did think she was going to commit harakiri because she had lost such face. As a result, we were given a huge feast on the house in which the centrepiece after several courses was a large whole fish with mountains of greenery and dry ice and a smoky volcano. The top side had been sliced, diced and replaced in the shape of the fish. It was brought in with a great deal of ceremony and a bottle of sake was poured down its mouth – at which point, to show it was really fresh, it came alive and waggled its tail" – ROBIN HANBURY-TENISON.

Buddhism for an afternoon. At this peaceful Buddhist temple (the only one of it's kind open to foreigners) nuns prepare shojin ryori (vegan Buddhist food). Float in to your private room and await the understated mouthfuls.

Ski resorts

NAEBA
A resort surrounded by luxury natural hot springs (après-ski in Japan consists of lolling around in a steaming bath). The Emperor visits annually.

SAPPORO
On the north island of Hokkaido, this resort has excellent snow and hot-spring bathing. Despite being difficult to get to and bitterly cold, it's getting as crowded as other resorts (beware squads of kamikaze skiers). Site of the celebrated annual Snow Festival and the world-renowned brewery (open to the public).

ZAO
A top ski resort, in one of Japan's most beautiful natural parks. Best hotel: the nearby **Yamagata Grand**.

KENYA

GIRAFFE MANOR, PO Box 15004, Langata, Nairobi ☎ (02) 891078. Reservations c/o AFEW, 1512 Bolton St, Baltimore, MD 21217 ☎ (301) 346 6146
"If you want something really unusual, you can be a PG here. It's a mock-Tudor mansion with views over the Ngong Hills, right near Karen Blixen's house. It's also a reserve for Rothschild giraffe, which wander around the mowed lawns . . . you are often woken up in the morning by Daisy, who is 18ft tall, sticking her head in your window. A very cute little place" – EDWARD CARTER. Being a registered charity, African Fund for Endangered Wildlife, about 60% of the room fee is tax-deductible.

LAMU
A small island and former trading port with Arabia, dating back to the 10C. Free from traffic (transport by dhow or donkey) and surrounded by deserted beach. Best hotel: **Peponi Hotel**, PO Box 24, Lamu ☎ (0121) 3029, small, informal and right on an 8-mile beach in Shella, a little fishing village with minareted mosques. Indulge in all water sports, deep-sea fishing, a dhow cruise, and a 'Neap Tide Goggling Trip'.

MASAI MARA GAME RESERVE
One of the greatest wildlife areas in the world, where a spectacular migration of wildebeest and zebras arrives from the Serengeti, accompanied by numerous predators. Best camp: **Kichwa Tembo Camp**.

🐾 MOUNT KENYA SAFARI CLUB, PO Box 35, Nanyuki ☎ (0176) 33323
One of the best hotels in Africa, a cameo of old colonial days. On the slopes of Mount Kenya, it's set in 200 acres of rolling turf with beautifully manicured flower-beds, a walled rose garden, ponds, vegetable and nursery gardens and a mountain stream with waterfalls. With its own airfield and satellite communications to the world, international VIPs can rest easy.

SAFARI HOTEL AND COUNTRY CLUB, PO Box 45038, Nairobi ☎ (02) 802493
"If you want to stay at a hotel in Nairobi, this is the one (the Norfolk is rather tired and tatty). It has the largest swimming pool in Africa" – EDWARD CARTER.

SAMBURU GAME RESERVE
A wild, semi-desert area bordering the Uaso

Nyiro River, where zillions of animals and birds drop in. Rare species include Grevy's zebra, oryx and the reticulated giraffe. Best hotels: **Samburu Lodge** and **Larsen's Camp**.

TSAVO NATIONAL PARK

The first and largest game park in Kenya where, on a clear night, you can observe wildlife at illuminated watering holes and, on a clear day, you can't miss the snow-capped summit of Mount Kilimanjaro. Best lodge: **Kilaguni Lodge**, c/o African Tours & Hotels, PO Box 30471, Nairobi ☎ (02) 336858; or London ☎ (01) 541 1199.

TREETOPS, c/o Block Hotels Central Reservations Office, Rehema House Arcade, PO Box 47447, Nairobi ☎ (02) 335807

The famous lodge on stilts where royals and other elevated guests dine at giraffe level overlooking water-holes and salt licks. An overnighter only, to observe game by night. A sheet of glass divides man and beast, for those pesky baboons have acquired more of a taste for Wallbangers than water.

———— *Tours* ————

See also **Silk Cut Travel**, **Tempo Travel** and **Tippett's Safaris** (Travel Directory).

ABERCROMBIE & KENT (see Travel Directory)

Particularly hot on Kenya. On top of the best land safaris, they arrange hot-air balloon trips, wing safaris, camel safaris, and stays in private homes and farms.

AIR KENYA, PO Box 30357, Nairobi ☎ (02) 501601 and SAFARI AIR, PO Box 41951, Nairobi ☎ (02) 501211

Flights to remote and inaccessible parts of Kenya.

EAST AFRICAN WILDLIFE SAFARIS (see Travel Directory)

Jock Anderson's Private Mobile Camping Safaris will convince you that camping knocks spots off a lodge-to-lodge safari. Luxury, tailor-made tours across all the best game reserves. Or fly over by plane or hot-air balloon. Clients have included John Travolta, Caroline Kennedy and Jackie Onassis.

> **"***In Uganda, the Queen Elizabeth game sanctuary at the foot of the Rwenzori Mountains is one of the most enjoyable in Africa. You never see a tourist . . .* "**

 QUENTIN CREWE

KOREA

HOTEL SHILLA, 202 2-Ga, Jangchung-Dong, Chung-Ku, Seoul ☎ (2) 233 3131

Set in 23 acres of sculpture-filled parkland, this modern hotel uses the traditional-style former state guest house as its annexe. Suites of immense grandeur, 7 restaurants with a range of cuisines from East and West (**Sorabol** serves classical Korean), health club and indoor pool. Interestingly, locals don't place it at the top.

THE WESTIN CHOSUN, CPO Box 3706, 87 Sogong-Dong, Chung-Ku, Seoul ☎ (2) 77105

This is the old favourite, set in the centre of the business district, beside a historic pagoda-like temple. High standards appeal to the biz crowd. No less than 8 restaurants, and the only outdoor pool in the city.

MALAYSIA

GENTING HIGHLANDS

GENTING HIGHLANDS RESORT, 69000 Pahang Darul Makmur ☎ (03) 211 1118

Extensive hill-station resort where high-rolling Singapore and Malay Chinese helicopter in to gamble away their weekends. 3 hotels, the Casino De Genting, Awana Golf & Country Club, dazzling Disco 6000 (that's the number of feet above sea level), horse ranch, bowling, squash, swimming, lakeside amusement park with rollercoaster, boating and mini railway – the number of thrilling ways to excite yourself here are inexhaustible.

KUALA LUMPUR

PARKROYAL, Jalan Sultan Ismail, 50250 ☎ (03) 242 5588

This fine hotel (the old Regent), with its beautiful hand-carved wooden lobby, has undergone a major refurbishment – additions include marble bathrooms, a new Cantonese restaurant, and the **Grill**.

REGENT OF KUALA LUMPUR, 160 Jalan Bukit Bintang, 55100 ☎ (03) 241 8000

A brand new, plushly appointed 470-room whopper, offering all you'd expect – spacious rooms, health club, pool and squash courts; Chinese, Japanese, Malay and Western cuisine.

SHANGRI-LA, 11 Jalan Sultan Ismail, 50250 ☎ (03) 232 2388
Roomy, flashy, busy...a 28-storey hotel with over 700 rooms and suites. Nancy Reagan took over several floors when she stayed with her entourage. The pretty blue and rose **Lafite** is one of the best Western restaurants in KL; **Nadaman** remains the best Japanese.

PENANG

EASTERN & ORIENTAL HOTEL, 10 Farquhar St, 10200 ☎ (04) 375322
One of the old colonial haunts of Somerset Maugham and Noel Coward. Set in mature gardens facing the Indian Ocean, it's still the place to meet for an E&O Colada or an E&O Sling. Dine in candlelit Victorian grandeur at the **1885 Grill**.

PENANG MUTIARA, Jalan Teluk Bahang, 11050 ☎ (04) 812828
The best beach hotel on the best beach in Penang. Addled expats come here to relax over a G&T in the pool bar. Service is as swish as the spacious surroundings. All water sports, tennis, fitness centre, and dining Japanese, Chinese or Italian style. Recommended by LORD LICHFIELD.

MEXICO

LAS BRISAS, PO Box 281, 39868 Acapulco ☎ (748) 41580
Glorious resort in gardens splurged with violet bougainvillaea and scarlet hibiscus, high in the hills above Acapulco Bay. The 300 individual 'casitas' have their own or shared pools, garnished daily with fresh flowers. *"My favourite hotel. It's terribly romantic, absolutely superb"* – ROSS BENSON. Catch a pink jeep down to the sea, skin-dive, waterski, take a yacht cruise or bask under open white tents.

❝I love Mexico in winter when it is cold everywhere else. The west coast has the most reliable winter climate in the whole world. The Mexicans are very friendly, warm people❞

 STANLEY MARCUS

HOTEL GARZA BLANCA, PO Box 58, Puerto Vallarta, Jalisco ☎ (322) 21023
The in place in the in place, near where Liz Taylor has a villa. Suites right on the little bleached sandy shore or Mexican villas with private garden and pool.

MOROCCO

— *Hotels* —

EL MINZAH, 85 Rue de la Liberté, Tangier ☎ (9) 35885
The best hotel in the heart of the only resort city where the Med and Atlantic meet. Moorish red salon; shady arcaded courtyard.

LA GAZELLE D'OR, PO Box 60, Taroudant ☎ (085) 2039
Extraordinary oasis resort near a fortified town in the Atlas mountains. A fantasyland of 30 bungalows, kitted out with a plethora of mosaics, antiques and marble, set in acres of orange groves and tropical gardens. Tennis, riding, lovely pool, starlit dining.

LA MAMOUNIA, Ave Bab Djedid, Marrakech ☎ (4) 48981
A Moorish extravaganza with intricate mosaics, acres of marble, painted cedar, and a wonderful Andalusian patio with fountains. Some feel it has lost some of its old magic after various unsympathetic revamps, but it is nevertheless an *experience*. Fab health and beauty facilities, with hammam and sauna.

PALAIS JAMAI, Bab-el-Guissa, Fez ☎ (06) 34331
This hotel is an old luxury favourite, once an 18C palace, in suave Moroccan style. The service, restaurants and garden bounded by the Medina walls are still sensational.

— *Restaurants* —

MOHAMED ZKHIRI KAWTAR, 79 Sidi Ahmed Soussi ☎ (4) 41903
"The best restaurant for local dishes" – MARIUCCIA MANDELLI. Try for tajine, couscous, salads, fish, pigeon and other traditional Moroccan food.

NEPAL

THE SOALTEE OBEROI, PO Box 97, Tahachal, Kathmandu ☎ (01) 211106
The best hotel in town, with the recent addition of 7 extremely plushy suites. Lovely pool, tennis and health club.

TIGER TOPS JUNGLE LODGE, PO Box 242, Kathmandu ☎ (01) 222706
Based in the great Royal Chitwan National Park, this famous lodge has hosted the British royal family, all earnestly safari-suited, and the elephant polo championships. Stay in thatched houses on stilts; search for the elusive Royal Bengal Tiger by elephant or Land-Rover, and spot the rare freshwater dolphin and fish-eating gharial croc by boat.

─────── *Tours* ───────

MOUNTAIN TRAVEL NEPAL, PO Box 170, Kathmandu ☎ (01) 414508
The oldest, highest-quality Himalayan trekking company, founded by ex-British Army officer and mountaineer Colonel Jimmy Roberts. Owners of the Tiger Tops clan that includes the Jungle Lodge (above), the **Tiger Tops Tented Camp**, on an island on the edge of the Chitwan park, and the **Tharu Village** for only 16, staying in a custom-made traditional longhouse, among the Tharu villagers. Also the new **Karnali Lodge** and **Tented Camp** with wildlife viewing by elephant and river rafting.

NETHERLANDS

AMSTERDAM

─── *Art and museums* ───

REMBRANDTHUIS, Jodenbreestraat 6, 1011 NK ☎ (020) 249486
Former home of the greatest Dutch artist. Virtually all his etchings and sketches remain in tribute.

RIJKSMUSEUM VINCENT VAN GOGH, Paulus Potterstraat 7, 1071 CX ☎ (020) 764881
About 200 paintings and 500 drawings by Van Gogh and co (*The Sower*, *Vincent's Bedroom*, a version of *Sunflowers*), plus memorabilia.

🐦 RIJKSMUSEUM, Stadhouderskade 42, 1071 ZD ☎ (020) 732121
Not only the unsurpassed collection of 17C Dutch paintings (plus 16C, 18C and 19C) but also sculpture, antique furniture, Delft pottery, silver, glassware and lace. See Rembrandt's *Jewish Bride* and the enormous *Night Watch*.

🐦 STEDELIJK MUSEUM, Paulus Potterstraat 13, 1071 CX ☎ (020) 573 2911
The national collection of modern (from 1850) and contemporary art, with fine examples of Matisse, Picasso, Rothko and Stella. Strong on artistic developments since 1950. Changing exhibitions.

─────── *Hotels* ───────

🐦 AMSTEL HOTEL, Professor Tulpplein 1, 1018 GX ☎ (020) 226060
Super-grand hotel run by Inter-Continental, right on the river. Impressive entrance with marble floor, Oriental carpets and magnificent stairway leading up to a balustraded balcony. Elegant library-like restaurant, **La Rive**; riverside terrace. Mammoth champagne brunch on Sundays.

HOTEL DE L'EUROPE, Nieuwe Doelenstraat 2-8, 1012 CP ☎ (020) 234836
Heineken-owned hotel by the River Amstel, with a lovely terrace, elegant rooms, and the marvellous restaurant, **Excelsior**, that refreshes the parts others cannot reach.

HOTEL PULITZER, Prinsengracht 315-331, 1016 GZ ☎ (020) 523 5235
Behind the façades of 24 narrow, gabled 17C-18C town houses is this charmingly converted hotel. Set between the canals Prinsengracht and Keizersgracht, it's a labyrinth of corridors and stairs and low-beamed rooms, with interior gardens and an art gallery. The brainchild of Peter Pulitzer, grandchild of Joseph, it feels like a private house in real old-fashioned Amsterdam.

─────── *Music* ───────

CONCERTGEBOUW, Concertgebouwplan 2-6, 1071 LN ☎ (020) 718345
Amsterdam's leading concert hall, among the top 4 in the world for ANDRE PREVIN (on a par with the Symphony Hall in Boston and Carnegie Hall, New York).

🐦 Buzzz Dutch art beat: Pay homage to Hals at the **Frans Hals Museum**, in the artist's home town of Haarlem – dozens of his works and changing exhibitions... For **decorative and applied arts** (from the 16C on), **Boymans van Beuningen** in Rotterdam is the place; also 17C-18C paintings and drawings🐦...... **Eat beat**: BARRY HUMPHRIES plumps for the **Oesterbar**, 10 Leidseplein, Amsterdam ☎ (020) 232988: *"Very good for fresh fish"*.................. 🐦

Restaurants

BISTRO KLEIN PAARDENBURG,
Amstelzijde 59, 1184 TZ Ouderkerk a/s
Amstel ☎ (02963) 1335
Ton Fagel's buzzing riverside bistro is in a village
a few miles outside Amsterdam. Classic cuisine
updated with flair – fresh meat, fish and seafood
and outstanding salads. Fine wines.

DE LUTTE, 26-28 Laleagracht
☎ (020) 258548
Unpretentious, cosy restaurant serving eclectic
European cuisine and delicious outsize salads.
Ever-changing menu. Trompe-l'oeil and film-set
décor.

🍴 DE TRECHTER, 63 Hobbemakade,
1071 XL ☎ (020) 711263
Tiny and cosy (only 8 tables), this is one of the
best in town, for haute French cuisine. Specializes in smoked foods, made into imaginative
dishes. Don't miss the divine lobster cappuccino
– a bisque topped with creamy froth.

HET SWARTE SCHAAP, 24 Korte
Ledsedwairsstriit ☎ (020) 223021
The Black Sheep is a smart local favourite, in an
old-fashioned rustic setting. French-based seasonal cuisine (great game in winter); 4- or 5-
course set meals featuring whatever's freshest
from the market.

· REST OF THE ·
NETHERLANDS

Art and museums

MAURITSHUIS, Kortd Viverberg 8, The
Hague 2513 AB ☎ (070) 346 9244
Important architecturally (as one of the finest
Dutch Palladian houses, built 1630s), it holds a
marvellous collection of 17C Dutch paintings,
including the best of Vermeer and some notable
Rembrandts. A favourite museum of VISCOUNT
HAMBLEDEN.

RIJKSMUSEUM KROLLER-MULLER,
Houtkampweg 6, 6731 AW Otterlo
☎ (0838) 21041
A large and stunning collection of Van Gogh
master works, nearly all from his peak period
($$$), plus a contemporary sculpture garden. "*A*
great museum. Beautiful things by Van Gogh
that you don't remember ever having seen; mar-
vellous Impressionist pictures, all kinds of in-
teresting things. It's in what I call the 'Dutch
Alps' – where there is a very slight rise in the
ground.... You go by train north from Amster-
dam, then catch a bus and then go by bicycle –
keeps you fit" – BARRY HUMPHRIES.

Hotels

HOTEL DES INDES, Lange Voorhout
54-56, The Hague 2514 EG ☎ (070) 346 9553
Stately mid-19C house on the loveliest square in
town, near the Queen's palaces. Stunning classi-
cal salons. The Imperial Suite, with its own roof
terrace, is one you could really settle in to.
Previous settlers ranged from Mata Hari and
Haile Selassie to Anna Pavlova (who died here).

KASTEEL WITTEM, Wittemer Allée 3,
6286 AA Wittem-Zuid Limburg
☎ (04450) 1208
Small medieval castle some 8 miles from
Maastricht. Only a dozen raftered bedrooms,
including a suite in the tower. Gourmet candlelit
dining and renowned wine cellar.

Restaurants

JEAN MARTIN, Groenewegje 115, The
Hague ☎ (070) 380 2895
A highlight in an otherwise unsavoury area.
Lovely restaurant for honest cooking...fresh-
as-fresh food that speaks for itself, with no heavy
sauces but bundles of flavour. The style is French
with Chinese and Indonesian accents.

NEW ZEALAND

AUCKLAND

Hotels

🍴 THE REGENT AUCKLAND, Albert St,
Private Bag ☎ (09) 398882
The best international city hotel in the country,
for business persons and travellers alike. "*An*
oasis. The Regent carries world-class standards.
Not only are the appointments really wonderful,
but the service and the food...I think it's terribly
important when you're travelling to be able to
rely on a certain level of service and quality" –
KEN HOM. "*Comfortable suites overlooking*
Auckland harbour and the piers" – ELISE
PASCOE. Fine restaurants too: "**Longchamp**
has a wine list that is an education in New
Zealand wine" – DON HEWITSON. "*Excellent food*
and a good wine list," echoes EP.

Restaurants

🍴 ANTOINE'S, 333 Parnell Rd, Parnell 1
☎ (09) 798756
Based in one of the earliest colonial houses, this

knockout restaurant is run by the passionate chef Tony Astle, *"who is just crazy about food. Something as simple as a wonderful roast lamb he does with imagination: he gets a very young lamb (which is difficult to find because most of them are sheep) and roasts it with fresh herbs. ...When you eat this you think 'my God I'm in France'"* – KEN HOM. *"Getting even better. It's the best in New Zealand. I particularly like the salmon and chive beurre blanc. It also has a good wine list"* – DON HEWITSON.

BELL HOUSE, Bells Rd, Lloyd Ellsmore Park, Pakuranga ☎ (09) 564015

Chef-restaurateur and bright young returnee Simon Gault runs a fine eatery, based in an authentic colonial house. His cuisine takes trad English/French and adds Pacific accents.

CIN CIN ON QUAY, 99 Quay St ☎ (09) 376966

Warwick Brown's buzzy brasserie offers Italian, French, Chinese and Japanese cuisine, plus char-grills and wood-fired pizzas. Nothing but glowing reports.

THE FORK 'N' VIEW, 473 Scenic Drive, Waiatarua ☎ (09) 814 9804

Scenic Drive's about right: sitting on the ridge line of Waitakere mountain range, this fine restaurant has stunning views. Decorated in blacks, reds and blues by the artist Graham Nash, it's terribly trendy with arty folk. The food is California-comes-to-New-Zealand with dishes like warm ox tongue with shaved parmesan and dried tomatoes, or rolled pavlova with fresh cream and passion fruit.

WELLINGTON

—— Restaurants ——

THE COACHMAN, 26 Allen St ☎ (04) 848200

Des Britten spearheaded the new wave of New Zealand cuisine (chefs like Tony Astle did their apprenticeship under his guidance). In a beautiful setting he serves light, individual dishes.

GRAIN OF SALT, 232 Oriental Parade ☎ (04) 848642

Romantic restaurant with a fab view over Wellington Harbour, the city lights glimmering on the water. Candlelit tables with pink cloths, blue napkins, crystal, the whole special-occasion dîner-à-deux set-up. New Zealand food of the nouvelle kind.

PIERRE'S, 342 Tinakori Rd, Thorndon ☎ (04) 726238

A French bistro that has been polled best eatery in Wellington and best BYO in NZ – *and* it's *"getting better"* – DON HEWITSON.

· REST OF ·

NEW ZEALAND

—— Hotels ——

🐟 HUKA LODGE, Huka Falls Rd, PO Box 95, Taupo, North Island ☎ (074) 85791

The best country hotel in New Zealand, a latter-day hunting lodge on the banks of the whooshing Waikato River near Huka Falls. No slacking here – you'll be fishing, deer hunting, horse-trekking, golfing, playing tennis, sailing, skiing, jet-boating, white-water rafting or helicopter sightseeing. No starving either – Huka has won a string of culinary awards (they'll even cook up what you've bagged) – and there's fruit and spicy biccies in the bedroom. The Queen Mother, clad in thigh waders, has cast her rod here. *"Excellent"* echoes DON HEWITSON. *"One of the most beautiful, most romantic and lovely places in the world. A collection of wooden huts cleverly decorated in soothing colours, each with a breathtaking view of the crystal green waters. The brilliant young New Zealand chef, Greg Heffernan, serves stunning food in a magical setting"* – ELISE PASCOE.

MOOSE LODGE, Whakatane Highway 30, RD 4 Rotorua ☎ (073) 27823

Angle to stay at this peaceful lodge by one of the best trout-fishing lakes in the country, twice visited by British royals. Top New Zealand cuisine and wines; hot mineral water pool; tennis; boating.

SOLITAIRE LODGE, Lake Tarawera, RD 5 Rotorua ☎ (073) 28208

Lovely lakeside retreat for the energetic – there's fishing, sailing, ballooning, waterskiing, white-water rafting, and outings to the hot pool, boiling mud and geyser 'activities' around Rotorua. Slap-up dinners on best New Zealand produce such as smoked rainbow trout, venison or lamb.

> ❝*The best art deco architecture in the world is in Napier, North Island. The town was destroyed by an earthquake in 1931 and rebuilt in a cohesive style to create the most complete group of art deco buildings in the world*❞
>
> ROBIN HANBURY-TENISON

TIMARA LODGE, RD 2 Blenheim, Marlborough ☎ (057) 28276

A property by a private lake, amid sweeping lawns and mature trees, with swimming pool and lawn tennis. Elegant dinners using produce from within a 10-mile radius and outstanding wines, many from local vineyards. Highly recommended by DON HEWITSON. Fishing, cruising and skindiving at nearby Marlborough Sounds, an area of drowned river valleys.

———— Ski resorts ————

MOUNT COOK
Fabulous ski resort with uncluttered slopes and exhilarating heli-skiing down the 8-mile Tasman Glacier. See the highest peak in New Zealand (in Maori, 'Aorangi' – 'Cloud Piercer'); ski the nearby Harris Mountains. Cheap ski passes and heli-hire. Skiwis and Euro pros visit July-Aug for training.

Best hotel: **The Hermitage**, Mount Cook National Park, Private Bag ☎ (05621) 809, a chalet hotel at the foot of the mountain. Here, cocktails are poured over ice from the highest, purest glaciers in the country.

MOUNT RUAPEHU
Where to go for wonderful spring snow. **Chateau Tongariro**, Mount Ruapehu, North Island ☎ (081223) 809, is the best hotel in the north, set in the mountains with marvellous views and its own ski lodge, 15 minutes from the glorious National Parkland.

QUEENSTOWN
The best base for skiers in the South Island, though in summer there's exhilarating jet-boating on Shotover River and white-water rafting. From the mountains around the lake, the Remarkables, you can shoot down metal slides into the icy water. **Queenstown Resort Hotel**, Marine Parade ☎ (0294) 27750, on the shores of Lake Wakatipu, is good for families, with local pistes for beginner and advanced skiers, plus a mine of activities.

———— *Wine* ————

New Zealand's best wines are the height of fashion. The country's natural gift is what the winemakers of Australia and California are constantly striving for: the growing conditions that give slowly ripened, highly aromatic grapes. SIMON LOFTUS thinks New Zealand's white wines will soon be challenging the very best in the world. GLYNN CHRISTIAN caps that: *"It's well established that New Zealand Sauvignon Blancs are the best in the world."* DON HEWITSON agrees: *"There has been a vast improvement in white wine, especially Sauvignon Blanc; there are also some excellent Chardonnays. Red wine has improved, too – there is quite a bit of competition as the vines have matured."*

Best whites: from the South Island, both recommended by MARGARET HARVEY for outstanding Sauvignon and Chardonnay, are **HUNTER ESTATE** and **CLOUDY BAY** (DON HEWITSON is also keen). In the North Island, look out for **NGATARAWA**'s unwooded dry Sauvignon and **BROOKFIELDS**'s wonderful wooded Sauvignon. **MISSION VINEYARDS** (the oldest vineyard in NZ, set up and still run by the order of Marist Brothers) and **SELAK** both do a fine Sauvignon/Semillon blend, tipped by DON HEWITSON.

Top Chardonnays include those of **TE MATA ESTATE** and the **Black Label** of **MORTON ESTATE** (on the Bay of Plenty: supplies are always good). **KUMEU RIVER**, Auckland, produce a celebrated barrel-fermented Chardonnay, the only one of its kind in NZ, and **VILLA MARIA**, Auckland, a wooded Chardonnay.

MATAWHERO WINES do a great Gewürztraminer; MARGARET HARVEY thinks **MATUA VALLEY WINES'** unique late-harvest Gewürztraminer is heaven.

🧥 **Buzzz** The finest walk in the world is the **Milford Track** (you have to book and pay to set foot on it), which winds up at Milford Sound, an equally magnificent fjord with cruise boats to take you gasp-makingly near the waterfalls that plummet down the sheer mountain walls🧥......ROBIN HANBURY-TENISON tips the high country of the South Island the best scenery in New Zealand (along with the better-known west coast)🧥......International yachties bob around the historic **Bay of Islands** area, where the best hotel is the exclusive **Okiato Lodge**, Old Russell Rd, Okiato Point, Russell ☎ (0885) 37948 – only 4 suites, modern rustic design, fine cuisine and wines – recommended by DON HEWITSON🧥...... **Christian values**: *"The best vintage of New Zealand wine so far is 1989. For me, a truly spectacular wine is the* **Noble Dry**, *made with Botrytis-affected grapes, which normally give you a sweet Sauternes, but are fermented out dry. So you have a wine which has the richness of a dessert wine but is dry. It's worth killing for a bottle"* – GLYNN CHRISTIAN.. 🧥

MONTANA (*"a very large winery with very good wine indeed"* – ROBERT MONDAVI) produce a spicy Riesling and, in conjunction with Deutz of France, the sparkling **Lindauer** that is, for GLYNN CHRISTIAN, *"the best champagne-style wine"*. DON H and MARGARET HARVEY second and third that (it's méthode champenoise – a blend of Chardonnay and Pinot Noir – and excellent value). Other buzz fizzes are those of **DANIEL LE BRUN** (of the Le Brun family from Champagne) and **MORTON ESTATE**.

REDWOOD VALLEY ESTATE, Nelson, is tops for Botritis Rhine Riesling (*the* NZ sweet white, says MARGARET HARVEY).

Best reds: **TE MATA** and **VIDAL**'s wonderful Cabernet/Merlot blends (tipped by DON HEWITSON); **MATUA VALLEY**'s Cabernet Sauvignon (arguably the best in NZ, produced in commercial qualities); the Pinot Noirs of **ST HELENA**, Canterbury, and **MARTINBOROUGH**.

STONYRIDGE, of Waiheke Island, do, according to MARGARET HARVEY, a *"stunning organic red wine,* **Cabernet La Rose** – *if you can get your hands on any"*.

PERU

GRAN BOLIVA HOTEL, Plaza San Martin
☎ **(014) 276400**
Traditional and well known, it's *the* place to stay. Recommended by ELISABETH LAMBERT ORTIZ.

SUN RESORT LAS DUNAS, c/o Lima offices, PO Box 4410, Lima 100
☎ **(014) 424180**
Resort designed as a small desert oasis in the coastal valley of Ica, between Paracas and Nazca, where the extraordinary Nazca Lines are cut into the landscape. Lovely pool, horse riding,

Peruvian restaurant and its own airstrip for viewing the Lines.

PORTUGAL

LISBON

—— *Art and museums* ——

GULBENKIAN MUSEUM, Avenida de Berna 45A ☎ (01) 735131
Calouste Gulbenkian's art collection contains 3,000 pieces, including some bought from the Hermitage in the 20s. *"My favourite art gallery, designed by Mies van der Rohe. It has exquisite things from many periods – painting, sculpture, furniture, porcelain and glass and a very important collection of Lalique jewellery. It is a beautiful museum"* – BARRY HUMPHRIES.

—— *Hotels* ——

AVENIDA PALACE, Rua 1 de Dezembro 123 ☎ (01) 366104
A turn-of-the-century hotel with that air of faded grandeur (all gilt, crystal and plush) that pleases regulars to the capital.

—— *Restaurants* ——

PAP' ACORDA, Rua da Atalaia 57
☎ **(01) 346 4811**
In the narrow streets of the up-and-coming Bairro Alto area, this is *"quite the most fashionable, fun and friendly place in Lisbon, jammed*

Topolski's Poland

"Warsaw is not a sparkling town – the economy is in dire straits and there's a certain downness and gréyness about the city – but the people are lovely. Particularly now, they'll be full of beans. Bars, cafés and jazz clubs will be buzzing with activity and enthusiasm and discussion and argument as people try to grasp the reality of what's going on. Warsaw will be a real buzz town over the next few years."

"For some of the most scenic areas of the country, drive either north to the lakes or south to Crakow, a fantastic city. Then go south from Crakow to Zakopane, up in the Tatra mountains, which span the border with Czechoslovakia. Another delightful place, 100 miles south-east of Warsaw, is Kazimierz. It's an artist colony, on the Wista river. I spent some of the happiest weeks of my life there, when my father first took the family back to Poland in 1961. I went back again the next summer on my own because it was such a pleasure and it made me Polish."

full of Portuguese – so be prepared to queue even if you have a booking. Very good food at Portuguese prices, which are not severe. One of the nicer restaurants dotted around the world that I have been to" – ALASTAIR LITTLE. The restaurant is named after their bread/egg/oil speciality, Açorda, which, according to AL is "like porridge and not very nice".

RISTORANTE TAVARES RICO, Rua da Misericordia 37 ☎ (01) 328942

The oldest restaurant in Lisbon, it grew out of a café that opened in 1784. Opulently restored, it is, for BARRY HUMPHRIES, "still my favourite restaurant in Europe. Have the ham or the very good trout, but don't forget to leave room for the anjelica soufflé".

· REST OF ·
PORTUGAL

HOTEL PALACIO, Parque Estoril, Estoril ☎ (01) 268 0400

Partly palatial, partly dated, this is nevertheless a top-class base for the best of city and sea – 30 minutes from Lisbon, 1 from the sea and about 5 from its own golf courses. Attentive staff.

HOTEL QUINTA DO LAGO, Quinta do Lago Almancil, 8100 Loulé, Algarve ☎ (089) 96666

Ritzy resort in hundreds of undulating acres, where the privileged play golf, play tennis, ride, windsurf on the saltwater lake, or dip a toe into the Atlantic. Part of the Orient-Express group, to assure high standards.

———— Wine ————

The Portuguese red wines are the best 'forgotten' wines of Europe. The Portuguese forgot about them, too, for as long as 10 years at a stretch, which is why, when they come to sell them, some of them are so good. "Portuguese reds are very good and cheap – warm and velvety" – SERENA SUTCLIFFE. One of the best, **BUCACO TINTO**, is made at the Palace Hotel in Buçaco and can only be drunk there and at its sister hotel near Lisbon. Nothing has changed in the way this wine is made for centuries. "The 1945 is exquisite, almost Lafite-like" – MICHAEL BROADBENT. He is also dazzled by **Ferreira's BARCA VELHA**: "One of the best Portuguese reds – outstanding."

Madeira

Vintage Madeira is among the world's best fortified wines, and will outlive vintage port. A vintage year, however, is rare. The best Madeiras – the 1795 and 1862 **TERRANTEZ**

---

enjoyed by MICHAEL BROADBENT ("both incredibly refined and concentrated"), or even the non-vintage **COSSART GORDON SERCIAL DUO CENTENARY** – command love, respect, devotion ... and, above all, further purchases.

Port

TAYLOR'S

The best: still foot-trodden, their ports are of unrivalled ripeness, depth and every other dimension. MICHAEL BROADBENT still thinks their 1935 the best he's ever tasted, while ANTON MOSIMANN's favourite is the 1945 and STEVEN SPURRIER's the 1977. The top vineyard is the Quinta de Vargellas, released in lesser years as a single-vineyard port and eagerly snapped up by AUBERON WAUGH ("about half the price of Taylor's vintage port and just as good").

Other houses worth a vintage detour are **GRAHAM, DOW, FONSECA, COCKBURN, WARRE** and **QUINTA DO NOVAL**. "The 1931 Quinta do Noval, the Everest of port, still stands supreme, but for style I prefer the 1955 Graham and 1963 Fonseca" – MICHAEL BROADBENT. He advises which vintages will make New Year's Eve 1999 go with a swing: 1977 is "great", 1982 and 1983 "good" and 1985 "very good".

SERENA SUTCLIFFE's tip for impatient port lovers is to try the slightly cheaper single Quinta wines such as **Graham's Quinta do Malvedos, Dow's Quinta do Bomfim** and **Fonseca's Quinta do Panascal**.

More Scenic Journeys

"The most scenic-dramatic area is the Arizona desert – the Painted Desert – it's probably more beautiful than anywhere in the world. The red rocks look like cathedrals. The Grand Canyon itself is remarkable. And if you drive from Wyoming and Idaho to Oregon, you drive through magnificent countryside" – VISCOUNT HAMBLEDEN. *"There are so many wonderful scenic drives in France – we drove from Marseilles right up through the Alps, which was beautiful. I used to love driving through the Black Mountains in Wales between Hay and Abergavenny. I now live in Kent and I think there are some wonderful, wonderful drives and walks through the Weald of Kent"* – ED VICTOR. *"Northern Portugal, Austria, and Bohemia in the area of Carlsbad. I like walking around the lakes in Austria in the summer. Also north-west Australia"* – BARRY HUMPHRIES. ELISABETH LAMBERT ORTIZ is less ambitious: *"The A30 is very charming and goes through the prettiest country in Cornwall and Devon. It's been my ambition for a long time now just to get on the A30 and stay there. Wouldn't it be the greatest fun?"*

RUSSIA

LENINGRAD

—— *Art and museums* ——

🐦 **HERMITAGE, Dvortsovaya Nab 34**
☎ **(0812) 212 9525**
Freshly modernized and expanded, this is the largest art gallery in the world, occupying the stupendous 18C Winter Palace of the Tsars, a symphony of gilt, marble and crystal. A rich collection of international art works, jewels, objects and silver, from primitive cultures through classical antiquity to the moderns. French art of the 19C-20C is brilliantly represented (Delacroix, Degas, Renoir, Bonnard, 35 Matisses...), as is virtually every other famous painter and sculptor – Titian, Raphael, Bernini, Rubens, Van Dyck, Rembrandt (x 26), Claude, Poussin.... *"Is there anything like the Hermitage?"* asks HELEN GURLEY BROWN, rhetorically. *"For me this has the most wonderful collection of art treasures in the world."*

—— *Ballet and opera* ——

🐦 **KIROV THEATRE OF OPERA AND BALLET, Leningrad Academic Theatre, Teatral'naya Pl 1** ☎ **(0812) 314 9083**
Some of the most splendid productions of classical ballet in the world, performed under the direction of Vinogradov. *"The former Imperial ballet company of the Tsars, it's the most aristocratic company, and still the arbiter of pure classicism – the one to which all other classic companies of the world look for perfection of technique"* – EDWARD THORPE. Choreography tends to be less adventurous than the Bolshoi, but athletic dancing always astonishes. Baryshnikov, Nureyev and Makarova are the Kirov's most famous defectors; nevertheless the ballet still makes frequent tours. Like the Bolshoi, an important ballet school and opera company that is *"streets ahead of the Bolshoi Opera. This is where the classical tradition rests in Russia"* – RODNEY MILNES.

—— *Hotels* ——

YEVROPEISKAYA (European Hotel), Ul Brodskovo 1-7 ☎ **(0812) 210 3295**
Standing off Nevsky Pr, this is Leningrad's equivalent to Moscow's National Hotel – old-fashioned (but recently renovated), with lots of character.

MOSCOW

—— *Art and museums* ——

ARMOURY PALACE, Kremlin
☎ **(095) 221 4720**
One of the oldest and most opulent museums in Russia, within the Kremlin walls. Armoury, natch, plus a magnificent array of Russian gold and silver, Fabergé eggs and jewellery, diplomatic gifts from all over Europe, and a knockout collection of rare 16C-17C English silver. *"A must – decadence preserved and beautifully presented"* – DAVID SHILLING.

PUSHKIN FINE ART MUSEUM, Ul Volkhonka 12 ☎ **(095) 203 7998**
Moscow's answer to the Hermitage, especially strong on Egyptian antiquities, the Impressionists and Post-Impressionists.

TRET'YAKOV GALLERY, Lavrushinskiy Per 10 ☎ (095) 231 1362
The finest collection of Russian icons in the world, plus Russian art of the 18C and 19C. The breakaway **Gallery of the USSR**, Ul Krymskiy Val 10, shows Soviet art of the first half of the 20C.

—— *Ballet and opera* ——

🐎 **BOLSHOI BALLET AND OPERA, Bolshoi Theatre, Ploshchad Sverdlova 2 ☎ (095) 292 9986**
One of the great classical ballet companies, where the great Grigorovich is still artistic director. Productions always pack a dramatic punch, with highly tuned choreography and technique. Frequent tours to the West. Their ballet school provides a massive pool of muscle-bound dancers. Also one of the world's largest resident orchestras and a fine opera company, *"famous for their old-fashioned productions and everything being run by the KGB"* – RODNEY MILNES. Glamorous neo-classical theatre.

——— *Hotels* ———

NATIONAL HOTEL, Pr Marksa 14/1 ☎ (095) 203 6539
Looking across to the Kremlin, this old hotel was once the British Embassy. A prime example of the faded-grandeur school. *"It is great. The best suites are on the third floor, with French furniture … really fabulous"* – DAVID SHILLING. Definitely worth paying the extra for a suite.

SAVOY HOTEL, Ul Rozhdestvenka 3 ☎ (095) 230 2625
An opulent new departure in a grey and gloomy world. The first 4-star hotel in Russia, it opened in 1912 and has now been restored and transformed into a Western-style delight. Not only such luxuries as room service, telephones that work and bathplugs, no less, but gilded ceilings, inlaid floors, marble bathrooms, US telly, the British pub-style Hermitage (built and stocked by Allied Breweries) and a restaurant featuring Russian, Scandinavian and French cuisines, with food flown in from the West. *"A European oasis. The bar is essential if you need a reviving shot of swags and tails [décor-wise], or draught beer, which is John Bull Export"* – DAVID SHILLING.

——— *Restaurants* ———

Visit the coffee houses on **Old Arbat Street**, a recently pedestrianized area bustling with performers, buskers, students and portraitists.

ARAGVI, Ul Gorkovo 6 ☎ (095) 229 3762
A well-known Georgian restaurant, full of life (most of it tourist, admittedly), with music playing and hearty food.

SLAVYANSKY BAZAAR, Ul 25-vo Oktyabrya 13 ☎ (095) 221 1872
For fine old Russian cuisine. The first restaurant in Moscow, open since the mid-19C, and a traditional meeting place for writers and artists. Binge on blinis and bortsch to the sound of balalaikas.

Iron Curtain-raisers
🐎

The East may be raising the curtain, but can you stay in the major cities in comfort? Our scouts czech 'em out. In **Prague**, the newly revamped **HOTEL PALACE**, Panská 12 ☎ (2) 236 0008, has Westerners most impressed. Art nouveau elegance, fine French cuisine, mod cons (messages flashed up on your TV screen), a direct line to the 'secret police' (actually the hotel detective) and a good position by Wenceslas Square. **U TRI PSTROSU** (Three Ostriches), Drazického námestí 12 ☎ (2) 536151, is as exclusive as they come – only 18 rooms in a renovated 17C house by the river. Of the city, DAN TOPOLSKI enthuses: *"Prague is very exciting and beautiful to wander round. It's so imposing … the architecture wasn't damaged during the war, so it retains its extraordinary beauty."*

Elsewhere, it's a toss up between rather down-at-heel trad hotels and the modern chains. In **Warsaw**, the brand new soaring **WARSAW MARRIOTT**, Aleje Jerozolimskie 65-79 ☎ (22) 283444, has all zippy bizwise facilities and a range of restaurants and bars. The **ORBIS EUROPEJSKI**, Ul Krakowskie Przedmiescie 13 ☎ (22) 265051 is a fine older faithful with tiptop service. In **Budapest**, on Castle Hill, overlooking the city, is the **BUDAPEST HILTON**, Hess András Tér 1-3 ☎ (1) 751000, a symphony of 70s brown PVC and hanging baubles, *but* a favourite none the less. The **GELLERT**, Szet Gellért Tér 1 ☎ (1) 852200 is a trad oasis; the smaller, cheaper **NEMZETI**, József Körút 4 ☎ (1) 339160, presides in delightful fin-de-siècle style.

SEYCHELLES

BIRD ISLAND
For bird-watchers and honeymooners – this, the most remote of the islands, is uninhabited except for millions of Fairy, Noddy and Sooty Terns, one 150-year-old giant tortoise, and one hotel, **Bird Island Lodge**, with just 25 thatched cottages. Translucent turquoise sea, superb snorkelling.

DENIS ISLAND
Private 350-acre island offering the exclusive hideaway **Denis Island Lodge**, a small bungalow resort with a French/creole restaurant and sea sports on tap.

MAHE
The largest of the archipelago, at 17 by 5 miles, an island of mountains, tropical vegetation and the proverbial palm-fringed shoreline. Best hotels: **Northolme**, hidden among the palms, with its own diving school; **Meridien Fisherman's Cove**, a select cottage resort set in tropical gardens on Beau Vallon Bay beach.

SINGAPORE

———— Clubs ————

ANYWHERE, 04-08 Tanglin Shopping Centre ☎ 734 8233
Where can you find a mischievous edge in an otherwise toe-the-line city? Not just anywhere, but Anywhere. The band Tania (they run the place) provides live music (cover versions of 70s hits), with their Shirley Basseyesque male lead camping it up to a swinging audience. Jam-packed, slightly seamy, and bags of fun.

Far East's Best Clubs

1	JJ's · Hong Kong
2	LEXINGTON QUEEN · Tokyo
3	TOP TEN · Singapore
4	DIANA'S · Bangkok
5	GOLD · Tokyo
6	ROME CLUB VIDEOTHEQUE · Bangkok
7	CANTON · Hong Kong
8	JAVA JIVE · Tokyo
9	INK STICK · Tokyo
10	HOT GOSSIP · Hong Kong

CHINOISERIE, Hyatt Regency, 10-12 Scotts Rd ☎ 733 1188
Swish, newish nightclub with dark mirrored walls that reflect a ravy clientele of bright young things and local jetsetters.

TOP TEN, 400 Orchard Rd ☎ 732 3077
No 1 in the chart hits, tops for locals and expats alike. The vast converted cinema has the Manhattan skyline scudding across the walls. Disco

Buzzz Singapore's national monument, **Raffles**, 1-3 Beach Rd ☎ 337 8041, re-opens in 1991 after a complete refit – the colonial part has been painstakingly restored (and a new wing for tourist groups added)..... The new **Regent Singapore**, 1 Cuscaden Rd ☎ 733 8888, starts its major 'enhancement' plan this year. Based in the old Pavilion Inter-Continental, the Regent is set to tackle its old rivals in a new location...... Swinging club? Golfers with plenty of sponduliks should be/seek out a member of the **Singapore Island Country Club**, 180 Island Club Rd ☎ 459 2222, for its 4 fantastic 18-holers (S$150,000-plus membership)...... Clubland 2: the private **Cricket Club** is the only club in Singapore not to have been ousted from its original colonial home. Set in the Padang, an inner-city Elysian field..... When the band stops playing at **Cheers** (in the Novotel Orchid Inn, 214 Dunearn Rd), the barmen and waiters burst into song. Best pair of lungs (in Barry White mode) belongs to the manager...... **Breath of fresh air**: non-smokers will love ash-free Singapore, where restaurants are now smoke-free zones – it's back to the bicycle sheds for nicotine addicts. . . . .

and live music (imported stars), superlative lighting.

XANADU, Shangri-La, 22 Orange Grove Rd ☎ 737 3644

Top of the bops – sleek, super-trendy disco with outsize videos, spectacular lighting and laser shows, and a wild female DJ. Bars and seats surround the sunken dance floor.

———— *Hotels* ————

GOODWOOD PARK, 22 Scotts Rd ☎ 737 7411

Much-loved white colonial building which began life as the Teutonia Club in 1900, now tastefully revamped. Apartment-sized Parklane suites, plus the most gorgeous suite in the East – the S$3,000 Brunei (the size of a ballroom, in Georgian style), where the Sultan himself often stays. There have been complaints about the lobby being full of tour luggage, but LEO COOPER is impressed: *"My son stayed there and they looked after him so well."* See also Restaurants.

🐟 THE ORIENTAL, 5 Raffles Ave, Marina Sq ☎ 338 0066

The most spectacular-looking hotel in the city, it's hot on the Shangri-La's heels for top slot – one group of discerning travellers even felt the general treatment and atmosphere here had the edge on the Oriental Bangkok. A 21-storey triangular-shaped harbourfront hotel, with smart health club and swimming pool that plays underwater classical music. *"The loveliest outdoor swimming pool and terrace overlooking Singapore harbour. Terrific for a relaxing poolside breakfast"* – ELISE PASCOE. Dining is among the best in town (see Restaurants).

🐟 SHANGRI-LA, 22 Orange Grove Rd ☎ 737 3644

The best in Singapore, for spectacular service (a low turnover of staff so that you are remembered and greeted with friendly smiles) and some of the most spacious rooms in the East (especially in the plush, secluded Valley Wing – where guests are also spoilt with complimentary drinks). The current S$30 million refurbishments should set the hotel back on top in the décor stakes. Exotic pool area, tropical gardens with waterfalls, outdoor spa bath, squash and tennis courts, putting green. *"The best hotel I've ever stayed in. Every day they put a different carpet in the lift with the day written on it. They're charming, charming people – very keen to please yet unsubservient at the same time"* – SIMON WILLIAMS. See also Restaurants.

———— *Restaurants* ————

BANANA LEAF APOLO, 56 Race Course Rd ☎ 293 8682

A true taste of Singapore. You eat with your fingers and food is served on a banana-leaf plate. Excellent Indian, fish and meat dishes (fish-head curry is a speciality).

CHAO PHAYA, 4272-A, Block 730, Ang Mo Kio Ave 6 ☎ 456 0119

First-rate Thai restaurant. You choose your garoupa, crab or lobster and vegetables from the market display, then watch your dinner being broiled, fried or steamed behind huge glass windows. Specialities are tom yam kung (spicy prawn soup) and green fish curry.

🐟 GOODWOOD PARK, see Hotels

Endless ways to titillate the palate, all artily presented. Superb Sichuan at **Min Jiang** (invariably full, so book), decorated in pale green with giant red Chinese lanterns drooping from the ceiling; service so fast you don't take a breath. Marvellous fresh seafood and dim sum at the **Garden Seafood Restaurant**. Shanghainese delicacies served in Western style in the newly decorated golden-yellow surroundings of **Chang Jiang**. Daintily designed Japanese nosh at **Shima**. The best straight steaks, great Continental and American cuisine and *kilted staff*, no less, at the **Gordon Grill**. Round it off by the best – and most impressively served – coffees at **Café L'Espresso**.

🐟 LE RESTAURANT DE FRANCE, Hotel Meridien Singapore, 100 Orchard Rd ☎ 733 8855

Very elegant and very Parisian, this is the one for French cuisine at its best. Formal by Singapore standards (don't forget that tie), it has arguably the best service in town, always with Singaporean friendliness. Decorated in warm peachy tones; a lush conservatory forms part of the dining room.

🐟 THE ORIENTAL, see Hotels

The **Cherry Garden** looks out onto a pebbled courtyard (murder on heels), a reproduction of the inner courtyard of a Ming dynasty nobleman's house. Elegant, pretty setting with subtle daylight-effect lighting and gentle swathes of cherry blossom. Excellent presentation enhances already knockout Sichuan and Hunan cooking. Private dining room, too. The Continental restaurant, **Fourchettes**, has a huge grill at the entrance and a mouth-watering display of hors d'oeuvres, including Chilean oysters. One of the best business buffet lunches in town – all the rage with Singaporeans, who savour the knowledge that they can pile up their plates again and again for a set price.

🐟 SHANGRI LA, see Hotels

Tops for Singaporean food and great salads is the **Waterfall Café**, surrounded by lush tropical vegetation and running water (a Chinese symbol of good fortune). Do the Continental (cuisine-wise) at the **Latour**, a dining room in deep pink with huge batiks of tropical flowers. Ice and butter sculptures make a spectacle of the lunchtime buffet; impressive wine cellars. **Shang Palace** has a dramatic Chinese entrance and dramatic Cantonese cuisine. **Nadaman**, on the 24th floor, serves superb Japanese food. 10-course monthly menu that reflects the Japanese food seasons, as well as sushi, sashimi, tempura, shabu-shabu, sukiyaki et al.

Food Markets

For typical ethnic cuisine at street level, go to the food markets, where hawkers each specialize in 1 or 2 dishes. *"The markets are a wonderful place to eat. You go on buying and eating until you've had enough and take a rickshaw home. The trouble is the rickshaw-puller is usually a quarter of my size and I feel like giving him a lift instead"* – SIMON WILLIAMS. The best market is **Newton Circus** with over 100 stalls; haunt of expat kids from the American school. Also try the seaside **Satay Club**, off the Padang, for nosh in the prettiest part of Singapore. *"Nonya cooking married with Malay food and the Chinese obsession for absolute freshness and subtleties of textures makes for one of the great Oriental cuisines. Don't miss the* **KK Markets**, *Serangoon Rd, where most of the cuisines of Asia are represented"* – ELISE PASCOE.

Shopping

In a duty-free city that is overloaded with European designer labels for the Japanese, and Japanese superstores for the locals, 2 stores excel: the pagoda-topped **C K Tang**, 320 Orchard Rd, housing Gucci, Dunhill, YSL and other Euro labels, plus batik and Chinese curios; and **Metro** (7 branches – the most upmarket are M. Grand and M. Paragon), with cool designer boutiques and own-label quality gear... much-patronized by locals. The Jap store **Isetan**, Orchard Rd, is crammed with designer labels (Gucci, Chanel, Burberry, Porsche Design). The Oriental's **Marina Square** complex claims to be the largest shopping complex in S E Asia. **Holland Village** is frequented by expats but not tourists for more local handicrafts, etc; try **Lim's Arts & Crafts**, Holland Rd Shopping Centre, for ceramics, wood carvings, chests, pictures, silk screens and all manner of goodies; **Tanglin Shopping Centre** is tops for Oriental antiques and carpets. *The* place for jewellery and stones (prices and authenticity are regulated) is the **South Bridge Centre**. And for electronic

gadgetry (especially computers, plus cosmetics, furnishings and more), go to the **Funan Centre**.

ALLAN CHAI FASHION DESIGN, 05-56 Peninsula Plaza, 110 N Bridge Rd ☎ 338 4330
Come armed with your Chanels and Saint Laurents, and Allan Chai will replicate them – some say his workmanship is better than the originals.

CENTREPOINT, 176 Orchard Rd
Homesick Brits find solace at Singapore's **St Michael** (Marks & Sparks to the rest of the world). Also Charles Jourdan, Benetton and **Robinsons'** – the original 'English' department store, for exquisite presents...

HILTON SHOPPING GALLERY, 581 Orchard Rd ☎ 737 2233
The best hotel shopping arcade with a handy supply of top European labels: Valentino, Ferré, Frizon, Cartier, Bulgari, Dunhill, Gucci, Vuitton, Lanvin, Davidoff and L'Ultima shoes, plus antiques, paintings, jewellery, leather goods and other temptations.

JUSTMENS, 01-36 Tanglin Shopping Centre, Tanglin Rd ☎ 737 4800
One of the most reliable tailors on the island, catering to Singaporean bigwigs and expat businessmen alike.

THE PROMENADE, 300 Orchard Rd
A great source of designer gear. In the boutique **Man & His Woman** are Miyake, Byblos, Matsuda, Tokio Kumagai, and the young creative French; at **Glamourette** are Ozbek, Gaultier and co. You can also promenade past the ranks of Féraud, Boss, Ralph Lauren and Basile.

SCOTTS SHOPPING CENTRE, Scotts Rd ☎ 235 5055
A S$200 million development offering some of the best shopping on the island. Etienne Aigner for clothes, handbags, shoes; a China Silk House; Tang Studio (for gimmicky/trendy clothes and accessories); Diane Freis; Fellini; Ellesse sportswear. Also Cost Plus Electronics, one of the most reputable firms in the city.

SOUTH AFRICA

The Cape of Good Hope is the most beautiful part of South Africa. On the Atlantic side of the Cape peninsula, the best beaches are Camps Bay, Llandudno Bay and Clifton Beach – for sun but not sea bathing (cold with dangerous undercurrents). On the Indian Ocean side, where the sea is warmer and safer, Muizenburg Beach is the best. Further along the Garden Route to the east are the 2 top resorts that attract local gentry: Hermanus (best hotel: **The Marine**, PO Box 9 ☎ (02831) 21112, a handsome whitewashed building overlooking Walker Bay) and Plettenberg Bay (**The Plettenberg**, PO Box 719 ☎ (04457) 32030, originally a 19C holiday mansion, done up in candy colours, right by the sea).

Hotels

MALA MALA, Rattray Reserves, PO Box 2575, Randburg ☎ (011) 789 2677
The luxurious main camp on the famous privately owned Mala Mala Game Reserve. A mere 86 visitors to 57,000 acres makes for peaceful game-viewing. Part of Rattray Reserves, which also include the Malachite Game Reserve in northern Natal and Mashatu Game Reserve in Botswana.

MOUNT NELSON HOTEL, Orange St Gdns, PO Box 2608, Cape Town ☎ (021) 231000
Recently renovated, this rose-pink building is the best hotel in town: old-fashioned, colonial, caringly run and beautifully kept. Gorgeous gardens.

Tours

See also **Tempo Travel** (Travel Directory).

BLUE TRAIN, c/o SARtravel (see below)
South Africa's answer to the Orient-Express. The streamlined steam train chugs at a stately 40 mph from Cape Town over the Hex River Mountain Pass, across the Karoo to Johannesburg and Pretoria. Fitting Cordon Bleu cuisine, a formidable cellar, private valets, and windows tinted with pure gold to tone down the glare.

GAMETRACKERS, PO Box 4245, Randburg ☎(011) 886 1810
Wing safaris in South and East Africa, tailor-made from a choice of camps.

SARTRAVEL, PO Box 1113, Johannesburg 2000 ☎ (011) 774 4504
Tours of the winelands – Stellenbosch Paarl and Franschoek Wine Estate, lunching and quaffing at wonderful farms such as the former home of Cecil Rhodes.

SOUTH AFRICAN AIR TOURS, PO Box 8, Lanseria 1748 ☎ (011) 659 1246
Personalized South African safaris.

SPRINGBOK ATLAS SAFARIS, Tollgate House, 183 Sir Lowry Rd, Cape Town 8001 ☎ (021) 455468
Variety of tours, from common-or-garden coach to specialist tours (eg for stud breeders, gemologists, botanists or sportsmen). Do the winelands, Table Mountain, Garden Route, wildlife (taking in Hluhluwe, Ubizane, Kruger and Sabi Sabi reserves), or SA highlights.

SPAIN

BARCELONA

Bars and cafés

LA FIRA, Provenzia 171 ☎ (93) 323 7271
All the fun of la fira: this wacky warehouse bar is full of funfair relics – sit in whip chairs or in hanging chair-o-plane seats up at the bar.

MIRABLAU, Plaza Dr Andreu ☎ (93) 418 5879
One of the most fashionable bars in Tibidabo, with knockout views. Take an aperitivo before dining at La Venta, or a few digestivos before dancing (downstairs) till dawn.

Clubs

OTTO ZUTZ, Calle Lincoln 15 ☎ (93) 238 0722
Young, fun, booming warehouse disco in the lively, old part of town, Gracia. Don't miss out on your siesta – here the action starts at 1am and continues through till 6.

UP AND DOWN, Numancia 179 ☎ (93) 204 8809
Smart underground nightclub in the Mayfair of Barcelona – olds go up, youngs go down.

Hotels

8 new first-class hotels are planned for the 1992 Olympics. Meanwhile, these are the best:

BARCELONA HILTON, Avenida Diagonal 589-591 ☎ (93) 410 7499
This brand-new Hilton, a chic tower-block in modern Catalan design, is going for gold. VIPs and stars have been quick to latch on....

HOTEL COLON, Avenida de la Catedral ☎ (93) 301 1404
A long-standing favourite, in the Gothic Quarter, stronger on charm and views than on luxury.

HOTEL MELIA, Avenida Sarria 48 ☎ (93) 410 6060
Another new hotel, all bright and beautifully designed. Locals and guests dig in to the endless Sunday brunchtime spread. The Princess Royal has stayed.

HOTEL RITZ, Gran Via 668 ☎ (93) 318 5200
The traditional best, this César Ritz creation has recently been restored to its original super-luxe state. International and Catalan cuisine.

——— *Restaurants* ———

BELTXENEA, Mallorca 275, Entlo
☎ (93) 215 3024
Wonderful old-established restaurant for Basque
country food by chef Miguel Ezcurra. Hidden
away behind a private entrance (you are let in
by intercom, then a maid or butler opens the
door), this restaurant has a country-house
atmosphere with a series of dining rooms, and
log fires in winter. Affluent Catalans grab any
excuse to celebrate here.

CANMAJO, Almirante Aixada 23
☎ (93) 310 1455
Serious seafood dining in the fishy area of Barce-
loneta, near the port. At this restaurant (unlike
some) you don't have to contend with waves
lashing at your feet, but join a smart crowd at
tables with pink cloths.

LA VENTA, Plaza Dr Andreu
☎ (93) 212 6455
Up at Tibidabo, overlooking the city, presides
this garden restaurant for nouvelle cuisine. Cool
in all senses of the word, and a wondrous panor-
ama. Take the tram up the mountain.

MADRID

—— *Art and museums* ——

🎎 **MUSEO DEL PRADO, Paseo del Prado**
☎ (91) 468 0950
One of the best national collections in the world,
covering 12C-19C Italian art, 15C-18C Dutch,
French, English and German art, plus, of course,
the Spanish school – Velázquez and his amigos.
Currently expanding and modernizing, it's always a high spot for HELEN ("*I could spend a
year here*") GURLEY BROWN, BARBARA TAYLOR
BRADFORD, JEFFREY ARCHER and LORD GOWRIE.

Pilgrim's Progress
——————— 🎎 ———————

"The best long-distance footpath and
bridlepath in Spain is the 500-mile Way of
St James to Compostela, from the Pyre-
nees to the Atlantic coast. It's easy to
follow because so many pilgrims do the
journey each year. It leads through glorious
scenery and past some of the finest medieval architecture in Europe. Walk, or ride
a horse or bicycle (the lazy can go by car).
Three of the best and most beautiful hotels
in Spain are paradors converted from
ancient monasteries or hospices for pilgrims – palaces with cloisters, comfort and
elegance. They are: **Parador de Santo
Domingo de la Calzada**, Plaza del Santo
3, S Domingo de la Calzada ☎ (941) 340300;
Parador San Marcos, Plaza de San
Marcos 7, León ☎ (987) 237300, with the
grandest façade in the world (built by de
Badajoz, architect of El Escorial); and the
15C **Hostal de los Reyes Católicos**,
Plaza de Espana 1, Santiago de Compostela ☎ (981) 582200, in the best urban
setting for a hotel in the world" – ROBIN
HANBURY-TENISON.

——————— *Hotels* ———————

🎎 **HOTEL RITZ, Plaza de la Lealtad 5**
☎ (91) 521 2857
The best hotel in Spain, for the beautifully
restored historic building (first opened in 1910),
the garden setting with flower-covered pergolas
and fountains, excellent management (under

🎎 **Buzzz** around Madrid🎎 . . . . . . In sum-
mer, the **Castellana** becomes *the* hang-out, lined with all-night open-air bars . . . Set
in front of the Royal Palace, **Café de Oriente**, Plaza de Oriente, is one of the loveliest
café-bars to sop up the sun . . . **La Trucha**, near Plaza Santa Ana, and **Bocaito**, 6
Libertad St, are among the tops for **tapas** – baby lamb chops, stuffed mussels, weeny
eels on toast, wild mountain strawberries . . . **Archie**, Marquis de Riscal, is the trendspot
for late-night drinking, with a disco downstairs (and if modish Madrileños aren't bopping
there, they'll be at **Nairobi** or **Amnesia**) . . . For SERENA SUTCLIFFE, "*the most
fascinating food market is* **Madrid fish market**, *the largest in the world after Tokyo.
Not bad for a land-locked capital*"🎎 . . . . . . **Spanish fizz:** the best sparkling wines go
under the generic name of **Cava**. The biggest house, **Codorniu**, also owns the **Raimat**
estate, whose sparkling Chardonnay is arguably the best in Spain. . . . . 🎎

THF) and a great location looking across to the Prado. Remarkable hand-woven bespoke carpets and fine tapestries. Margaret Thatcher joins the dignitaries that have stayed over the years. Devoted fans include BARBARA CARTLAND, BRUCE OLDFIELD and NICHOLAS VILLIERS ("*it's outstanding*"). Locals go for Sunday brunch on the terrace.

PALACE, Plaza de las Cortes 7
☎ **(91) 429 4144**
A firm favourite. Though not in quite such spanking condition as the nearby Ritz, it's another beauty from the belle époque, exalted for its dazzling domed foyer where elegant locals sip pre-prandials.

—— Restaurants ——

CASA PACO, Puerta Cerrada 11
☎ **(91) 266 3166**
Real Madrid...in the heart of the old town, this spit 'n' sawdust joint is packed with Spaniards who come for near-raw rump steaks that are served up on a sizzling hot plate for them to cook to their taste.

JOCKEY, Amador de los Rios 6
☎ **(91) 319 1003**
An air of the private club – lots of dark wood, antiques, soft carpeting – this is the place business whizzes go to impress each other. Monstrously expensive, but worth it for creative cuisine – sea urchin soup, partridge and mushrooms en croûte. "*A wonderful restaurant. Excellent fish – the best in Europe except for Tavares in Lisbon*" – BARRY HUMPHRIES.

LA DORADA, Orense 64 ☎ **(91) 270 2004**
Rigged out in shipshape style (whitewashed walls, wooden beams, round windows), this fish restaurant is one *everybody* loves (expense accounts and personal wallets alike). Seafood,

flown in fresh from Málaga, is served up in deliciously simple fashion – try sea bream baked in salt, hammered open in front of you.

ZALACAIN, Alvarez de Baena 4
☎ **(91) 261 4840**
The most highly renowned restaurant in Spain, excellent in every respect. A blend of the hearty Spanish and exquisite modern – red mullet with olive oil and herbs, roast duck with cream of black olives.

—————— *Wine* ——————

"*Like Italy, Spain is now developing its own native grape varieties rather than relying on French ones. It results in a more interesting national/regional identity. Spain is beginning to show signs of producing quality wines at a high level. A particularly interesting area is the north-west – the districts of Ribera del Duero, Toro, Rueda and, in a smaller way, Galicia*" – SIMON LOFTUS.

*P*enedès

In terms of the best table wines, Penedès means **TORRES**. Every year Torres himself produces a portfolio of wines from different classic and native grape varieties – and he then rushes off to the family's vineyards in Chile to do the same thing there. The best Torres wine is undoubtedly **Gran Coronas 'Black Label'**.

*R*ibera del Duero

The renowned **VEGA SICILIA** is 10 years in the making. Knife-edge stuff – it's kept in the wood almost too long. **Valbuena**, the second wine, makes less demands on time and wallet

🐦 **Buzzz** 🐦......Second only to the Prado on the culture beat is the Moorish fortress and palace of the **Alhambra**, Granada, an exotic world of domes and mosaics and fountains 🐦...... **Pilgrimage to the Paseo del Prado**: the arrival of 787 paintings on loan from the priceless **Thyssen-Bornemisza** collection makes this one of the hottest spots in the land for art lovers. Conversion of the **Palacio de Villahermosa** (opposite the Prado) will be complete by 30 June 1991, giving you 9 years 6 months of gawping before the loan period expires 🐦...... **Homage to the Masters**: in El Greco's home-town of Toledo is the **Museo del Greco**, El Paseo del Transito, a lovely little town house with interior courtyards and balconies (though he didn't actually live there) 🐦...... In Dalí's birthplace of Figueras is the **Museo Dalí**, Plaza Gala-Dalí, a walk-in Surrealist experience 🐦...... In Barcelona, where the great Pablo spent his formative years, is the **Museo Picasso**, Montcada 15, containing paintings, engravings and drawings....................... 🐦

and is considered by some aficionados a better wine.

Pesquera from **BODEGAS ALEJANDRO FERNANDEZ** is the wine of the moment, even if it has been overpraised by some.

Rioja

MARQUES DE RISCAL is the best-known name, especially among claret-lovers, though its elegant modern wines are almost too light to take seriously. **MARQUES DE MURRIETA** is a more powerful and altogether more serious wine. **MARQUES DE CACERES** is more modern and very reliable. SERENA SUTCLIFFE adores the white **Tondonia** from **BODEGAS LOPEZ DE HEREDIA**. LIZ BERRY recommends **CVNE** across the board, **BODEGAS RIOJANAS**, and the **Vina Ardanza Reserva 904** from **BODEGAS LA RIOJA ALTA**.

Sherry

Good sherry is smart again. Just as mouldy grapes make some of the world's best sweet wines, so mouldy white wine makes one of the world's best apéritifs: dry sherry. The thicker the fur of *flor* across the wine in cask, the drier the finished sherry. The most brilliant Finos and Olorosos are greatly undervalued, selling at a fraction of the price of their equivalents in Burgundy or Madeira. **Barbadillo's SANLUCAR MANZANILLA, Domecq's LA INA** and the famous **TIO PEPE** of **Gonzàles Byass** would make a Fino start to any meal (Gonzàles B's **APOSTOLES** – dry oloroso – is another treat). SERENA SUTCLIFFE also votes for **Valdespino's INOCENTE FINO**. The new **Harvey's 1796 PALO CORTADO** is a rare dry sherry of outstanding quality.

SWEDEN

STOCKHOLM

DROTTNINGHOLM PALACE
☎ **(08) 759 0380**
The official residence of the Swedish royal family, a magnificent 17C palace with formal gardens, known as the Versailles of the North. In the grounds are Marie Antoinette-style follies, the China House and a 'tent' of wood and iron. Don't miss the perfect 18C **Court Theatre**, unchanged since it was built for Queen Lovisa Ulrika. Scenery is still manoeuvred by hand and the original sets for *Cosi Fan Tutte* and *The Magic Flute* are still used (as are the original musical instruments). "*The most beautiful*

theatre in the world ... in Swedish taste – austere, restrained neo-classicism. I would give that the prize for the place to see an opera" – LORD GOWRIE. A chorus of approval from BARBARA CARTLAND and JULIAN LLOYD WEBBER: "It just has to be seen to be believed. It's quite extraordinary." Make your pilgrimage for the summer **Drottningholm Festival** of opera, PO Box 27050 ☎ (08) 665 1100.

———— *Hotels* ————

GRAND HOTEL, S Blasieholmshamnen 8, PO Box 16424 ☎ (08) 221020
Sweden's swankiest hotel, opened in 1874 and now restored to its original opulence. On the harbourside, with views of the Royal Palace and the old town, it's a favourite port of call for yachties (tempted by smorgasbord and home-made pastries on the verandah). Fine dining at the **Franska Matsalen**. Luxy suites at the adjacent Bolinder Palace, a replica of a Venetian palazzo.

SWITZERLAND

GENEVA

———— *Hotels* ————

BEAU RIVAGE, 13 quai du Mont-Blanc, CH-1201 ☎ (022) 731 0221
Immaculate, grand, family-run hotel where the Duke of Brunswick once lived. Dine on the terrace looking over the lake.

HOTEL DE LA PAIX, 11 quai du Mont-Blanc, CH-1211 ☎ (022) 732 6150
More lakeside grandeur, with lovely views of Mont Blanc and distant Alpine peaks.

LE RICHEMOND, Jardin Brunswick, CH-1211 ☎ (022) 731 1400
The best of the Geneva trio, owned and run by 4 generations of Armleders, the original of whom set up the revered Ecole Hôtelière. With the air of a private mansion, it is filled with paintings and antiques. In the visitors' book, the Livre d'Or, are priceless comments and scribbles from Colette, Miró, Walt Disney, Chagall....

———— *Restaurants* ————

LE DUC, 7 quai du Mont Blanc, CH-1201 ☎ (022) 317330
Run by the Michelli brothers, who hold the key to simplicity. Fish and shellfish specialities.

More Best Advice

Continuing our contribs' tales of the best advice they have been given: *"My father taught me from the time we were knee-high that there were 3 golden rules in life: never to accept anything at face value, never to succumb to blind obedience and to remember that while I owed first allegiance to myself, my family and those I loved, I was also a child of the world"* – MARIE HELVIN. *"I remember my mother saying, always look for the best in someone"* – CAROLINE HUNT. *"Always think of the other person as being better than you are"* – QUENTIN CRISP. *"'The heights by great men reached and kept were not attained by sudden flight, but they, while their companions slept, were toiling upward in the night' (The Ladder of St Augustine – Longfellow)"* – JEFFREY ARCHER. *"My father used to say that quality is remembered long after the price is forgotten"* – STANLEY MARCUS. *"Never be photographed with a drink or a cigarette in my hand"* – BRUCE OLDFIELD. *"There is no free lunch"* – HELEN GURLEY BROWN. *"Don't take men seriously"* – DIANE FREIS. *"Enjoy life"* – SHAKIRA CAINE. *"Stick to it. Stick with something until you've made it work for you"* – BILL BLASS. *"On my opening night of my first important play, my father gave me a little cigarette case, and inside was an inscription from Hamlet: 'Let your own discretion be your tutor'"* – DOUGLAS FAIRBANKS JR. *"The best advice is not to heed advice"* – PETER USTINOV.

LA PERLE DU LAC, 128 route de Lausanne, CH-1202 ☎ (022) 731 7935
One of the prettiest lakeside garden restaurants, with lovely views and exquisite food – try lobster ravioli with mustard and thyme, mille-feuilles with seasonal fruits.

ZURICH

—— Bars and Cafés ——

CAFE SCHOBER, Napfgasse 4, CH-8001 ☎ (01) 251 8060
A delightful old coffee house that appeals to PETER USTINOV: *"absolutely sensational because it rambles all over the place. This kind of café develops a special kind of waitress who is maternal and feminine at the same time. They sell Teuscher chocolates, which are the best in the world, perhaps even in Switzerland!"* In summer, you can sit outside and watch the world go by and buskers busk.

CONFISERIE SPRUNGLI, Am Paradeplatz, Bahnhofstrasse 21, CH-8001 ☎ (01) 221 1722
The biggest and best chocolatiers in Switzerland, as ANTON MOSIMANN vouches: *"You can't beat it ...quality made with fresh Swiss milk and cream – just gorgeous."* A celebrated café-restaurant, too. *"Go for coffee and a chocolate fix – melt-in-the-mouth creamy Swiss chocolates, fabulous teardrop cachous [little bonbons] and gorgeous pâtisseries"* – ELISE PASCOE.

—— Hotels ——

BAUR AU LAC, 1 Talstrasse, CH-8022 ☎ (01) 221 1650
An air of quiet dignity, with courteous staff and one of the best concierges in the world, Albert Ostertag (president of the Clefs d'Or Internationales, the respected society of concierges). The **Pavillon**, overlooking the river, is a smart lunch spot. BARBARA TAYLOR BRADFORD and MARK MCCORMACK drop in.

—— Restaurants ——

AGNES AMBERG, Hottingerstrasse 5, CH-8032 ☎ (01) 251 2626
Fashionable eatery where arty-media types go for cleverly concocted dishes using fresh-as-fresh ingredients. Fine presentation.

CHEZ MAX, Seestrasse 53, CH-8702 Zollekon ☎ (01) 391 8877
A synthesis of French and Eastern aesthetics, this is eye- and palate-stroking fodder. Max Kehl bakes a mean feuilleté, and makes wonderful use of fruits, Oriental seasonings and uncommon combinations.

· REST OF ·
SWITZERLAND

—— Art and museums ——

THYSSEN-BORNEMISZA COLLECTION, Villa Favorita, CH-6976 Castagnola ☎ (091) 521741
While the larger part of his magnificent collection wings its way to the Villahermosa Palace in Madrid, Baron Heini Thyssen's lakeside villa and gardens remain open (Easter to Oct), with some

400 works on show. As a private collection, his is second only to the Queen of England's in quality and quantity, with some 550 Old Masters (from Holbein and Van Eyck through Titian and Rembrandt to the 18C rococo) and 800 modern works (Impressionists, Picasso, Cézanne, Van Gogh and the German Expressionists). Beautifully displayed in calm surroundings.

Hotels

HOTEL HAUS PARADIES, CH-7551 Ftan ☎ (084) 91325

Sunny, salubrious Alpine retreat highly rated by FRANK BOWLING. Only 21 rooms with really dumbfounding views of the peaks and meadows of the Lower Engadine. Non-skiers/riders/ hikers / tennis players / golfers can bury their heads in the fascinating library. Culinary works of art from chef-proprietor Roland Jöhri, using super-fresh vegetables and herbs from their garden, and fish and crustaceans from clear mountain reservoirs.

🍴 RHEINHOTEL FISCHERZUNFT, Rheinquai 8, CH-8200 Schaffhausen ☎ (053) 253281

A 15C German guild house on the banks of the Rhine, run by André and Doreen Jaeger (he Swiss, ex-Peninsula Hong Kong, she Cantonese). *"Only 8 rooms which are just amazing ...upholstered walls, the kind of thing you'd expect in a grand English country house. Extraordinary Japanese toilets where they don't use paper – you press a button and a mechanical arm comes out and you get squirted and blown dry. But what is really extraordinary is the food. It is fabulous international food presented in a Chinese way. A delight to the eye... one of the most memorable meals I have ever had in my life"* – EDWARD CARTER. *"It's right on the Rhine where the terrific waterfalls occur. The chef is fascinating, determined to do his own particular blend of exotic Oriental and the best of European food. Quite apart from the taste, it's the most ravishing sight I have ever seen on a plate"* – SERENA SUTCLIFFE.

Music

FESTIVAL DE MUSIQUE MONTREUX-VEVEY, ave des Alpes 14, CH-1820 Montreux ☎ (021) 635450

A calm, glimmering lakeside setting for the classical music festival that runs from end-Aug to end-Sept, filling concert halls, châteaux and churches with its vibes.

MONTREUX JAZZ FESTIVAL, Service de Location, Case 97, CH-1820 Montreux; tickets c/o Tourist Office ☎ (021) 631212

More famous and more rowdy than its classical counterpart, it's an international mix of jazz and rock.

Restaurants

STUCKI BRUDERHOLZ, Bruderholzallee 42, CH-4059 Basle ☎ (061) 358222

Fine French cuisine by Hans Stucki. Fish and seafood are his love – rouget marinated in coriander, oyster consommé with ginger, frogs' legs in sweet peppers. Fine wines include Swiss 'uns.

🍴 GIRARDET, 1 rue d'Yverdon, Crissier, CH-1023 Lausanne ☎ (021) 341514

Renowned the foodie world over, thought by many to be the best restaurant in Europe. Girardet conjures with super-fresh ingredients; brilliant inventiveness and perfectionist execution – who else could dream up and bake sea urchin soufflé with such precision?

Ski resorts

CRANS

Très snob resort, drawing royals and aristos from Benelux, Denmark and Italy. Spectacular views over the Rhône Valley and, since it's all south-facing, hours more sun than most resorts. Best shopping in the Swiss Alps in rue du Golf. Best Alpine glühwein (fruity and spicy, served in a silver teapot): **Des Vignettes**. Best fondue and raclette: **Le Cave**.

GSTAAD

The best haunt for nightclub skiers, who by day wear their skis on their shoulders rather than their feet. Nevertheless, it's a pretty little rustic village where you're as likely to see cartloads of manure as the furred and bejewelled jetset – Prince Rainier et famille, Audrey Hepburn, Roger Moore, Lynn Wyatt, Boucherons, Bulgaris and Buckleys (Pat gives the most splendid parties). Best hotel: **Palace Hotel** ☎ (030) 83131, a splendid, turretted affair peeping above the pines. LORD DONOUGHUE loves staying in the *"birthday cake"*. This is the hub of Alpine society in February, though there's a summer season too for healthy walks, swimming and tennis. Go-go down at the **Green Go** disco. PS Check out the annual **Menuhin Festival**, YEHUDI MENUHIN's favourite music festival – *"but then I'm biased"*.

KLOSTERS

Small, smart, old-fashioned resort where the younger British royals – the Waleses, the Yorks and the Gloucesters – still love to ski, staying in a friend's private chalet. Best choice of slopes at nearby Davos. Best hotels: **Wynegg** (excellent cuisine); the small **Chesa Grischuna**.

ST MORITZ

Grand Victorian resort with enough activities to keep you run off your feet. The Cresta Run, of course, the treacherous, terrifying, men-only toboggan run that could only have been invented by the Brits; bobsleighing, curling, heli-skiing,

---

Best Bedding

You can lay your head on the best pillows at the **Mandarin Oriental**, Hong Kong: *"They are made of beautiful down and really are comfortable. So often you get these horrid little foam-filled pads"* – CAROL WRIGHT. Joint honours must go to the **Schweizerhof**, Via dal Bagn 54, CH-7500 St Moritz ☎ (082) 22171, whose goose down duvets and pillows in soft sateen-linen covers are blissfully sleep-conducive. Votes also go to the warm, cocoon-like

Scandia Down duvets of **Le Meridien Chicago at 21 East Kempinski**, Chicago. CAROL WRIGHT thinks **Reid's**, Estrada Monumental, Funchal, Madeira ☎ (091) 23000, has *"the most glorious beautiful bedlinen, really old-fashioned heavy stuff. Also beautiful towels..."*. For EDWARD CARTER, *"the most attractive bedlinen is at* **Le Manoir Aux Quat' Saisons**, *Oxfordshire. They have lovely antique Irish linen and lace"*.

---

and, on the frozen lake, racing, polo and the mad mountain sport skikjöring, where a 'jockey' is towed, water-ski style, behind a riderless horse. February is non-stop party month, for jetsetters who wing in in their G3s and Falcon 50s – the Aga Khan, Gianni Agnelli, Fredy Heineken, Stavros Niarchos et al. Best club: **Corviglia** (for mountain lunches). Best nightspots: Gunther Sachs's private **Dracula Club** (at the Kulm) and **Kings'** (at Badrutt's Palace). Best hotels: CLARE FRANCIS's fave, **Badrutt's Palace** ☎ (082) 21101, a towering hotel with strains of the baronial hunting lodge. In high season, this is where it's at for the flasher crowd. **Suvretta House** ☎ (082) 21121, under the new management of Vic and Helen Jacob. The most discreet of the grand-scale St Moritz hotels, it's out of town with gorgeous Christmas card views. Virtually self-sufficient and family-orientated, with private ski lift and ski school, own post office, and creative, classical cuisine. ANTON MOSIMANN is a long-time fan. Best Alpine nosh: **La Marmite** ☎ (082) 36355. Hartly Mathis and son Reto produce such mind-bending dishes as duck's liver drowned in sauce Périgord with truffles, mushrooms and tagliatelle in a cream sauce and *"a steak tartare which is literally covered with caviare"* – BARBARA KAFKA. Try skiing after that.

VERBIER
Sunny chalet resort teeming with bright and noisy young Brits. Challenging skiing – black runs and terrain for powder buffs and mogul bashers. Late-night drinks at **La Luge**. Best hotels: **Rosalp**, **Rhodania** (dancing in the basement **Farm Club** – best nightspot in the Alps), **Le Mazot**. Best restaurant: **Upstairs at the Rosalp** – *"one of the best in Switzerland. Very smart with a champagne bar attached; beautiful cuisine and a fine wine cellar"* – JANE LINDQUIST.

ZERMATT
Romantic setting beneath zer Matterhorn. Only horse-drawn sleighs and electric taxis allowed in town. Brilliant, varied skiing; some of the best heli-skiing in Europe. Best café-bar: **Elsie's Bar** – Irish coffee, oysters, escargots. Best res-

taurant: **Le Mazot**. Best discos: at **Hotel Alex; Le Village** and the **Broken Bar** at the Hotel Post. Best nightclub: **Zermatt Yacht Club**. Best hotels: **Mont Cervin; Zermatterhof**. MARIUCCIA MANDELLI and ROBERT SANGSTER's favourite resort.

TAIWAN

GRAND HYATT TAIPEI, 2 Sung Shou Rd, Taipei ☎ (2) 720 1234
This vast new 1,000-room hotel has gone straight to the top of the tree. Based in the Taipei World Trade Centre, it boasts no less than 9 restaurants and bars (including Cantonese, Shanghainese, Japanese, Californian – and an English pub) and a splendiferous fitness centre.

Topolski on Taiwan

"Taiwan is different from China, because people are attuned to American ways, more used to visitors. Driving is pretty simple, with modern roads and hotels. In the centre of Taiwan, there are some wonderful lakes – the Sun Moon Lake is absolutely spectacular – and on the east coast, there are rainforests. In Taipei, the downtown hotel area seems to stay open all night. The stalls are out on the sidewalk and you might find yourself sitting next to a businessman or a prostitute or a taxi driver eating at 5 o'clock in the morning, with a great sense of busyness going on all the time" – DAN TOPOLSKI.

TANZANIA

A vast country south of Kenya and equally rich in national parkland and game reserves, including the famous Serengeti National Park and the Ngorongoro Crater, enclave of a fascinating animal community (stay at the rim of the crater at **Ngorongoro Crater Lodge**). **Abercrombie & Kent**, **East African Wildlife Safaris**, etc (see Travel Directory), run a number of joint safaris in Kenya and Tanzania.

"In Tanzania, I photographed the trees and the nature and that wild look of Africa and the air...to me these looks have a primitive type of chic. They have inspired my latest line of clothes"

 BIJAN

ZANZIBAR
Instant immersion in the evocative history of East Africa and the slave trade. On this legendary island you can visit the houses of Dr Livingstone and of the notorious slave trader Tippu Tip. Best hotel: **Bhawani**, PO Box 670 ☎ (054) 30200.

THAILAND

BANGKOK

—— *Art and museums* ——

GRAND PALACE
Home of the royal family, a gaudy golden wonderland of wats (temples) plus the palace itself, a blend of Thai and colonial/Mediterranean styles. The best temples are that of the diminutive **Emerald Buddha**, the most sacred image of Buddha in Thailand, whose outfit changes with the seasons, and that of the **Reclining Buddha**, a golden statue that is, by contrast, astonishingly large – 160 ft long, taking up the entire temple.

JIM THOMPSON'S HOUSE, 6 Soi Kasemsan 2, Rama 1 Rd
A delightful taste of old Thailand. Silk king Jim Thompson reconstructed 6 trad Thai houses from the ancient capital of Ayutthaya to form one rambling canal-side house. The beautiful polished teak structures on stilts contain his impressive collection of fine art, porcelain and furniture.

—— *Clubs* ——

Patpong is the famous centre of all hustling, colourful, crazy, straight or kinky Oriental night-life – jazz clubs, discos, hostess bars, sex shops, sex shows, massage parlours, go-go bars where numbered bikini-clad dancers aerobicize up on the counters (pick a number...) – and plenty of deviations in between. Best bar: **King's Castle**. Mosey along to the new Patpong, **Soi Cowboy**, off Soi 23 Sukhumvit Rd, a narrow lane full of rowdy saloons. **Silom Plaza** is a more civilized late-night drinking spot, with a bevy of bustling café-bars that spill out on to a central outdoor area.

BROWN SUGAR, 231/20 Sarasin Rd
Bubbling Brown Sugar is a live jazz and blues joint, with a good mix of biz kids and more arty-intellectual types. Laid-back atmosphere, spontaneous music.

BUBBLES, Dusit Thani, Rama IV Rd
☎ (02) 233 1130
A typical hotel disco, similar to Diana's, but *always* packed mainly because it's easier to park. Smart but informal; smart crowd.

DIANA'S, Oriental Plaza, 48 Oriental Ave ☎ (02) 234 1327
The Annabel's of Thailand, an exclusive, pukka club which hosts the royal family and old school Thais from Harrow and Eton.

NASA SPACEDROME, 999 Ramkhamhang Rd ☎ (02) 314 4024
Colossal ravy disco, jam-packed to its 4,000 capacity. At 11pm you can have a close encounter with a spaceship, which glides in and hovers above the dance floor.

ROME CLUB VIDEOTHEQUE, Soi 4, 90-96 Silom Rd ☎ (02) 233 8836
Thronging bar, with an OTT transvestite show at 1am featuring glitteringly costumed boys miming to pop soundtracks. If the spectacle's too much for you, take a breather over coffee at the Rome Club café on the other side of the soi.

—— *Hotels* ——

HILTON INTERNATIONAL, 2 Wireless Rd ☎ (02) 253 0123
A high-rating Hilton, occupying 8 acres of prime space in the crowded city. Low-rise crescent-shaped building in landscaped Nai Lert Park, with canal, waterfalls and bridges. Ultra-spacious bedrooms, plus the palatial Presidential and Thai-style Royal suites, designed by fashion supremo Valentino. See also Restaurants.

THE ORIENTAL, 48 Oriental Ave
☎ **(02) 236 0400**
One of the best-known and best-loved hotels in the world, sending contributors such as PETER USTINOV, BARBARA CARTLAND, GLYNN CHRISTIAN, ANTON MOSIMANN, SERENA SUTCLIFFE and MADHUR JAFFREY into ecstasies. The Authors' Residence is the place to stay for the old colonial atmos, but the modern block boasts the most splendid suites. Best is the Oriental Suite, with a US$ 500,000 injection of silks, teak, marble and hand-cut crystal, and wraparound balcony. TERRY HOLMES goes for the Sunset Moon Suite, *"one of the loveliest I have ever stayed in anywhere. The attention we were given was incredible, really special."* Superlative eating (see Restaurants). *"The best in the world – for its views across the river and fireworks displays on New Year's Eve"* – DIANE FREIS. *"Gorgeous, the orchids in the room were beyond fabulous"* – STEPHEN JONES. *"I like the nostalgic atmosphere and breakfasts on the terrace overlooking the River of the Kings"* – ELISE PASCOE. *"Still the best floor service in the East. At first it's hard to believe it is going to last one's stay. It does"* – JEREMIAH TOWER. If we're being picky, one group of discerning travellers felt it had slipped a fraction – niggles such as losing some of its discreet charm because tourists pour through just to gawp, and maintenance needing a bit more attention.... However, if we're talking caring service, KEN HOM has this to say: *"I had an incident there which was really wonderful: I arrived to find they had mistakenly redirected my work permit. They were so sorry that they made my stay complimentary. Then when I got to London, there was my permit! They must have made 50 calls to track it down. That's the hallmark of service and quality. I'm committed to them for ever."*

Far East's Best Hotels

1	THE REGENT · Hong Kong
2	THE ORIENTAL · Bangkok
3	HOTEL SEIYO · Tokyo
4	MANDARIN ORIENTAL · Hong Kong
5	THE PENINSULA · Hong Kong
6	THE REGENT · Bangkok
7	GRAND HYATT · Hong Kong
8	SHANGRI-LA · Singapore
9	THE ORIENTAL · Singapore
10	SHANGRI-LA · Hong Kong

THE REGENT, 155 Rajadamri Rd
☎ **(02) 251 6127**
This swanky hotel has truly joined the ranks of the Oriental, with its own devotees. A central building is flanked by 2 blocks with hollow cores containing tropical gardens, so that you can look down from galleries at all levels. Arrival is a satisfying affair as you sweep around ponds and fountains to be greeted by a white-uniformed doorman with sola topee or pill-box hat. The lobby has a ceiling of hand-painted silk; all around are Thai carvings, hangings and antiques. Deferential service (*"the best in the world"* – ELISE PASCOE), beautiful fitness centre, and fine dining (see Restaurants). PS The best hotel drivers to show you the *real* Bangkok.

Buzzz Top-hole watering holes: ranked among the finest drinking and dining establishments in Bangkok are the **Polo Club**, **Royal Bangkok Sports Club** and the **British Club**...... CAROL WRIGHT checks out the market place: *"The* **Sunday Market** *in Bangkok is wonderful. Also once a year, in February, they have a* **Prisoners' Market**, *where all the things made by prisoners in Thailand are sold; the money goes to them and their families. The goods – furniture, carved items – are absolutely superb. It's a very big event, held in the grounds of the royal palace and opened by the King"*...... Market too: MARIUCCIA MANDELLI dilly-dallies at her favourite, the **Floating Market**......The **Dusit Thani** hotel group's new hotels in the north mean you can start your jungle treks in style: at Chiang Mai, the **Dusit Inn** and, at the gateway to the Golden Triangle in Chiang Rai, the **Dusit Island Resort**, on an island in the Mae Kok River. Also just opened is the **Dusit Resort & Polo Club** at the royal seaside town of Hua Hin, south of Bangkok. Book via Dusit Thani, Rama IV Rd, Bangkok ☎ (02) 236 0450......
The most splendiferous hotel in Pattaya is the mammoth **Royal Cliff Beach Resort**, near Pattaya City ☎ (038) 421421; stay in the peerless Royal Wing...................

—— *Restaurants* ——

BUSSARACUM, 35 Soi Pipat 2, Convent Rd ☎ (02) 235 8915
A reliable old favourite for beautifully presented trad Thai food. Wonderful tom yam kung.

HILTON INTERNATIONAL, see Hotels
Dine on classic Continental cuisine at **Ma Maison**. The German chef, a great character, is the only hotel chef to have cooked for the King and Queen of Thailand. **Genji**, one of the best Japanese restaurants in town, has stupendous daily displays of fish, and pits around the tables for those unaccustomed to low-level dining.

🍴 LE BANYAN, Soi 8, 59 Sukhumvit Rd ☎ (02) 253 5556
Bruno Bishoff, late of the Oriental's Normandie, has opened his own French restaurant with partner Michel Binaus. Currently considered the best fine French in town, it's in a lovely wooden Thai house with a garden.

🍴 LEMON GRASS, 5/1 Soi, 24 Sukhumvit Rd ☎ (02) 258 8637
Arguably the best Thai restaurant in the country. It's like dining in a private house, very 'in'. Consistently brilliant food – never an off-day nor an off-dish. Regional specialities, particularly from southern Thailand. *"Some of the best Thai food I've ever eaten anywhere in the world. It takes the best of the Thai tradition and brings it into the modern era. It is absolutely delightful and really cheap"* – KEN HOM. *"The best restaurant I know in Bangkok. Their plate-cooked seafood is exquisite and I adore their goong soam – prawns cooked in coconut oil. Excellent coffee for a Thai restaurant"* – ELISE PASCOE. Also a twin Lemon Grass in Chiang Mai.

MAYFLOWER, Dusit Thani Hotel, Rama IV Rd ☎ (02) 233 1130
The best Chinese restaurant in Bangkok, in an elegant Western-style environment.

🍴 THE ORIENTAL, see Hotels
A gamut for gourmets, starting at the top with the **Normandie**, for exquisite French cuisine and top-floor river views. The much-lauded **Lord Jim's** for local seafood in a 19C steamship state-room setting (this is the one Thais will take you to). **Sala Rim Naam** for trad Thai food, classical Thai music and dance. Or follow ELISE PASCOE's advice: *"The very best Thai food is at The Oriental Thai Cooking School at lunch, after a morning class with Chalie Amatyakul, on the verandah of the wooden school house across the river from the hotel."* The **Authors' Lounge**, in the original wing, is the place for civilized teas, and the **Riverside Terrace** for cocktails (fab Oriental Slings) and nightly barbecue.

🍴 THE REGENT, see Hotels
The newly refurbished **Le Cristal** still serves the same excellent European/French cuisine. **La Brasserie** is a more informal restaurant for Continental cuisine. Get a seat around the tropical pool and admire the fat goldfish. The superb **Spice Market** is in a pseudo-rustic Thai bazaar setting, with spice sacks lining the walls. Classic national cuisine with fiery regional specialities. Try the green rice pudding.

THANYING RESTAURANT, 10 Pramuan St, Off Silom Rd ☎ (02) 236 4361
Excellent Thai restaurant in a homely setting. Locals and foreigners relish its typical cuisine.

TUMNAK THAI, 131 Ratchadapisek Rd ☎ (02) 276 1810
A phenomenon. this 10-acre complex seats 3,000, is served by waiters on roller-skates and run by computer. Set in Thai-style houses around a pond with a stage for classical dance shows. The most OTT eating experience in Bangkok.

—— *Shopping* ——

Peninsula Plaza, Rajadamri Rd, is home to Bualaad Jewellery and Frank's Jewellery, who bejewel high-society necks, and Chailai, a treasure trove of ethnic pieces sought out from northern Thailand by Princess Chailai, and creatively restructured. The **Regent** and **Oriental** arcades are further homes to the chic set.

Bangkok is the leading city for tailor-made women's clothes, completed in double-quick time for a pittance (try **Burlington Tailor**, Cloen Ploenchit Arcade). At the designer end of the scale, **Kai Guerlain**, 2-14 N Wireless Rd ☎ (02) 253 2998, continues his mini-fashion dictatorship, fitting a loyal clientele. The best of young design is on the 2nd floor of the swanky **Charn Isala Tower**, Rama V Rd. Seek out **Teeraphan Wanarat**, who dresses society ladies; **Daung Jai Bis**, **Urai Risa** and **Venick**.

More top shopping at the new **World Trade Center**, the **Mah-Boon Krong** area, and the **Siam Center**, a maze of shoplets for cheapish young designer wear and other trend purchases. Good-quality fake designer goods from around **Silom Village** in Silom Rd, street 'bazaars' between **Sois 7 and 11 off Sukhumvit Road**, and the **Gaysorn** area. **Thai Home Industries**, 35 Oriental Ave, has ethnic craftware. **Chatuchak Park**, off Phalan Yothin Rd, is a weekend market for all things weird and wonderful, especially good for Thai antiques and bric-à-brac. 'Antiques' can be checked for authenticity by the Fine Arts Department ☎ (02) 233 0977.

JIM THOMPSON, 9 Surawong Rd ☎ (02) 234 4900
The best silk spot in the world for lustrous Thai silks in jewel and iridescent colours – Parma violet, sky blue, emerald, peacock, flame. Cotton furnishing fabrics too in the same vibrant palette. Enormous but elegant cushions, chic ready-to-wear, and zingy silken accessories.

KRISHNA'S, 137-6-7 Sukhumvit Rd (btwn Soi 9 and 11) ☎ (02) 254 9944
An Aladdin's cave of handicrafts, Burmese tapestries, pottery, lacquerware, wood carvings, elephant chairs, etc, on 3 floors. Run by an Indian family, who are experts on the finer points of shipping – so you can be sure everything will arrive safely.

LOTUS, Kannika Court, The Regent, 155 Rajadamri Rd ☎ (02) 250 0732
For the most exquisite Oriental trinkets and antiques. You must remove your shoes before stepping on the raised antique teak floor. Semi-precious carved stones, small presents, antique embroidery and tribal rugs.

· REST OF ·
THAILAND

Phuket, the nearby islands, and **Pattaya** boast some of the most beautiful natural beaches in the world, though the ever-developing tourist industry has spoilt some out of all recognition, and encouraged seamy living (under-age 'escorts' and unattractive Western businessmen, all on the pick-up).

——— *Hotels* ———

🏊 **AMANPURI, Pansea Beach, Phuket ☎ (076) 311394**
A stunner, like staying in your own mini Jim Thompson's House. 40 private pavilions made of local teak, raised on stilts, with temple roofs and their own sala – a shrine-like open sundeck looking over the coconut grove out to the Andaman Sea. The brainchild of Adrian Zecha, a founder of the Regent group, with 3 partners. Guests are assigned an assistant manager to attend their every whim. 2 restaurants for spicy Thai or tamer Italian dishes; large pool, tennis and squash courts, gym, sauna and library. Cruises take you snorkelling, scuba diving, game fishing or simply exploring. Michael J Fox and Sean Penn stayed here between locations for *Casualties of War*. It's JEREMIAH TOWER's joint-best getaway in the Far East.

PANSEA HOTEL, 118 Moo 3, Surin Beach, Phuket ☎ (076) 216137
A cluster of traditional thatched cottages in a hilly coconut grove with private beach. SERENA SUTCLIFFE recommends their seafood buffets and Chinese cuisine.

PHUKET YACHT CLUB, Nai Harn Beach, Phuket ☎ (076) 381156
Secluded beach paradise away from the action. Nautical theme, though it's not actually a yacht club. Terraced rooms cut into the hillside and surrounded by foliage. Tennis, shimmering pool,

and water sports on tap. *"A wonderful setting – watch the sunsets and drink pink gins or Singapore Slings on the pool terrace dripping with rich purple bougainvillaea. Idyllic and beautiful"* – ELISE PASCOE.

TURKEY

Sailing is still the best way to do Turkey, though Bodrum is old hat – smarties now seek quieter ports such as Gocek. On your travels, don't miss the knockout ancient sites of **Aphrodisias** and **Ephesus**, or the fantasy rock formations and hot springs of **Pamukkale**.

ISTANBUL
——— *Hotels* ———

Until the Regent of Istanbul comes to fruition (now planned for 1991) the best international hotel is the **Istanbul Sheraton**, Taksim Park ☎ (1) 131 2121, overlooking the sea and the minarets and domes.

HIDIV KASRI, Cubuklu-Kanlica ☎ (1) 331 2651
In a beautiful setting above the Bosphorus, this former summer palace of the last Viceroy of Egypt is decorated in a fantastic mishmash of styles. Stay in the Viceroy's Suite, with its own terrace. Pretty wooded grounds. Arrive by boat (a 2-hour trip from the city centre).

YESIL EV, Kabasakal Craddesi 5, Sultanahmed ☎ (1) 511 1150
'The Greenhouse' is an old Ottoman mansion, converted into a hotel but retaining the feel of a private house, replete with Victorian details such as velveteen chaises-longues and dim lamps. Beautiful walled garden, good food, and a lovely situation near the mosques.

> **❝The Egyptian Market in Istanbul sells everything, but mainly wonderful spices and all sorts of aphrodisiacs. There's a tremendous aroma❞**
>
> CAROL WRIGHT

—— *Tours, yachts, villas* ——

Abercrombie & Kent organize guided or independent Turkish programmes, in hotels and/or aboard the historic MY *Halas*. **Yachtclub Charter Co** arrange not only yachts and crewed schooners but overland tours with driver and guide to mainland villages, ancient sites, secluded bays, etc. **Top Yacht Charter**, **Continental Villas**, etc, arrange holidays in yachts, old-style wooden gulets and/or villas. See Travel Directory.

VENEZUELA

HATO PINERO, Av La Estancia, Torre Diamen, Piso 1, Ofic 19, Chuao, Caracas 1060 ☎ (02) 916854
The equivalent of a game reserve, this cattle ranch, bounded by rivers and ancient rocky outcrops, is a dream for nature-lovers. Some of the best bird-watching in the world – over 300 species of bird, plus rare animals such as the jaguar, puma, crab-eating fox, ocelot, anteater and crab-eating racoon. Go in May, when the first rains mean an explosion of floral life, or later in winter (until Sept) when the land is verdant and alive with birdsong, and lagoons are navigable. Boat rides and safaris.

LOS FRAILES, c/o Avensa, Centro Comercial Tamanaco, Nivil C2, Caracas ☎ (02) 563 3020
Between Santo Domingo and Laguna Mucubaji is this hidden discovery of EDWARD CARTER: *"You fly out of Caracas to Mérida, then drive white-knuckled along the most incredible twisting road with precipices on both sides for two hours up to 13,500 ft, over the top and down again to 10,000 ft, to a monastery created in 1643, now a government-run inn. You live in converted monks' quarters and can see mountains ranging away and llamas drinking from ice-cold rivulets. The food is not fabulous, but good considering where the hell it is....Just wonderful, a terrific secret."*

ZAMBIA

The South Luangwa National Park boasts perhaps the highest concentration and variety of wildlife in Africa.

KAPANI SAFARI LODGE, PO Box 100, Mufuwe ☎ (062) 45015
Exclusive camp on the edge of a sheltered lagoon, with a viewing platform overlooking the water. *"Super little place, with lovely thatched native-style lodges and a bar and fridge on the*

Yugo – Do Go

"There is a spectacular part of Yugoslavia called Slovenija, in the north-west corner on the Austrian border, up around Ljubljana and Lake Bled. There's some wonderful walking in the hills. The Yugoslavs are terribly attractive, nice people. On Lake Bled, there's a lovely hotel, **Toplice Grand**, Resort Bled, Cesta Svobode 12 ☎ (64) 77222. It's rather old-world, and you must get a room that overlooks the lake. There are wonderful castles and churches perched high above the lakes. The currency is extraordinary – it increases as you stand and pay the bill – but it doesn't affect you very much... you just have to carry a lot of money around" – DAN TOPOLSKI.

---

verandah, which makes it comfortable" – CAROL WRIGHT. She also loves Kapani's nearby little sister, **LOUWI RIVER CAMP**: *"One of the best bush camps. It's dead simple – little bamboo huts, in the middle of nowhere. Run by Norman Carr, a leading naturalist. Absolutely magic and it's tiny tiny. You have to walk, following the lion tracks, and you see hippos fighting!"*

ZIMBABWE

—— *Hotels and camps* ——

BUMI HILLS SAFARI LODGE, PO Box 41, Kariba ☎ (161) 2353
Fan-cooled rooms are set at the edge of a cliff overlooking Lake Kariba. You can go fishing, game viewing or try a Water Wilderness safari, in houseboats that are purportedly insect-proof.

MEIKLES HOTEL, PO Box 594, Stanley Ave, Harare ☎ (4) 707721
Perhaps a little jaded on a world scale, nevertheless it's Zimbabwe's first 5-star hotel, and one of Africa's best.

RUCKOMECHI CAMP, c/o Shearwater
A Utopian camp in perfect peaceful position, with only 8 cottages. Despite private showers, guests swoon over the bathroom which opens on one side to the river. Walking, canoeing and vehicle safaris.

VICTORIA FALLS HOTEL, PO Box 10, Victoria Falls ☎ (113) 4203

Elegant and colonial, with lovely verandahs and gardens. The doorman is virtually a national monument, with badges from top to toe. Nightly African dance displays, brilliantly staged in a floodlit amphitheatre.

—— Tours and charters ——

See also Travel Directory.

SHEARWATER, 5th Fl, Karigamombe Centre, PO Box 3961, Harare ☎ (4) 735712

Daredevil adventures on the Zambezi: a) White water canoe safaris between Kazungula and Vic Falls, alternately drifting and 'bracing muscle and sinew' against rapids. A vehicle provides luxury back-up... meals at long tables under acacia and ebony trees on riverbank; b) Canoeing in Red Indian-style craft on the lower, less rabid part of the river. Stay at Ruckomechi; c) Rafting down gorges below Victoria Falls, some of the biggest white-water rapids in the world. Exhilaration isn't the word. Do the 8-mile grade 3-4 run or the 13-mile grade 5. The rapid scale is 1-6. Six is unrunnable.

UNITED AIR CHARTERS, PO Box AP 50, Harare Airport, Harare ☎ (4) 731713; bookings (113) 4530

The famous Flight of Angels: on seeing Victoria Falls, Livingstone described *"scenes so lovely they must have been gazed upon by angels in their flight...."* Now you can wing your way over the 5 separate waterfalls – the Devil's Cataract, Main Falls, Horseshoe Falls, Rainbow Falls and the Eastern Cataract – that make up the Mosi oa Tunya (Smoke that Thunders). Also air safaris over game parks.

TRAVEL DIRECTORY

—— Airlines ——

All airlines have their fans; here is a list of those that our contributors recommend. In general, Oriental airlines come out tops for pampering, pandering service, while Swiss, German and Scandinavian airlines are exceptional for their reliability. British Airways is, once again, the most talked-about airline. It wins for overall reliability, good service, good food, and for its vast network of routes.

AIR FRANCE

Gastronomic appeal. Support from GLYNN CHRISTIAN, HILARY RUBINSTEIN, LORD MONTAGU OF BEAULIEU and BARBARA CARTLAND.

AIR INDIA

"Air India has come up a lot. The service is now excellent and they're the only airline to have several non-stop flights a week to India" – SERENA FASS. *"Economy class from London to New York is excellent"* – DON HEWITSON.

AIR NEW ZEALAND

Patriotic cheers from GLYNN CHRISTIAN for the hospitality, space and food... and from DON HEWITSON for *"the best business class. You don't need to waste your money on first class."*

AMERICAN AIRLINES

Waving the banner are OLIVIER COQUELIN (*"I think it's the best airline in the world"*) and LARRY KING (*"My favourite airline, I like their service, their on-time record – for a company as large, they really give personal service"*), BILL BLASS (*"our best airline"*), HELEN GURLEY BROWN and CAROLINE HUNT.

✈ BRITISH AIRWAYS

Still comes out bubble and wings above the others. Frequent flyers are still talking in terms of *improvement*. Take KEN HOM: *"From top to bottom they are getting better. People used to make jokes about them, but they have really picked themselves up and are up there with the best in the world."* Among those who used to despise it and now prize it are EDWARD CARTER (*"phenomenal improvement"*), RICHARD COMPTON-MILLER (*"greatly improved"*) and LOYD GROSSMAN (*"improved beyond recognition"*). Which class to pick? *"I've heard nothing but amazement and praise. They so improved club class that everyone from first went down to club, so they relaunched first to make it more luxurious..."* – LORD LICHFIELD. *"I think it is superb now (it used not to be)... you can't beat them in club and first"* – JOHN TOVEY. *"BA is the best international airline that I know. BA club class is the best because they have the old first-class seats"* – BOB PAYTON. For DON HEWITSON, however, *"you have to go first class or nothing. The business class is crap."* TERRY HOLMES thinks BA and Qantas tie for the best first class. JOSEPH, STANLEY MARCUS and MARIO BUATTA agree it's tops for transatlantic flights; PATRICIA HODGE for long-haul trips. Other loyal supporters include FRANK LOWE (*"mainly for the leg room"*), CAROL WRIGHT (*"for the bread and butter pudding – businessmen love it"*), JOAN BURSTEIN (*"my favourite... I really do enjoy travelling with BA"*), JOHN GOLD (*"they always look after me extremely well"*), TESSA DAHL (*"I love BA"*), ANDRE PREVIN (*"a great airline"*), PETER STRINGFELLOW (*"for reliability"*), BARRY HUMPHRIES, GILES SHEPARD, JEFFERY TOLMAN, NICHOLAS VILLIERS, ROSS BENSON, KEITH FLOYD, HELEN GURLEY BROWN, BIJAN, VISCOUNT HAMBLEDEN, YEHUDI MENUHIN and ED VICTOR. Just 2 alarm signals: from JULIAN LLOYD WEBBER, *"I would say BA still, but with a slight question mark creeping in. I personally feel they reached a peak of efficiency and politeness, which is perhaps in

danger of being dissipated." And from JAMES
BURKE: *"I think BA is having a wobbly time.
They were on the up and up, but they have
levelled out. They need constant reminders...."*

♠ CATHAY PACIFIC
Hong Kong's airline, part of the Swire Group.
*"Some of the best food in the air and of course
the best service. I would really vote it one of the
best airlines"* – KEN HOM. *"Of all the Oriental
airlines, it's the best"* – LORD LICHFIELD. So say
BARRY HUMPHRIES and EDWARD CARTER.

♠ CONCORDE
*"My ideal way to travel would be Concorde –
speed, comfort, no hassle"* – NED SHERRIN. *"My
ideal way,"* echoes GILES SHEPARD, *"because you
go with fewer people – a maximum of 100 arrive
at any one time and it makes movement through
the airport much less tiresome." "I find that
British Concorde is much better than French
Concorde. Service is really first class, as it
should be. You feel as though you're pampered
from beginning to end. It is a miracle that they
can keep that standard still"* – JOAN BURSTEIN.
"Concorde is just bliss" – SIMON WILLIAMS.
*"There is no comparison. I'm always astonished
that they can serve such good food, because there
is so little room"* – PETER STRINGFELLOW. Not
everyone is keen on Concorde cuisine: *"I'm
disappointed in the food. Just because you're
going so fast doesn't mean you can't have good
food"* – KEN HOM. *"I still think Concorde is the
best form of travel, in spite of the fact that the
food isn't as good as it used to be..."* – FREDERIC
RAPHAEL. JAMES BURKE would like to *own* a
Concorde: *"It's a perfect-sized aeroplane for one
person. I do like it, but you're cheek by jowl..."*
Meanwhile, it's supreme for the transatlantic
gang – STANLEY MARCUS, BARBARA TAYLOR
BRADFORD, BILL BLASS and BIJAN.

JAPAN AIR LINES
Top service and exquisite food. Votes from
ANDRE PREVIN and STEPHEN JONES.

LUFTHANSA
Teutonic precision gains them valuable points.
*"Undoubtedly the most efficient airline in the
world..."* – ROSS BENSON. STEVE MADOFF, DEREK
MALCOLM and ANDRE PREVIN add support.

MGM GRAND AIR
New York to LA daily – in style. The converted
727s offer all 33 passengers first-class luxe (of
the disco plush kind). Stand-up bar and lounge,
squashy armchairs in a heady shade of raspberry
crush, private sleeping compartments, gourmet
cuisine, choice of 6 movies, papers and mags,
s-p-a-c-e. *"A very luxurious and comfortable
way to fly coast to coast. You don't have to worry
about your luggage – you just give it in and it's
there waiting for you when you get off the plane.
It's almost like travelling on a private jet"* –
BARBARA TAYLOR BRADFORD. *"I love flying with
them"* – TESSA DAHL.

Anti-jetlag Jag
In the never-ending quest to combat jetlag, our contributors submit their ideas:
*"I've tried everything. I take potassium
tablets, bananas and lots of water. Don't
eat! Sleep. But you still get jetlag....The
best solution is to try to have a rest before
the flight. Get everything done a few days
before. It's the tension before leaving that
gives you the jetlag"* – BARRY HUMPHRIES.
*"Eat as little as possible and certainly
don't drink any alcohol. Drink water –
plain is better than gassy. Adjust to the
new time zone as soon as possible"* –
BARBARA TAYLOR BRADFORD. *"I think it's a
question of mind over matter, really. If
you've got something to do, you just bat on
and do it. Fly at night and sleep"* – SIMON
WILLIAMS. Alternatively, try **Danièle
Ryman**'s aromatherapy products, available at Heathrow Terminal 4 or c/o Park
Lane Hotel, Piccadilly, London W1 ☎
(071) 753 6707. Or take JOHN GOLD's advice:
"Don't go! Keep off the plane, kid."

♠ QANTAS
Continues to boast an impeccable safety record.
LORD LICHFIELD notices *"everyone is saying that
they have got so good"*. TERRY HOLMES goes for
their first class: *"Along with BA, it has to be the
best."* ELISE PASCOE applauds their new frequent-
flyer club, *"which rewards you for being faithful.
Well worthwhile."*

SAS (SCANDINAVIAN AIRLINE SYSTEMS)
The airline of Denmark, Norway and Sweden.
Punctual and reliable, they're the businessman's
dream – they'll send luggage direct to your hotel,
and you can check in from your hotel. STEVE
MADOFF is keen.

♠ SINGAPORE AIRLINES
High flyers find them a joy to travel with – they
attend your every whim and dish out lots of
luxury goodies. The buzz aircraft is the new
Boeing 747-400 or, in SA-speak, 'Megatop',
which flies non-stop Singapore to London (head
winds prevented the fuel-greedy 747-300 from
doing the 13-hour flight). *"I still recommend
Singapore Airlines as the best – in fact it's better
than before. I went on the Megatop, and you'd
think with the extra supplies and crew [they
work on a rota], standards would fall, but
they've got better. A marvellous airline"* – JAMES
BURKE. *"One of the most agreeably different...
just the costumes they wear..."* – DOUGLAS FAIR-

BANKS JR. *"Truly one of the great airlines of the world. They are terribly attentive and they have new planes which are very clean – one thing which impresses me is how the stewards constantly clean the WC. It's very important on long flights"* – KEN HOM. *"Service with a smile and on time!!"* – BENNY ONG. Tops for DEREK MALCOLM.

✈ SWISSAIR
Very highly regarded (it's the inimitable Swiss precision, inherent also in their hoteliers and timepieces), with a comforting safety record. *"I don't know if it's psychological, but one always feels one can trust Swissair. They are going to be on time, they are not going to lose your luggage..."* – LOYD GROSSMAN. *"I think you get better food on an ordinary Swissair flight than on French or British Concorde"* – JAMES BURKE. A winner for LORD LICHFIELD (*"purely in Europe, because of their punctuality and precision"*), PETER USTINOV (*"for sheer quality"*), BIJAN, ANDRE PREVIN, STEVE MADOFF, BARBARA TAYLOR BRADFORD and VISCOUNT HAMBLEDEN (*"Swissair is always impeccable"*).

THAI AIRWAYS INTERNATIONAL
"An airline that is, in its own way, better than BA (though it is not really fair to compare it because it is government sponsored and flies fewer routes)" – JAMES BURKE.

VIRGIN ATLANTIC AIRWAYS
One of the best carriers across the Atlantic. 'Upper' (business) class provides seats you can actually sleep in, excellent food, and the best in-flight entertainment, including personal video walkmans.

Cruises

CLUB MED 1, Club Med, 106-110 Brompton Rd, London SW3, England ☎ (071) 225 1066
Club Med's new £50 million sailing yacht is the largest ever to exist, a splendiferous 5-masted, 10,000-ton, 614-ft vessel, with 7 decks of Burmese teak. Yet she's still neat enough to enter small harbours and marinas. 425 guests lap up the usual Club Med fun and games and brilliant cuisine: a platform descends to sea level to provide a sun deck and marina from which to windsurf, waterski, snorkel or scuba dive.

ROYAL VIKING LINE, 95 Merrick Way, Coral Gables, FL 33134, USA ☎ (305) 447 9660
Classy cruises all over the globe, from the Norwegian fjords to the balmy South Pacific. Go for a week, or opt for a 109-day world trip, visiting 36 ports. As slick as a first-class hotel, RVL is voted No 1 by LORD LICHFIELD. *"A lot of fun"* – AUBERON WAUGH.

SEA GODDESS CRUISES, Cunard, South Western House, Canute Rd, Southampton,

England ☎ (0703) 634166; 30A Pall Mall, London SW1 ☎ (071) 491 3930
A plushy line with 2 identical small ships, more like floating clubs, carrying about 100 guests apiece (with 86 staff). They visit the ports other ships cannot reach – Portofino, Puerto Banus, Tobago Cays, Virgin Gorda. Swimming pool, spa, windsurfers, snorkelling equipment and waterskiing. Al fresco breakfasts and lunches, formal dinners and nightclub-casino. *"The best cruises – not just because we own them, but I don't ever hear any complaints. They are very special, and the food is worthy of Michelin stars"* – TERRY HOLMES.

WINDSTAR SAIL CRUISES, 300 Elliott Ave W, Seattle, WA 98119, USA ☎ (206) 286 3210
Lavish week-long cruises aboard stunning 4-masted sailing vessels – *Wind Star* in the Caribbean and Mediterranean, *Wind Song* in the Society Islands (strains of *High Society* or *South Pacific*?) and *Wind Spirit* in the Caribbean and Alaska. Norwegian officers and European hotel staff form the 84-strong crew serving 148 (mainly American) passengers.

Rail

PALACE ON WHEELS, Central Reservation House, 36 Chandralok, Janpath, New Delhi 110001, India ☎ (011) 322332
A luxurious (by Indian standards) steam train that takes in all the sights of Rajasthan, with overnight stops at top-class hotels. Lovely atmosphere of faded grandeur, in tiny carriages that once belonged to Maharajas.

✈ VENICE SIMPLON ORIENT-EXPRESS, Sea Containers House, 20 Upper Ground, London SE1, England ☎ (071) 928 6000
The legendary train still delights all who travel in it. Still coal-stoked, the Orient-Express remains as it was in the 20s, with pretty cabins (polished mahogany, marquetry, brass fittings, glowing table lamps) and beautiful dining cars (one decorated with glass panels of dancing nudes by Lalique). Cuisine would be Michelin-starred if it weren't served in motion – lobster for brunch, filet de boeuf for dinner, irresistible herby bread rolls, flavoured with spinach, olive or tomato. Added to the Venice- or Vienna-to-London trip is a new Oriental run between Bangkok and Singapore. Dig-a-dig-diggers include CLARE FRANCIS and LORD LICHFIELD.

– Tours, villas and agents –

See also Australia, Brazil, Britain, Canada, Caribbean, Egypt, Greece, India, Italy, Kenya, Malawi, Nepal, South Africa and Zimbabwe.

ABERCROMBIE & KENT, Sloane Square House, Holbein Place, London SW1, England ☎ (071) 730 9600; 1420 Kensington Rd, Suite 111, Oakbrook, IL 60521, USA ☎ (312) 954 2944
One of the most extensive and very best tour companies in the world. All sorts of luxury tours, staying in the smartest hotels. Hot on Africa and the Far East. Efficient, knowledgeable guides.

AFRO VENTURES, 61 Bond St, Ferndale (PO Box 2339), Randburg, South Africa ☎ (011) 789 1078
Acknowledged specialists in overland tours in Zimbabwe and Botswana.

ART STUDY TOURS & COUNTRY TRAVELS, c/o Serena Fass, 2 Chesil Court, Chelsea Manor St, London SW3, England ☎ (071) 352 9769
Worldwide cultural tours, organized by Serena Fass (ex-Serenissima) and accompanied by a lecturer. Egypt, Ladakh, Russia, etc. Also property lets in France, Portugal and Spain.

BALES TOURS, Bales House, Junction Rd, Dorking, Surrey RH4 3HB, England ☎ (0306) 885923 (brochures); 885991 (reservations)
Specialists in Egypt, the Middle East and Africa, from budget to luxury holidays.

BUTTERFIELD & ROBINSON, 70 Bond St, Toronto, M5B 1X3, Canada ☎ (416) 864 1354
Luxury biking and hiking through France, Italy and northern Spain: 5-star hotels, award-winning restaurants and tours of local vineyards revive saddle-sore cyclists. Also Bali by bike and family trips to France, Austria, Tanzania and the Canadian Rockies.

CARIBBEAN CONNECTION, Concorde House, Forest St, Chester, England ☎ (0224) 41131; 93 Newman St, London W1 ☎ (071) 631 4482
Carefully vetted upmarket hotels and villas in the Caribbean. Also **Pacific Connection**, to Australia, New Zealand and the South Pacific.

CONTINENTAL VILLAS, Eagle House, 58 Blythe Rd, London W14, England ☎ (071) 371 1313
Luxury villas, old and modern, mostly with pools, in the South of France, Spain, Majorca, Ibiza, Italy, Portugal, Greece, Turkey, Palm Beach and the West Indies.

CV TRAVEL, 43 Cadogan St, London SW3, England ☎ (071) 581 0851
The smartest villas (and villa girls) on Corfu and Paxos – the Duchess of Kent stayed in one. Also beautifully decorated privately owned villas in Majorca, the Algarve, the Riviera and Italy. Maids and often cooks. Their **Different World** takes you to the best, most tasteful resort hotels in the Caribbean and Africa.

EAST AFRICAN WILDLIFE SAFARIS, PO Box 43747, Nairobi, Kenya ☎ (02) 331228
Luxury, tailor-made safaris in Kenya, Tanzania, Zimbabwe and Botswana.

EQUINOX TRAVEL, King's Mead House, 250 King's Rd, London SW3, England ☎ (071) 352 1672
Small company specializing in tailor-made tours for individuals in India, Pakistan, eastern Thailand and Burma. Good connections with maharajahs, so you can visit palaces and private villas. Adventure tours too (from camel to bicycle safaris) and VIP treks in Thailand. No brochures, but they will compile a tailor-made guide book for you.

EXPLORASIA, 13 Chapter St, London SW1, England ☎ (071) 630 7102
Smart, pioneering treks in India, Nepal, Kashmir, Ladakh, Tibet, Ecuador and Peru. Go off the beaten track to new trekking areas, to Everest Base Camp, the finest Indian and Nepalese game parks or trout fishing in Kashmir.

FOUR CORNERS, 127 Kensington High St, London W8, England ☎ (071) 376 1077 and branches
The new British Airways designer travel agency-cum-store. "*Spectacular, brilliant if you want a complicated tailor-made tour. I had to do 32 take-offs and landings in 10 days as ambassador for VSO. They structured it brilliantly, minimum hassle, first class. The more complicated the better!*" – LORD LICHFIELD.

GAMETRACKERS, PO Box 4245, Randburg, South Africa ☎ (011) 886 1810
Wing safaris in South and East Africa, tailor-made from a choice of camps.

HEMPHILL HARRIS, 16000 Ventura Blvd, Suite 200, Encino, CA 91436, USA ☎ (818) 906 8086
Highly exclusive tours for rich old fogeys. Guarantee the best of everything. Trips all over the world (except for North America) include heli cruises, ballooning and a world tour in a private jet.

KUONI TRAVEL, Kuoni House, Dorking, Surrey RH5 4AZ, England ☎ (0306) 740500
Vast range of worldwide holidays, from lazing in a Caribbean club to trekking, river-rafting and searching for the Royal Bengal tiger in the Himalayas. Also round the world on Concorde – for c. £12,000.

LINDBLAD TRAVEL, 1 Sylvan North, PO Box 912, Westport, CT 06881, USA ☎ (203) 226 8531
Fabulously expensive trips for the intelligent élite. Conservation-minded regulars have formed an exclusive travellers' club, the Intrepids. Their Masai Mara safari has the most

luxurious tented camp in Africa, staying in 4-poster beds. Cruises are a speciality.

MARY ROSSI TRAVEL, Suite 3, Gr Fl, The Denison, 65 Berry St, N Sydney, NSW 2060, Australia ☎ (02) 957 4511
All arrangements for upmarket globetrotters are made by Mary and 6 members of her family.

REEF AND RAINFOREST TOURS/ ECOSAFARIS, 146 Gloucester Rd, London SW8, England ☎ (071) 370 5032
Conservation-biased safaris to southern Africa, India, Central and South America. Visit their own conservation camp, Kasanka, in Zambia.

SERENISSIMA TRAVEL, 21 Dorset Square, London NW1, England ☎ (071) 730 9841
Under the Voyages Jules Verne umbrella. Cultural tours accompanied by a scholarly lecturer, sometimes in association with the Friends of the Royal Academy. Take a journey by sea through the Spice Islands of Indonesia; go to North Yemen; the Sultanate of Oman; Mexico and Guatemala. NB Not all are cocoons of luxury.

SILK CUT TRAVEL, Meon House, Petersfield, Hampshire, England ☎ (0730) 65211
Upmarket tours, cruises and hotels in the Caribbean, South America, Far East and Africa – a blend of safari/Indian Ocean or jungle/Galapagos, say, or the Mayan and Andean Explorer tours for real travellers.

SPECIALTOURS, 81A Elizabeth St, London SW1, England ☎ (071) 730 2297
Cultural tours (often for Friends of museums and societies), such as the sites and sights of northern Cyprus, the Villas of the Veneto, a Pilgrimage to Santiago de Compostela, or Houses of the Hudson. *"They run extremely proficient, efficient, happy tours"* – SERENA FASS.

TEMPO TRAVEL, Brunswick House, 91 Brunswick Crescent, London N11, England ☎ (081) 361 1131
African specialists, from Botswana to the Seychelles – safaris, cruises, simple lodges, first-class hotels. Particularly good on South Africa.

TIPPETT'S SAFARIS, PO Box 43806, Nairobi, Kenya ☎ (02) 332132; 14E Paveley Drive, London SW11, England ☎ (071) 223 3187
Private tented trips off the beaten track in East Africa. *"The very best safaris"* – SERENA FASS.

TRAILFINDERS, 194 Kensington High St, London W8, England ☎ (071) 938 3939 (long-haul); (071) 938 3232 (transatlantic and Europe); (071) 938 3444 (first and business class); 42-48 Earl's Court Rd, W8
The full service for travellers. The cheapest reliable flights, on-the-spot ticketing, insurance,

immunization and medical advice, travellers' cheques and currency, maps and books.

TRAVEL ASSOCIATES, 178 Jersey Rd, Woollahra, NSW 2025, Australia ☎ (02) 328 7377
Tailor-made travel by Warwick Vyner, *"a sensational travel agent, at home and overseas"* – DORIAN WILD. Takes care of all the arrangements for the social Sydney set.

TWICKERS WORLD, 22 Church St Twickenham, Middlesex, England ☎ (081) 892 7606
A massive selection of tours and treks to outlandish places with the accent on wildlife, wilderness, adventure, action and culture. Take off to Africa, the Far East, Falkland Islands, Oman, Guatemalan Markets and Villages; go Kjolur Horse Trekking in Iceland, or Dog Sledding in Greenland.

VACANZE IN ITALIA, Bignor, Nr Pulborough, W Sussex, England ☎ (07987) 426
Superb privately owned villas and châteaux for hire in Italy and France (☎ 433). Also English/Scottish/Welsh cottages ☎ (0328) 851155.

── *Yacht charter* ──

See also Australia.

CAMPER & NICHOLSONS, BP 183, Port Pierre Canto, 06407 Cannes, France ☎ 9343 1675
Over 400 luxury crewed yachts, motor and sailing, modern and old-fashioned, steered where you will. Nothing much below US$5,000, rising to c. US$170,000 for the deluxe *Katalina*.

TOP YACHT, Andrew Hill Lane, Hedgerley, Buckinghamshire, England ☎ (02814) 6636
With bases at buzzy Bodrum and tiny Gocek, they arrange bareboat and crewed yacht or gulet cruising in Greek and Turkish waters. Can be combined with self-drive mainland tour.

WINDSOR YACHTS, c/o Navtol Agencies, 65 Broadway, 10th Fl, New York, NY 10006, USA ☎ (212) 363 7990
The Bermuda-based yachts, *Lady Diana* and *Lady Sarah* (a third is due...), have almost 60 crew to 54 guests and can be chartered in any waters for around US$2,000 a head per day.

YACHTCLUB CHARTER CO, 307 New King's Rd, London SW6, England ☎ (071) 731 0826
Operating now from unspoilt Gocek, this smart young company has a fine fleet of sailing yachts for charter, with or without crew. Specialists in luxury crewed Turkish schooners – even the most fanatical of sailors cast off any yearning to hoist the main. Also new overland safaris.

INDEX